Tort

AUSTRALIA
Law Book Co.
Sydney

CANADA and USA
Carswell
Toronto

HONG KONG
Sweet & Maxwell Asia

NEW ZEALAND
Brookers
Auckland

SINGAPORE and MALAYSIA
Sweet & Maxwell Asia
Singapore and Kuala Lumpur

TORT

Sweet & Maxwell's Textbook Series

Paula Giliker, M.A. (Oxon.), B.C.L., Ph.D. (Cantab.)
Barrister, Senior Lecturer in Law, Queen Mary,
University of London

and

Silas Beckwith, LL.B (Lond.)

Barrister, Senior Lecturer in Law, London Metropolitan University

LONDON
SWEET & MAXWELL
2004

Published in 2004 by
Sweet & Maxwell Limited of
100 Avenue Road, London NW3 3PF
(http://www.sweetandmaxwell.co.uk)
Typeset by LBJ Typesetting Ltd of Kingsclere
Printed in Great Britain by CPI Bath

Reprinted 2005, 2006

No natural forests were destroyed to make this product;
only farmed timber was used and replanted

A CIP catalogue record for this book
is available from the British Library

ISBN 0421 859 806

Preface

This book is designed for readers approaching tort law for the first time. We have sought to set out clearly and succinctly the rules applicable to each tort and illustrate how they work in practice by reference to case law. Whilst our discussion of case law can by no means replace reading the cases themselves, we have set out the salient points to serve as an *aide memoire* and to enable the reader to consider the law in a factual context. Similarly, we have outlined the main statutory provisions in this area of law and have sought to help the reader understand the wording and impact of these provisions.

The book has a traditional structure. In the first chapter, we give an overview of tort liability and consider its aims and objectives, the interests it seeks to protect, and its role in modern society. In Chapters 2 to 6, we examine the tort of negligence. Negligence is the most commonly used tort and forms an essential part of any tort law course. It is therefore considered in some detail and is divided into a number of issues which tend to be studied separately. Chapter 6 examines the law relating to causation. This is dealt with in the context of negligence, although it is relevant to all torts. The second half of the book deals with negligence-related liability, strict liability and other torts. Chapter 7 explores tort liability arising in an employment relationship, whilst Chapter 8 examines tort liability arising from occupation of land. Chapter 9 considers two examples of strict liability statutes—the Consumer Protection Act 1987 and the Animals Act 1971—and their role within the law of tort. The book then deals with other torts, namely nuisance (and associated liability under the rule in *Rylands v Fletcher*), trespass and defamation. Our final two chapters deal with the important subjects of defences and remedies.

No understanding of the law is complete without an appreciation of possible reforms and changes. In particular, we note the recommendations of the Law Commission and the impact of the implementation of the Human Rights Act 1998 in 2000. As we noted in our first edition, the latter has brought enormous potential for change in English law by allowing litigants to bring a claim for breach of the European Convention on Human Rights in the English courts. Until October 2000, litigants were forced to bring their claims in the European Court of Human Rights in Strasbourg, but implementation of the 1998 Act brings the Convention "close to home". Notably in our chapters on negligence, but also inevitably in relation to other torts, we have highlighted the impact of the Act on the English law of tort, and the ways in which the law is likely to change. As will be seen, the protection given by the Convention to the rights to life (Article 2), not to suffer inhuman or degrading treatment (Article 3), liberty and security (Article 5), access to a court (Article 6), respect for private and family life (Article 8), and of freedom of expression (Article 10) have all had some impact on the current rules of tort law.

In writing this book, we have received considerable support from our colleagues and friends, to whom we express our thanks. We would particularly like to thank Susan and Keith for their help and encouragement, and Tracy Elliott, whose assistance was invaluable. We would also like to thank all at Sweet & Maxwell. In a book of this kind, inevitably work must be divided. Silas has therefore taken primary responsibility for chapters on negligence, whilst Paula has done so in respect of chapters on negligence-related liability, nuisance, trespass, defamation, defences and remedies. The book remains, however, a joint effort. Needless to say, any errors therein are ours alone. We have attempted to state the law as it stood on May 1, 2004, but have been able to incorporate some more recent developments at proof stage.

One final point of terminology: the Woolf reforms were implemented in the Civil Procedure Rules 1998 which came into force on April 26, 1999. The aim of the rules is to speed up and simplify civil litigation. Accordingly, in an effort to demystify the law, the term the "plaintiff" was replaced with the term "claimant". We therefore use the latter term when discussing principles of law and recent cases. The term "plaintiff", however, is used when discussing cases decided prior to the date of the change.

Paula Giliker
Silas Beckwith
London, May 2004

Table of Contents

2   Negligence: The Duty of Care

3 Negligence: Economic Loss

6 Causation and Remoteness

7 Employers' Liability

8 Occupiers' Liability

10   Nuisance and the Rule in *Rylands v Fletcher*

11 Trespass

15 Remedies

TABLE OF CASES

TABLE OF STATUTES

TABLE OF STATUTORY INSTRUMENTS

TABLE OF EC AND INTERNATIONAL LEGISLATION

Chapter 1

THE NATURE OF TORTIOUS LIABILITY

Liability in tort can be imposed for a diverse range of conduct, extending from **1–001** negligent behaviour to attacking a person's reputation or limiting a person's freedom of movement. This book aims to provide an understanding of the nature of tortious liability by explaining how and why a defendant can be liable in these and other situations. This chapter provides a starting point. Here, we shall examine what is meant by "tort", the aims and objectives of the current system of tort law, and the factors that seem to influence tortious liability. We shall also consider how tort law fits in with other forms of civil liability, namely contract and restitution. The second part of this chapter addresses some different questions: How well does tort law fulfil its role in English law? Are there any alternatives to tort law which could or should be adopted? By gaining a basic understanding of the scope and nature of tort, the reader will be better able to understand the law in following chapters.

What is tort?

Tort takes many forms. It includes, for example, negligence, nuisance, libel, slander, **1–002** trespass, assault and battery. It is therefore more accurate to speak of a "Law of Torts", rather than a "Law of Tort". To provide a definition which encompasses the whole of this area of law is impossible. Each tort has its own particular characteristics. Some torts, such as negligence, require proof of damage, whilst others, such as trespass and libel, are actionable without proof of damage. Whilst the tort of negligence obviously requires "negligent" behaviour, other torts, such as trespass, require intentional behaviour or at least recklessness. It is best, therefore, to confine ourselves to a statement that the law of tort is the law of *civil wrongs*[1] that is to say, it is concerned with behaviour which is legally classified as "wrong" or "tortious", so as to entitle the claimant to a remedy.

It must be conceded that this definition is somewhat circular, but it is the only one that will suffice. More precise definitions, such as that of the great tort lawyer Professor Winfield, have been widely criticised. Winfield defined tort as arising "from the breach of a duty primarily fixed by law; this duty is towards persons generally and

---

[1] The word "tort" is in fact Norman-French for "harm" or "wrong". It dates from the times when Norman-French was used within the English judicial system.

its breach is redressible by an action for unliquidated damages".[2] This definition has been criticised because it ignores the fact that some tortious duties arise by consent,[3] some are owed only to specific individuals,[4] and a breach of duty does not automatically make the defendant liable.

Whilst it may not be possible to provide a precise definition of "tort", it is certainly possible to identify a number of principles that determine when liability in tort will arise. It is to these that we now turn.

PRINCIPLES OF LIABILITY

1–003   Tort law determines who bears the loss which results from the defendant's actions. For example, driver A knocks down pedestrian B in the street. B suffers personal injury. Tort law will determine who bears the loss suffered by B. If A is not liable, B bears the loss. If A is liable, A (or rather his or her insurance company) will bear the loss. The aim of shifting loss does not tell us, however, what makes a court choose between A and B. A number of principles seem to underlie the decision whether or not to impose liability on A, and it is important to note that no one principle predominates. These principles may be broadly summarised as:

- compensation
- fault
- retributive justice (punishment)
- deterrence
- economic efficiency (market deterrence)
- loss distribution (spreading losses in a socially fair way)

We examine each principle below.

(1) Compensation

1–004   Perhaps the most obvious objective of tort law is to award compensation for loss. In doing so, the courts are guided by the principle known as *restitutio in integrum*. Lord Blackburn, in *Livingstone v Rawyards Coal Co.*,[5] explained the meaning of this principle when he said that compensation in tort should take the form of:

> "the sum of money which will put the party who has been injured, or who has suffered, in the same position as he would have been in if he had not sustained the wrong for which he is now getting his compensation or reparation."

---

[2] *The Province of the Law of Tort* (1931), p.32.
[3] *e.g.* if you invite someone into your home (see Occupiers' Liability, discussed in Ch. 8).
[4] *e.g.* duties owed to employees (see Employers' Liability, discussed in Ch. 7).
[5] (1880) 5 App. Cas. 25 at 39 *per* Lord Blackburn.

The goal of compensation, of course, is subject to practical constraints. For example, where the claimant has lost an arm, the best tort law can do is to provide a sum of money which represents that loss. Tort law has also recognised that liability must be subject to certain rules which limit the availability of compensation. Fears of indeterminate liability (the so-called "floodgates of litigation") and of disproportionate liability (or "crushing liability") have dictated that tort law must set limits to the types of loss it will compensate. Thus, for example, compensation for mental distress is rarely awarded, and a restrictive approach is adopted towards liability for "pure economic loss" and psychiatric illness. The idea of full compensation, therefore, translates into "compensation within reason".

Tort law has been supported in its compensatory goal by the growth of the insurance industry.[6] Statistically, most tort claims for personal injury arise from road traffic accidents or accidents in the workplace. In both cases it is compulsory for the defendant to insure against liability. The Road Traffic Act 1988 makes liability insurance compulsory for motorists[7] and its objectives are underpinned by the existence of the Motor Insurers Bureau, which administers schemes to compensate victims of uninsured drivers and hit-and-run incidents. Similarly, the Employers' Liability (Compulsory) Insurance Act 1969 provides that employers must be insured against accidents in the workplace. In these areas, then, legislation and the law of tort work in tandem. The legislation ensures that deserving claimants are guaranteed compensation (rather than being at the mercy of the defendant's resources), whilst the law of tort provides the mechanism through which they can obtain it.

Of course, compensating misfortune is not an objective peculiar to the law of tort. Tort operates in the context of a wider regime which includes statutory compensation schemes such as the Criminal Injuries Compensation Scheme and, ultimately, the cushion of social security payments. The law's efforts to reconcile the relationship between these different ways of providing compensation are examined in Ch. 15. What should be noted here, however, is that the existence of tort law means that society applies the principle of full compensation selectively. In the absence of a universal system of compensation for all accident injuries, successful tort claimants are likely to receive substantial compensation, whilst victims of naturally occurring accidents (unless they are privately insured) receive no compensation, except possibly low-level social security payments.

(2) Fault

Fault is the idea most commonly used to *justify* an award of compensation. Fault-based **1–005** liability embodies the idea of taking personal responsibility for one's own conduct and may serve as a deterrent. It also serves a retributive purpose—a claimant's anger at being the victim of a wrong is more likely to be placated if he or she receives compensation from the person who has been at fault, rather than from an alternative source. Both of these matters are considered in later sections.

Liability for fault has become particularly significant because of the growth of the tort of negligence. As we shall see in Ch. 2, liability for negligence was opposed by

[6] See Davies (1989) 9 L.S. 67.
[7] See ss.143 and 145.

most of the judges in the nineteenth century, because it ran contrary to the ideas of individualism and laissez-faire that dominated the political philosophy of the age. But this philosophy gradually changed, so that in 1932, Lord Atkin in *Donoghue v Stevenson*[8] was able to justify fault-based liability by saying that members of society ought to take reasonable care to avoid harming their "neighbours". The idea of fault nowadays pervades many areas of tort law, but it is not to be thought that all torts are fault-based. In libel, for example, a defendant who writes a defamatory article in a newspaper may be liable even if he or she has taken all due care in researching the article.

It should be noted that the context in which tort law operates in modern society means that, whilst the notion of "fault" is used to justify imposing liability, often, legal "fault" does not equate with moral blame. In relation to driving accidents, for example, the administrative advantages for the law in being able to settle claims easily have triumphed over moral considerations. Thus, as we shall see in Ch. 5, a driver can be held legally at "fault" for a mistake that by the standards of society is morally excusable. Moreover, in many areas of tort law, the widespread practice of insuring against liability means that, in reality, it is an insurer rather than a morally guilty defendant who foots the bill for compensation. The fault principle is similarly undermined by the doctrine of vicarious liability.[9] Vicarious liability renders one person responsible for the torts committed by another. The most common example is that of employer and employee. If an employee commits a tort in the course of employment, the claimant is perfectly entitled to sue the employer for damages in tort. In these circumstances, then, the burden of the wrong done may be shouldered by the innocent employer, rather than by the employee who is to blame. Insurance and vicarious liability subordinate the fault principle to the overriding need to compensate victims of accidents. In the light of this, fault can be only *one* possible explanation of how the tort system works.[10]

(3) Retributive justice

1–006   Vengeance or retribution is the most ancient justification for imposing liability on a defendant who has committed a wrong. It was to fulfil the objective of preventing "blood feuds" that the law developed an action for compensating harm, which eventually became the law of torts. In modern times, perhaps, this objective is less relevant. Even today, though, it should be recognised, for example, that a person is less likely to commit an act of "road rage" against a driver who has dented his or her bumper if a tort claim (settled by insurers) will pay for a new one.

Nowadays, the idea of retribution as an objective of tort sits very uneasily with the existence of the criminal law. It is the function of the criminal law to punish the wrong-doer and see that he gets his "just deserts". It is hard to justify importing the concept of punishment into civil proceedings for two reasons. First, in a civil trial, the

[8] [1932] A.C. 562 at 580. See also *Sedleigh-Denfield v O'Callaghan* [1940] A.C. 880 (expanding the tort of nuisance on the basis of fault).
[9] See Ch. 7.
[10] For a more detailed critique of the fault principle, see Cane, *Atiyah's Accidents, Compensation and the Law* (6th ed., 1999), Ch. 7.

punishment may be meted out in the absence of the evidential and procedural safeguards to which a defendant is entitled in criminal proceedings. Secondly, because tort law and criminal law operate concurrently, the defendant may receive "double punishment" for a single wrong. Nevertheless, in the modern law of tort there are certain circumstances where the courts may punish a defendant by an award of "punitive" damages. Such damages are justified on the basis of their deterrent effect. This is discussed below.

(4) Deterrence

In its basic form, the concept of tort liability acting as a deterrent is a simple one: if I **1–007** cause harm through my actions or inaction and have to pay compensation, I will try to behave differently next time. We can see the deterrence principle at work in various contexts. Publishers, for example, aware of the high cost of compensation if they publish defamatory material, often employ lawyers to screen publications so as to avoid liability. Equally, professionals such as doctors and lawyers may be encouraged to take care in their work because they fear the consequences of liability—not just in terms of financial cost, but in terms of the harm litigation may cause to their professional reputations.

The objective of deterrence is supported by the courts' power to award "exemplary" or "punitive" damages in tort.[11] These are damages which seek not to compensate the claimant, but to punish a defendant for acting deliberately with a view to profiting from his or her tort, or to punish the executive arm of government for acting in an arbitrary, oppressive or unconstitutional manner.[12] Their goal is to show that tort does not pay and thereby deter the defendant from contemplating such conduct in future.[13] A good example is the American case of *Grimshaw v Ford Motor Co.*[14] concerning the Ford Pinto. Here, Ford was alleged to have discovered a defect in the car which rendered it susceptible to explosion when struck from the rear. Nevertheless, it continued to market the car on the basis that it would be cheaper to pay compensation to victims of the defect than to redesign the car. Such cynical disregard for human safety led a jury[15] to award exemplary damages of $125 million, reduced to $3.5 million on appeal.

In the tort of negligence, however, deterrence theory has limited application. This is because, in a case where A has injured B by simple *inadvertence* (which the law may call "negligence"), it is difficult to see how making A liable can alter the behaviour of a person in A's position. A is liable because he or she has failed to meet the standard of behaviour expected of the "reasonable person". As we shall see in Ch. 5, this is an *objective* standard—which means that in applying it the court takes little account of the personal characteristics of the defendant. What this means is that a defendant can be held liable even though he or she is already taking all the care which he or she could possibly take in pursuing a particular activity. The point is well illustrated by the

---

[11] Discussed more fully in Ch. 15.
[12] See *Rookes v Barnard* [1964] A.C. 1129.
[13] [1964] A.C. 1129 at 1228 *per* Lord Devlin.
[14] 119 Cal. App. 3d 757 (1981).
[15] Juries are still used in tort cases in the US, but are rarely used in English courts, save for torts such as defamation, fraud and false imprisonment: see Supreme Court Act 1981, s.69.

decision of the Court of Appeal in *Nettleship v Weston*[16] (discussed further in Ch. 5). Here, a learner driver on her third lesson was held liable in negligence for driving below the standard of the "reasonable driver"—which was set at the standard of an ordinary, competent, qualified driver. No concession was made to the fact that she was a learner (or even that she was being sued by her instructor—arguably the very person whose skill was supposed to prevent the accident!).

There are further objections to regarding deterrence as an important aim of tort law—a deterrent can only work if the people whose actions or inaction cause damage are the same people who have to pay for that damage. We have seen that the doctrine of vicarious liability means that the employer pays for the damage, rather than the negligent employee. In such circumstances, it cannot be said that the prospect of having to pay compensation has an effect on the amount of care taken by the employee in his or her work. Similarly, the existence of liability insurance removes the sting of arguments based on deterrence. When a motorist gets in a car, it is rather far-fetched to say that his or her mind is concentrated by the prospect of civil liability for careless driving, because that is a prospect against which he or she is insured. To the careless motorist, the cost of a car crash is likely to be no more than the loss of a "no-claims bonus", entailing a small increase in premiums (against which, nowadays, it is even possible to insure). In the context of employers' liability to their employees, whilst it is true that the threat of liability may provide an incentive for employers to adopt safer working practices, in a commercial world, these will only be adopted where they are cost effective. Moreover, because of the way the insurance industry works—spreading the cost of accidents amongst all policyholders—the full force of the incentive is seldom brought to bear on employers.

All of the problems with deterrence theory we have examined, then, are really part of the same problem: the objective of deterrence is accorded less importance in tort law than the objective of compensation. This is so for two reasons. First, by social consensus, vicarious liability and insurance make compensation available at the expense of deterrence. Secondly, there are limits to the extent to which deterrence arguments can be considered in the context of a tort trial. If a court seeks to deter a whole class of potential defendants from wrongful conduct by imposing liability on the particular defendant in the case (or by awarding punitive damages), then the result of the case may be unjust—the particular defendant is singled out to pay the price for wrongful conduct that may be the common practice of his or her peers, and (in the case of punitive damages) the particular claimant receives a windfall in addition to compensation.[17] Similarly, effective deterrence requires that potential defendants be given guidance about how to avoid liability. Whilst the courts occasionally provide such guidance, constraints of time and resources prevent them from going into details. Moreover, because the guidance is given in the context of a particular case, it may be difficult to interpret in terms of general application. In the light of these factors, such guidance is better provided by statute (for example, health and safety legislation) than by ad hoc decisions in tort.

---

[16] [1971] 2 Q.B. 691.
[17] But note that the Law Commission in its report No. 247 "Aggravated, Exemplary and Restitutionary Damages" (1997) recommended a more generous approach to punitive damages, which will be discussed in Ch. 15.

(5) Economic efficiency (market deterrence)

If, through the operation of law, a manufacturer of products (for example) is forced to **1–008** bear the cost of harm caused by those products, and to pass that cost on to consumers, he or she will seek to maximise the safety of the products in order to obtain the best price in the marketplace. Logically, therefore, as a result of this process the safest products will become the cheapest, and market competition should operate to reduce the *total amount* of harm caused in society by all products on the market. This idea is known as the principle of "market deterrence".

Once we start to explore such arguments, we venture into the difficult realm of economic analysis of law. To use the language of economists, every product (or activity) has the potential to produce "externalities" ("extra costs" not reflected in the price) when either it causes harm, or necessitates precautions to prevent harm from arising. Economic analysis of law seeks to discover how these "externalities" are paid for. Economists argue that the framework of any legal system should be such as to ensure that externalities are paid for in a way that maximises "efficiency". In economic language, the most "efficient" way of doing things is the way that produces the least cost to society as a whole. What all this means for the law of tort is that the courts should seek to develop rules under which the risk of harm in any given situation is borne by the person who will expend the least amount of society's resources in taking precautions against it. This person is sometimes known as the "best cost-avoider".

We can see that this principle already operates in the law to some extent by considering a simple example. Suppose that a number of televisions are sold with wrongly wired mains plugs, presenting risks of fire and electric shock. It is likely that tort law will make the manufacturer of the televisions liable if these risks materialise. Whilst this result will accord with the principles of compensation and fault, it will also fulfil the objective of efficiency. This is because, whilst it will be relatively inexpensive for the manufacturer to change his or her production methods so that the wires are put in the plug the right way round, it would be relatively expensive (in terms of missed opportunities to create wealth) if all of the individuals affected by the problem had to rewire a plug themselves.

Whilst it is clear that tort law can be analysed in terms of economics, economic concepts are seldom referred to by English judges.[18] This might be explained by the fact that the "economics and law" debate is largely an American one,[19] and reflects the political trends of that country, namely right of centre market economics. It is sometimes also suggested that much of the academic commentary on the subject may be rather impenetrable to non-economist judges—yet it should be remembered that the current House of Lords comprises a large number of commercial judges who are undoubtedly familiar with economic concepts. Perhaps the true explanation for the lack of judicial enthusiasm in this area is that economic analysis of tort law cannot in many cases be reconciled with more pressing objectives of the tort system. Economic analysis takes as its starting point the assumption that in most, if not all cases, the potential human cost of the defendant's actions can be given a monetary value. Whilst,

[18] But see, *e.g.* the analysis of Lord Hoffmann in *Stovin v Wise* [1996] 1 A.C. 923 at 944 in the context of liability for omissions.
[19] Most of the relevant academic commentary is American. See, *e.g.*, R. Posner, *Economic Analysis of Law*, (4th ed., 1992).

arguably, this is just a cold fact of life, it is one which society and the judiciary are understandably reluctant to face. Society may not be prepared to quantify in monetary terms the cost of a young child being hideously disfigured, so as to weigh it against the purely financial cost of preventing such an occurrence. Equally, whilst an economic perspective can be instructive in explaining decisions in negligence and nuisance[20] cases, it is less helpful in explaining torts like trespass and defamation, whose primary aim is to protect the integrity of the individual.

(6) Loss distribution

1–009   As stated earlier, tort law shifts loss from the victim to the tortfeasor by imposing liability. In a broader context, however, it can be seen that tort law operates to shift losses so that they are borne by the whole (or large sections) of society. This function of tort law is known as "loss spreading" or simply "loss distribution". It is fulfilled mainly through vicarious liability—part of tort law itself—and through liability insurance—part of the context in which it operates.

Vicarious liability makes employers liable for accidents caused by their employees, but employers cover themselves by insurance and pass the cost of the premiums on to consumers in the prices of their goods and services. In this way, the cost of compensating accident victims is spread throughout the community, in much the same way that social security payments, funded by taxation, spread the cost of compensating social need. Similarly, because the legislature has imposed compulsory liability insurance for road traffic accidents, the cost of accidents will be met first by insurance companies, who will then pass on this cost in the form of premiums paid by their clients. The cost of accidents is thereby spread amongst the (insured) driving community.

Clearly, "loss distribution" can be criticised for a number of reasons. It can be criticised for ignoring the importance of fault and undermining the objective of deterrence. It can also be criticised as unjust: why should a careful driver or employer subsidise the cost of accidents caused by the tortious activities of others? It can only be justified by acceptance of its underlying rationale—that a certain amount of "distributive justice" is desirable in a civilised society.[21]

Conclusions

1–010   Tort law is an amalgam of all six of the concepts considered above. Its mixed aims are the inevitable result of the common law system of justice where law is developed on a case-by-case basis. Although compensation is the most common reason for bringing a tort action, claimants may have a number of other reasons, including deterrence and retribution. In *Hill v Chief Constable of West Yorkshire*,[22] for example,

[20] The role of economic deterrence in the tort of nuisance is discussed in the influential article of A. Ogus and G. Richardson [1977] C.L.J. 284.
[21] The concept of "distributive justice" is referred to in a number of negligence cases, most notably *McFarlane v Tayside Health Board* [2000] 2 A.C. 59 (discussed in Ch. 2) and *White v Chief Constable of South Yorkshire* [1999] 2 A.C. 455 (discussed in Ch. 4).
[22] [1989] A.C. 53.

the mother of the last victim of Peter Sutcliffe (a serial killer known as the "Yorkshire Ripper") sued the police for negligence, mainly in order to criticise their carelessness in failing to apprehend the murderer soon enough, and to make the point that police practices should be improved. In Lord Templeman's view, the action was misconceived. His Lordship pointed out that "an action for damages for alleged acts of negligence by individual police officers in 1980 could not determine whether and in what respects the West Yorkshire police force can be improved in 1988". Lord Templeman's remarks emphasise that an adversarial system is ill-suited to a proper consideration of broad questions of social and economic policy. The focus of the courts' attention is whether compensation should be awarded to do justice in the particular cases before them. This does not prevent courts using their skill and experience to address broader concerns, but it is important to recognise that there are constraints on their ability to do so.

THE INTERESTS PROTECTED BY TORT

Tort law aims to protect the individual from actual or threatened harm to certain specific interests. In this section, we examine the degree of protection afforded to each interest. Tort law does not protect *all* interests from harm, and certain interests, such as personal safety, receive better protection than others. As tort law has developed, the nature of protection offered to each interest has reflected the importance of that interest to society at the relevant period in history. Thus, whilst in feudal times trespass to land was the most sophisticated and important tort, in the modern industrial age protection against personal injury has dominated the agenda.

1–011

(1) Personal harm

The industrial revolution brought with it new threats to the safety of individuals with the introduction of heavy machinery, motor vehicles and railways. Tort law responded by developing the tort of negligence. This supplemented the existing protection provided by trespass to the person, where the torts of assault, battery and false imprisonment serve to protect individuals from intentional interference with their personal freedom and bodily integrity.[23] Yet, whilst tort law has clearly offered protection against physical injury, the judiciary has been reluctant to offer protection against other forms of personal harm, such as psychiatric illness and distress. Considerable scepticism was expressed in the nineteenth century towards claims for "nervous shock", on the basis that they would leave "a wide field open for imaginary claims".[24] Although claims for psychiatric illness may now be brought, the law still adopts a restrictive regime of recovery, as will be seen in Ch. 4. Claims for mental distress still cannot be brought in their own right,[25] although this is a developing area of the law. The problem of harassment has become more significant in recent times

1–012

---

[23] See Ch. 11.
[24] See *Victorian Railway Commissioners v Coultas* (1888) 13 App. Cas. 222 at 226.
[25] On claims for mental distress in tort generally, see Giliker (2000) 20 L.S. 19.

and developments in tort law have now been replaced by a statutory tort under the Protection from Harassment Act 1997. We shall see in Ch. 2 that the Human Rights Act 1998, which safeguards fundamental rights (such as the right of access to a court, and the right to respect for family life) has recently had an effect on the scope of the tort of negligence.

(2) Harm to property

1–013   Protection against harm to property remains important, but no longer has the primacy accorded to it during feudal times. "Property" here is used to signify both personal property and land (real property). Personal property is protected by the torts of trespass to goods and conversion (civil theft). Real property is protected by a number of torts, including trespass to land, nuisance, and the rule in *Rylands v Fletcher*, which are discussed in Chs 10 and 11. Property loss is also recoverable in other torts such as negligence.

(3) Harm to reputation

1–014   Reputation is protected by the tort of defamation, which creates liability for untrue statements which diminish the claimant's reputation in the eyes of right-thinking members of society. Defamation is examined in Chs 12 and 13 of this book. It should be noted that defamation protects the claimant's *reputation* and not his or her *feelings*, so that there will be no action for defamation if the claimant is insulted in private or if the statement fails to diminish his or her reputation. As will be discussed, protection of reputation must be weighed against the public interest in free speech and a free press. In practice, this balance is far from easy to achieve.

(4) Harm to financial interests

1–015   Tort law gives limited protection to financial interests. Such interests are usually protected outside tort law, for example by contract law or by legislation such as the Competition Act 1998 and the Enterprise Act 2002. In this area, tort law is particularly conscious of the potential number of claims and the threat of "liability in an indeterminate amount for an indeterminate time to an indeterminate class".[26] Whereas the cost of compensating physical injury tends to be limited, the potential for "crushing liability", resulting from a flood of claims for financial loss, presents a problem for the law. Courts are therefore reluctant to impose liability for *negligent* infliction of financial loss, save in the specific situations where the defendant has voluntarily assumed responsibility for the claimant's interests, or where the loss is consequential on physical damage.[27]

However, tort law does offer some protection where the defendant has *intentionally* interfered with the claimant's economic and trading interests. The tort of deceit

---

[26] See Cardozo C.J. in *Ultramares Corp.Touche* 255 N.Y. Rep. 170 at 179 (1931); 174 N.E. Rep. 441 at 444 (1931).
[27] See Ch. 3.

(fraud) imposes liability where the defendant has made a false statement[28] to the claimant in the knowledge that it is false, or reckless as to its truth, with the intention that the claimant will act on it.[29] The claimant may recover damages for economic loss suffered by acting on the statement.[30] Likewise, there are torts (sometimes called "economic torts") which impose liability for interference with business interests.[31] These include the torts of intentional interference with contractual relations,[32] conspiracy to injure[33] or use unlawful means intentionally to injure another,[34] intimidation,[35] and passing off one's goods as those of the claimant.[36] All these torts, which arguably form a common tort of unlawful interference with the trade or business of another,[37] are founded on intentional conduct which causes economic loss to the claimant.

The limited protection given to economic and trading interests by these torts can only be appreciated properly by considering them in their wider context. Torts such as intentional interference with contractual relations, conspiracy and intimidation largely arise in the context of labour disputes and are therefore best understood as part of labour law. Equally, the protection given by the law to intellectual property rights is usually taught as a subject in its own right. For these reasons, these torts are not explored in this book. Readers are advised to consult textbooks on labour law, intellectual property law and competition law.

(5) Harm to the due process of law

This will be dealt with briefly. Certain torts seek to protect the claimant against misuse of the legal system. In this book, we refer specifically to one such tort: malicious prosecution.[38] In a system where the criminal law permits individuals to instigate prosecutions, this tort affords the claimant valuable protection against prosecutions which are brought maliciously without reasonable and probable cause. In the leading case of *Martin v Watson*[39] the tort was used to protect the plaintiff where the defendant had maliciously made a groundless accusation of indecent exposure against the plaintiff, leading to his prosecution. Although it is a difficult tort to prove, it demonstrates the willingness of the English legal system to intervene to prevent abuse of the law.

1–016

---

[28] Which must be of an existing fact: *Edgington v Fitzmaurice* (1885) 29 Ch. D. 459.

[29] See *Derry v Peek* (1889) 14 App. Cas. 337.

[30] The claimant can recover for all the losses directly flowing from the fraudulent misstatement: *Doyle v Olby (Ironmongers) Ltd* [1969] 2 Q.B. 158. Deceit or fraud generally appears in the context of contract law and reference should be made to works on contract law.

[31] See H. Carty, *An Analysis of the Economic Torts* (2001, OUP) and T. Weir, *Economic Torts* (1997, Clarendon Press).

[32] See *Allen v Flood* [1898] A.C. 1.

[33] See *Crofter Hand Woven Harris Tweed Co. v Veitch* [1942] A.C. 435.

[34] Unlike conspiracy to injure where the predominant purpose must be to injure the claimant, where the conspirators use unlawful means it is sufficient that the parties intended to hurt the claimant by directing or aiming their pressure at him or her: *Lonrho v Fayed* [1992] 1 A.C. 448.

[35] See *Rookes v Barnard* [1964] A.C. 1129.

[36] See *Warnink v Townend* [1979] A.C 731.

[37] See Lord Diplock in *Merkur Island Shipping Corp. v Laughton* [1983] 2 A.C. 570 at 608 and Carty (1988) 104 L.Q.R. 250.

[38] See Ch. 11.

[39] [1996] 1 A.C. 74.

THE ROLE OF TORT IN THE LAW OF OBLIGATIONS

1–017   In this section, we compare the role of tort with two other aspects of civil law, namely the law of contract and the law of restitution (or unjust enrichment). Together with tort, these heads of liability are sometimes referred to as the "Law of Obligations". In English law, the same defendant may be liable under more than one of these heads of liability. This is known as "concurrent liability". A claimant is not obliged to choose between bringing an action in contract, tort or restitution[40] and may plead all three. Nevertheless, the three causes of action perform different roles in English law, which are examined below.

The distinction between tort and contract

1–018   The role of contract law is, put simply, the enforcement of promises.[41] Liability is therefore centred around the contract itself: Has it been formed? What are its terms? Have they been breached? Contractual remedies seek to place the claimant in the position, so far as money can do it, that he or she would have been in had the contract been performed.[42] By contrast, tort is concerned with compensating the victim who has suffered injury as a result of conduct classified as a civil wrong by law. The aim here is not to enforce a bargain, but to compensate the victim for his or her out-of-pocket expenses, thereby placing the victim in the same position as he or she would have been in had the victim not sustained the wrong for which compensation is being awarded.[43]

     Readers should be wary of attempts to distinguish contract and tort on the basis that contract consists of obligations imposed by consent and tort consists of obligations imposed by law. Contract law is subject to considerable legislative and judicial intervention and terms may be imposed by statute[44] or by the courts. Equally, the defendant in tort law may, in a sense, agree to undertake certain tortious responsibilities, for example by inviting a guest into his or her household[45] or by undertaking to advise the claimant on the merits of a particular business transaction.[46] Such a theory, therefore, is really too general to be of much use. In practice, the distinction between contract and tort is determined simply by asking the question: "Have the rules of contract law been complied with?" If the answer is "no", the obligation or wrong in question cannot be classified as contractual, but may be classified as tortious.

The distinction between tort and restitution

1–019   Restitution is a growing area of civil liability, the proper scope of which remains unclear. The law of restitution intervenes where the defendant has been unjustly enriched at the expense of the claimant. Rather than compensating the claimant, it

---

[40] See *Henderson v Merrett Syndicates Ltd* [1995] 2 A.C. 145, overturning the doubts experienced following Lord Scarman's equivocal judgment in *Tai Hing Cotton Mill Ltd v Liu Chong Hing Bank Ltd* [1986] A.C. 80 at 107. This is not the case in all jurisdictions. The position is different, *e.g.* in France.
[41] Although it has been argued that its real role is in the protection of detrimental reliance: see, *e.g.*, Atiyah (1978) 94 L.Q.R 193 and in P.S. Atiyah, *Essays on Contract* (1990, Clarendon Press).
[42] *Robinson v Harman* (1848) 1 Exch. 850 at 855 *per* Parke B.
[43] Lord Blackburn in *Livingstone v Rawyards Coal Co.* (1880) 5 App. Cas. 25 at 39.
[44] *e.g.* under the Sale of Goods Act 1979.
[45] See Ch. 8.
[46] See Ch. 3.

seeks to restore to the claimant the amount by which the defendant has been wrongfully enriched. Whilst its goal is therefore distinct from that of tort, it is clear that restitutionary damages may be awarded as an alternative to tort in certain limited circumstances. These are discussed in Ch. 14.[47]

THE IMPACT OF EUROPEAN AND HUMAN RIGHTS LAW

In examining the English law of torts, it is important to recognise the impact of European law and policy. Sometimes this impact is direct. For example, in Ch. 9, we examine liability for defective products, which is now largely dealt with under the Consumer Protection Act 1987. This was introduced to comply with Directive 85/374 on liability for defective products. In other cases, the impact is indirect—there is a body of case law which states that certain breaches of European Community law may be actionable in the national courts of Member States. Where a provision of community law (contained either in a treaty or in secondary legislation) has direct effect, giving claimants a remedy in national law,[48] actions by such claimants have been recognised as falling within the tort of breach of statutory duty.[49] This area — sometimes referred to as the law of "Eurotorts"—is likely to become increasingly significant.[50] **1–020**

The European Convention on Human Rights, incorporated into English law by the Human Rights Act 1998, has also had some impact on the development of tort law[51] and has broadened the circumstances in which claimants are entitled to sue in the tort of negligence. Litigants are no longer required to pursue their case before the European Court of Human Rights in Strasbourg. They are able to raise breaches of the Convention in the English courts. Section 6 of the Act provides that public bodies, including courts[52] must not act in a way which is incompatible with a Convention right. This means that courts must take account of the rights established in the Convention and by the case law of the Strasbourg court. If they do not, proceedings may be brought in English law for damages.[53] Where legislation is concerned, s.3(1) of the Act provides: "So far as it is possible to do so, primary legislation and subordinate legislation must be read and given effect in a way which is compatible with the Convention rights". However, the Act does not affect the validity of any incompatible primary legislation,[54] although a court may make a declaration of incompatibility.[55]

---

[47] For a more detailed discussion, see Jackman [1989] C.L.J. 302; Birks, "Civil wrongs: a new world", Butterworths Lectures 1990–1 (1992) and leading texts on the law of restitution.
[48] The concept of direct effect has been developed by the European Court of Justice from the case of *Van Gend en Loos v Nederlandse Administratie der Belastingen* [1963] C.M.L.R. 105.
[49] *Garden Cottage Foods Ltd v Milk Marketing Board* [1984] A.C. 130, HL: breach of Art. 86, Treaty of Rome (now Art. 82).
[50] Consider, *e.g. Francovich v Italian Republic* [1993] 2 C.M.L.R. 66 and, more recently, *Brasserie du Pecheur v Germany; R.Secretary of State for Transport, ex p. Factortame (No. 4)* [1996] 1 C.M.L.R. 889. See Downes (1997) 17 L.S. 286 and Craig (1997) 113 L.Q.R. 67.
[51] See, *e.g. Osman v United Kingdom* (1998) 5 B.H.R.C. 293 and *Z v United Kingdom* (2002) 34 E.H.R.R. 3, discussed in Ch. 2.
[52] See *Aston Cantlow v Wallbank* [2004] 1 A.C. 546, H.L., discussed by F. Meisel [2004] P.L. 2.
[53] See ss.7 and 8.
[54] S.3(2). It also does not affect the validity, continuing operation or enforcement of any incompatible subordinate legislation if (disregarding any possibility of revocation) primary legislation prevents removal of the incompatibility.
[55] S.4(2).

The question for us to consider in this book, of course, is the impact of the Human Rights Act 1998 on the law of torts. We shall see in Ch. 2 how Art. 6 (right to a fair trial) has affected the courts' practice of "striking out" cases where the claimant has no real prospect of success, and how the decisions in these cases may have had a lasting effect on the substance of negligence liability. We shall also see how Art. 3 (right not to be subject to inhuman or degrading treatment) has given child abuse victims an action against local authorities in respect of their child welfare functions. Art. 6 (right to a fair trial) is likely to affect all civil cases, and Arts 2 (right to life) and 5 (right to liberty and security) will be especially relevant to actions for trespass to the person. We also discuss the potential effect of the 1998 Act on other torts, for example nuisance (in Ch. 10) and in Ch. 13 we specifically consider the effect Art. 10 (the right to freedom of expression) on the tort of defamation.

TORT IN MODERN SOCIETY

1–021   Detailed study of tort law sometimes tends to obscure the fact that, especially in personal injury cases, there are often other means by which a claimant may be compensated for his or her loss. It is appropriate, therefore, to say something about tort law in its wider social context, to give the reader a clearer view of where it fits in modern society. In this section, we explore the role of tort in providing compensation and consider proposals for its reform, focusing particularly on the New Zealand experience of replacing tort with a no-fault system of accident compensation.

Tort and other compensation systems

1–022   It is important to realise that in practice tort law plays a minor role in compensating accident victims. The Pearson Commission,[56] which undertook a survey of accident compensation in England and Wales in the 1970s, reported that only 6.5 per cent of accident victims received any form of tort damages.[57] This means that the bulk of compensation comes from sources outside the tort system. These include payments from employers, from insurance, from schemes such as the Criminal Injuries Compensation Scheme, and social security payments. Whilst the level of such payments is usually well below that of tort damages, which are unique in seeking to provide full compensation for the victim, in practice they provide financial assistance for the majority of accident victims. This assistance is supplemented by the provision of publicly funded health care under the National Health Service. As we shall see in Ch. 15, there are sometimes problems involving "double-counting" where a claimant has received tort damages and also benefits from insurance, or perhaps a charitable donation. The courts (with the help of legislation) have evolved a number of complicated rules which govern the relationship between different sources of compensation.

The importance of these alternative sources of compensation varies. Social security payments are obviously significant, particularly for those on low incomes. However, the

---

[56] Royal Commission on Civil Liability and Compensation for Personal Injury (Cmnd 7054).
[57] *ibid.*, Vol. 1, Table 5(i).

amounts are relatively small. As at June 2003, income support for a single person over 25 was set at £54.65 per week with housing benefit also set at £54.65 per week.[58] Insurance is also important, particularly in respect of property damage, where tort actions are rarely brought.[59] Health insurance, critical or terminal illness cover, and unemployment insurance are also significant, as are payments from the accident victim's employer, such as occupational sick pay and pensions. The Criminal Injuries Compensation Scheme makes provision for victims of crimes of violence and those sustaining injuries in the course of apprehending an offender, although a tariff system is adopted and compensation in respect of a single injury is capped at £500,000.[60] Criminal courts also have the power to make compensation orders when sentencing in a criminal court,[61] but the amounts awarded tend to be nominal and the awards have limited impact if the convicted defendant does not have the means to pay.

Why not tort?

Given that tort compensation tends to be paid at a higher level than the other forms of   **1–023** compensation, why is it that the majority of claimants do not bring an action in tort? One reason is that, in many circumstances, the rules of tort are well established. This means that whilst a tort *claim* may be made (perhaps on a very informal basis) and quickly settled, it is unnecessary to bring a tort *action*. The Pearson Commission found that 86 per cent of tort claims were disposed of without the issue of writ or summons, and that, of the total number of claims made (including those where no legal proceedings were commenced) only 1 per cent actually reached the courts. There are, however, a number of additional reasons why tort litigation is seldom used.

Cost

Litigation is extremely expensive. A claimant must be able to fund litigation and take   **1–024** the risk that if he or she loses, the court is likely to order the claimant to pay not only his or her own costs, but also those of the defendant. The burden of cost has to some extent been alleviated by the introduction of conditional fees. Under this system, a solicitor agrees to take on a client's case on the basis that no fee will be charged if the client loses[62] , but a larger fee will be charged if the client succeeds in his or her action. This is not, however, a universal panacea: a solicitor is only likely to take on cases with reasonable prospects of success, and may be reluctant to take on complicated and time-consuming cases.

Time

Litigation moves very slowly (which of course adds to its cost). Despite the attempts of   **1–025** the Woolf reforms to speed up litigation[63] and despite time limits (set under the Limitation Act 1980) within which actions must be brought, it remains the fact that

---

[58] See *www.dss.gov.uk/hq/pubs/benefits/rates.htm.*
[59] See Cane, *Atiyah's Accidents, Compensation and the Law*, (6th ed., 1999), p.423.
[60] See Criminal Injuries Compensation Act 1995. See generally Cane, *op. cit.*, Ch. 12.
[61] Powers of Criminal Courts (Sentencing) Act 2000.
[62] Subject to charges for disbursements and insurance premiums. See Access to Justice Act 1999 and the Conditional Fee Agreements Regulations 2000 (SI 2000/692) as amended by Conditional Fee Agreements (Miscellaneous Amendments) Regulations 2003 (SI 2003/1240).
[63] See the final report of Lord Woolf, *Access to Justice* (1996).

many cases take years to get to court, during which the claimant will generally have to wait to receive any compensation.

Risk

1–026   The adversarial system makes litigation a risky option. Indeed, the risk of litigation is often used by defendants to force the claimant to settle, rather than face the possibility of losing everything in a court of law.

Difficulty

1–027   Despite the intervention of Lord Woolf, going to law is often a complicated process. The workings of the law seem impenetrable to many lay people. Few would attempt a claim in tort without the assistance of qualified lawyers, and getting this assistance may be expensive, time-consuming and often alienating to an individual who simply wishes to be compensated for his or her injury.

Absence of litigation consciousness

1–028   Traditionally, there has been a lack of litigation awareness in this country. Accident victims have been far more likely to contact their insurers, or blame bad luck, than seek a possible defendant on whom to transfer their loss.[64] This, however, seems to have changed in recent years with the introduction of conditional fees. Few can have missed the aggressive advertising of numerous firms offering to take on personal injury claims. Such advertising has raised litigation awareness, but its effect must, of course, be balanced against the other problems with litigation which we have considered. Datamonitor, an organisation which tracks personal injury litigation, has found a static level of personal injury claims in recent years, running at around 688,000 a year, although in 2002–3 it records that public liability claims did increase by 8.7 per cent.[65] It is important, therefore, not to exaggerate the impact of "litigation culture". Nevertheless, as we shall see in Chs 2 and 8, the House of Lords has on a number of occasions expressed concern that the *fear* of litigation might induce public authorities to act in an over-defensive manner, for example, by closing down a popular public beach to avoid any risk of drowning.[66] The courts have also been concerned that a culture of litigation should not encourage individuals to rely on tort law to avoid responsibility for their own actions.[67]

Proposals for reform

1–029   It is clear that tort law is far from perfect. A number of suggestions for reform have been made, which we consider below. These suggestions are not without problems and all require the legislature to take tough political decisions about the aims of any reformed compensation system. On current thinking, the possibilities for reform are threefold:

[64] A survey conducted by researchers at the Centre for Socio-Legal Studies in Oxford in 1976 found that only 14% of personal injury victims consulted a lawyer: *Harris et al.*, Compensation and Support for Illness and Injury (1984).
[65] *UK Personal Injury Litigation* (Datamonitor, 2003). See also the report of the government's Better Regulation Task Force (May 2004): *www.brtf.gov.uk*
[66] *Tomlinson v Congleton BC* [2004] 1 A.C. 46, discussed in Ch. 8.
[67] See, for example, the recent case of *Gorringe v Calderdale MBC* [2004] 1 W.L.R. 1057.

(1) A mixed system

The Pearson Commission made a number of recommendations about reforming the   **1–030**
system of compensation in England and Wales.[68] Its main proposal was that a mixed
system of tort law and social security should be retained, but with greater emphasis on
the role of social security payments.[69] Greater attention would also be paid to how tort
and social security worked together. For certain accidents, such as road traffic
accidents[70] (which represent a large proportion of total accident claims) special
provision would be made. The Commission proposed a no-fault system for road traffic
accidents funded by a 1p tariff per gallon of petrol.[71] This would spread the cost of
such accidents, whilst placing the greatest burden on those who consume the most
petrol. This was justified on the basis that drivers who use the most petrol—either by
driving long distances or by driving vehicles with high petrol consumption—are those
most likely to cause an accident.

The proposals were criticised for singling out road traffic accident victims and giving
them preferential treatment over victims of other types of accident.[72] They can also be
criticised, of course, for ignoring the functions of tort law in terms of deterrence and
retribution (although the Commission felt that these ends could be adequately served
if tort law were retained concurrently with a no-fault scheme). Delivered in 1978,
immediately prior to the election of the new Thatcher Conservative government, a
plan of reform based on increasing state involvement in individual welfare stood little
chance of success. In the event, of the Commission's 188 recommendations, only a
handful have been implemented.[73] It is most unlikely that this situation will change
under the present Labour government.

(2) No-fault liability

This is a more radical proposal. It is based on the proposition that if tort law primarily   **1–031**
aims to compensate victims, it achieves this in an inefficient and often arbitrary way.
Tort law is inefficient because of the sheer costs of administering the system. The
Pearson Commission reported that the operating costs of the tort system amounted to
a figure representing about 85 per cent of the money paid out in compensation. In
other words, for every £100 paid out, it costs about £85 (in insurers' handling fees,
lawyers' fees, etc.) just to make the payment. Clearly this can be seen as a waste of
society's resources. The costs of running a no-fault scheme may be much lower.

Tort is arbitrary in the sense that only those victims who can point to a tortfeasor
can recover full compensation. All other accident victims must fall back on other forms
of compensation which are likely to be paid at a lower level. By contrast, no-fault
liability seeks to compensate all accident victims on the basis of need.

---

[68] See J. Fleming (1979) 42 M.L.R. 249.
[69] Vol. 1, para.275, on the basis that social security payments were quick, certain and inexpensive to
administer and already covered the majority of accident victims.
[70] Specific proposals were also suggested for airline and vaccination accidents, defective products and
extraordinary risks.
[71] Vol. 1, Ch. 18.
[72] See, *e.g.* Ogus, Corfield and Harris (1978) 7 I.L.J. 143.
[73] *e.g.* special treatment for vaccine-damaged children was implemented in the Vaccine Damage Payments
Act 1979, which provides for a tax-free lump-sum payment of £100,000 where serious mental or physical
damage has been caused by the administration of specified vaccines.

Although the Pearson Commission felt that the adoption of a comprehensive no-fault scheme to the exclusion of tort was beyond their terms of reference,[74] a different view was taken by the Woodhouse Commission in New Zealand, which in 1967 recommended that such a scheme should be adopted in that country.[75] A comprehensive system of state-run compensation for all "accidents" causing personal injury and death was brought in by the New Zealand Labour government in 1974 and tort actions for personal injury were abolished. The term "accident" has been extended to cover medical misadventure and intentional acts such as battery and rape. With its five aims of community responsibility, comprehensive entitlement, real compensation, complete rehabilitation and administrative efficiency, the system provides a dramatic contrast to our own system of tort law. The scheme is funded by citizens paying premiums into relevant funds. Accordingly, employers and the self-employed pay to cover work-related injuries, and drivers to cover road traffic accidents.[76] Accidents which occur outside of these contexts are funded by general taxation.

The New Zealand scheme has run for 30 years, and the New Zealand experience is useful in evaluating our own system.[77] A number of conclusions can be drawn. First, a comprehensive system which seeks to replace tort law damages in every respect is inevitably expensive.[78] The escalating cost of the New Zealand scheme led to the passing of legislation to curtail the scheme and reduce the level of benefits available to accident victims. Generally speaking, the scheme now compensates only lost earnings, although additional lump-sum payments for victims with permanent disability have been recently re-introduced, in response to criticism from claimants that the scheme was unfair by comparison to a tort action. Compensation for non-financial loss (such as pain and suffering), however, is not available. The scheme is administered by the Accident Compensation Corporation, whose tasks now include the promotion of accident-prevention measures (such as speed limits) and the promotion of rehabilitation of accident victims.

Secondly, it is clear that the success of a no-fault scheme depends on the political mood of the country. This, of course, may change over time. In the early 1970s, many contemplated that the New Zealand scheme would expand, but in fact it has contracted. In the United Kingdom, the political mood is not in favour of the no-fault option, which requires a dominant philosophy of state intervention and responsibility. In 2003, the Chief Medical Officer rejected the option of a comprehensive no-fault compensation scheme for treatment under the NHS, when faced with an estimated cost of £4 billion a year.[79] In recommending more limited measures which aimed to

[74] Vol. 1, para.274, although it may be questioned whether this was an excuse to avoid discussion due to the obvious disagreement within the Commission as to the relationship between tort and no-fault liability.
[75] See Report of the Royal Commission of Inquiry on Compensation for Personal Injury in New Zealand (1967).
[76] By means of part of the motor vehicle registration fee and a percentage of petrol sales.
[77] Information can be gathered from the website of the Accident Compensation Corporation which administers the scheme: *http://www.acc.co.nz*. Although accident insurance for work-related injuries was, between July 1, 1999 and March 31, 2000, provided in a competitive marketplace, new legislation provides that the ACC should become the single provider once again for accident insurance for all work and non work-related injuries: see the New Zealand Injury Prevention, Rehabilitation and Compensation Act 2001.
[78] The ACC spends about $1.4 billion each year on rehabilitation, treatment and weekly compensation: *www.acc.co.nz/about-acc/acc-funding/*. Proposals to replace "medical misadventure" claims with a broader category of "treatment injury", which does not require proof of medical error or mishap, would increase this category from $47 million to $55.69 million.
[79] See *Making Amends* (NHS, 2003): *www.doh.gov.uk/makingamends*.

address serious shortcomings in the NHS,[80] Sir Liam Donaldson regarded any other option as unaffordable.

(3) Insurance

This proposal is perhaps more consistent with current political views on free market   **1–032**
economics. It is primarily advanced by Professor Atiyah, who explains it in his book *The Damages Lottery*.[81] Insurance, as we have seen, is an important adjunct to the law of tort, yet the influence of insurance on the law of tort is a matter of some dispute.[82] Whilst the orthodox position is that the courts should ignore the presence of insurance cover,[83] judges such as Lord Denning have used the presence of insurance cover to justify developments in the law aimed at achieving the principle of loss distribution.[84] Professor Atiyah's approach is more radical. Put simply, he argues that the tort system should be replaced by a system of first party insurance. By purchasing "first party" insurance, a person insures himself or herself against suffering *harm*. (It should be distinguished from "third party" insurance, where a person insures against *liability* for harm suffered by others.) The argument runs that, if everyone were covered by first party insurance, there would be no need for an inefficient system of tort law. Accident compensation and prevention could be dealt with through the more efficient medium of the market.

There are a number of objections to this suggestion,[85] the strongest of which is that not everyone in society has the means to pay for first party insurance. One must also have doubts about the morality and the wisdom of placing all accident compensation in the hands of insurers. At present, tort law provides the benchmark against which the appropriate levels of compensation for personal injuries are assessed. It is questionable whether justice would be seen to be done if this function were removed from the judiciary and placed in the hands of insurance companies.

Tortious liability: conclusion

Tort law is a stimulating, if sometimes complicated and often frustrating subject to   **1–033**
study. It faces a number of challenges, some of which are of quite recent origin. The effects of the Human Rights Act 1998, a growing body of European law, and the Woolf reforms on civil litigation are now beginning to be felt. Despite its failings, tort law continues to offer a humane and pragmatic response to the problems of twenty-first century life.

---

[80] Parallel to the tort system, it was recommended that there should be redress for low value claims where the patient had been injured by "seriously substandard" NHS care and compensation packages for brain damaged babies who suffer severe neurological impairments related to or resulting from birth, irrespective of proof of fault (the NHS Redress Scheme). See M. Jones, *Medical Negligence* (3rd ed., 2003, Sweet & Maxwell).
[81] (Hart, 1997).
[82] See Stapleton (1995) 58 M.L.R. 820 and Morgan (2004) 67 M.L.R. 384.
[83] See Lord Bridge in *Hunt v Severs* [1994] 2 A.C. 350 at 363 who held that at common law the fact that the defendant is insured can have no relevance in assessing damages. See also Viscount Simonds in *Lister v Romford Ice and Cold Storage Co. Ltd* [1957] A.C. 555 at 576–577.
[84] See, *e.g. Nettleship v Weston* [1971] 2 Q.B. 691 at 700.
[85] See the excellent review of Professor Atiyah's book by Conaghan and Mansell (1998) 25 J.L.S. 284.

Chapter Two

NEGLIGENCE: THE DUTY OF CARE

Introduction

The tort of negligence is the most frequently used of all the torts and is therefore **2–001** perhaps the most important. It has flourished in the latter part of the twentieth century, rising to a dominant position because of the flexible nature of its rules, which have allowed the judges to expand the tort to protect many claimants who would otherwise have been left unprotected by the law. Unfortunately for the law student, however, this broadness of judicial approach can make the principles of the tort seem frustratingly vague.

This book explores negligence over five chapters, taking each ingredient of the tort in turn. This chapter introduces these ingredients and then, from a general perspective, discusses the first of them, namely the duty of care. The next two chapters explore some of the special difficulties the courts have encountered in deciding whether a duty of care should exist in relation to economic loss and psychiatric illness. The last two chapters on negligence deal with the remaining ingredients of the tort, namely breach of duty and causation.

This chapter begins with a basic definition. There then follows a short section describing the correct approach to be taken when studying negligence and a section giving a brief overview of the tort. These sections introduce certain important ideas which, once grasped, will help dispel some of the frustration often experienced by those who approach the subject for the first time.

Definition of "negligence"

The tort of negligence has been usefully defined as: **2–002**

". . . a breach of a legal duty to take care which results in damage to the claimant."[1]

The tort is not usually concerned with harm inflicted *intentionally*. Rather, it is concerned with harm inflicted "accidentally" or through want of care. We shall see, however, that establishing negligence involves much more than simply showing that the defendant behaved "carelessly"—careless behaviour is only one ingredient of the tort.

---

[1] W.H. Rogers, *Winfield and Jolowicz on Tort*, 16th ed. (2002), p.103.

To establish the tort of negligence, the claimant must prove three things:

(1) the defendant owes the claimant a duty of care;

(2) the defendant has acted in breach of that duty, and

(3) as a result, the claimant has suffered damage which is not too remote a consequence of the defendant's breach.

For the purpose of learning the law, it is convenient to consider each element of the tort in turn. Rarely in practice, however, will disputes ever involve all three elements. In a dispute involving a carelessly driven car, for example, the court will not embark on a detailed inquiry as to whether the defendant motorist owes a duty not to be careless, because the duty of care owed in this situation is well established. Rather, the question for the court is likely to be whether the defendant *was*, in fact, careless (*breach* of the duty of care), or perhaps the crucial question will be whether the defendant's carelessness was the legal *cause* of the claimant's loss (causation and remoteness of damage).

It should also be noted that in practice the courts have a tendency to blur the distinctions between each of the separate elements of negligence. Quite often, therefore, a judgment may indicate that the defendant is not liable but may fail to make it entirely clear which of the three separate requirements of the tort has not been fulfilled. This difficulty stems from the fact that, as we shall see, the concept of "reasonable foreseeability" is used by the courts in establishing all three of the elements of the tort.

A further difficulty stems from the way in which lawyers use the word "negligence". In ordinary language, of course, the word "negligent" means "careless". For present purposes, however, we need to treat the word as having a special meaning: what tort lawyers usually mean when they say that a person has been "negligent" is that the person has *committed the tort of negligence*—they mean that all three of the ingredients of the tort have been established.

Yet the ordinary meaning of the word "negligent" (in the sense of "careless") is still important for tort lawyers. This is for two reasons. First, it is not only the tort of negligence that can be committed "negligently". When establishing liability for other torts, such as nuisance, it is often relevant to ask whether the defendant has behaved "negligently", in the sense of "carelessly". Secondly, even in the context of the tort of negligence, lawyers, confusingly, sometimes say that a defendant has been "negligent" when all they really mean is that the defendant was in breach of the duty of care.

STUDYING NEGLIGENCE

2–003   The tort of negligence covers such a wide range of factual situations that the search for a single "set of rules", applicable to all types of negligence case, will be fruitless. The correct approach, then, is to focus on the *type of interest* which the claimant is trying to use the tort to protect (physical safety, the safety of property, financial well-being, or psychological well-being), and then to think about the *policy reasons* why the courts have felt either able or unable to extend the scope of negligence to protect that interest in particular situations. The language of the judges, and the pattern of their decision-making, will only begin to make real sense when considered alongside the political and economic forces which motivate decisions in negligence cases.

When one looks at what negligence is trying to achieve within society—the redistribution of certain risks associated with day-to-day activities—it becomes clear why the judges have had such difficulty in formulating workable rules for the tort. The point to grasp is that negligence is essentially concerned with a conflict of values within society. The driver of a car, for example, wishes to go fast to reach his destination, but the pedestrian crossing the road wishes the driver were going more slowly so as to lessen the likelihood of being knocked down. In essence, therefore, in order to decide the question of negligence, the judge must make a *political and moral value-judgment* as to the relative merits of fast driving and road safety in society. Making this sort of judgment, however, is not a task with which judges feel very comfortable, because it is one for which the British Constitution does not equip them. As Lord Scarman put it in *McLoughlin v O'Brian*[2]:

> ". . . the policy issue where to draw the line is not justiciable. The problem is one of social, economic and financial policy. The considerations relevant to a decision are not such as to be capable of being handled within the limits of the forensic process."

Clearly, his Lordship is referring to the fact that, in constitutional theory, the role of the judge is not to make law, but only to interpret it. Much of the interest in studying negligence, however, comes from exploring the way in which the judges have managed to make new law, usually without explicitly stating that they have done so. For constitutional reasons, the judges are not able to use the explicit language of politicians or economists in their judgments. This means that where the relevant political and economic reasoning is present in cases, it is often encoded in "judicial", rather than "political" language. A proper understanding of the tort of negligence, then, requires a good deal of "reading between the lines".

AN OVERVIEW OF NEGLIGENCE

In 1932, Lord Atkin, in the landmark case of *Donoghue v Stevenson*,[3] formulated a **2–004** general principle (known as the "neighbour principle") by which the existence of a legal duty to take care could be determined, thus effectively inventing the modern tort of negligence. The problem with Lord Atkin's general principle, however, was that it contained too little by which, on the basis of logic, the limits of the tort could ever be confined.

As the tort of negligence developed, the courts sought to qualify Lord Atkin's general principle with a number of complex, inherently vague and sometimes rather arbitrary rules. These rules were necessary in order to keep the scope of negligence

[2] [1983] 1 A.C. 410 at 431.
[3] [1932] A.C. 562.

within acceptable bounds. In particular, the courts felt it important to avoid being overrun with a multiplicity of negligence claims (they were afraid to open the so-called "floodgates of litigation") because, as was noted in Ch. 1, the tort system is very costly to administer. The courts were also afraid of allowing what is sometimes called "crushing liability". Crushing liability would occur if one particular defendant were made liable for a very large amount of loss, of which the defendant's actions were the logical cause, but for which it would be unfair or economically inefficient to make the defendant responsible in law.

In studying negligence, we shall see how, during the period from 1963 until the mid-1980s, the House of Lords was willing to apply Lord Atkin's "neighbour principle" fairly broadly, so that, from its beginnings in *Donoghue v Stevenson*, it came to be applied to factual situations which were far removed from the facts of that case. During this period, the tort of negligence grew from a tort protecting only property and physical well-being into one which, to a limited extent, now protects the financial and psychological well-being of claimants. We shall then see how, in recent years, faced with the problems of indeterminate and crushing liability, their Lordships have retraced their steps, diminishing the scope of the tort.

To some extent, it can be seen that the expansion of negligence, and its subsequent contraction, have mirrored certain changes in political thought that took place in the latter half of the twentieth century. This period saw a gradual change away from a philosophy of welfarism and state control towards a philosophy of individualism and contraction of state responsibility. The long rule of a Conservative government, from 1979 to 1997, brought arguments about economic efficiency into tighter focus than ever before. It is likely that these arguments have influenced the courts, resulting in their reluctance to make people responsible for certain types of loss when, under a contract, the risk of that loss (and the reward for taking that risk) has been allocated to someone else. This point is further explored in Ch. 3.

THE DUTY OF CARE

An overview

2–005   As the courts have struggled to determine the proper scope of negligence, they have used each of its three ingredients—duty, breach and causation—as a *control mechanism* to set limits to the tort. This multi-faceted approach can sometimes be rather confusing. What is clear, however, is that in recent times there has been a marked tendency to deal with the question of liability by reference to the scope of the duty of care. Logically, establishing the existence of a duty of care is the first hurdle a claimant must overcome. It therefore makes sense for a court to deal with this first, because it simplifies the decision-making process.

In many situations it will be obvious from established case law that the defendant owes the claimant a duty of care. The real problem for the courts has been to decide whether a duty of care should be owed in novel factual situations which are not covered by authority. Because of the political and economic considerations involved, the courts have found it difficult both to decide this question and to express their decisions in appropriate language. In order to limit the scope of the duty of care, they have repeatedly asserted the importance of the *relationship* between the defendant and the claimant. This approach, however, has not resulted in a universally applicable test for determining the existence of a duty of care in all cases. The qualifications on Lord Atkin's "neighbour principle" have become so numerous that the House of Lords has been forced to abandon the search for a single workable test. Thus, in *Caparo v Dickman*,[4] Lord Roskill concluded:

"It has now to be accepted that there is no simple formula or touchstone to which recourse can be had in order to provide in every case a ready answer."

With this in mind, we can now examine more closely the historical development of the duty of care, and the modern approach to deciding whether it exists.

The historical background

Negligence was not regarded as a tort in its own right until the late nineteenth century. **2–006** The traditional system of writs, under which claims would not be recognised unless they had been made in the prescribed form, did not include a specific writ for negligence. Early case law, however, did suggest that in certain situations liability based on carelessness could arise. For example, it was established from early times that innkeepers and common carriers could be liable for the careless performance of a specific task. Later, in the seventeenth century, it became established that a surgeon or an attorney would be liable if his conduct was less than that expected of a reasonably skilled professional. Although, at the time, such cases were not considered in terms of a separate tort of negligence, with hindsight they show us how the courts came gradually to accept that liability could arise where a defendant had merely been careless, as opposed to having committed an intentional act of wrongdoing.

   In the nineteenth century, the technology of the industrial revolution brought with it great potential for personal injury. In addition, as urban areas became more densely populated, congestion on city streets led to an increase in the number of "running down" cases. These factors brought about a change in judicial attitudes. As Professor Winfield observes:

"Early railway trains, in particular, were notable neither for speed nor for safety. They killed any object from a Minister of State to a wandering cow, and this naturally reacted on the law."[5]

The stage was set for the emergence of a new tort which could meet the needs of claimants in an increasingly dangerous age.

The first step: identifying a general principle

Whilst, in the nineteenth century, the courts came to recognise that liability could be **2–007** based on careless conduct, there was no general principle of law applicable to these situations. Instead, a body of case law emerged consisting of a collection of isolated

---

[4] [1990] 2 A.C. 605 at 628.
[5] Winfield (1926) 42 L.Q.R. 184 at 195.

instances where such liability had been imposed. The major obstacle to the development of a general principle seems to have been the Victorian belief that individuals should bear all responsibility for their own welfare and that they could not be expected to look out for the welfare of others unless they were being paid to do so. The concept of "collectivism"—the idea that every member of society can benefit if each member takes some responsibility for the well-being of others—whilst central to our modern way of thinking, was alien to Victorian political culture. Thus, whilst the courts were happy to make defendants liable where they had *assumed* responsibility for the care of another by entering into a contract with that other for reward, they were less happy about *imposing* on defendants a gratuitous duty to look after others.

This attitude was apparent in the decision in *Winterbottom v Wright*.[6] The plaintiff was a coach driver, employed by the Postmaster-General, who suffered serious injuries when he fell from a coach that had been defectively built by the defendants. It was held that the driver could not recover compensation from the builders of the coach because he was not a party to the contract with the Postmaster-General, under which the defendants had supplied the coach. The idea, of course, was that since it was the Postmaster-General, rather than the coach driver, who had paid the coach builders to assume responsibility for the safety of the coach, there was no reason why the coach driver should benefit when the coach proved dangerous.

In *Winterbottom v Wright*, then, it was decided that where a person had assumed responsibility under a contract for the quality of a thing supplied, and that thing turned out to be defective, he would be liable only to the person to whom he had supplied it under a contract. He could not also be liable for damage suffered by a third party who was not privy to the contract. This idea later became known as the "privity of contract fallacy". It persisted in the law until it was overturned by the decision in *Donoghue v Stevenson*[7] in 1932.

The first real suggestion that there could be a general principle of law governing the existence of the duty of care came in 1883. Brett M.R., in *Heaven v Pender*,[8] observed that the following proposition appeared to cover all of the recognised cases of liability for careless conduct:

> " . . . whenever one person is by circumstances placed in such a position with regard to another that everyone of ordinary sense who did think would at once recognise that if he did not use ordinary care and skill in his own conduct with regard to those circumstances he would cause danger of injury to the person or property of the other, a duty arises to use ordinary care and skill to avoid such danger."

The majority of the Court of Appeal, however, were unwilling to adopt such a broad principle of liability,[9] and in his later decision in *Le Lievre v Gould*,[10] Brett M.R. (now Lord Esher M.R.), declined to apply the principle to a case involving purely financial loss. In a sense, Brett M.R.'s formulation of a general principle came before its time. It was not until 1932 that a change in judicial attitudes, which mirrored the political and

[6] (1842) 10 M. & W. 109.
[7] [1932] A.C. 562.
[8] (1883) 11 Q.B.D. 503 at 509.
[9] *ibid.*, at 516 *per* Cotton and Bowen L.JJ.
[10] [1893] 1 Q.B. 491 at 497.

economic changes that had taken place in society, allowed for a unified approach to cases of careless conduct.

A further problem with Brett M.R.'s formulation of the principle was that, although it referred to the "position" of one person "with regard to another" as giving rise to a duty of care, it did not go very far in describing the nature of the relationship which had to exist between the claimant and the defendant. This meant that, on the face of it, Brett M.R.'s general principle would have given rise to liability in any case where a person should have foreseen that his conduct might cause harm to another. We shall see that Lord Atkin's reformulation of the principle in *Donoghue v Stevenson*[11] makes it much clearer that foreseeability of harm alone should not be sufficient to establish the existence of a duty of care.

Lord Atkin's "neighbour principle"

In 1932, the House of Lords decided the famous case of *Donoghue v Stevenson*.[12] The **2–008** facts of the case have become legendary,[13] although it should be noted that, because the case was decided by the House of Lords on a point of law and was then settled before going to trial, these facts were never actually proved. It was alleged that Mrs Donoghue and her friend visited Minchella's Wellmeadow Café, in Paisley.[14] At the café, the friend bought for Mrs Donoghue a "ginger beer float", consisting of ginger beer, supplied in an opaque bottle, and ice-cream. Mrs Donoghue drank some of the mixture, and when her friend topped up the drink, out of the ginger beer bottle floated the decomposed remains of a snail. Mrs Donoghue claimed that the sight of the snail, together with the ginger beer she had already drunk, made her ill.

Now, Mrs Donoghue, of course, could not sue the retailer of the ginger beer for breach of contract because, not having bought the ginger beer herself, she was not in a contractual relationship with him. The contract had been made between the retailer and her friend. She therefore brought an action in tort against the manufacturer of the ginger beer. It was not worthwhile suing the *retailer* in tort, because he was not at fault. The ginger beer had been supplied to him in an opaque bottle, so that he could not have looked inside the bottle to check that its contents were wholesome, and there was no possibility that the snail could have entered the bottle at any stage after it had been supplied by the manufacturer.

Mrs Donoghue's position, however, was very similar to that of the coach driver in *Winterbottom v Wright*. She had been the victim of a defective product that had been supplied to another person under a contract to which she was not a party. According to *Winterbottom v Wright*, it appeared that the manufacturer would only be liable under his contract with the retailer. Yet Mrs Donoghue succeeded in her claim. A majority of the House of Lords distinguished *Winterbottom v Wright*, holding that a manufacturer of products, which he sells in such a form as to show that he intends them to reach the ultimate consumer in the form in which they left him, with no reasonable possibility of intermediate examination before the products are consumed, would be liable to the consumer in tort if he failed to take reasonable care to ensure that the products were

---

[11] [1932] A.C. 562.
[12] *ibid*.
[13] For an entertaining review of the case, see Rodgers Q.C. [1988] C.L.P. 1.
[14] Paisley is in Scotland and the case was therefore brought in Scots law. The House of Lords accepted that no difference existed between English and Scots law in this instance.

safe. Their Lordships rejected the so-called "privity of contract fallacy" of *Winterbottom*—privity of contract did not prevent a third party bringing an action in tort.

At first sight, it seemed that the decision in *Donoghue v Stevenson* had simply added yet another category to the separate instances of negligence recognised by the law. What has become significant about the case, however, is Lord Atkin's analysis of the law and his subsequent formulation of a general principle for determining the existence of a duty of care. This is what Lord Atkin said[15]:

> ". . . in English law there must be, and is, some general conception of relations giving rise to a duty of care, of which the particular cases found in the books are but instances. The liability for negligence . . . is no doubt based upon a general public sentiment of moral wrongdoing for which the offender must pay. But acts or omissions which any moral code would censure cannot in a practical world be treated so as to give a right to every person injured by them to demand relief. In this way rules of law arise which limit the range of complainants and the extent of their remedy. The rule that you are to love your neighbour becomes, in law, you must not injure your neighbour; and the lawyer's question who is my neighbour? receives a restricted reply. You must take reasonable care to avoid acts or omissions which you can reasonably foresee would be likely to injure your neighbour. Who then, in law is my neighbour? The answer seems to be—persons who are so closely and directly affected by my act that I ought reasonably to have them in contemplation as being so affected when I am directing my mind to the acts or omissions which are called in question."

Lord Atkin's general principle contained two elements. First, there was the element of "reasonable foreseeability". Thus, a duty of care would be owed where the defendant ought reasonably to foresee that his failure to take care may cause injury to another. (This, of course, is the same as what Brett M.R. had said in *Heaven v Pender*.) The second element was the test of "neighbourhood"—a duty of care would be owed only where the claimant was "closely and directly" affected by the defendant's conduct. Brett M.R.'s simple test of foreseeability of harm, therefore, became qualified by the additional need to show, as Lord Atkin put it, a degree of "proximity"[16] between the claimant and the defendant, not in the sense of physical proximity, but in the sense of "close and direct relations".

Lord Atkin's general test of foreseeability plus "proximity", then, gave the courts a basis on which the existence of a duty of care could be decided in all cases. It allowed them to view negligence as a tort in its own right, capable of being developed to meet any new factual situation which arose.

It is important, however, not to overestimate the significance of Lord Atkin's general principle. It has already been noted that, in modern times, it is recognised that this principle alone fails to provide a workable solution to the problem of imposing a duty of care. The principle suffers from a number of fundamental flaws. First, although

---

[15] [1932] A.C. 562 at 580.
[16] Interestingly, the term "proximity'" was first used by Brett M.R. in *Thomas v Quartermaine* (1887) 18 Q.B.D. 685 at 688.

Lord Atkin speaks of "acts or omissions", we shall see that the law treats liability for acts very differently from liability for omissions. Secondly, as the law has developed, it has become clear that, besides identifying the defendant's "neighbour", it is also necessary to identify the *type of loss* which the "neighbour" is likely to suffer (or, in other words, the *type of interest* which the claimant is seeking to use the law to protect) before any decision can be made about whether to impose a duty of care. Lord Atkin's words, spoken in the context of personal injury caused by a defective product, gave little indication of the degree of "proximity" which would be required in other factual situations. We shall see that, especially where other types of harm are in issue, the courts, for policy reasons, have had to say that a far greater degree of "proximity" is required in some situations than in others. In *Donoghue v Stevenson*, Lord Atkin observed: "There will no doubt arise cases where it will be difficult to determine whether the contemplated relationship is so close that the duty arises".[17] Such prescience, it will be seen, was all too accurate.

The second step: applying the general principle

Without Lord Atkin's "neighbour principle", the decision in *Donoghue v Stevenson* would simply have been another isolated example of negligence liability. (The case did indeed establish liability in English law for defective products, which is discussed in Ch. 9.) It should be noted that Lord Atkin's principle did not form part of the *ratio* of the case, because the two other majority judges in the case refrained from adopting it. As might be expected, then, the first response of the courts was to treat the case as a narrow example of liability. The judges were particularly reluctant to apply the principle in situations where there was clear authority which excluded liability in negligence, such as where the claimant suffered financial loss because of a carelessly made statement. And so things might have remained, but for a number of radical decisions in the 1960s and 1970s, in which the House of Lords was prepared to overturn previous authority to extend the scope of the duty of care.

2–009

The decision in Hedley Byrne

The first of these cases came in 1964. The decision in *Hedley Byrne v Heller and Partners*[18] established, contrary to previous authority, that there could be liability in English law in respect of financial loss caused by negligent misstatement. The case is examined more fully in Ch. 3, but it will be convenient to state the facts here.

2–010

Hedley Byrne, who were advertising agents, were about to enter into certain contracts on behalf of one of their clients—a company called Easipower—on terms which meant that, if Easipower failed to honour its obligations under the contracts, Hedley Byrne would become liable to pay Easipower's debts. Hedley Byrne therefore wished to find out whether Easipower was creditworthy, so, through their own bankers, they sought a reference from Easipower's bankers, Heller and Partners. Heller and Partners wrote saying that although the amounts in question were larger than they were accustomed to see, they considered Easipower to be good for the ordinary course of business. But they made it clear that they were providing this advice "without responsibility" on their part. In other words, they included a disclaimer of liability.

---

[17] [1932] A.C. 562 at 582.
[18] [1964] A.C. 465.

On the basis of the favourable credit reference, Hedley Byrne went ahead with the advertising contracts. It turned out, however, that Heller and Partners had carelessly failed to realise that, at the time they gave the reference, Easipower was in a very bad way financially. Easipower went into liquidation shortly after the contracts had been made, so that Hedley Byrne became liable to pay Easipower's debts. Hedley Byrne therefore brought an action against Heller and Partners for the negligently given advice.

Two major problems faced Hedley Byrne. First, their action concerned a statement which had been made carelessly, but previous authority had decided that there could only be liability where a statement had been made fraudulently.[19] Secondly, their action was for financial loss, rather than for personal injury or damage to property—the areas where the courts had so far been willing to impose negligence liability.

Nevertheless, the House of Lords was prepared to hold that, but for the disclaimer of liability, Heller and Partners would have been liable for their negligent statement. Whilst their Lordships were prepared to use Lord Atkin's "neighbour principle" as a starting point in establishing liability, they were not prepared to decide the case purely by analogy to the facts of *Donoghue v Stevenson*. Their Lordships made it clear that there were important differences between negligently made statements causing financial loss and negligently manufactured products causing personal injury. These differences meant that Lord Atkin's principle could not be applied without qualification in negligent misstatement cases. The reasoning in *Hedley Byrne v Heller and Partners* is considered more fully in Ch. 3. For present purposes, however, it is sufficient to note that, in order to avoid the problems of indeterminate and "crushing" liability, their Lordships held that in negligent misstatement cases a high degree of "proximity", or closeness of relationship, would be required. It was held that for liability to arise, a "special relationship" had to be shown between the maker of the statement and the person who subsequently relied on it.

The decision in Dorset Yacht

2–011   The next landmark case was *Home Office v Dorset Yacht*.[20] This case was important because it imposed a duty of care on the defendant to prevent damage being caused by the actions of others. Liability for the acts of third parties has proved to be a difficult area for the courts and is further discussed later in this chapter.

In *Home Office v Dorset Yacht*, the Home Office had established a Borstal (a prison training camp for young male offenders) on an island off the Dorset coast. One night, because of the carelessness of the guards, a number of the prisoners escaped and caused damage to some yachts moored in the harbour. The House of Lords was prepared to impose liability on the guards (for whom the Home Office was responsible in law), holding that there were "special relations" between the Home Office and Borstal boys, so that the Home Office could be liable for its failure to prevent the boys from causing damage. This, together with a high degree of foreseeability—escaping and causing the damage was the "very kind of thing" the boys were likely to do—made the Home Office liable.

---

[19] See *Derry v Peek* (1889) 14 App. Cas. 337 and *Candler v Crane, Christmas & Co.* [1951] K.B. 164 (discussed in Ch. 3).
[20] [1970] A.C. 1004.

Lord Reid made the following observation:

"*Donoghue v Stevenson* may be regarded as a milestone, and the well-known passage in Lord Atkin's speech should, I think, be regarded as a statement of principle. It is not to be treated as if it were a statutory definition. It will require qualification in new circumstances. But I think the time has come when we can and should say that it ought to apply unless there is some justification or valid explanation for its exclusion."[21]

Lord Wilberforce's "two stage test"

This positive affirmation of Lord Atkin's principle was approved by the House of **2–012** Lords in the next important case—the now discredited case of *Anns v Merton LBC*.[22] Here, a local authority had failed to notice that the foundations of a new block of maisonettes had not been dug to an adequate depth. The plaintiffs, who had taken long leases of the maisonettes, found that cracks appeared in the walls. They sued the local authority for the cost of rebuilding. (Nowadays, this case is regarded as one of economic loss. It was overruled in 1990 by the decision in *Murphy v Brentwood DC*,[23] discussed in Ch. 3.).

In *Anns*,[24] Lord Wilberforce reformulated the test for determining the existence of a duty of care. According to his Lordship, the judges should ask themselves two questions, one after the other. This became known as Lord Wilberforce's "two stage test" and can be summarised as follows:

Stage one: is there, between the claimant and defendant, a sufficient relationship of "proximity or neighbourhood" such that the defendant can reasonably foresee that carelessness on his or her part would be likely to cause damage to the claimant? If the answer to this question is "yes", then a prima facie duty of care arises.

Stage two: are there any considerations which should nevertheless lead the court to deny a duty of care, or to limit its scope, in these particular circumstances?

This straightforward test had the appeal of simplicity, but unfortunately was flawed. Essentially, the problem was that it was unclear what Lord Wilberforce meant by the word "proximity" in stage one of the test. We have seen that Lord Atkin thought that "foreseeability" and "proximity" were two separate things. Foreseeability of harm alone would not give rise to a duty of care—there had also to be "close and direct relations" between the claimant and the defendant. Lord Wilberforce, on the other hand, now appeared to say that foreseeability *was* the test for proximity. This meant that, in applying the two stage test, if a judge felt that, although harm was foreseeable, liability should not be imposed because the relationship between the claimant and the defendant was not sufficiently close, the judge would have to find some way of expressing this idea by answering Lord Wilberforce's second question, *i.e.* by explicitly stating a policy reason for denying the existence of a duty of care.

Lord Wilberforce's approach proved difficult, and was eventually abandoned, because, on this interpretation, it did not truly reflect the way the courts decide the existence of the duty of care. The courts do not assume a duty of care and then

---

[21] [1970] A.C. 1004 at 1027. Contrast the more reserved approach of Lord Diplock at 1060.
[22] [1978] A.C. 728.
[23] [1991] A.C. 398.
[24] [1978] A.C. 728 at 751.

consider, as a matter of policy, whether in the circumstances the type of damage in question should be compensated. Rather, the policy question of whether certain types of damage should be recoverable in certain circumstances goes to the central question of whether, in each case, a duty should exist in the first place. Reading between the lines, we might observe that the problem with Lord Wilberforce's formulation was that it made it difficult for judges to avoid explicit reference to *political* and *economic* considerations when answering the second question in the two stage test. Although there is no logical reason why liability cannot depend on a composite test of foreseeability plus politics and economics, the judges have not felt able to adopt such a direct approach.

Lord Wilberforce's two stage test, then, embodied a more generous approach to the duty of care issue—a *presumption* that a duty of care would exist unless clear policy objections could be found. This approach was adopted in *Junior Books Ltd v Veitchi & Co. Ltd*[25] (discussed in Ch. 3), where the majority of the House of Lords supported a claim brought by factory-owners against specialist sub-contractors who had negligently installed a floor in their factory. By so doing, their Lordships extended the tort of negligence so that, in special circumstances, it would provide a remedy not just for damage to property caused by the supply of a defective product, but for the cost of replacing the defective product itself. This was important because, previously, only contract law had provided a remedy for defects in the quality of products.

Following *Junior Books*, however, the courts began to express concern about the way in which the duty of care was expanding. Insufficient attention seemed to be given to the problems of indeterminate and crushing liability. Moreover, if tort were prepared to intervene and upset the delicate contractual allocation of risk between a main contractor and a sub-contractor, this would have implications for the prices charged by sub-contractors: if the law said that sub-contractors could be liable in tort for financial losses, even though they had expressly excluded this sort of liability in contract, they would need to take out insurance, and it was unclear whether, in terms of economic efficiency, these sub-contractors were always the best people to do so. Therefore, the courts have declined to follow the decision in *Junior Books*.

In *Donoghue v Stevenson*, Lord Atkin had recognised these problems when he said:

> " . . . it is of particular importance to guard against the danger of stating propositions of law in wider terms than is necessary, lest essential factors be omitted in the wider survey."[26]

From the mid-1980s, then, the courts began to examine these "essential factors" more closely and to stress their importance in limiting the scope of the duty of care.

The third step: refining the principle

2–013   In a series of decisions, from 1985 onwards, the House of Lords began to reject Lord Wilberforce's broad approach to the duty of care. Lord Keith in *Governors of the Peabody Donation Fund v Sir Lindsay Parkinson & Co. Ltd*[27] criticised the tendency to

---

[25] [1983] 1 A.C. 520.
[26] [1932] A.C. 562 at 583.
[27] [1985] A.C. 210 at 240. See also Lord Bridge in *Curran v Northern Ireland Co-ownership Housing Association Ltd* [1987] A.C. 718.

treat Lord Wilberforce's simple two stage test as a definitive formula, saying that the temptation to do so should be resisted. In *Leigh & Sillavan Ltd v Aliakmon Shipping Co. Ltd (The Aliakmon)*,[28] Lord Brandon stated that Lord Wilberforce's two stage test should only be applied in novel factual situations where the courts had not previously ruled on the existence of a duty of care. Where a precedent existed (either directly or by analogy), the court should follow it, rather than apply the test. In *The Aliakmon*, this approach allowed the House of Lords to reject a claim by a buyer for damage caused by the negligent stowage of goods on board a ship. Whilst the claim may well have satisfied Lord Wilberforce's criteria, their Lordships preferred to follow previous authority which excluded such claims where the buyer had not yet acquired a proprietary interest in the goods.

In 1988, the Privy Council, deciding *Yuen Kun Yeu v Att.Gen. of Hong Kong*,[29] was openly critical of the approach adopted in *Anns*. Lord Keith commented that the two stage test appeared to have been elevated to a degree of importance that it did not deserve and that it should not in all circumstances be regarded as a suitable guide to determining the existence of a duty of care. His Lordship highlighted the danger of misinterpreting stage one of the Wilberforce test as a simple test of foreseeability and stated that, henceforth, it should be presumed that by using the expression "proximity or neighbourhood" in stage one, Lord Wilberforce had intended to import into stage one of the test all of the ideas about "close and direct relations" that Lord Atkin had expressed in *Donoghue v Stevenson*. This meant that stage two would be reserved for considerations of "public policy", such as whether a common law duty of care would be inconsistent with the purpose of legislation, or would not be in the public interest.

In the light of their Lordships' growing reservations about Lord Wilberforce's approach, it was perhaps unsurprising that in 1990, a seven-member House of Lords took the unusual step of using the 1966 Practice Statement[30] to overturn its own decision in *Anns*. In *Murphy v Brentwood DC*,[31] their Lordships expressed their concerns about the potentially extensive liability permitted under the two stage test, and asserted that *Anns* should no longer be regarded as good law.[32] Instead, the courts should favour the approach suggested by Brennan J., an Australian judge, in *Sutherland Shire Council v Heyman*,[33] that is to say, novel categories of negligence should be developed incrementally and by analogy with established categories, rather than under a general principle which permits a massive extension of a prima facie duty of care, restrained only by indefinable policy considerations. This "incremental" approach is now the accepted means of finding a duty of care in English law.

The modern approach

The leading case is now *Caparo v Dickman*.[34] This case concerned a claim for financial loss which resulted when an investor relied on published annual accounts and a company report that had been prepared carelessly by the company's auditor. The

2–014

[28] [1986] A.C. 785 at 815.
[29] [1988] A.C. 175. Applied in *Davies v Radcliffe* [1990] 1 W.L.R. 821 at 826.
[30] Practice Statement (Judicial Precedent) [1966] 1 W.L.R. 1234.
[31] [1991] 1 A.C. 398.
[32] Contrast the position in Canada, where the Supreme Court retained the *Anns* test and declined to follow *Murphy*, although its recent reformulation of the *Anns* test in *Cooper v Hobart* (2002) 206 D.L.R. (4th) 193 has brought it closer to the position in English law.
[33] (1985) 60 A.L.R. 1 at 43; (1985) 157 C.L.R. 424 at 480.
[34] [1990] 2 A.C. 605.

significance of *Caparo* in terms of claims for negligent misstatement will be discussed in Ch. 3. For present purposes, we need to note that the House of Lords gave guidance as to how to decide whether a duty of care should exist.

Their Lordships rejected as impractical the task of articulating a single general principle for the existence of a duty of care and concluded that, in future, to establish a duty of care, either:

(1) the claimant must point to a direct precedent, or to a closely analogous precedent, where a duty of care had been imposed, or

(2) in cases where no relevant authority exists, the court should apply three criteria (which their Lordships identified) to determine whether there is a duty of care.

The *Caparo* criteria

2–015 According to the dicta in *Caparo*, in novel factual situations all of the following three criteria must be satisfied before a court should be willing to impose a duty of care:

(1) the damage must be foreseeable;

(2) there must be a sufficiently proximate relationship between the parties;

(3) it must be "fair, just and reasonable" for the court to impose a duty of care in the light of policy considerations with which the court is concerned.

The application of the three *Caparo* criteria is sometimes referred to as a "three stage test", but this, it is submitted, is rather a misnomer. This is because, unlike the "two stage test" put forward by Lord Wilberforce in *Anns*, the *Caparo* criteria are designed to be considered all at once, not one after the other. This follows from the fact that the criteria cannot be precisely defined or evaluated in isolation from one another. As Lord Oliver noted in *Caparo* itself, the three criteria are, in most cases, "facets of the same thing".[35] On this basis, then, it might be said that the more foreseeable the harm suffered by the claimant, the closer the proximity of the parties, and vice versa. Equally, the closer the proximity, or the more foreseeable the damage, the more likely it is that the third criterion will be satisfied.

It will be appreciated that the *Caparo* criteria are somewhat vague.[36] On one view, though, it is this very vagueness which makes them so useful. We have seen that the problem with the approach in *Anns* was that it required the judges openly to refer to policy considerations in their judgments. Their reluctance to rule on policy meant that the expansion of the duty of care was inevitable. Under the modern approach, however, judges are no longer forced to confront policy issues so directly. Of course, they continue to make decisions based on policy, but they are now able to frame those decisions in appropriate judicial language by finding that there is insufficient proximity between the parties, or by declaring that the imposition of a duty would not be "fair, just and reasonable".

---

[35] *ibid.*, at 633.
[36] The *Caparo* test has recently been rejected by the High Court of Australia in favour of a multi-faceted approach which addresses the policy issues arising in the case itself: see *Perre v Apand Pty Ltd.* (1999) 198 C.L.R. 108, and *Sullivan v Moody* (2001) 207 C.L.R. 562.

Although each of the *Caparo* criteria is a "facet of the same thing", it is nevertheless possible to say something about each criterion in turn:

(1) Foreseeability

It should be remembered that the relevant question is not what the defendant *actually*   **2–016**
did foresee, but what a "reasonable person" in the circumstances of the defendant *ought to have foreseen*. The duty of care can only be owed in respect of preventing loss if the type of loss in question is "reasonably foreseeable". Implicit in this idea is that it must be reasonably foreseeable that the conduct of the defendant will affect the *particular claimant* in the case. This point is examined below:

The foreseeable claimant

In English law, it is said that negligence cannot exist "in the air". This is simply   **2–017**
another way of saying that the particular claimant in the case must be, as Lord Atkin put it, someone who is "closely and directly affected" by the defendant's conduct. Thus, it is not sufficient to say that the defendant breached a duty of care owed to person A and the claimant (person B) was affected because he or she happened to be in the general area of the negligence.

This principle is illustrated by the House of Lords' decision in *Bourhill v Young*.[37] A heavily pregnant woman was descending from a tram when she heard a road traffic accident some 50 feet away from her, caused by the defendant's negligence. She arrived at the scene of the accident and saw blood on the road where a motorist had been killed (although his body had been removed) and subsequently suffered a miscarriage and psychiatric illness. Their Lordships were unsympathetic. Whilst the defendant would be liable for damage suffered by other road-users, the claimant was too far removed from the scene of the accident to be a reasonably foreseeable victim.

A more graphic illustration is the well-known United States case of *Palsgraf v Long Island Railroad*,[38] where the negligence of railway employees caused a passenger to drop a box of fireworks as he was boarding a moving train. The fireworks exploded and knocked over some heavy metal scales several feet away, which struck the plaintiff. The New York Court of Appeals rejected her claim for damages, holding that if any wrong had been committed, it had not been committed against *her*, because she was not a foreseeable victim of the railway company's negligence.

Is an unborn child a "foreseeable claimant"?

Obviously, the "no negligence in the air" principle serves to prevent indeterminate   **2–018**
liability by restricting the range of claims that can result from a single negligent act. Its distinguishing feature is that it will not allow a claimant to base his or her claim on a wrong done to someone else. A difficult question of policy has arisen, however, in determining how far this principle should be applied in respect of children who are born disabled because of a wrong done to one of their parents before they are born.

For people born on or after July 22, 1976, the sort of claim that can be made is determined by the provisions of the Congenital Disabilities (Civil Liability) Act 1976.[39]

---

[37] [1943] A.C. 92.
[38] 248 N.Y. 339 (1928); 162 N.E. 99.
[39] As amended by the Human Fertilisation and Embryology Act 1990. Note that in 1992, *Burton v Islington Health Authority* [1993] Q.B. 204 finally established that a duty of care could be owed at common law to an unborn child, even though a foetus has no independent legal personality. It was held that the wrong done to the parent would "crystallise" into a cause of action, maintainable at the suit of the child, once the child was born.

In summary, this states that if a child is born disabled as a result of an injury to either parent which affects that parent's ability to have a normal child, or which affects the mother during pregnancy, or affects the mother or child during birth, the child may sue for his or her resulting disability.[40] It is not necessary to show that the parent has suffered personal injury of a type which would enable the parent to maintain an action in his or her own right.[41] However, any defences (and the principle of contributory negligence) which would apply if the parent were suing for injuries to himself or herself will be available to the defendant in fighting the child's claim.[42] It should be remembered that the Act not only covers injury to the foetus, it extends to cover situations where, before a child is conceived, a wrong is done to either of the parents which prevents them from conceiving a normal baby.

For policy reasons, the Act does not allow children to bring claims against their mothers, except in one particular situation, namely where the mother injures the child by negligently driving a motor vehicle when she knows (or ought to know) that she is pregnant.[43] The moral objections against children suing their mothers are overcome in this situation because the mother is, by law, obliged to be insured.[44] In such cases, the insurance company will meet or defend the child's claim. It should be noted that the general immunity granted to mothers does not extend to fathers.[45]

Moral objections have prevented the courts from holding that an unborn child is a foreseeable claimant in so-called "wrongful life" cases. These are cases in which disabled claimants argue, in effect, that they should never have been born, and were only born because of the defendant's negligence. The defendant may, for example, have failed to recommend an abortion to the mother, in circumstances where it was likely that the claimant would be born disabled. In *McKay v Essex Area Health Authority*,[46] the court struck out such a claim as contrary to public policy. It was not prepared to state that in law a disabled life was to be regarded as less valuable than that of an able-bodied person. Equally, the court was reluctant to set a precedent under which an action might be maintained by a child against a mother who, knowing of the risk of the child's disability, refused to have an abortion.[47]

Although children themselves have not been allowed to sue for "wrongful life", the courts have in the past been prepared to allow *parents* to sue for the cost of bringing up "unintended children" where the negligence of the defendant has prevented them from choosing not to conceive, or choosing to terminate the pregnancy. In recent times, however, the House of Lords has declined, for public policy reasons, to allow such claims to succeed. The relevant cases are considered later in this chapter, in the context of the liability of the NHS.

---

[40] Congenital Disabilities (Civil Liability) Act 1976, s.1. See also Consumer Protection Act 1987, s.6(3) (specific application of the 1976 Act to situations where the parent is affected by a defect in a product, *e.g.* a drug).
[41] *ibid.*, s.1(3).
[42] *ibid.*, ss.1(4), 1(6), and 1(7). Note, however, that contractual exclusions or limitations cannot be relied on where the case concerns the supply of a defective product: Consumer Protection Act 1987, s.6(3).
[43] *ibid.*, s.2.
[44] Road Traffic Act 1988, s.143.
[45] Although the Pearson Commission thought that it should (see Cmnd 7034, Vol.1, para.1471).
[46] [1982] Q.B. 1166 at 1180. The court, obiter, also ruled out any claim under the 1976 Act. See also Symmons (1987) 50 M.L.R. 269.
[47] The difficulty of assessing the level of damages also concerned the court.

(2) Proximity

It is impossible to define the concept of "proximity" in concrete terms. What can be   **2–019**
said, however, is that it refers to the *closeness of the relationship* between the defendant
and the claimant. The degree of closeness which the law will require before imposing a
duty of care differs according to the *type of damage* for which the claimant is seeking
redress. Therefore, as we shall see, in cases of economic loss and psychiatric illness, the
courts require a very close relationship between the parties, whilst in cases of physical
injury, the requirement of proximity is more easily satisfied.[48] Thus, if I negligently
make a statement causing you financial loss, I must (generally speaking) know who you
are and how you will rely on that statement before I can be made liable, but if I
negligently drive my car, causing you personal injury, I will be liable to you without
knowing who you are or that you, in particular, were relying on me to drive carefully.

The fact that the courts' insistence on "proximity" appears to be confined to certain
types of situation, then, indicates that questions of *policy* are relevant to the question
of whether or not, in a given situation, the required degree of proximity exists. As Lord
Oliver put it, in *Alcock v Chief Constable of South Yorkshire*[49]:

> ". . . no doubt 'policy', if that is the right word, or perhaps more properly, the
> impracticability or unreasonableness of entertaining claims to the ultimate limits of
> the consequences of human activity, necessarily plays a part in the court's
> perception of what is sufficiently proximate . . . in the end, it has to be accepted that
> the concept of 'proximity' is an artificial one which depends more upon the court's
> perception of what is the reasonable area for the imposition of liability than upon
> any logical process of analogical deduction."

(3) "Fair, just and reasonable"

Because policy concerns are relevant to the degree of proximity required, it is often   **2–020**
unclear what useful purpose is served by an additional consideration of whether the
imposition of a duty of care is "fair, just and reasonable". In *Marc Rich & Co. A.G. v
Bishop Rock Marine Company (The Nicholas H)*,[50] Balcombe L.J. doubted whether the
criterion added anything to the requirement of proximity. There may be exceptional
cases, however (such as the old cases of advocates' immunity, discussed elsewhere in
this chapter) where the courts wish to deny the existence of a duty of care, but where it
will be a nonsense for them to speak in terms of an insufficiently close relationship
between the parties. In such cases, the "fair, just and reasonable" criterion provides a
"long stop", enabling the courts to determine liability on the basis of policy.

Applying the *Caparo* criteria: factors relevant to the imposition of a duty of care

To understand how the *Caparo* criteria are applied in practice, it is useful to identify a   **2–021**
number of factors which the courts take into account in deciding whether to impose a
duty of care. We have already noted that the *type of harm* the claimant has suffered

---

[48] See Lord Oliver in *Murphy v Brentwood DC* [1991] 1 A.C. 398 at 487; *Mobil Oil Hong Kong Ltd v Hong
Kong United Dockyards Ltd (The Hua Lien)* [1991] 1 Lloyd's Rep. 309 at 368; *Perrett v Collins* [1998] 2
Lloyd's Rep. 255; *Pearson v Lightning* (1998) 95(20) L.S.G. 33.
[49] [1992] 1 A.C. 310 at 410.
[50] [1994] 1 W.L.R. 1071.

(physical, financial, or psychiatric) has a profound effect on whether a duty of care will be owed. This factor is further considered in Chs 3 and 4. In the following sections of this chapter, we examine two other relevant factors:

- whether the damage in question is caused by a positive act (misfeasance), or by an omission (non-feasance);

- the *type of defendant* who is being sued.

MISFEASANCE AND NON-FEASANCE

2–022   It will be recalled that Lord Atkin, in *Donoghue v Stevenson*, spoke of a duty of care arising in respect of "acts or omissions", yet, as Lord Goff notes in *Smith v Littlewoods Organisation Ltd*[51]:

"... the common law does not impose liability for what are called pure omissions."

The law draws a distinction between a positive act which causes harm (misfeasance) and a mere failure to prevent harm from arising (non-feasance), there being no liability for the latter. The distinction between misfeasance and non-feasance is sometimes very difficult to draw and has given rise to problems. A motorist who causes an accident by failing to stop at a red light is guilty of an omission, but the law says that he or she is liable because this omission cannot be considered in isolation from the positive act of driving. The key question, therefore, is whether the "omission" in question can be seen as having been made *in the course of doing some positive act*. In a number of cases concerning the liability of local authorities, the courts have explored this question and have used the distinction between misfeasance and non-feasance to justify findings of no liability.

In *Curran v Northern Ireland Co-ownership Housing Association*,[52] Lord Bridge endorsed academic commentary which had pointed out that duties to *prevent* harm (as opposed to duties to *refrain from causing* harm) would normally only arise where one person, under a contract, had promised to make another person better off, and that it may not be appropriate for such duties to be imposed in tort.[53] In *Curran*, their Lordships held that a local authority was not liable for its failure to prevent financial loss caused by a defective part of a building. The plaintiffs had bought a house on which an extension had been built, by the former owners, with the help of a home improvement grant from the local authority. When the extension proved defective and had to be rebuilt, the plaintiffs sued the authority, arguing that it had been negligent in failing to supervise the building works. It was held that the purpose of the statutory powers under which the authority had acted was to ensure that public funds were well spent, rather than to protect individuals from the financial consequences of poor workmanship. It followed that if the local authority was not engaged in any positive

[51] [1987] A.C. 241 at 271.
[52] [1987] A.C. 718.
[53] Smith and Burns (1983) 46 M.L.R. 147.

supervisory activity for the benefit of the plaintiffs, the plaintiffs' case must fail, because it was an allegation of mere non-feasance, for which there could be no liability.

In *Stovin v Wise*,[54] which is discussed later in this chapter, Lord Hoffmann made the following important observations about liability for omissions:[55]

"There are sound reasons why omissions require different treatment from positive conduct. It is one thing for the law to say that a person who undertakes some activity shall take reasonable care not to cause damage to others. It is another thing for the law to require that a person who is doing nothing in particular shall take steps to prevent another from suffering harm . . . One can put the matter in political, moral or economic terms. In political terms it is less of an invasion of freedom for the law to require him to consider the safety of others in his actions than to impose upon him a duty to rescue or protect. A moral version of this point may be called the "why pick on me?" argument. A duty to prevent harm to others or to render assistance to a person in danger or distress may apply to a large and indeterminate class of people who happen to be able to do something. Why should one be held liable rather than another? In economic terms, the efficient allocation of resources usually requires an activity should bear its own costs. If it benefits from being able to impose all or some of its costs on other people (what economists call 'externalities') the market is distorted because the activity appears cheaper than it really is. So liability to pay compensation for loss caused by negligent conduct acts as a deterrent against increasing the cost of the activity to the community and reduces externalities. But there is no similar justification for requiring a person who is not doing anything to spend money on behalf of someone else."

It can be seen from the reasoning in these cases that whether a case is one of misfeasance or non-feasance depends essentially on the *nature of the relationship* between the claimant and the defendant. The issue therefore overlaps with the idea of "proximity". This is illustrated by the decision in *Yuen Kun Yeu v Att.-Gen. of Hong Kong*.[56] Here, the plaintiffs alleged that the Commissioner of Deposit-Taking Companies in Hong Kong had failed to prevent them from losing their investments, because he had negligently granted a licence to a fraudulent deposit-taking company, and had failed to stop that company from continuing to trade when he had reasonable grounds to suspect it was trading fraudulently. The Privy Council held that there could be no liability. The key finding was that there was insufficient proximity between the Commissioner and the investors, but the case might equally be regarded as one of non-feasance. The Commissioner's statutory powers did not require him to take steps actively to safeguard the financial well-being of investors. It followed that he could not be liable for his omission to act. Lord Keith noted that negligence liability is not based solely on foreseeability of harm. There is, for example, no liability "on the part of one who sees another about to walk over a cliff with his head in the air, and forbears to shout a warning".[57] His Lordship was here citing a classic example of non-feasance—in

---

[54] [1996] A.C. 923. See also *Gorringe v Calderdale M.B.C.* [2004] 1 W.L.R. 1057.
[55] *ibid.*, at 943.
[56] [1988] A.C. 175.
[57] *ibid.*, at 192.

the absence of a "special relationship", there is no duty to go to the rescue of another. By analogy, the Commissioner owed no duty to save the investors from their fate, or, for that matter, to prevent a third party (the fraudulent company) from acting so as to cause them loss.

The rule against liability for non-feasance, then, gives rise to two important propositions:

- in English law, in contrast to civil law jurisdictions,[58] there is no general duty to rescue another;
- there is no *general* duty to prevent other people from causing damage.

These matters are considered below.

Non-feasance: no duty to rescue

2–023 In *Smith v Littlewoods Organisation Ltd*,[59] Lord Goff stated that the refusal of English law to impose liability for mere omissions might one day need to be reconsidered, in the light of the "affirmative duties of good neighbourliness" imposed in other countries.[60] It seems, however, that that day is still some way off. In order for a duty to rescue to arise in English law, a prior relationship of care must exist between the defendant and the person who needs rescuing. Thus, whilst parents may be liable in negligence if they stand by and let their children drown in shallow water, the same cannot be said of a mere bystander at a swimming pool.[61] There is a related point that should be noted here: because there is no duty to rescue, it follows that in cases where a rescuer chooses to intervene, he or she cannot be liable in negligence unless it can be said that the intervention has made the claimant's position worse than if it had not taken place.[62]

Non-feasance: no general duty to prevent others from causing damage

2–024 In the same way that there is no duty to save others from natural perils, there is, generally speaking, no duty to save them from perils arising from the actions of others. This was affirmed by Lord Goff in *Smith v Littlewoods Organisation Ltd*. The defendants had acquired a disused cinema, intending to develop the land where it stood. Shortly after they had taken possession of the cinema, vagrants occupied the building. On two occasions, small fires had been started using rubbish that had been left lying outside the cinema, but these fires had not been reported to the defendants or to the police. Then, one evening, the cinema was set on fire, damaging the plaintiffs'

---

[58] See, *e.g.* Art. 233–6 of the French Penal Code, which punishes (with corresponding tortious liability) anyone who wilfully refrains from assisting a person in danger, when he or she could have done so without risk to himself or herself or to third parties.
[59] [1987] A.C. 241 at 271.
[60] Citing Fleming, *The Law of Torts* (6th ed., 1983) at 138.
[61] *per* Lord Nicholls in *Stovin v Wise* [1996] A.C. 923 at 931.
[62] *Horsley v MacLaren (The Ogopogo)* [1971] 2 Lloyd's Rep. 410, applied in *Capital & Counties v Hampshire CC* [1997] Q.B. 1004.

neighbouring property. The plaintiffs argued that the defendants ought to have prevented the vagrants from starting the fire. It was held that whilst the defendants were under a duty to prevent their property from becoming a source of danger to neighbouring property, on the facts, this duty did not extend to controlling the activities of the vagrants. Because the defendants had not known about the previous fires, it was not reasonably foreseeable that a fire would be started that would damage neighbouring property.

The decision in *Smith v Littlewoods* represented the culmination of a number of judicial attempts to identify the legal basis on which a defendant should be absolved from liability for the consequences of a wrong committed by a third party. Previously, there had been three Court of Appeal decisions on similar facts to *Smith v Littlewoods*, each of which had used a different element of the tort of negligence to deny liability. In *Lamb v Camden LBC*[63] it had been held that the third party's actions were too remote a consequence of the defendant's breach, whilst in *P.Perl (Exporters) Ltd v Camden LBC*[64] it had been held that, because the defendant could not be expected to control the third party, no duty of care was owed, and in *King v Liverpool CC*[65] it had been held that although a duty was owed, the defendants were not in breach of their duty because there was nothing they could reasonably have done to prevent the third parties from causing the damage.

The reasoning in *Smith v Littlewoods*, however, does little to clarify the question of which approach should be adopted. This is because, whilst Lord Goff approaches the question of liability from the point of view of the duty of care, the other Law Lords speak in terms of breach of duty. It is submitted, however, that Lord Goff's approach is to be preferred, because it introduces some clarity into this area of the law. His Lordship took as a starting point the proposition that, as a general rule, there is no duty of care owed to prevent third parties from causing damage, but acknowledged that there appear to be certain exceptions to this rule. His Lordship went on to identify four particular situations where liability for the acts of third parties can arise. These can be summarised as follows:

(1) Special relationship between the defendant and the claimant

The first situation is where the defendant has assumed responsibility to look after the claimant's property. Thus, in *Stansbie v Troman*,[66] the plaintiff employed a decorator who went out and left the premises unsecured. The decorator was held liable for losses caused by a thief who entered the premises and stole some of the plaintiff's property. The contractual relationship between the plaintiff and the decorator justified the imposition of liability—the decorator had agreed to look after the premises.   2–025

(2) Special relationship between the defendant and the third party

In *Home Office v Dorset Yacht* (discussed above), the defendants were liable because they had a relationship of control over the third parties who caused the damage.   2–026

(3) Creating a source of danger "sparked off" by a third party

The defendant may be liable for creating a dangerous situation which is subsequently "sparked off" by the foreseeable actions of third parties. This principle may apply, for example, to a defendant who keeps an unsecured shed full of fireworks that are   2–027

---

[63] [1981] Q.B. 625.
[64] [1984] Q.B. 342.
[65] [1986] 3 All E.R. 544.
[66] [1948] 2 K.B. 48.

subsequently ignited by mischievous children.[67] The principle was applied in *Haynes v Harwood*,[68] where the defendants left their horses unattended in the street and a boy threw a stone at them and caused them to bolt. The defendants were liable when the plaintiff was injured trying to save people from being injured by the horses.

(4) Failing to take reasonable steps to abate a danger created by a third party

2–028   Where the defendant knows, or reasonably ought to know, that third parties are creating a danger on his or her premises, the defendant is under a duty to take reasonable steps to abate that danger. Thus, in *Clark Fixing Ltd v Dudley Metropolitan Borough Council*[69], where known trespassers on a vacant development site started a fire which burned down neighbouring property, the Court of Appeal, distinguishing *Smith v Littlewoods*, held the defendant council liable for failing to remove combustible material from the site, so as to prevent the spread of fire. If, in *Smith v Littlewoods*, the previous fires had been reported to the defendants, they too may have been held liable on this principle.

THE TYPE OF DEFENDANT

2–029   It goes without saying that before imposing liability on a particular defendant the court will look beyond the individual case to the broad consequences of establishing that a duty is owed by this type of defendant. If the defendant is a member of a particular profession or group, a precedent will be set fixing all members of that profession or group with the duty in question. Decisions on liability can have far-reaching implications about the allocation of financial resources by potential defendants. This is of particular concern where the defendant in question is providing a public service. For example, if Doctor X is held liable to Patient Y in undertaking a certain procedure, then in future, all doctors will be liable in similar circumstances. This may increase the insurance costs of the hospitals employing the doctors and may even lead to doctors becoming reluctant to undertake the procedure in question, or to their insisting that excessive safeguards be taken. The cost of the safeguards will increase the cost of the procedure and may reduce its availability in a financially-constrained health service.

The problem of increasing the scope of negligence liability affects a number of different professions and groups. In relation to each of these, the courts have adopted a slightly different approach. In relation to NHS medical services, for example, the usual mechanism for limiting negligence liability is not to restrict the scope of the duty of care. Rather, it is to hold that a doctor (or other medical professional) will not be in *breach* of the duty of care if his or her behaviour lives up to the standard of other responsible medical professionals.[70] In relation to some other public services, however, the courts are at times prepared to hold that, for policy reasons, no duty of care is owed. This discrepancy in approach between different types of defendant has attracted judicial comment,[71] but it remains the case that certain types of defendant may escape

---

[67] *per* Lord Goff in *Smith v Littlewoods* [1987] A.C. 241 at 273.
[68] [1935] 1 K.B. 146.
[69] [2001] EWCA Civ 1898.
[70] *Bolam v Friern Barnet Hospital Management Committee* [1957] 1 W.L.R. 582 (discussed in Ch. 5).
[71] See *Capital and Counties plc v Hampshire CC* [1997] Q.B. 1004 *per* Stuart-Smith L.J. at 1040.

negligence liability because they owe no duty, whilst others are judged by the standard of their profession.

For the sake of convenience, we deal with different types of defendant under four headings:

- local authorities

- other public servants

- private regulators

- lawyers

(1) Local authorities

Actions against local authorities are common. Often, a claimant will seek to show that   **2–030**
he or she is owed a duty of care by a local authority, even though its contribution to the damage has been minor, because the authority has the funds to pay compensation. To succeed, however, a claimant must overcome a number of hurdles. In exploring these hurdles, it is helpful to appreciate that, in essence, the courts are here faced with the difficult task of determining the terms of the "social contract" under which taxpayers pay for the services the authorities provide. The fundamental question in most local authority cases is simply this: how far is it appropriate to provide a remedy in negligence where the state fails to confer a benefit on an individual?

Policy arguments

There are a number of policy objections to the imposition of a duty of care on local   **2–031**
authorities. A common objection is that the threat of liability may lead to the local authority adopting overly cautious practices at the public expense. Another objection is that allowing liability in tort will undermine or distort the framework of public protection provided by statute[72] or available in another area of the common law. In many cases, the claimant will have an alternative means of redress. He or she may be able to seek judicial review, or take advantage of a remedy provided by the statute under which the local authority has acted. Sometimes, compensation will be available from a publicly funded body such as the Criminal Injuries Compensation Board, or by invoking other torts such as breach of statutory duty and misfeasance in public office. Moreover, it is argued that making a local authority pay compensation is contrary to the general public interest, because it forces the authority to divert scarce financial resources away from general public welfare, reallocating them to a small number of litigants.

In recent years, the courts have been keen to stress the distinction between contract and tort and have made it clear that there are political, moral and economic reasons why tort should not be used to impose a duty to confer a benefit on others, as opposed to a duty to refrain from causing harm. These reasons were cogently enunciated by Lord Hoffmann in *Stovin v Wise* (the relevant passage is set out earlier in this chapter.)

---

[72] See *X v Bedfordshire CC* [1995] 2 A.C. 633 at 750; *Yuen Kun-Yeu v Att.-Gen. of Hong Kong* [1988] A.C. 175 at 198; *Harris v Evans* [1998] 3 All E.R. 522.

The question arises, however, whether it is appropriate to maintain this sharp distinction in the context of the welfare state, when to do so may create an unacceptable social divide between those who rely on the state for their welfare and those who look after themselves privately. In the context of the National Health Service (discussed later), the courts have clearly found such a divide unacceptable— therefore an NHS patient has substantially the same remedy in tort as a private patient would have for breach of contract.

Similarly, in the context of state education, the House of Lords has held in *Phelps v Hillingdon LBC*[73] that a local authority can owe a duty of care when providing educational services. This mirrors the legal position which would arise if the pupil (or his or her parents) had contracted privately for educational services. In relation to other state services, however, such as the provision of safe roads (*Stovin v Wise*), the courts have been unwilling to hold that a local authority owes a duty of care. Arguably, the courts have only been able to deny a duty of care in these cases because this does not create an obvious contrast with services provided in the private sector. With this in mind, we can now examine some of the reasoning the courts have employed to determine liability.

It should be noted that, in line with the courts' general opposition to claims for pure economic loss, such claims against local authorities will normally be disallowed.[74] The problem of economic loss is considered in Ch. 3. Here, we concentrate on other issues, and examine the extent to which a local authority owes a duty of care in relation to physical and psychiatric harm.

"Powers" and "duties"

2–032   The damage in suit will usually have resulted from a local authority's exercise of a statutory power or duty. In deciding the question of liability, the court will examine the wording of the statute under which the local authority has acted and determine whether the power or duty in question has been given for the benefit of individuals, or whether it serves only a general governmental purpose.[75] In the latter case, there may be no liability, because it cannot be said that the authority has assumed responsibility to the aggrieved individual.

The leading authority on statutory *powers* is *Stovin v Wise*.[76] Here, the plaintiff was involved in a road traffic accident at a dangerous junction. The question arose whether the local authority, which had resolved to carry out improvements to the junction, could be liable for its failure to do so. By a 3:2 majority, the House of Lords held that the local authority was not liable for its omission to act. The local authority had a statutory power to improve the junction, but not a duty to do so. Thus, its omission to improve the junction could not be seen as having occurred in the context of any positive obligation to protect the plaintiff from harm.

Their Lordships held that, normally, there could be no liability for failure to exercise a statutory *power*—the absence of a *duty* in the statute would exclude the existence of a

---

[73] [2001] 2 A.C. 619.
[74] *Murphy v Brentwood D.C.* [1991] 1 A.C. 398 (discussed in Ch. 3).
[75] See, *e.g. Governors of the Peabody Donation Fund v Sir Lindsay Parkinson & Co. Ltd* [1985] A.C. 210, *Yuen Kun-Yeu v Att.-Gen. of Hong Kong* [1988] A.C. 175 and *Curran v Northern Ireland Co-ownership Housing Association Ltd* [1987] A.C. 718.
[76] [1996] A.C. 923.

common law duty of care. However, there could be liability for failure to exercise a mere power in very exceptional circumstances, namely where it could be said that the authority's decision not to exercise the power had been *irrational*, and where there were exceptional grounds for holding that the policy of the statute required compensation to be paid to persons who suffered loss because the power was not exercised. Such was the case in *Kane v New Forest District Council*.[77] Here, the claimant was seriously injured when he emerged from a footpath on to a main road and was hit by an oncoming car. The council had required the construction of the footpath as a condition of planning permission for surrounding development. It had intended to see that the main road was widened, so that people emerging from the footpath could be seen by drivers, but at the time of the accident this had not been done. Since the footpath was a source of danger that had been *created* by the council's positive act (insisting that it be built), the court was able to distinguish *Stovin v Wise* (which concerned a mere failure to act). Their Lordships went on to hold that it was irrational for the council not to have exercised its power to prohibit the opening of the footpath until it was safe to use—the circumstances were such as effectively to place the council under a duty to exercise this power for the benefit of the claimant. It had assumed an obligation to protect the claimant from harm. Simon Brown L.J. rejected the council's submission that it was entitled to avail itself of a blanket immunity in respect of its planning functions, as being inconsistent with recent developments in the law (which we discuss below).[78]

Where the provision in question is a statutory *duty* (as opposed to a *power*), an important factor will be *whether the statute expressly provides for compensation* to be paid to individuals affected by failure to fulfil the duty. If this is the case, there may be a claim for breach of statutory duty (a separate tort, considered in Ch. 7), but the courts may disallow negligence liability, so as not to create an overlap with another cause of action. If this is not the case, the courts may, in any event, decline to impose negligence liability, for fear of disturbing the intention of Parliament. As Lord Hoffmann put it, in *Stovin v Wise*:   **2–033**

"Whether a statutory duty gives rise to a private cause of action is a question of construction . . . if the policy of the Act is not to create a statutory liability to pay compensation, the same policy should ordinarily exclude the existence of a common law duty of care."[79]

"General reliance" on the exercise of statutory powers

As has been said, *Stovin v Wise* concerned the exercise of a statutory *power* — the local authority had a power to improve the road junction, had made a decision to do so, but had then let the matter go to sleep. We have already noted that Lord Hoffmann regarded this as a case of non-feasance. His Lordship did recognise, however, that in   **2–034**

---

[77] [2002] 1 W.L.R. 312. It has been pointed out that this decision places a very onerous burden on planning authorities to monitor and enforce planning conditions where a source of danger may have been created. See Pether, [2003] J.P.I. Law 48.

[78] His Lordship referred to *Barrett v Enfield LBC* [2001] 2 A.C. 550 and *Osman v United Kingdom* (1998) 29 E.H.R.R. 245.

[79] *ibid.*, at 952. Compare this with the opinion of Lord Nicholls (at 940) who thought that where public law is unable to provide a remedy, a "concurrent common law duty is needed to fill the gap".

certain cases, where a section of the public placed "general reliance" on the exercise of a power by a public body, this reliance could create a degree of proximity that would justify regarding the omission to exercise the power as misfeasance.[80] But in his Lordship's view, in order for the doctrine of "general reliance" to assist a claimant, it had to be shown that the authority had arbitrarily denied a benefit to the claimant that was routinely and consistently provided to a distinct and limited class of individuals. This could not be shown on the facts: the improvement of road junctions was not a uniform and identifiable service, and the plaintiff was in the same position as all other road-users. Lord Nicholls, on the other hand, who delivered a powerful dissenting opinion (with which Lord Slynn agreed), thought that "general reliance" by road users on the authority to provide safe road junctions should be an important factor in establishing liability.[81]

2–035   **Human rights cases.**   It should be noted that their Lordships' assertion, in *Stovin v Wise*, that there can generally be no liability for failure to exercise a statutory power must now be seen in the context of the Human Rights Act 1998. Where (as in the "child abuse" cases discussed below) the failure to exercise the power would result in a violation of human rights, it is doubtful that the courts will allow the arguments that succeeded in *Stovin v Wise* to preclude the existence of a duty of care. The same might be said for cases where failure to comply with a statutory *duty* causes human rights violations, but the statute does not provide for compensation. The correct approach in such cases, however, remains a little unclear. This is because the courts have not yet expressed with certainty their view about the mechanism by which breaches of human rights should be redressed. In the meantime, as we shall see, the courts have been reluctant to apply the broader aspects of the reasoning in *Stovin v Wise* in the context of negligence claims involving allegations of breaches of human rights by local authorities.

"Policy matters" and "operational matters"

2–036   In many cases, the courts draw a distinction between activities involving matters of "policy" and activities which can be regarded as "operational" (*i.e.* activities which *implement* policy). This distinction is a persistent feature of the reasoning in local authority cases, and was explored at some length in *Anns v Merton LBC*. On the basis of the policy/operational distinction, so the argument ran, it could be said that the way in which buildings were inspected was an "operational" activity, to which negligence liability might attach, whilst a decision to allocate financial resources which resulted in too few building inspectors being appointed would be immune from a negligence suit, because such policy decisions are not justiciable.

The problem with the policy/operational distinction, however, is that it is difficult logically to identify "operational" activities which do not involve any element of "policy". This is because, whenever a person exercises *discretion* in the performance of a task, some element of "policy" will be involved. Is this task to be done quickly or slowly? How much money will be spent in performing this task? Logically, these

---

[80] See *Invercargill City Council v Hamlin* [1996] A.C. 624.
[81] [1996] A.C. 923 at 939. It has been noted, however, that the doctrine of "general reliance" does not seem to have gained wider acceptance by the UK courts. See Lunney and Oliphant, *Tort Law Text and Materials*, 2nd ed. (2003) at p.498.

matters are just as much matters of "policy" as resolutions passed in committee meetings. As Lord Slynn noted in *Barrett v Enfield LBC*,[82] "even knocking a nail into a piece of wood involves the exercise of some choice or discretion".

The attempt in *Anns v Merton LBC*[83] to assert the relevance of a policy/operational distinction met with considerable criticism. In *Rowling v Takaro Properties*,[84] Lord Keith observed:

"... this distinction does not provide a touchstone of liability, but rather is expressive of the need to exclude altogether those cases in which the decision under attack is of such a kind that a question whether it has been made negligently is unsuitable for judicial resolution, of which notable examples are discretionary decisions on the allocation of scarce resources or the distribution of risks."

Whilst the distinction is attractive, because it enables the court to wash its hands of political matters by declaring them not justiciable, the impossibility of drawing a logical distinction between, on the one hand, matters of "high policy", and, on the other hand, "operational" matters involving the exercise of discretion, makes the distinction problematic. Nevertheless, despite its imperfections, the distinction is still occasionally used by the courts, largely one suspects because they have no better means of avoiding conflict with the legislature.

Human rights: the child abuse cases

In recent years, a number of cases have arisen in which claimants have sought damages   **2–037** for psychiatric harm, alleging that this has been caused by the negligence of local authorities in the exercise of their statutory functions in protecting child welfare. The initial response of the courts was to dismiss such claims, holding that, for policy reasons, the local authorities could owe no duty of care. It soon became clear, however, that this approach was incompatible with the European Convention on Human Rights. In many of the cases, the claimants had been subjected to "inhuman or degrading treatment", contrary to Art. 3 of the Convention, and the danger was, that if the courts said no duty of care was owed to these claimants, they would be denied an effective remedy.

The courts' initial approach to the child abuse cases (and to the "education cases"— discussed later) is illustrated by the reasoning of Lord Browne-Wilkinson in *X v Bedfordshire CC*.[85] In *X*, the House of Lords considered five consolidated appeals. In the first group of cases, it was alleged that a local authority had negligently failed to take children into care, with the result that they suffered neglect and abuse at home and, conversely, that a local authority had wrongly decided to take a child into care, causing psychiatric harm to the child and its mother. The second group of cases concerned allegations that the local authority had negligently failed to provide adequate education for children with special needs.

On the facts of these cases, Lord Browne-Wilkinson thought that it would not be fair, just and reasonable to impose a duty of care. In the abuse cases, a duty of care

[82] [2001] 2 A.C. 550.
[83] [1978] A.C. 728 at 754.
[84] [1988] A.C. 473 at 501.
[85] [1995] 2 A.C. 633.

would have been inconsistent with the operation of the statutory system set up for the protection of children at risk. This system involved a number of agencies besides the local authority, and to place liability only on one agency would be manifestly unjust. Equally, to state that all parties owed a duty of care would cause untold problems in ascertaining which party had been in breach or had caused the damage. In the education cases, the claimants had access to a statutory appeals procedure, and their Lordships felt that this, rather than litigation, was the most appropriate way of dealing with the claimants' problems.[86] As we shall see, however, the courts have subsequently changed their approach both to the child abuse cases (which involved human rights violations) and to the education cases, discussed separately below.

A central part of Lord Brown-Wilkinson's reasoning in *X v Bedfordshire CC* was that, if the actions alleged to be negligent had resulted from a local authority properly exercising its discretion in pursuing a particular course of conduct (*e.g.* taking a child into care) the exercise of that discretion could not give rise to liability in negligence. As his Lordship put it:

"... the local authority cannot be liable in damages for doing that which Parliament has authorised. Therefore if the decisions complained of fall within the ambit of such statutory discretion they cannot be actionable in common law."[87]

In *Barrett v Enfield LBC*,[88] however, the House of Lords took the opportunity to refine and clarify this idea. *Barrett* was a case in which it was alleged that, having taken a child into care, the local authority had been negligent in looking after the child's welfare, causing the child to grow up with a number of problems, including alcoholism and a predisposition towards criminal activity and self-harm. Lord Slynn emphasised that Lord Browne-Wilkinson's view that a local authority could not be liable for the *proper* exercise of its discretion did not, of course, mean that liability in negligence was ruled out just because the actions of the authority *involved* the exercise of discretion. Therefore, in an application to strike out a case as disclosing no cause of action (which was the issue both in *X* and in *Barrett*) it would not be appropriate to do so, because the question whether the local authority had exercised its discretion *properly* could only be answered once the facts of the case had been fully considered.[89]

The decision in Z v United Kingdom[90]

2–038   Some of the claimants in *X v Bedfordshire CC*, having failed in the House of Lords, took their claims to the European Court of Human Rights, where the case proceeded under the name of *Z v United Kingdom*.[91] These claimants were four siblings who had suffered terrible abuse at the hands of their mother—they had, for example, been locked in filthy unlit bedrooms, which they had been forced to use as toilets, and had been left so hungry that they had had to scavenge for apple cores in dustbins. The local

---

[86] Compare Lord Templeman's view in *Hill v Chief Constable of West Yorkshire* [1989] A.C. 53.
[87] *X v Bedfordshire CC* [1995] 2 A.C. 633 at 736.
[88] [2001] 2 A.C. 550.
[89] In this context, see also *W. v Essex CC* [2001] 2 A.C. 592.
[90] *Z v United Kingdom* is also an important case on the interpretation of Art. 6.1 and is discussed later in that context.
[91] (2002) 34 E.H.R.R. 3.

authority had repeatedly decided not to appoint a social worker for the children and had declined to place them on the Child Protection Register. The E.C.H.R. was prepared to award the claimants compensation, to be paid by the UK Government, on the basis that the UK had breached two of its obligations under the European Convention on Human Rights—it had allowed the claimants to be subjected to "inhuman and degrading treatment" (contrary to Art. 3) when it failed to act to ensure their welfare, and it had denied them a right to an effective remedy in respect of that treatment (contrary to Art. 13).

It is important to understand, however, that in coming to this decision, the E.C.H.R. did *not* hold that the "effective remedy" which ought to have been provided should *necessarily* have taken the form of a duty of care in negligence. There were other ways in which such a remedy could be provided, not least of which would be an award of compensation by a UK court for breach of the Human Rights Act 1998.[92] Under the Act, it is "unlawful for a public authority [*e.g.* a local authority] to act in a way which is incompatible with a Convention right".[93] An "act" includes a "failure to act"[94], and victims of a breach of a Convention right by a public authority are entitled to bring proceedings against that authority.[95] The UK courts are empowered to grant such relief or remedy as they see fit, including damages.[96] The Act therefore creates statutory rights that individuals can enforce directly against local authorities, without needing to invoke the tort of negligence. Thus, strictly speaking, nothing said by the E.C.H.R. in *Z v United Kingdom* contradicts the proposition that local authority liability in negligence can be confined for policy reasons by using the *Caparo* criteria (as it was in *X v Bedfordshire CC*), so long as, in appropriate cases (like *X*) the court is prepared to grant an alternative remedy under human rights law.[97]

One of the important issues in the recent development of the duty of care has been the question of whether, in cases like *X*, the duty of care concept should be extended so that the tort of negligence accommodates human rights law, or whether negligence claims should remain confined on traditional policy principles, with claimants being allowed an alternative remedy instead. There is, of course, much to be said for developing the tort of negligence so that it encompasses human rights law in appropriate cases. Without such a development, one is faced with a rather unsatisfactory dilemma: on the one hand, a public authority might have no duty of care in negligence, yet on the other hand it might be ordered to pay damages for breach of Convention rights. The incoherence of this result becomes clear when one considers that the foundation of this latter liability, put in plain terms, is the state's failure to have taken reasonable care for the welfare of its citizens. It would seem rather artificial to suggest that such liability might arise without someone acting on behalf of the state having committed the tort of negligence. At present, however, because of the reasoning in *Z*, this remains a theoretical possibility.

---

[92] Although at the time when *X* was decided such compensation was not available, because the Act was not in force.

[93] Human Rights Act 1998, s.6(1).

[94] *ibid.,* s.6(6).

[95] *ibid.,* s.7.

[96] *ibid.,* s.8. Damages under the Human Rights Act 1998 are discussed in Ch. 15.

[97] An alternative view would be that, since the court itself is a "public authority", it would be unlawful for it to apply the *Caparo* criteria inconsistently with Convention rights, even where it is willing to provide an alternative remedy. This appears to be the view taken, in essence, by the Court of Appeal in *D v East Berkshire Community Health NHS Trust* [2004] 2 W.L.R. 58.

Since most of the relevant cases have only concerned preliminary rulings about whether claimants have an "arguable case" that a duty of care *might* arise, it is too early to predict how this issue will unfold. Only, perhaps, when claimants and their lawyers get used to relying on breach of the Human Rights Act 1998 as a cause of action will a clear picture emerge of how negligence claims and human rights litigation are to sit alongside one another. However, the approach taken by the Court of Appeal in *D v East Berkshire Community Health NHS Trust*[98]—a case decided after *Z*—is instructive. Here, in refusing to strike out a number of claims, the court held that the policy reasons that had been advanced in *X* to deny a duty of care could not survive the passing of the Human Rights Act 1998, and that in local authority child abuse cases involving possible human rights violations, where the claim is brought by the child[99], the question whether the authority owed a duty of care should not be decided without a full trial. Although the point is not put beyond doubt[1], central to the court's reasoning seems to be the idea that, if, in the course of that trial, breaches of human rights are indeed established, a court must *inevitably find that a duty of care exists in negligence to avoid causing those breaches*, no matter how persuasive the policy arguments against liability. Such an approach, of course, means that, in these types of cases, traditional policy arguments are now displaced by the need to accommodate human rights law within the tort of negligence.

The education cases

2–039   In *Phelps v Hillingdon LBC*,[2] the House of Lords was prepared to hold that, in certain circumstances, a local authority could owe a duty of care in respect of the provision of educational services. In *Phelps*, the claimant had suffered from dyslexia as a child, causing her severe learning difficulties when she was at school. She had been referred to an educational psychologist when she was 11, but the psychologist failed to notice her dyslexia. She subsequently left school with no qualifications, and later sued the local authority for negligence in having failed to provide her with an appropriate education. The appeal in *Phelps* was consolidated with three other cases in which it was alleged that local authorities had been negligent in its provision of education for children with special needs. The House of Lords found in favour of all the claimants[3], emphasising that *X v Bedfordshire* did not lay down any principle that there should be a blanket immunity in respect of local authority liability for the provision of educational services.

The decision in *Phelps*, then, marked a significant shift away from the idea of using policy arguments to afford immunity to local authorities.[4] The gist of the decision is

---

[98] [2004] 2 W.L.R. 58. Note that the case is also known as *JD v East Berkshire Community Health NHS Trust*.
[99] The court held that public policy dictated that no common law duty of care could be owed to *parents* in respect local authority decisions as to whether to take a child into care–if it were otherwise, the authority might be faced with a conflict of interests where it had to remove a child from its parents to protect the child from degrading treatment, yet doing this would interfere with the parents' right to family life.
[1] The court conceded: "It is possible that there will be factual situations where it is not fair, just or reasonable to impose a duty of care, but each case will fall to be determined on its individual facts." [2004] 2 W.L.R. 58 at 87, *per* Lord Phillips M.R.
[2] [2001] 2 A.C. 619.
[3] Note that in only one of the appeals (*Phelps* itself) did this mean that the claimant won the case. In the other cases, the issue was simply whether they should be allowed to proceed to trial.
[4] See also *S v Gloucestershire CC* [2001] Fam. 313; *A v Essex CC* [2003] EWCA Civ 1848, (2004) F.C.R. 660; *D v East Berkshire Community Health NHS Trust* [2004] 2 W.L.R. 58.

that each case of this type should be carefully considered on its merits, and that, although there are certainly important policy arguments why local authorities should be protected from a flood of negligence claims, the courts should be reluctant to rule that these arguments justify the denial of a duty of care. The effect of *Phelps*, therefore, is to shift emphasis away from using the duty of care as a control mechanism to limit the scope of liability in local authority cases. As Lord Nicholls put it: "Denial of a cause of action is seldom, if ever, appropriate response to fear of its abuse."[5] With this in mind, we can perhaps expect greater emphasis to be placed on questions of breach of duty and causation in the future.

In the wake of *Phelps*, it seems that a general duty of care on the part of local authorities to look after the welfare of children in state schools is becoming firmly established. Thus, in *Kearn-Price v Kent CC*[6] a local authority was liable when the claimant, a boy of 14, was struck in the eye by a leather football. The school had banned the use of such footballs, because of the potential danger to pupils, but had done little to enforce the ban. The claimant was injured in the playground shortly before the start of the school day. The Court of Appeal dismissed the local authority's argument that it could not be expected to supervise the welfare of pupils outside of school hours. In the particular circumstances, a duty of care was owed and had been breached. It is clear, however, that the scope of a local authority's "out of school" supervisory duty is limited. Thus, in *Bradford-Smart v West Sussex CC*,[7] Garland J. held that it would not be fair, just and reasonable to hold that the duty extended to protecting a child from bullying outside school. Reading between the lines, we can see that in all of these "educational welfare" cases the courts are concerned not to create a socially unacceptable divide between private educational services (where contractual liability might arise) and educational services provided by the state.

(2) Other public servants

In this section, we consider the duty of care in relation to the following types of   **2–040**
defendant:

- the police
- the fire brigade
- the coastguard
- the ambulance service
- the NHS
- the armed forces

The police

Where a claimant suffers loss as a direct result of police negligence in the day-to-day   **2–041**
conduct of their operations, this will be treated in the same way as any other claim.
Thus, in *Rigby v Chief Constable of Northamptonshire*,[8] the plaintiff's gun shop had

---

[5] *Phelps v Hillingdon LBC* [2001] 2 A.C. 619 at 667.
[6] [2003] P.I.Q.R. P11 (CA).
[7] [2002] EWCA Civ 7; (2002) 1 F.C.R. 425.
[8] [1985] 1 W.L.R. 1242. See also *Knightley v Johns* [1982] 1 W.L.R. 349.

been under siege and the police had negligently fired a canister of C.S. gas into the shop without taking adequate precautions against the high risk of fire. When a fire occurred, the plaintiff was successful in his negligence claim.

The position is different, however, where the complaint is that the police have been negligent in their investigations. In *Hill v Chief Constable of West Yorkshire*,[9] the mother of the last victim killed by Peter Sutcliffe (a serial killer known as the "Yorkshire Ripper") sued the police authority for negligence, alleging that it had failed to use reasonable care in apprehending him. Sutcliffe had been interviewed by the police and subsequently released. It was argued that the police had carelessly failed to realise, at an earlier stage in their investigations, that Sutcliffe was the murderer. Had they done so, his last victim, Jacqueline Hill, would not have died.

The House of Lords refused to impose a duty of care. Lord Keith held that, since it could not be shown that there was any exceptional risk to Jacqueline Hill personally, there was insufficient proximity between her, as the potential victim of a crime, and the police.[10] His Lordship also objected to liability on policy grounds. Policy considerations dictated that liability in such cases would be counter-productive: the threat of liability would lead to defensive practices which would absorb limited public resources, causing the police to divert manpower and attention from their most important function—the suppression of crime. Lord Templeman commented that the courts were an inappropriate forum for the claim. If Mrs Hill wished to criticise the way the police had conducted the case, the matter would be best dealt with by a public inquiry instituted by national or local authorities responsible to the electorate.[11]

The application of the police "immunity" established in *Hill* was subsequently challenged before the E.C.H.R. in *Osman v United Kingdom*[12] as being contrary to Article 6.1 of the European Convention on Human Rights (right of access to a court). It was this litigation that gave rise to the "Article 6.1 controversy", and threatened to curtail the UK courts' practice of striking out claims where the *Caparo* criteria indicated that the defendants did not owe a duty of care. Although the claimants in *Osman* were successful, the E.C.H.R. subsequently conceded —in *Z v United Kingdom* — that its approach in *Osman* was wrong. This issue is discussed further in a section at the end of this chapter.

The approach in *Hill* was followed in *Cowan v Chief Constable of Avon & Somerset*.[13] Here, a landlord was threatening to commit the criminal offence of evicting a tenant, contrary to section 1 of the Protection from Eviction Act 1977. The police arrived at the scene in order to prevent a breach of the peace, but the eviction went ahead. The tenant brought an action against the police, arguing that the officers at the scene

---

[9] [1989] A.C. 53. See also *Ancell v McDermott* [1993] 4 All E.R. 355, applied by analogy to the Crown Prosecution Service in *Elguzouli-Daf v Commissioner of Police of the Metropolis* [1995] Q.B. 335, but contrast *Welsh v Chief Constable of the Merseyside Police* [1993] 1 All E.R. 692 where the Crown Prosecution Service were liable when they had assumed responsibility for informing the magistrates that the charge had been dealt with in the Crown Court, but had negligently failed to do so because of an administrative mix-up. Compare *Quinland v Governor of Swaleside Prison* [2003] Q.B. 306.
[10] *Hill v Chief Constable of West Yorkshire* [1989] A.C. 53 at 62. See also *Alexandrou v Oxford* [1993] 4 All E.R. 328, CA, where the police were held not to owe a duty to the owners of business premises who had a burglar alarm system connected to a police station. There was insufficient proximity between the police and a member of the public who informed them of a crime.
[11] *Hill v Chief Constable of West Yorkshire* [1989] A.C. 53 at 65.
[12] (1998) 5 B.H.R.C. 293.
[13] [2002] H.L.R. 44.

should have prevented the eviction, because they owed a duty of care to protect him from the landlord's commission of a criminal offence. It was held that the police owed no general duty to individual members of the public in exercising their functions, and that their presence at the scene did not in itself create a relationship of sufficient proximity with members of the public who might be the victims of crime. To hold otherwise would not be in the public interest, because it would mean that, in order to protect themselves from liability, the police would have to take time to analyse all relevant legal information before responding to urgent calls for assistance.

Where the case concerns the protection of a police informant, however, there is some indication that the courts have been willing to balance the *Hill* "immunity" arguments against countervailing considerations. In *Swinney v Chief Constable of Northumbria Police*,[14] a police informant had given information to the police about an individual who was known to be violent and ruthless. Subsequently, this individual made threats against her and her husband, following the theft of her details from an unattended police car. In an application to strike out the case before trial, it was held that the informant had an arguable case in negligence. There was a sufficient degree of proximity between the police and the informant because the risk to her was clear. The court was conscious of the strong public policy argument in favour of allowing liability in such cases, so that informants would be encouraged to give information vital to the suppression of crime. At the full hearing, however, the Swinneys lost their case. On the facts, the police had not been in breach of their duty of care.[15]

The courts have held that the arguments advanced in *Hill* do not necessarily preclude a duty of care owed by the police authority to its own employees. Thus, in *Costello v Chief Constable of Northumbria Police*[16] the Court of Appeal held that countervailing arguments in favour of liability justified holding a police officer liable for standing by whilst his colleague suffered personal injury. Similarly, in *Mullaney v Chief Constable of West Midlands*[17] the police authority was liable when a probationary constable suffered serious injury whilst attempting an arrest, in circumstances where fellow officers had failed to respond to his calls for assistance. The police have also been held liable where their negligence has allowed people to commit suicide while in custody.[18] In cases where the courts have found it necessary to distinguish *Hill*, however, they have stressed that their decisions should not be interpreted as undermining the general principle of immunity laid down in that case.

In the light of the positive obligations now placed on public authorities by the Human Rights Act 1998, and the recent general decline in the courts' willingness to entertain public policy immunity arguments, it is questionable how long the "*Hill* immunity" can survive. We can perhaps expect a more open evaluation by the courts

[14] [1997] Q.B. 464.
[15] *Swinney v Chief Constable of Northumbria Police (No.2)* (1999) 11 Admin. L.R. 811.
[16] [1999] 1 All E.R. 550. See also *Waters v Commissioner of Police of the Metropolis* [2000] 1 W.L.R. 1607 (HL).
[17] [2001] EWCA Civ 700, *The Independent*, July 9, 2001. Compare *Leach v Chief Constable of Gloucestershire Constabulary* [1999] 1 All E.R. 215 where, by a majority, the Court of Appeal struck out a claim by the appropriate adult who had sat with Frederick West (a serial killer) in police interviews. The police had not assumed responsibility for her psychological well-being. Their only obligation was to provide counselling during or within a short time of the interviews.
[18] See *Reeves v Commissioner of Police of the Metropolis* [2000] A.C. 360; *Keenan v United Kingdom* (2001) 33 E.H.R.R. 38. Compare *Orange v Chief Constable of West Yorkshire* [2002] Q.B. 347 and *Vellino v Chief Constable of Greater Manchester* [2002] 1 W.L.R. 218.

of the policy issues underlying police immunity. In any event, it is questionable whether the broad policy objections advanced in *Hill* can be justified. Would imposing a duty of care on the police lead to unduly defensive practices, or would it encourage the force to take more care? The courts have been rightly criticised for omitting any sociological or statistical analysis from their deliberations on this matter, and they risk being accused of too readily protecting the police in the vague pursuit of the common good.

The fire brigade

2–042   In *Capital & Counties plc v Hampshire CC*,[19] the idea that the fire brigade should be immune from liability on public policy grounds was examined by the Court of Appeal. The case was consolidated with three other appeals in which it was alleged that the fire brigade had been negligent in tackling fires. In the first two cases (*Capital & Counties* and *Digital Equipment*), the alleged negligence consisted of ordering that a sprinkler system, which had been operating at the location of the fire, be turned off. In the third case (*John Munroe*), it was alleged that, after fighting a fire on adjacent premises, the fire brigade left the scene without ensuring that the fire was properly extinguished, with the result that it re-ignited, damaging the plaintiff's premises. In the fourth case (*Church of Jesus Christ of Latter-Day Saints*), it was alleged that the fire brigade had negligently failed to take proper steps to ensure that an adequate supply of water was available at the scene of the fire.

The plaintiffs faced two main problems. First, they faced policy objections that were similar to those advanced in *Hill*—for example that making the fire brigade liable for negligence in the course of its duties would lead to defensive practices, diverting resources away from the task of fighting fires. Secondly, they faced the reluctance of the courts to find that a sufficient degree of proximity exists where the case is one of "general reliance" by the public on services provided by a public body.

Stuart-Smith L.J., giving the judgment of the Court of Appeal, held that the fire brigade's attendance at the scene of a fire did not, of itself, give rise to the requisite degree of proximity. In the court's view, this followed from the fact that the fire brigade was under no duty to attend the fire in the first place. As Stuart-Smith L.J. put it:

"... the fire brigade are not under a common law duty to answer the call for help, and are not under a duty to take care to do so. If, therefore, they fail to turn up, or fail to turn up in time, because they have carelessly misunderstood the message, get lost on the way or run into a tree, they are not liable."[20]

It would be strange, therefore, if, being under no duty to attend, the fire brigade could be liable where it had attended but had not made a claimant's position any worse. Accordingly, the plaintiffs in *John Munroe* and *Church of Jesus Christ of Latter Day Saints* could not succeed because, although the fire brigade had intervened, its actions

---

[19] [1997] Q.B. 1004. Consolidated with *Digital Equipment Co. Ltd v Hampshire CC*, *John Munroe (Acrylics) Ltd v London Fire and Civil Defence Authority* and *Church of Jesus Christ of Latter-Day Saints (Great Britain) v West Yorkshire Fire and Civil Defence Authority*.
[20] *Capital and Counties plc v Hampshire CC* [1997] Q.B. 1004 at 1030. See also *Alexandrou v Oxford* [1993] 4 All E.R. 328.

had not caused any damage that would not have occurred had it failed to attend the fire. In the first two cases, however, the position was different. Here, it could be said that the incompetence of the fire brigade in ordering the sprinklers to be turned off had created a fresh source of danger, making the plaintiffs' position worse. So their claims succeeded.

So far as public policy immunity arguments were concerned, the court did not accept that the arguments which had been used in *Hill* were applicable, finding no close analogy between the activities of the fire brigade and the function of the police in investigating and suppressing crime. Neither did the court accept arguments based on the fear of indeterminate liability and the fact that property owners should bear the risk of fire because they are generally insured against it.

The coastguard

The familiar policy arguments for immunity have been applied to the coastguard,   **2–043** which has been held not to owe a duty of care in respect of its watching, search and rescue functions. In *O.L.L. v Secretary of State for the Home Department*,[21] it was alleged that the coastguard, by misdirecting a rescue operation, had substantially increased the risk of injury to those in peril and that it should therefore be liable on the same basis that the fire brigade had been liable in *Capital & Counties*. It was held, somewhat questionably perhaps, that on the facts this had not been the case. The coastguard had not directly inflicted physical injury on those who were lost at sea, and May J. declined to draw an arbitrary distinction between situations where the coastguard had misdirected itself (for which, in the light of *Capital & Counties*, it would not be liable) and situations where it had misdirected other organisations such as the Royal Navy. Clearly, though, his Lordship's decision reflected sympathy for a publicly funded service partly staffed by volunteers.[22]

The ambulance service

In *Kent v Griffiths*,[23] the Court of Appeal held that the policy arguments applicable to   **2–044** the police, and the "no liability unless the claimant's position is made worse than by failing to attend" argument, applicable to the fire brigade, had no general application to the ambulance service. The ambulance service was to be regarded as part of the health service rather than as a "rescue" service. The claimant suffered an asthma attack, and her doctor called an ambulance which took 40 minutes to arrive. Whilst waiting for the ambulance, she suffered a respiratory arrest, which would probably have been prevented if the ambulance had arrived within a reasonable time. Lord Woolf M.R., giving the judgment of the court, stated that the acceptance of the 999 call established a duty of care. Although cases might arise where policy considerations could exclude a duty of care—such as where the ambulance service had properly exercised its discretion to deal with a more pressing emergency before attending the claimant, or where it had made a choice about the allocation of resources—this was not such a case.

The decision in *Kent v Griffiths*, then, illustrates the idea that the courts are unwilling to deny a duty of care where this would create a divide between the

---

[21] [1997] 3 All E.R. 897. See also *Skinner v Secretary of State for Transport, The Times*, January 3, 1995.
[22] *O.L.L. v Secretary of State for the Home Department* [1997] 3 All E.R. 897 at 907.
[23] [2000] 2 All E.R. 474. Compare *King v Sussex Ambulance NHS Trust* [2002] EWCA Civ 953, [2002] I.C.R. 1413.

standards to be expected from public and private sector service providers. Had Mrs Kent contracted privately for health care services including emergency ambulance provision, she would have been able to claim for breach of contract. It would be socially unacceptable if she were placed in a worse position because of her reliance on the National Health Service. In relation to firefighting and the suppression of crime, however, such arguments do not arise, because people do not commonly contract privately for those services.[24]

The National Health Service

2–045   The normal way for a claimant to proceed in a medical negligence case is to allege that a medical professional has been negligent and that an NHS provider (*e.g.* an NHS Trust or Health Board) is vicariously liable.[25] In most cases, the duty of care owed by such professionals is well established. The courts therefore confine the scope of negligence liability by reference to the concept of breach of duty. This is discussed in Ch. 5. There is one group of cases, however, in which the courts have been willing to limit NHS negligence liability by using the scope of the duty of care as a control mechanism—the "unintended children" cases.

2–046   **The "unintended children" cases.** Until quite recently, the courts had been prepared to entertain claims against the NHS for the cost of bringing up children born as a result of negligent advice or treatment having been given to the parents.[26] Then, in *McFarlane v Tayside Health Board*,[27] the House of Lords decided that, in the case of healthy, able-bodied children, the law would no longer entertain such claims. In rejecting a claim in respect of a healthy baby girl, who was conceived as a result of wrong advice that a vasectomy had been successful, Lord Millett said that "the law must take the birth of a normal, healthy baby to be a blessing, not a detriment".[28] Their Lordships declined to compensate the claimant for the cost of bringing up the child—damages were to be confined to compensating the pain and suffering endured as a result of the pregnancy. Various reasons were advanced by their Lordships for reaching this conclusion. In particular, their Lordships were unwilling to accept that the law might regard a baby as being "more trouble than it was worth"[29]—parenthood had its burdens but also its rewards, and since the rewards of parenthood were incalculable, they could not sensibly be weighed up against the burdens, so it was impossible to quantify what the parents had lost by having a child. Their Lordships were also conscious of the fact that awarding compensation to the parents of a healthy child, at the expense of a financially constrained NHS, might offend against ordinary people's views of how public money should be spent.

---

[24] In this context, it is also worth considering whether *Alexandrou v Oxford* [1993] 4 All ER 328 (no liability where police failed properly to inspect premises after a burglar alarm had sounded) might have been decided differently had the defendants been a private security firm, or had the plaintiff been in a contractual relationship with the police. See the remarks of Glidewell L.J. in that case at 338, and compare *Bailey v HSS Alarms The Times*, 20 June, 2000 (2000 WL 345011).
[25] Vicarious liability is discussed in Ch. 7.
[26] See, for example, *Emeh v Kensington & Chelsea A.H.A.* [1985] Q.B. 1012; *Thake v Maurice* [1986] Q.B. 644; *Benarr v Kettering Health Board* (1988) 138 N.L.J. 179; *Nunnerley v Warrington Health Authority* [2000] P.I.Q.R. Q69.
[27] [2000] 2 A.C. 59. Compare the approach of the High Court of Australia in *Cattanach v Melchior* [2003] HCA 38.
[28] *ibid.*, at 113–114.
[29] *ibid.*, at 82 (*per* Lord Steyn) and 114 (*per* Lord Millett).

The decision in *McFarlane* did not resolve the question of whether compensation should be available for the costs of bringing up a *disabled* child. In *Parkinson v St James NHS Trust*[30] the claimant, who already had four children, underwent a sterilisation operation. The operation was carelessly performed and she subsequently became pregnant. She eventually gave birth to a child with significant disabilities. The Court of Appeal, mindful of *McFarlane*, could not award the claimant the normal costs associated with bringing up a child. Nevertheless, it felt able to award damages in respect of the *additional costs* associated with providing for a disabled child's special needs. This was so, even though the negligence of the doctors in performing the sterilisation operation had not been the cause of the child's disabilities.

Hale L.J. justified a departure from the approach taken in *McFarlane* by saying that, whatever ordinary people might think about the NHS having to pay the costs of bringing up a normal, able-bodied child, they would not regard it as unfair that where the NHS had undertaken to prevent the birth of further children, and had negligently failed to do so, it should meet the additional costs of bringing up a disabled child.[31] A departure from the *McFarlane* principle in such circumstances did not entail a suggestion that a disabled child was any less valued by its parents than an able-bodied one. It simply reflected the reality of the situation, which was that significant extra expenses were incurred by parents of disabled children in seeking to provide them with an upbringing comparable with that of an able-bodied child.[32]

In *Rees v Darlington Memorial Hospital NHS Trust*[33], the House of Lords was faced with a new factual variation. Here, a healthy, able-bodied child was born to a blind mother, as a result of a negligently performed sterilisation. The mother claimed the additional costs of bringing up the child that would be attributable to *her* disability. By a 4:3 majority, a seven-member House of Lords held that no exception to the principle in *McFarlane* was justified in such circumstances—the task of bringing up a normal, healthy baby could not be regarded as a loss that deserved compensation. In reaffirming this principle, however, their Lordships held that the law set out in *McFarlane* should be changed to a limited extent—there should be an award of a modest sum in all cases where negligence had caused an unintended pregnancy. The purpose of this award—which their Lordships called a "conventional award"—was to mark the courts' recognition of the fact that a legal wrong had been done, and to compensate the parents for having lost their right to limit the size of their family. The level of the award was fixed at £15,000.

In the light of *Rees* the status of the decision in *Parkinson* is uncertain. Three of their Lordships broadly endorsed the decision[34], whilst three doubted its correctness.[35] The remaining Law Lord, Lord Millett, expressly stated that the question whether

---

[30] [2002] Q.B. 266. See also *Hardman v Amin* [2000] Lloyd's Rep. Med. 498; *Groom v Selby* [2001] Lloyd's Rep. Med. 39; *Greenfield v Irwin* [2001] 1 W.L.R. 1279 (causing an unwanted child involves no breach of Art. 8 of the European Convention on Human Rights).

[31] *Parkinson v St James NHS Trust* [2002] Q.B. 266 at 295.

[32] *ibid.*, at 293.

[33] [2004] 1 A.C. 309. *Rees* was applied by the Court of Appeal in *AD v East Kent Community NHS Trust* [2003] 3 All E.R. 1167.

[34] Lords Steyn, Hope and Hutton.

[35] Lords Bingham and Nicholls were in favour of a conventional award in all cases, whilst Lord Scott thought that the additional costs of bringing up a disabled child might be recoverable where the reason for seeking the advice or treatment was precisely to avoid having a disabled child (*e.g.* where there was a likelihood of congenital abnormalities).

Parkinson was correct should be left open. Thus, the decision in *Rees* did not overrule *Parkinson*, so future claims for the additional costs of bringing up a *disabled child* remain a possibility.

The armed forces

2–047   The armed forces have never been treated as ordinary employers. Thus, in *Mulcahy v Ministry of Defence*,[36] the Court of Appeal held that, in battle conditions, common sense and sound policy dictated that the army could not owe a duty of care to its members. The plaintiff had been injured during the Gulf War, his injury being due to the negligence of his sergeant in causing a gun to fire whilst he was in front of it fetching water, rather than to active enemy involvement. The court accepted the argument that a duty of care would lead to defensive practices and undue caution, which would be wholly inappropriate to battle conditions. Whilst the immunity is likely to apply to all war-time activities, it is unlikely to apply to activities in peace-time. Thus, in *Jebson v Ministry of Defence*[37], where the claimant was injured as a result of drunken horseplay in the back of an army truck, on the way back from an organised social event, the Court of Appeal held that the defendants were in breach of their duty to provide suitable transport and supervision for soldiers in high spirits.

(3) **Private regulators**

2–048   In this section, we consider the liability of private regulatory bodies. These bodies are essentially "clubs" formed for the promotion and protection of private interests, although in some cases they perform a role akin to public service organisations.

Ship classification societies

2–049   The same kind of arguments that were employed in *Hill* and elsewhere to deny liability have been applied in relation to ship classification societies. Thus, in *Marc Rich & Co. v Bishop Rock Marine Co. Ltd (The Nicholas H)*,[38] a classification society issued a certificate which indicated the seaworthiness of a ship. The ship subsequently sank. The House of Lords asserted that despite the presence of physical loss resulting from the carelessly-made report of the society's surveyor, and despite the fact that the loss was clearly foreseeable, no duty of care was owed to the owner of the cargo that was lost. The classification society was an independent and non-profit-making entity, created and operating for the sole purpose of promoting the safety of lives and ships at sea. In this way, it fulfilled a role akin to a public service which would otherwise have to be fulfilled by individual states. In this light, it would not be fair, just and reasonable to impose a duty of care.

There are suggestions, however, that the courts may be willing to overcome traditional policy objections where a classification society inflicts physical loss in a

[36] [1996] 2 All E.R. 758.
[37] [2000] 1 W.L.R. 2055. See also *Barrett v Ministry of Defence* [1995] 1 W.L.R. 1217 and *Bici v Ministry of Defence, The Times,* June 11, 2004 (peacekeeping and policing functions in Kosovo). Note that in respect of incidents occurring before 1987, s.10 Crown Proceedings Act 1947 confers immunity. In *Matthews v Ministry of Defence* [2003] 1 All E.R. 689, the House of Lords held that preserving this immunity does not involve violation of Art. 6(1) of the European Convention on Human Rights.
[38] [1996] 1 A.C. 211. See also *Reeman v Department of Transport* [1997] 2 Lloyd's Rep. 648 (Department of Transport surveyor causing economic loss).

more direct way. Lord Steyn commented in *The Nicholas H*[39] that if the surveyor had caused an explosion by carelessly dropping a lighted cigarette into a hold known to contain combustible cargo, he would have been more willing to find that the society owed a duty of care. This approach was followed by the Court of Appeal in *Perrett v Collins*[40] where an inspector's role in certifying the airworthiness of light aircraft was critical, and, as a direct result of his negligence, the plaintiff suffered personal injury. The court saw no reason why the inspector should not owe the plaintiff a duty of care. Although the inspector worked for the Popular Flying Association, whose aim was to facilitate the construction and flying of light aircraft by amateurs, the imposition of a duty of care was not inconsistent with this aim. More recently, in *Grinstead v Lywood*[41], the High Court refused to strike out a claim that an employee of the Auto Cycle Union, a club formed to regulate motorcycle racing, could be liable in respect of personal injury caused by approving a dangerous race track.

Sports regulators

In *Watson v British Boxing Board of Control*[42], the Court of Appeal was prepared to **2–050** hold that the BBBC, a private organisation formed for the regulation of boxing, owed a duty of care to ensure an adequate standard of ringside medical treatment for an injured boxer. The case was novel because the claimant's allegation was that the defendant had been negligent in failing to formulate satisfactory rules for the conduct of the sport. The case arose as a consequence of the world super-middleweight title fight between Chris Eubank and Michael Watson. In the final round, the referee stopped the fight when it appeared that Watson was unable to defend himself. He had, in fact, suffered a brain haemorrhage. He was examined by a doctor at the ringside, and subsequently taken to hospital where he was given resuscitation treatment, but by this time he had already suffered permanent brain damage leading to disability. Watson claimed that immediate resuscitation treatment should have been available at the ringside, and that the BBBC was in breach of its duty of care by not providing for this in its rules.

Lord Phillips M.R., giving the judgment of the court, dismissed the BBBC's argument that Watson, knowing of the rules, had been the author of his own misfortune by consenting to box in accordance with them. His Lordship also regarded the fact that the BBBC was a non-profit-making organisation, without insurance, as irrelevant to its liability. Finding that there was a sufficient degree of proximity between Watson and the BBBC, his Lordship pointed out that Watson was one of only a limited class of individuals affected by the rules, so there could be no question of indeterminate liability.[43] Moreover, the BBBC had exclusive control over the provision of ringside medical assistance. Accordingly, it was fair just and reasonable for Watson to rely on the BBBC to look after his safety.

In *Vowles v Evans*[44], the issue was not whether the rules of the game were adequate to protect the claimant, but whether they had been properly applied by the referee.

---

[39] [1996] 1 A.C. 211 at 237.
[40] [1998] 2 Lloyd's Rep 255.
[41] 2002 WL 31397573.
[42] [2001] 2 W.L.R. 1256. See George, (2000) 65 M.L.R. 106.
[43] The High Court of Australia had found this a bar to liability in *Agar v Hyde* [2000] H.C.A. 41, where the allegation was that inadequate rules governing rugby scrums had exposed the claimants to injury.
[44] [2003] 1 W.L.R. 1607.

The claimant was left confined to a wheelchair as a result of an injury he sustained during an amateur game of rugby. The injury had occurred when the referee had decided to allow the game to continue with "contestable scrummages" (in which the players are allowed to push against one another to gain possession of the ball) even though the substitution of an inexperienced player by one of the teams meant that this could not be done safely. The Court of Appeal saw no reason why the referee should not owe a duty of care. Even though the referee was acting in an amateur capacity, the second defendants (Welsh Rugby Union Ltd.) who had appointed him could be expected to take out insurance against the negligence of their referees. The fact that serious injuries of this kind were comparatively rare meant that this would not create an unfair financial burden, or discourage amateurs from volunteering to act as referees.

(4) The legal profession

2–051   Generally, judges[45] and arbitrators[46] cannot be sued in respect of their activities during a case. Prior to the decision of the House of Lords in *Hall v Simons*,[47] barristers and solicitor advocates enjoyed a similar immunity—they could not be sued for negligently conducting a case in court, or for matters intimately connected with the conduct of the case in court.[48] In *Hall v Simons*, however, their Lordships abolished advocates' immunity, stating that the traditional arguments used to support it could no longer be sustained.

Although the immunity has been abolished, it remains difficult for a claimant who feels he or she has been the victim of incompetent advocacy to succeed in negligence against an advocate. For reasons we explore below, this is especially true in criminal cases where the claimant has been convicted. In all cases, of course, the claimant must show that the advocate is in breach of the duty of care, and that his or her negligence caused the loss suffered. As we shall see in Chs 5 and 6, this can be difficult to establish.

The old law

2–052   Under the old law, the immunity enjoyed by barristers and solicitor advocates[49] applied only in the context of litigation. Where non-litigious work was concerned, a duty of care was owed. The immunity granted to lawyers had somewhat different justifications from the restrictions on liability of the police and public bodies we have considered above, and its existence had been questioned by academics and practitioners alike.[50] Moreover, the distinction between "litigious" and "non-litigious" work proved very difficult to draw in practice and led to a lack of clarity in the law. In order to appreciate the modern law, it is convenient to set out below the arguments that were formerly used to support advocates' immunity[51] and to explore how each was addressed by their Lordships in *Hall v Simons*.

[45] *Sirros v Moore* [1975] Q.B. 118.
[46] *Arenson v Arenson* [1977] A.C. 405. (Provided they are acting in an arbitral capacity. The immunity does not extend to mutual valuers.)
[47] [2002] 1 A.C. 615.
[48] *Saif Ali v Sydney Mitchell & Co (a firm)* [1980] A.C. 198.
[49] See s.62(1) Courts and Legal Services Act 1990.
[50] See Hill (1986) 6 O.J.L.S. 183 and D. Pannick, *Advocates* (OUP, 1992).
[51] The leading case was *Rondel v Worsley* [1969] 1 A.C. 191, in which the relevant arguments were set out by Lord Reid.

Arguments for advocates' immunity

(1) The advocate's duty to the court. The integrity of our legal system relies on advocates adhering to their overriding duty to the court whilst representing their clients' interests. Thus, the advocate must not mislead the court, cast aspersions on the other party or its witnesses for which there is insufficient evidence, or withhold authorities or documents relevant to the case. In this context, then, it was argued that the immunity helped to ensure that advocates did not succumb, through fear of being sued, to pressure from their clients to breach their duties as officers of the court. Whilst the chief guarantee of integrity was the ethical code of the advocate's profession, it was argued that the existence of the immunity served to underpin this code, ensuring that advocates could carry out their duties "fearlessly" without "looking over their shoulders" for the reaction of their clients, who may feel that their interests are better served by breaking or bending the rules.   2–053

In *Hall v Simons*, their Lordships dismissed this "divided loyalty" argument.[52] Lord Steyn pointed out that it was difficult to see how the argument could justify the immunity of advocates when doctors, for example, enjoyed no such immunity, even though they too could be faced with questions of "divided loyalty", as where a patient with Aids asks his doctor not to disclose this fact to his wife. Moreover, their Lordships noted that there was no evidence to suggest that in jurisdictions where advocates had no immunity (Canada, for example) their overriding duty to the court was compromised.

(2) The "cab-rank" rule and "vexatious" clients. Barristers (but not solicitor advocates) are obliged to act for any client who requests their services, provided that the client's claim is within their field of expertise and a proper fee is offered. This is known as the "cab-rank" rule. It was traditionally thought that the operation of this rule justified advocates' immunity because, if a barrister could not stop representing a client, even when that client threatened to sue the barrister for refusing to behave unethically, it was only fair that the barrister should be immune from suit. It was argued that were matters otherwise, barristers might be beset with unmeritorious negligence claims from "vexatious" clients whose cases they had no choice but to take.   2–054

This argument, too, was dismissed in *Hall v Simons*. Lord Hope said of the cab-rank rule that "its significance in daily practice is not great".[53] Lord Steyn went so far, perhaps, as to hint that the rule is more often honoured in its breach than its observance when he noted that "in real life" barristers' clerks were free, within limits, to raise the fees for unwanted briefs (*i.e.* so as to discourage clients from briefing the barrister of their choice).[54] Lord Hoffmann thought that although there could be a number of reasons why a barrister might not wish to take on a particular client, for example because the client was "tiresome or disgusting", the barrister's fear of an unwarranted and vexatious negligence action was seldom one of those reasons.[55]

In any event, their Lordships thought that the Civil Procedure Rules, which allow for "summary disposal" of claims where "the claimant has no real prospect of

[52] A minority of judges believed, however, that it still had force in relation to criminal cases.
[53] [2002] 1 A.C. 615 at 714.
[54] *ibid.*, at 678.
[55] *ibid.*, at 696.

succeeding"[56] would ensure that barristers were not subject to a flood of unmeritorious claims following the abolition of advocates' immunity. It was also observed that recent reforms of the legal aid system, under which negligence claims are dealt with by way of conditional fee agreements, should prove a substantial obstacle to "vexatious" litigants—they will have to convince another lawyer to take on their case, and, according to Lord Hoffmann, a fellow lawyer "will be able to recognise a vexatious claim when he sees one".[57]

2–055   **(3) The need to avoid a retrial.**   To sue successfully for compensation resulting from an advocate's negligence, the claimant must show that the advocate's negligence has caused him or her to lose the case. To assess whether the unfavourable outcome of the trial was in fact the consequence of the advocate's negligence (or whether the client would have lost in any event), a court would effectively have to re-hear the case, evaluating the effect of the advocate's contribution to its outcome in the light of all the evidence. Clearly, permitting the courts to do this does little to uphold the certainty of the judicial process and the finality of justice.

Although the avoidance of re-trials was often used as an argument to support advocates' immunity, in fact, the "no re-trial" objective was already met in the law by different means. The House of Lords' decision in *Hunter v Chief Constable of the West Midlands Police*[58] confirmed that, at least in criminal cases, a collateral attack on the correctness of the final decision of a court would be struck out as an abuse of process where the claimant had had the opportunity of appealing against that decision. *Hunter* was a case in which six convicted I.R.A. terrorists (the "Birmingham Six") had alleged at their trial that the police had beaten them to extract confessions. The trial judge had found that this had not been the case, and they were convicted. They applied for leave to appeal (on other grounds) and this was refused. Whilst in prison, they brought proceedings for assault against the police, alleging the same beatings that had been alleged at the criminal trial. The House of Lords struck out their claim as an abuse of process, because the men were attempting to relitigate issues which had already been decided at their trial.

The rule in *Hunter* reflects considerations of public policy, namely the importance of finality in litigation, the affront to a coherent system of justice which would arise if there subsisted two inconsistent decisions of the courts, and the virtual impossibility of fairly re-trying, at a later date, issues of fact a court had decided on an earlier occasion.[59] Their Lordships in *Hall v Simons* stressed the importance of maintaining the prohibition on collateral attacks on judicial decisions in criminal cases, but felt that this concern was relatively unimportant in relation to civil cases.

2–056   **(4) Other grounds: the length of trials and the "witness analogy".**   It was traditionally argued that advocates' immunity ensured that trials were not unnecessarily prolonged by defensive conduct by the advocate, such as over-cautious questioning. Equally, it was asserted that the immunity was consistent with the general immunity

---

[56] Civil Procedure Rules 1999, rule 24.2, applied in *Hussain v Cuddy Woods* [2001] Lloyd's Rep. P.N. 134.
[57] [2002] 1 A.C. 615 at 692.
[58] [1982] A.C. 529. For an explanation of the *Hunter* principle, see *R v Belmarsh Magistrates' Court, ex parte Watts* [1999] 2 Cr. App. R. 188.
[59] *Smith v Linskills* [1996] 1 W.L.R. 763.

from civil liability that attaches to all persons participating in court proceedings, such as the judge, court officials, witnesses and parties.

Both of these arguments were addressed in *Hall v Simons*. In relation to the first, it was noted by Lord Hoffmann that lengthy submissions by advocates were a problem even with the immunity in place. His Lordship thought that the disapproval of the court, together with the possibility of the judge making a wasted costs order against the advocate in question, would be sufficient to contain the length of trials in the absence of advocates' immunity. In relation to the second argument, their Lordships thought that advocates' immunity was an unwarranted extension of the protection of free speech given to witnesses. The rationale for witness immunity was that, without it, witnesses might be less willing to assist the court. The same could not be said for advocates.

The decision in Hall v Simons

In *Hall v Simons* the House of Lords considered a number of appeals in which it was 2–057 alleged that solicitors had been negligent in reaching settlements subsequently approved by the court. Since none of the appeals involved solicitors acting in the capacity of advocates, it was, as Lord Hope pointed out,[60] not strictly necessary to question the fundamental rule of advocates' immunity. Nevertheless, the seven-member House of Lords ruled unanimously that the immunity could no longer stand in civil cases, dismissing the traditional arguments, for the reasons we have examined above. By a majority, their Lordships also held that the immunity should be abolished in criminal cases, although a minority of three[61] thought that it should be preserved in such cases, because the conduct of criminal trials made advocates particularly vulnerable to unmeritorious complaints and the risk of "divided loyalties".

The majority thought that the rule against collateral attack, established in *Hunter*, would be sufficient to prevent the administration of justice being brought into disrepute by negligence claims against advocates. They noted that the rule in *Hunter* will operate differently in relation to criminal and civil cases. In relation to civil cases, it will seldom be possible to say that an action for negligence against a legal representative will bring the administration of justice into disrepute. This is because the correctness of the decision in a civil trial is a matter of concern only to the parties. Unlike a decision in a criminal court, it serves no wider purpose. Therefore, according to Lord Hoffmann, the rule in *Hunter* is unlikely to be used in a civil context, except in rare cases where allowing an action to proceed against an advocate would be unfair to a third party, for example, where a defence of justification[62] has been rejected in a defamation action.

In relation to criminal cases, a distinction was to be drawn between, on the one hand, cases where the accused has been convicted—either after a trial or a guilty plea—and, on the other hand, cases where the accused has had the conviction set aside after a successful appeal. Where the accused still stands convicted of the offence, any attempt to challenge the competence of his or her advocate will generally fall foul of *Hunter* and will be struck out as a collateral attack on the correctness of the conviction.

[60] *Hall v Simons* [2002] 1 A.C. 615 at 709.
[61] Lords Hope, Hutton and Hobhouse.
[62] See Ch. 13.

The appropriate way for the accused to challenge a conviction is by an appeal rather than a negligence action against an advocate. On the other hand, if the accused has had his or her conviction set aside on appeal, there can be no such objection to a negligence action.

THE ARTICLE 6.1 CONTROVERSY

2–058   We have already noted that, under the Human Rights Act 1998, which incorporates the European Convention on Human Rights into UK law, individuals who have their convention rights violated by a public authority can apply to a UK court for compensation. We have also noted that one of the important issues for the development of the tort of negligence is whether, in the light of this, the scope of the duty of care should expand to accommodate human rights law.

In this section, we are concerned with a slightly different but related point, namely the extent to which Art. 6.1 of the convention (the right of access to a court) has been regarded as inconsistent with the UK courts' practice of striking out negligence claims. By this practice, the courts refuse to allow a full trial in cases where application of the third *Caparo* criterion ("fair, just and reasonable") indicates that no duty of care should be owed. In *Osman v United Kingdom*, the E.C.H.R. held that this striking-out procedure denied the litigants proper access to a court, and so constituted a breach of Art. 6.1. Subsequently, however, in *Z v United Kingdom*, the E.C.H.R. retreated from this position. We shall see that, as a result of the confusion this produced, a number of cases, which on traditional principles would probably have been struck out for want of a duty of care, were allowed to proceed to trial.

Few of these cases, however, have yet been heard in a full trial, and some of them may have been settled or discontinued, and so never will be heard. The result of this is to make it difficult to define with precision the scope of the duty of care in the modern law. We are left with a number of "striking out" cases, in which much has been said about the *potential* scope of the duty of care in local authority cases. These cases, however, cannot be read as authority for the proposition that a duty of care actually exists in the circumstances in question, only that it *might* exist. All that can be said is that, by informing the debate about the relationship between the duty of care and human rights, the "Article 6.1 controversy" seems to have led the courts to adopt a more expansive general approach to the existence of a duty of care.

Article 6.1 states:

> "In the determination of his civil rights and obligations . . . everyone is entitled to a fair and public hearing within a reasonable time by an independent and impartial tribunal established by law. . .."

The controversy surrounding the implications of Art. 6.1 began with the decision of the Court of Appeal in *Osman v Ferguson*.[63] Ahmet Osman was a school pupil. One of his teachers, who was psychologically disturbed, formed an obsessive attachment to

---

[63] [1993] 4 All E.R. 344.

Ahmet, giving him money, following him home, and even changing his own name by deed poll to "Ahmet Osman". When Ahmet's father asked for him to be moved to another school, the teacher began a campaign of violence against the Osman family, smashing the windows of their house and car. After each incident, the police questioned the teacher, but failed to arrest him. Eventually, the teacher went to the Osmans' house with a stolen gun, shot and injured Ahmet, and shot and killed Ahmet's father.

The Osmans sued the police in negligence, but the Court of Appeal struck out their claim. McCowan L.J. stated that, in the light of *Hill v Chief Constable of West Yorkshire*, their case was "doomed" to fail[64]—for policy reasons, the police enjoyed an immunity from negligence claims in respect of their investigation and suppression of crime. The Osmans then applied to the European Court of Human Rights, arguing, *inter alia*, that by striking out their claim, the Court of Appeal had denied them their human right to a fair and public hearing, as guaranteed by Art. 6.1.

In *Osman v United Kingdom*, the E.C.H.R. upheld this claim, stating that striking out the case on the basis of the police immunity rule established in *Hill* had constituted a disproportionate restriction of the Osmans' right of access to a court. In the E.C.H.R's view, the Court of Appeal should have given proper consideration to countervailing arguments that liability was in the public interest, and balanced these against the arguments for immunity before reaching its decision. The court pointed out that the Osmans had satisfied the rigorous "proximity" test, that this was an allegation of grave negligence in failing to protect the life of a child, and that it was alleged that the police had assumed responsibility for the victims' safety. The Osmans were awarded compensation for their lost opportunity to have their case considered in a full trial.

Unsurprisingly, in the wake of *Osman v United Kingdom*, there followed a line of cases in which the courts were reluctant to strike out negligence claims, for fear that this behaviour would be seen by the E.C.H.R. as the application of a "blanket immunity" rule, falling foul of Article 6.1. (Most of the relevant cases concerned the duties of local authorities in relation to children. See, for example, *Barrett v Enfield LBC* and *Phelps v Hillingdon LBC*, considered above.[65]) In *Barrett v Enfield LBC*, however, Lord Browne-Wilkinson was critical of the E.C.H.R's decision in *Osman*. The gist of his Lordship's opinion was that the E.C.H.R's view (*i.e.* that the applicability of a policy-based exclusionary rule should be decided afresh in every case) represented a failure to understand the operation of precedent in UK law, and a failure to appreciate the legal mechanisms by which negligence cases are decided.

His Lordship pointed out that, although the word "immunity" is often used in an imprecise way, it is not wholly accurate to say that a finding that, on policy grounds, it is not "fair, just and reasonable" to hold a certain class of defendants liable, amounts to granting "immunity" to those defendants. Rather, it represents the proper application of the rules of negligence liability. His Lordship expressed the hope that the decision in *Osman* would be reconsidered by the E.C.H.R. (as indeed it subsequently was, in *Z v United Kingdom*) and expressed the view that, in the meantime, the courts had little choice but to be wary of striking out negligence claims, lest they fall foul of

---

[64] [1993] 4 All E.R. 354.
[65] See also *W v Essex CC* [1998] 3 All E.R. 111 (CA) and [2001] 2 A.C. 592 (HL); *S v Gloucester CC* [2001] Fam 313 (CA). Contrast *Palmer v Tees Health Authority* [2000] P.I.Q.R. P1 (CA) (*Osman* did not prevent striking out for lack of proximity).

Osman.[66] The decision in *Osman* undoubtedly influenced the House of Lords' decision in *Hall v Simons* to abolish advocates immunity, and, for a time, it looked as if the E.C.H.R's dim view of policy-based exemptions from negligence liability might effectively put a stop to any line of reasoning which would deny negligence liability on the basis of policy-based "immunities".

Then came the decision of the E.C.H.R. in *Z v United Kingdom*.[67] This case arose out of the *X v Bedfordshire* litigation, and has already been considered in that context. In *Z*, the E.C.H.R. stated, in effect, that it had changed its mind about what it had said in *Osman*. It was now persuaded that the UK courts' practice of striking out negligence claims, where the third *Caparo* criterion indicated the claims could not succeed, did not amount to a breach of Article 6.1. The court conceded that, in deciding *Osman*, it had misunderstood the effect of the *Caparo* criteria. The application of the *Caparo* criteria did not, in fact, operate to exclude claimants from the courts, or mean that certain types of defendant were above the law because they were exempt from legal proceedings. Rather, the *Caparo* criteria served to define what the law was. If, having applied those criteria, a court came to the conclusion that the law could not possibly assist the claimant, it was not a breach of Art. 6.1 for the court to save time and expense by declaring that proceedings should be discontinued.

After *Z v United Kingdom*, it might be thought that the courts would revert to their former approach in striking out negligence actions. In fact, they do not appear to have done so. The Article 6.1 controversy appears to have left a lasting mark on the substance of negligence liability. In cases like *D v East Berkshire Community Health NHS Trust*, the courts now seem concerned to accommodate human rights law within the tort of negligence, and, in cases like *Phelps v Hillingdon LBC* and *Hall v Simons*, there is a new-found reluctance to restrict the scope of the duty of care by granting policy-based exemptions to particular classes of defendant.

Duty of care: conclusion

2–059   We have seen that the duty of care is one of the most important tools available to the courts in determining the scope of the modern tort of negligence, and that the question whether a duty should exist in a given situation is answered by reference to a number of considerations, in particular the ideas of ensuring that liability remains proportionate to the defendant's fault, yet consistent with the structure and general objectives of the law. In the chapters which follow, we shall explore the way the courts have incorporated these considerations into their decisions in cases of economic loss and psychiatric illness.

---

[66] Compare the approach of Lord Woolf M.R. in *Kent v Griffiths* [2000] 2 All E.R. 474 at 484.
[67] (2002) 34 EHRR 3. See also *TP v United Kingdom* [2001] 2 F.C.R. 289, where the E.C.H.R. rejected a claim of breach of Art. 6 for similar reasons to those given in *Z*.

Chapter 3

NEGLIGENCE: ECONOMIC LOSS

Introduction

We have seen that it is generally much more difficult to establish a duty of care in   **3–001**
respect of "economic loss" than in respect of damage to property or personal injury.
This chapter examines the reasons why this is so. We shall see that, broadly speaking,
no duty of care is owed to avoid causing economic loss by careless activities, but that
very different rules apply to careless statements, making it easier for a claimant to
recover. The division between the two situations is largely a matter of historical
accident in the way the law has developed, but it also has to do with the fact that, in
the "activity" cases, the courts have been more heavily influenced by public policy
arguments, in particular the need to limit the liability of local authorities.

Definition of "economic loss"

"Economic loss" may be defined as *loss that is purely financial, in the sense that it does*   **3–002**
not result from damage to the claimant's property or injury to the claimant's person.
    For the non-lawyer, many losses resulting from negligence might appear to deserve
the title "economic"— if a claimant's car is "written off" by a negligent driver, for
example, a lay person might call the loss "economic" because the claimant has lost a
financial asset. Similarly, a claimant who is seriously injured and must give up work
suffers a financial loss. In tort law, however, the term "economic loss" has a more
precise meaning. It is used to describe losses which are "purely" financial, in the sense
that the claimant has suffered "damage to the pocket" without suffering personal
injury or property damage. This is the case, for example, where a person buys a
product which is defective, although it does not cause personal injury or damage to
property. The person is said to have suffered "economic loss" because the only loss in
question is the cost of repairing or replacing the product.

"Pure" and "consequential" economic loss

Tort lawyers generally use the term "economic loss" as shorthand for "pure economic   **3–003**
loss" (of the type described above) but they sometimes need to draw a distinction
between this type of loss and what they call "consequential" economic loss. The term

"consequential economic loss" simply means financial loss that is *consequent upon damage to property owned by the claimant*. (Lost profits, for example, resulting from damage to a profit-making machine.) Whilst this sort of loss is, of course, "damage to the pocket", the law has little difficulty in holding that it is recoverable, because it results directly from damage to the claimant's property. As a rule of thumb, then, we can say that "consequential economic loss" is recoverable, but "pure economic loss" (except where it results from negligent misstatement or negligent provision of services) is not.

An illustration: *Spartan Steel*

3–004   The distinctions between "(pure) economic loss", "consequential economic loss" and "damage to property" are neatly illustrated by the decision in *Spartan Steel & Alloys Ltd. v Martin & Co. (Contractors) Ltd.*[1] The defendants, who were construction workers, negligently cut through a cable which supplied power to the plaintiffs' factory, causing a power cut which lasted for $14^{1}/_{2}$ hours. Without electricity, the plaintiffs' furnace could not operate and they had to close their factory. The metal that was in the furnace at the time the power went off (the "melt") began to solidify, and to save damaging the furnace the plaintiffs had to throw it away. The plaintiffs brought an action for three types of loss:

- damage to the melt that was in the furnace at the time of the power cut (physical damage to property);

- loss of the profit which would have been made on the sale of that melt (consequential economic loss resulting from property damage);

- loss of profits on four further melts which would have been processed during the $14^{1}/_{2}$ hours the factory was closed because of the power cut (pure economic loss).

A majority of the Court of Appeal held that the first two claims were recoverable, but the third claim was not. The defendants owed the plaintiffs a duty not to damage their property, and therefore had to pay for the damaged metal and the loss of profit resulting directly from that damage, but they did not owe a duty of care in respect of the further lost profits, because these did not result from the fact that the plaintiffs' property had been damaged.

Lord Denning M.R. was unsure whether to approach the question from the point of view of duty of care or remoteness of damage. His Lordship observed:

"At bottom I think the question of recovering economic loss is one of policy. Whenever the courts draw a line to mark out the bounds of duty, they do it as matter of policy so as to limit the responsibility of the defendant. Whenever the courts set bounds to the damages recoverable—saying that they are, or are not, too remote—they do it as matter of policy so as to limit the liability of the defendant."[2]

[1] [1973] Q.B. 27.
[2] *ibid.*, at 36.

His Lordship then referred to the policy considerations which precluded liability for the further loss of profits. Observing that power cuts are a fact of life and that they can often cause economic loss, his Lordship stated that people should bear that loss themselves, either by taking out insurance or by installing emergency generators, concluding: " . . . the risk of economic loss should be suffered by the whole community. . . rather than be placed on one pair of shoulders". His Lordship also noted that if claims for pure economic loss due to power cuts were allowed, it would be very easy to make inflated claims—plaintiffs could assert that they had intended to use their machinery for the duration of a power cut, but it would be impossible to prove whether, in fact, they really would have done so. If the courts simply took the plaintiffs' word for it, exaggerated damages awards would result.

Policy considerations

The reasoning of the majority in *Spartan Steel*, then, reflects the two central policy considerations that have traditionally made pure economic loss non-recoverable in tort: **3–005**

(1) Tort law should not undermine contract law

Those who contract for the installation and maintenance of emergency generators, for example, have a contractual remedy if they break down during a power cut causing economic loss. It would therefore be inconsistent to give a remedy in tort to others who have not so contracted.   **3–006**

(2) The desire to avoid "crushing liability"

Whilst a negligent act is likely to cause personal injury or property damage only to a limited number of people, the same act may cause an enormous number of people to suffer pure economic loss. The classic illustration of the point is that of a defendant who crashes his car, blocking a busy tunnel. This may cause a plumber on his way to work to be late and lose pay. In turn, the plumber's lateness may cause financial loss to others—a builder, for example, who is waiting for the plumber to complete his tasks before starting his own—and then to a property developer who misses a market opportunity by waiting for the completion of the building works. People's financial interests are so closely interrelated that causing economic loss to one person usually produces a "domino effect". The law's way of dealing with this phenomenon is to allow people, through the mechanism of contract law, to fix the extent of their economic liabilities to others—they will only be liable to others with whom they have contracted. This prevents one defendant from being liable for an indeterminate amount of loss.   **3–007**

   From a moral standpoint, it may be thought objectionable that a defendant who has caused foreseeable loss is allowed to escape liability. We have seen in Ch. 2, however, that countervailing considerations sometimes dictate that a defendant should not be liable in tort without having accepted responsibility for the welfare of others. These considerations also have moral weight, in the sense that the law is regarded as just only if it recognises that people's willingness to look after the interests of others is limited. People are generally more willing to assume a duty to look after the physical safety and property of others than to look after the financial wellbeing of others. In denying recovery for economic loss, then, it may be argued that tort law simply reflects the feelings of society.

Whilst moral justification may be found, it is harder to find a justification in logic for the way in which the courts have sought to limit liability for economic loss. As can be seen from *Spartan Steel*, the courts have drawn a rather arbitrary line between economic loss resulting from damage to the claimant's *own* property (which they call "consequential") and economic loss resulting from damage to property in which the claimant only has a *contractual interest* (non-recoverable "pure" economic loss). In *Spartan Steel*, Edmund-Davies L.J., dissenting, objected to this arbitrary distinction. In his Lordship's view, the law would be clearer if it stated that all foreseeable economic loss was recoverable. His Lordship could not see why the recovery of economic loss should depend on the purely fortuitous circumstance of who happened to own the piece of property that was damaged.[3] The gist of his Lordship's argument, it is submitted, is this: suppose that the contractors had *entered the factory*, perhaps in pursuance of a statutory power, and had damaged a part of the power cable that *belonged to the plaintiffs*—all the economic loss would then have been recoverable, because it would have resulted from damage to the plaintiffs' own property. There is no logical basis on which to distinguish this type of situation from what happened in *Spartan Steel*. Despite its logical force, however, Edmund-Davies L.J.'s view has not found favour with the courts.

With the law's policy objectives in mind, it is now appropriate to examine the relevant case law in more detail. We shall begin with the "activity" cases and then consider the question of liability for economic loss caused by statements, and the extension of such liability to the negligent provision of services.

ECONOMIC LOSS CAUSED BY NEGLIGENT ACTIVITIES

The traditional approach

3–008   A convenient place to start is *Cattle v Stockton Waterworks*.[4] Here, the defendants, who had laid a pipe under land belonging to a certain Mr Knight, were under a statutory duty to keep the pipe in good repair. A road ran through Mr Knight's land which made it difficult for him to get easily from one side to the other, so he contracted with the plaintiff, Mr Cattle, to have a tunnel dug underneath the road. Mr Cattle agreed to do this for a fixed price, but after he had started work, he noticed that the land was becoming hard to excavate because it was waterlogged. He realised that the defendants' pipe was leaking and contacted them about this, but they negligently failed to repair it. The result of this negligence was that Mr Cattle lost profit on his contract, so he sought to recover this from the defendants.

Blackburn J. held that Mr Cattle could not sue in his own name for damage that had been done to land belonging to Mr Knight. In other words, because Mr Cattle had no proprietary interest in the damaged land, he had no cause of action. In modern terms, we should say that Mr Cattle's loss was purely economic. Blackburn J. made reference to what we now call the "floodgates" argument, or the argument against "crushing

---

[3] [1973] Q.B. 27 at 41.
[4] (1875) L.R. 10 Q.B. 453.

liability". Considering his earlier (and more famous) decision in the case of *Rylands v Fletcher*,[5] where the defendant flooded the plaintiff's mine, his Lordship noted that if liability for damaged contractual interests were allowed in tort, then in *Rylands v Fletcher* it would have meant that not only could the owner of the flooded mine sue, but so could every workman who lost wages as a result of the flood. This would clearly be unacceptable because it would place the defendant under a financial liability disproportionate to his fault.

The *Stockton Waterworks* case, then, established that a claimant could not recover economic loss resulting from damage to property in which he or she had only a contractual interest. The point was tested again, however, in *Weller & Co. v Foot and Mouth Disease Research Institute*.[6] (In 1963, the House of Lords, in *Hedley Byrne v Heller & Partners*, had radically extended the scope of the duty of care in respect of economic loss, as will be discussed below. It was in the wake of this expansion that the plaintiffs in *Weller* felt able to bring their case.) The plaintiffs were auctioneers of cattle. The defendants, by their carelessness, allowed an imported African virus to escape from their research institute and infect cows in the vicinity. This led the Minister of Agriculture to order the closure of all local cattle markets, with the result that the plaintiffs lost profit. It was held that, whilst the Institute might be liable to the owners of infected cows (i.e. for property that had been damaged by the virus), it could not be liable to the auctioneers because they did not have a proprietary interest in anything that had been physically damaged. It was true that they had such an interest in the premises in which cattle markets were held, but it could not really be said that these premises had been "damaged" by the virus. At best, it could be said that the plaintiffs had missed an opportunity to contract to sell the cows, but this missed opportunity was the same sort of loss that would be suffered by all other local traders—owners of shops and pubs, for example—while the cattle market was closed. Policy dictated that a line must be drawn somewhere, otherwise all of these traders would be able to claim compensation. This policy of avoiding wide and disproportionate liability was subsequently confirmed in *Spartan Steel*, which we have already examined.

A brief period of expansion: *Anns* and *Junior Books*

At the beginning of this chapter, it was stated that where a person buys a product, and that product suffers from a defect in quality (although it does not damage anything or injure anyone), the cost of repairing or replacing the product is a classic example of economic loss. This type of loss (commonly called "defective product economic loss") is recoverable under a contract, but is not normally recoverable in tort. In the late 1970s and early 1980s, however, the House of Lords chose to depart from this long-standing rule in two important cases: *Anns v Merton LBC*[7] (which has now been overruled) and *Junior Books v Veitchi*[8] (which is nowadays unlikely to be followed). These cases were part of the general expansion of negligence liability during that period, discussed in Ch. 2.

3–009

[5] (1868) L.R. 3 H.L. 330. (discussed in Ch. 10)
[6] [1966] 1 Q.B. 569.
[7] [1978] A.C. 728.
[8] [1983] 1 A.C. 520.

The decision in Anns

3–010   It will be recalled that *Anns* involved a claim against a local authority which, it was alleged, had failed properly to supervise the construction of a building, so that cracks appeared in the walls of the building. Lord Wilberforce took the unusual step of categorising these cracks as "damage to property",[9] apparently ignoring (or intending to displace) the distinction tort lawyers had always made between situations where a defect in a product *caused damage to other property*, and situations where the claim was for the cost of remedying the *defect itself*. The traditional position had been that if a defective building fell down, for example smashing furniture inside it, then a claim for replacing the furniture would be allowed (this would be a claim for "damage to property") but a tort claim for the cost of replacing the building itself would fail—it would be a claim for "defective product economic loss". Before *Anns*, a building that was defective, in the sense that it failed to meet the contract specification, could not properly be said to be "damaged". Lord Wilberforce, however, appeared to use that word in the very much looser sense that the building contained a defect which made it less valuable (*i.e.* in the sense that a lay person might complain that he or she has been supplied with "damaged goods"). As we shall see, in *Murphy v Brentwood DC*,[10] the House of Lords rejected this broad analysis, stating that the loss in *Anns* had been wrongly categorised, and restored the traditional distinction between defects in quality and "damage to property".

The decision in Junior Books

3–011   The decision in *Junior Books v Veitchi*,[11] which followed similar reasoning to that in *Anns*, marked the high point of the expansion of the duty to avoid causing economic loss by supplying a defective product. The plaintiffs entered into a contract with a firm of contractors ("the main contractors") for the construction of a factory. The factory needed a special floor to support heavy machinery, so the plaintiffs instructed the main contractors to sub-contract the flooring work to the defendants, who were flooring specialists. There was, therefore, a contract between the plaintiffs and the main contractors, and a contract between the main contractors and the defendants, but there was no contractual relationship between the plaintiffs and the defendants. The floor turned out to be defective and had to be rebuilt, necessitating a temporary closure of the plaintiffs' factory. For reasons which were unknown, the plaintiffs did not pursue their contractual remedy against the main contractors (who were perhaps insolvent), but instead brought a claim against the defendant sub-contractors, claiming the cost of re-laying the floor and lost profits while this was done.

In the House of Lords, it was observed (apparently without noticing any inconsistency with the way the loss had been categorised in *Anns*) that the claim in *Junior Books* was a claim for economic loss caused by the supply of a defective product. It was not a "damage to property" claim. Nor, indeed, was there any suggestion that the floor presented a danger to other property or a risk of personal injury (which might have made the plaintiffs' task a little easier). Regarding the case squarely as one of economic loss, their Lordships recognised that the question for the House was whether

[9] *Anns v Merton LBC* [1978] A.C. 728 at 759.
[10] [1991] 1 A.C. 398.
[11] [1983] 1 A.C. 520.

to extend the scope of the duty of care beyond a duty to prevent harm being done by faulty work, to a duty to avoid defects *being present in the work itself*. Normally, such a duty would only be owed in contract. By a 4:1 majority, the House of Lords held that the special circumstances of the case meant that the defendants owed such a duty in tort. Their Lordships gave a number of reasons why this should be so. The gist of their Lordships' argument was that Veitchi had "assumed responsibility" towards the plaintiffs for the quality of the floor, that the plaintiffs had "reasonably relied" on Veitchi's special skill, and that, because Veitchi were nominated sub-contractors, the relationship between the parties was "almost as close a commercial relationship . . . as it is possible to envisage short of privity of contract".[12]

Lord Roskill gave eight specific reasons why the plaintiffs should succeed:

"(1) The appellants were nominated sub-contractors. (2) The appellants were specialists in flooring. (3) The appellants knew what products were required by the respondents and their main contractors and specialised in the production of those products. (4) The appellants alone were responsible for the composition and construction of the flooring. (5) The respondents relied upon the appellants' skill and experience. (6) The appellants as nominated sub-contractors must have known that the respondents relied upon their skill and experience. (7) The relationship between the parties was as close as it could be short of actual privity of contract. (8) The appellants must be taken to have known that if they did the work negligently . . . the respondents would suffer financial or economic loss."[13]

His Lordship was careful to observe that the circumstances of *Junior Books* were to be distinguished from:

". . . the ordinary everyday transaction of purchasing chattels when it is obvious that in truth the real reliance was upon the immediate vendor and not upon the manufacturer."[14]

Thus, the reasoning in *Junior Books* did not mean, for example, that Mrs Donoghue should have been able to recover in tort the cost of a replacement bottle of ginger beer. It should be noted, however, that Lord Roskill's justification for excluding "everyday transactions" from the scope of *Junior Books* makes use of a legal fiction— the truth of the matter is that there are many occasions on which a consumer will walk into any nearby shop and buy a particular brand of product, putting his or her faith in the product's manufacturer, rather than in the shop. Clearly, then, Lord Roskill's interpretation of "reliance" was heavily influenced by policy considerations, namely the need to avoid widespread liability.

Lord Brandon dissented, arguing that the majority's decision created, between parties who were not in a contractual relationship, the sort of liability that should only arise in the law of contract. We shall see that it has proved very difficult to extract the *ratio* of *Junior Books*, and that the case has met with considerable judicial criticism. In

[12] *per* Lord Roskill in *Junior Books v Veitchi ibid.*, at 542.
[13] *ibid.*, at 546.
[14] *ibid.*, at 547.

D. & F. Estates Ltd v Church Commissioners,[15] for example, Lord Bridge gave his support to Lord Brandon's dissenting view, stating that his Lordship had enunciated principles of "fundamental importance" and that the decision in *Junior Books* could not be regarded as laying down any principle of general application.[16] Although *Junior Books* has never been overruled, it is nowadays regarded as having turned on its own special facts, and is unlikely to be followed.

The liberal approach to economic loss, then, exemplified by *Junior Books* and *Anns*, was short-lived. The courts quickly came to see that those decisions threatened to undermine the principles of contract law. Moreover, they were concerned that the prospect of widespread local authority liability raised by *Anns* might lead to an unacceptable drain on the public purse. These matters are considered below.

THE "ACTIVITY" CASES: PRINCIPLES OF THE MODERN LAW

3–012   The courts now adopt a more restrictive approach to economic loss. Although the law is complex, it is possible clearly to identify three guiding principles which limit the scope of the duty of care. These principles, which all concern the problem of drawing a boundary between contract law and tort law, can be summarised as follows:

- economic loss is not generally recoverable in tort where this would undermine contractual intentions;

- "defective product economic loss" is not generally recoverable;

- a claimant cannot generally recover in respect of damage to property unless he or she has a proprietary interest in the property which is damaged.

Each principle is examined below.

(1) No recovery where contractual intentions are undermined

3–013   There are a number of good reasons why tort law should not be allowed to circumvent the expressed intentions of contracting parties. First, it is arguable that allowing the parties, through contracts, to determine where liability will fall if things go wrong makes for economic efficiency. This is because the parties may choose to allocate risk to the person who can absorb that risk at least cost, perhaps by obtaining the cheapest insurance policy. Certainly, where all of the risk is allocated to a main contractor, who then employs sub-contractors, the transaction costs involved in taking out multiple insurance policies are avoided. Secondly, it is obvious that the quality of a product must be related to the price a person has paid for it. It makes little sense for the law of tort to regulate the quality of products (except to prevent them causing personal injury or damage to other property) because this is a matter for the market and for the rules of contract law. Freedom of contract exists precisely to allow the parties to trade off

[15] [1989] A.C. 177.
[16] *ibid.*, at 202.

quality against price. If tort law begins to impose obligations to supply goods of a certain quality, it interferes with this process of bargaining, rendering the rules of contract law redundant.

Contracts (Rights of Third Parties) Act 1999

In *Junior Books*, tort law was used, in effect, to circumvent the strict rules of privity of contract. If the case were to arise today, there is a possibility that a court might impose liability via an alternative route that does not require recourse to the tort of negligence. This is because the rules of privity have been reformed. The Contracts (Rights of Third Parties) Act 1999 provides that where a third party is *expressly identified* in a contract (either by name or as a member of a class) and that contract either: **3–014**

- expressly states that its terms are enforceable by the third party, *or*

- purports to confer a benefit on the third party, and, on a proper construction of the contract, it appears that the parties intend the contract to be enforceable by the third party,

the third party may sue on the contract as if he had been a party to it.[17]

It seems probable that Junior Books would have been identified in the contract between the main contractor and Veitchi. It is uncertain, however, whether on a proper construction of that contract, a court would feel able to say that the parties to the contract intended that it should be enforceable by Junior Books. It is important to note that the provisions of the Act place the emphasis firmly on the intentions of the contracting parties. The Act does not allow the courts to *impose* obligations on contracting parties in spite of their intentions. Arguably, this was what happened in *Junior Books*. In a line of subsequent cases, however, the Court of Appeal has repeatedly affirmed that it will not permit tort law to be used in this way.

The retreat from Junior Books

In *Muirhead v Industrial Tank Specialities*,[18] an enterprising fishmonger conceived a plan to buy lobsters during the summer months, when they were cheap, and resell them on the lucrative Christmas market. In order to store the lobsters, he contracted with the first defendants to build him a tank. The lobsters were stacked in the tank and kept alive in a semi-refrigerated immobile state. Sea-water had to be re-circulated through the tank in order to oxygenate it. This was achieved using a number of pumps which, though installed by the defendants, had been supplied to them by a third party. Because the motors driving the pumps had been made in France and were unsuitable for United Kingdom mains voltage, the pumps failed, causing the death of the lobsters.   **3–015**

Mr Muirhead successfully sued the first defendants for breach of contract, but they went into liquidation and were unable to satisfy the judgment. He therefore brought a claim in tort against the manufacturer of the pumps, claiming compensation for a number of things including: (1) the loss of the lobsters in the tank; (2) loss of profit consequent on loss of those lobsters; (3) expenditure incurred in trying to correct the

---

[17] Contracts (Rights of Third Parties) Act 1999, s.1.
[18] [1986] Q.B. 507.

fault with the pumps; (4) the cost of the pumps. The Court of Appeal, following the reasoning in *Spartan Steel*, held that Mr Muirhead could recover only for the damage to his property (the dead lobsters) and for the loss of profits consequent on that damage. He could not recover for the cost of the pumps or for the expenditure wasted in trying to fix them.

Relying on *Junior Books*, Mr Muirhead had argued that he had placed "reliance" on the manufacturer of the pumps and that the manufacturer had "assumed responsibility" for their quality. Robert Goff L.J., however, confessed difficulty in understanding the *ratio* of *Junior Books*. His Lordship said that the majority in *Junior Books* appeared to have stated that Veitchi had accepted a direct responsibility towards Junior Books for the quality of the floor, but pointed out that this proposition was very difficult to reconcile with the facts of the case—in fact, the parties had, through their contracts, deliberately structured their relationships so that Veitchi assumed responsibility only towards the main contractor, and the main contractor then assumed responsibility towards Junior Books.[19] Clearly, the parties *could* have structured their contractual relationships in such a way that Veitchi would have been directly responsible to Junior Books, but they had chosen not to do so. Thus, it was difficult to accept an argument based on "assumption of responsibility".

In any event, Robert Goff L.J. found it impossible to say that Mr Muirhead had relied on the manufacturer of the pumps in the same way that Junior Books had relied on Veitchi—he had not nominated the manufacturer to supply the pumps. On the contrary, he had never even heard of the pump manufacturer at the time the pumps were supplied. Here, therefore, there was no close, quasi-contractual relationship. In the light of these difficulties, the Court of Appeal thought that the safest course of action was to treat *Junior Books* as a decision confined to its own facts. The decision in *Muirhead*, then, reflected a policy shift towards reaffirming the sharp distinction between contractual and tortious obligations—only contract would provide a remedy for "defective product economic loss".

This policy shift was further evidenced by the Court of Appeal's decision in *Greater Nottingham Co-operative Society v Cementation Piling Ltd*.[20] Here, the plaintiffs had employed contractors to build an extension to one of their buildings and the defendants were nominated sub-contractors, responsible for pile driving. They did this negligently so that completion of the building was delayed, causing the plaintiffs economic loss. Although there was a collateral contract between the plaintiffs and the defendants, the Court of Appeal was not prepared to find liability under *Junior Books*. Woolf L.J. stated:

> "Where, as here, the sub-contractor has entered into a direct contract and expressly undertaken a direct but limited contractual responsibility to the building owner, I regard the direct contract as being inconsistent with any assumption of responsibility beyond that which has been expressly undertaken."[21]

The contract, in setting out which materials were to be used and the design of the piles, therefore set out the sum total of the obligations which the defendants intended

---

[19] [1986] Q.B. 528.
[20] [1989] Q.B. 71.
[21] *ibid.*, at 106.

to assume towards the plaintiffs. This restrictive approach may also be seen in the Court of Appeal decisions in *Simaan v Pilkington Glass Ltd (No. 2)*[22] and *Pacific Associates v Baxter*.[23] In both these cases, the courts held that in view of the way in which the parties had structured their contractual relationships, liability in tort would be inappropriate. The court in *Simaan* rejected the argument that a sub-contractor who had failed to provide the correct shade of glass should be liable to the plaintiffs, who, as main contractors, had suffered economic loss when their client refused to pay.[24] Dillon L.J. dismissed arguments that the principles of *Junior Books* should apply to allow the plaintiffs to sue a sub-contractor for supplying a defective product: "I find it difficult to see that future citation from the *Junior Books* case can ever serve any useful purpose".[25]

Similarly, in *Pacific Associates v Baxter*, the Court of Appeal rejected a claim by the plaintiffs, who had been employed to undertake certain dredging work, against an engineer who had been retained by their employer to supervise the work. The substance of the claim was that the engineer had failed to certify that the plaintiffs were entitled to extra payments when they met with hard material in the course of dredging which made the work more difficult. The Court of Appeal held that in the light of the way the parties had structured their contractual relationships—there was no contract between the engineer and the plaintiffs; his contract was with the employers and contained a general disclaimer of liability[26]—it would be inconsistent to hold that the engineer owed a duty in tort to avoid causing the plaintiffs economic loss. All of these decisions, then, show that under the modern law the courts are unwilling to allow economic loss claims where to do so would interfere with expressed contractual intentions.

(2) "Defective product economic loss" generally not recoverable

We have seen that in *Muirhead* the cost of replacing the pumps was not recoverable in tort. This was a claim for "defective product economic loss"—whilst the pumps had caused damage to *other property* (the lobsters), they were not themselves "damaged" in the tort lawyers' sense of the word; they were simply defective. The issue of "defective product economic loss" has arisen most frequently in relation to defective buildings (*i.e.* where the "product" in question is a building). We have seen that in the 1970s, the House of Lords was prepared to allow such a claim in *Anns*. In subsequent cases, however, their Lordships were reluctant to apply the principles in *Anns* with a broad brush, eventually overruling their decision in that case.

In *D. & F. Estates Ltd v Church Commissioners*,[27] the plaintiffs brought an action against sub-contractors who had negligently plastered the walls of a flat. They claimed

3–016

---

[22] [1988] 2 W.L.R. 761.
[23] [1990] 1 Q.B. 993.
[24] The client (Sheikh Al-Oteiba) had specified that panels of green glass should be incorporated into the curtain wall of the building; green being the colour of peace in Islam. The panels, on arrival, were found to contain shades of red.
[25] *Simaan v Pilkington Glass Ltd (No. 2)* [1988] 2 W.L.R. 761 at 778.
[26] Compare *J. Jarvis & Sons Ltd v Castle Wharf Developments Ltd* [2001] EWCA Civ 19; [2001] Lloyd's Rep P. N. 308.
[27] [1989] A.C. 177.

for the cost of renewing the plaster and for the consequent disruption and loss of rent while the work took place. The House of Lords held that the claim failed because it was for economic loss, which was only recoverable in contract. A number of important points emerged from the decision. First, their Lordships saw a clear difference between, on the one hand, situations where a latent (undiscovered) defect materialised, causing damage to other property or personal injury, and, on the other hand, situations where a dangerous defect is discovered by the building owner before any such damage has occurred. In the latter case, the cost of remedying the defect—even where this is necessary in order to obviate an immediate threat of personal injury or damage to other property—was to be regarded as non-recoverable economic loss. This observation, although *obiter* to the decision in *D. & F. Estates*, did much to settle previous debate about whether a duty of care could be owed in respect of defects that posed an imminent danger, but had not yet caused any damage. The approach suggested in *D. & F. Estates* was subsequently applied in *Murphy v Brentwood DC*. The second point of importance was their Lordships' reference to what has become known as the "complex structure theory". This is dealt with below.

On the question of whether tort law should be used to impose obligations of a contractual nature, their Lordships were clear: the plasterers could not be liable to the plaintiffs, with whom they had no contractual relationship, simply for a defect in the quality of their workmanship. Lord Oliver stated that, in English law, there were no such things as "transmissible warranties" of quality,[28] and Lord Bridge did not consider that tort should be used to impose " . . . the obligation of one who warranted the quality of the plaster as regards materials, workmanship and fitness for purpose."[29] Dealing with *Anns*, Lord Oliver commented that the "underlying logical basis" of the case was "not entirely clear".[30]

The leading case is now *Murphy v Brentwood DC*.[31] Here, Brentwood Council, relying on the negligent advice of its consulting engineers, approved the building plans for a house. There were certain errors in the design of the foundations which made them defective. Mr Murphy subsequently bought the house, and, while he was in occupation, the foundations cracked, causing extensive damage. The gas, water and sewage pipes underneath the house began to rupture, posing a danger to Mr Murphy and his family and forcing them to move out. Instead of repairing the house, Mr Murphy sold it to a builder for considerably less than he had paid for it. He then sued the council for his financial loss.

The claim failed. The House of Lords held that Mr Murphy could not recover his economic loss. On the question of whether the law would allow claims for damage to "other property" caused by a defective building, their Lordships held that, whilst a local authority (or a builder) might be liable in tort if a *latent* (undiscovered) defect suddenly materialised, causing personal injury, or damage to property other than the building itself, no duty of care was owed in respect of damage caused by a defect that

[28] [1989] A.C. 214. Note that "transmissible warranties" are now, of course, provided for under the Contracts (Rights of Third Parties) Act 1999.
[29] *ibid.*, at 207.
[30] *ibid*. at 216.
[31] [1991] 1 A.C. 398. The reasoning in *Murphy* was applied in *Department of Environment v Thomas Bates & Son Ltd.* [1991] A.C. 499, an opinion handed down on the same day. For examples of how *Murphy* has subsequently been applied, see *Blaxhall Securities Ltd v Sheard Walshaw Partnership* [2001] B.L.R. 36; *Payne v John Setchell Ltd* [2002] B.L.R. 489.

had become *apparent*. "Apparent", in this context, meant that the defect had already been discovered by the claimant, or that he or she ought reasonably to have discovered it. The cost of replacing "other property" damaged by an apparent defect was, like the defect itself, to be regarded as economic loss.

Apparent defects: exceptions to the general rule

There appear to be two exceptions to the principle stated in *Murphy* that there can be no liability in tort for damage caused by a defect in a building once that defect has been discovered. One of these exceptions arises from the subsequent decision of the Court of Appeal in *Targett v Torfaen BC*.[32] Another arises from certain observations made in *Murphy* itself: **3–017**

(i) A claimant may recover for injury caused by an apparent defect where it is unreasonable to expect the claimant to repair the defect or vacate the building

In *Targett v Torfaen BC* a council tenant was injured when he fell down some steps that had been poorly designed and were not adequately lit. When he sued the council, the defence was raised that because the defect in the steps was apparent, it was a matter of economic loss—the tenancy was simply less valuable than it might have been. It was argued that, because there was no liability for the defect, it followed that that there could be no liability for the injury it had caused. To put it another way, the tenant should be regarded as the author of his own misfortune by failing either to remedy the defect or to vacate the property.   **3–018**

   The Court of Appeal rejected the council's argument, holding that *Murphy* did not lay down any absolute rule to the effect that a claimant who suffered personal injury because of a defect was automatically barred from recovery because of his or her knowledge of the defect.[33] In the case of many householders, it would be quite unrealistic to expect them to vacate their homes for fear of being injured by a relatively small defect. Therefore, liability should be decided by reference to whether, in the circumstances, it was reasonable to expect the householder to remain in the building.

(ii) A claimant may recover where the defect is a potential source of liability to neighbouring landowners

In *Murphy*, Lord Bridge suggested that: **3–019**

   ". . . if a building stands so close to the boundary of the building owner's land that after discovery of the dangerous defect it remains a potential source of injury to persons or property on neighbouring land or on the highway, the building owner ought, in principle, to be entitled to recover in tort from the negligent builder the cost of obviating the danger . . . so far as that cost is necessarily incurred in order to protect himself from potential liability to third parties."[34]

His Lordship did not explain the reasoning behind this exception to the general rule, but it has been suggested that it might be explained on the basis that such a building would

---

[32] [1992] 3 All E.R. 27.
[33] Such a proposition would have been inconsistent with the Court of Appeal's decision in *Rimmer v Liverpool City Council* [1985] Q.B. 1, which had not been referred to in *Murphy*.
[34] *Murphy v Brentwood D.C.* [1991] 1 A.C. 398 at 475.

also constitute a nuisance, entitling the neighbouring land-owner to an injunction ordering that it be demolished or made safe.[35] It is possible, of course, that his Lordship's intention was to create a general exception, going beyond the case of neighbouring land-owners, to the effect that any expenditure in repairing a defective building might be recoverable where it was necessary to avoid liability to a third party. This is unlikely, however, because the implications of such a rule would be, for example, that Mr Murphy could have recovered the cost of repairing his house by arguing that this was necessary to protect himself from a law suit by his family or his visitors.

The "complex structure theory"

3–020   In *D. & F. Estates*, Lords Bridge and Oliver, seeking to distinguish *Anns*, appeared to suggest that the decision might be explained on the basis of the "complex structure theory". Before we consider this, it is important to emphasise that, in the light of *Murphy*, the theory has no application where a defect in property has already been discovered.[36] Rather, the theory may be advanced as a way of explaining how damage to some parts of a building (or product), caused by an undiscovered defect materialising, might be recoverable, even though the cost of replacing the *defect itself* is not.

According to the "complex structure" theory, it might be possible to regard the constituent parts of a building as *separate items of property*, instead of regarding the whole building as a distinct and indivisible entity. On this basis, their Lordships in *D. & F. Estates* thought it might be possible to say that the defective foundations in *Anns* were separate from the rest of the building, and that they had caused damage to "other property", namely the walls. It followed that there would be no objection to liability for the cost of repairing the walls, and, of course, to repair the cracked walls properly it would be necessary to rebuild the building, replacing the defective foundations themselves.

In *Murphy*, however, the House of Lords rejected the "complex structure theory" as an explanation for *Anns* — it was wholly unrealistic to view a building as distinct from its foundations. Lords Keith, Bridge and Jauncey did not, however, rule out the application of a limited version of the theory in appropriate cases. Thus, in a case where a defective central heating boiler (unexpectedly) exploded and damaged a house, or where a defective electrical installation set a house on fire, Lord Bridge thought that the owner of the house could recover damages against a builder on the basis that damage had been caused by one piece of property (for example, the boiler) to "other property" (the house).[37] Lord Jauncey, whilst agreeing that the theory could apply to the examples given by Lord Bridge, went further, stating that the theory might operate where:

> " . . . one integral component of the structure was built by a separate contractor and where a defect in such a component had caused damage to other parts of the structure, *e.g.* a steel frame erected by a specialist contractor which failed to give adequate support to floors and walls."[38]

---

[35] Rogers, *Winfield & Jolowicz on Tort* (16th ed., Sweet & Maxwell, 2002) p.333.
[36] This proposition, of course, is subject to the reasoning in *Targett v Torfaen BC* [1992] 3 All E.R. 27, *viz.* that there might be liability for damage caused by an apparent defect which the householder cannot reasonably be expected to fix. It is unclear, however, whether the reasoning in *Targett* would be extended to cover cases of property damage.
[37] *Murphy v Brentwood D.C.* [1991] 1 A.C. 398 at 478.
[38] *ibid.*, at 497.

In Lord Jauncey's example, then, the presence of a separate contractor is the crucial feature which brings the theory into play. The limits of the theory, however, remain unexplored.[39]

Defective Premises Act 1972

It is appropriate here to mention the Defective Premises Act 1972. At the same time that the judges had been considering liability for defective premises at common law, the matter was being considered by the Law Commission, whose conclusions led to the passing of the Act. In the more recent cases, therefore, the courts, in developing this area of law, have been concerned not to create liability that is wider than that provided for by Parliament. The Act provides for the liability of builders and other professionals involved in the construction of "dwellings", but the extent of their liability is much more restricted than that which had been envisaged in *Anns*. For a time, the decision in *Anns* had the effect of making the Act something of a dead letter, but the decision in *Murphy* restored its importance.

3–021

Under the Act, persons who undertake work for, or in connection with, the provision of a dwelling have a statutory duty to see that the work is done in a workmanlike or professional manner and with proper materials so that, as regards that work, the dwelling will be fit for habitation when completed.[40] The duty is imposed not only on the builders of dwellings, but also, for example, on the architects, surveyors and sub-contractors involved. Moreover, the duty is owed not only to a person commissioning the work, but also to every person who later acquires an interest (whether legal or equitable) in the dwelling. The Act provides a remedy for mere defects in quality (provided they make the house unfit for habitation) without the claimant having to show an imminent danger of personal injury or damage to other property.

For many years, the effect of the Act was substantially curtailed. This was because the Act does not apply to houses protected by an "approved scheme". Most newly constructed dwelling houses are built under a scheme operated by the National House Building Council (NHBC), and until the late 1980s, the NHBC scheme was an "approved scheme", so that most new houses were not covered by the Act. But now that the NHBC no longer submits its scheme for approval by the Secretary of State, the Act has a wider field of application.[41] Under the Act, however, a claimant's position is much less favourable than under the common law as it was developed in *Anns*. This is because a six-year limitation period begins to run when the dwelling is completed.[42] If the common law in *Anns* had remained unchanged, the claimant could have taken advantage of a limitation period that started to run only when symptoms of the defect became reasonably discoverable.[43]

---

[39] See, however, *Aswan Engineering Establishment Co. v Lupdine Ltd* [1987] 1 All E.R. 135, where defective containers caused damage to the proofing compound they contained. Lloyd L.J. was of the "provisional view" that the proofing compound was "other property", even though it had been bought in the containers from the same supplier.

[40] Defective Premises Act 1972, s.1.

[41] It should be noted, however, that the NHBC scheme generally provides superior cover in comparison with the Act because claims for major structural defects may be made for up to 10 years.

[42] Defective Premises Act 1972, s.1(5).

[43] The Latent Damage Act 1986 made the claimant's position more favourable in building cases at common law by providing a limitation period of three years running from the date damage was reasonably discoverable. The Act is now a dead letter in this regard, however, because, under *Murphy*, claimants have no cause of action in the first place.

(3) No recovery unless claimant has proprietary interest in damaged property[44]

3-022   The principles enunciated in *Cattle*, *Weller*, and *Spartan Steel* remain an important feature of the modern law. Thus, in *Candlewood Navigation Corp. Ltd v Mitsui O.S.K. Lines*,[45] one ship, the Mineral Transporter, collided with another, the Ibaraki Maru, because of the negligence of the Mineral Transporter's crew. The first plaintiffs, who were in fact the owners of the Ibaraki Maru, had let it on a charterparty to the second plaintiffs. The second plaintiffs had then re-let it back to the first plaintiffs. When the first plaintiffs—not in their capacity as *owners* but as *charterers* of the ship—sued for economic loss caused while the ship was being repaired, the Privy Council held that they had no cause of action, re-affirming the principle established in *Cattle v Stockton Waterworks* that a person cannot sue in respect of damage to property in which he or she has only a contractual interest.

In *Leigh and Sillavan Ltd v Aliakmon Shipping Co. Ltd. (The Aliakmon)*,[46] the plaintiffs had contracted to buy a cargo of steel coils to be shipped from Korea. The arrangements between the plaintiffs and the sellers of the coils were such that, although the *risk* in the cargo had passed to the plaintiffs, the *ownership* of the coils had not. When the coils were damaged at sea by the defendant shippers' negligence, the plaintiffs, who had to pay for the damaged goods, sought to recover their financial loss from the negligent shippers. The loss to the plaintiffs was clearly foreseeable, and in arrangements for the carriage of goods by sea, situations where the party likely to suffer loss is not the owner of the cargo are quite common. Nevertheless, the House of Lords denied the plaintiffs a remedy, holding that because they had had only a contractual interest in the coils at the time they were damaged, they were unable to recover.[47] This resulted in the somewhat bizarre situation that the person who had suffered the loss had no remedy, whilst the person who had a remedy (the owner of the coils) had suffered no loss (he had been paid for the damaged goods). As we shall see below, however, in the context of solicitors drafting wills, it is precisely this dilemma that has prompted the House of Lords to allow disappointed beneficiaries to recover economic loss.

THE "WILL DRAFTING" CASES

3-023   There is one type of "activity" case that defies analysis in terms of the principles we have so far examined. The courts have held that a solicitor, in preparing a will for a testator, owes a duty of care to intended beneficiaries of the will to prevent them from suffering economic loss.

[44] Contrast the position in Canada: *The Norsk (Canadian National Railway Co. v Norsk Pacific Steamship Co.)* (1992) 91 D.L.R. (4th) 289; *Bow Valley Husky (Bermuda) v Saint John Shipbuilding Ltd* (1998) 153 D.L.R. (4th) 385.
[45] [1986] A.C. 1.
[46] [1986] A.C. 785. Applied recently in *Homburg Houtimport BV v Agrosin Private Ltd (The Starsin)* [2003] 2 W.L.R. 711.
[47] Note that the Carriage of Goods by Sea Act 1992 introduced certain amendments to the law which would nowadays enable claimants to recover.

The decision in *Ross v Caunters*

In *Ross v Caunters*,[48] the defendant solicitor failed to tell a testator that if his will was   **3–024**
witnessed by the spouse of a beneficiary, any gift to that beneficiary would be void. The
plaintiff, whose husband had witnessed the will, sued the solicitor for the loss of her
gift under the will. Sir Robert Megarry V.-C. held that the solicitor owed the plaintiff a
duty of care and was liable. His Lordship found assistance in the decision of the High
Court of Australia in *Caltex Oil (Australia) Pty Ltd v Dredge "Willemstad"*.[49] In that
case, the owner of a dredger, which fractured a submerged oil pipeline, was held liable
to an oil company. The oil company was not the owner of the pipeline, but it had the
right to receive oil through it, and therefore incurred expense in transporting the oil by
other means while the pipeline was being repaired. Mason and Gibbs JJ. were
prepared to depart from the rule against recovery for damage to property belonging to
others because, in this case, the negligence in question affected only a single clearly
foreseeable plaintiff—it followed that the "floodgates" objection to economic loss
claims did not apply. Applying similar reasoning, Sir Robert Megarry V.-C. was
prepared to say that liability in *Ross v Caunters* should follow, either by an extension of
the "*Hedley Byrne* principle" (discussed later in this chapter), or by a direct application
of the principle of *Donoghue v Stevenson*.[50] In any event, the decision was not likely to
lead to indeterminate liability, because the duty of care would only arise where the
defendant actually *knew* (or ought to have known) that the claimant, for whose benefit
he or she was supposed to draft the will, would be affected by his or her negligence—
there was no question of liability to a large or unascertainable class of claimants.

After the decision in *Ross v Caunters*, a number of cases seemed to cast doubt on
whether it had been correctly decided. In *The Aliakmon*, for example, Robert Goff
L.J., in the Court of Appeal, confessed difficulty in accepting the principle put forward
in the *Caltex Oil* case, on which Sir Robert Megarry V.-C. had relied. Similarly, in *The
Mineral Transporter* (discussed above), the Privy Council considered the *Caltex* case,
but were unable to extract any clear *ratio* from it and declined to apply it. In *White v
Jones*,[51] however, the House of Lords (employing different reasoning) upheld the
decision in *Ross v Caunters*.

The decision in *White v Jones*

In *White v Jones*, a testator had quarrelled with his two daughters and had made a will   **3–025**
cutting them out of their inheritance. Subsequently, he became reconciled with them,
so he instructed the defendants to prepare a new will under which they were to be left
£9,000 each. The defendants failed to act promptly on these instructions. The solicitor
dealing with the matter arranged to meet the testator three times, but failed to keep
the appointments. He then went on holiday. When he returned, he made a further
appointment to see the testator, but unfortunately the testator, who was 78, died three
days before the meeting. The estate was distributed according to the old will, depriving

---

[48] [1980] Ch. 297.
[49] (1976) 136 C.L.R. 529.
[50] [1980] Ch. 297 at 322.
[51] [1995] 2 A.C. 207.

the daughters of their intended legacies. They brought an action against the defendants, claiming £9,000 each in damages.

By a bare majority, the House of Lords upheld the daughters' claims. Lord Goff was content to decide the case by a very broad application of the principle laid down in *Hedley Byrne v Heller & Partners* (discussed below), but declined to follow the reasoning in *Ross v Caunters*, stating that that case had raised a number of conceptual difficulties. Lords Browne-Wilkinson and Nolan held that the defendants had *assumed responsibility* for the task of preparing the new will and that, as a matter of law, this meant that they had assumed responsibility to the plaintiffs. Lord Nolan also thought that the plaintiffs could be said to have *relied* on the defendants, who were acting as family solicitors. Lords Keith and Mustill dissented. Lord Keith stated that to allow the claim would, in effect, be to give the plaintiffs the benefit of a contract (between the testator and the defendants) to which they were not parties.

The overriding factor that seemed to influence the decisions in *Ross v Caunters* and *White v Jones* was the need to do practical justice in the circumstances. In such cases, the courts are faced with an exceptional situation where the only people who suffer loss (the intended beneficiaries) would, on traditional principles, be denied a remedy, but the only person who has a traditional remedy (the estate) suffers no loss. This situation leaves, as Lord Goff put it in *White v Jones*, "a lacuna in the law which needs to be filled".[52] It is interesting to note, however, that the decisions in these cases produce, arguably, injustice of a different kind. This is because those legally entitled to the deceased's estate receive a windfall, in the sense that the deceased does not intend that the money should go to them, while those to whom the money *should* have gone recover from the negligent solicitor. It may be argued that a truly coherent legal system should find a way of giving effect to the testator's intentions without causing this enrichment of the estate—after all (as we can see from the early behaviour of the testator in *White v Jones*) an intention to deprive may sometimes be just as important as an intention to bequeath!

The limits of the "*Ross v Caunters* principle"

3–026   Subsequent cases have made it clear that the *ratios* of *Ross v Caunters* and *White v Jones* are limited in a number of respects. First, it is unlikely that the cases have any application to gifts made between living persons.[53] Thus, in *Hemmens v Wilson Browne*,[54] a certain Mr Panter, who was having an affair with the plaintiff, instructed his solicitors to draft a document that would entitle her to call upon him for the sum of £110,000 at any time in the future. The solicitors drafted a document which had no legal effect—it was not a deed (because it was not under seal) and it was not a contract (because there was no consideration). When the plaintiff asked Mr Panter to fulfil his promise, he refused to pay, having gone back to his wife. Unable to enforce the terms of the document, the plaintiff sued the solicitors, arguing that their negligent drafting

---

[52] 1995] 2 A.C. 260.
[53] Although both Sir Donald Nicholls V.-C. in the Court of Appeal in *White v Jones* [1995] 2 A.C. 207 (at 227) and Sir Robert Megarry V.-C. in *Ross v Caunters* [1980] Ch. 297 (at 322) thought that the principle could be applied to *inter vivos* gifts.
[54] [1993] 4 All E.R. 826.

had caused her to lose her gift. It was held that the special policy considerations which had dictated the outcomes in *Ross v Caunters* and *White v Jones*[55] did not apply here— Mr Panter, being still alive, would be able to rectify the situation, if he so wished, by instructing a solicitor to re-draft the document properly.

Secondly, it has been held that the *Ross v Caunters* principle can only be invoked in situations where the claimant has exhausted his or her other remedies. Thus, in *Walker v Geo. H. Medlicott & Son*,[56] the claimant sued solicitors who had been instructed to include a gift to him in a client's will, but had negligently failed to do so. The circumstances were such that the claimant was entitled to have the will rectified under section 20 of the Administration of Justice Act 1982. The Court of Appeal held that he could not bring an alternative claim in negligence.[57]

In *Worby v Rosser*[58] an attempt was made to apply the *Ross v Caunters* principle in a novel context. The testator had made a will in 1983, leaving money to the plaintiffs. Subsequently, he came under the influence of an associate who acted fraudulently in persuading him to make a new will, in 1989, under which the associate stood to benefit substantially. The plaintiffs successfully contested the new will, and it was refused probate, the 1983 will being admitted in its place. The plaintiffs brought an action against the solicitor who had drafted the new will, seeking to recover the legal costs they had incurred in disproving it. They argued that the solicitor had been negligent in failing to realise that the testator had lacked testamentary capacity and had been acting under undue influence. The Court of Appeal held that the *Ross v Caunters* principle could not be extended to cover such a situation. There was no authority to suggest that a solicitor owed a duty of care to beneficiaries of an earlier will. Moreover, the special circumstances in *Ross* and *White* were not present here. The expense of contesting the new will was a loss suffered by the *estate*, which it could recover from the solicitor. Therefore it could not be said that the person suffering the loss had no remedy.[59]

ECONOMIC LOSS CAUSED BY NEGLIGENT STATEMENTS AND SERVICES

The law on negligent misstatement has developed differently from the law relating to negligent activities (although certain concepts were borrowed by the latter during its development). This divergence in the law produces a somewhat uneasy result. For example, a surveyor who negligently advises on the purchase of a defective house may, as we shall see, be liable for economic loss caused as a result of his advice, whilst a

3–027

---

[55] *White v Jones* was a Court of Appeal decision at the time.
[56] [1999] 1 W.L.R. 727.
[57] Compare *Horsefall v Haywards* [1999] 1 F.L.R. 1182. (There can be no objection to a negligence action where there is little likelihood that rectification will succeed.)
[58] *The Times*, June 9, 1999; [1999] Lloyd's Rep. P.N. 972.
[59] Compare *Farah v British Airways plc*, *The Times*, January 26, 2000 (1999 WL 1142461). The Court of Appeal refused to strike out an action by a number of immigrants who alleged economic loss as a result of the actions of British Airways, who had acted in reliance on negligent advice given by the Home Office. If the claimants could not sue the Home Office, they would have no effective remedy. British Airways had a remedy, but had suffered no loss. The case was an example of the unusual tripartite situation that had existed in *White v Jones* and *Spring v Guardian Assurance plc* [1995] 2 A.C. 296 (discussed below), in which the plaintiffs were affected by advice communicated to a third party.

builder who causes economic loss by constructing a house negligently may escape liability.[60] It must be admitted that it is almost impossible to reconcile the two branches of the law, more especially because, as we point out in the conclusion to this chapter, the distinction between "activity" and "statement" cases is often extremely fine. The lack of clarity in the law is compounded by the fact that, as we shall see, the House of Lords has been prepared to extend the principle developed in negligent misstatement cases to cases involving the negligent provision of services.

The old law

3–028   In 1951, the Court of Appeal decided *Candler v Crane, Christmas & Co.*[61] Here, the defendants, a firm of accountants, prepared the accounts of a company knowing that the figures they produced would be relied on by the plaintiff in deciding whether to invest in the company. The accounts were prepared negligently, causing the plaintiff financial loss. The majority of the Court of Appeal reaffirmed existing precedent, holding that liability for a careless (as opposed to fraudulent) statement could only arise where the maker of the statement had a contractual or fiduciary relationship with the plaintiff. Denning L.J. dissented. In his Lordship's view, existing precedent was inapplicable, because it was based on the idea that the existence of a contractual relationship would prevent a duty of care from being owed to third parties—and this was a myth that had been exploded by the decision in *Donoghue v Stevenson*. Denning L.J.'s dissenting view, then, paved the way for the change in the law that was to take place in *Hedley Byrne & Co. v Heller & Partners*.[62]

The "*Hedley Byrne* principle"

3–029   The facts of *Hedley Byrne* were set out in Ch. 2. It will be recalled that the claim was in respect of a negligently given banking reference (accompanied by a disclaimer) on which the plaintiffs relied, suffering financial loss. The House of Lords held that, in view of the disclaimer, the defendants had not accepted any legal responsibility towards the plaintiffs, so the claim failed. What is important, however, is that their Lordships went on to consider what the position would have been in the absence of the disclaimer, holding that there was no reason in principle why a duty of care should not be owed in respect of careless statements. Their Lordships held that the majority in *Candler* had wrongly decided that case, and that the view of Denning L.J. was to be preferred.

The decision in *Hedley Byrne* represented a radical change in the law, because it was the first time that the duty of care had been extended to cover pure economic loss. The House of Lords was not, however, prepared to decide the case simply by extending the principle of *Donoghue v Stevenson*. Their Lordships noted that because statements may be repeated, and then relied on by an unlimited number of people, the effects of negligent statements have a much greater propensity to spread throughout society than

---

[60] For further discussion of this anomaly, see Stapleton (1991) 107 L.Q.R. 249 and Markesinis and Deakin (1992) 55 M.L.R. 619.
[61] [1951] 2 K.B. 164.
[62] [1964] A.C. 465.

do the effects of negligently manufactured products. In the case of statements, therefore, the law had to impose tighter controls on the scope of liability. Accordingly, their Lordships laid down two requirements which a claimant will need to satisfy to establish a duty of care in respect of a statement. These may be summarised as follows:

- the existence of a "special relationship" between the claimant and the defendant, involving an "assumption of responsibility" by the defendant;

- "reasonable reliance" by the claimant.

Taken together, these factors may be referred to as the *"Hedley Byrne* principle". We have seen that the factors in question were used to establish liability in *Junior Books*. We have also seen that in *Muirhead*, and in subsequent "careless activity" cases, the courts were critical of the way they had been applied in *Junior Books*, pointing out that where contracts exist, setting out the nature of the relationships between parties, it is inappropriate to talk about "special relationships" existing independently of those contracts. In negligent misstatement cases, however, the *"Hedley Byrne* principle" has continued to be regarded as important, although it is noteworthy that it has not escaped academic criticism.[63] In particular, it has been pointed out that in *Hedley Byrne*, the plaintiffs, in effect, were given the benefit of a contractual warranty for which they had not paid—there was nothing to stop the plaintiffs from protecting themselves in law by entering into a contract with the defendant bank for the supply of the advice, but instead they sought to "freeload" on the bank's advice, and then to impose a contractual type of liability when the advice proved wrong. Below, we explore each element of the *"Hedley Byrne* principle" in turn.

(1) "Special relationship" and "assumption of responsibility"

The ideas of "special relationship" and "assumption of responsibility" cannot really be examined in isolation from one another, because both phrases are ways of saying the same thing, namely that there is a sufficient degree of "proximity" between the claimant and the defendant. This is a rather complex area of the law, but it can be broken down into a number of discrete issues, which are considered below.   **3–030**

When will a "special relationship" normally arise?

In *Hedley Byrne*, Lord Reid thought that a "special relationship" would arise where "it is plain that the party seeking information or advice was trusting the other to exercise such a degree of care as the circumstances required, where it was reasonable for him to do that, and where the other gave the information or advice when he knew or ought to have known that the inquirer was relying on him".[64]   **3–031**

His Lordship went on to say that a reasonable man, when asked for advice, and realising that his skill and judgment might be relied on, would have three options open to him: he could keep silent; he could give an answer with a clear qualification that he accepted no responsibility for it (a disclaimer); or he could simply answer without any such qualification. A person who chose the last option would be held to have assumed

---

[63] See, *e.g.* Weir [1963] C.L.J. 216.
[64] [1964] A.C. 465 at 486.

responsibility for his or her answer being given carefully, and therefore would owe a duty of care to the recipient of the advice.

Can a "special relationship" arise in a purely social context?

3–032   Lord Reid, in *Hedley Byrne*, made it clear that a "special relationship" could only arise where the statement was made in a "business connection". There would be no liability for statements made on purely social occasions. This was because, as his Lordship observed:

> "Quite careful people often express definite opinions on social or informal occasions even when they see that others are likely to be influenced by them; and they often do that without taking that care which they would take if asked for their opinion professionally or in a business connection."[65]

Interestingly, the Court of Appeal seemed to depart from this fundamental principle in *Chaudhry v Prabhakar*.[66] Here, a family friend agreed to help the plaintiff find a second-hand car, telling her that she could rely on him and that she need not have the car inspected by a mechanic. The defendant, through his negligence, advised the plaintiff to buy a car which, it turned out, was unroadworthy and practically worthless. Before the trial, the defendant conceded that he owed a duty of care to the plaintiff. A majority of the court held that this concession had been rightly made, and that the plaintiff was able to recover her economic loss. May L.J., however, dissented. His Lordship doubted that any duty of care was owed. In May L.J.'s view, to impose liability in such a situation was undesirable, because it would make social relations between friends unnecessarily hazardous.

   What makes the decision in *Chaudhry v Prabhakar* so extraordinary is that there was no suggestion that the defendant, Mr Prabhakar, was securing any benefit to himself by offering the free advice—he offered his services on a purely gratuitous basis. Thus, the situation is to be contrasted with *Hedley Byrne*, where the bank, although not of course paid for the advice, nevertheless supplied it to further their general business interests. As Lord Devlin observed, in *Hedley Byrne*:

> "It may often be material to consider whether the adviser is acting purely out of good nature or whether he is getting his reward in some indirect form. The service that a bank performs in giving a reference is not done simply out of a desire to assist commerce. It would discourage the customers of the bank if their deals fell through because the bank had refused to testify to their credit when it was good."[67]

The majority of the Court of Appeal in *Chaudhry v Prabhakar* did not appear to think it relevant that the defendant was acting "purely out of good nature". Reading between the lines, however, it might be possible to explain the decision on the basis that Mr Prabhakar's conduct clearly involved a risk of injury to Miss Chaudhry.

Must the defendant be "in the business of giving advice"?

3–033   The Privy Council, in *Mutual Life and Citizens' Assurance Co. v Evatt*,[68] took a somewhat restricted view of the circumstances in which a "special relationship" could arise. Here, the plaintiff sought advice from his insurance company about the wisdom

[65] [1964] A.C. 482.
[66] [1989] 1 W.L.R. 29.
[67] [1964] A.C. 465 at 529.
[68] [1971] A.C. 793.

of investing in a company with which it was associated. He was given certain information that turned out to be false, and sought to recover the money he lost on his investment. The majority held that the *Hedley Byrne* principle should be confined to cases involving defendants whose profession includes the giving of advice, such as accountants, surveyors and lawyers. Since the defendants were in the business of providing insurance cover, not investment advice, they could not be liable. Lords Reid and Morris, however, dissented, holding that it was sufficient for the *Hedley Byrne* principle to apply if the advice was sought from a business person in the course of business. It is this minority view in *Mutual Life* which has found favour with the courts. Thus, in *Esso Petroleum Co. Ltd v Mardon*[69] (discussed below), Ormrod L.J. remarked that if the majority opinion were accepted, "the effect of *Hedley Byrne* would be so radically curtailed as to be virtually eliminated",[70] and in *Howard Marine and Dredging Co. Ltd v Ogden & Sons Ltd*[71] (discussed later), both Lord Denning M.R. and Shaw L.J. made it clear that they preferred the minority view.

In *Esso v Mardon*, the plaintiff leased a filling station on the strength of Esso's advice that he could expect to sell at least 200,000 gallons of petrol a year. This forecast had been based on an assumption that the petrol pumps would be located at the front of the filling station on the main road. It then transpired that the local planning authority in fact required the pumps to be at the back of the filling station, where they would attract much less passing trade. Esso failed to revise its forecast in the light of that fact. The plaintiff sold only 78,000 gallons in 15 months, and sued Esso for his financial loss. In allowing the claim, the Court of Appeal held that Esso had assumed responsibility for the accuracy of its forecast and that it had been reasonable for Mr Mardon to rely on Esso's skill in predicting likely petrol sales.

Employment references

The decision in *Spring v Guardian Assurance plc*[72] makes it clear that a "special relationship" will exist between an employer and an employee who asks for a job reference. Here, the plaintiff, Mr Spring, had been employed by the defendants but subsequently dismissed. He sought work with one of the defendants' competitors, but received such a bad reference that he failed to get the job. The statements in the reference, although made honestly, had given a misleading impression of the circumstances surrounding Mr Spring's dismissal, and had been made without a proper investigation of the facts. The House of Lords held that the defendants owed a duty of care in preparing the reference and, accordingly, were liable. It made no difference that if Mr Spring had sued in defamation, the defendants would have had the defence of qualified privilege.[73] The existence of this defence did not prevent liability in negligence. Nor, apparently, did it matter that this was a case where, exceptionally, the plaintiff was seeking to recover in respect of a statement that had not been made to *him* but to *someone else*.[74]

3–034

---

[69] [1976] 1 Q.B. 801.
[70] *ibid.*, at 827.
[71] [1978] 2 All E.R. 1134.
[72] [1995] 2 A.C. 296. See also *Cox v Sun Alliance Life Ltd* [2001] I.R.L.R. 448. Compare *Kapfunde v Abbey National plc* [1999] I.C.R. 1 (no duty owed by a doctor retained by a prospective employer who had no professional relationship with the plaintiff) and *Legal & General Assurance plc* v Kirk [2002] I.R.L.R. 124 (no liability for negligent statements not amounting to a reference).
[73] See Ch. 13.
[74] On this point, see also *Farah v British Airways plc, The Times*, January 26, 2000.

Provision of services (the "extended Hedley Byrne principle")[75]

3–035   In *Spring v Guardian Assurance plc*, Lord Goff, with whom Lord Lowry agreed, stated that, in appropriate cases, the *Hedley Byrne* principle should not be limited to the provision of advice, but could be applied more generally to situations involving the provision of services. The proper interpretation of *Hedley Byrne*, according to Lord Goff, was that "where the plaintiff entrusts the defendant with the conduct of his affairs, in general or in particular, the defendant may be held to have assumed responsibility to the plaintiff. . ."[76] His Lordship approved Lord Morris's assertion in *Hedley Byrne* that: "The fact that the service is to be given by means of or by the instrumentality of words can make no difference".[77]

This wider application of the *Hedley Byrne* principle was also seen in *Henderson v Merrett Syndicates Ltd*.[78] The action, which involved five appeals, arose in the following way: in the early 1990s, there were a number of unusually large claims made against the Lloyds insurance organisation. These losses had to be borne by people known as "Names", who invest in Lloyds by underwriting their insurance policies. The Names are grouped into syndicates. The plaintiffs alleged that the agents who had organised their syndicates had been negligent in handling their affairs.

Without having to refer to a specific statement or piece of advice, the House of Lords was able to say that a duty of care was owed because the agents had assumed responsibility for the financial welfare of the Names. Their Lordships also confirmed that the existence of a contractual relationship between the claimant and the defendant does not preclude the existence of a "special relationship", giving rise to liability in tort. Many of the Names had contracts with the defendant agents, but sought to sue in tort because the limitation period for actions in contract had expired. Their Lordships held that they were entitled to take advantage of a longer limitation period which (for reasons that do not concern us here) was applicable in tort.

Pensions Advice

3–036   In *Gorham v British Telecommunications plc*[79], the Court of Appeal was prepared to hold that the *Hedley Byrne* principle could, in appropriate cases, make providers of financial services liable to the dependants of a deceased person who had been wrongly advised about how to make provision for them. Mr Gorham had opted out of his employer's pension scheme and had sought the advice of the Standard Life Assurance Co., making it clear that his first priority was to make provision for his wife and children in the event of his death. The company negligently failed to advise him that his employer's pension scheme might provide superior cover, and instead sold him one of its personal pension plans. Some months later, the company admitted its mistake

---

[75] This expression was used by Lord Steyn in *Williams and Reid v Natural Life Health Foods Ltd and Mistlin* [1998] 1 W.L.R. 830 at 835 *et seq.*
[76] *Spring v Guardian Assurance plc* [1995] 2 A.C. 296 at 318.
[77] [1964] A.C. 465 at 503.
[78] [1995] 2 A.C. 145. See also *Welton v North Cornwall D.C.* [1997] 1 W.L.R. 1397. The defendants' environmental health officer had imposed excessive hygiene requirements on a guest house. The claim was held to be well within the *Hedley Byrne* principle, even though it could not be described as a case involving negligent "advice".
[79] [2000] 1 W.L.R. 2129. See also *Wheldon v GRE Linked Life Assurance Ltd* [2000] 2 All E.R. (Comm.) 914 (Life insurance company liable for presenting a direct debit mandate to the wrong branch of a bank, so that premiums were not collected and the policy lapsed.)

and correctly advised Mr Gorham that his employer's scheme was better. Unfortunately, however, Mr Gorham did not re-join his employer's scheme, mistakenly believing that he was already a member. This meant that his dependants were not provided for when he died. The court upheld an action by the wife and children for loss of the pension rights to which they would have been entitled had Mr Gorham been correctly advised in the first place and remained a member of his employer's scheme. Their Lordships took the view that the situation was directly analogous to that in *White v Jones* (discussed above) and that, just as a solicitor owed a duty to see that a testator's intentions were given effect so as to provide for beneficiaries, a company selling a pension plan had a duty not to give negligent advice to a customer which adversely affected the interests of his dependants as he intended them to be.

How do the courts justify the "assumption of responsibility" doctrine?

In recent cases, then, the courts have increasingly used the concept of "assumption of responsibility" to justify imposing a duty of care on the defendant to protect the claimant from economic loss. This concept lies at the heart of the decisions in *Henderson* and *Spring* (discussed above). Yet the concept has not escaped criticism. In *Henderson*, Lord Goff noted that there had been a tendency for the courts to criticise the notion of "assumption of responsibility" on the basis that it was inconsistent with contractual arrangements between the parties.[80] His Lordship noted that in *Smith v Eric Bush* (discussed later) Lord Griffiths had said that the idea was "unlikely to be a helpful or realistic test in most cases" and that in *Caparo v Dickman*, Lord Roskill had expressed a similar view. Lord Goff pointed out, however, that in those cases, the criticism had been made by their Lordships in an effort to contain the scope of liability under *Hedley Byrne* (*i.e.* to avoid opening the floodgates of litigation). His Lordship thought that in a case like *Henderson*, where there was no danger of liability to an indeterminate class of claimants, there was no reason why the idea of "assumption of responsibility" should not be applied.

A similar approach was taken by Lord Steyn in *Williams and Reid v Natural Life Health Foods Ltd and Mistlin*[81] (discussed later). Delivering the opinion of the House of Lords, his Lordship dealt specifically with academic criticism that had been levied against the principle of assumption of responsibility (on the basis that it rested on a fiction used to justify a conclusion that a duty of care existed)[82] and said: "In my view the general criticism is overstated. Coherence must sometimes yield to practical justice". Lord Steyn explained that *Hedley Byrne* and subsequent cases had been decided using the principle because of the restrictive nature of the doctrines of privity and consideration in English contract law. His Lordship noted that in *The Pioneer Container*[83] Lord Goff had said that it was open to question how long the principles of consideration and privity would be maintained. Lord Steyn concluded:

" . . . while the present structure of English contract law remains intact the law of tort, as the general law, has to fulfil an essential gap-filling role. In these

3–037

---

[80] *Henderson v Merrett Syndicates Ltd* [1995] 2 A.C. 145 at 181.
[81] [1998] 1 W.L.R. 830.
[82] *ibid.*, at 837. His Lordship specifically refers to Barker (1993) 109 L.Q.R. 461; Hepple (1997) 50 C. L. P. 69 at 88, and Cane, *Tort Law and Economic Interests*, (2nd ed., 1996, O.U.P.), pp. 177 and 200.
[83] [1994] 2 A.C. 324.

circumstances there . . . is no better rationalisation for the relevant head of tort liability than assumption of responsibility."

Can there be an "assumption of responsibility" where the defendant expressly disclaims responsibility?

3–038   Whilst the question of "assumption of responsibility" is decided by reference to things said or done by the defendant, it is clear, of course, that the term does *not* imply that the defendant has *expressly indicated* acceptance of legal responsibility. Liability is imposed on the basis of an objective test, to which the expressed intentions of the defendant are only partly relevant. It follows that although a disclaimer will normally work to absolve the defendant from liability (as in *Hedley Byrne*), there may be exceptional circumstances in which liability will be imposed in spite of an assertion that the defendant accepts no legal responsibility for the advice in question. Such was the case in *Smith v Eric Bush*.[84]

Here, the House of Lords decided two appeals in which the plaintiffs had suffered economic loss as a result of negligent surveys. In the first appeal (which serves to illustrate the decision), the plaintiff, Mrs Smith, wished to buy a house, and approached a building society for a mortgage. The building society instructed the defendants, a firm of surveyors, to carry out a visual inspection of the house in order to confirm that it was worth at least the money which they were proposing to lend. The defendants' valuer noticed that two chimney breasts had been removed, but he failed to check whether the chimneys had been left adequately supported. His report stated that no essential repairs were necessary.

The mortgage application form and the valuation report contained a disclaimer of liability. Mrs Smith was also informed that the report was not a structural survey and she was advised to obtain independent professional advice. The building society, pursuant to an agreement with Mrs Smith, who had paid an inspection fee, supplied her with a copy of the report. She, like many purchasers of modest houses, relied on it and purchased the house without any further survey. The chimneys were not adequately supported and one of them subsequently collapsed.

When Mrs Smith sought to recover her financial loss, the defendants argued that the disclaimer exempted them from liability. The House of Lords, however, held that the disclaimer was invalid under s.2 of the Unfair Contract Terms Act 1977. It did not satisfy the requirement of reasonableness set out in s.11(3) of that Act. Since the valuer was a professional, whose services were paid for (albeit indirectly) by Mrs Smith, and since he was aware that Mrs Smith would probably purchase the house in reliance on his valuation without an independent survey, it would not be fair and reasonable to allow the valuer to rely on the disclaimer. Accordingly, the valuer had assumed responsibility to Mrs Smith and was liable in negligence. Lord Griffiths observed:

> " . . . the phrase 'assumption of responsibility' can only have any real meaning if it is understood as referring to the circumstances in which the law will *deem* the maker of the statement to have assumed responsibility. . ."[85]

---

[84] [1990] 1 A.C. 831.
[85] *ibid*., at 862. See also Lord Slynn, in *Phelps v Hillingdon LBC* [2001] 2 A.C. 619 at 654: "The phrase simply means that the law recognises that there is a duty of care. It is not so much that responsibility is assumed as that it is recognised or imposed by the law."

Faced with the familiar "floodgates" argument, their Lordships chose to confine the *ratio* of their decision to situations where a private purchaser was buying a *modest house*. Commercial purchasers, or purchasers of more expensive houses, could be expected to instruct their own independent surveyors. In this way, the decision would not expose surveyors to liability for very large losses, and would have only a small effect on their insurance premiums and the cost of surveys.

The decision in *Smith v Eric Bush* was subsequently applied in *Merrett v Babb*.[86] Here, the claimant applied to a building society for a mortgage, and the building society commissioned a survey from a firm of which the defendant was an employee. By the time the claimant discovered that the survey had been conducted negligently, causing her economic loss, the firm had gone into liquidation. However, by a majority, the Court of Appeal held that the negligent surveyor, by signing the mortgage valuation report for the building society, had assumed a *personal* responsibility to the claimant for its accuracy. A majority of the court was prepared to hold that the claimant had reasonably relied on the surveyor's professional skill, even though the claimant was unaware of who had conducted the survey, because the copy of the survey she had been shown had omitted all references to the firm and the surveyor who had provided it. This decision seemed to produce a rather harsh result for the surveyor, and should be contrasted with the decision of the House of Lords in *Williams and Reid v Natural Life Health Foods Ltd. and Mistlin*, discussed below.

Policy considerations: the limits of the "assumption of responsibility" doctrine

In *Williams and Reid v Natural Life Health Foods Ltd. and Mistlin*,[87] the plaintiffs had **3–039** obtained a franchise from a company (the first defendant) to run a health food shop. They had relied on representations made in the company's literature about the likelihood of their shop being successful. In the event, the turnover of the shop proved to be substantially less that the company had predicted—in fact it traded at a loss for 18 months. The plaintiffs sought to recover their financial losses from the company, but the company went into liquidation, so they pursued their action against its managing director, Mr Mistlin. The plaintiffs argued that he had assumed personal responsibility towards them, because the company literature had made it plain that the predictions about profit were based on Mr Mistlin's personal expertise and experience in the health food trade. The House of Lords held, however, that nothing that had been said or done by Mr Mistlin showed that he had assumed responsibility towards the plaintiffs in a personal capacity. The representations on which they had relied had been made by the *company*. It was particularly important, in the context of small businesses, that the court should not be too ready to "lift the corporate veil" and undermine the protection of limited liability conferred by establishing a company.

In *Caparo v Dickman*,[88] Lord Bridge examined the authorities and drew an important distinction between, on the one hand, cases like *Smith v Eric Bush* and *Hedley Byrne*, and, on the other hand, a case like *Caparo*. In *Caparo* the plaintiffs took over a company called Fidelity, relying on figures contained in an audit which had been prepared by the defendants, a firm of accountants. The plaintiffs alleged that the audit

---

[86] [2001] Q.B. 1174.
[87] [1998] 1 W.L.R. 830.
[88] [1990] 2 A.C. 605.

had been prepared negligently, causing them financial loss. The House of Lords held that the accountants owed them no duty of care. Lord Bridge made it clear that in deciding whether a sufficient relationship of proximity existed between the plaintiffs and the defendants, it was important to consider the *size of the class* to which the plaintiffs belonged. Here, although the plaintiffs were existing shareholders, for the purposes of the decision, they should be regarded as being in the same position as any other person who might wish to buy shares in Fidelity. In other words, they belonged to a class of persons the size of which could not be ascertained and which was potentially very large. It followed that making the accountants liable would set a precedent that would expose accountants to enormous liability.[89] (It was also important that, whilst the audit had been prepared for *one purpose*, it had been relied on by the plaintiffs for *another purpose*. This point is discussed later.)

Reading between the lines, we can see that their Lordships' decision in *Caparo* was underpinned by considerations of policy. If the case had been decided the other way, accountants' insurance premiums would have increased dramatically, leading to a rise in the cost of accounting. This in turn would have placed a great burden on businesses and might have had a depressing effect on the national economy.[90]

Dealing with *Hedley Byrne* and *Smith v Eric Bush*, Lord Bridge noted that, in those and similar cases:

" . . . the defendant giving advice or information was fully aware of the nature of the transaction which the plaintiff had in contemplation, knew that the advice or information would be communicated to him directly or indirectly and knew that it was very likely that the plaintiff would rely on that advice or information in deciding whether or not to engage in the transaction in contemplation."[91]

His Lordship said that this was entirely different from the situation in a case like *Caparo*, where:

" . . . a statement is put into more or less general circulation and may foreseeably be relied on by strangers to the maker of the statement for any one of a variety of different purposes which the maker of the statement has no specific reason to anticipate."[92]

To impose liability in the latter situation would subject the maker of the statement to indeterminate liability and would, as Lord Bridge put it, "confer on the world at large a quite unwarranted entitlement to appropriate for their own purposes the benefit of the expert knowledge or professional expertise attributed to the maker of the

---

[89] Compare *Law Society v KPMG Peat Marwick* [2000] 1 W.L.R. 1921, where the Court of Appeal upheld a preliminary ruling that accountants, in auditing solicitors' firms, owed a duty of care to the Law Society in respect of compensation payments made by the Society because the accountants had failed to detect fraud. Here, the scope of potential liability was limited and could arise only during the year for which the audit had been prepared.

[90] Hoffmann J., in *Morgan Crucible Co. v Hill Samuel & Co.* [1991] 2 W.L.R. 655 at 662, said that ". . . if the decision in *Caparo*'s case had gone the other way, firms of accountants below a certain size may have been deterred by insurance costs from competing for the audit work of public limited companies potentially liable to take-over bids. This would have driven such companies into the hands of the largest firms".

[91] *Caparo v Dickman* [1990] 2 A.C. 605 at 620.

[92] *ibid.*, at 621.

statement".[93] Therefore, in order to limit the scope of the duty of care for negligent misstatement, it was necessary for the plaintiff to show a very high degree of "proximity" with the maker of the statement. In his Lordship's view, this could only be achieved where:

> ". . . the defendant knew that his statement would be communicated to the plaintiff, either as an individual or as a member of an identifiable class, specifically in connection with a particular transaction or transactions of a particular kind . . . and that the plaintiff would be very likely to rely on it for the purpose of deciding whether or not to enter upon that transaction or upon a transaction of that kind."[94]

This formulation of the test for proximity (or "special relationship") may be taken to encapsulate the modern approach to applying the *"Hedley Byrne* principle".

The judgment of Hoffmann J., in *Morgan Crucible plc v Hill Samuel & Co.*,[95] provides a helpful insight into the policy reasons which influence the courts in negligent misstatement cases. *Morgan Crucible* was a case in which the accountants, directors and financial advisers of a target company were being sued by disappointed take-over bidders. Hoffmann J. undertook a comparison of the decisions in *Caparo* and *Smith v Eric Bush*. His Lordship started by noting the similarity between the cases. In both cases the statements in question had been prepared to fulfil a statutory purpose (under the Companies Act 1985 and the Building Societies Act 1986 respectively), and in both cases the person making the statement had had no wider purpose in mind. In both cases reliance on the statement by the defendant was regarded as highly foreseeable.

In answering the question why the House of Lords had felt able to find liability in *Smith v Eric Bush*, but not in *Caparo*, Hoffmann J. went on to identify a number of differences between the cases. First, in *Smith* the plaintiff had paid for the survey, but the plaintiffs in *Caparo* had not paid for the audit. Secondly, the plaintiff in *Smith* was a person of modest means making the most expensive purchase of her life, whilst the take-over bidders in *Caparo* were entrepreneurs taking high risks for high rewards. Thirdly, it was to be noted that the imposition of liability on surveyors would not be likely to result in a great increase in their insurance costs and in the cost of surveys. The same could not be said about the insurance costs of accountants if *Caparo* had been decided the other way. In Hoffmann J.'s view, then, the different results in the two cases could be justified in terms of the "different economic relationships between the parties and the nature of the markets in which they were operating".[96] His Lordship did point out, however, that "the courts do not have the information on which to form anything more than a broad view of the economic consequences of their decisions", and that consequently, "they are more concerned with what appears to be fair and reasonable than with wider utilitarian calculations".

[93] *Caparo v Dickman* [1990] 2 A.C. 605 at 621.
[94] *ibid.,* at 621. Lord Bridge gives the example of "a prospectus inviting investment" as likely to give rise to a duty of care, as to which, see *Possfund Custodian Trustee Ltd v Diamond* [1996] 1 W.L.R. 1351, where the court refused to strike out a claim against those responsible for preparing a prospectus for general public circulation after the floatation of a company—it was arguable that the claimants' reliance might be reasonable if it could be shown that the authors of the prospectus intended the public to rely on it.
[95] [1991] 2 W.L.R. 655.
[96] *ibid.,* at 662.

A summary of the current law

3–040   In *James McNaughton Paper Group v Hicks, Anderson & Co.*,[97] Neill L.J., in the Court of Appeal, considered *Caparo* and provided a useful analysis of the modern law.[98] The case was brought against a firm of accountants that had been instructed to prepare the accounts of a company, knowing that they were going to be relied on by a take-over bidder. The accounts proved inaccurate and the take-over bidder suffered economic loss. In denying the existence of a duty of care, Neill L.J. stated that the law was nowadays reluctant to extend the scope of the duty of care to protect claimants other than persons whom the maker of the statement *directly intended should rely on the statement*. His Lordship then said that, in deciding whether a duty of care existed, it was necessary to take into account all the circumstances of the particular case. Nevertheless, it was possible to identify certain matters that, in most cases, were likely to be of importance in deciding whether to impose a duty of care. His Lordship went on to enumerate six such matters:[99]

(i) The purpose for which the statement was made

3–041   Where the primary purpose in making a statement is to *advise the "advisee"*, it may be easy to conclude that he or she is owed a duty of care. However, in cases where a statement is made primarily for a *different* purpose, it becomes necessary to look carefully at the purpose for which the statement was *communicated* to the advisee and the purpose for which it was *used*.

(ii) The purpose for which the statement was communicated

3–042   Under this heading, Neill L.J. observed:

> ". . . it will be necessary to consider the purpose of, and the circumstances surrounding, the communication. Was the communication made for information only? Was it made for some action to be taken and, if so, what action and by whom? Who requested the communication to be made? These are some of the questions which may have to be addressed."

(iii) The relationship between the adviser, the advisee and any relevant third party

3–043   Where the statement is made primarily for the benefit of someone other than the advisee, the courts will consider the relationship between the parties in the case. In some cases, the advisee will receive information from an adviser via a third party (as in *Smith v Eric Bush*—where the valuer's advice was passed on by the building society). In such cases, the court must ask whether it is reasonable for the claimant to look *through the third party* to the adviser for advice.

(iv) The size of any class to which the advisee belongs

3–044   Under this heading, his Lordship said:

[97] [1991] 2 W.L.R. 641.
[98] *ibid.*, at 651.
[99] His Lordship's headings are repeated in the text, whilst the gist of his Lordship's observations is presented in summary form. Compare Lord Oliver's distillation of the *Hedley Byrne* principle in *Caparo v Dickman* [1990] 2 A.C. 605 at 638.

"Where there is a single advisee or he is a member of only a small class it may sometimes be simple to infer that a duty of care was owed to him. Membership of a large class, however, may make such an inference more difficult, particularly where the statement was made in the first instance for someone outside the class."

We have seen that in *Caparo v Dickman* the size of the class to which the plaintiffs belonged was a crucial factor in denying liability.

(v) The state of knowledge of the adviser

According to Neill L.J., this is one of the most important matters to consider. When   **3–045**
the statement is made, does the adviser know, or ought he or she to know:

- the purpose for which the statement is being made?
- the purpose for which it may be communicated to the advisee?
- that the advisee will probably rely on the statement without obtaining independent advice?

Under this heading, his Lordship made it clear that a duty of care can be owed only in respect of transactions or types of transaction of which the adviser has knowledge.

(vi) Reliance by the advisee

Under this heading, the courts will consider whether the advisee did in fact rely on the   **3–046**
statement, as opposed to acting on his or her own judgement (even though this accorded with the advice given). They will also consider whether, and in what way, it was *reasonable* for the advisee to rely on the statement. This matters are considered below.

(2) "Reasonable reliance"

There are two issues to consider here: **3–047**

- was reliance reasonable in the circumstances?
- did reliance actually take place?

Reliance must be reasonable

The decision of the Court of Appeal, in *Howard Marine and Dredging Co. Ltd v Ogden*   **3–048**
& Sons Ltd,[1] is a good example of how the question of whether a claimant's reliance on advice is "reasonable" in the circumstances can be a complex one, giving rise to judicial disagreement.

Ogden & Sons ("Ogdens") were about to put in a tender for dredging works, which involved carrying a large quantity of clay out to sea and dumping it. In order to carry the clay, they needed to hire a number of barges. In the course of negotiations with Howard Marine, they were on a number of occasions wrongly informed that the carrying capacity of the barges they intended to hire was greater than it actually was.

---

[1] [1978] 2 All E.R. 1134. Compare *Fashion Brokers Ltd v Clarke Hayes* [2000] P.N.L.R. 473.

Howard Marine's representative had based his answers to their questions on his recollection of a figure entered in Lloyd's Register. In fact, Lloyd's had made a mistake—the correct carrying capacity was stated in the ships' documents, written in German, which the representative had access to, but either did not consult or chose to disregard. Ogdens put in their tender in reliance on the defendants' advice, only to find that they had underestimated the expense involved in disposing of the clay. They sued for their financial loss.

A majority of the Court of Appeal held that Howard Marine were liable. Lord Denning M.R. dissented, however, holding that in the circumstances the only duty which Howard Marine had owed in responding to Ogdens' inquiries was a duty to act honestly. Their representative had discharged this duty when he had quoted the carrying capacity of the barges from memory, twice on the telephone and once at a meeting. His Lordship pointed out that in *Hedley Byrne*, Lord Pearce had thought that for a duty of care to arise, the statement in question had to be made in the context of a business or professional transaction "whose nature makes clear the gravity of the inquiry and the importance and influence attached to the answer".[2] Similarly, in *Mutual Life v Evatt*, Lords Reid and Morris, whose dissenting opinions were to be preferred, had discussed liability in terms of situations where a plaintiff "makes it plain . . . that he is seeking considered advice and intends to act on it in a particular way".[3] In Lord Denning M.R.'s view, Ogdens had not done enough to emphasise that they intended to rely on the figures quoted by the representative. They could easily have made plain the "gravity of their enquiry", for example by asking him to put the figures in writing. It was therefore unreasonable for them to rely on the figures without making their own inquiries.

Bridge L.J., having reviewed the evidence given at the trial, concluded that Howard Marine's representative had, in fact, read the figures contained in the ships' documents and had not shown reasonable grounds for disregarding them and basing his advice on the Lloyd's Register figures instead. Accordingly, Howard Marine were liable under the Misrepresentation Act 1967, having made a false pre-contractual statement without reasonable grounds to believe it was true. Bridge L.J. found it unnecessary to decide the question of negligence liability, but doubted whether a duty of care arose in the circumstances. Shaw L.J. on the other hand, whilst agreeing with Bridge L.J. about liability for misrepresentation, thought that Howard Marine were also liable in negligence. On Shaw L.J.'s view, the carrying capacity of the barges was such an important and fundamental fact that the gravity of Ogdens' inquiries must have been *obvious*. Moreover, Howard Marine were in a better position than Ogdens to find out the carrying capacity of the barges. It followed that it was reasonable for Ogdens to rely on their advice without making inquiries of their own.

3–049   **The purpose for which the statement is made.** Although the issue of "reasonable reliance" arises in all negligent misstatement cases, the courts have particularly focused on the issue in cases where the statement in question has been made for one purpose, but is relied on by the claimant for another purpose. Thus, in *Caparo v Dickman*, it was important that, whilst the accounts had been prepared for the purpose of fulfilling

---

[2] *Hedley Byrne v Heller & Partners* [1964] A.C. 465 at 539.
[3] *Mutual Life v Evatt* [1971] A.C. 793 at 812.

certain statutory duties placed on auditors for the benefit of shareholders (including the plaintiffs), the plaintiffs had relied on the accounts as a general guide to the performance of investments—a purpose for which they had not been designed. It followed that in the circumstances the plaintiffs' reliance on the accounts was unreasonable.

Similar reasoning was applied in *Reeman v Department of Transport*.[4] Here, the plaintiff was the owner of a fishing boat that required an annual certificate of seaworthiness from the Department of Transport. The boat had been covered by a certificate when Mr Reeman had bought it, but he later discovered that the surveyor who had inspected the boat had been negligent. In fact, the boat was unseaworthy. The certificate should never have been issued and could not be renewed. This meant the boat was practically worthless. When Mr Reeman sued for his financial loss, the Court of Appeal, following *Caparo*, held that it had not been reasonable for him to rely on the certificate as a means of establishing the boat's commercial value. The certificate had not been provided for this purpose. It had been issued to promote safety at sea.

Reliance must, in fact, take place

Generally, a successful claimant must show that he or she has, in fact, relied on the defendant's advice or services (rather than acting in reliance on his or her own views or the views of another)—otherwise the advice or services cannot be said to be the cause of the claimant's loss.[5] The decision in *Abbott v Strong*[6] illustrates the idea that a claimant cannot be said to have placed reliance on a defendant unless the claimant knows (or acts reasonably in assuming) that the statement in question has been made *by the defendant*.[7] Here, the plaintiffs had been encouraged to invest in a company by a circular that had been sent to them by the company's directors. The circular contained inaccurate profit forecasts, and the company subsequently went into receivership. When the plaintiffs sued the accountants who had prepared the profit forecasts, it was held that the plaintiffs had not relied on the accountants, because, at the time they had acted on the information in the circular, they had thought that it had come solely from the directors of the company.

The "will drafting" cases: an apparent exception. It should be noted that in the "will drafting" cases (discussed earlier in this chapter), which represent an extension of the "*Hedley Byrne* principle" to cover negligent services, the fact of reliance does not seem to be a prerequisite of liability. Thus, a negligent solicitor may be liable to a disappointed beneficiary, even in cases where the beneficiary is not aware, at the time the negligence occurs, that but for the negligence he or she would be entitled to a legacy. In these circumstances it cannot be said that the disappointed beneficiary is "relying" on the skill of the solicitor, except in the very general sense that all members of society, some of whom may unknowingly be intended beneficiaries, rely on solicitors to get things right. The anomaly produced by the "will drafting" cases, however, may

3–050

3–051

[4] [1997] 2 Lloyds's Rep. 648.
[5] *Bristol & West Building Society v Mothew* [1996] 4 All E.R. 698.
[6] [1998] B.C.L.C. 420.
[7] Note, however, that the claimant need not necessarily know the precise identity of the defendant. It may suffice if, as in *Merrett v Babb* (discussed above), the claimant reasonably assumes that the statement must have been prepared by a defendant of a particular type.

be explained on the basis that these cases fall into a special category where, for policy reasons, reliance is not regarded as important.

Economic loss: conclusion

3–052   We have seen that, over the years, the courts have vacillated on the question of economic loss. This has resulted in a body of law that lacks coherence. The main problem is that it is difficult to find any logical principle on which to justify the distinction between the "statement" cases and the "activity" cases. Consider *Murphy v Brentwood*. We can see that only a small adjustment of the facts might have brought the case closer to the authorities stemming from *Hedley Byrne*, perhaps with very different results. Suppose that Mr Murphy, before buying his house, had contacted the council about its structural integrity and had been sent a letter confirming its soundness. In this situation, he might have framed his case in negligent misstatement, but it is hard to see how the gist of his complaint would have been any different.

Although the modern trend, in cases like *Murphy*, has been to restrict the scope of liability for careless activities, at the same time, the reasoning in cases like *Spring v Guardian Assurance*, *Smith v Eric Bush* and *Henderson v Merrett* has marked a clear extension of the *Hedley Byrne* principle into the realm of services. This threatens to undermine the traditional distinction between statements and acts. In spite of the delicate reasoning the courts have employed, at bottom, there is very little in principle to differentiate, say, the services of a bank (owing a duty of care in *Hedley Byrne*) from the services of a glass manufacturer (owing no duty of care in *Simaan*). Moreover, it remains to be seen whether a liberal interpretation of the Contracts (Rights of Third Parties) Act 1999 will further erode the distinction between statements and acts, by undermining the policy considerations that prompted decisions like *Simaan*.

Finally, it is noteworthy that in Commonwealth jurisdictions, particularly in Australia, New Zealand and Canada, the United Kingdom's restrictive approach to economic loss has not been whole-heartedly embraced. Commonwealth courts have, for example, been more willing to allow recovery where the claimant has only a contractual interest in damaged property, and have taken a more liberal approach to the liability of builders and local authorities for defective premises.[8] Whilst (as we saw in Ch. 2) the United Kingdom courts have rejected Lord Wilberforce's broad "two-stage test" for finding the duty of care, Commonwealth courts, in economic loss cases, have often chosen to apply it, in conjunction with a close examination of the economic and political relationships between the parties.[9] Academic commentators have pointed out that this approach makes much more sense, and that the incoherence of UK law derives from the courts' continued analysis of economic loss questions "not on the basis of common policy concerns but in pockets according to how the loss [has] been caused".[10]

---

[8] See *Kamloops (City) v Nielsen* (1984) 10 D.L.R. (4th) 641 (Supreme Court of Canada); *Bryan v Maloney* (1994–5) 182 C.L.R. 609 (High Court of Australia); *Invercargill v Hamlin* [1996] A.C. 624 (Privy Council).
[9] In Canada, for example, the *Anns* test is still applied, although it has recently been "revisited". See *Cooper v Hobart* (2002) 206 D.L.R. (4th) 193 and *Edwards v Law Society of Upper Canada* (2002) 206 D.L.R. (4th) 211, but contrast the more flexible approach adopted by the High Court of Australia in *Perre v Apand Pty Ltd* (1999) 198 C.L.R. 180.
[10] See J. Stapleton (1991) 107 L.Q.R. 249, and more recently [2002] UCLA L Rev. 531.

Chapter 4

NEGLIGENCE: PSYCHIATRIC ILLNESS

Introduction

This chapter deals with the circumstances in which a duty of care will be imposed to **4–001** avoid causing psychiatric illness. In *White v Chief Constable of South Yorkshire*,[1] a recent House of Lords case that we shall examine in due course, Lord Steyn noted that the law in this area is "a patchwork quilt of distinctions which are difficult to justify".[2] That case, like *Alcock v Chief Constable of South Yorkshire*,[3] another important House of Lords authority, arose from events which happened at the Hillsborough football stadium in April 1989, when police negligence caused the overcrowding of spectator stands, crushing 95 people to death and injuring hundreds more.

The claims in these cases were brought by people who, though not physically injured, suffered psychiatric illness as a result of the tragedy. In *Alcock*, claims were brought by relatives who had witnessed or heard about the death or injury of their loved ones. In *White*, claims were brought by police officers who had assisted in the aftermath of the disaster. In deciding that no duty of care was owed to any of these plaintiffs, the House of Lords developed and applied a set of rules that are hard to justify in terms of logic and morality. The area has been the subject of a recent report by the Law Commission, whose recommendations are considered at the end of this chapter.

Definition of "psychiatric illness"

It important to understand that the courts draw a distinction between claims in respect **4–002** of *medically recognised psychiatric illness*[4] and claims for mere grief, sorrow and distress. The latter, being unfortunate but commonplace symptoms of the human condition, are generally afforded no remedy at law.[5] In psychiatric illness cases,

---

[1] [1999] 2 A.C. 455.
[2] *Alcock v Chief Constable of South Yorkshire* [1992] 1 A.C. 310 at 418 and 419.
[3] [1992] 1 A.C. 310.
[4] For comprehensive discussion of the types of psychiatric illness that can found an action, see Law Com. 249 Part III (paras 3.1–3.33).
[5] Lord Denning M.R., in *Hinz v Berry* [1970] Q.B. 40 made it clear that "in English law no damages are awarded for grief or sorrow caused by a person's death". Subsequent to that decision, however, a modest sum has become payable for bereavement, in limited circumstances, under the Fatal Accidents Act 1976. (See Ch. 15).

successful claimants must establish that they are suffering from medical conditions such as "post-traumatic stress disorder (PTSD)",[6] "organic depression and a change of personality",[7] or "pathological grief disorder".[8] The law recognises that these conditions can be just as serious and debilitating as physical injuries. As we shall see, however, for policy reasons it limits the circumstances in which they can give rise to claims for compensation.

Until very recently, claims for psychiatric illness were described as claims for "nervous shock". This rather quaint terminology served to emphasise the idea that the law would only entertain such claims in cases where psychiatric illness resulted from the "sudden shock" of witnessing or participating in a *specific single event*. Although, in the modern law, the position remains uncertain,[9] it is generally thought that an element of "sudden shock" remains an essential ingredient of the cause of action. Thus, a person whose psychiatric illness is brought on by the cumulative effect of prolonged exposure to distressing circumstances (by caring for a brain-damaged accident victim, for example) will normally have no cause of action.[10]

Once the claimant has established that he or she is suffering from a psychiatric condition which the law will recognise as actionable, there are a number of additional hurdles that must be overcome in order to succeed. As in cases of economic loss, the law uses the concept of the duty of care as the mechanism to control the scope of liability. The nature of the hurdles which a particular claimant will have to overcome depends on the *type of situation* that has given rise to the psychiatric illness. The law divides claimants into a number of categories, with very different rules applying to each category.

Types of Claimant

4–003   Broadly speaking, and in the light of the decision in *White v Chief Constable of South Yorkshire*, it can be said that there are nowadays three categories of claimant in psychiatric illness cases[11]:

- claimants who suffer psychiatric illness as a result of having been physically injured by the defendant's negligence;

---

[6] As in *White v Chief Constable of South Yorkshire* [1999] 2 A.C. 455.

[7] As in *McLoughlin v O' Brian* [1983] 1 A.C. 410 (*per* Lord Wilberforce at 417).

[8] As in *Vernon v Boseley (No.1)* [1997] 1 All E.R. 577.

[9] See the observations of Lord Slynn in *W. v Essex CC* [2000] 2 All E.R. 237 at 240. See also *Vernon v Boseley (No. 1)* [1997] 1 All E.R. 577 (where the claimant's condition results from a combination of grief and "sudden shock", the court will not attempt to draw a fine distinction between the two).

[10] See *Alcock v Chief Constable of South Yorkshire* [1992] 1 A.C. 310 at 396, 401 and 416. Note, however, that the position may be different where the defendant has a contractual relationship which requires him or her to exercise reasonable care in respect of the claimant's health. Thus, in *Walker v Northumberland CC* [1995] I.C.R. 702, discussed in Ch. 7, an employer was liable for imposing an excessive work load which caused psychiatric illness.

[11] In addition to the three categories listed here, there are other situations where psychiatric illness may be recoverable in negligence. These include situations where psychiatric illness is induced by stress at work (discussed in Ch. 7) and a group of situations which the Law Commission classified as "miscellaneous" (see Law Com. 249, para.2.51). These include: where a patient suffers psychiatric illness at the hands of a negligent psychiatrist; and where a prisoner suffers psychiatric illness as a result of ill-treatment in prison. Such cases, however, fall outside the traditional focus of psychiatric illness liability and are beyond the scope of this chapter.

- claimants who are put in physical danger, but who in fact suffer only psychiatric illness (these claimants are known as "primary victims"[12]);

- claimants who, though not in any physical danger themselves, suffer psychiatric illness as a result of *witnessing the death, injury or imperilment of another person* (known as the "immediate victim") with whom they have a close relationship of love and affection (these claimants are known as "secondary victims").

Arguably, there remains an additional category, namely claimants who suffer psychiatric illness as a result of witnessing the destruction of their property. Such a claim succeeded in *Attia v British Gas plc*,[13] which is discussed later in this chapter. It should be remembered, however, that this decision was taken in the 1980s, at a time when the courts were in the last throes of expanding the duty of care in negligence, and before the modern rules relating to psychiatric illness had been clearly defined. It is therefore uncertain whether it would nowadays be followed.

HISTORICAL DEVELOPMENT

The old law

Unsurprisingly, perhaps, the law was slow to recognise claims for psychiatric illness. **4–004** The approach of the courts in the nineteenth century is exemplified by the decision of the Privy Council in *Victorian Railway Commissioners v Coultas*.[14] Here, the defendants' gate-keeper had carelessly allowed a carriage to enter a railway crossing when a train was about to pass. Although no physical injury occurred, the plaintiff, who was pregnant and a passenger in the carriage, suffered severe shock—thinking she would be killed by the oncoming train—and subsequently miscarried her child. The Privy Council denied that there could be liability for psychiatric illness in the absence of physical injury. As Lord Hoffmann pointed out in *White*,[15] the main reason their Lordships gave for this restricted approach was the evidential difficulty of deciding on the causes of psychiatric illness at a time when so little was known about the workings of the mind. The Privy Council thought that opening the doors to psychiatric illness liability might have led to a large number of "imaginary claims".

The "impact theory"

In 1901, however, the courts adopted a more liberal approach in deciding *Dulieu v* **4–005** *White & Sons*.[16] Here, the plaintiff, a pregnant barmaid, was behind the bar in a pub when a negligently driven carriage came off the road and crashed into the pub,

---

[12] We use the term "primary victims" here in its "narrow" post-*White* sense. Contrast this with the sense in which it was used by Lord Oliver in *Alcock v Chief Constable of South Yorkshire* [1992] 1 A.C. 310 at 407.
[13] [1988] Q.B. 304.
[14] (1888) 13 App. Cas. 222.
[15] *White v Chief Constable of South Yorkshire* [1999] 2 A.C. 455 at 501.
[16] [1901] 2 K.B. 669.

entering the room where she was standing. She suffered shock and a subsequent miscarriage. Kennedy J. upheld her claim. Dealing with *Victorian Railway Commissioners v Coultas*, Kennedy J. thought that the problem of exaggerated or fraudulent claims was not a good enough reason for simply denying the existence of a duty of care in respect of psychiatric harm, observing: "Such a course involves the denial of redress in meritorious cases, and it necessarily implies a certain degree of distrust, which I do not share, in the capacity of legal tribunals to get at the truth in this class of claim".[17]

In allowing liability for psychiatric illness in negligence, Kennedy J. was influenced by the case of *Wilkinson v Downton*,[18] which had been decided four years earlier. Here, the defendant, in the exercise of what he regarded as a practical joke, had arrived at the plaintiff's front door and announced that her husband had been involved in a serious accident and had broken both his legs. When the plaintiff suffered shock, accompanied by vomiting and other physical symptoms, the defendant was held liable for the effect of his statement, on the basis that he had perpetrated an *intentional act of wrongdoing*. (Liability under the "rule in *Wilkinson v Downton*", as it is known, is discussed more fully in Ch. 11. It should not be confused with liability in *negligence*.)

In *Dulieu v White & Sons*, then, and in a number of similar cases, the courts sought to control the scope of liability by using what became known as the "impact theory", according to which a plaintiff would be allowed to recover for psychiatric illness provided that this was caused by reasonable fear of being physically injured by the defendant's negligence.

The law expands: *Hambrook v Stokes*

4–006 In later cases, the courts abandoned the "impact theory", extending the law to cover plaintiffs who had not been in danger, but had suffered psychiatric illness as a result of witnessing a loved one being injured or placed in peril by a defendant's negligence. (We now call such plaintiffs "secondary victims".)

Such was the case in *Hambrook v Stokes*.[19] Here, a pregnant mother had accompanied her three children part of the way on their journey to school and then, as usual, had left them to walk a short way by themselves along the bend of a road. The children had passed out of sight when, owing to the defendants' negligence, an out-of-control lorry came down a hill at speed and went round the bend. The mother was afraid that her children would be killed by the lorry (in fact, however, two of them were unharmed, whilst the third was taken to hospital with injuries). She suffered shock which led to a miscarriage with medical complications, causing her death. A majority of the Court of Appeal held the defendants liable. But in extending the law to cover this situation, Bankes L.J. was careful to point out that the *ratio* of the decision was to be confined to situations where the plaintiff suffered psychiatric illness because of fear for the safety of her children. The decision was not intended to overturn previous authority to the effect that a plaintiff could not recover in respect of psychiatric illness caused by witnessing physical injury to a person with whom the plaintiff had no relationship of love and affection.[20]

[17] [1901] 2 K.B. 681.
[18] [1897] 2 Q.B. 57.
[19] [1925] 1 K.B. 141.
[20] *e.g. Smith v Johnson & Co.* (unreported, but considered in *Wilkinson v Downton* [1897] 2 Q.B. 57 and *Dulieu v White* [1901] 2 K.B. 669).

No further expansion: *Bourhill v Young*

Nearly 20 years later, in *Bourhill v Young*,[21] the question of psychiatric illness liability **4–007** came before the House of Lords for the first time. The facts of this case were noted in Ch. 2. It will be recalled that it concerned a pregnant woman who, while descending from a tram, heard a road accident occur some distance away. She later attended the scene of the accident, saw blood on the road, and subsequently suffered a miscarriage produced by shock. As was noted in Ch. 2, the House of Lords held, in effect, that the woman was not a "foreseeable claimant". In other words, she could not base her action on a wrong done to someone else.

In arriving at this conclusion, their Lordships considered a number of points. First, there was the question of whether the woman might be regarded as being peculiarly susceptible to psychiatric illness because of her pregnant condition (Lord Wright appeared to think this was likely). If so, then she could only recover if it could be said that, in the circumstances, psychiatric illness was reasonably foreseeable *in a person of ordinary fortitude*. On the facts, their Lordships did not think this was the case—ordinary people could be expected to withstand the rigours of witnessing injury to a stranger on the roads without suffering psychiatric illness. Secondly, there was the question of whether it mattered that the plaintiff had not feared for her own physical safety. A majority of their Lordships appeared to answer this question by resurrecting the "impact theory" and holding that she could not recover because she was outside the area of foreseeable physical impact. Their Lordships held that *Hambrook v Stokes* was to be regarded as a special case and was of limited application.

Initially, then, the courts took a narrow view of the decision in *Hambrook v Stokes*. In *King v Phillips*,[22] for example, the Court of Appeal denied recovery to a mother who suffered psychiatric illness when, from an upstairs window some 70 yards away, she saw her son's tricycle disappear under a reversing taxi and heard the boy scream. The decision in *Hambrook v Stokes* was distinguished on the basis that the mother in *King v Phillips* was too far away from the scene of the accident—like the plaintiff in *Bourhill v Young*, she was not, in effect, a "foreseeable claimant".

In the 1960s, however, the courts began to take a more liberal approach, holding in *Boardman v Sanderson*[23] that a plaintiff who suffered psychiatric illness when his son was involved in an accident could recover even though he had not seen the accident but had only *heard* it from some distance away, and had come to the scene of the accident shortly after its occurrence. This approach was developed a stage further by the House of Lords in 1982, when it decided the landmark case of *McLoughlin v O'Brian*.

The emergence of the modern law: *McLoughlin v O'Brian*

In *McLoughlin v O'Brian*,[24] the plaintiff's husband and three of her children were **4–008** involved in a serious road accident, caused by the defendants' negligence. The plaintiff did not witness the accident, being, at the time, at home about two miles away. About

---

[21] [1943] A.C. 92.
[22] [1953] 1 Q.B. 429.
[23] [1964] 1 W.L.R. 1317.
[24] [1983] A.C. 410.

an hour after the accident, it was reported to her by a family friend that her 17–year-old son, George (who had been driving the car), was dying. The friend then drove her to a local hospital where she was told that her three year-old daughter had died. She could hear George shouting and screaming in an adjoining room. She saw her husband and seven year-old daughter, who were in a distressed state, covered with oil and mud. She was then taken to see George, who appeared to recognise her before lapsing into unconsciousness. These events caused her to suffer psychiatric illness.

In holding the defendants liable, the House of Lords extended the law to cover a situation where the plaintiff had not seen or heard the accident itself, but had come upon its "immediate aftermath". Their Lordships declined to say, in precise terms, what could constitute the "immediate aftermath" of an accident. But it was significant that the plaintiff in *McLoughlin v O'Brian* had seen her family within a fairly short time of the accident, and that, when she saw them, they had not been "cleaned up" and remained in more or less the same condition they had been in immediately after the accident. She had therefore witnessed scenes which went to "make up the accident as an entire event".[25] Lord Wilberforce thought that extending liability in these circumstances was "on the margin of what the process of logical progression [from previous authority] would allow".[26] His Lordship thought that the High Court of Australia's decision in *Chester v Waverly Municipal Council*,[27] where a child's body was found floating in a trench after a prolonged search, might "perhaps be placed on the other side of a recognisable line".[28] As we shall see, the question of what can constitute the "immediate aftermath" was considered again in *Alcock v Chief Constable of South Yorkshire*, but was left unresolved.[29]

The speech of Lord Wilberforce, then, laid the foundation for the modern approach of the courts in psychiatric illness cases. Whilst his Lordship thought that extending previous authority to assist the plaintiff was a "logical progression", he noted that, because psychiatric illness was capable of affecting such a large number of potential plaintiffs, there was "a real need for the law to place some limitation on the extent of admissible claims".[30]

Lord Wilberforce's "control mechanisms"

4–009   In *McLoughlin v O'Brian*, Lord Wilberforce identified three factors that would need to be considered in every case:

- the class of persons whose claims should be recognised;
- the proximity of such persons to the accident;
- the means by which the psychiatric illness was caused.

These three "control mechanisms" suggested by Lord Wilberforce were subsequently reformulated and applied by a unanimous House of Lords in *Alcock*.

[25] [1983] A.C. 422 (as in *Benson v Lee* [1972] V.R. 879, to which Lord Wilberforce referred).
[26] *ibid.*, at 419.
[27] (1939) 62 C.L.R. 1. Compare *Vernon v Boseley (No.1)* [1997] 1 All E.R. 577.
[28] *McLoughlin v O'Brian* [1983] A.C. 410 at 422.
[29] A point confirmed by Lord Slynn in *W. v Essex CC* [2000] 2 All E.R. 237 at 244.
[30] *McLoughlin v O'Brian* [1983] A.C. 410 at 422.

In relation to the class of persons who might claim, Lord Wilberforce recognised that "the possible range is between the closest of family ties, of parent and child, or husband and wife, and the ordinary bystander". He noted that the law, as in *Bourhill v Young*, had always denied recovery to mere "bystanders" who suffered psychiatric illness as a result of witnessing accidents. According to Lord Wilberforce, the law's justification for this approach was either that "such persons must be assumed to be possessed of fortitude sufficient to enable them to endure the calamities of modern life", or that "defendants cannot be expected to compensate the world at large".[31] His Lordship thought that cases brought by plaintiffs who did not have a very close family relationship with the "immediate victim" of the accident would have to be "very carefully scrutinised".

As regards proximity to the accident, this had to be "close in both time and space", but it would be impractical and unjust to insist that plaintiffs must be present at the scene of the accident. As regards the means by which the psychiatric illness was caused, his Lordship noted that there had thus far been no negligence case in which the law had compensated psychiatric illness brought about by mere communication to the plaintiff of distressing news. There was no justification for departing from this position. It followed that the psychiatric illness must arise through direct perception of the accident, or its immediate aftermath, by sight or hearing. Lord Wilberforce left open the question of whether "some equivalent of sight or hearing, *e.g.* through simultaneous television", would suffice. (This point, as we shall see, was subsequently considered by the House of Lords in *Alcock*.)

Although, as has been said, the "control mechanisms" suggested by Lord Wilberforce in *McLoughlin v O'Brian* were subsequently endorsed in *Alcock*, it was initially unclear whether they formed part of the *ratio* of the case. This was because other members of the House of Lords did not view them in the same way. Whilst Lord Wilberforce (with whom Lord Edmund-Davies agreed) appeared to think that the "control mechanisms" should be satisfied in addition to a test of reasonable foreseeability, Lords Bridge and Scarman appeared to think that liability for psychiatric illness should be decided by applying a broad test of foreseeability, and that, although the factors suggested by Lord Wilberforce were to be considered in applying that test, they did not exclusively define the circumstances in which psychiatric illness could be recoverable. (Lord Russell's opinion on the point was not clear.) This is why the plaintiffs in *Alcock* felt able to pursue their claims.

The House of Lords in *Alcock*, however, unanimously adopted Lord Wilberforce's approach. After *Alcock* came the important decision in *Page v Smith*,[32] a case involving a "primary victim" of psychiatric illness. Next came the case of *White v Chief Constable of South Yorkshire*.[33] The reasoning of the House of Lords in these three cases forms the core of the modern law and is considered, in a number of sections, below.

ELEMENTS OF THE MODERN LAW

In this section, we examine certain elements of the modern law. We begin by dealing **4–010** with the position of claimants who suffer psychiatric illness as a result of suffering physical injury, or through witnessing damage to their property. The position of such

[31] *McLoughlin v O'Brien* [1983] A.C. 410 at 422.
[32] [1996] A.C. 155.
[33] [1999] 2 A.C. 455.

claimants can be shortly stated, and should not be the focus of too much of our attention. Next, we examine the more important issue of the role of policy in psychiatric illness cases. Then, we consider the courts' use of "reasonable foreseeability" in establishing the duty of care.

Psychiatric illness resulting from personal injury

4–011   Where a claimant has suffered bodily injury as a result of the defendant's negligence, the courts have no difficulty in allowing recovery in respect of psychiatric illness resulting from the injury. (Such claimants are sometimes referred to as "primary victims", although their position is conceptually distinct from that of the plaintiff in *Page v Smith*—discussed later—who did not suffer physical injury, though he had been placed in physical danger.) The ability of such claimants to recover for psychiatric illness follows from the fact that the law has traditionally allowed them to recover damages for pain and suffering consequent upon their injuries. Such damages were awarded, for example, in *Kralj v McGrath*,[34] where the negligence of a defendant obstetrician resulted in the plaintiff suffering psychiatric trauma and losing her baby shortly after its birth. (Woolf J. was careful to point out, however, that these damages were to be distinguished from damages awarded because of natural grief and sorrow resulting from the death of her child, which the law would not compensate.)

Psychiatric illness resulting from property damage

4–012   In *Attia v British Gas plc*,[35] the Court of Appeal was asked to decide, as a preliminary issue, whether a duty of care could arise where the plaintiff had witnessed the destruction of her home, as opposed to injury to a loved one. Their Lordships held that it could. The defendants, by negligently installing a central heating system, had caused a fire which destroyed the plaintiff's house. The plaintiff suffered psychiatric illness when she returned home one day to witness the blaze. Bingham L.J., holding that a duty of care could exist in such a situation, cited other possible examples, such as where "a scholar's life's work of research or composition were destroyed before his eyes as a result of a defendant's careless conduct".[36] The decision in *Attia*, however, is not considered in any of the three modern leading cases on psychiatric illness.[37] Therefore, as has already been noted, its status remains uncertain.[38]

Policy considerations

4–013   In *White v Chief Constable of South Yorkshire*, Lord Steyn provided a useful summary of the main policy considerations that dictate that claims for psychiatric illness should be treated differently from claims for physical injury.[39] His Lordship identified four

---

[34] [1986] 1 All E.R. 54.
[35] [1988] Q.B. 304.
[36] *ibid.*, at 320.
[37] The decision is not mentioned in *Alcock* or *White*, although in *Page v Smith* [1996] A.C. 155 at 179 it is referred to in passing by Lord Jauncey (dissenting) as an illustration of foreseeable damage.
[38] It has been suggested that the decisions in *Attia v British Gas* and in similar cases might be explained on the basis that a contractual relationship between the defendant and the claimant gave rise to an "assumption of responsibility"' for the claimant's psychiatric well-being: see Deakin, Johnston and Markesinis, *Markesinis and Deakin's Tort Law* (5th ed., 2003), p.107.
[39] *White v Chief Constable of South Yorkshire* [1999] 2 A.C. 455 at 493. For further discussion of relevant policy considerations, see Law Com. 249, paras 6.5–6.8.

such considerations. First, there is the difficulty of drawing the line between acute grief and psychiatric illness.[40] It is difficult to draw this line because the symptoms of both conditions are often the same, but it is necessary to differentiate between them because, as we have noted, the law provides no compensation for the former. Lord Steyn pointed out that establishing psychiatric illness by expert evidence was a costly and time-consuming exercise, so that if claims for psychiatric illness were to be treated as generally on a par with physical injury cases there would be adverse economic implications for the administration of justice.

Secondly, Lord Steyn thought it was important to consider the effect on people who had witnessed gruesome events of increasing the availability of compensation. His Lordship did not have in mind fraudulent or bogus claims, saying that it ought to be possible for the courts to expose such claims. Rather, he thought that the prospect of compensation might sometimes be an *unconscious disincentive to rehabilitation*. His Lordship noted that in cases where there was generally no prospect of compensation for psychiatric illness, such as where injury had been sustained while playing sport, reports of psychiatric illness were uncommon. On the other hand, in industrial accident cases, where there was often a prospect of compensation, psychiatric illness was repeatedly encountered.

The third policy consideration was that relaxing the special rules governing compensation for psychiatric harm would greatly increase the class of persons who could recover damages in tort. (In other words, it would open the "floodgates of litigation".) Fourthly, his Lordship thought that expanding liability for psychiatric harm might result in liability which was disproportionate to the tortious conduct involved— perhaps only a momentary lapse of concentration, for example in a road traffic accident. (In other words, it would result in "crushing liability".)

Bearing these policy considerations in mind, we can now examine the various rules that the courts apply in order to limit the scope of the duty of care. The first of these, as may be expected, is the requirement that some harm (either physical or psychiatric, depending on the type of claim) must be reasonably foreseeable.

Foreseeability of psychiatric illness

As in all negligence actions, reasonable foreseeability of damage is an essential   **4–014**
ingredient of the duty of care in psychiatric illness cases. In this area of the law, however, the question of foreseeability can sometimes be a source of confusion. This is because different rules apply in relation to "primary victims" and "secondary victims".

Foreseeability: primary victims

In relation to "primary victims" (victims who are placed in physical danger), provided   **4–015**
physical harm is reasonably foreseeable, *it is unnecessary to establish that psychiatric illness is reasonably foreseeable*. In *Page v Smith*,[41] the plaintiff was involved in a relatively minor car accident, but was not physically injured. Prior to the accident, he had for about 20 years suffered from a condition variously described as myalgic encephalomyelitis (M.E.), chronic fatigue syndrome, or post-viral fatigue syndrome.

---

[40] See Hedley [1997] C.L.J. 254, to which his Lordship refers.
[41] [1996] A.C. 155.

This had manifested itself from time to time with different degrees of severity. The illness had been in remission at the time of the accident and the plaintiff was expecting to return to work after a period of convalescence, but the crash triggered a recurrence of the disease, which became chronic and permanent, so that it was unlikely he would be able to take up full-time employment again.

In the Court of Appeal, it was held that the defendant driver was not liable, because he could not reasonably have foreseen that his negligence would cause psychiatric illness. A majority of the House of Lords, however, overturned this decision and held that reasonable foreseeability of psychiatric illness need not be established when physical injury was reasonably foreseeable. As Lord Lloyd put it: "Since the defendant was admittedly under a duty of care not to cause the plaintiff foreseeable physical injury, it was unnecessary to ask whether he was under a separate duty of care not to cause foreseeable psychiatric injury".[42] Lord Lloyd reasoned that if a plaintiff could recover for psychiatric illness in a case where he or she had *actually suffered* physical harm, it should follow that where the plaintiff had, by good luck, escaped reasonably foreseeable physical harm, he should not be deprived of compensation by the existence of this purely fortuitous fact.

The reasoning in *Page v Smith* is quite difficult to understand. In essence, however, their Lordships held that, where there is a danger of physical injury, the law should regard physical and psychiatric injury as the same kind of harm. Then, applying the so-called "eggshell skull rule", their Lordships reasoned that, because it was foreseeable that some (minor) harm of a relevant kind would be caused (being "shaken up" by the car crash), the defendant was liable for the full extent of the harm that was actually suffered. The "eggshell skull" rule is considered more fully in Ch. 6. In summary, it provides that where an injured claimant suffers serious medical consequences, the defendant may be liable for *all* of those consequences, even though they could not all have been reasonably foreseen.

Lords Keith and Jauncey dissented in *Page v Smith*, on the basis that the defendant could not reasonably have foreseen that a person of ordinary fortitude would suffer psychiatric illness as a result of a minor car accident. Lord Jauncey appeared to think the "eggshell skull" rule was not relevant where what was in issue was the existence of a duty of care to avoid causing a particular kind of damage—it was only relevant to the *extent* of the damage which occurred, once an established duty of care had been breached.[43] Similar criticism of the approach of the majority in *Page v Smith* was articulated by Lord Goff in his dissenting judgment in *White v Chief Constable of South Yorkshire*. His Lordship observed that the "eggshell skull" rule was "a principle of compensation, not of liability"[44] and concluded that "Lord Lloyd appears to have taken an exceptional rule relating to compensation and treated it as being of general application, thereby creating a wider principle of liability".[45] Lord Griffiths, in *White*, appeared to take the same view, stating: "The law expects reasonable fortitude and

---

[42] [1996] A.C. 187.

[43] *ibid.*, at 176. Lord Ackner, whilst approving Lord Lloyd's analysis, was content to decide the appeal on the basis that psychiatric illness (as opposed to physical injury) was reasonably foreseeable in the circumstances, and suggested (at 170) that consideration of the eggshell skull rule was "nothing to the point". In the light of Lord Ackner's position, then, it is unclear whether the extended application of the rule forms part of the true ratio of *Page v Smith*.

[44] *White v Chief Constable of South Yorkshire* [1999] 2 A.C. 455 at 470.

[45] *ibid.*, at 476.

robustness of its citizens and will not impose liability for the exceptional frailty of certain individuals. This is not to be confused with the 'eggshell skull' situation, where as a result of a breach of duty the damage inflicted proves to be more serious than expected".[46] Despite these criticisms, the majority in *White* were content to accept that *Page v Smith* had been correctly decided.

Foreseeability: secondary victims

In relation to "secondary victims" (those suffering psychiatric illness because of **4–016** *witnessing* an event, though they are not themselves in any danger), the claimant must establish that psychiatric illness was reasonably foreseeable. This involves showing that a person of ordinary fortitude or "customary phlegm"[47] might reasonably have suffered psychiatric illness in the circumstances. In other words, no duty of care is owed to avoid causing psychiatric harm to people who are "peculiarly susceptible" to such harm because they have a nervous or emotional disposition. (This is one of the reasons the plaintiff in *Bourhill v Young* did not succeed.)

It is important to understand, however, that the differing relevance of foreseeability **4–017** in relation to primary and secondary victims does *not* amount to saying that "in the case of secondary victims the 'eggshell skull' rule does not apply". In the case of "secondary victims", reasonable foreseeability of psychiatric illness to a person of ordinary fortitude is part of the test for the existence of the duty of care. But once it is shown that this duty exists, and has been breached, the defendant will be liable for all of the psychiatric illness that results, even though the precise nature and the seriousness of the claimant's particular illness may not have been foreseen. This means that a defendant who could reasonably foresee that his or her negligence might cause a person of ordinary fortitude to suffer from post-traumatic stress disorder, and require, say, two years off work to recuperate, cannot argue that his liability is limited to the cost of that period of recuperation when the claimant, because of his or her special susceptibility to psychiatric illness, will take 10 years to recover. Thus, in *Brice v Brown*,[48] where it was reasonably foreseeable that a mother of "customary phlegm" might suffer some psychiatric illness on witnessing injuries to her daughter, the plaintiff was able to recover for the full extent of her psychiatric illness even though the illness was made more severe by the fact that she had an underlying personality disorder.

Primary and Secondary Victims

We have, of course, already noted the distinction between "primary" and "secondary" **4–018** victims of psychiatric illness. In this section, we consider in more detail how this distinction is drawn, and explore a little further the law relating to recovery by each type of claimant. This provides the background for detailed consideration of the law relating to "secondary victims" (examined in the next section) and for consideration of the law relating to certain claimants who, prior to the decision in *White v Chief Constable of South Yorkshire*, were traditionally regarded as "primary victims".

---

[46] *White v Chief Constable of South Yorkshire* [1999] 2 A.C. 455 at 463.
[47] This colourful phrase was coined by Lord Porter in *Bourhill v Young* [1943] A.C. 92 at 117.
[48] [1984] 1 W.L.R. 997.

"Primary victims"

4–019   The decision in *White* seems to make it clear that in order to qualify as a "primary victim", the claimant must establish that he or she has been placed in physical danger by the defendant's negligence (or at least has been put in reasonable fear for his or her physical safety). The position of "primary victims" is governed by the decision in *Page v Smith*, which has already been discussed. Thus, such a claimant may recover for *psychiatric* harm, even though the threatened *physical* harm does not materialise. This was established in the early case of *Dulieu v White & Sons* (discussed above) and was confirmed in *Page v Smith*.

It appears from the reasoning of the majority in *White*, that although physical imperilment is a precondition of qualifying as a "primary victim", it is not necessary to show that fear of physical harm is the *cause* of the primary victim's psychiatric illness. (Thus, where the primary victim is a "rescuer", although the element of physical danger—or reasonable fear thereof—must be present, the cause of the psychiatric illness may be witnessing the imperilment of those being rescued.)

The decision in *White* is important because, before that decision, it had been unclear whether the category of "primary victims" could be said to encompass a miscellaneous group of claimants, namely employees, rescuers and other "participants" in the circumstances of an accident who, *although placed in no physical danger*, were able to take advantage of liberal rules in recovering for psychiatric illness. *White* seems to make it clear that such claimants are not to be regarded as "primary victims".[49] This aspect of the decision is controversial, and its effects on the position of this group of claimants are discussed later. Here, however, two further points should be noted.

There may be a requirement of "actual danger"

4–020   In most cases, of course, a claimant's reasonable grounds for fearing for his or her safety will derive from the fact that he or she is in actual danger. Nevertheless, it is possible to imagine a case where a claimant *reasonably thinks* that he or she is in danger when, as a matter of fact, no such danger exists. The position of such claimants is unclear because the two leading opinions in *White* do not deal with the point in the same way. Lord Steyn thought that an additional requirement of actual danger was not necessary, saying that it would be sufficient if a claimant had "objectively exposed himself to danger or reasonably believed that he was doing so".[50] According to Lord Hoffmann, however, claimants have to be "within the range of foreseeable physical injury"[51] to qualify as primary victims—it is unclear whether his Lordship meant by this that they must be in actual danger. The point therefore remains unresolved.[52]

---

[49] Although this effect of *White* does not seem to have been wholly accepted by the courts. See, for example, the strange case of *Farrell v Avon Health Authority* [2001] Lloyd's Rep. Med 458 where a claimant not in physical danger succeeded as "primary victim" and *Salter v UB Frozen and Chilled Foods Ltd* [2003] S.L.T. 1011, where it was held that a claimant employee not in danger had an arguable case under *Dooley v Cammell Laird & Co. Ltd* [1951] 1 Lloyd's Rep. 271 (discussed later), notwithstanding the way that case had been dealt with in *White*.

[50] *White v Chief Constable of South Yorkshire* [1999] 2 A.C. 455 at 499.

[51] *ibid.*, at 504, 505 and 509.

[52] Note that the Law Commission suggested that it should be a precondition of recovery by secondary victims that the immediate victim be in actual danger. See Law Com. 249, para.6.18 (discussed below).

In any event, the claimant's fear for his or her own safety must be reasonable

Whether or not there is a requirement of "actual danger", the decision of the Court of Appeal, in *McFarlane v E.E. Caledonia*,[53] makes it clear that claimants who seek to qualify as "primary victims" because they have been put in fear for their physical safety must have some reasonable basis for that fear. Here, the plaintiff alleged psychiatric illness brought on by his involvement in the Piper Alpha oil rig disaster—the rig exploded, causing the death of many workers on board. His claim as a "primary victim" failed, however, because at the time of the disaster he had been working in a support boat about 50 yards away from the rig and it was obvious that the boat had never been in any danger. It followed that his fear for his safety was unreasonable. (The plaintiff could not recover as a "secondary victim", for reasons which are considered below.)   **4–021**

"Secondary victims"

The position of "secondary victims" is governed by the decision in *Alcock v Chief Constable of South Yorkshire*, which must now be examined in detail. The claims in *Alcock* (and in *White*) arose from the tragic events that took place during the 1989 F.A. Cup semi-final between Liverpool and Nottingham Forest. Tickets to the Hillsborough football stadium were sold out, and the match was being shown on live television. After six minutes of play, however, it had to be stopped because, owing to negligent crowd control, too many spectators had been allowed on to the terraces. It became apparent that some were being crushed against the high fences erected between the terraces and the pitch.   **4–022**

South Yorkshire police admitted that the death of 95 spectators, and injuries to a further 400, were caused by their negligence in allowing too many people into the stadium. Claims for physical injury and death were settled by the police, as were certain psychiatric illness claims by police officers who had dragged bodies from the scene of the danger, risking physical injury to themselves. Psychiatric illness claims were then brought by two groups of people who had not been in physical danger: relatives (and a fiancée) who had in various ways witnessed or heard about the death or injury of their loved ones (the plaintiffs in *Alcock*) and police officers who had assisted in the aftermath of the tragedy (the plaintiffs in *White*).

The question for the House of Lords in *Alcock* was whether the plaintiffs were owed a duty of care on the basis that their psychiatric illness was reasonably foreseeable, applying the reasoning of Lords Bridge and Scarman in *McLoughlin v O'Brian*, or whether, *in addition*, their claims should be governed by the "control mechanisms" which had been suggested by Lord Wilberforce in that case. *Alcock* was a test case in which the specific plaintiffs had been chosen because their situations—in terms of closeness of relationship to the dead and injured and proximity to the disaster in time and space—were similar to those of about 150 other people who also wished to claim for psychiatric illness. Their Lordships held that none of the plaintiffs could succeed. Each of the plaintiffs, in one way or another, failed to satisfy the stringent criteria that their Lordships laid down for recovery by "secondary victims".

---

[53] [1994] 2 All E.R. 1. See also *Fagan v Goodman* (2001) WL 1476185.

SECONDARY VICTIMS: THE *ALCOCK* "CONTROL MECHANISMS"

4–023   In *Alcock*, following the approach of Lord Wilberforce in *McLoughlin v O'Brian*, their Lordships held that "secondary victims" of psychiatric illness had to show not only that their injuries were reasonably foreseeable; they had to satisfy three additional "control mechanisms", designed to restrict the scope of liability, as follows:

- proximity of relationship with the "immediate victim";

- proximity in "time and space" to the events causing the psychiatric illness;

- the means by which the psychiatric illness is caused.

It should be noted that some elements of the second and third "control mechanisms" are sometimes called "proximity of perception". Each is considered in turn below.

(1) Proximity of relationship

4–024   The plaintiffs in *Alcock* were parents, brothers, sisters, a brother-in-law, a grandparent and a fiancée of the immediate victims. Their Lordships refused to define rigid categories of relationship into which secondary victims of psychiatric illness must fall. Instead, they held that there must generally be a *close relationship of love and affection* between the "secondary victim" and the "immediate victim" of the accident. According to their Lordships, such a relationship could be *presumed* to exist in the case of spouses, parents and children. (But, of course, the presumption could be rebutted by evidence in an appropriate case, such as where the parties were estranged.) Lord Keith thought that the presumption relating to spouses should also extend to fiancé(e)s, or, at least, that it should be extended to the plaintiff in *Alcock* who had lost her fiancé, whom she had known for four years.[54] Siblings and other relatives (such as grandparents, uncles and aunts) would *not* normally be regarded as having the requisite closeness of relationship, unless they could show that, because of special factors, such a relationship did in fact exist. (For example, because they had brought up the immediate victim as their own child.) Dealing with the position of the plaintiff who had lost his brother in the disaster, Lord Ackner pointed out: "The quality of brotherly love is well known to differ widely".[55] It followed that this plaintiff did not satisfy the "close tie of love and affection" test in the absence of evidence that his relationship with his brother had been particularly close.

Whilst holding that closeness of relationship was an important factor to consider, their Lordships declined to hold that it was an *absolute prerequisite* of recovery in every case, leaving open the possibility that a mere "bystander" who witnessed a catastrophe which was *exceptionally horrifying* might be able to recover for psychiatric illness without showing any relationship at all with the immediate victim of the catastrophe. Lord Ackner gave the example of a bystander witnessing a petrol tanker careering out of control into a school in session and bursting into flames. Subsequent to the decision

---

[54] *Alcock v Chief Constable of South Yorkshire* [1992] 1 A.C. 310 at 398.
[55] *ibid.*, at 406.

in *Alcock*, however, this point was tested in the Court of Appeal in *McFarlane v E.E. Caledonia Ltd*.[56] When his claim as a "primary victim" failed, the plaintiff, who had been in the support boat when the Piper Alpha oil rig had exploded, claimed to be a "secondary victim", on the basis that he had witnessed the death of fellow workers in exceptionally horrific circumstances. His claim failed. In holding that it was not reasonably foreseeable that a mere "bystander" would suffer psychiatric illness in such circumstances, Stuart-Smith L.J. noted that people's reactions to horrific events were "entirely subjective".[57] This meant that there were serious practical and policy objections to allowing recovery by mere bystanders. The reasoning in *McFarlane*, then, has probably excluded the possibility of such claims in the future.

(2) Proximity in time and space

The various plaintiffs in *Alcock* had witnessed the injury or death of their loved ones in different ways. Some had been in other stands inside the ground and had seen the disaster happen, others had only seen the events on television, or heard about them on the radio. After the disaster had occurred, some of the plaintiffs had gone to the ground to search for their relatives, or had identified their bodies in a mortuary.   **4–025**

Their Lordships held that, to succeed as a secondary victim, a plaintiff had to show a high degree of proximity to the accident in time and space. Thus, the plaintiff must normally witness the accident as it actually occurs, or must come upon its "immediate aftermath" within a very short space of time. Whilst conceding that subsequent identification of the body of an accident victim might, in some circumstances, be regarded as part of the "immediate aftermath", Lord Ackner thought that Mr Alcock, who had identified his brother-in-law in a bad condition in a mortuary some eight hours after the disaster, could not be described as having come upon its *immediate* aftermath.[58] The decision in *Alcock*, then, took the law on the meaning of "immediate aftermath" little further than it had been taken in *McLoughlin v O'Brian*.

However, in *Galli-Atkinson v Seghal*[59] the Court of Appeal was prepared, on the facts, to take a more generous view of the circumstances in which a subsequent visit to a mortuary could constitute the "immediate aftermath" of an accident. Here, the claimant was a mother whose daughter had been involved in a road accident. The claimant arrived at the scene just over one hour later and was told by a police officer that her daughter had been killed. She then attended the mortuary and saw her daughter's body which, although it had been cleaned-up, had been badly disfigured by the accident. The trial judge had not been prepared to accept that the visit to the mortuary had formed part of the aftermath, and had disallowed the mother's claim because her psychiatric illness had resulted from what she had been told, rather than from witnessing the accident. In allowing her appeal, however, Latham L.J. thought that the visit to the mortuary was not, as it had been in *Alcock*, a separate event, taking place after the horror of the accident had unfolded. Rather, it was the last in a

---

[56] [1994] 2 All E.R. 1.
[57] *ibid.*, at 14.
[58] *Alcock v Chief Constable of South Yorkshire* [1992] 1 A.C. 310 at 405. Compare the view of Lord Keith, at 397, who appears to endorse the view of Deane J. in *Jaensch v Coffey* (1984) 155 C.L.R. 549, viz. that the "immediate aftermath" will continue for as long as the victim remains in the state caused by the accident.
[59] [2003] Lloyd's Rep. Med 285.

sequence of uninterrupted events which went to make up the entirety of the claimant's perception of the tragedy. His Lordship pointed out that the mortuary visit had been made not merely to identify the body, but to "complete the story so far as the appellant was concerned, who clearly at that stage did not want—and one can understand this—to believe that her child was dead".[60]

Simultaneous live television

4–026   If the plaintiffs had only seen *pre-recorded* television pictures of the disaster, they clearly would not have satisfied the requirement of temporal proximity. However, in *Alcock*, some of the plaintiffs had seen a simultaneous live broadcast of the disaster. The position of these plaintiffs required careful consideration. It will be recalled that in *McLoughlin v O'Brian*, Lord Wilberforce had left open the question of whether live television could sometimes be treated as the equivalent of being present at the scene of a disaster. Their Lordships held that, in the circumstances of the *Alcock* case, it could not. This was for two reasons. First, broadcasters had not shown the suffering of recognisable individuals—this was prohibited by their professional code of ethics. (If they had done this, then the broadcasters, rather than the police, might have been regarded as the legal cause of the plaintiffs' psychiatric illness.) Secondly, the pictures transmitted from Hillsborough had been taken by cameras from many different view points. They therefore showed a combination of scenes which no one individual present at the ground would have been likely to see. Their Lordships held, therefore, that it was normally a prerequisite of liability that claimants should perceive the events in question with their "own unaided senses". But they were reluctant to lay down an inflexible rule on this point, holding that there might be very exceptional circumstances where a simultaneous broadcast of a disaster would equate with direct perception. Lord Ackner (approving the example given by Nolan L.J. in the Court of Appeal) thought that this might be the case where a publicity-seeking organisation had made arrangements for children to go up in a hot air balloon, and the children's parents, watching a live broadcast of the event, suffered psychiatric illness on seeing the balloon suddenly burst into flames.[61]

(3) The means by which the psychiatric illness is caused

4–027   In *Alcock*, Lord Jauncey observed:

"The means by which the shock is caused constitutes a third control, although in these appeals I find it difficult to separate this from proximity."[62]

Despite their conceptual similarity to the requirements of "proximity in time and space" considered above, their Lordships chose to consider a number of additional points under this third heading.

The "sudden shock" requirement

4–028   It was reaffirmed in *Alcock* that the psychiatric illness in question must result from the sudden psychological impact of witnessing a single event or its immediate aftermath, as opposed to being caused by subsequent reflection on an event,[63] or prolonged exposure

---

[60] [2003] Lloyd's Rep. Med 285 para.26.
[61] *Alcock v Chief Constable of South Yorkshire* [1992] 1 A.C. 310 at 405.
[62] *ibid.*, at 420.
[63] Note, however, that in *W. v Essex CC* [2000] 2 All E.R. 237 (discussed later in this chapter) the House of Lords refused to say that a claim in such circumstances would be unarguable.

to distressing circumstances. Thus, although two of the plaintiffs had been present at the ground and had witnessed obviously distressing scenes, their claims were rejected because their perception of the consequences of the disaster for their relatives was, as Lord Oliver put it, "gradual".[64] Similarly, those who had seen the disaster on television had not satisfied the "sudden shock" requirement because the psychological trauma in each case had not arisen purely from the impact of the transmitted images. Rather, it had been caused by a combination of two things: first, the plaintiffs had seen the images—which, as Lord Oliver put it, provided "the matrix for imagined consequences"—and secondly, they had had their worst fears confirmed by subsequently hearing about the death of a loved one or identifying his or her body.

The "sudden shock" requirement prevented recovery by the claimant in *Sion v. Hampstead Health Authority*.[65] The claimant, a father whose son had been injured in a motorcycle accident, stayed by his son's bedside for 14 days, watching his son deteriorate, go into a coma and die. The Court of Appeal denied the father's claim, because his psychiatric illness had not resulted from the sudden appreciation of a horrifying event. (By the time the son died, his death was expected.) This decision should be contrasted with the Court of Appeal's approach in the more recent case of *North Glamorgan NHS Trust v Walters*.[66] Here, the claimant was a mother whose baby, following negligent treatment at a hospital, suffered an epileptic fit leading to a coma and, some 36 hours later, his death in his mother's arms. The Court of Appeal was prepared to hold that the 36 hours during which the claimant had been subjected to trauma could be regarded as a single event for the purpose of satisfying the sudden shock requirement.

No liability where the claimant is merely informed about the accident

In *Alcock*, their Lordships affirmed that a defendant who causes harm or imperilment to an "immediate victim" will not be liable to a claimant who is *merely informed about this* by a third party.[67] This rule, of course, may produce some bizarre results. Consider a claimant who, very shortly after an accident, is informed by a friend that his or her loved-one is dying in hospital. If the claimant suffers psychiatric illness there and then and faints on the spot, he or she will have no claim. But if the friend has the legal acumen to revive the claimant and take him or her to the hospital, the claimant may be compensated under the "immediate aftermath" doctrine, as was the plaintiff in *McLoughlin v O'Brian*. We shall see that the Law Commission has suggested that this restrictive rule, like many others, should be abolished.   4–029

It is important to understand that this rule does not mean that there can never be liability where a claimant suffers psychiatric illness as the result of hearing distressing news. The person who *communicates* the news (as opposed to the person who caused the harm the news is about) *may* be liable if the news is broken in a negligently insensitive manner. In *AB v Tameside and Glossop Health Authority*,[68] the defendants

---

[64] *Alcock v Chief Constable of South Yorkshire* [1992] 1 A.C. 310 at 417.
[65] [1994] 5 Med L.R. 170.
[66] [2003] P.I.Q.R. P16.
[67] Their Lordships doubted the correctness of *Hevican v Ruane* [1991] 3 All E.R. 65 and *Ravenscroft v Rederi AB Transatlantic* [1991] 3 All E.R. 73, which had appeared to decide that receiving news of a son's death could be an effective cause of psychiatric illness. (The latter decision was subsequently reversed by the Court of Appeal: [1992] 2 All E.R. 470).
[68] [1997] 8 Med. L.R. 91.

sent out letters warning former patients that they were at risk of having contracted HIV, because a health worker who had treated them had tested positive for the disease. The plaintiffs alleged they had suffered psychiatric illness as a result of hearing the news in this way, and argued that they should have been told face-to-face. The Court of Appeal held that the defendants had not been negligent in choosing to communicate the information by letter, but their Lordships made no comment on the fact that counsel in the case had conceded that a duty of care was owed.[69]

Psychiatric illness caused by a defendant harming or imperilling himself or herself

4–030   One further point was considered, *obiter*, in *Alcock*, but was left undecided. This was whether the law would allow a claim in circumstances where a defendant had caused psychiatric illness to a secondary victim by negligently placing *himself or herself* in danger, or causing *self-inflicted* harm. To take the example given by Lord Oliver, would a mother be able to bring a claim against her son for psychiatric illness caused by witnessing his imperilment when he negligently walked in front of an oncoming car? His Lordship thought that if such a claim were denied, the denial had to be based on policy rather than logic, because it would be difficult to imagine a case in which the elements of foreseeability of psychiatric harm and proximity were more clearly established. Whilst declining expressly to decide the point, Lord Oliver suspected that liability in such a situation would be barred as a matter of policy, noting that this view had been expressed by Deane J. in the Australian case of *Jaensch v Coffey*.[70]

The issue subsequently arose for consideration in the extraordinary case of *Greatorex v. Greatorex*.[71] Here, the defendant, John Greatorex, had been out drinking with his friend and had then crashed his friend's car while driving on the wrong side of the road. He was trapped in the car, injured and unconscious, when the fire brigade arrived. By co-incidence, the leading fire-officer at the scene was Christopher Greatorex, the defendant's father. Christopher Greatorex suffered psychiatric illness as a result of witnessing his son's injuries, and so brought an action against his son. In denying the father's claim, Cazalet J. reasoned that, since the defendant's injuries were self-inflicted, to make him liable to those who witnessed the injuries would be contrary to public policy. The policy consideration in question was that making a person liable in such a situation would restrict his or her right to self-determination—*i.e.* a person ought to be free to choose to incur personal risks, without exposing himself or herself to liability to others. (This point is considered further in the context of the Law Commission's proposals.) The issue was complicated by the fact that the claimant and defendant were father and son. On this point, Cazalet J. thought that an additional policy consideration precluded liability—causing distress to members of one's family was a normal part of family life, and for the law to allow a remedy for psychiatric illness caused by another family member would open the way for undesirable litigation within the family involving questions of relative fault as between its members. The gist of his Lordship's view was that, if such litigation were allowed, contrived and ill-founded claims might be used to prolong and aggravate family conflicts which might otherwise resolve themselves. Therefore, the law should only provide a remedy for

---

[69] See also the reasoning of Morland J. in *CJD Group B Plaintiffs v Medical Research Council* [2000] Lloyd's Rep. Med. 161 and Mullany (1998) 114 L.Q.R. 381.
[70] (1984) 155 C.L.R. 549.
[71] [2000] 1 W.L.R. 1970.

psychiatric illness caused when a loved one is harmed by a defendant who is not a family member.

THE IMPACT OF *WHITE*

The limits of the decision in *Alcock* were explored in *White v Chief Constable of South Yorkshire*. Here, as has been said, the plaintiffs were police officers who had suffered psychiatric illness as a result of their professional involvement in the Hillsborough disaster. Subsequent to the full height of the disaster, five of the six plaintiffs had assisted the injured and had worked to ensure that there was no further danger to those leaving the stadium. The sixth plaintiff had been on duty at a temporary mortuary which had been set up near the ground. None of the plaintiffs had been in physical danger. A majority of the Court of Appeal held that the five plaintiffs present at the stadium could recover in respect of their psychiatric illness.[72] This decision provoked outrage from the relatives of those killed and injured at Hillsborough, who had recently been refused compensation by the decision in *Alcock*. It was subsequently overturned by the House of Lords, which openly acknowledged the argument that the public would think it unacceptable to compensate police officers at the ground for psychiatric illness sustained simply in the course of doing their jobs, when compensation had been denied to the relatives in *Alcock*.

4–031

In the Court of Appeal, it was said that the police officers might be regarded as "primary victims" of the Chief Constable's negligence. This was because previous authority had suggested that the category of "primary victims" included plaintiffs who, though not in any physical danger, had *participated* in the events giving rise to their psychiatric illness. In *Alcock*, their Lordships had been content to divide psychiatric illness claimants into two broad categories—on the one hand, claimants who were *directly involved* in the accident (Lord Oliver thought that such claimants should be regarded as "primary victims") and, on the other hand, claimants who were only "passive and unwilling" witnesses of injury to others (who should be regarded as "secondary victims"). By the time the Court of Appeal came to decide *White*, however, the House of Lords, in *Page v Smith*, appeared to have suggested that only claimants who had been in physical danger could be regarded as "primary victims". This, as Henry L.J. recognised in the Court of Appeal, cast doubt on whether the police officers could be regarded as "primary victims".

The Court of Appeal thought, however, that even if there was doubt about their classification as "primary victims", the officers present at the stadium were entitled to succeed without needing to meet the *Alcock* criteria. Their Lordships drew this conclusion from previous authority (which we shall examine later) that appeared to establish that special rules applied where a psychiatric illness claimant was a "rescuer" or an employee, holding that the officers in question were both.[73] But the House of Lords in *White* took a very different approach, holding that no special rules applied to

---

[72] See *Frost v Chief Constable of South Yorkshire* [1998] Q.B. 254 (from which the appeal to the House of Lords in *White* was made).

[73] Technically, a police officer's relationship with a Chief Constable is not one of employment, but the courts were prepared to treat it as such in *White*.

"rescuers" or employees. The police officers did not qualify as "primary victims"—this classification was to be reserved for people who had been placed in physical danger (or who reasonably believed themselves to be in danger). All other psychiatric illness claimants were "secondary victims", and had to bring themselves within the *Alcock* criteria in order to succeed. On the facts, these criteria had obviously not been met, not least because none of the officers at the scene had a close relationship of love and affection with the dead and injured.

Clearly, the decision in *White* has implications for the general law relating to employers' liability. It also appears to be contrary to the general attitude of the courts towards rescuers. The decision in *White* also leaves unresolved the law relating to so-called "unwitting agents"—that is to say, claimants who, because of the defendant's negligence, are placed in a position where they themselves bring about the death, injury, or imperilment of the "immediate victim". Below, then, we consider the implications of *White* for three types of claimant:

- employees
- unwitting agents
- rescuers

The general law of employers' liability is considered in Ch. 7, so discussion of it here is omitted. The general law on rescuers, however, is considered here in some detail.

(1) Employees

4–032   In *Dooley v Cammell Laird & Co. Ltd*[74] (a case decided before *Alcock* and *White*), a crane driver was operating a crane at the docks where he worked when, through the fault of his employers, the sling connecting the load to the crane-hooks snapped, causing the load to fall into the hold of a ship where men were working. The crane driver suffered psychiatric illness, resulting from his fear that the falling load would injure or kill some of his fellow workmen. Donovan J., whilst drawing the inference that the men in the ship were friends of the plaintiff, was prepared to decide liability without requiring the plaintiff to establish any closer degree of relationship with the imperilled workers—the plaintiff's relationship of employment with the defendant created the necessary degree of "proximity" for his negligence action to succeed. Before the decision in *White*, it was thought that this case, and a number of similar decisions,[75] might have established that an employee had a right to recover for psychiatric illness caused by witnessing or fearing injury to fellow workers as a result of an employer's negligence.

In *White*, however, their Lordships held that no such independent right existed. An employer's duty to safeguard employees from psychiatric harm was no different from the general duty of care owed by all people to others whom their conduct might affect. It followed that in cases where an employee suffered psychiatric illness through

---

[74] [1951] 1 Lloyd's Rep. 271.
[75] See *Galt v British Railways Board* (1983) 133 N.L.J. 870; *Wigg v British Railways Board, The Times,* February 4, 1986; *Mount Isa Mines Ltd v Pusey* (1970) 125 C.L.R 383.

witnessing the death, injury or imperilment of others, the ordinary rules of tort applied, namely those laid down in *Alcock*. Therefore, there was no advantage to be gained by the police officers framing their action as a case of employers' liability. Their Lordships found little assistance in *Dooley v Cammell Laird & Co. Ltd* and similar decisions. Dealing with these cases, Lord Hoffmann said:

"I think that, on a fair reading, they were each regarded by the judges who decided them as raising one question of fact, namely whether psychiatric illness to the plaintiff was a foreseeable consequence of the defendant's negligent conduct. This was in accordance with the law as it was thought to be at the time. There was no reference to the control mechanisms, which had not yet been invented."[76]

(2) "Unwitting agents"

Although *White* makes it clear that employees are not to be regarded as a special group of psychiatric illness claimants, what remains unclear is whether cases like *Dooley v Cammell Laird & Co. Ltd* are still good authority for a different proposition, namely that special treatment should be given to claimants who, because of a defendant's negligence, are placed in circumstances where they accidentally cause the death, injury or imperilment of another through no fault of their own (or reasonably think that they have done so). In *White*, Lord Hoffmann acknowledged that "there may be grounds for treating such a rare category of case as exceptional and exempt from the *Alcock* control mechanisms".[77]

4–033

In this context, the decision of the House of Lords in *W. v Essex CC*[78] should be noted. Here, an action for psychiatric illness was brought by foster parents against a local authority. The foster parents, who had four young children of their own, had made it clear to the authority that they would not be willing to foster a child who had a history of carrying out sexual abuse. Nevertheless, the authority placed such a child in their care. It was alleged that the child had perpetrated acts of indecency against the claimants' children. The substance of the foster parents' claim was that their psychiatric illness had been caused, not just by discovering the abuse, but also by feelings of guilt that they, by being parties to a decision to bring their children into contact with a child abuser, had unwittingly *caused* harm to their children.

The local authority applied to have the claim struck out as disclosing no cause of action, but the House of Lords refused to do this. Lord Slynn, delivering the unanimous opinion of the House, thought that although the claimants might have difficulty in succeeding, their claim could not be said to be unarguable. His Lordship observed: ". . . the categorisation of those claiming to be included as primary or secondary victims is not as I read the cases finally closed".[79]

[76] *White v Chief Constable of South Yorkshire* [1999] 2 A.C. 455 at 507. Compare the analysis of Judge Gordon Reid Q.C. in *Salter v UB Frozen and Chilled Foods Ltd* [2003] S.L.T. 1011.
[77] *ibid.*, at 508.
[78] [2000] 2 All E.R. 237.
[79] *ibid.*, at 243. In *Salter v UB Frozen and Chilled Foods Ltd* [2003] S.L.T. 1011, it was pointed out by counsel that in *W v Essex* the claimants' relationship with the local authority had a "contractual flavour". This might have allowed them to succeed as primary victims without being in physical danger (see *Walker v Northumberland C.C.* [1995] I.C.R. 702, discussed in Ch. 7).

(3) Rescuers

4–034   First, in this section, it is necessary to consider at some length the approach of the courts towards "rescuers" who suffer physical injury. This provides an understanding of the legal background against which the decision in *White* may seem controversial. We then go on to consider the implications of *White* for "rescuers" who suffer only psychiatric harm.

Rescuers who suffer physical injury

4–035   We have seen in Ch. 2 that in English law there is generally no duty to go to the rescue of a person in peril. Here, we are considering a different point: if a person does go to the rescue of another, and suffers physical harm in attempting the rescue, can that person (the "rescuer") claim compensation from the defendant who negligently endangered the person being rescued?

In 1934, the courts answered this question in the affirmative, and they have done so ever since. The relevant case is *Haynes v Harwood*.[80] In Ch. 2, we considered this case in the context of liability for creating a "source of danger" that is "sparked off" by the actions of a third party. Here, we consider it in a different context. The plaintiff was a police constable who was on duty inside a police station in a street where there were a large number of people, including children. The defendants had left their horses unattended in the street. A boy threw a stone at the horses and caused them to bolt ("sparking off" the danger). Seeing the defendants' horses coming down the street, the plaintiff rushed out of the police station and eventually stopped them, sustaining injuries in the process. The question for the Court of Appeal was whether, in the circumstances, physical harm to the plaintiff was reasonably foreseeable by the defendants. The court rejected arguments that rescuers were not, in effect, "foreseeable claimants", holding that a person who can reasonably foresee that his act or omission may imperil another will also be taken to foresee that it may imperil a rescuer. This idea is encapsulated by the well-known words of the American judge, Cardozo J., who, in *Wagner v International Railway Co.*,[81] said: "Danger invites rescue. The cry of distress is a summons to relief".

Cardozo J.'s words were cited and approved by the Court of Appeal in *Baker v T.E. Hopkins and Son Ltd*,[82] a case which clearly illustrates the approach of the courts in this area. The defendant company was engaged to clean a well, and used a petrol-driven pump to clear out the water. The defendant's managing director realised that this would create carbon monoxide fumes inside the well, which could be a danger to his employees. He therefore instructed them not to go down the well until the next day, by which time, he assumed, the fumes would have dispersed. In fact, when the employees went down the well the next morning, the danger had not passed. They were overcome by the fumes and eventually died. The plaintiff, who was a doctor, was summoned to the scene by concerned farm workers. People who had gathered at the top of the well urged him not to go down, and to wait for the arrival of the fire brigade, but he insisted, saying, "There are two men down there. I must see what I can do for

---

[80] [1935] 1 K.B. 146.
[81] 232 NY Rep. 176 at 180 (1921).
[82] [1959] 1 W.L.R. 966.

them". Having tied a rope around his waist and asked the people at the top of the well to hold one end of it, and pull him up if he felt ill, he descended the well. He was heard to call up that there was nothing he could do for the men. He had started to climb up again when he was overcome by the fumes and collapsed. The people at the top tried to haul him up, but the rope became caught in a pipe or cross-member of the well and they were unable to raise him. Soon afterwards, the fire brigade arrived and the doctor was brought to the surface. He was unconscious, and died before reaching hospital.

The doctor's estate succeeded in its claim. The Court of Appeal (as it had done in *Haynes v Harwood*) rejected the suggestion that a rescuer, by intervening, should be regarded as having caused his or her own loss, or as having voluntarily accepted the risk of injury. Willmer L.J. made it clear that, provided the rescue attempt was not foolhardy or "wanton", the presence of a rescuer at the scene of an accident should be regarded as reasonably foreseeable. His Lordship cited with approval some additional words of Cardozo J. in *Wagner v International Railway Co.*: "The risk of rescue, if only it be not wanton, is born of the occasion. The emergency begets the man. The wrongdoer may not have foreseen the coming of a deliverer. He is accountable as if he had".

The courts, then, have taken the view that as a matter of policy rescue attempts should be encouraged and rewarded. This has led them to hold that a duty may be owed to a rescuer even in circumstances where no duty is owed to the person being rescued. Such was the case in *Videan v British Transport Commission*.[83] Here, a two-year-old boy, who, being the son of a village stationmaster, lived in a house adjoining the platform, strayed on to the railway track. The stationmaster saw his son standing on the track and at the same time saw a power-driven trolley approaching on the track at considerable speed. He signalled to the driver of the trolley to stop, but the driver did not understand the signals and did not see the child until it was too late to pull up. In a desperate effort to rescue his son, the stationmaster leapt from the platform on to the track in front of the trolley, and in so doing was killed. (The child, though saved by this act, suffered severe injuries.)

In an action by the stationmaster's widow in respect of the death of her husband and on behalf her injured son, the court found that the trolley driver had been careless. He had driven too fast in wet conditions, and had failed to keep a proper look-out. But the claim in respect of the child's injuries *failed*, because, at the time the case was decided, only very limited duties were owed to trespassers. This, however, did not prevent a successful claim in respect of the stationmaster's death. Harman and Pearson L.JJ. based their decision on the fact that, because the stationmaster had a duty to rescue trespassers on the line (even though he was off duty at the time), his presence on the track dealing with an emergency was reasonably foreseeable by the trolley driver. Lord Denning M.R. went a stage further, however, holding that the position would have been the same if the rescuer had been a mere passer-by and not the stationmaster rescuing his son—a person who negligently created a situation of peril should answer for it to anyone who attempted a rescue, whether or not the *victim rescued* had a cause of action.

A number of additional points should be noted about rescuers. First, where a defendant negligently imperils *himself or herself*, as opposed to a third party, a rescuer

[83] [1963] 2 Q.B. 650.

who suffers *physical injury* will have a cause of action against the defendant,[84] although *Greatorex* suggests that this will not be the case where the rescuer suffers only psychiatric illness.[85] Secondly, it is clear that rescuers have a cause of action where what has been put in peril is not a person, but property. Thus, in *Haynes v Harwood*, it was accepted that the objects of the rescue were not only the people in the street who were endangered by the runaway horses, but the horses themselves. Similarly, in *Ogwo v Taylor*,[86] a fireman succeeded when he was injured trying to save the defendant's property from a fire. Where property is the object of the rescue, however, the question of whether it is reasonable for the rescuer to intervene and risk his own safety will have to be very carefully considered[87] (whereas, in the case of people, rescue attempts are normally regarded as reasonable, provided they are not reckless or "wanton"). Thirdly, the decision in *Ogwo v Taylor* confirmed that in English law there is no equivalent of the "firemen's rule" which obtains in some parts of the United States. This rule provides that, because members of the emergency services are employed to act as rescuers, defendants cannot be liable to them in respect of the very dangers they are paid to incur. In English law, however, (subject to the qualification that defendants are entitled to expect professional rescuers to use professional skill) professional rescuers are treated in the same way as public-spirited lay rescuers.

Rescuers who suffer only psychiatric harm

4–036   Prior to *White*, by way of an extension of their general approach to rescuers, the courts appeared to have developed a special approach to cases where rescuers suffered only psychiatric harm. The leading case here was *Chadwick v British Transport Commission*.[88] The case arose from the events of a serious train crash which occurred in December 1957 in Lewisham, South London. Mr Chadwick, who lived about 200 yards from the scene of the accident, went to the scene to do what he could to help, and worked all through the night giving assistance to the injured and dying. The key witness at the trial—a woman trapped in the wreckage who had been given an injection by Mr Chadwick at the request of a doctor, who was himself too large to enter the wrecked carriage—described the horrors of the tragedy to which Mr Chadwick had been exposed: there had been a "sea of bodies" and people had been screaming in pain and fear. Before the incident, Mr Chadwick had been a cheerful and active member of the local community and had run a successful window-cleaning business, but as a result of his involvement in the tragedy, he developed severe anxiety and neurosis. Waller J. held that the defendants (who admitted the train collision was caused by their negligence) were liable for Mr Chadwick's psychiatric illness.

Before *White*, it was widely thought that the decision in *Chadwick* meant that rescuers were to be given special treatment for the purposes of psychiatric illness claims. In particular, they did not need to establish that they had been in physical danger to qualify as "primary victims". Certainly, this was the view taken by the Law

---

[84] *Harrison v British Railways Board* [1981] 3 All E.R. 679.
[85] See *Greatorex v Greatorex* [2000] 1 W.L.R. 1970; the observations of Lord Oliver in *Alcock v Chief Constable of South Yorkshire* [1992] 1 A.C. 310 at 418 (discussed above); and Law Com. 249, para.6.18 (discussed below).
[86] [1998] A.C. 431.
[87] See *Hyett v Great Western Railway* [1948] 1 K.B. 345.
[88] [1967] 1 W.L.R. 912.

Commission in March 1998, who expressed concern about aspects of the Court of Appeal's reasoning in *McFarlane v E.E. Caledonia* that might have suggested otherwise.[89] We have seen that the majority of the Court of Appeal in *White* held that the police officers at the scene were entitled to recover for psychiatric illness as rescuers, even though they had not been in physical danger. By a bare 3:2 majority, however, the House of Lords disagreed. Whilst Lords Goff and Griffiths (dissenting) thought that rescuers were entitled to special treatment, the majority held that rescuers must either satisfy the "narrow" definition of "primary victims" (*i.e.* by being in physical danger) or must bring their claims as "secondary victims" and satisfy the *Alcock* criteria.

Lord Hoffmann gave two reasons why the law should not give special treatment to rescuers unless they had been placed in physical danger. The first was that, if the control mechanism of physical danger were removed, it would become difficult to define the concept of a "rescuer"—would the term then apply to a bystander who had rendered only some trivial assistance? The second (and in his Lordship's view more important) reason was that removing the control mechanism of physical danger would produce a result in *White* that would be "unacceptable", in the sense that it would offend against the ordinary person's notions of distributive justice. His Lordship said that the ordinary person: ". . .would think it wrong that policemen, even as part of a general class of persons who rendered assistance, should have the right to compensation for psychiatric injury out of public funds while the bereaved relatives are sent away with nothing".[90]

In *White*, then, the majority of the House of Lords distinguished *Chadwick* on its facts, saying that the situation of Mr Chadwick differed from the situation of the police officers at Hillsborough because Mr Chadwick, by entering wrecked train carriages, had been "within the range of foreseeable personal injury". This made him a "primary victim" (in the narrow *Page v Smith* sense). Lords Goff and Griffiths, however, disagreed with the majority about the *ratio* of *Chadwick*. Lord Goff pointed out that although Mr Chadwick had been exposed to some physical danger, "the trial judge [Waller J.] treated that as irrelevant".[91] Lord Steyn, on the other hand (speaking with the majority), thought that the fact that Mr Chadwick had been exposed to personal danger had influenced Waller J.'s decision, albeit that his Lordship had not held that fear of personal injury was the *cause* of Mr Chadwick's psychiatric illness.[92] Lord Hoffmann was also prepared to take a restricted view of *Chadwick*, stating that the case could be subjected to an "ex post facto rationalisation"[93] and should be regarded as one turning on the presence of physical danger:

In his powerful dissenting speech, Lord Goff clearly stated that he regarded the reasoning of the majority as contrary to the existing authority of *Chadwick*, and noted that introducing what his Lordship saw as a new requirement that rescuers had to be in physical danger could produce very unjust results. His Lordship put forward an extreme example to illustrate the point[94]:

"Suppose that there was a terrible train crash and that there were two Chadwick brothers living nearby, both of them small and agile window cleaners distinguished

---

[89] See Law Com. 249, para.7.3.
[90] *White v Chief Constable of South Yorkshire* [1999] 2 A.C. 455 at 500.
[91] *ibid.*, at 484.
[92] *ibid.*, at 499.
[93] *ibid.*, at 509.
[94] *ibid.*, at 487.

by their courage and humanity. Mr. A. Chadwick worked on the front half of the train, and Mr. B. Chadwick on the rear half. It so happened that, although there was some physical danger present in the front half of the train, there was none in the rear. Both worked for 12 hours or so bringing aid and comfort to the victims. Both suffered P.T.S.D. in consequence of the general horror of the situation. On the new control mechanism now proposed, Mr. A. would recover but Mr. B. would not. To make things worse, the same conclusion must follow even if Mr. A. was unaware of the existence of the physical danger present in his half of the train. This is surely unacceptable."

Despite Lord Goff's objection, the decision of the majority of the House of Lords in *White* has effectively closed the door on future claims by rescuers who have not been placed in physical peril.[95] It remains to be seen, however, whether, in line with their general approach to rescue cases, the courts will adopt a liberal interpretation of this requirement in order to do justice in meritorious cases. In this context, it is interesting to note the (possible) combined effect of the decisions in *White* and *Page v Smith*. This is that if rescuers in physical peril are now to be regarded as "primary victims" (in the narrow *Page v Smith* sense), they may be able to take advantage of the "eggshell skull" reasoning in *Page v Smith* to establish a duty of care. Thus (arguably) in a case like *Chadwick*, provided it could be shown that some very minor personal injury to the claimant was reasonably foreseeable, the law would then proceed to regard personal injury and psychiatric injury as the same kind of damage. The "eggshell skull" rule would then apply, so that the claimant could recover even if he or she were "peculiarly susceptible" to psychiatric illness. This consequence of their Lordship's interpretation of *Chadwick* has the effect of *widening* the scope of liability to rescuers for psychiatric illness—a point that does not appear to have been specifically addressed in *White*.[96]

PSYCHIATRIC ILLNESS LAW: PROPOSALS FOR REFORM

4–037   In March 1998, the Law Commission published a report which recommended some important changes to the law.[97] In summary, the report concluded that, in relation to secondary victims, whilst the "control mechanism" of "close ties of love and affection" should remain, all of the other *Alcock* "control mechanisms" should be abolished. The Law Commission expressed the view that, with the decision in *Alcock*, the common law had in some respects "taken a wrong turn".[98] The Commission did not think it appropriate, however, to codify *all* of the common law on psychiatric illness—this was not a sensible option, because the flexibility of the common law would allow new areas of liability to develop incrementally, as experts learned more about psychiatric illness, and society further recognised its debilitating consequences. Therefore, the Commission proposed a strategy of minimal legislative intervention to modify and clarify the

---

[95] Thus, the fireman father in *Greatorex v Greatorex* [2000] 1 W.L.R. 1970, although a rescuer, could not succeed as a primary victim because he was not in physical danger.
[96] Although it is alluded to by Lord Goff at 479–480.
[97] "Liability for Psychiatric Illness" Law Com. 249 (available from *http://www.open.gov.uk/lawcomm/*).
[98] *ibid.*, para.4.2.

common law. A draft Bill forms part of the Law Commission's report. With the help of consultants from the insurance industry, the Commission was able to estimate (very roughly and in relation to motor vehicle insurance only) that its proposals to expand the scope of liability might lead to an increase in insurance premiums of between 2 and 5 per cent.[99]

The most radical proposal, then, is that two of the *Alcock* "control mechanisms" should be abolished. Thus, it would no longer be necessary for secondary victims to show proximity to the accident in time and space,[1] or that they had perceived the accident or its aftermath by their "own unaided senses". This would mean that, provided they could show closeness of relationship with the "immediate victim" (see below), people in the position of the plaintiffs in *Alcock* would be able to succeed, as would claimants whose psychiatric illness resulted from merely being *told* about the accident. The requirement that the claimant's psychiatric illness must be produced by a "sudden shock" would be abolished. This would allow recovery, for example, by a long-term carer who developed psychiatric illness because of the emotional strain of looking after the victim of the defendant's negligence.

"Close ties of love and affection": the "fixed list"

In deciding to retain the requirement of "close ties of love and affection" between a secondary victim and the immediate victim, the Commission noted that policy considerations dictated limits to recovery by secondary victims, and felt that the requirement operated as an appropriate control mechanism. It thought, however, that in *Alcock* the requirement had been too narrowly drawn. Under its proposals, therefore, the *rebuttable* common law presumptions governing spouses, parents and children would be replaced with *conclusive* statutory presumptions in respect of a wider class of relationships. Thus, there would be a statutory "fixed list" of relationships in which close ties of love and affection would be *deemed* to exist.[2] These relationships would be: parent, child, sibling, spouse, and cohabitant (whether heterosexual or homosexual) for a period of two or more years. (Thus, the list is wider than the categories of presumed close relationships in *Alcock*, because it includes siblings and cohabitants.) Persons outside the "fixed list" would remain in the hands of the common law. Thus, they would not be barred from making a claim, but would be required to establish the necessary ties of love and affection by evidence. (In this context, the Commission thought that the class of potential claimants might extend to non-relatives who could establish a "relationship of care"—such as might exist between a schoolteacher and a pupil.) The Commission saw no need for legislation relating to mere "bystanders", leaving their position to the common law (so the reasoning in *McFarlane v E.E. Caledonia* would probably prevent them recovering).

4–038

---

[99] "Liability for Psychiatric Illness" Law Com. 249 para.1.13 (available from *http:/www.open.gov.uk/lawcomm/*).
[1] At para.6.12, the report cites *Taylor v Somerset Health Authority* (1993) 4 Med. L.R. 34 and *Taylorson v Shieldness Produce Ltd* [1994] P.I.Q.R. P329 as examples where the requirement has produced unjust results.
[2] Note, however, as the report points out (at para.6.25), it would still be open to the court to hold that the absence of a *de facto* close relationship meant that psychiatric illness to the claimant was not reasonably foreseeable, as, for example, where a mother, who had abandoned her son at birth, suffered psychiatric illness on reading about his death in a newspaper many years later.

The Commission also recommended that legislation should provide that the requirement of a close relationship could be satisfied by the existence of such a relationship *either* at the time of the accident, *or* at the onset of the claimant's psychiatric illness. This provision would be necessary to accommodate, for example, the case of a carer who, whilst having no ties of love and affection with the victim at the time of the accident, subsequently developed such ties in the course of looking after the victim, and suffered psychiatric illness as a result of this task.

The "just and reasonable" proviso

4–039   The report points out that the duty of care owed by a defendant to a secondary victim is an *independent duty* — its existence does not depend on a duty of care being owed to the immediate victim. (For example, where the immediate "victim" is placed in danger but not actually injured, there may be no tort committed against him or her.) The Law Commission recognised, however, that in certain circumstances it might be undesirable to impose liability on a defendant towards a secondary victim if the defendant would not be liable to the immediate victim (for example because the immediate victim had consented to the risk of injury). To accommodate such circumstances, the Commission proposed a legislative provision stating that defendants should not be liable to secondary victims in cases where the court considers that such liability would not be "just and reasonable".

Such a provision would also cover situations where the immediate victim was the defendant—in other words, where the defendant had injured or imperilled himself or herself, causing a secondary victim psychiatric illness. We have seen that, in *Alcock*, Lord Oliver thought that policy considerations would probably preclude the liability of such a defendant, and that in *Greatorex* v. *Greatorex* such considerations formed part of the reasoning in denying liability. The Law Commission, however, thought that there was no good reason why, generally speaking, a defendant who injured or imperilled himself or herself should not owe a duty of care to others. The Commission was conscious, however, that the imposition of such a duty in all circumstances might severely restrict a person's right to self-determination. For example, it would mean that a person could not, without exposing himself or herself to potential liability, choose to engage in a dangerous sport, or refuse medical treatment for religious reasons. The Commission noted: "there is a difficult balance to be arrived at between respecting self-determination and requiring proper concern to be shown for the consequences for others of choosing to harm or incur the risk of harm to oneself".[3] Regarding this as a matter for the courts, it proposed that, whilst the absolute bar to liability in such cases (if it existed) should be removed, the imposition of a duty should be qualified by a requirement that it must be "just and reasonable" in the circumstances.

The "actual danger" proviso

4–040   The Law Commission noted that whilst it was not in doubt that, under existing law, a secondary victim who satisfied the *Alcock* criteria would be able to recover where the immediate victim had been *placed in danger* but had not actually been *injured*, some

---

[3] Law Com. 249, para.5.42.

doubt existed as to whether a secondary victim could recover in a situation where he or she *reasonably believed* that the "victim" was in danger, whereas, as a matter of fact, he or she was not. The Commission thought that, if liability were allowed in such a situation, "the policy against opening the floodgates of litigation would be undermined".[4] It therefore proposed that "legislation should draw the line at where the loved one has in fact been killed, injured or imperilled by the defendant". Thus, to take the Law Commission's example,[5] there would be no liability in a situation where a wife suffers psychiatric illness after watching evening news reports of a train crash, believing that her husband is on the train, when, in fact, he has been delayed at work and taken a later train, arriving home safely that night.

Rescuers, "participants" and "unwitting agents"

The Commission's report (dated March 1998) suggested that the position of "rescuers" and "involuntary participants" should be left to the common law. The decision in *White* (in 1999) has, of course, settled the position of rescuers. However, in the light of Lord Hoffmann's remarks in that case (noted earlier) to the effect that "unwitting agent" cases may be exempt from the normal control mechanisms, there appears to remain some scope for the courts to develop the law in situations where the claimant is either an "unwitting agent" (the involuntary cause of the death, injury or imperilment of the immediate victim) or is otherwise intimately involved as a "participant" in the events which give rise to the harm to the immediate victim.   **4–041**

Such a claim succeeded in the Scottish case of *Salter v UB Frozen and Chilled Foods Ltd*.[6] Here, the claimant was a forklift-truck driver engaged in a stock-taking exercise in a warehouse whereby he drove along carrying his workmate in a cage at the top of the truck. The workmate was fatally injured when he failed to duck to avoid a roof-beam while checking stock on the upper shelves, and the claimant suffered psychiatric illness as a result of witnessing the incident. The claimant had not himself been in physical danger. In an action against his employer, however, he was able to succeed on the basis that he was so intimately involved in the incident that (unlike the police constables in *White*) he could be regarded as a "participant" in the tragic event. Judge Gordon Reid Q.C. pointed out that this was not the same as saying that he was the *cause* of the tragedy—the true cause was the employers' unsafe working practices (as it had been in *Dooley*).

Defences

Finally, it should be noted that the Law Commission's proposals would preserve certain defences.[7] Thus, there would be no liability to a secondary victim who had voluntarily assumed the risk of suffering psychiatric illness, or in relation to whom a defendant had excluded his or her duty not to cause psychiatric illness (for example by a contract term[8]), or in situations where it would be unjust to allow the secondary   **4–042**

---

[4] Law Com. 249, para.6.18.
[5] *ibid.*, para.6.69.
[6] [2003] S.L.T. 1011.
[7] *ibid.*, para.6.42.
[8] Unfair Contract Terms Act 1977, s.2(1) prohibits the valid exclusion of negligence liability for personal injury and death where the liability in question is "business liability".

victim to recover because he or she was involved in conduct that was illegal or contrary to public policy.

Liability for psychiatric illness: conclusion

4–043   Clearly, the law on psychiatric illness, like the law on economic loss, suffers from a lack of coherence. It is an emotionally charged area of liability which raises acute moral problems. The rules developed in *Alcock* and *White* seem to deny liability to many genuinely deserving claimants. Moreover, the application of those rules compounds the moral dilemma. As Lord Hoffmann noted in *Alcock* (echoing the views of the Law Commission)[9]:

> ". . . the spectacle of a plaintiff who has, ex hypothesi, suffered psychiatric illness in consequence of his brother's death or injury, being cross-examined on the closeness of their ties of love and affection and then perhaps contradicted by the evidence of a private investigator, might not be to everyone's taste."[10]

It is the prospect of such an undignified spectacle, of course, which has led the Law Commission to recommend replacing the rebuttable common law presumptions of close ties of love and affection with conclusive presumptions in statutory form.

In conclusion, we can do little more than endorse the sentiments of Lord Oliver, who stated in *Alcock*: ". . . I cannot, for my part, regard the present state of the law as either entirely satisfactory or as logically defensible", and, after acknowledging that the answers in this area of the law were to be found "not in logic but in policy", concluded that the relevant policy considerations would be "much better accommodated if the rights of persons injured in this way were to be enshrined in and limited by legislation".[11]

---

[9] Law Com. 249, para.6.24.
[10] *Alcock v Chief Constable of South Yorkshire* [1992] 1 A.C. 310 at 503. His Lordship also refers to J. Stapleton, "In Restraint of Tort" in *The Frontiers of Liability* (1994, O.U.P.), Vol. 2, p.84, who says that a mother who suffers psychiatric illness after finding her child's mangled body in a mortuary "might wonder why the law rules her child's blood too dry to found an action".
[11] *Alcock v Chief Constable of South Yorkshire* [1992] 1 A.C. 310 at 418 and 419.

Chapter 5

NEGLIGENCE: BREACH OF DUTY

Introduction

Once it has been established that the defendant owes the claimant a duty of care, it **5–001** must next be established that the defendant has breached that duty. In practical terms, breach of duty is the most important element of the tort of negligence, because in everyday cases the existence of a duty of care and questions of causation and remoteness are rarely in issue.

Establishing breach of duty involves showing that the defendant's conduct has fallen below the *standard of care* required in all the circumstances. The standard set by the law is one of "reasonableness". The flexibility inherent in the concept of "reasonableness" is necessary to accommodate the infinite variety of cases that may arise. Thus, for example, the law says that motorists must drive with "reasonable care in all the circumstances" because it cannot possibly prescribe the precise speed at which motorists must drive in each and every possible set of road conditions. In the case of driving, of course, the law makes some attempt to reduce the requirement of "reasonableness" into a set of concrete "rules"—in the form of speed limits and the rules of the Highway Code—but generally speaking the courts have resisted attempts to boil down the requirement of "reasonableness" into a series of precise and definite obligations. Decisions in individual cases as to what amounts to "reasonable conduct" are regarded only as useful guides. To treat them otherwise would introduce a rigidity into the law that might produce injustice.

In this chapter, then, we are not concerned with learning a multiplicity of specific "rules" about what defendants must or must not do in various sets of circumstances. Although it is possible to enumerate a great number of fairly definite "rules" about what the law considers "reasonable" in specific situations (for example, when driving, looking after another's property, or carrying passengers on a ship), it is not usual to consider all of these rules in a book of this kind. The only specific obligations we do consider are those owed by an employer to an employee (see Ch. 7) and by an occupier to persons on his or her premises (see Ch. 8). This chapter deals with the *general principles* the courts employ in setting the standard of care. It begins by exploring these principles. It then discusses the extent to which the law expects special standards of care from special categories of defendant (for example from children, or professionals). Finally, it considers the problem of *proving* breach of duty.

"Duties" and the standard of care

5–002   Before we commence our analysis, it is important to clarify the terminology we can expect to encounter. Confusingly, lawyers have a tendency to speak of the standard of care owed by different types of defendant in different situations by using the word "duty". For example, it may be said that a motorist has a "duty" to keep a safe stopping distance from the car in front, or (as we shall see in Ch. 7) that an employer has a "duty" to provide a safe place of work for his or her employees. It should not be forgotten that when the word "duty" is used in this context, it is being used to describe the *standard of care required*. In other words, what is in issue is not the existence of a duty of care—there is no doubt that a motorist owes a duty of care to other road users—but the *nature and scope* of that duty. Because of the terminology used, and because the idea of "reasonable foreseeability" is used in establishing both the existence of a duty and breach of that duty, the distinction between the two issues can easily become blurred, but it is important, where possible, to think of each issue separately.

The "reasonable person"

5–003   The law's starting point in deciding breach of duty is to judge the defendant's conduct by the standard of the hypothetical "reasonable person" (in older cases referred to as the "reasonable man"). The most famous example of the "reasonable person" being used to define the standard of care comes from the judgment of Alderson B. in *Blyth v Birmingham Waterworks Co*.[1] His Lordship said:

> "Negligence is the omission to do something which a reasonable man, guided upon those considerations which ordinarily regulate the conduct of human affairs, would do, or doing something which a prudent and reasonable man would not do."

Two important points must be noted about the standard of the "reasonable person":

- the standard is objective

- the standard does not always reflect "average" behaviour

The standard of care is objective

5–004   The first point to note, then, is that the judgment as to whether the defendant has behaved like a "reasonable person" is an objective one. That is to say, the question for the court is not: "What could we have expected *this particular defendant* to do in the circumstances?" Rather, the question is: "What could we expect a 'reasonable person' to do?" Thus, a defendant who is unusually clumsy or slow-witted cannot succeed by arguing that his or her conduct amounts to an "incompetent best". The defendant will be judged according to the best efforts of the hypothetical "reasonable person".
    The objective nature of the "reasonable person" test was explained by Lord Macmillan in *Glasgow Corp. v Muir*.[2] Here, the manageress of the defendants' tea-

---

[1] (1856) 11 Ex. 781 at 784.
[2] [1943] 2 A.C. 448.

room, to which access was obtained by way of a small shop, gave a picnic party permission to use the tea-room when rain prevented them from eating their food outside. She allowed two members of the party to carry a tea urn through the shop. Despite taking all due care, one of the carriers let go of the urn, so that tea was spilt, severely scalding several children who were buying sweets at the counter of the shop. The plaintiffs argued that the manageress had been negligent in giving permission for the tea urn to be brought in without first clearing the children out of the shop. On the facts, the defendants were not liable, because the risk of injury was not so high that a reasonable person would have done this in the circumstances. Dealing with the "reasonable person" standard, Lord Macmillan said:

"The standard of foresight of the reasonable man is in one sense an impersonal test. It eliminates the personal equation and is independent of the idiosyncrasies of the particular person whose conduct is in question. Some persons are by nature unduly timorous and imagine every path beset with lions; others, of more robust temperament, fail to foresee or nonchalantly disregard even the most obvious dangers. The reasonable man is presumed to be free both from over-apprehension and from over-confidence."[3]

His Lordship conceded, however, that the test for breach of duty does contain a certain subjective element. This is because the question for the court is: what would the reasonable person have done in the defendant's circumstances? However, although the defendant's conduct must be judged in the light of "all the circumstances of the case", it is important to distinguish between, on the one hand, external circumstances (for example, the defendant was acting in an emergency) and, on the other hand, "circumstances" which are personal characteristics of the particular defendant (for example, the defendant's "circumstances" were that he or she happened to be a novice or a half-wit). Whilst the law will adapt the standard of care to take account of external circumstances, it will not, generally speaking, take account of the defendant's personal characteristics.

The case of *Nettleship v Weston*[4] provides perhaps the most famous illustration of the objective standard of care. The defendant was a learner driver. The plaintiff, a family friend, had agreed to give her driving lessons. On her third lesson, when the car was moving very slowly, with the plaintiff moving the gear lever and the defendant steering, the defendant panicked. The car mounted the pavement and struck a lamp-post, causing the plaintiff to suffer a broken knee cap. He sued the defendant for personal injury.

The Court of Appeal held the defendant liable. The majority of the Court held that her conduct was not to be judged, as she argued, by the standard of a learner driver, but by the standard of a reasonably competent and experienced one. Lord Denning M.R. stated that, although the defendant was not *morally* at fault, she should be regarded as *legally* at fault. Since she was legally required to be insured, it made sense that she should bear the risk of her driving. Megaw L.J. pointed out that, once the law accepted the principle that the standard of care could be varied according to the

---

[3] [1943] 2 A.C. 457.
[4] [1971] 2 Q.B. 691.

experience of the particular defendant, it would be logically impossible to confine application of the principle to cases of driving. This would mean that in every negligence case, the court would be obliged to hear evidence about the level of competence to be expected of a "reasonable person" with the same level of experience as the defendant. Such an exercise would be costly and time-consuming and would undoubtedly produce unpredictability and uncertainty in the law. His Lordship concluded, therefore, that "the certainty of a general standard is preferable to the vagaries of a fluctuating standard".[5]

The standard of care is a "hypothetical", not an "average" standard

5–005   Although the "reasonable person" is sometimes personified as the "man on the Clapham omnibus",[6] or the "man on the Underground",[7] it is important to appreciate that the standard of care the law requires is sometimes a poor reflection of the standard such a man would probably, in fact, exercise. Whilst evidence of the fact that most people behave in a certain way may, in appropriate cases, be relevant in setting the legal standard of care, the law will not always regard such evidence as conclusive. This is because there are situations where, as a matter of policy, very high standards of care are imposed for the purpose of shifting losses on to defendants, with little regard for fault. In such cases, the idea of fault is subordinated to the objectives of compensation and loss distribution, discussed in Ch. 1. Below, we discuss how this is achieved in the context of road traffic accidents, but the reader should also consider the issue in the context of the high standards of care required of employers, discussed in Ch. 7.

Because the "reasonable person" is a mythical judicial creation, then, he or she may sometimes be credited with a level of skill and prudence that is seldom attainable in the real world. The Pearson Commission, which in 1978 reported on civil liability for personal injury, noted:

> "Even good drivers make mistakes. A study by the World Health Organisation in 1962 found that a good driver makes a mistake every two miles; and an American study in 1964 suggested that on average a good driver makes nine mistakes every five minutes."[8]

Yet, many of the "mistakes" good drivers make are regarded by the law as conduct falling below the standard expected of a "reasonable driver". This means, in effect, that the standard of care in relation to driving is so high that in certain situations there is almost strict liability (liability without fault) for driving. The reason why this is so has partly to do with historical accident (the rules on driving were developed when many fewer cars were on the roads), but it also has to do with particular policy considerations which apply in road traffic cases. The most important goal of tort law in the context of driving accidents is to provide compensation for victims. The issue of fault, therefore, is subordinated to achieving this goal. As was noted in Ch. 1, the law is

---

[5] [1971] 2 Q.B. 707.
[6] *per* Greer L.J. in *Hall v Brooklands Auto Racing Club* [1933] 1 K.B. 205 at 224.
[7] *per* Lord Steyn in *White v Chief Constable of South Yorkshire* [1999] 2 A.C. 455 at 495.
[8] Report of the Royal Commission on Civil Liability and Compensation for Personal Injury, Vol. 1, Ch. 18, para.983.

assisted in this regard by the availability of third party insurance, which is compulsory for motorists.

It should be noted, however, that whilst the standard of care in relation to driving is very high, the courts have stopped short of holding that liability for driving is entirely divorced from fault. In *Mansfield v Weetabix Ltd*,[9] the Court of Appeal held that a driver who becomes unable to control a vehicle will not be liable for damage caused by his or her loss of control if the driver is unaware (and should not reasonably have been aware) of a disabling condition from which he or she is suffering, which suddenly manifests itself, causing the loss of control. Prior to this decision, Neill J. had held, in *Roberts v Ramsbottom*,[10] that a driver who suffered a stroke at the wheel remained liable. His Lordship had suggested that this would be so even if the driver had been unaware that he had a medical condition likely to lead to a loss of control. In *Mansfield v Weetabix Ltd*, however, the Court of Appeal held that *Roberts v. Ramsbottom* was wrongly decided on this point, although the decision could be supported on the alternative ground that the defendant had carried on driving when he felt strange and ought to have known that he was probably unfit to drive.

Now that we are familiar with the standard of the "reasonable person", it is appropriate to explore the various factors which the courts take into account in deciding whether this standard has been met.

FACTORS RELEVANT TO THE STANDARD OF CARE

The relevant factors can be stated as follows: 5–006

- foreseeability of harm;
- magnitude of the risk;
- burden of taking precautions;
- utility of the defendant's conduct;
- common practice.

Below, we consider each of these in turn. We then look at how some of them may be considered together in a quasi-mathematical way, using what is known as the "Learned Hand test".

Foreseeability of harm

If the particular harm the claimant suffers is not foreseeable, the defendant will not be   5–007
liable. This is because, rather obviously, the "reasonable person" cannot be expected to take any precautions against unforeseeable risks. The point is illustrated by the decision of the Court of Appeal in *Roe v. Minister of Health*.[11] In 1947, the plaintiff

[9] [1998] 1 W.L.R. 1263.
[10] [1980] 1 All E.R. 7.
[11] [1954] 2 Q.B. 66.

went into hospital for a minor operation. He suffered permanent paralysis as a result of being given a spinal anaesthetic which was contaminated with phenol. The contamination had occurred when glass ampoules containing the anaesthetic had been stored in the phenol, which was used as a disinfectant, and the phenol had seeped through invisible cracks in the glass. At the time, it was not known that contamination could occur in this way. The action came to trial in 1954, by which time the dangers had become known. The defendants were not liable. Denning L.J. made the point that, although in 1954 it would be regarded as negligent to store anaesthetic in phenol, the court "must not look at the 1947 accident with 1954 spectacles".[12]

Whilst the defendant will escape liability where the risk is unforeseeable, it does not follow that he or she will automatically be liable for all risks that are foreseeable. The law insists that a risk must be *reasonably* foreseeable before making a defendant liable. This point is explored below.

The magnitude of the risk

5–008   The "reasonable person" does not take precautions against risks that are very small. Assessing the "magnitude" of any risk involves consideration of two factors. First, there is the likelihood that harm will occur. Secondly, there is the question of how serious the consequences will be if harm *does* occur.

(1) The likelihood of harm

5–009   In *Bolton v Stone*,[13] the plaintiff, who was standing outside her house on a quiet street, was hit by a cricket ball which came from a nearby cricket ground. It was clear that the defendant cricketers could have foreseen that a ball might be hit out of the ground, because this had happened before, but it was a very rare occurrence. The evidence established that cricket balls had been hit out of the ground on about six occasions in the previous 30 years. There was a fence around the ground which was seven feet high and, due to the slope of the ground, the top of the fence was some 17 feet above the level of the pitch. The fence was some 80 yards away from where the batsman stood. The House of Lords held that, in these circumstances, the chance of an injury occurring to someone who was standing in the position of the plaintiff was so slight that the defendants were not negligent in continuing to play cricket without taking additional precautions. Lord Oaksey said that "an ordinarily careful man does not take precautions against every foreseeable risk. He can, of course, foresee the possibility of many risks, but life would be almost impossible if he were to attempt to take precautions against every risk which he can foresee".[14] Similarly, Lord Radcliffe thought that a reasonable person, taking account of the chances against such an accident occurring, "would have done what the appellants did: in other words, he would have done nothing".[15]

It is useful to compare *Bolton v Stone* with the decision of Ashworth J. in *Hilder v Associated Portland Cement Manufacturers Ltd.*[16] Here, the defendants were the

---

[12] [1954] 2 Q.B. 84.
[13] [1951] A.C. 850.
[14] *ibid.*, at 863.
[15] *ibid.*, at 869.
[16] [1961] 1 W.L.R. 1434. *Bolton v Stone* was applied, for example, in *Zucchi v Waitrose Ltd* 2000 WL 345171 where the risk of customers being injured by a collapsing stack of plastic bottles was so small that the store had acted reasonably in disregarding it.

occupiers of some grassland on which they permitted some small boys to play football. One of the boys kicked the ball over a low wall into the adjoining road where it caused the plaintiff, a passing motorcyclist, to fall off his motorbike and suffer fatal injuries. The defendants were held liable. Because the risk of injury to a road user was much greater than the risk in *Bolton v Stone*—the land was only some 15 yards from the road—it was not a risk that the reasonable person would have disregarded.

In *Haley v London Electricity Board*,[17] the House of Lords was presented with detailed statistical evidence about the likelihood of harm occurring. The plaintiff, who was blind, fell into a hole in the pavement that had been dug by the defendants. As a result of the fall he became deaf. The precautions taken to guard the hole were sufficient for sighted people but were insufficient for the blind. Their Lordships considered evidence relating to the number of blind people who lived in the same London borough as the plaintiff, and concluded that the likelihood of a blind person falling into the hole was not so small that the defendants could ignore it. The case is authority for the proposition that the reasonable person must tailor his conduct in the light of the characteristics of the people whom he knows it might affect. Thus (as we shall see in Ch. 7), a defendant employer has been held liable for causing psychiatric illness to an employee whom he ought to have known was likely to suffer a nervous breakdown,[18] but in other cases, where the risk of psychiatric illness to the particular employee could not reasonably have been known, employers have escaped liability.

(2) The seriousness of the consequences

The decision in *Bolton v Stone* does not mean that a reasonable person is *always* 5–010
justified in ignoring a very small risk. The risk of harm materialising must be weighed against other factors, including the seriousness of the consequences if the harm does materialise. The more serious the consequences, the greater the obligations of the defendant. This point is neatly illustrated by the decision in *Paris v Stepney Borough Council*.[19] The plaintiff, who was blind in one eye, was employed by the defendants in a garage. One day he was called upon to dismantle the chassis of a large vehicle and had to use a hammer to knock out a rusty bolt. A fragment of metal came off the bolt and hit him in his good eye, causing him to become totally blind. The risk of such an injury occurring was extremely small and did not justify the use of goggles by ordinary workers. Nevertheless, a majority of the House of Lords held that the defendants were liable for failing to provide this particular worker with goggles, knowing that he might suffer such serious consequences if the small risk materialised.

The burden of taking precautions

The court will take account of the cost and practicality of taking precautions against a 5–011
risk. If the burden of taking steps to eliminate a risk is far greater than the benefit obtained by its elimination, then failure to take those steps will not generally amount to negligence. Thus, one factor which influenced the House of Lords in deciding *Bolton v Stone* was that the only practical way the defendant cricketers could have

---

[17] [1965] A.C. 778.
[18] *Walker v Northumberland CC* [1995] 1 All E.R. 737.
[19] [1951] A.C. 367.

prevented balls from going out of the ground would have been to erect an extremely high fence—wind conditions made this very difficult, if not impossible. Alternatively, they could simply have stopped playing cricket. In either case, taking precautions against the risk would have placed a burden on the defendants that was out of all proportion to the risk the precautions would avoid.

The case most often cited in this context is *Latimer v AEC Ltd.*[20] Here, the floor of the defendants' factory was flooded by an exceptionally heavy rainstorm. As a result, an oily cooling mixture, which was normally contained in a channel in the floor, mixed with the flood waters. When the flood subsided, the floor was left in a slippery state. The defendants spread sawdust on the floor, but did not have enough sawdust to go round, so some areas were left untreated. The plaintiff, who was working in an area which had not been treated with sawdust, was attempting to load a heavy barrel on to a trolley when he slipped and injured his ankle. The House of Lords held that the defendants had not been negligent. They had done all that reasonable employers could be expected to do for the safety of their workers. The only way the defendants could have eliminated the risk entirely would have been to close the factory, and this would have been a precaution out of all proportion to the risk in question.

It is useful to compare *Bolton* and *Latimer* with the decision of the Privy Council in *The Wagon Mound (No.2)*.[21] Here, the defendants negligently discharged a quantity of furnace oil into the sea. The evidence in the case established that there was an extremely small risk that the oil might ignite in very unusual circumstances. (These circumstances are explained in Ch. 6, because the incident also gave rise to another case—*The Wagon Mound (No.1)*—which is the leading authority on remoteness of damage.) The oil ignited, causing damage to the plaintiffs' ships. The defendants argued that, because the risk of damage was very small, they were justified in disregarding it. The Privy Council was unimpressed by this argument. The burden of eliminating the risk in this case was minimal—all the defendants had to do was ensure that the oil did not discharge into the harbour by keeping a tap turned off. Their Lordships pointed out that a reasonable person would not ignore even a very small risk, "if action to eliminate it presented no difficulty, involved no disadvantage and required no expense".[22] In *The Wagon Mound (No.2)*, it was also relevant to a finding of liability that the defendants, in discharging the oil, were not doing anything worthwhile—they were committing an act of pollution. In other words, their act had no "utility". This issue is considered further elsewhere.

The defendant's financial circumstances

5–012   A difficult issue is whether the financial resources available to the defendant should be taken into account in deciding whether the defendant should take precautions against a risk. Where the defendant can be said to have a choice about whether or not to engage in the activity which creates the risk, he or she cannot argue lack of resources as a reason for failing to meet the standard of care. The Australian case of *P.Q. v Australian Red Cross Society*[23] serves as a vivid illustration. Here, the Australian court firmly rejected the argument that the standard to be expected of the Red Cross in

[20] [1953] A.C. 643.
[21] *Overseas Tankship (UK) v Miller Steamship Co. Pty. Ltd, The Wagon Mound (No.2)* [1967] 1 A.C. 617.
[22] *ibid.*, at 642.
[23] [1992] 1 V.R. 19.

testing blood donations for the AIDS virus should be determined in the light of the financial constraints of the charity. The charity had a choice. If it lacked adequate financial resources to collect blood donations properly, it should choose not to provide that service.

By contrast, there are situations where the defendant's lack of choice in pursuing a certain course of action justifies taking financial constraints into account. Such is the case where an occupier comes under an affirmative duty of care to prevent others being harmed by a natural hazard arising on his land.[24] Acting in an emergency may be regarded as another "no choice" situation in which the actor can only be expected to make use of the financial resources immediately available.

Decisions concerning the standard of care required of public authorities indicate that the financial resources available to the authority are a relevant consideration in setting the standard of care.[25] Thus, for example, in *Knight v Home Office*[26] it was held that the prison authorities were not negligent in failing to provide the same level of care for prisoners suffering from psychiatric illness that could be expected in a psychiatric hospital outside prison. Pill J., however, noted that there were limits to this approach. Lack of financial resources could not operate as a complete defence. Taking an extreme example, his Lordship said that, "if the evidence was that no funds were available to provide any medical facilities in a large prison there would be a failure to achieve the standard of care appropriate for prisoners".

The utility of the defendant's conduct

The greater the social utility of the defendant's conduct, the less likely it is that the defendant will be held to be negligent. The classic case which illustrates this is *Daborn v Bath Tramways Motor Co. Ltd*.[27] The relevant issue was whether, in wartime, the driver of a left-hand drive ambulance had been negligent in turning into a road without giving a hand signal. The Court of Appeal held that she was not liable. During wartime, it was necessary for many highly important operations to be carried out by means of vehicles with left-hand drives, and it was impossible for the drivers of such vehicles to give the warning signals which drivers might normally have been expected to give. Asquith L.J. noted that the utility of the defendant's act had to be weighed against the risks it created, saying:

5–013

"... if all the trains in this country were restricted to a speed of five miles an hour, there would be fewer accidents, but our national life would be intolerably slowed down. The purpose to be served, if sufficiently important, justified the assumption of abnormal risk."[28]

His Lordship concluded that, because ambulance drivers were performing a valuable service in a time of national emergency, it would be demanding too high a standard of

[24] See *Goldman v Hargrave* [1967] 1 A.C. 645 and *Leakey v National Trust* [1980] Q.B. 485, discussed in Ch. 10.
[25] At least, this appears to be so where the authority is in a "no choice" situation, in the sense that it is fulfilling a statutory duty rather than exercising a power. There is some obvious overlap here with the question of when the authority will owe a duty of care, which has been explored in Ch. 2.
[26] [1990] 3 All E.R. 237.
[27] [1946] 2 All E.R. 333.
[28] *ibid.*, at 336.

care from them to say: "Either you must give signals which the structure of your vehicle renders impossible or you must not drive at all".

Similar reasoning was adopted in *Watt v Hertfordshire CC*.[29] Here, the plaintiff was a fireman, who was injured when travelling to rescue a woman reported to have been trapped under a heavy lorry. In the haste of the rescue, the plaintiff's colleagues picked up a jack, which was needed to save the woman's life, and put it into the lorry in which they were travelling. The lorry was not equipped for carrying the jack and the plaintiff was injured when the driver of the lorry braked suddenly and the jack fell on him. It was held that the defendant employers were not negligent because the need to act speedily in an attempt to save the woman's life outweighed the risk to the plaintiff. It should be noted, however, that this decision does not mean that the emergency services will always escape liability for accidents occurring in the haste of a rescue. The court will have regard to all of the circumstances of the particular case. Thus, for example, in *Ward v London CC*[30] the driver of a fire engine was held to have been negligent in driving through a red traffic light.

Common practice

5–014   Failure to conform to a common practice of taking safety precautions is strong evidence of negligence because it suggests that the defendant did not do what others in the community regard as reasonable. It must be remembered, however, that such a failure is not conclusive evidence of negligence. This is because the claimant must also prove that the failure to adopt the safety precautions in question was the *cause* of his or her loss. Thus, in *Brown v Rolls Royce Ltd*,[31] the plaintiff contracted dermatitis from contact with grease during the course of her work. She claimed that this was caused by the negligence of her employers, who had not supplied a barrier cream which was commonly supplied by other employers to people doing the same type of work. However, whilst it was the common practice to use this cream, there was conflicting evidence about its efficacy. The plaintiff's action failed because she could not prove that, had the defendants supplied the cream, it would have prevented her from contracting dermatitis.

Conversely, where it can be shown that the defendant *has* complied with a common practice in relation to safety precautions, this is very good evidence that the defendant has not been negligent. Again, however, such evidence cannot be regarded as conclusive. This is because a particular course of conduct may be negligent despite its being common practice. As Lord Tomlin succinctly put it in *Bank of Montreal v Dominion Gresham*: "Neglect of duty does not cease by repetition to be neglect of duty".[32] The question of common practice assumes enormous significance in cases involving professional negligence and is discussed more fully in that context later in this chapter.

[29] [1954] 1 W.L.R. 835.
[30] [1938] 2 All E.R. 341. See also *Nelson v Chief Constable of Cumbria* [2000] C.L.Y. 4217.
[31] [1960] 1 W.L.R. 210.
[32] [1930] A.C. 659 at 666.

The "Learned Hand" test

It is clear that in deciding breach of duty, the courts "balance" all of the factors we have considered above. In *United States v Carroll Towing Co*,[33] an American case, Learned Hand J. provided a useful insight into the way the courts may perform this "balancing act" in some cases. He suggested that some of the factors relevant to breach of duty might be given a notional statistical value, so that the problem could be approached in a quasi-mathematical way. Taking B as the "burden of taking precautions", P as the "probability that the risk will materialise", and L as the "loss which will occur if the risk does materialise", one can express the courts' approach in terms of two "equations":

$$B < P \times L = \text{Liability}$$
$$B > P \times L = \text{No Liability}$$

Expressed in words, these "equations" mean that, where the "burden" on the defendant (in terms of taking precautions) *is less than* the notional value achieved by multiplying the "probability" and the "loss", the court will be likely to find the defendant liable. Conversely, where the "burden" on the defendant *is greater than* the product of the "probability" and the "loss", a finding of no liability is likely.

We can see how these "equations" might work by analysing two cases—*Bolton v Stone* and *The Wagon Mound (No. 2)*. In *Bolton*, a finding of no liability resulted from the fact that a low value could be given to the probability of the risk materialising (six times in 30 years) and a relatively low value could be given to the loss in question (at worst, injury of one individual). The burden on the defendants (giving up cricket) could be given a high value. By contrast, in *The Wagon Mound (No. 2)*, whilst the probability of the risk materialising could also be given a low value, the loss in question (at worst, the complete destruction of Sydney Harbour) would have to be given a relatively high value, whilst the slight burden on the defendants (retaining the oil onboard ship) would obviously be given a very low value. Thus, a finding of liability resulted.

SPECIAL STANDARDS OF CARE

There are certain types of defendant to whom additional special rules apply in determining the standard of care required of them. These are:

- children;
- defendants acting in an emergency;
- defendants engaged in sport;
- defendants claiming to have special or professional skill.

In this section, we consider the standard of care required of the first three of these special types of defendant. The standard of care required of professionals warrants more lengthy discussion and is dealt with in a later section.

5–015

5–016

---

[33] 159 F. 2d 169 (1947).

Children

5–017   The conduct of a child defendant is judged by reference to the standard of conduct that can be expected of a reasonable child of the defendant's own age. For many years, there was no English authority on the point, but it was assumed that the courts would adopt the reasoning of Kitto J. in the Australian case of *McHale v Watson*.[34] Here, the defendant was a 12-year-old boy. He threw a sharp rod which ricocheted off a post and hit a nine-year-old girl. The High Court of Australia declined to apply the standard of the "reasonable person" to cases involving children, and applied a lower standard which was appropriate to the defendant's age. Applying that standard, it was held that the boy was not negligent. It should be noted, however, that the standard of care applied to children remains an objective one. As Kitto J. remarked: "It is no answer for [a child], any more than it is for an adult to say that the harm he caused was due to his being abnormally slow-witted, quick tempered, absent minded or inexperienced".

In England, the same approach was adopted by the Court of Appeal in *Mullin v Richards*.[35] Here, the defendant and the plaintiff were 15–year-old schoolgirls. They were fencing with plastic rulers during a lesson, when one of the rulers snapped and a piece of plastic flew into the plaintiff's eye, causing blindness. It was held that the proper test to apply was whether an ordinarily careful and reasonable 15–year-old would have foreseen that the game carried a risk of injury. On the facts, the injury was held to be not reasonably foreseeable by such a child—the game was common and the girls had never been warned that it could be dangerous.

Defendants acting in an emergency

5–018   Where the defendant is forced to act quickly "in the heat of the moment", the standard of care is relaxed to take account of the exigencies of the situation. This was established long ago in the case of *Jones v Boyce*[36] (a case concerned with contributory negligence). Here, the issue was whether a passenger on a coach had acted reasonably when, thinking that the coach was about to overturn, he jumped off in order to save himself, breaking his leg. The jury found in the man's favour, Lord Ellenborough C.J. having directed them that the man was not guilty of negligence just because he had selected the more perilous of two alternatives with which he was confronted in an emergency. It made no difference that, with the benefit of hindsight, it was obvious the man had made the wrong decision.

A more modern example of the principle is the case of *Ng Chun Pui v Lee Chuen Tat*.[37] Here, the defendant was driving a coach on a dual carriageway when another vehicle cut in front of him without warning, forcing him to brake suddenly. The coach swerved and skidded across the central reservation, where it collided with a bus travelling in the opposite direction, injuring the plaintiffs, who were passengers on the bus. The Privy Council held that the driver's actions had been reasonable, given the emergency with which he was faced.

[34] [1966] A.L.R. 513.
[35] [1998] 1 W.L.R. 1304. *Mullin v Richards* was applied in *Etheridge v K* [1999] Ed. C.R. 550 where a teacher was injured by a basketball thrown by a 13 year-old boy.
[36] (1816) 1 Stark. 493.
[37] [1988] R.T.R. 298.

It appears from the decision in *Marshall v Osmond*[38] that where the police are chasing a suspected criminal, this may count as an emergency situation. Here, the plaintiff, a suspect, was injured when a police car drew up alongside the car from which he was attempting to run away. It was held that in these circumstances the actions of the police could not be judged by the same standard of care that would apply had there been time for reflection. This decision, however, should be compared with *Rigby v Chief Constable of Northamptonshire*.[39] Here, the police were held liable for fire damage to the plaintiff's shop when they fired a canister of CS gas into the shop to flush out a dangerous psychopath. The nature of the situation did not justify the police's failure to ensure that fire-fighting equipment was at hand.

Participants in sport

It is clear that those engaged in sport owe a duty of care both to other competitors in the sporting event and to spectators. The courts have recognised, however, that a participant in sporting activity is in a similar position to a person faced with an emergency, in the sense that he or she may have to take a decision in the heat of the moment. The required standard of care takes account of this.   5–019

In the well-known case of *Wooldridge v Sumner*,[40] the Court of Appeal laid down a test for the sporting standard of care that meant that a participant in sport would only be liable to spectators if he or she had "acted in reckless disregard of the spectators' safety". This test, however, was subjected to severe academic criticism on the basis that the need to show "recklessness" seemed too favourable to the defendant. The courts appear to have responded to this criticism. Thus, in *Wilks v Cheltenham Cycle Club*,[41] the Court of Appeal applied the test suggested by Professor Goodhart in his commentary on *Wooldridge*, namely that there was negligence if injury was caused "by an error of judgment that a reasonable competitor, being the reasonable man of the sporting world, would not have made".[42] Applying this test, it was held that the defendant, a participant in a motorcycle scramble, was not negligent when his bike left the course and hit a spectator. The standard of care would be adjusted to take account of the fact that a competitor could reasonably be expected to "go all out to win", even if this meant exposing others to some risk. This did not mean, however, that it was acceptable for a competitor to expose others to danger by conduct that was "foolhardy".[43]

It is clear that the mere fact that a competitor has broken the rules of a game will not, of itself, provide a conclusive indication of negligence. This point is illustrated by the decision of the Court of Appeal in *Caldwell v Maguire*.[44] The claimant, a professional jockey, was injured when the defendants, two other jockeys, rode in such a

---

[38] [1983] Q.B. 1034. Compare *Nelson v Chief Constable of Cumbria* [2000] C.L.Y. 4217 (police driver *causing a crash* to be judged by the same standard as an ordinary driver unless in a situation of pursuit at speed).
[39] [1985] 1 W.L.R. 1242.
[40] [1963] 2 Q.B. 43.
[41] [1971] 1 W.L.R. 668.
[42] Goodhart (1962) 78 L.Q.R. 490 at 496.
[43] *per* Lord Denning M.R. at p.670. Compare the behaviour of the defendant in *Condon v Basi* [1985] 1 W.L.R 866 who was liable for a rugby tackle made in a "reckless and dangerous manner".
[44] [2001] EWCA Civ 1054; [2002] P.I.Q.R. P6.

way as to cause an accident. The defendants' conduct was investigated by the Jockey Club and found to amount to "careless riding" in breach of its rules. However, the Court of Appeal drew a distinction between a finding of carelessness by a regulatory body and a finding of negligence by a court of law. In the circumstances, it was not possible to characterise the defendants' momentary carelessness as negligence.

Where referees put competitors at risk by failing to enforce the rules of the game, they may be liable where this causes injury to the competitors. Thus, in *Vowles v Evans*[45] a rugby referee was held liable when a player was injured by a scrummage collapsing in circumstances where the referee should not have allowed the game to continue with contestable scrummages after the substitution of an untrained player. The court was careful to point out, however, that the threshold of referee liability should be a high one, and that the standard of care expected of referees depended on all the circumstances of the case. One of those circumstances was the nature of the game. Thus, in a fast-moving game, a referee could not be expected to avoid some oversight and error of judgment when supervising the game. Moreover, the standard of care demanded of a referee would depend on the grade of the referee and the level of the game in question. In other words, rather than apply the usual objective standard of care, the law would adopt the unusual practice of adjusting the standard of care in the light of the referee's qualifications. Clearly, the Court of Appeal thought that this approach was necessary so as not to discourage amateurs from volunteering as referees.

The Professional Standard of Care

5–020   In this section, we consider the standard of care demanded of people who, by following a particular trade or profession, hold themselves out as having special skills. In relation to such people, the question of breach of duty is decided by applying the so-called "*Bolam* test".

The *Bolam* test

5–021   The case of *Bolam v Friern Hospital Management Committee*[46] (the facts of which we shall discuss later) confirmed the application of two important principles, which can be summarised as follows:

- Where the defendant purports to have a special skill, the defendant's conduct is judged according to the standard of a reasonable person having the skill the defendant claims to possess. It is not judged by the standard of the reasonable lay person.

- The law will not regard a professional defendant as having fallen below the required standard of care if it is shown that the defendant's conduct is regarded

---

[45] [2003] 1 W.L.R. 1607. See also *Smolden v Whitworth* [1997] P.I.Q.R. P 133.
[46] [1957] 1 W.L.R. 582.

as proper by one responsible body of professional opinion. (Even though some other members of the defendant's profession may think the conduct is negligent.)

It is convenient to explore each principle in turn.

The standard of the "reasonable skilled person"

This first element of the "*Bolam* test" is straightforward. The obvious point here is that the law expects a member of a trade or profession to live up to the standard of an ordinary skilled member of the trade or profession in question. As McNair J. put it in *Bolam*:

5–022

> "Where you get a situation which involves the use of some special skill or competence, then the test as to whether there has been negligence or not is not the test of the man on the top of the Clapham omnibus, because he has not got this special skill. The test is the standard of the ordinary skilled man exercising and professing to have that special skill."[47]

Accordingly, the law will not judge a surgeon performing an operation by the standard of a reasonable lay person performing that operation (to do so would be absurd) but by the standard of the "reasonable surgeon". Although most cases of interest in this area concern allegations of medical negligence, it should be remembered that the relevant principles apply equally in other contexts. Thus, a lawyer is judged by the standard of a "reasonable lawyer", an accountant by the standard of a "reasonable accountant", and so on. Similarly, in *Gates v McKenna*,[48] Paul McKenna, the well-known stage hypnotist, was judged by the standard of a "reasonably careful exponent of stage hypnotism".

It is important to note that the relevant issue is not whether the defendant is in fact a member of a trade or profession, but whether, in all the circumstances, by undertaking a particular task, the defendant has held himself or herself out as possessing a trade or professional skill. There are cases, however, where the fact that the defendant is *not* a member of a relevant trade or profession has been seen as important in determining whether the defendant has held himself or herself out as possessing a particular level of skill. In *Philips v William Whitely Ltd*,[49] for example, it was held that the plaintiff, who had had her ears pierced by the defendants, who were jewellers, could not expect them to exercise the same degree of care and skill that would be exercised by a qualified surgeon. Similarly, in *Wells v Cooper*,[50] where the plaintiff suffered injury when a door handle came off in his hand, it was held that, although householders who decide to carry out work on their property involving carpentry skills must achieve the standards of a reasonably competent amateur carpenter, the safety of their work was not to be judged by reference to the contractual obligations that might be owed by a professional carpenter working for reward, since this would be too high a standard.[51]

---

[47] [1957] 1 W.L.R. 586.
[48] [1998] Lloyd's Rep. Med. 405.
[49] [1938] 1 All E.R. 566.
[50] [1958] 2 Q.B. 265.
[51] *ibid., per* Jenkins L.J. at 271.

In *Wilsher v Essex Area Health Authority*[52] it was confirmed that the standard of care to be expected from a professionally qualified defendant is to be determined by considering the nature of his or her "post" and the tasks which it involves. The professional standard of care is objective in the sense that the same standard of care will be required of all professionals holding the same "post". In *Wilsher*, therefore, where a number of medical professionals professed expertise in the care of premature babies, the Court of Appeal held that each of them could be expected to exercise a degree of care and skill appropriate to the tasks usually undertaken by a person holding his or her post. The defendant's "post" was to be distinguished from the defendant's "rank" or "status". This meant that, where a junior doctor was filling a "post" involving the performance of tasks more usually undertaken by someone more senior, the junior doctor would be judged by exactly the same standards as a senior doctor. Dealing with the argument that this placed too great a burden on young doctors, Mustill L.J. commented:

"To my mind, it would be a false step to subordinate the legitimate expectation of the patient that he will receive from each person concerned with his care a degree of skill appropriate to the task which he undertakes, to an understandable wish to minimise the psychological and financial pressures on hard-pressed young doctors."[53]

The apparent harshness of this rule, however, is mitigated to some extent by the Court of Appeal's assertion in *Wilsher* that where an inexperienced doctor is called upon to perform a task in which he or she lacks expertise, it is sufficient for the doctor to discharge the duty of care to the patient if he or she seeks and acts on the advice of a more senior colleague.

In this context, it should also be noted that a doctor or other professional may, in certain circumstances, discharge the duty of care by simply refusing to act. In certain professions, the position is straightforward. Barristers, for example, have a professional duty to decline cases that are beyond their competence. In the context of the medical profession, however, the position is more complicated. Junior doctors on duty in casualty departments, for example, cannot, without breaching their duty of care, decline to treat patients whose conditions call for expertise they do not possess. On the other hand, it is clear that a general practitioner, unskilled in open heart surgery, can and should decline to perform that task.

The relevance of common practice and professional opinion

5–023   The second element of the *"Bolam* test"—namely that a professional will escape liability if his or her conduct accords with *one* view of responsible common practice—has proved controversial. Before considering the nature of this controversy, it is useful to explore the facts of *Bolam*, which neatly illustrate the problem which this part of the test was designed to solve.

Mr Bolam was a mental patient suffering from acute depression. One of the accepted forms of treatment for this condition was (and still is today) to administer

[52] [1987] Q.B. 730. The facts of *Wilsher* are considered in Ch. 6. The case eventually went to the House of Lords and is important in the context of causation.
[53] *ibid.*, at 751.

electro-convulsive therapy (ECT). The treatment involves the patient being given a brief but severe electric shock. An unfortunate side effect, however, is that the shock causes muscle spasms. These can sometimes be of such magnitude as to break the patient's bones. Mr Bolam suffered a fractured pelvis during a bout of ECT treatment. He contended that the doctor who administered the treatment had been negligent in a number of respects. First, he argued that he should have been given relaxant drugs prior to the treatment. Secondly, he argued that a restraining sheet should have been used to hold him down whilst the shock was being given. His third argument related not to the way in which the treatment was administered, but to the doctor's failure to warn him of the danger of broken bones so that he could decide for himself whether or not to undergo the treatment. (The issue of whether doctors have a duty to disclose the risks of treatment is considered in more detail later.)

At the trial, the expert evidence given showed a marked difference of opinion within the medical profession as to the correct procedure for administering E.C.T. It became clear that some doctors favoured relaxant drugs, whilst others preferred not to use them because they could depress the respiratory system, causing the patient to stop breathing. Whilst some doctors favoured restraining sheets, others preferred to leave the limbs free during the treatment (as the doctor in this case had done), arguing that if bones were trapped under a sheet, they were, in fact, more likely to break.

In summing up the case for the jury (the case was decided when juries were used in negligence trials), McNair J. pointed out that ECT was a "progressive science", on which responsible medical opinion differed. His Lordship stated that, according to the law, a doctor will not be liable in negligence if, "he has acted in accordance with a practice accepted as proper by a responsible body of medical men skilled in that particular art". He went on to say that a professional person would not be liable "merely because there is a body of opinion which would take a contrary view".[54] Unsurprisingly, in the light of this direction, the jury in *Bolam* returned a verdict in favour of the defendant doctor.

The controversial aspect of the approach taken in *Bolam*, which has been followed in subsequent cases, is that, to a great extent, it allows the professions to be "self-regulating"—if the conduct required of a doctor is to be determined, not by a judge, but by evidence of what some other doctors do, then it can be argued that doctors are not truly answerable to their patients through the courts, because they are allowed to set their own standards of care.[55] We shall see, however, that there are limits to the extent to which doctors and other professionals can place themselves "above the law" in this way. These limits were re-affirmed by the House of Lords in the important case of *Bolitho v City and Hackney Health Authority*.[56] Nevertheless, the "*Bolam* test" makes it very difficult for a claimant to prove negligence against a professional person.

It is important to recognise that the "*Bolam* test" means that a judge is not normally permitted to substitute his or her own views for the views of the defendant's responsible expert witnesses. In other words, even though a judge, as a lay person in medical (or other professional) terms, may strongly prefer a form of practice advocated by the claimant's expert witnesses, and may instinctively feel that the

---

[54] *Bolam v Friern Hospital Management Committee* [1957] 1 W.L.R 582 at 587–588.
[55] See Grubb [1988] C.L.J. 12.
[56] [1998] A.C. 232.

defendant's way of doing things was wrong, he or she must resist the temptation to choose between two competing "responsible" schools of professional thought.

This point is clearly illustrated by *Maynard v West Midlands Health Authority*.[57] Here, the defendants carried out a diagnostic procedure, in the nature of a biopsy, on the plaintiff's throat. The procedure was performed with all due care and skill, but it carried a small risk of damage to the vocal chords. This risk materialised, and the plaintiff brought a negligence action alleging that the biopsy had been unnecessary. The defendants contended that they had acted properly in deciding to perform the procedure, because it was required in order to exclude the possibility (albeit remote) that the plaintiff was suffering from Hodgkin's Disease. The trial judge preferred the view of the plaintiff's experts—who would have waited for the results of blood tests to come through instead of carrying out a biopsy—and held the defendants liable. His Lordship's judgment, however, was overruled by the Court of Appeal and the House of Lords. Lord Scarman said: "a judge's 'preference' for one body of distinguished professional opinion to another also professionally distinguished is not sufficient to establish negligence in a practitioner".

The practical result of Lord Scarman's approach, then, is that it is extremely difficult for a claimant to prove professional negligence—he or she must effectively show that no responsible body of professional opinion would have supported what the defendant did. Whilst showing this may be difficult, however, it is not always impossible. This is because the cases have repeatedly made it clear that a judge is only obliged to accept the views of the defendant's experts if those views are "responsible".

The limits of the "Bolam principle"

5–024   As we have already noted, the fact that the defendant has conformed with common practice cannot be regarded as *conclusive* evidence that he or she has met the standard of care, because the common practice in question may itself be negligent. Thus, in *Edward Wong Finance Co. Ltd v Johnson, Stokes & Master*,[58] the Privy Council held that a conveyancing practice which involved a risk to the client was negligent, despite its widespread adoption by the legal profession in Hong Kong. The courts clearly have a part to play in setting standards of professional conduct. Were it otherwise, certain professionals might persist with outdated or clearly indefensible practices, and escape justice by saying that are only doing what some other professionals do. This would amount to an abuse of their position in society.

In *Bolam* itself, McNair J. made it clear that, "mere personal belief that a particular technique is best is no defence unless that belief is based on reasonable grounds".[59] His Lordship went on to explain that it had long been the law, for example, that a doctor who obstinately refused to use anaesthetics or antiseptics could not escape liability simply by calling as witnesses colleagues who took a similarly stubborn and irrational view. More recently, in *Bolitho v City and Hackney Health Authority*,[60] Lord Browne-Wilkinson, delivering the opinion of a unanimous House of Lords, took the opportunity to clarify the circumstances in which a court was entitled to reject the professional opinions of the defendant's experts.

---

[57] [1984] 1 W.L.R. 634. It is important to distinguish this type of case from a case such as *Penney v East Kent Health Authority* [2000] Lloyd's Rep. Med. 41 where the expert witnesses agree that the defendant's conduct was wrong but give conflicting opinions about whether it is "excusable". See de Prez (2001) 17 P.N. 75.
[58] [1984] A.C. 1269.
[59] *Bolam v Friern Hospital Management Committee* [1957] 1 W.L.R 582 at 587.
[60] [1998] A.C. 232.

Bolitho is a rather complicated case, because it involves issues of causation as well as issues of breach of duty. It is further considered in Ch. 6. For present purposes it is sufficient to note that the case concerned a two-year-old boy who was admitted to hospital suffering from breathing difficulties. In the events which happened, the boy suffered cardiac arrest leading to brain damage, and his mother brought a negligence action on his behalf. One of the questions for the court was whether the doctor in charge should have intubated the child (put a tube down his throat to assist his breathing) or whether, given the boy's symptoms, she would have been justified in taking no such action. At the trial, the judge heard evidence from eight different experts. Five of them (called for the plaintiff) said that, in the circumstances, any competent doctor should have intubated the boy. Three of them (called for the defendant doctor) said that intubation would not have been appropriate, and referred to the fact that intubation carried a very small risk of injuring the child's throat. The trial judge held that the doctor was not liable. Although, having listened to the experts, as a lay person he felt persuaded that intubation would have been the right course of action, he felt bound to hold that the defendant escaped liability because her failure to intubate was endorsed by *one* responsible body of medical opinion. To hold otherwise would amount to substituting his own views for the views of the defendant's expert witnesses, and the "*Bolam* test" did not allow him to do this.

The House of Lords confirmed the judge's approach as correct. What is important to note, however, is that Lord Browne-Wilkinson made it clear that in some circumstances a judge *would* be entitled to reject the opinions of professional experts, if he or she felt that their opinions had no *logical basis*. Thus, where (as in this case) the expert evidence was concerned with the question of weighing up the risks presented by different forms of treatment, the experts, in order to have their evidence accepted, had to show that they had directed their minds to this question and had reached a conclusion that was logically defensible.

On one view, it can be argued that Lord Browne-Wilkinson's approach entails a slight modification of the "*Bolam* test". That is to say, whilst McNair J. had made it clear in *Bolam* that expert evidence could be rejected if *the person giving it* was not "responsible", *Bolitho* now makes it clear that expert evidence, even when given by a responsible and respected expert, can be rejected *if the evidence itself* is not "responsible", in the sense that it does not withstand logical analysis. The distinction between the credibility of the evidence and the credibility of the person giving it is, of course, an extremely fine one. This point did not escape Lord Browne-Wilkinson, who thought that, in most cases, the fact that an opinion was held by a responsible medical expert would, in itself, demonstrate that the opinion was a reasonable one. His Lordship was careful to point out that, this being the case, it would be only in very rare cases that a judge would be justified in rejecting professional expert opinion as unreasonable.

Lord Browne-Wilkinson went on to conclude that the case before him was not, in fact, one of these rare cases. On the facts of *Bolitho*, the trial judge had been right in accepting the defendant's expert evidence, because the experts had given a logical justification for their opinion that intubating the child was not appropriate—namely that intubation involved a small risk of injury. Accordingly, because the defendant doctor's failure to intubate had been endorsed by one body of reasonable medical thought, she escaped liability.

It is clear from *Bolitho*, then, that a doctor cannot escape liability for his or her conduct unless that conduct has a rational justification. But the limits of this rule remain untested.[61] In particular, one thorny problem remains to be directly addressed by the courts: suppose the defendant's experts say that he or she was justified in withholding a very expensive drug from a patient, on the basis that it is common medical practice to have regard to budgetary constraints in administering treatment. Would a judge be entitled to reject this view because, in the words of Lord Browne-Wilkinson, it "does not withstand logical analysis"?[62]

Disclosure of the risks of treatment

5–025   Here, we consider the extent to which the standard of care expected of doctors requires them to disclose to a patient the risks of treatment, so that the patient can make an informed choice about whether to consent to that treatment. (It will be recalled that this was one of the issues in *Bolam*.) Where the treatment in question involves physical contact (as opposed to taking a drug orally, for example), absence of consent on the part of the patient may render the doctor liable in the tort of battery. This issue is discussed in Ch. 11, where we shall see that so long as the claimant has given consent to the procedure in broad terms, no action in battery will lie. Here, we are concerned with liability in negligence.

The leading case is the House of Lords decision in *Sidaway v Bethlem Royal Hospital Governors*.[63] The plaintiff, who was suffering from pain in her neck and shoulders, was advised by her surgeon to have an operation on her back. The surgeon did not warn her that there was a very small risk (around 1 per cent) of damage being done to her spine, due to the fact that he would be operating within less than three millimetres of her spinal cord. The plaintiff consented to the operation and it was performed with all due care and skill. But the risk of injury materialised, leaving the plaintiff disabled. She claimed that the surgeon had been negligent in failing to tell her about the risk, and that had she known about it, she would not have agreed to the operation.

The House of Lords (Lord Scarman dissenting) held that the surgeon was not liable. Lords Diplock and Bridge, who gave the leading speeches for the majority, both thought that the "*Bolam* test" applied in this context. Accordingly, because the surgeon had conformed with a responsible body of medical opinion which would not have disclosed the risk, he escaped liability. Lord Bridge was careful to point out, however, that the decision did not amount to handing over to the medical profession complete control over the practice of disclosure. His Lordship said that a judge, ". . . might in certain circumstances come to the conclusion that disclosure of a particular risk was so obviously necessary to an informed choice on the part of the patient that no reasonably prudent medical man would fail to make it".[64] As an example of the type of

obiter →

---

[61] See, however, *Wisniewski v Central Manchester Health Authority* [1998] P.I.Q.R. P324, where the Court of Appeal rejected a finding by the trial judge that because the defendant's witness failed to give oral evidence at the trial, his view was not logically supported.
[62] Note that in *Hucks v Cole* (1968) (1993) 4 Med. L.R. 393 the court was prepared to say that the relatively *low* cost of administering penicillin to prevent septicaemia was a relevant reason for rejecting the defendant's evidence that it was reasonable not to administer the drug—but this, of course, is a slightly different issue.
[63] [1985] A.C. 871.
[64] *ibid.*, at 900.

case he had in mind, Lord Bridge referred to an operation involving "a substantial risk of grave adverse consequences, as for example the 10 per cent risk of a stroke".

In *Sidaway*, then, the majority declined to adopt a strict doctrine of "informed consent". The reasons for this refusal were clearly enunciated by Lord Bridge:

> "The doctor cannot set out to educate the patient to his own standard of medical knowledge of all the relevant factors involved. He may take the view, certainly with some patients, that the very fact of his volunteering, without being asked, information of some remote risk involved in the treatment proposed, even though he describes it as remote, may lead to that risk assuming an undue significance in the patient's calculations."[65]

According to the majority in *Sidaway*, then, it is for doctors to decide whether, and how much, information to reveal to a patient, having regard to the best interests of the particular patient. Lord Scarman, however, took a different view. His Lordship thought that the question of disclosure should be decided by the courts, using an objective test. On Lord Scarman's view, doctors should be placed under a duty to disclose all "material" risks, and the question for the judge (in deciding whether a risk was "material") would be whether or not a reasonable person in the patient's position would be likely to attach significance to the risk. If the answer to this question was "yes", then a doctor who failed to disclose that risk would be in breach of duty.

Lords Bridge and Templeman, in *Sidaway*, placed great emphasis on the fact that Mrs Sidaway had not specifically asked the surgeon about the risks of the operation. Lord Bridge thought that, in a case where a doctor was questioned specifically by the ← obiter dicta. patient, the doctor would be obliged to answer "both truthfully and as fully as the questioner requires".[66] This principle was applied in *Chester v Afshar*.[67] The claimant, who was considering an operation on her spine, specifically asked her consultant about the risks inherent the operation. The defendant was held to be in breach of duty when, instead of explaining that the operation carried a small but inherent risk, he merely gave the light-hearted reply: "Well, I have never crippled anybody yet".

Policy issues in medical negligence cases

It is possible to discern a number of policy considerations underlying the decisions we **5–026** have examined in this section. First, the courts are concerned that their decisions should not encourage the practice of "defensive medicine", *i.e.* medical care which involves a "belt and braces" approach to treating patients, motivated by the desire to avoid negligence liability. There is some concern in the United States that doctors are adopting this sort of approach, which is not always in the best interests of the patient.

In *Whitehouse v Jordan*,[68] Lord Denning M.R., in the Court of Appeal, warned of the dangers of following the American example. The case involved an allegation of

---

[65] *Sidaway v Bethlem Royal Hospital Governors* [1985] A.C. 871 at 899.
[66] *ibid.*, at 898.
[67] [2002] 3 All E.R. 552.
[68] [1980] 1 All E.R. 650, CA. The decision was subsequently upheld by the House of Lords at [1981] 1 W.L.R. 246.

negligence against a senior registrar who, it was argued, had wrongly persisted in delivering a baby by forceps when a Caesarean section was called for. In holding the defendant not liable, Lord Denning M.R. expressed the view that if too high a standard of care were demanded of doctors, experienced practitioners might refuse to treat certain patients, and young people might be deterred from entering the medical profession because of the high insurance premiums that would be required to meet professional negligence claims.

In the factual context of *Whitehouse v Jordan*, the gist of Lord Denning's argument is that a finding of liability might have led doctors to "err on the side of caution" when delivering babies, and opt for Caesarean section, even where this was not in the best interests of the mother or the child. It should also be noted that the practice of "defensive medicine" is expensive, because it requires the administration of "precautionary" tests and treatments to exclude remote risks. The courts' attempts to contain the scope of liability for medical negligence may reflect concern about the proper allocation of scarce NHS resources.

The second policy issue to note is that the courts may be anxious not to encourage a "culture of litigation" in medical cases, because of the harm that unjustified allegations of negligence can do to a defendant's reputation. It was noted in Ch. 1 that a professional person's fear of having his or her reputation tarnished by a negligence action may serve as a deterrent to negligent conduct. But it must be remembered that, because many people may take the view that there is "no smoke without fire", a professional's reputation may be unjustly tarnished by a mere allegation of negligence, even though the professional is eventually absolved of fault.

This problem was recognised by Kilner Brown J. in *Ashcroft v Mersey Regional Health Authority*.[69] Here, an allegation was made against a much respected senior surgeon, who had carried out an operation on the plaintiff's inner ear involving a small risk of injury to her facial nerve. This injury materialised despite his having performed the operation with all due care and skill. In holding him not liable, Kilner Brown J. stated the case for no-fault compensation in cases of medical mishap. His Lordship observed:

> ". . . this claim reveals a disgraceful state of affairs. Where an injury is caused which never should have been caused, common sense and natural justice indicate that some degree of compensation ought to be paid by someone. As the law stands, in order to obtain compensation an injured person is compelled to allege negligence against a surgeon who may, as in this case, be a careful, dedicated person of the highest skill and reputation. If ever there was a case in which some reasonable compromise was called for, which would provide some amount of solace for the injured person and avoid the pillorying of a distinguished surgeon, this was such a case."[70]

PROOF OF BREACH

5–027   Although the claimant bears the burden of proving breach of duty, there are certain circumstances in which special rules will assist in discharging this burden.

---

[69] [1983] 2 All E.R. 245, affirmed on appeal [1985] 2 All E.R. 96.
[70] [1983] 2 All E.R. 245 at 246.

Civil Evidence Act 1968

Section 11(1) of the Civil Evidence Act 1968 provides that, in a civil trial, proof that a person has been convicted of a criminal offence shall be taken as proof that he or she committed the offence, unless the contrary is proved. What this means in the context of a negligence trial is that, if the claimant shows that the defendant has been convicted of an offence arising out of the same facts as those in issue at the trial, the burden of proof is reversed, so that the defendant will have to disprove negligence. Thus, in *Wauchope v Mordecai*,[71] the plaintiff was injured by being knocked off his bicycle when the defendant suddenly opened the door of a parked car. The defendant was convicted of an offence arising out of the incident. The Court of Appeal held that the effect of s.11 of the 1968 Act was to shift the burden of proof to the defendant. Since the defendant had failed to prove that he had *not* been negligent, the trial judge had been wrong to dismiss the plaintiff's case on a finding that the plaintiff had not proved negligence.

5–028

Res ipsa loquitur

The maxim *res ipsa loquitur* means "the thing speaks for itself". Where the maxim applies, the court is prepared to draw an inference that the defendant has been negligent without requiring the claimant to bring evidence about the precise way in which the negligence occurred. This idea originates from the judgment of Erle C.J. in *Scott v London and St Katherine Docks Co.*,[72] a case which provides a good example of when the maxim will apply.

5–029

The plaintiff was passing the defendants' warehouse when six bags of sugar, which were being hoisted by the defendant's crane, fell on him. The plaintiff could not prove *how and why* this happened—the only thing he could prove was that the bags fell and caused him injury. It was held, however, that these facts were sufficient to give rise to an inference of negligence. Bags of sugar do not usually fall from a crane unless someone *has* been negligent, so the fact of negligence "spoke for itself". Since the defendants had failed to provide an innocent explanation of how the incident had occurred, they were held liable.

When does the maxim apply?

There are three conditions which must be satisfied before *res ipsa loquitur* can apply:

5–030

(1) The occurrence must be one that will not normally happen without negligence
This requirement was clearly met on the facts of *Scott v London and St Katherine Docks*—there was no obvious alternative explanation why the bags fell off the crane. Similarly, in *Byrne v Boodle*[73] the maxim was held to apply when a barrel of flour fell on the plaintiff as he was passing underneath the defendant's window. The cases in which the requirement has been met are many and varied. In *Chapronière v Mason*[74], for example, the court was prepared to infer negligence when a stone was found in a

---

[71] [1970] 1 W.L.R. 317.
[72] (1865) 3 H. & C. 596.
[73] (1863) 2 H. & C. 722.
[74] (1905) 21 T.L.R. 633.

bun, and in *Ward v Tesco Stores Ltd*,[75] negligence was inferred when the plaintiff slipped on a spillage of yoghurt on a supermarket floor, which the defendants had failed to clean up.

As the reliability of machines has improved, the courts have become increasingly willing to conclude that accidents involving machines are more probably due to the negligence of their operators than to mechanical failure. Thus, the courts have been willing to invoke the maxim in road traffic cases where cars skid,[76] or veer on to the pavement[77] or into the opposite carriageway.[78] In a medical context, *res ipsa loquitur* has been applied, for example, to a case where a surgeon left a swab inside a patient's body.[79] It has also been applied in the context of failed treatment. Thus, in *Cassidy v Ministry of Health*,[80] as Denning L.J. put it, the plaintiff was entitled to say: "I went into hospital to be cured of two stiff fingers. I have come out with four stiff fingers and my hand is useless. That should not happen if due care had been used. Explain it if you can".

(2) The defendant must have control of the thing which causes the harm

5–031   This requirement can be illustrated by comparing two cases involving railway accidents. In *Gee v Metropolitan Railway*,[81] the plaintiff was injured when he fell out of an underground train, having leaned against a door. Because the train had only just left the station, it could be inferred that the defendants, who clearly had a duty to see that the door was closed before the train departed, had been in control of the door at the time it flew open. By contrast, in *Easson v London and North Eastern Ry. Co.*,[82] where a four year-old boy fell through an unsecured train door, it was held that *res ipsa loquitur* did not apply. At the time of the accident, the train was seven miles beyond its last stopping place. In these circumstances, although the accident *might* have been due to the defendants' negligence, it was not appropriate to infer that it was, because the door might have been opened by a passenger, rather than by one of the defendants' employees.

(3) The cause of the occurrence must be unknown to the claimant

5–032   This requirement is not of any great practical significance. All it means is that, where the facts are sufficiently known, there is no need to invoke the maxim because the claimant can prove what actually happened. Thus, in *Bolton v Stone*,[83] the maxim was held to have no application, because it was obvious that the cricket ball must have been hit over the fence by the batsman. In *Barkway v South Wales Transport Co. Ltd*,[84] where a burst tyre on a bus caused an accident, it was held that the maxim should not be applied. There was some evidence that the bus company might have prevented the accident if it had told its drivers to report incidents involving blown tyres, and it had failed to do so. Accordingly, the plaintiff was required to investigate this issue, rather than rely on *res ipsa loquitur*.

[75] [1976] 1 W.L.R. 810. Applied in *Dobson v Asda Stores* [2002] C.L.Y. 4551.
[76] *Richley v Faull* [1965] 1 W.L.R. 1454.
[77] *Ellor v Selfridge & Co. Ltd* (1930) 46 T.L.R. 236.
[78] *Ng Chun Pui v Lee Chuen Tat* [1988] R.T.R. 298.
[79] *Mahon v Osborne* [1939] 2 K.B. 14.
[80] [1951] 2 K.B. 343 at 365.
[81] (1873) L.R. 8 Q.B. 161.
[82] [1944] 2 K.B. 421.
[83] [1951] A.C. 850
[84] [1950] 1 All E.R. 392.

What is the effect of the maxim?

There has been some debate about whether the effect of *res ipsa loquitur* is to reverse   **5–033**
the legal burden of proof, or whether it places only an *evidential* burden on the
defendant to rebut the inference of negligence.[85] In most cases, the point is of little
practical importance, but in one circumstance it may be significant. Suppose that, after
hearing the defendant's explanation, the judge finds that the balance of probabilities is
equal as between a negligent and an innocent explanation of the occurrence in
question. Who should win the case? If the effect of the maxim is to reverse the legal
burden of proof, the claimant should win, because the defendant has not proved, on
the balance of probabilities, that he or she has *not* been negligent. On the other hand,
if the burden of proof stays with the claimant, the defendant should win, unless the
claimant can adduce further evidence to tip the scales in his or her favour.

In *Colvilles Ltd v Devine*,[86] Lord Donovan in the House of Lords said that the maxim
had no effect on the legal burden of proof. However, a year later, the House of Lords
appeared to take a different approach in the case of *Henderson v Henry E. Jenkins &
Sons*.[87] Here, the plaintiff's husband was killed when the brakes of the defendants'
lorry failed. The failure was caused by corrosion of a brake fluid pipe. In answer to the
plaintiff's claim of *res ipsa loquitur*, the defendants gave evidence that they had
maintained the lorry in accordance with common practice. They had had the lorry
regularly inspected, but the pipe in question could only be fully inspected by removing
it from the lorry, and this was not recommended by the manufacturers until the lorry
had done a certain mileage. In spite of this, the House of Lords held that the
defendants had failed to rebut the inference of negligence—they should have gone on
to show that there was nothing in the history of the lorry that would have caused
abnormal corrosion and required a special inspection. Thus, although the point was
not entirely clear, their Lordships appeared to say that it was for the *defendants* to
prove that they were *not* negligent. As Lord Pearson put it, the defendants lost the case
because "their answer was incomplete".[88]

More recently, however, in *Ng Chun Pui v Lee Chuen Tat*,[89] the Privy Council has
reasserted that in *res ipsa loquitur* cases the burden of proof does not switch to the
defendant. Here, a coach veered across a central reservation into the opposite
carriageway, where it collided with oncoming traffic. This fact alone would have
justified a finding of negligence, so the plaintiff called no evidence. The defendants,
however, explained that a car had suddenly cut across the driver's path, causing him to
brake suddenly and skid. In the light of this explanation, the Privy Council held that
there could be no inference of negligence, because the driver's actions in such an
emergency had not been negligent. What is important is that, rather than saying that
the defendants *had discharged the burden of proof*, their Lordships said, in effect, that
the explanation had tilted the balance of probabilities against the plaintiff. The burden
of proof remained with the plaintiff, who was entitled to bring further evidence to
show that the defendants had been negligent. But since he could not do so, he lost the

---

[85] See, *e.g.* P.S. Atiyah (1972) 35 M.L.R. 337.
[86] [1969] 1 W.L.R. 475.
[87] [1970] A.C. 282. A similar approach was taken by the Court of Appeal in *Ward v Tesco Stores Ltd* [1976] 1
W.L.R. 810.
[88] [1970] A.C. 282 at 303.
[89] [1988] R.T.R. 298.

case. Lord Griffiths, delivering the opinion of the Privy Council, said that it was misleading to talk of the burden of proof shifting to the defendant in a *res ipsa loquitur* situation. The burden of proving negligence rests throughout the case on the plaintiff. Although *Ng Chun Pui v Lee Chuen Tat* is a Privy Council decision, and therefore not technically binding, it is probable that this approach will be followed in future cases.

Breach of duty: conclusion

5-034   We have seen that breach of duty is in most respects a relatively straightforward element of the tort of negligence, but one where policy nevertheless plays an important part in the courts' decisions. In Chs 7 and 8, we shall explore breach of duty again in the specific contexts of employers' liability and occupiers' liability. First, however, it is appropriate to examine two further elements of the tort of negligence, namely causation and remoteness.

Chapter 6

CAUSATION AND REMOTENESS

Introduction

This chapter deals with the question of whether the defendant's actions can be said to be the legal cause of a claimant's loss. Essentially, in answering this question, two separate issues need to be considered. First, there is the issue of whether what the defendant did was the *factual cause* of the defendant's loss (or whether the loss was caused by something else). Secondly, there is the issue of whether, in certain cases, although the claimant's loss is the factual result of the defendant's actions, the law should nevertheless say that the defendant is not liable because that loss is too "remote"—in the sense that it is too unusual or "far removed" a consequence of the defendant's actions. We explore each of these issues in turn.

6–001

FACTUAL CAUSATION

Factual causation is a difficult subject. It divides into a number of separate issues, but there is a considerable degree of conceptual overlap between these issues. Often, when a court focuses on one particular issue, it is merely selecting one particular approach from a number of alternatives. In some cases, a number of approaches are adopted concurrently, and it may be difficult to classify a given case as turning on one issue rather than another.[1] The root of all the confusion is the difficult nature of causation as a philosophical problem. We begin by examining this problem and noting, in general terms, the law's response to it.

6–002

The Pragmatic Approach

The relationship between "cause" and "effect" is complex. Philosophically speaking, every "effect" is produced by the coming together of many different "causes". Moreover, all of these "causes" will, in truth, themselves be "effects" produced by

6–003

---

[1] For more detailed discussion of causation, see Hart and Honoré, *Causation in the Law* (2nd ed., Oxford: Clarendon Press, 1985).

other "causes". Take an example: I light a cigarette and carelessly discard my lighted match in your waste paper basket, which results in a fire burning down your house. Who is to blame? Legally speaking, the answer is pretty obvious—it is my carelessness that has caused the fire. But philosophically speaking, the fire has many causes. A philosopher might say that there are many "conditions" without which the fire might not have happened. It might not have happened had you not allowed the waste paper basket to become so full with paper. It certainly would not have happened without your inviting me to your house in the first place, and allowing me to smoke there. Do these factors mean that you are the cause of your own loss? Alternatively, we might say that there would have been no fire if I were not an addicted smoker. Therefore, can we not blame the person who offered me my first cigarette? Ultimately, if I had not been born, your house would not have burned down. Does this mean we can blame my parents? How about fixing the blame on my distant ancestors? Clearly, the law cannot take a philosophical approach to causation. If it did, nobody could ever be said to have caused *anything*. Defendants could always "pass the buck", or, as a lawyer might say, fix responsibility on a person or an event further back in the "chain of causation". Therefore, the law takes a pragmatic, or "common sense" view of causation. As Lord Wright put it, in *Yorkshire Dale Steamship Co. Ltd v. Minister of War Transport*: "Causation is to be understood as the man in the street, and not as either the scientist or the metaphysician, would understand it".[2] But this approach, of course, can leave us in a position where the reasoning in the cases defies analysis in terms of logical principle. Another unfortunate consequence of the "common sense" approach is that, in causation cases, legal language is particularly apt to produce confusion. For example, judges and writers may say that a defendant is not liable unless he has "caused" the damage; on the other hand, they may say that a defendant is not liable for all of the damage that he has "caused". Qualifying the word "cause" with adjectives such as "legal", "proximate" or "remote" does little to unravel the mysteries of the topic.[3]

In most cases, the application of the "man in the street" approach reveals that there is only one activity or event that can be sensibly regarded as the cause of the claimant's loss, so the issue is straightforward. In a small minority of cases, however, the law must somehow choose between two or more competing causes of the claimant's loss. These problematic cases are the focus of this chapter. We shall consider them once we have examined in more detail the test the courts apply in straightforward cases.

The "but for" test

6–004   The law's starting point in determining causation is to apply the "but for" test.[4] In other words, to ask the question, "Can it be said that 'but for' the defendant's conduct, the claimant's loss would not have occurred?" Another way of putting this is to ask, "Would the claimant's loss have occurred *in any event*, even without the defendant's conduct?" If the answer to this question is "yes", then the defendant will not have caused the claimant's loss. The classic illustration of the application of the "but for"

[2] [1942] A.C. 691 at 706.
[3] Hepple, Howarth and Mathews, *Tort: Cases and Materials* (5th ed., Butterworths, 2000) p.345.
[4] *Cork v Kirby MacLean Ltd* [1952] 2 All E.R. 402.

test is the case of *Barnett v. Chelsea and Kensington Hospital Management Committee*.[5] Here, a man went to a casualty department feeling unwell after having drunk some tea. The doctor in charge sent him away without treatment, telling him to see his own doctor. He subsequently died from arsenic poisoning. It was held that the doctor was in breach of his duty of care in failing to examine the man, but expert evidence indicated that, having drunk the arsenic, the man was beyond help when he arrived at the hospital and would have died in any event. Therefore, the doctor's breach of duty had not caused the man's death.

In applying the "but for" test, the courts take into account not only *existing* causes that might have produced the claimant's loss (for example, the arsenic in *Barnett*), but also *hypothetical* causes that might have produced the loss. For example, in *McWilliams v. Sir William Arrol Ltd*,[6] a steel erector fell to his death at work. The defendants were in breach of their statutory duty in failing to provide him with a safety harness, but the evidence was that he had rarely used such a harness in the past. In the House of Lords, the defendants successfully argued that this meant he would not have worn a harness even if one had been provided. This being the case, it followed that the defendants were not liable because the man would probably have died in any event.

Bolitho v. City and Hackney Health Authority[7] (considered in Ch. 5) was another case in which the House of Lords had to consider the causal effect of a hypothetical omission. Here, a two-year-old boy was admitted to hospital suffering from breathing difficulties and was kept under observation. His condition deteriorated and on two occasions a nurse contacted the doctor in charge, asking her to attend, but she failed to do so. The child subsequently suffered cardiac arrest leading to brain damage. The doctor had clearly been negligent in failing to attend, but the doctor argued that her non-attendance had not caused the child's death. She maintained that, given the child's symptoms, even if she had attended and examined the child, she would not have taken any action, but would have left the child for a further period of observation. The plaintiff countered this argument by saying that such a course of action would have been negligent—given the symptoms, a competent doctor should have "intubated" (inserted a tube) to assist the child's breathing.

As was noted in Ch. 5, the House of Lords held that the doctor's failure to intubate would not have been negligent, because her reasons for not doing so were supported by a body of responsible medical opinion. What is relevant here, however, is to note that in deciding the question of causation, the House of Lords was prepared to ask not simply, "Would the doctor have intubated if she had attended?", but "*Should* the doctor have intubated in such circumstances?" As Lord Browne-Wilkinson put it: "A defendant [who is in breach of duty] cannot escape liability by saying that the damage would have occurred in any event because he would have committed some other breach of duty thereafter."[8]

---

[5] [1969] 1 Q.B. 428.
[6] [1962] 1 All E.R. 623.
[7] [1998] A.C. 232. For further discussion of *Bolitho*, see Giliker (1998–99) 9 K.C.L.J. 109 and Scott (1998) 148 N.L.J. 64.
[8] *Bolitho v City and Hackney Health Authority* [1998] A.C. 232 at 240.

Problems with the "but for" test

6–005 The "but for" test works well enough in the majority of cases, but in cases where there are "multiple causes" it runs into problems. The celebrated example is that of two fires—Fire A and Fire B—both started negligently on different pieces of neighbouring land, which each are capable of burning down the claimant's house.[9] The fires converge and destroy the house. If the claimant sues the creator of Fire A, the creator of Fire A can argue that the loss would have happened in any event, because of the existence of Fire B. If the creator of Fire B is sued, he can employ a similar argument. Thus, applying the "but for" test, neither defendant is liable. It is doubtful that the courts would countenance such an unjust result. They would (probably) treat the case as one involving "cumulative causes" (discussed below), making both defendants jointly liable for the full extent of the damage.[10]

In the sections below, we consider the courts' approach to different types of cases involving multiple causes. It is traditional to classify such cases under a number of headings. But this classification, and the traditional accompanying analysis of the various "rules" governing each class of case, can give the misleading impression that causation is a rather "technical" or "evidential" branch of the law, in which policy plays only a minor role. It should not be forgotten that, as in other areas of tort law, the rules are flexible. We shall see that they have often been stretched to accommodate policy concerns. Indeed, they have sometimes been stretched so far that they cease to withstand clear analysis.

CONCURRENT CAUSES

6–006 Certain cases are traditionally described as involving "concurrent causes", by which is meant simply that the causes in question occur more or less simultaneously, as opposed to one after another. As a means of classification, the expression is rather inadequate, because, as we shall see, it might equally be applied to certain cases traditionally described as involving "consecutive causes", in which the causes occur at different times but their *effects* operate at the same time. Nevertheless, it is traditional to consider the so-called "concurrent cause" cases separately.

"Concurrent cause" cases can be divided into two groups, as follows:

"Indeterminate cause"

6–007 In these cases, there is more than one defendant, but there is only one "operative cause" of the claimant's loss, it being unclear which of the defendants' acts produced this cause. Such is the case, for example, where a claimant has *one* bullet in his leg, but several defendants have been negligent in shooting their guns in the claimant's direction. (As in *Cook v Lewis* and *Summers v Tice*, considered below.)

"Cumulative cause"

6–008 In these cases, there is more than one "operative cause" of the claimant's loss, each produced by the act of a different defendant, but the problem is, these causes have combined inextricably to produce the same damage. Such is the case, for example,

---

[9] See P. Cane, *Atiyah's Accidents, Compensation and the Law* (6th ed., Butterworths, 1999), p.95.
[10] Alternatively, the courts might apportion liability equally between the two defendants.

where a claimant has *two* bullets in his leg, each fired by a different defendant, and as a result of this predicament has to have his leg amputated.

We consider each type of case in turn.

"Indeterminate Cause"

The relevant principles here can be understood by considering the Canadian case of **6–009** *Cook v Lewis*[11] and the American case of *Summers v Tice*.[12] Both cases involved hunting accidents in which the plaintiff had been shot by *one* bullet, fired by one of two defendants, each of whom had been careless in aiming his gun in the plaintiff's direction. The evidence could not establish from whose gun the shot had been fired. The courts adopted the pragmatic approach of reversing the burden of proof. Thus, in the absence of evidence from either defendant that he had *not* been responsible for the bullet, both defendants were held liable as joint tortfeasors. Joint tortfeasors are each potentially liable for the whole of the claimant's loss. Each defendant can then seek a contribution from the other, but that is a separate question relating to damages rather than to liability (see Ch. 15). A similar approach was adopted by the House of Lords in *Fairchild v Glenhaven Funeral Services Ltd.*[13] (discussed later under the heading "proof of causation"). Here, the claimants contracted mesothelioma, a disease that might have been caused by contact with a single fibre of asbestos. It was impossible to determine which of the defendant employers had exposed the claimants to the fibre(s) in question. Their Lordships therefore made all the employers liable for the full amount of the claimants' losses. It is clear, however, that this approach will only be adopted in special circumstances, where considerations of policy and justice demand that the "but for" test should be relaxed. This issue is examined more fully in a later section.

In *Sindell v Abbott Laboratories*,[14] another American case, the court adopted a more radical solution. The case concerned the liability of manufacturers for a defective pregnancy drug which caused cancer in the female children of mothers who had taken it. The problem did not become apparent until the children had reached puberty and it was then impossible to show which of several hundred manufacturers had produced the particular drug taken by the plaintiffs' mothers. It was known, however, that the drug was inherently defective, so that any one of the manufacturers could have been responsible. The court rejected the solution of imposing joint liability, as in *Summers v Tice*, because only a few of those potentially responsible were defendants before the court and it was unfair to make them responsible to the full extent. Instead, the court held each defendant liable according to the degree of its share of the market for the drug at the relevant time, on the basis that this was the best approximation that could be made of each defendant's likely responsibility.

In the cases discussed above, the courts had to decide which of two human actions produced the claimant's loss. The solutions adopted in these cases, however, have not been favoured by the English courts in cases where the fault of one defendant is

[11] [1951] S.C.R. 830.
[12] 119 P.2d 1 (1948).
[13] [2003] 1 A.C. 32.
[14] 607 P.2d 924 (1980).

competing with one or more "innocent" or "natural" explanations for the claimant's loss. The leading authorities here are *Wilsher v Essex Area Health Authority*[15] and *Hotson v East Berkshire Area Health Authority*.[16] In these cases, the courts have not been prepared to make a defendant liable unless the claimant can show that, on the balance of probabilities, his or her loss was caused by the defendant's fault rather than by a natural occurrence. In such cases, the standard of proof required of the claimant assumes enormous significance. For this reason, these cases are worthy of separate consideration and are discussed in a later section of this chapter, under the heading "proof of causation".

"Cumulative cause"

6–010   We have already considered a good example of a "cumulative cause" situation—that of two negligently started fires, each capable of burning down the claimant's house, which converge and destroy the house. We have noted that in such situations, applying the "but for" test would result in neither defendant being liable. Therefore, the usual approach of the courts is to say that, because either negligent act would have produced the same damage, each defendant is liable for the whole of the damage.[17] This is what happened in *The Koursk*,[18] where two ships collided because both were simultaneously subject to negligent navigation.

In the example above, we have made the assumption that the act of one defendant alone would have given rise to the whole of the damage. If we cast aside this assumption, however, we are left with a slightly different and more complex type of "cumulative cause" case. This is the sort of case where one defendant (the "first defendant") commits a tortious act, and then, very shortly afterwards, and before the force of that act is spent, a second defendant commits an act which *combines* with it, producing a single result that might not have occurred without the operation of the second act. In such cases, both the first and the second defendant may be liable for the result produced. Take an example: negligent driver A causes his vehicle to obstruct the highway, and subsequently negligent driver B crashes into it, causing injury to a bystander, C. Here, driver A may be held to have caused C's injuries, and may be jointly liable with driver B.[19] This is so, even though it cannot be said that driver A's negligence alone would have caused the accident.

One of the best known examples of this type of "cumulative cause" case is *Fitzgerald v. Lane*.[20] Here, the plaintiff was crossing a pelican crossing when the lights showed green for cars, but red for pedestrians. He was hit by a car driven negligently by the first defendant. The force of the collision threw him up on the bonnet and propelled

---

[15] [1988] A.C. 1074.

[16] [1987] A.C. 750.

[17] Note, however, that where the evidence shows that one defendant is more responsible than another, the court will apportion liability between them in proportion to their fault. See *Holtby v Brigham & Cowan (Hull) Ltd* [2000] 3 All E.R. 421 and *Allen v British Rail Engineering Ltd* [2001] I.C.R. 942.

[18] [1924] P. 140.

[19] See *Rouse v Squires* [1973] Q.B. 889, *per* Cairns L.J. at 898, but see also *Wright v Lodge* [1993] 4 All E.R. 299 (discussed below) for a restriction on the application of this principle, namely that subsequent "reckless" conduct by the second driver will exculpate the first driver.

[20] [1987] Q.B. 781, CA. There was an appeal to the House of Lords, but only on the question of apportionment of damages, which is discussed in Ch. 15.

him into the middle of the road. He was then hit by a car driven negligently by the second defendant. He suffered severe injuries to his spine resulting in tetraplegia. At the trial, the evidence could not establish whether his tetraplegia resulted from impact with the first car or from impact with the second car. Moreover, it was impossible to say whether the tetraplegia had only one (indeterminate) cause, or whether it was the result of the combined effect of being hit by both cars. It was clear, however, that the plaintiff had himself been careless in crossing when the lights were against him. The judge held that all three parties involved had been negligent and that, since it was impossible to say that one of the parties was more or less to blame than the other, the responsibility should be borne equally by all three. Therefore, both defendants were held liable and the plaintiff was held contributorily negligent.

In *Fitzgerald v. Lane*, one of the reasons why the first driver was held liable was that his negligence had exposed the plaintiff to a risk of further damage. This sort of reasoning, however, has not found favour with the courts in commercial cases involving economic loss. Consider *South Australia Asset Management Corp. v. York Montague Ltd.*[21] Here, the House of Lords heard three consolidated appeals. In each, the defendants were surveyors who had been asked by the plaintiffs to value property, on the security of which the plaintiffs were proposing to lend money. The surveyors negligently overvalued the property, and, on the strength of their statements, the plaintiffs made loans which they would not have made if they had known the true value of the property. In the first appeal, for example, the surveyors stated that the property was worth £15 million when in fact it was worth only £5 million, and the plaintiffs advanced a loan of £11 million. When the debtors defaulted, the plaintiffs sought to recover their money by selling the property, but, of course, they could not realise the full amount of the money they had lent. In fact, they only managed to sell the property for £2,477,000.

The question for the House of Lords was whether the *total amount* of the shortfall—*i.e.* the difference between the £2,477,000 recovered and the £11 million lent—had been caused by the defendants' negligence. The issue was problematic because there had been a fall in the property market in the period between the negligent valuation and the subsequent sale. This meant that the defendants could argue that, whilst the difference between £11 million and £5 million might be their fault, the *additional* shortfall had been caused not by their negligence, but by the fall in the property market. In reply, the plaintiffs argued that they would not have been exposed to the market falls at all if they had known the property's true value, because they would not have made the loans. Thus, applying the "but for" test, the defendants ought to be liable for the additional shortfall. The House of Lords rejected this argument, however, holding that the defendants' liability was limited to the difference between the amount of the negligent over-valuation and the actual value of the property at the time of the valuation—the additional loss was attributable solely to another cause, namely the collapse of the property market.

It should be noted, however, that Lord Hoffmann, who delivered the opinion of the House of Lords in the *York Montague* case, appeared to regard the question of causation as inseparable from the question of the scope of the duty of care owed by the defendants. Thus, in the final analysis, the defendants could not be liable because they

[21] [1997] A.C. 191.

had only undertaken to provide the plaintiffs with *information* as to the value of the properties, not *advice* as to the wisdom of acting on that information.[22] The risk of the market was not something against which the imposition of the duty of care was designed to guard. Thus, the result in the case might be explained equally in terms of absence of duty or absence of causation.

CONSECUTIVE CAUSES

6–011 In so-called "consecutive cause" cases, the key issue is whether, where one act succeeds another, there are circumstances where the effect of the first act can be said to have become "overtaken" or "obliterated" by the effect of the second act, in such a way that the first act ceases to be a cause of the claimant's loss. The classic illustration of this sort of situation is this: Imagine that a man is about to set out on a journey across the desert. He has a lethal dose of poison put into his water bottle by one of his enemies. Later, the bottle is emptied by a second enemy. Ignorant of these events, he sets out on his journey during the course of which he dies of thirst.

Now, in theory we might absolve the second enemy by pointing to the fact that, if the water bottle had not been emptied, the man would have died in any event from poison. But we could also absolve the poisoner by pointing out that, if the water had not been poisoned, the man would still have died of thirst. Thus, applying the "but for" test makes nobody liable. This sort of situation, however, is different from the example of the converging fires, where the law, unable to determine which action caused the loss, may make both actors liable. Here, the factual cause of the traveller's death is clear—he died of thirst and not of poison. In cases of this sort, then, we might say that the effect of the poisoner's act was "overtaken" or "obliterated" by the act of the second enemy. In other words, in the light of what the second enemy did, the act of the poisoner had no effect.

Situations like that in the example above, however, must be distinguished from cases where the effect of the first wrongful act is said to continue, in spite of the effect of the second. Such was the case in *Performance Cars v Abraham*.[23] The plaintiff's Rolls-Royce was involved in two collisions in the space of a fortnight. After the first collision, the car was in need of a respray. It was then hit by a second driver (the defendant), sustaining the sort of damage that would also necessitate a respray. In an action against the second driver, the Court of Appeal rejected the owner's claim for the cost of a respray on the grounds that the loss did not flow from the defendant's wrongdoing—at the time of the second collision, the vehicle was already in need of a respray. Here, then, rather than saying that effect of the first tort was obliterated by the second, the court applied exactly the opposite sort of reasoning: the second tort had no effect, given the continuing effect of the first.

Broadly similar reasoning was applied by the House of Lords in *Baker v Willoughby*.[24] The plaintiff was run down by the defendant's negligent driving, suffering a stiff leg which caused him loss of mobility and a consequent reduction in his earning

[22] [1997] A.C. 214.
[23] [1962] 1 Q.B. 33.
[24] [1970] A.C. 467.

capacity. Before the action came to trial, the plaintiff was shot in the same leg by armed robbers, after which the leg had to be amputated. The defendant driver argued that his liability should be limited to the loss caused by the original injury up to the date of the robbery—any loss of mobility and reduction in earning capacity thereafter had been caused, not by him, but by the amputation of the leg. In other words, it was argued that the effect of the original injury had been submerged or obliterated by the second. The defendant also argued that, because, in assessing the amount of damages, it is the courts' practice to discount the award to take account of the hypothetical "vicissitudes of life" that a claimant may suffer in the future, it followed that where these "vicissitudes" had become *actual*, the damages should be reduced accordingly.

The House of Lords rejected these arguments. Treating the case as one where the plaintiff's continuing loss of amenity had *concurrent* causes, Lord Reid, speaking for the majority, held the defendant liable for *all* of the consequences of the first injury, just as if the second injury had not occurred. In Lord Pearson's view, this result was necessary in order to avoid "manifest injustice" and could be achieved by taking a "comprehensive and unitary view of the damage caused by the original accident".[25] In other words, as Lord Reid put it: "A man is not compensated for the physical injury: he is compensated for the loss which he suffers as a result of that injury".[26] Because the second injury had not diminished the loss the plaintiff would continue to suffer, it could not be regarded as having "submerged" or "obliterated" the effects of the first injury.

Their Lordships were influenced by the need to do practical justice. The thieves who had shot the plaintiff could not be found, and even if they could be found and sued in tort, it would be unlikely that they would be able to pay compensation. Moreover, if the thieves were sued in tort, they would be entitled to "take their victim as they found him". This meant that they could not be liable for the whole of the plaintiff's loss of amenity, but only for the extent to which they had made his condition worse. In this light, it would be very unfair to say that the first tortfeasor could not be fully liable either, because this would leave the plaintiff under-compensated. He would "fall between two defendants". Policy therefore dictated that a first tortfeasor should remain liable for the continuing effects of his or her tort, even where a second tort produced the same (or worse) effects.

The decision in *Baker v Willoughby* should be contrasted with that in *Jobling v Associated Dairies Ltd*.[27] In *Jobling*, the defendant employers had been responsible for injuring the plaintiff's back, causing him loss of mobility and reduced earning capacity. Before the action came to trial, the plaintiff succumbed to a crippling back disease, completely unrelated to his accident, which rendered him totally unfit for work. As in *Baker*, the House of Lords had to decide whether, in the light of a supervening event giving rise to the same loss, the defendants could remain liable for the plaintiff's reduced earning capacity in the future. Here, however, the supervening event in question was a disease rather than a tort. Their Lordships reached the opposite conclusion from that in *Baker*. Taking account of the aim of an award of damages, their Lordships held that the plaintiff would be over-compensated if he were able to

---

[25] [1970] A.C. 496.
[26] *ibid.*, at 492.
[27] [1982] A.C. 794.

recover from the defendants. It was held, therefore, that the defendants' liability ceased at the time of the onset of the disease.

In *Jobling*, Lord Bridge felt unable to accept the approach that had been adopted in *Baker*. His Lordship pointed out that the decision in *Baker* appeared to ignore the fundamental principle that the aim of a damages award in tort is to put the claimant in the same position he or she would have been in had the tort not occurred. On Lord Bridge's analysis of *Baker*, it could be said that, had the first tort not occurred, the plaintiff would have suffered the same sort of loss *in any event* when he was shot by the thieves. Thus, the outcome of the decision was one which actually put him in a *better* position than he would have been in had the first tort never occurred.[28] Arguably, however, on the facts of *Baker*, this analysis is not entirely accurate: the only reason why the plaintiff happened to be where he was when he was shot—sorting scrap metal in a yard—was that he was forced to accept such a menial job by the first tortfeasor's negligence, which had rendered him unfit for other types of work. But for the first tort, therefore, he might never have been shot.

Lord Edmund-Davies, acknowledging academic criticism of the decision in *Baker*,[29] pointed out that the decision had appeared to overlook the fact that the plaintiff could be compensated under the Criminal Injuries Compensation Scheme in respect of the actions of the thieves. This meant that the "injustice" the decision sought to avoid "did not, at least in its full dimensions, exist".[30] Both Lord Edmund-Davies and Lord Wilberforce thought that the decision in *Baker* could not be properly analysed in terms of legal principle and that the case had been decided on policy grounds. Lord Edmund-Davies concluded:

> "My Lords, it is a truism that cases of cumulative causation of damage can present problems of great complexity. I can formulate no convincing juristic or logical principles supportive of the decision of this House in *Baker v. Willoughby*, and none were there propounded."[31]

Although, in *Jobling*, their Lordships criticised the decision in *Baker*, they were not prepared to overrule it and accepted that the case might have been correctly decided on its facts. Lords Keith and Russell drew a distinction between a supervening illness, which would obliterate the effect of a previous tortious act, and a supervening tort, which might not.[32] This distinction is hard to justify. At bottom, it must be admitted that the decisions in *Baker* and in *Jobling* cannot be satisfactorily reconciled. The decisions show us that the answers to causation questions are heavily dependent on a pragmatic, policy-driven approach.

PROOF OF CAUSATION

6–012   In this section we are concerned with the difficult question of how, in cases where the defendant's conduct competes with other possible explanations of the claimant's loss, the courts approach the question of requiring the claimant to *prove* that the claimant's

---

[28] [1982] A.C. 820.
[29] See Atiyah (1969) 85 L.Q.R. 475.
[30] *Jobling v Associated Dairies* [1982] A.C. 794 at 807.
[31] *ibid.*, at 808.
[32] In *Heil v Rankin* [2001] P.I.Q.R. 3 the Court of Appeal affirmed that there was no absolute rule that the effect of a supervening tort would obliterate the effect of a previous tort.

breach is the cause of his or her loss. The nature of the approach the courts will take depends on the type of case with which they are concerned, and here, again, we can see that the courts' decisions seem heavily influenced by policy considerations. Two very different approaches can be discerned, each of which is supported by a number of House of Lords decisions. These two approaches may be described as:

- the "all or nothing" approach;
- the "material increase in risk" approach.

Like the different approaches taken in *Jobling* and *Baker*, which we have just examined, the two approaches in the "proof of causation" cases are not possible to reconcile with one another on the basis of coherent principle. Each is simply a pragmatic response to what the courts perceive as the broad demands of justice in particular circumstances.

The "all or nothing" approach

The "all or nothing" approach is the approach that will be applied in most cases. It   **6–013** takes as its starting point the proposition that the claimant, who bears the burden of proof in a civil trial, must discharge that burden by meeting the normal civil standard of proof. Thus, the claimant must show that, on the balance of probabilities, it was the claimant's breach (rather than some other event) that caused the loss. This is known as an "all or nothing" approach because, where a claimant succeeds in showing that it is probable (at least 51 per cent likely) that the breach caused the loss, the law will treat this probability as a certainty, so the claimant will win the case and recover in respect of *all* of his or her loss. If, on the other hand, a claimant can only show, say, a 25 per cent likelihood that the breach caused the loss, he or she will lose the case and leave court with nothing. The approach is exemplified by the decisions of the House of Lords in *Hotson* v. *East Berkshire Area Health Authority*[33] and *Wilsher* v. *Essex Area Health Authority*,[34] both of which were cases where medical negligence was alleged to be the cause of the plaintiffs' loss.

In *Hotson*, the plaintiff, when aged 13, fell while climbing a tree and sustained injury to his hip. He was taken to hospital, but his injury was not correctly diagnosed or treated for five days. In the event, he suffered avascular necrosis—a condition that left him with severe and permanent disability by the time he was 20. Had the hospital treated him promptly when he was first admitted, the plaintiff would have had a 25 per cent chance of making a full recovery, but the effect of the delay in treatment was that the plaintiff lost that 25 per cent chance.

The trial judge (Simon Brown J.) awarded the plaintiff a sum in damages which reflected 25 per cent of the damages which might have been awarded had the hospital's negligence been the only possible cause of his disability. This decision was affirmed by the Court of Appeal, but was reversed by the House of Lords. The key finding of the House of Lords was that the plaintiff had failed to prove his case on the

---

[33] [1987] A.C. 750.
[34] [1988] A.C. 1074.

balance of probabilities. Simon Brown J., assessing the medical evidence, had found, of course, that there had been a 75 per cent chance that avascular necrosis would have resulted *in any event*, even if the plaintiff had been treated promptly. This meant, in their Lordships' view, that on the balance of probabilities the plaintiff's disability had been caused when he fell out of the tree. In these circumstances, Simon Brown J. had been wrong to embark on a "quantification" of the loss caused by the defendant—the issue of quantifying the loss could only arise once the hurdle of causation had been overcome, and this the plaintiff had failed to do.

Whilst their Lordships did not rule out the possibility that damages in medical negligence cases could sometimes be awarded for "loss of a chance" (discussed in a separate section below) they did not think that the circumstances of *Hotson* warranted such an approach. This was because the evidence as to when the plaintiff's disability occurred was clear—when he fell from the tree, he was, on the balance of probabilities, disabled; the law would treat this probability as a factual certainty, which meant that, by the time the plaintiff arrived at the hospital he was *as a matter of decided fact* already disabled. Thus, in effect, at this point in time the plaintiff had had no chance to lose.

In *Wilsher v Essex Area Health Authority* the plaintiff was a premature baby who suffered from oxygen deficiency. In monitoring the levels of oxygen in his blood, one of the doctors employed by the defendants negligently failed to notice that a catheter had been wrongly placed into a vein instead of an artery. This meant that the monitoring equipment gave a misleading reading, resulting in the plaintiff being given too much oxygen. The plaintiff developed retrolental fibroplasia (RLF)—a condition permanently affecting his retina—which left him almost totally blind. The expert evidence suggested that excess oxygen was a *possible* cause of RLF. But RLF was a condition that occurred even in premature babies who did not receive oxygen, and there was a causal link between RLF and at least five conditions that were very common in premature babies.

The trial judge and the Court of Appeal (relying on the House of Lords' decision in *McGhee v National Coal Board*—discussed below) had held the defendants liable on the basis that, by supplying excess oxygen, they had "materially increased the risk" that the plaintiff would succumb to RLF. The House of Lords, however, rejected this liberal approach to causation and substituted the "all or nothing" approach, holding that the plaintiff had failed to establish, on the balance of probabilities, that his RLF had been produced by the excess oxygen, rather than by one of the five other possible common causes of RLF. Lord Bridge, who delivered the unanimous opinion of the House of Lords, acknowledged that the application of the "all or nothing" approach had produced a harsh result for the plaintiff. His Lordship said:

"Many may feel that [ordering a retrial] serves only to highlight the shortcomings of a system in which the victim of some grievous misfortune will recover substantial compensation or none at all according to the unpredictable hazards of the forensic process. But, whether we like it or not, the law, which only Parliament can change, requires proof of fault causing damage as the basis of liability in tort. We should do society nothing but disservice if we made the forensic process still more unpredictable and hazardous by distorting the law to accommodate the exigencies of what may seem hard cases."[35]

[35] [1988] A.C. 1092.

Despite Lord Bridge's assertion that the "all or nothing" approach should not be displaced to accommodate "hard cases", this is precisely what appears to have happened in the two cases we examine next—*McGhee* and *Fairchild*. Both of these cases concern the liability of employers for industrial disease, and in both the House of Lords was prepared to relax the strict requirements of the "all or nothing" approach in order to produce what was perceived as a just result.

The "material increase in risk" approach

In *McGhee* v. *National Coal Board*,[36] the plaintiff contracted the skin disease dermatitis   **6–014** from the presence of abrasive brick dust on his skin. Some exposure to brick dust was an inevitable part of his job—he worked in brick kilns. It was accepted that the defendants were not negligent in exposing him to brick dust during his working day. The plaintiff's argument, however, was that because no washing facilities were provided at his place of work, throughout his working life he had had to cycle home each day with his skin coated with the dust. He argued that, without this additional and unnecessary exposure to the dust, he would not have contracted dermatitis. The defendants admitted that they had been negligent in failing to provide washing facilities, but they argued that their negligence was not the cause of the plaintiff's disease. The medical evidence established that exposure to brick dust caused dermatitis, but the experts were unable to say that, on the balance of probabilities, the *additional* negligent exposure to brick dust had been the cause of plaintiff's condition—it might have occurred in any event, given that he was daily exposed to the "innocent" dust.

The House of Lords held the defendants liable. Their Lordships did not expect the plaintiff to establish, on the balance of probabilities, that the absence of washing facilities was the *actual cause* of his dermatitis. It was sufficient that, by failing to provide washing facilities, the defendants had "materially increased the risk" of the plaintiff contracting the disease. Their Lordships justified this conclusion in different ways. Thus, at the time *McGhee* was decided, it was not altogether clear what the *ratio* of the case was, or in what other factual circumstances its liberal approach to proof of causation might apply. According to Lord Wilberforce, in *McGhee*, the outcome was dictated by policy. The defendants, by their negligence, had created a risk of a particular kind of damage, and when damage of that very kind materialised, they should not be allowed to escape liability because of the claimant's "evidential difficulties" in proving causation. In appropriate cases, where such difficulties became apparent they should, as a matter of policy and justice, be borne by the person who created the risk. As his Lordship put it:

> ". . . it is a sound principle that where a person has, by breach of a duty of care, created a risk, and injury occurs within the area of that risk, the loss should be borne by him unless he shows that it had some other cause."[37]

The logical objection to Lord Wilberforce's approach, of course, was that it appeared to ignore the fundamental principle that the claimant must prove his case. There was

---

[36] [1973] 1 W.L.R. 1. For a detailed and entertaining account of the case, see Lord Hope of Craighead, (2003) 63 C.L.J. 587.

[37] [1973] 1 W.L.R. 1 at 6.

really no evidence to suggest that the plaintiff's damage materialised "within the area of risk" created by the defendants' negligence. (It might have materialised within the area of risk created by his doing his job, for which it was accepted that the defendants could not be liable.) Clearly, Lord Wilberforce's attempt to elide what were, in fact, two distinct "areas of risk" owed much to the broad policy consideration that, as a matter of justice, large employers should be made to compensate their employees for all injuries and diseases occurring in the workplace.

When the House of Lords came to decide *Wilsher*, Lord Bridge, no doubt mindful of this logical objection, sought to explain the decision in *McGhee* by saying that the case had "laid down no new principle of law whatever"—on a proper interpretation, it was simply a case where their Lordships had, in the light of the evidence, felt able to draw a "legitimate inference of fact",[38] namely that the absence of washing facilities had *actually been one of the causes* contributing to the plaintiff's dermatitis. In *Fairchild v Glenhaven Funeral Services Ltd*,[39] however, the House of Lords rejected this explanation of *McGhee*, stating that there had been no evidence in the case from which their Lordships could have legitimately inferred that the defendant's conduct was an *actual cause* of the dermatitis—all the defendants had done was to create an *increased risk* of dermatitis. Accordingly, the decision in *McGhee* should indeed be seen as having laid down a new principle of law, namely that, in appropriate cases, a claimant will succeed by merely establishing a "material increase in risk".

The approach in *McGhee* was followed in *Fairchild v Glenhaven Funeral Services Ltd*. This was a case concerning a number of claimants who had contracted mesothelioma (a lung tumor) as a result of exposure to asbestos, over a lifetime of work for different employers. All the employers admitted they were in breach of their duty of care to protect the claimants against exposure to asbestos. The problem for the claimants, however, was that they could not establish which of their different employers had exposed them to the particular asbestos that had caused their disease. The medical evidence was that the disease did not necessarily build up gradually with continued exposure to asbestos, but could be triggered suddenly at any time, perhaps by one single fibre causing a cell to become malignant. It followed that, while all the employers could be said to have increased the *risk* of mesothelioma, it was not possible to say that all of them had been responsible for *cumulatively causing* the disease. And, of course, it was not possible to say which of them had been responsible for the particular fibre(s) that had suddenly triggered the disease.

The solution adopted by the House of Lords was to make all of the employers liable, on the basis that each had increased the risk of mesothelioma, without requiring the claimants to prove which of the employers had been responsible for causing it. Each employer was made liable for the total amount of the claimants' loss (they could then seek to determine, between themselves, how much each should pay).[40] Their Lordships affirmed the principle laid down in *McGhee* that, in appropriate cases, merely

---

[38] [1988] 1 A.C. 1074 at 1090.
[39] [2003] 1 A.C. 32.
[40] See also *Barker v Saint Gobain Pipelines plc* [2004] EWCA Civ 545. (*Fairchild* applied even where exposure was due to the negligence of the claimant's employers and of himself during a substantial period of self-employment.) Their Lordships in *Fairchild* gave no guidance as to the basis on which the contribution problem might be resolved—an omission that has met with academic criticism. See, for example, J. Stapleton (2002) 10 Torts L.J. 276.

establishing a "material increase in risk" would be sufficient to discharge the claimant's burden of proving causation.

When will the "material increase in risk approach" apply?

There is, of course, an obvious conflict between the two different approaches we have considered. If the claimants in *Fairchild* could succeed simply by showing that exposure to asbestos had increased the risk of mesothelioma, why was it that the plaintiff in *Wilsher* could not succeed by showing that exposure to excess oxygen had increased the risk that he would contract RLF? Their Lordships in *Fairchild* were content to say that *Wilsher* had been correctly decided, the majority basing this assertion on the factual differences between that case and cases like *McGhee* and *Fairchild*. The key difference is that, in the latter type of case, there is only one "causal agent" of the claimant's injury (brick dust in *McGhee* and asbestos in *Fairchild*) whereas, in a case like *Wilsher*, there are many competing "causal agents" (oxygen and the other possible natural causes of RLF).

6–015

This rather technical distinction, based on the number of "causal agents" present in a case, does not provide a very satisfying or coherent justification for adopting different approaches to proof of causation in the two types of case. Indeed, it was not a distinction that Lord Hoffmann in *Fairchild* was prepared to accept. His Lordship stated that he regarded the distinction as "unprincipled"[41] and doubted whether, if the claimants had been exposed to two different types of dust—asbestos and another kind of dust known to cause mesothelioma —it should make any difference. Lord Roger took an alternative line. Although not requiring the existence of a *single* "causal agent" for the application of the "material increase in risk" approach, his Lordship thought it would be necessary to show that, where there were a number of "causal agents", they all "operated in substantially the same way".[42] Thus, the approach could not apply in a case like *Wilsher*, where the possible causes of the plaintiff's blindness would have *operated in different ways* to produce that result.

The reasoning in *Fairchild* has been subject to academic criticism for failing to define with sufficient clarity the circumstances in which the "material increase in risk approach" might apply in other cases.[43] The problem, in essence, is that whilst their Lordships acknowledged that the question whether to adopt the approach depended on considerations of policy, they declined to state specifically what those policy considerations might be. In the light of this problem, it is impossible to state precisely the criteria which must be met before the courts can apply the "material increase in risk" approach to proof of causation. The following points, however, should be borne in mind:

- The application of the approach is probably confined to cases where there is only one "causal agent" of the claimant's loss (*e.g.* brick dust or asbestos dust), or, at least, to cases where, if there is more that one "causal agent", all of them operate in substantially the same way to produce the claimant's loss.

[41] *Fairchild v Glenhaven Funeral Services Ltd* [2003] 1 A.C. 32 at 77.
[42] *ibid.*, at 118.
[43] See, *e.g.* J. Morgan, (2003) 66 M.L.R. 277 and J. Stapleton (2002) 10 Torts L.J. 276.

- The approach will have no application in cases where evidence can be produced to show that particular defendants are probably responsible for making *distinct and quantifiable causal contributions* to the claimant's loss. In such cases, the courts will apportion liability to each defendant in accordance with his or her degree of fault. This is what happened in *Holtby* v. *Brigham & Cowan (Hull) Ltd*.[44] Here, the claimant contracted asbestosis. Unlike mesothelioma, asbestosis is a disease that can get progressively worse the more a person is exposed to asbestos. The claimant had been exposed to asbestos for most of his working life, but had only been employed by the defendants for about half that time. The medical evidence stated that if the claimant's exposure to asbestos had been limited to that caused by the defendants, his condition would not be so bad. The Court of Appeal therefore reduced the claimant's damages, holding that the defendants could only be liable to the extent that their fault had made a causal contribution to the claimant's condition.

- The truth of the matter may be that the application of the approach is limited to cases where the defendants are employers with deep enough pockets to make it seem just that they should compensate the claimant. On this view, it is unlikely that the approach will be used in medical negligence cases against the NHS.[45] Lord Hoffmann, in *Fairchild*, relied on the medical negligence context to distinguish *Wilsher*, and was the only member of the House to allude specifically to the sort of policy considerations that might influence the courts in deciding whether to adopt the "material increase in risk" approach. His Lordship said:[46]

". . . the political and economic arguments involved in the massive increase in the liability of the National Health Service which would have been a consequence of the broad rule favoured by the Court of Appeal in *Wilsher's* case are far more complicated than the reasons given by Lord Wilberforce [in *McGhee*] for imposing liability upon an employer who has failed to take simple precautions."

Recovery for "loss of a chance"

6–016   Whilst there is no doubt that damages can be awarded for "loss of a chance" in contract,[47] the position in tort is far less certain. We have seen that in *Hotson*, the court applied the "all or nothing" approach to deny recovery for a lost chance, holding that the plaintiff had failed to establish causation. By contrast, in a number of cases involving economic loss, the courts have held that loss of a chance of financial gain is recoverable. Such was the case, for example, in *Allied Maples Group Ltd v Simmons & Simmons*.[48] Here, the plaintiffs were purchasers of a business and the defendants, a

---

[44] [2000] 3 All E.R. 421. See also *Allen v British Rail Engineering Ltd* [2001] P.I.Q.R. 10.
[45] In *Gregg v Scott* [2002] EWCA Civ 1471, (2003) Lloyd's Rep. Med. 105, the Court of Appeal declined to extend the *Fairchild* approach to a case involving medical negligence. The case is currently under appeal in the House of Lords.
[46] *Fairchild v Glenhaven Funeral Services Ltd* [2003] A.C. 32 at 77
[47] See, *e.g. Chaplin v Hicks* [1911] 2 K.B. 786.
[48] [1995] 1 W.L.R. 1602. See also *Normans Bay Ltd v Coudert Brothers* [2003] EWCA Civ 215, *The Times*, March 24, 2004.

firm of solicitors, were responsible for drafting the contracts of sale. They negligently replaced a certain clause in the sale agreement with a different one, which failed to give the plaintiffs protection against certain liabilities attaching to the business. The solicitors argued that it could not be shown that their negligence had caused the plaintiffs any loss. In order to show this, they argued, it would be necessary to prove that, on the balance of probabilities, had the proper effect of the new clause been pointed out, the plaintiffs would have successfully re-negotiated the sale with the vendors of the business, to achieve the protection from liability which they sought.

A unanimous Court of Appeal held that, in cases where a claimant's loss depended on the hypothetical action of a third party, the claimant was entitled to succeed if he or she could show that there was a real or substantial, rather than a speculative, chance that the third party would have acted so as to confer a benefit on or avoid a risk to the claimant. A majority of the Court of Appeal held that there was ample evidence to support the judge's finding of fact that, but for the defendants' negligence, the plaintiffs would have had a realistic chance that the vendor would have agreed to a clause giving them protection from the liabilities in question. Accordingly, having proved that they had lost such a chance, the plaintiffs had established causation.

This difference in outcome between economic loss cases and cases involving personal injury suggests that recovery for loss of a chance depends on policy considerations. It may make more sense to award damages for loss of a chance in economic loss cases (and in contract cases), because, in such cases, the lost chance *already has an economic value*. This avoids the artificiality involved in translating a chance of, say, losing a limb, into a sum of money.[49] Yet, if this consideration underpins the difference of approach in economic loss cases, it means that, surprisingly, in this context the law is prepared to give greater protection to financial interests than to physical well-being.[50]

An alternative explanation for the different approaches taken in *Allied Maples* and in *Hotson* is to be found in the opinion of Lord Mackay in *Hotson*. In answer to the question why the damage in that case could not be formulated in terms of a lost chance, his Lordship asserted (as we have noted) that, in effect, on the evidence, once the plaintiff had fallen from the tree, he had no "chance" to lose—he either had sufficient blood vessels alive to make a complete recovery or he did not—and this was a question of fact to be determined on the balance of probabilities. Thus, a distinction can be drawn between cases where the uncertainty or "chance" involves a hypothetical future occurrence (re-negotiating the deal in the *Allied Maples* case) and cases where, albeit that the cause of the damage is uncertain at the time of the trial, there was a time in the past when the uncertainty in the case might have been resolved.

The obvious conceptual difficulty for the courts is that of reconciling damages for loss of a chance with the idea that, in a civil trial, once the burden of probabilities has been satisfied, "the winner takes all". If loss of a chance generally amounted to actionable damage, then a claimant who, through medical negligence, lost a 40 per cent chance of recovering from illness, would be able to receive 40 per cent of the appropriate award where medical negligence had been the total or only cause of his or her illness. But, if that were so, where would be the justice in allowing a claimant who

---

[49] Coote (1988) A.L.J. 761 at 772.
[50] Lunney and Oliphant, *Tort Law Text and Materials*, 2nd ed. (2003), p.197.

had lost a 51 per cent chance of recovery (thereby satisfying the standard of proof) to recover 100 per cent of the damages? Since, under our present system, this predicament seems insoluble, it is likely that the law on loss of a chance, at least in cases that depend on past uncertainties rather than hypothetical future occurrences, will remain undeveloped.[51]

NOVUS ACTUS INTERVENIENS

6–017   In certain circumstances, where one act follows another, the law will say that the second act (the "new intervening act") is to be regarded as the true cause of the damage, because it has "broken the chain of causation" and has extinguished the effect of the first act. This idea, known as the doctrine of *novus actus interveniens*, is explored here. It should be noted that the essence of the doctrine overlaps not only with the reasoning in "consecutive cause" cases, which we have already examined, but with other areas of the law—in particular, the question of whether a person owes a duty to prevent a third party from causing damage (considered in Ch. 2) and the defences of act of God, *volenti non fit injuria*, and act of stranger, which are considered in later chapters. Each area of the law simply represents a different way of determining liability. The fact that some cases are decided using the concepts of "duty" or "defence", rather than causation, is sometimes the result of historical accident in the way the law has developed, and sometimes the product of a judicial search for clarity.

It should also be noted that many writers and judges treat the idea of *novus actus interveniens* as part of the test for "remoteness of damage".[52] This is mainly because, as we shall see later, the test for "remoteness" is whether the kind of damage in question is reasonably foreseeable, and the same issue arises when considering whether a defendant is liable in spite of an intervening act. Some writers, on the other hand (ourselves included), reserve the phrase "remoteness of damage" for a slightly different problem, namely, where, on any sensible view, there is only one true cause of the claimant's loss, but where the loss caused seems too bizarre or "far removed" to be recoverable. This problem is explored in a later section.

It is convenient to place the relevant cases into two groups—intervening act of a third party and intervening act of the claimant.

Intervening act of a third party

6–018   It is useful to draw a distinction between three different ways in which a third party may interfere with a course of events—natural (or "instinctive") intervention; negligent intervention; and intervention in the form of intentional wrongdoing. We consider each type of intervention in turn.

---

[51] For further consideration of all these issues, see J. Stapleton (1988) L.Q.R. 389 and H. Reece (1996) 59 M.L.R. 188. See also *Gregg v Scott* [2002] EWCA Civ 1471 where a majority of the Court of Appeal (including Simon Brown L.J., who had been the first instance judge in *Hotson*) reluctantly applied *Hotson* to a case where the claimant had lost a chance of recovery through negligent treatment. The case is currently under appeal in the House of Lords.
[52] See, *e.g.* the terminology used by the Court of Appeal in *Lamb v Camden LBC* [1981] Q.B. 625.

Natural or "instinctive" intervention

The classic example of "instinctive" human conduct failing to amount to a *novus actus*   **6–019**
interveniens is the very old case of *Scott v Shepherd*.[53] Here, the defendant threw a
lighted firework into a market place. It landed on a stall belonging to a third party, A,
who threw it on so that it landed on the stall of a fourth party, B, who reacted in a
similar way. The firework ultimately hit the plaintiff and injured him. It was held that
neither the intervening act of A or B broke the causal connection between the
defendant's act and the subsequent damage. Both A and B had acted in an instinctive
and natural way to avoid damage to themselves and their property.

It is clear from *Scott v Shepherd*, then, that a third party's intervention will not break
the chain of causation where it is an involuntary reaction in the "heat of the moment".
But the same sort of reasoning appears to apply in cases where the third party has
some opportunity to reflect before taking action. Consider, for example, *The Oropesa*.[54]
Here, because of the defendants' negligence, a ship of that name collided with a ship
called the *Manchester Regiment*. The captain of the *Manchester Regiment* set out in a
life boat to consult the captain of *The Oropesa* about how best to save his crew. The
life boat capsized, causing the death of many of those aboard. The captain's
intervention did not break the chain of causation.

Negligent intervention

It is impossible to state with clarity the circumstances in which the negligent conduct of   **6–020**
a third party will break the chain of causation. Where A commits a tort, and B
commits a subsequent tort, the key question is whether the nature of B's tort is so
powerful that it ought to be regarded as rendering A's tort merely part of the
surrounding historical circumstances—the backdrop against which B's tort occurred.
Thus, negligent conduct will not always break the chain of causation. For example, in
Roberts v Bettany[55] the defendant negligently started an underground fire, and was
ordered by the council to extinguish it. He failed to comply with this order, so the
council intervened to extinguish the fire. Unfortunately, owing to the council's
negligence in so doing, subsidence occurred under the claimant's house. The Court of
Appeal held that the council's negligence did not break the chain of causation, so the
defendant was liable for the subsidence. The defendant's having started the fire could
not be said to be merely part of the "surrounding circumstances" of the council's
negligence—it being the direct cause of the council's forseeable and necessary
intervention.

Some flavour of the courts' approach can be gained by considering a number of
cases involving negligent driving. In *Knightley v Johns*,[56] for example, the defendant
negligently overturned his car in a tunnel. A police inspector then arrived at the scene
to take charge of the situation, and negligently ordered a police motorcyclist to secure
the closure of the tunnel by riding against the traffic towards its entrance. The
motorcyclist collided with the plaintiff's oncoming car. In holding the defendant not
liable for this accident, the Court of Appeal stated that the relevant question to ask

[53] (1773) 2 Wm. Bl. 892.
[54] [1943] P. 32.
[55] [2001] EWCA Civ 109; [2001] N.P.C. 45.
[56] [1982] 1 All E.R. 851.

was whether the whole sequence of events was a natural and probable consequence of the defendant's negligence, so that it should have been reasonably foreseen by the defendant, or whether the events were foreseeable only as a mere possibility. In answering this question, it was helpful to consider whether the third party's negligent intervention had involved a deliberate choice to do a positive act, as opposed to an error of judgment in the course of performing an act in which the third party was already engaged. Here, the conduct of the police had taken the form of a deliberate positive act, and was not reasonably foreseeable by the defendant.

It is useful to compare *Knightley v Johns* with the decision in *Rouse v Squires*.[57] Here, the defendant lorry driver negligently caused an accident which blocked two lanes of a motorway. The plaintiff, who was assisting at the scene, was killed when a second lorry driver negligently drove into the obstruction. The Court of Appeal held that the defendant was 25 per cent to blame. The negligent driving of the second lorry driver did not break the chain of causation between the original accident and the plaintiff's death—a driver who caused an obstruction could be taken reasonably to foresee that a further accident might be caused by other drivers negligently colliding with the obstruction.

Whilst an act of *negligent* driving may not break the chain of causation, then, *reckless* driving may amount to a *novus actus interveniens*, because such driving is not normally foreseeable. Such was the case in *Wright v Lodge*.[58] Here, the second defendant was driving her Mini at night along a dual carriageway. It was foggy and the road was unlit. The Mini broke down and came to a stop in the near side lane. A few minutes later, as she was trying to restart her car, it was hit from behind by an articulated lorry being driven at 60 mph by the first defendant. After hitting the Mini, the lorry careered across the central reservation. It ended up on its side, blocking the opposite carriageway, and four oncoming vehicles collided with it. One driver died of his injuries and another was seriously injured. The Court of Appeal accepted that the Mini driver had been negligent in failing to push her car off the road before trying to restart it—which she could easily have done with the help of her passengers—but held that the lorry driver's dangerous driving was to be regarded as the true cause of the plaintiffs' injuries.

A particularly difficult question is whether, when a claimant is injured by a defendant's negligence and subsequently undergoes negligent medical treatment, the latter can be regarded as a *novus actus interveniens*. This should not be confused with the more straightforward question of whether a defendant remains liable when non-negligent medical treatment makes a claimant's position worse because of the claimant's pre-disposition to respond adversely to treatment. This point is discussed in a later section.

The circumstances in which negligent treatment will break the chain of causation cannot be stated with certainty. Assistance, however, may be found from the decision of the House of Lords in *Hogan v Bentinck West Hartley Collieries (Owners) Ltd*.[59] The case concerned a miner who injured his thumb at work. He was taken to hospital, where, initial treatment having failed to relieve his pain, doctors negligently decided to

[57] [1973] Q.B. 889.
[58] [1993] 4 All E.R. 299.
[59] [1949] 1 All E.R. 588. The case decided a claim under the Workmen's Compensation Act 1925. It is only of persuasive authority in the tort of negligence.

amputate part of his thumb. This reduced his earning capacity, because it left him able to do only light work. The question before the House of Lords was whether the man's incapacity resulted from the original injury or the operation. The case was complicated by the fact that the man had a congenital abnormality (an additional top joint to his thumb) for which amputation in the event of pain was considered a reasonable form of treatment. By a 3:2 majority, their Lordships held that the amputation amounted to a *novus actus interveniens*, absolving the defendant employers from liability. Lord Reid, however, in a powerful dissenting speech, thought that subsequent medical treatment should only break the chain of causation where there was a "grave lack of skill and care" on the part of the doctors. It should not do so in this case, because it was not abundantly clear that an alternative form of treatment would have cured the plaintiff of his condition. It has been suggested that, nowadays, only where the treatment in question is "so grossly negligent as to be a completely inappropriate response to the injury inflicted by the defendant" should it operate to break the chain of causation.[60]

Intentional acts of wrongdoing

Where a third party's intervention takes the form of a deliberate act of wrongdoing, **6–021** the courts are very reluctant to hold a defendant liable, and will usually say that the third party's act has broken the chain of causation. However, much will depend on the particular circumstances of the case. In *H.M. Att-Gen v Hartwell*[61] an emotionally disturbed police officer in the British Virgin Islands, whom the defendant police authority had given access to a gun, deserted his post and travelled to a bar where he shot and injured a British tourist. The Privy Council, whilst conceding that the case was a "closely balanced" one, held that this action did not break the chain of causation. The defendant authority was liable for the tourist's injuries. The standard of diligence expected of the authority in supervising the use of firearms was a high one, in view of the grave risks involved. Moreover, given that the authority knew about the officer's disturbed emotional state, his actions were sufficiently foreseeable.

The case of *Home Office v Dorset Yacht Co. Ltd*[62] (discussed in Ch. 2) is a further example of a situation where criminal intervention did not break the chain of causation. Its outcome was justified on the basis that the wrongful intervention of the Borstal boys was extremely foreseeable by the defendants—there was a close relationship between the negligent guards and the boys, and their actions were the "very kind of thing" that was likely to happen if the guards allowed them to escape.

The "foreseeability-based" approach to liability for the criminal acts of third parties caused some difficulty for the Court of Appeal, however, in *Lamb v Camden LBC*.[63] This case suggests that the issue is ultimately one of pure policy. Here, a burst water main, for which the defendant council was responsible, had caused the plaintiff's house to become flooded. The plaintiff, who was living abroad at the time, moved her furniture out of the house and made arrangements for repairing the damage. Whilst the house was left unoccupied, squatters moved in and caused extensive damage to the

[60] *Clerk & Lindsell on Torts* (18th ed., 2000), para.2–55. See also *Webb v Barclays Bank plc* [2002] P.I.Q.R. P8; *Mitchell v Rahman* (2002) 209 D.L.R. (4th) 621; *Conley v Strain* [1988] I.R. 628.
[61] [2004] 1 W.L.R. 1273.
[62] [1970] A.C. 1004.
[63] [1981] Q.B. 625. Compare *Clark Fixing Ltd v Dudley Metropolitan Borough Council* [2001] EWCA Civ 1898 (discussed in Ch. 2).

house. The plaintiff's action in respect of this damage failed. The council was not liable for the squatters' antisocial and criminal behaviour. This was so even though (according to the majority) in modern times the actions of the squatters could be regarded as highly foreseeable.

In *Lamb*, their Lordships arrived at their decision by slightly different routes. Lord Denning M.R. thought that, as a matter of policy, the responsibility for keeping the squatters out lay with the plaintiff and not the council and that the loss they had caused should be borne by the plaintiff's insurers. (We can see at work here the economic and political consideration that loss should not be transferred from a private insurance arrangement to a publicly-funded authority.) His Lordship thought that in *Home Office v Dorset Yacht* Lord Reid had been wrong to decide the question of *novus actus interveniens* using a test of foreseeability, and that it was not helpful to attempt to distinguish between different degrees of foreseeability. To illustrate the point, Lord Denning M.R. put forward an example: Suppose a prisoner escapes and steals a car. He then drives many miles, abandons the car, breaks into a house to steal a change of clothes, gets a lift in a lorry and continues with his criminal activities. On Lord Reid's test of "very likely to happen", none of the prisoner's intervening acts would break the chain of causation, so that the Home Office would be liable for all of the damage caused by escaped convicts. As a matter of policy, this was unacceptable.

Oliver L.J., on the other hand, was content to say that the squatters' intervention was not reasonably foreseeable (although it was foreseeable as a mere possibility). Watkins L.J. thought that, in addition to foreseeability, the court should consider a number of other factors, including "the nature of the event or act, the time it occurred, the place where it occurred, the identity of the perpetrator and his intentions and responsibility, if any, for taking measures to avoid the occurrence and matters of public policy".[64]

The authorities suggest that the nature of the relationship between the defendant and the third party is an important consideration for the courts. In *Lamb*, the third parties were strangers to the defendant, whereas in *Dorset Yacht* there was a relationship of supervision and care. The relationship between the defendant and the claimant may also be important. Thus, in *Stansbie v Troman*[65] (considered in Ch. 2), the decorator who had impliedly agreed to look after the plaintiff's house was liable for the actions of the thief who broke in—the thief's action did not amount to a *novus actus interveniens*. Applying both of these "relationship" considerations, we can explain why, for example, in *Topp v London Country Bus (South West) Ltd*,[66] the defendants were not liable when a bus driver, for whose actions the defendants were responsible, left his bus unattended with the keys in the ignition and it was stolen by a third party whose careless driving caused injury to the plaintiff.

In the final analysis, it seems that both "relationship" and "degree of foreseeability" play a part in the courts' reasoning in these cases. Both concepts are the servants of policy, judicial "common sense" and judicial "instinct". (Thus, in *Lamb v Camden*, Watkins L.J. famously concluded: "I have the instinctive feeling that the squatters' damage is too remote".)[67] Given that policy considerations are so fundamental to the

---

[64] [1981] Q.B. 647.
[65] [1948] 2 K.B. 48.
[66] [1993] 1 W.L.R. 976.
[67] *Lamb v Camden LBC* [1981] Q.B. 625 at 647.

courts' assessment of when a defendant will be liable for the intervening act of a third party, the question, as we have suggested in Ch. 2, is perhaps better framed as one relating to the scope of the duty of care owed by the defendant.[68] Arguably, this allows the relevant policy concerns to be accommodated with greater coherence.

Intervening act of the claimant

In appropriate circumstances, the actions of the claimant can break the chain of causation, so that he or she, rather than the defendant, is to be regarded as the operative cause of his or her own loss. This question overlaps with the question of when a claimant can be regarded as having caused his or her own loss by accepting the risk of injury. This idea, known as the defence of *volenti non fit injuria*, is considered in Ch. 14. The question also overlaps with the rules on "contributory negligence" (also discussed in Ch. 14) under which a claimant can have his or her damages award reduced because he or she has been partly to blame. **6–022**

It should be noted that the "all or nothing" approach to causation, which depends on the balance of probabilities, sits somewhat uneasily alongside the fact that a claimant may be regarded by the law as so contributorily negligent that his or her damages are reduced by an amount greater than 50 per cent. Where this is so, why does the law not regard the claimant, rather than the defendant as the true cause of the loss? There is no clear answer to this question, save to say that the law places the question of contributory negligence in a separate "conceptual compartment" from factual causation, and sees it as a matter relating to the quantification of damages, rather than as a matter relating to the determination of liability in the first place.[69]

The courts' general approach to deciding whether a claimant's own act breaks the chain of causation can be illustrated by comparing two cases: *McKew v Holland and Hannens and Cubitts (Scotland) Ltd*[70] and *Wieland v Cyril Lord Carpets Ltd*.[71]

In *McKew*, the plaintiff suffered a slight injury to his leg as a result of the defendant's negligence, so that it had a tendency to give way when he was walking. Shortly afterwards, he went with his family to look at a flat. He descended a steep staircase with no handrail, ahead of his family, and holding a child by the hand. His injured leg gave way and he fell, fracturing his ankle. The House of Lords held that the plaintiff's unreasonable behaviour was a *novus actus interveniens*. He, not the defendant, had caused his injury by descending the staircase without waiting for the assistance of his wife or brother-in-law, knowing that his leg might give way at any moment.

A claimant's act will only break the chain of causation when it is unreasonable. Thus, in *Wieland v Cyril Lord Carpets Ltd*, although the facts were similar to those in *McKew*, the court reached a different conclusion. The plaintiff suffered an injury to her neck, caused by the defendant's negligence. Shortly after this, the plaintiff, who wore bi-focal spectacles, returned to the hospital where she had originally been taken and was fitted

---

[68] See Lord Goff's analysis of the problem in *Smith v Littlewoods* [1987] A.C. 241, considered in Ch. 2.
[69] See, *e.g. Stapley v Gypsum Mines* [1953] A.C. 663 where the damages were reduced by 80% because of contributory negligence. See also P.S. Atiyah (1965) 43 Can. Bar. Rev. 609.
[70] [1969] 3 All E.R. 1621.
[71] [1969] 3 All E.R. 1006.

with a surgical collar. The position of her neck in the collar deprived her of her usual ability to use her bi-focals—she could not easily adjust the position of her head. After leaving the hospital, the plaintiff was in a nervous state because of the trauma of the visit, and this, together with the problem with her bi-focals, made her unsteady on her feet. She went to her son's office to ask him to take her home. He accompanied her down the stairs of the office building, but when she neared the bottom she fell and injured her ankles. Eveleigh J. held that these injuries were caused by the defendant's negligence, which had impaired her ability to negotiate the stairs. Her actions in descending the stairs had been reasonable and could not be regarded as a *novus actus interveniens*.

In a number of cases, the question has arisen whether a claimant's taking his or her own life will break the chain of causation. The courts' approach has been to hold that where the defendant's negligence creates a risk of psychiatric illness leading to suicide, the suicide does not constitute a *novus actus interveniens*. Thus, in *Pigney v Pointer's Transport Services Ltd*,[72] the plaintiff suffered severe head injuries as a result of the defendants' negligence. He succumbed to severe depression and neurosis and eventually killed himself. In an action by his widow, it was held that his suicide, although "irrational and, no doubt, felonious",[73] did not break the chain of causation.

More recently, a similar conclusion was reached by the House of Lords in *Reeves v Metropolitan Police Commissioner*.[74] Here, the deceased was in police custody. Taking advantage of the police officers' inadvertence in leaving the flap of his cell door open, he hanged himself by tying his shirt through the spy hole on the outside of the door. It had been noted in police records that the deceased was a suicide risk, having made two previous attempts to kill himself whilst in custody. The doctor who had examined him on his arrival at the police station, whilst finding no evidence of psychiatric illness, had noted that he should be kept under frequent observation in the light of his previous suicide attempts. By a 3:2 majority, the House of Lords held that the suicide, although a deliberate and informed act, could not be regarded as having broken the chain of causation, given that the police were under a specific legal duty to guard against the commission of that very act.

REMOTENESS OF DAMAGE

6–023   Here, we are not concerned with whether the claimant's loss may have an alternative cause. Rather, the question is whether the law will deny recovery on the basis that the loss in question is a very unusual result of the defendant's conduct.

The old law

6–024   Before 1961, the law was dominated by the decision of the Court of Appeal in *Re Polemis and Furness, Withy & Co.*,[75] in 1921. Here, a ship had been loaded with a quantity of petrol, which, unbeknown to any of the parties, had leaked, causing the

---

[72] [1957] 1 W.L.R. 1121. See also *Kirkham v Chief Constable of Greater Manchester* [1990] 2 Q.B. 283.
[73] *ibid.*, *per* Pilcher J. at 1126. Note that, following the Suicide Act 1961, suicide is no longer a crime.
[74] [2000] 1 A.C. 360.
[75] [1921] 3 K.B. 560.

hold of the ship to fill with vapour. A dock worker employed by the defendants negligently allowed a wooden plank to drop into the hold, where it somehow caused a spark that ignited the petrol vapour, causing the ship to be lost by fire. The Court of Appeal held the defendants liable. Whilst the worker could not have foreseen that the falling plank would cause a fire, he could have foreseen that it might cause *some* damage to the ship (such as a scratch on the paint work). Given that this was so, the defendants were liable for all of the damage that was a direct factual consequence of the worker's negligence.

The exact *ratio* of *Re Polemis* is a matter of some confusion. It is often argued that there are two possible interpretations of the decision. On the first interpretation, their Lordships appear to have held that because *some* damage *of the relevant kind* was reasonably foreseeable, the defendants were liable for all damage *of that kind*. In other words, they were liable for the fire because "damage to a ship", whether by fire or by a scratch in the paintwork, was the same kind of damage—damage to property. According to this interpretation, then, all that their Lordships did in *Re Polemis* was to draw a distinction between "damage to property" on the one hand, and other "kinds" of damage (economic loss and personal injury) on the other. The second, wider, interpretation of the case, however, is that so long as *some* damage (of whatever "kind") was the foreseeable result of the defendant's conduct, he or she would be liable for any damage that was a "direct" consequence of his or her conduct (including damage of a different "kind", and even damage to an "unforeseeable claimant").

In the subsequent case of *The Wagon Mound (No.1)*, which is now the leading authority on remoteness of damage, the Privy Council appeared to treat *Re Polemis* as authority for this second, wider, proposition. Their Lordships held that the "rule" in the case—that a defendant was to be liable for all the direct consequences of his or her actions—was wrong, because, if it were right, it would mean that a defendant could be liable even for damage that could not be reasonably foreseen.[76] Such a proposition could not be reconciled with important cases that had been decided after *Re Polemis*, not least of which was *Donoghue v Stevenson*.

The modern law: *The Wagon Mound (No.1)*

The decision in *Overseas Tankship (UK) Ltd v Morts Dock & Engineering Co. Ltd*[77] is   **6–025** known as *The Wagon Mound (No.1)* because it is the first of two cases involving a ship of that name. It will be recalled that the second of these cases—*The Wagon Mound (No.2)*—has already been considered in Ch. 5 as a case involving breach of duty. It is important not to confuse the two cases. The difference between them lies in the fact that, whereas in *The Wagon Mound (No.2)* the evidence before the court showed there was a foreseeable risk (albeit a small one) that the oil would ignite, in *The Wagon Mound (No.1)*—the case we are now concerned with—the evidence was that the oil catching fire was unforeseeable. This rather surprising difference is explained by the fact that, at the time *The Wagon Mound (No.1)* was brought to trial in New South Wales, contributory negligence was a complete defence. This meant that the plaintiffs in *The Wagon Mound (No.1)* did not dare allege that it was reasonably foreseeable that

[76] *The Wagon Mound (No.1)* [1961] A.C. 388 at 398. See also Dias [1962] C.L.J. 178.
[77] [1961] A.C. 388.

the oil might catch fire, for fear that they might be held contributorily negligent in continuing with their welding operations.

It will be recalled that in the *Wagon Mound* litigation the defendants negligently allowed some furnace oil to spill on to the sea while their ship was in Sydney Harbour. In *The Wagon Mound (No.1)*, the plaintiffs were ship repairers. The oil was washed by the tide so that it fouled the plaintiffs' slipways, causing them to stop work. However, having been assured that there was no chance of the oil igniting, the plaintiffs resumed their welding operations. It was not clear what happened next, but it was assumed that some cotton waste, which was floating on the water, was ignited by a fragment of molten metal from the welding operations. The cotton waste, acting as a sort of wick, allowed the oil to ignite, and the plaintiffs' wharf and equipment were extensively damaged in the ensuing blaze. As has been said, the important finding of fact, on which the Privy Council based its decision, was that the occurrence of the fire was not reasonably foreseeable. But it was reasonably foreseeable, of course, that the oil might cause *some* damage to the plaintiffs' wharf by fouling it.

The Privy Council held that the defendants were not liable. Declaring *Re Polemis* to have been wrongly decided, their Lordships held that the proper test for remoteness of damage was whether the defendant could have reasonably foreseen the *kind of damage* for which the plaintiffs were suing. Their Lordships thought that "damage by fire" should be regarded as a different "kind" of damage from "damage by fouling", and since the former could not have been foreseen, the defendants were not answerable for it. Viscount Simonds explained the basis for decision, saying:

> "It does not seem consonant with current ideas of justice or morality that for an act of negligence, however slight or venial, which results in some trivial foreseeable damage the actor should be liable for all consequences however unforeseeable and however grave. . ."[78]

It may be argued, of course, that his Lordship's explanation is not wholly satisfactory. It views the matter exclusively from the defendant's point of view, and imports into tort law the penal idea that the "punishment" should fit the wrong, ignoring the idea that the traditional role of tort is to compensate the victim. It has been rightly asked: why should the claimant, who has not been to blame, be made to shoulder the whole loss rather than the defendant, who has been to blame at least in some degree?[79] Such considerations have doubtless influenced the courts in their interpretation of the decision in *The Wagon Mound (No.1)*, especially in the context of personal injury cases. This we explore below.

The principle in *The Wagon Mound (No.1)* contains a number of elements, which (as in the following sections) are traditionally considered in turn. It should be noted, however, that the elements overlap considerably. We shall see that this area of the law is beset with uncertainty and contains many decisions that are quite hard to reconcile.

Foreseeability of the "kind of damage"

6–026   In *Hughes v Lord Advocate*,[80] the Post Office, in breach of its duty, left a manhole open in the street during the course of its work on some telephone cables. The manhole was covered with a tent and, in the evening, left unguarded but surrounded by warning

[78] [1961] A.C. 422.
[79] *Clerk & Lindsell on Torts* (18th ed., 2000), para.7–141.
[80] [1963] A.C. 837.

paraffin lamps. The plaintiff was an eight year-old boy who had picked up one of the lamps and clambered down the manhole. Because of a very unusual set of scientific circumstances, an explosion occurred, causing him severe burns. The House of Lords held that the Post Office was liable, even though it could not reasonably have foreseen that anyone might be burned by an explosion in the manhole. It was sufficient to found liability that there was a reasonably foreseeable risk of the boy being burned by the paraffin lamp. In other words, "damage by burning" was the "kind" of damage in question, there being no distinction between burning caused by the flame of the lamp and burning caused by an unforeseeable explosion.

Similar reasoning was applied in *Bradford Corp. v Robinson Rentals Ltd.*[81] Here, the plaintiff suffered frostbite when he was sent on a journey by his employer in a van without a heater. It was held that, although frostbite was a rather unusual consequence in the circumstances (it was practically unheard of in Britain), it was nevertheless "of the type and kind of injury which was reasonably foreseeable".[82]

Both of these cases, then, suggest that the courts are happy to view personal injury as a single and indivisible "kind" of damage. Whilst the decision in *The Wagon Mound (No.1)* shows us that the courts will subdivide "damage to property" into different "kinds" of damage—such as "damage by fire" and "damage by fouling"—the courts appear not to apply the same sort of reasoning in personal injury cases. The difference in approach can be explained in terms of policy. First, the law has always been more anxious to protect physical wellbeing than to protect property. Secondly, if "damage to property" were regarded as a single, indivisible "kind" of damage, defendants might be exposed to "crushing liability" for very large amounts of loss. By contrast, in personal injury cases, losses are generally likely to be less expensive to compensate.

There is one well-known case, however, that appears to conflict with a general proposition that personal injury is an indivisible "kind" of damage. In *Tremain v Pike*[83] the plaintiff was a herdsman employed by the defendants, who were farmers. The farm became infested with rats and the plaintiff contracted Weil's disease—a rare disease that is caught by coming into contact with rats' urine. Payne J. held that, even on the assumption that the defendants had been negligent in failing to control the rat population, the plaintiff could not succeed. His Lordship thought that Weil's disease was both unforeseeable and "entirely different in kind" from the foreseeable consequences of contact with rats, such as food poisoning or the effects of a rat-bite. The status of *Tremain v Pike* is uncertain, especially in the light of *Parsons v Uttley Ingham* (discussed later), where the Court of Appeal implicitly rejected its reasoning.

So far as property damage is concerned, whilst it is clear that *The Wagon Mound (No.1)* allows the courts to subdivide property damage into different "kinds" of damage, the limitations (if any) on their ability to do so remain unclear. Analysis of the issue is difficult for a number of reasons. First, the answer to the question: "what is the kind of damage in suit?" is inextricably bound up with the problems (considered below) of whether the *extent* of the damage, and the *way it is caused*, have to be foreseeable. Secondly, the issue is often difficult to separate from the issue of the *measure of damages* necessary to compensate a foreseeable kind of loss. It is well

---

[81] [1967] 1 W.L.R. 337.
[82] *ibid., per* Rees J. at 344.
[83] [1969] 3 All E.R. 1303.

established that if a defendant injures a person with a high earning capacity, or damages a valuable piece of property, he or she cannot object to paying damages on the basis that the cost of compensation is greater than it might have been if the person had had a low income, or if the property had been less valuable.[84] But, suppose that (for some reasonable purpose) you leave a priceless Ming vase on your coffee table and I negligently break it. In such bizarre circumstances, can I not argue that, whilst "damage to a household ornament" might have been a foreseeable consequence of my negligence, "damage to a priceless antique" is an unforeseeable "kind" of damage? Or will the court say that "damage to a vase" was the foreseeable "kind" of damage, and that it matters not that the cost of replacing the vase is much greater than I could have expected?

To make matters worse, all of these issues are difficult to separate from the questions of whether, and how, the "eggshell skull" rule applies in the context of property damage (considered in a later section). In the final analysis, one is left with the suspicion that the courts are reluctant to rule authoritatively on the subdivision of property damage into different "kinds", so as to preserve the flexibility necessary to do justice whilst containing the scope of liability in appropriate cases.

Foreseeability of the "way the damage is caused"

6–027   In *Hughes v Lord Advocate* it was held that the precise manner in which the damage was caused did not have to be reasonably foreseen. So long as the defendant could reasonably foresee damage of the relevant "kind", the damage would not be too remote. In *Hughes*, therefore, the Post Office was liable even though it could not have foreseen the scientific circumstances which led to an underground explosion injuring the plaintiff. The same approach was adopted in *The Trecarrell*.[85] Here, the defendants were held liable when one of their employees, whilst working in a ship yard, carelessly dropped a drum of inflammable lacquer. The drum fell on a temporary electricity cable and severed it, causing a short circuit which ignited the lacquer. The plaintiffs' ship was damaged in the resulting blaze.

There are, however, two cases where precisely the opposite reasoning has been applied—the defendants were not liable because they could not have foreseen harm caused in such an unusual way. In *Doughty v Turner Manufacturing Ltd*,[86] workmen employed by the defendants had allowed an asbestos cover to drop into a vat of very hot liquid. The cover slid in at an angle and did not cause a splash. A few minutes later, however, chemical changes in the asbestos brought about by the high temperature caused an eruption of the liquid, which splashed out of the vat burning the plaintiff. The possibility of an eruption occurring in this way was unknown at the time. The Court of Appeal, following *The Wagon Mound (No.1)*,[87] held that the defendants were not liable. *Hughes* was distinguished on the basis that, in *Doughty*, the risk which materialised was very substantially different from any that could be foreseen.

This narrow view of risk was also adopted by the Divisional Court in *Crossley v Rawlinson*.[88] Here, the defendant had stopped his lorry when, as a result of his

[84] *Smith v London & South Western Railway Co.* (1870) L.R. 6. C.P. 14.
[85] [1973] 1 Lloyd's Rep. 402.
[86] [1964] 1 Q.B. 518.
[87] [1961] A.C. 388.
[88] [1982] 1 W.L.R. 369.

negligence, a tarpaulin covering the body of the lorry had caught fire. The plaintiff, an A.A. patrolman, who was on duty at a nearby A.A. service centre, saw the fire and ran out to assist. Whilst running towards the lorry on a rough path, he caught his foot in a concealed hole and fell. His claim for personal injury was dismissed on the basis that his being injured in this way was not reasonably foreseeable. The court drew a fine distinction between injury occurring during the course of tackling the fire (which was foreseeable) and injury occurring on the way to tackle the fire (which was not). Bearing in mind that the plaintiff was a rescuer, and that rescuers usually receive more sympathetic treatment from the courts, this seems a particularly harsh decision which has received considerable criticism.[89]

The validity of such reasoning must now be questioned in the light of the House of Lords' decision in *Jolley v Sutton LBC*.[90] Here, a 14 year old boy had been severely injured when a boat, abandoned on council land, had fallen upon him, breaking his back. He and his friend had been attempting to repair the boat to take it to Cornwall to sail it. Although the council, as occupier, owed him a duty of care, the Court of Appeal had rejected his claim on the basis that whilst it was foreseeable that children playing on the boat might suffer some minor injuries, it was *not* foreseeable that a teenager would attempt to reconstruct the boat. The House of Lords disagreed. *Hughes* required the court to judge foresight according to the nature of the risk which ought to have been foreseen. Here, in view of the known ingenuity of children in finding unexpected ways of doing mischief to themselves, and the fact that the council had conceded that it was under a duty to remove the boat to avoid the risk of minor injuries—which would have cost it no more than removing it to avoid the injuries that actually occurred[91]—their Lordships adopted a broad view of risk: was it foreseeable that children would meddle with the boat causing some physical injury? On this basis, the council was found liable for the claimant's injuries.

Their Lordships in *Jolley*, then, adopted a far more generous interpretation of risk than that seen in *Doughty* and *Crossley* above, although they did stress that much would depend on the individual facts of each case. Nevertheless, Lord Nicholls, delivering the opinion of the Privy Council in *HM Att-Gen v Hartwell*,[92] doubted whether the reasoning in *Doughty* would find favour with modern courts, and suggested that courts now take a more liberal approach in determining whether the way in which the damage is caused is foreseeable.

Foreseeability of the "extent" of the damage

In *Hughes v Lord Advocate*, Lord Reid made it clear that a defendant can be liable even when the damage caused is greater in extent than was reasonably foreseeable. Only where the damage is different in "kind" can the defendant escape liability.[93] This approach was followed in *Vacwell Engineering Co. Ltd v B.D.H. Chemicals Ltd.*[94] The

6–028

---

[89] For example, Jones, *Textbook on Torts* (OUP, 8th ed, 2002) p.269 finds the decision "arbitrary and inconsistent with *Hughes*".

[90] [2000] 1 W.L.R. 1082. This decision concerns occupiers' liability and will be considered further in Ch. 8. The principles of causation and remoteness are the same, however, for common law negligence and under the occupiers' liability statutes.

[91] See Lord Hoffmann *ibid.*, at 1093,

[92] [2004] 1 W.L.R. 1273.

[93] *Hughes v Lord Advocate* [1963] A.C. 837 at 845.

[94] [1971] 1 Q.B. 88.

defendants manufactured and supplied a chemical that was liable to explode in contact with water, but they gave no warning of this hazard to the plaintiffs. The plaintiffs bought a quantity of the chemical and a scientist who worked for them put the ampoules containing the chemical in the sink. A violent explosion resulted, causing extensive damage to the plaintiffs' premises. Rees J., whilst holding that an explosion of the magnitude which occurred was not reasonably foreseeable, thought that, given that a *small* explosion was foreseeable, the damage was not too remote. The damage was of a foreseeable kind, and it did not matter that it was greater in extent than could have been foreseen.

Similarly, in *Parsons v Uttley Ingham & Co. Ltd*,[95] the defendants installed a feed hopper for the plaintiffs' pigs, but negligently failed to leave open the ventilator, so that the nuts stored inside became mouldy. On eating the nuts, the pigs contracted a rare disease and a number of them died. The Court of Appeal held that, provided *some* damage of the relevant kind was reasonably foreseeable (in the form of mild illness of the pigs), the plaintiffs could recover for the more serious and unforeseeable consequence resulting from the defendants' negligence.

THE "EGGSHELL SKULL" RULE

6–029   Before the decision in *The Wagon Mound (No.1)*, it was established law that where an injured claimant suffered from some peculiar hypersensitivity which exacerbated his or her loss, then, provided the defendant could reasonably foresee *some* injury to a *normal* claimant,[96] the defendant would be liable for the full extent of the loss. Thus, in *Dulieu v White & Sons*,[97] Kennedy J. stated:

> "If a man is negligently run over or otherwise negligently injured in his body, it is no answer to the sufferer's claim for damages that he would have suffered less injury, or no injury at all, if he had not had an unusually thin skull or an unusually weak heart."[98]

The "eggshell skull" rule is sometimes also referred to as the maxim that "the defendant must take his victim as he finds him".

For a short time, it was uncertain whether the reasoning in *The Wagon Mound (No.1)* had displaced the rule. The matter was quickly settled, however, by the decision in *Smith v Leech Brain & Co. Ltd*.[99] The plaintiff's husband was burned on the lip at

---

[95] [1978] Q.B. 791. The action was for breach of contract but was decided on the basis that the rules of remoteness being considered were equally applicable in tort.
[96] It should be remembered that the rule does not come into play unless the claimant first establishes that a duty of care was owed and breached. Thus, in *Bourhill v Young* [1943] A.C. 92 Lord Wright, at 109, correctly stated: "One who suffers from the terrible tendency to bleed on slight contact, which is denoted by the term 'a bleeder', cannot complain if he mixes with the crowd and suffers severely, perhaps fatally, from being merely brushed against. There is no wrong done there." In the context of psychiatric illness, however, consider Lord Lloyd's reasoning in *Page v Smith* [1996] A.C. 155 (explored in Ch. 4).
[97] [1901] 2 K.B. 669.
[98] *ibid.*, at 679. Note, however, that his Lordship's reference to "no injury at all" seems inconsistent with the modern approach to the rule.
[99] [1962] 2 Q.B. 405.

work by a splash of molten metal. At the time of the accident, it was not known that he had a form of pre-malignant cancer. The burn triggered the onset of the cancer, from which he died three years later. Lord Parker C.J. stated that, in *The Wagon Mound*, whilst the Privy Council had held that a defendant must foresee the kind of damage in suit, their Lordships had not meant to hold that the *extent* of the damage had to be foreseeable. It followed that the "eggshell skull" rule had not been displaced. Thus, apparently regarding "damage by burning" and "damage by cancer" as the same "kind" of damage (personal injury caused by an accident at work), his Lordship held the defendants liable.

It is clear that the rule will apply in cases where the particular characteristics of the claimant act in combination with surrounding circumstances (including the reasonable action of a third party) to exacerbate the claimant's loss. Thus, in *Robinson v Post Office*,[1] owing to the defendant's negligence, the plaintiff slipped and wounded his leg at work. He was subsequently given an anti-tetanus injection and developed encephalitis because of an unforeseeable reaction to the serum. The defendants were held liable for this consequence.

What is less clear is whether the "eggshell skull" rule applies to claims in respect of damage to "hypersensitive" property as well as to hypersensitive people. It has been convincingly suggested that it should. Thus, for example, where a defendant drops a lighted cigarette on an unexpectedly "hypersensitive" carpet, which catches fire and is destroyed, he or she should be liable for the full extent of the damage, even though the reasonably foreseeable damage is no more than a small hole. It has been suggested that to hold otherwise would present the impossible difficulty of determining the extent of the "foreseeable" damage in circumstances where that damage has been "swallowed up" by events—if the carpet is completely destroyed, how can a court quantify the damage which would have been caused by a mere hole? Damages would have to be awarded by guesswork, rather than to compensate losses proved to have been suffered by the claimant.[2]

It is also unclear whether the "eggshell skull" rule can be properly thought of as applying to situations where the claimant's loss is exacerbated *only by surrounding circumstances*, rather than by *inherent* hypersensitive characteristics of the claimant's person or property. Some writers and judges appear to think that such cases can be analysed in terms of the rule.[3] Others tend to classify such cases as turning on the elements of the *Wagon Mound* principle we have considered above.[4] Analysis of certain cases in terms of the "eggshell skull" rule, however, gives us the broad proposition that "the defendant takes as he finds them, not only the physical state of the damaged person or property, but also the surrounding external physical circumstances".[5] On this basis, a case like *Great Lakes Steamship Co. v Maple Leaf Milling Co.*[6] can be explained by reference to the rule. Here, because of the defendant's negligence in failing to lighten a ship, it settled on a submerged anchor. The defendants were held liable for

---

[1] [1974] 1 W.L.R. 1176.
[2] *Clerk & Lindsell on Torts* (18th ed., 2000), para.7–148.
[3] See, *e.g.* Murphy, *Street on Torts* (11th ed., 2003).
[4] See, *e.g. Clerk & Lindsell on Torts*.
[5] Murphy, *Street on Torts* (11th ed., 2003), p.305.
[6] (1924) 41 T.L.R. 21 This was a contract case, but it is generally accepted that the relevant principle may apply in tort.

the full extent of the damage, even though they could not have known the anchor was there. Having created a risk of foreseeable damage of the relevant kind (the ship hitting the bottom), they had to take all the circumstances as they found them. The decision in *Parsons v Uttley Ingham & Co. Ltd* (considered above) can also be explained using this version of the "eggshell skull" rule.

Until recently, however, the courts refused to apply the "eggshell skull" rule to losses which were caused by the claimant's own lack of funds. In *Liesbosch Dredger v S.S. Edison*,[7] the House of Lords had restricted the plaintiffs' claim for losses caused by the sinking of their dredger due to the defendants' negligence, to exclude the additional costs incurred by hiring a replacement dredger at an exorbitant rate to fulfil an existing contract. Their Lordships awarded the lesser cost of buying a comparable dredger, and refused to recognise that, due to the plaintiffs' impecuniosity, such a purchase had been a financial impossibility. The additional costs incurred in hiring a replacement vessel had an "extraneous cause",[8] namely the plaintiffs' financial circumstances, and were therefore too remote.

This decision received considerable academic criticism,[9] and subsequent courts sought to distinguish it. For example, in *Dodd Properties (Kent) Ltd v Canterbury CC*,[10] it was held that *The Liesbosch* did not govern a situation where the claimant, because of "commercial prudence" rather than impecuniosity, made a decision not to undertake prompt repairs to damaged property. In view of such criticism, the House of Lords in *Lagden v O'Connor*[11] in 2003 finally accepted that *The Liesbosch* should no longer be viewed as good law. In the words of Lord Hope:

> "the law has moved on, and . . . the correct test of remoteness today is whether the loss was reasonably foreseeable. The wrongdoer must take his victim as he finds him . . . This rule applies to the economic state of the victim in the same way as it applies to his physical and mental vulnerability."[12]

Causation and remoteness: conclusion

6–030   In concluding, it is important to note that although the law we have examined in this chapter has developed as part of the tort of negligence (and most of the cases we have discussed are negligence cases), the rules relating to factual causation are applicable to all torts (except, of course, those actionable *per se*, where no damage need be proved) and the rules relating to remoteness are applicable to most.[13]

We have seen that causation and remoteness are difficult areas, where the courts, in a sense, are faced with the tricky problem of "what to do when the rules run out". The apparent absence of logical rules leaves one with the impression that in many cases the

---

[7] (*The Liesbosch*) [1933] A.C. 449.
[8] *ibid., per* Lord Wright at 460.
[9] See, for example, Coote [2001] C.L.J. 511.
[10] [1980] 1 W.L.R. 433. See also *Mattocks v Mann* [1993] R.T.R. 13.
[11] [2003] 3 W.L.R. 1571.
[12] *ibid.,* at 1590.
[13] Note that usual rules on remoteness do not apply, *e.g.* to the tort of deceit (see *Doyle v Olby (Ironmongers) Ltd* [1969] 2 Q.B. 158; *Shelley v Paddock* [1980] Q.B. 348). Uncertainty about the application of *The Wagon Mound (No.1)* to the rule in *Rylands v Fletcher* has been removed by the decision of the House of Lords in *Cambridge Water Co. Ltd v Eastern Counties Leather plc* [1994] 2 A.C. 264 (considered in Ch. 10).

judges adopt a practice of "reasoning backwards". In other words, they decide what is a fair and just outcome for the case at hand, and then select an appropriate set of rules to justify that decision.

Chapter 7

EMPLOYERS' LIABILITY

Introduction

Injury in the workplace is a significant problem. The Health and Safety Executive **7–001** reported in 2003 that over 250 people in Great Britain lose their lives at work each year.[1] The legal response to such injury takes a number of forms. For many injured employees, the simplest option is to turn to social security, which provides specific benefits for industrial injuries. Since 1948,[2] such compensation has been part of the welfare state. Therefore, victims who suffer personal injury due to an industrial accident[3] are entitled to claim benefits from the Department for Work and Pensions. Such benefits are inevitably not as high as any tort award and are subject to restrictions, but for many victims provide a simpler and cheaper way of gaining compensation. Readers are advised to consult textbooks on labour law generally for employers' liability outside tort law[4] and in particular should consider the provisions of the Health and Safety at Work etc. Act 1974, which applies to all persons at work in Great Britain, and recent regulations such as the Management of Health and Safety at Work Regulations 1999[5] and the Provision and Use of Work Equipment Regulations 1998.[6]

We concentrate here on an employer's liability in tort. This can take three forms:

- personal liability in negligence;
- liability for breach of statutory duty;

[1] Health and Safety Executive, *Health and Safety in Small Businesses*: (*http://www.hse.gov.uk/pubns*). Around 156,000 non-fatal injuries are reported each year and an estimated 2.3 million suffer from ill health caused or made worse by work.
[2] Industrial benefits first appeared in 1897 (see Workmen's Compensation Acts 1897, 1925 and 1943), but the changes in 1948 led to industrial benefits being integrated into the welfare state.
[3] This includes certain industrial diseases.
[4] See, *e.g.* S. Deakin and G.S. Morris, *Labour law* (3rd ed., Butterworths, 2001) or G. Pitt, *Employment law* (5th ed., Sweet & Maxwell, 2003).
[5] SI 1999/3242, which replace the Management of Health and Safety at Work Regulations 1992. These are part of significant EC developments to improve workplace conditions. Note, in particular, the amendments made by The Management of Health and Safety at Work and Fire Precautions (Workplace) (Amendment) Regulations SI 2003/2457 which now permit employees to bring civil claims against their employers where they are in breach of duties imposed by the 1999 Regulations (but as respects claims by non-employees the exclusion of civil liability for breach of duties imposed by the 1999 Regulations remains).
[6] SI 1998/2306, as amended.

- vicarious liability for the torts of employees committed in the course of their employment.[7]

Employers are popular targets for tort claims. As insurance is compulsory,[8] claimants know that if they succeed, the employer is likely to be able to meet their claim and may, for the sake of labour relations or to avoid adverse publicity, be willing to settle. Although we examine all three forms of liability below, we spend more time discussing vicarious liability, which plays a significant role in distributing loss and ensuring that claimants receive adequate compensation.

First of all, we examine the historical development of employers' liability. In seeking to understand the current law, it is particularly important to understand its historical background and why the rules have developed in their present form. For example, it may be questioned why there are three forms of liability and not simply one head of employers' liability. The answer lies in the historical development of the law, which we outline below.

The development of employers' liability

7–002 The law on employers' liability reflects the economic and political trends of the last 200 years. Courts have always been aware, even if this has not been admitted openly, that their decisions affect the relationship between employers and employees and, more bluntly, the amount of money employers will have to spend on employee protection. It is perhaps unsurprising that in the early nineteenth century, at a time of increasing industrialisation, and with the insurance industry still embryonic, the courts were not prepared to impose a heavy burden of liability on employers and strove instead to urge employees to take responsibility for their own safety. In *Priestley v Fowler*,[9] the Court of Exchequer introduced what became known as the doctrine of common employment. This prevented an employee from suing his or her employer for injury negligently caused by a fellow employee. The courts held that it was implied in the employee's contract of employment that he or she would assume the risk of injury caused by the negligence of fellow employees, provided they had been selected with due care by the employer.[10] Liability was further restricted by the fact that contributory negligence at that time was an absolute bar to any claim in negligence[11]—however minimal the negligence of the claimant—and the fact that the courts were willing to apply the defence of voluntary assumption of risk to tasks undertaken in the workplace.[12] The result of this "unholy trinity" was very limited liability on the employer.

However, as the century progressed (and insurance began to develop by which employers could protect themselves against legal claims), attitudes changed. The

---

[7] These heads impose specific duties on employers in tort. This is of course in addition to any general liability in tort, *e.g.* for negligence or nuisance.

[8] Employers' Liability (Compulsory Insurance) Act 1969. The Employers' Liability (Compulsory Insurance) Regulations 1998 (SI 1998/2573) raise the sum to be insured to not less than £5 million.

[9] (1837) 3 M. & W. 1; 150 E.R. 1030. B.A. Hepple and M. Matthews, *Tort: Cases and Materials* (4th ed., Butterworths, 1991) p.566, report that in addition to losing his case, Priestley spent some years in a debtors' prison because he could not pay the costs of his unsuccessful action.

[10] See *Bartonshill Coal Co. v Reid* (1858) 3 Macq. 266; *Johnson v Lindsay & Co.* [1891] A.C. 371.

[11] See *Senior v Ward* (1859) 1 El. & El. 385; 120 E.R. 954.

[12] This is discussed more fully in Ch. 14.

judiciary and legislature began to take note of the hardship suffered by employees injured by new machinery and the introduction of the railways. New concepts were developed to circumvent the obstacles to recovery. Vicarious liability continued to grow,[13] but this could not overcome the obstacle of the doctrine of common employment. The courts therefore developed the idea of a *personal* duty on the employer which was *non-delegable*, *i.e.* responsibility could not be displaced onto another party. Personal liability allowed claimants to sue the employer for damages, even if the injury had been caused by another employee, and provided a means of circumventing the barriers to liability. *Groves v Lord Wimborne*[14] also established that the doctrine of common employment did not apply to the tort of breach of statutory duty, and therefore boosted the use of this tort to permit an injured employee to sue for an award of damages.

Unsurprisingly, in the twentieth century, the three barriers to employers' liability have come under attack. The doctrine of common employment was abolished under the Law Reform (Personal Injuries) Act 1948, and the Law Reform (Contributory Negligence) Act 1945 permitted the courts to apportion liability where the claimant had been contributorily negligent.[15] In *Smith v Charles Baker & Sons*,[16] the House of Lords had already expressed its reluctance to apply the defence of voluntary assumption of risk to employees, and so by 1948, all three obstacles had either been abolished or tightly confined.

Despite these changes, the distinction between personal and vicarious liability remains,[17] although personal liability and breach of statutory duty are obviously less important nowadays than in the past. Having considered the historical development of liability, we shall now consider the three forms of tortious liability in turn.

PERSONAL LIABILITY

To understand the nature of the employer's personal liability, it is necessary to remember that it was developed to circumvent the doctrine of common employment. As a result of this doctrine—which prevented claims against the employer in respect of a fellow employee's negligence—where an employee (X) brought an action against his employer (Y) for negligent injury in the workplace, X ran the risk that Y could simply claim that he was not liable because:

7–003

(a) the injury was caused by the action of a fellow employee; *and*

(b) Y had taken reasonable care in choosing the employee in question.

Having delegated the duty, Y would therefore not have been responsible for how this duty was carried out. The victim would therefore be left with an action against a fellow

---

[13] See D. Ibbetson, *A Historical Introduction to the Law of Obligations* (Oxford, 1999), pp.181–184.

[14] [1895–99] All E.R. Rep. 147.

[15] See Ch. 14.

[16] [1891] A.C. 325, HL, unless the job of necessity involved risk. For full discussion, see Ch. 14.

[17] See *Staveley Iron & Chemical Co. v Jones* [1956] A.C. 627. This has nevertheless been the subject of extensive academic debate—see G. Williams (1957) 72 L.Q.R. 522 and F.H. Newark (1954) 17 M.L.R. 102—and it is not always clearly expressed by the judiciary—see, for example, Lord Hobhouse in *Lister v Hesley Hall Ltd* [2002] 1 A.C. 215.

employee, which would be difficult to establish and in all probability worthless. The leading case of *Wilson and Clyde Coal Co. v English*[18] resolved this difficulty by making the duty on the employer non-delegable. "Non-delegable" here does not mean that the employer cannot delegate its health and safety tasks (this would simply be impracticable in modern employment conditions), but that it cannot delegate *responsibility at law*. It is no excuse that the employer has taken care to ensure a competent fellow employee deals with safety: if the employee is injured due to lack of care, the employer is liable.

The facts of *Wilson and Clyde Coal Co. v English*[19] illustrate this point. A miner had been crushed in a mining accident, and had sued the mine-owners, on the basis that a safe system of work had not been adopted. The defendants argued that they had delegated pit safety to a qualified manager, as required by statute, and should not be held liable. Lord Wright, in the House of Lords, held that it was not enough for an employer to entrust the fulfilment of its duty of care to its employees, even when they had been selected with due care and skill.[20] The employer retained responsibility to provide a competent staff, adequate plant and equipment and effective supervision. If these were not provided with reasonable care and skill, the employer would be liable. Here, the system of working had not been reasonably safe and so the employers were liable.

The nature of the duty

7–004   In this section, we shall examine the nature of the non-delegable duty placed on the employer. An employer's personal duty is a duty to see that reasonable care is taken.[21] This will also apply to analogous relationships, for example the relationship between the Chief Constable of Police and police officers, although the courts do consider the demands of public policy in this context.[22] To comply with this duty, case law indicates that the employers should take care in the provision of:

- competent staff;
- adequate plant and equipment;
- a safe place of work;
- a safe system of work.

Each of these matters will be examined in more detail below.

---

[18] [1938] A.C. 57. See G. Williams [1956] C.L.J. 180, 190–192.
[19] [1938] A.C. 57
[20] *ibid.*, at 78. See also Lord Herschell in *Smith v Baker* [1891] A.C. 325 at 362.
[21] As stated in Ch. 5, readers should note the distinction between the employer's duty of care and breach of that duty. The duty is to see that reasonable care is taken. Breach of duty can be shown by evidence that the employer had failed to take reasonable steps to provide competent staff or a safe system of work.
[22] See *W v Commissioner of Police for the Metropolis* [2000] 1 W.L.R. 1607 and *Mullaney v Chief Constable of West Midlands Police* (CA) [2001] EWCA Civ 700; *Independent*, July 9 2001, where the courts continue to take note of the policy factors discussed in *Hill v Chief Constable of West Yorkshire* [1989] 1 A.C. 53 discussed in Ch. 2. Consider also *Mulcahy v Ministry of Defence* [1996] Q.B. 732 (no duty on Ministry of Defence to maintain a safe system of work in battle situations).

(1) Provision of competent staff

This was obviously important when the doctrine of common employment barred the **7–005**
employer's responsibility for the negligence of fellow employees. It meant that the
employer would be personally responsible for providing such incompetent staff. It still
has some modern relevance, however. A good example is *Hudson v Ridge Manufacturing Co*.[23] An employee had for nearly four years persistently engaged in practical jokes,
such as tripping up fellow employees, and had been reprimanded many times. His
employers were found to be personally liable when he tripped up the plaintiff and
caused him injury. They had failed to exercise reasonable care to put an end to such
conduct, which was a potential danger to other employees.[24] Equally an employer may
find itself liable for failing to prevent a campaign of sustained bullying when it was in
its power to do so.[25]

(2) Provision of adequate plant and equipment and a safe place of work

The employer should take reasonable care to ensure that the employee's place of work **7–006**
is safe, which extends to access to the premises.[26] In addition, the employer must take
reasonable care to provide all necessary equipment and to maintain it in a reasonable
condition. An interesting point was raised by *Davie v New Merton Board Mills*.[27] In this
case, the plaintiff lost the sight in his left eye when a particle of metal chipped off a
tool he was using, due to a fault in its manufacture. The tool had been provided by his
employers, who had bought it from a reputable supplier, and the defect could not be
detected by reasonable inspection. The House of Lords held that his employers were
not liable. Although they had a duty to take reasonable care to provide a reasonably
safe tool, this had been discharged[28]—they had bought the tool from a reputable
source and they had no means of discovering that it contained a latent defect. The
court held that if liability was imposed in such circumstances, any employer "employing another and supplying him with tools for his job acts at his peril".[29]

This decision, which obviously favoured employers, was reversed by the Employer's
Liability (Defective Equipment) Act 1969. Section 1 provides that where an employee
is injured in the course of his or her employment in consequence of a defect in
equipment provided by the employer for the purposes of the employer's business, and
the defect is due (wholly or partly) to the fault of a third party, then the injury will be
attributed to the fault of the employer. This applies regardless of whether the third
party is identified or not and extends to plant, machinery, vehicles, aircraft and even

---

[23] [1957] 2 Q.B. 348. See also *Smith v Crossley Brothers Ltd* (1951) 95 Sol. Jo. 655 and Sir Nicolas Browne-
Wilkinson V.-C. in *Wilsher v Essex Area Health Authority* [1987] Q.B. 730, CA at 778: "In my judgment, a
health authority which so conducts its hospital that it fails to provide doctors of sufficient skill and
experience to give the treatment offered at the hospital may be directly liable in negligence to the patient".
[24] The employer here is unlikely to be vicariously liable for the "playful" activities of such an employee as it
is doubtful whether a court would find such conduct to be in the course of his or her employment.
[25] See *W v Commissioner of Police for the Metropolis* [2000] 1 W.L.R. 1607 (breach of duty found to be
arguable).
[26] See *Ashdown v Samuel Williams & Sons Ltd* [1957] 1 Q.B. 409, CA.
[27] [1959] A.C. 604.
[28] The court held that the employer could not be found to have delegated its duty of care to the
manufacturer.
[29] Viscount Simonds [1959] A.C. 604 at 618. See C.J. Hamson [1959] C.L.J. 157.

clothing.[30] This provision is obviously intended to make it easier for an employee to sue. He or she is no longer required to pursue a manufacturer[31] who may be overseas, but can sue his or her employer. The employee must nevertheless show that:

(1) a defect in equipment caused the accident; *and*

(2) the defect, on the balance of probabilities, was due to some fault in its manufacture.

These matters are not always easy to prove. The Act also provides that the rules relating to contributory negligence still apply.

(3) Provision of a safe system of work

7–007   This is difficult to define, but essentially refers to decisions adopted by the employer on the method of working.[32] Employers are required to take reasonable steps to organise and supervise the work of their employees, and to give proper instructions and guidance to employees and check that it is adhered to. Employers must take account of the fact that employees are often heedless of their own safety and so the system of work adopted should, so far as possible, minimise the danger of the employee's own foreseeable carelessness. For example, in *General Cleaning Contractors v Christmas*,[33] there was an obvious danger that if window cleaners stood on the sill to clean the outside of the window, they might suffer injury if the window closed. By failing to instruct the window cleaners to take precautions, their employers had failed to provide a safe system of work. Particular care must be taken if the work is complex or involves a large number of personnel.

The modern scope of personal liability

7–008   It can be seen that the personal liability of an employer in negligence differs from the ordinary duty of care we have examined earlier in this book. Rather than being a duty to take care, it is perhaps more accurately described as *a duty to see that reasonable care is taken*. This duty extends not only to actual work of employees, but to all such acts as are normally and reasonably incidental to a day's work, such as making a cup of tea or going to the toilet.[34] Yet, apart from this, the ordinary rules of negligence apply. The employee must show that the duty of care has been breached and that breach caused the loss suffered. The duty is owed to the individual employee. We have seen in Ch. 5 that the particular characteristics of an employee may require extra care to be taken. In *Paris v Stepney B.C.*,[35] the court held that the employer was required to

---

[30] *Coltman v Bibby Tankers Ltd (The Derbyshire)* [1988] A.C. 276 even extended the Act to a ship which had sunk off the coast of Japan with the loss of all hands. See also *Knowles v Liverpool City Council* [1993] 1 W.L.R. 1428 (not restricted to tools and plant and could include flagstone which broke injuring workman laying the pavement).

[31] The employee still has a right to sue the manufacturer. Liability of manufacturers in tort will be discussed in Ch. 9.

[32] Consider *McGhee v National Coal Board* [1973] 1 W.L.R. 1 discussed in Ch. 6 (failure to provide adequate washing facilities).

[33] [1953] A.C. 180, see in particular Lord Oaksey at 189–190.

[34] *Davidson v Handley Page Ltd* [1945] 1 All E.R. 235.

[35] [1951] A.C. 367.

undertake extra safety precautions in respect of a one-eyed employee. The defendants were therefore liable for not providing safety goggles, even though they were not required to provide them to two-eyed employees.

Case law suggests that the courts are prepared to adopt a very generous approach towards the personal liability of employers. In *McDermid v Nash Dredging and Reclamation Co. Ltd*,[36] the plaintiff was an employee of the defendants, which were a wholly-owned subsidiary of a Dutch company, Stevin. The function of the defendants was to provide and pay the staff engaged in Stevin's operation in Sweden. The plaintiff had been injured whilst working on the deck of a tug owned by Stevin, due to the negligence of one of Stevin's employees. The question was whether the defendants (the subsidiary company) could be liable in such circumstances. The House of Lords held that the defendants could not effectively delegate the task of providing a safe system of work to the Dutch company and its employees and therefore retained personal responsibility for any lack of care which injured the plaintiff.

This decision stretches personal liability very far, but may be explained by the close connection between the Dutch company and the defendants. It should also be noted that the House of Lords was quite happy to base a failure to provide a safe system of work on a negligent failure to devise such a system or negligence *in its operation*.[37] It has been observed that this represented an extension of existing legal principles.[38]

Stress in the workplace

A similarly generous approach was adopted in the context of psychiatric illness in *Walker v Northumberland CC*.[39] In this case, Colman J. held that there was no logical reason for excluding the risk of psychiatric damage from the scope of an employer's duty to provide a safe system of work. Here, the plaintiff, the defendants' area social services manager, suffered a second nervous breakdown due to stress and pressure at work. The plaintiff had suffered an earlier breakdown due to stress at work and it was therefore reasonably foreseeable that a failure to lessen his work load might lead to a second breakdown.

Colman J. in *Walker* applied the ordinary principles of employers' liability. No mention was made of the House of Lords' decision in *Alcock v Chief Constable of South Yorkshire*[40] (discussed in Ch. 4) which stipulated that a restrictive approach should be taken towards psychiatric damage. The status of *Walker* has therefore been questioned, particularly in the light of the more recent case of *White v Chief Constable*

7–009

---

[36] [1987] A.C. 906. For a discussion of the case, see JD Fleming [1988] C.L.J. 11. Consider also *Johnstone v Bloomsbury Area Health Authority* [1992] Q.B. 333 (although this was only a striking-out case and so weak authority).

[37] See also *Mullaney v Chief Constable of West Midlands Police* (CA) [2001] EWCA Civ 700; *Independent*, July 9 2001 (failure to operate a safe system of work where distress calls from a police officer had not been monitored as instructed with the result that the officer received severe head injuries from an assailant).

[38] See E. McKendrick (1990) 53 M.L.R. 770 at 773–774 who remarks that the effect of the decision is as if vicarious liability had been imposed.

[39] [1995] I.C.R. 702; [1995] 1 All E.R. 737. Comment D. Nolan (1995) 24 I.L.J. 280. Contrast *Petch v Customs and Excise Commissioners* [1993] I.C.R. 789. See also *Young v Post Office* [2002] I.R.L.R. 660 and *W v Commissioner of Police for the Metropolis* [2000] 1 W.L.R. 1607. This generous approach does not seem to extend to economic loss: see *Reid v Rush and Tompkins Group plc* [1989] 1 W.L.R. 212, CA, although contrast the generous use of implied terms in *Scally v Southern Health and Social Services Board* [1992] 1 A.C. 294.

[40] [1992] 1 A.C. 310.

of South Yorkshire,[41] where the House of Lords held that police attending the victims of the Hillsborough disaster could not claim against their employers for psychiatric illness suffered as a result.[42] Although the majority of the House of Lords expressed no clear view on *Walker*, some comments were made. Lord Hoffmann suggested that a distinction may be drawn between claims arising from *the work itself* and claims due to *witnessing injury to others* in the course of work.[43] Lord Steyn, however, did seem to advocate that the ordinary rules of tort, which restrict recovery for psychiatric damage, should apply to all employee claims.

Subsequent case-law has confirmed the status of *Walker* and attempted to clarify exactly *when* employers will find themselves liable for psychiatric injury arising from stress or harassment in the workplace. The leading decision is currently that of *Sutherland v Hatton*.[44] In this case, the Court of Appeal, dealing with four conjoined appeals, sought to give employers guidance. It distinguished:

(a) cases where the harm suffered was the reasonably foreseeable product of specific breaches of a contractual duty of care between the defendant and a known primary victim (*e.g.* the employee in *Walker*);

(b) cases where the relationship was only in tort (*e.g. Page v Smith*,[45] *Alcock v Chief Constable of South Yorkshire Police*[46]) *and*

(c) cases where there was a contractual claim by a secondary victim (*e.g.* the police officer witnessing the Hillsborough disaster in *White v Chief Constable of South Yorkshire*).

The control mechanisms of *White* and *Alcock* would only apply under (b) and (c), and not where the employee was a primary victim under (a). This seems a rather fine distinction and is clearly introduced to maintain the *Walker* line of authority for potential claimants. Nevertheless, *Hatton* has been welcomed by employers primarily due its acceptance that an employer is entitled, unless he knows otherwise, to assume that the employee can cope. This is obviously in the employer's favour.[47] Only if the employer knows, or should know, of some particular problem or vulnerability will the employer be liable. This will require the court to look at a number of relevant factors, including the nature and amount of work undertaken by the employee (is the employee overworked or placed under unreasonable pressure?) and signs of stress in the employee. The indications that a person is about to suffer harm from stress at work must be plain enough for any reasonable employer to realise something should be done about it. Even if the risk of harm is foreseeable, the court must in every case examine what the employer could and should have done, bearing in mind the size and scope of the operation, its resources, whether it is in the public or private sector, and

---

[41] [1999] 2 A.C. 455.
[42] By a majority of 4 to 1, Lord Goff dissenting. Nevertheless, the Law Commission (Law Commission Report No. 249 *Liability for Psychiatric Illness* (1998), para.7.22) had found that *Walker* represented "a just development in the law."
[43] See Lord Hoffmann [1999] 2 A.C. 455 at 506.
[44] [2002] 2 All E.R. 1. Applied in *Foumeny v University of Leeds* [2003] EWCA Civ 557; [2003] E.L.R. 443. Hale L.J. at 11 cites *Walker* and Lord Hoffmann's judgment in *White* above with approval.
[45] [1996] A.C. 155.
[46] [1992] 1 A.C. 310.
[47] See N.J. Mullany "Containing claims for workplace mental illness" (2002) 118 L.Q.R. 373.

other demands placed upon it. The "threshold question" is whether this kind of harm to this particular employee was reasonably foreseeable.[48]

In the case of *Hatton*, Mrs Hatton had suffered a stress-related psychiatric illness whilst teaching at a comprehensive school. However, like many people, she had struggled to cope and did not complain to her superiors or ask for help. Yet, the fact that she had struggled on without complaint led the court to conclude that there was no clear indication that she was likely to suffer from psychiatric injury and that the school should not be liable.[49] In contrast, in the conjoined case, *Barber v Somerset County Council*,[50] another school teacher, Mr Barber, had been forced to take three weeks off school, which had been certified by his GP as due to depression and stress, and could point to several meetings in which he had expressed concern as to his workload and its effect on his health. Although the Court of Appeal had taken the robust view that these meetings had taken place before the summer vacation ("usually a source of relaxation and recuperation for hard-pressed teachers") and that his actual breakdown had taken place the following November, the House of Lords (on appeal) overturned its view that "it is expecting too much to expect school authorities to pick up the fact that the problems were continuing without some such indication."[51] Although the Court of Appeal guidelines in *Hatton* were not appealed,[52] Lord Walker, giving the leading judgment, chose to adopt a change of emphasis. His Lordship found that although the *Hatton* guidelines provided practical assistance, the overall test remains "the conduct of the reasonable and prudent employer, taking positive thought for the safety of his workers in the light of what he knows or ought to know."[53] On this basis, although this case was close to the borderline, the school had been negligent in failing to make ongoing inquiries as to Mr Barber's health and in not taking any measures to ease the problem.

As may be seen, complaints to one's employer seem to form the basis for any claim for liability. Yet, few employees in such circumstances will wish to alert their superiors to the fact that they are not doing their job properly. The Court of Appeal in *Hatton* recognised this, but insisted that it is difficult in such circumstances to blame the employer for failing to act. Any stricter regime would be better implemented by way of regulations imposing specific statutory duties.[54] The approach taken by the majority of the House of Lords in *Barber* does seem to be more "employee-friendly", but still requires some signs to be evident to the reasonable employer that a problem exists. Only in these circumstances will the court be able to impose a positive duty on the employer to act.

[48] See Hale L.J. above at 12. Her Ladyship lists 16 practical propositions at 18–19 which aim to provide clear guidance for employers in future.

[49] See also *Pratley v Surrey CC* [2003] EWCA Civ 1067, [2003] I.R.L.R. 794 (foresight of risk of illness arising from continuing overwork in the future not sufficient).

[50] [2004] 1 W.L.R. 1089, HL; [2002] 2 All E.R. 1, CA.

[51] *ibid.*, at 22.

[52] Lord Walker, giving the leading judgment, describes them at 1109 as "a valuable contribution to the development of the law" and "useful practical guidance, but . . . not . . . having anything like statutory force".

[53] Quoting Swanwick J. in *Stokes v Guest, Keen and Nettlefold (Bolts and Nuts) Ltd* [1968] 1 W.L.R. 1776, 1783. His judgment is heavily criticised by Lord Scott dissenting for setting an unrealistically high standard of care on the school.

[54] Hale L.J. above at 9–10. The Court of Appeal further indicated that should the employer set up a confidential advice service, with referral to appropriate counselling or treatment services, it would be unlikely to be found liable. This point was not addressed by their Lordships in *Barber*.

BREACH OF STATUTORY DUTY

7–010   This is a tort in its own right.[55] Although, as we shall see below, breach of statutory
duty is not confined to the employment context, its main application is in the
employment field, particularly in relation to matters of industrial safety.[56] It therefore
forms a part of the potential liability of employers in tort and it is appropriate to deal
with it in this chapter. Breach of statutory duty gives a remedy in tort for breach of
certain statutory duties where the legislature intended that, in addition to any criminal
or administrative penalties, the injured party should have a right to sue in tort. The
House of Lords, in *Lonrho Ltd v Shell Petroleum Co. Ltd (No. 2)*,[57] declined to accept
the broader notion that liability could arise whenever damage results from a
contravention of a statutory duty. The question, therefore, is *when* does Parliament
intend such a right to exist? Unfortunately, very few statutes expressly deal with this
issue.[58] In the absence of an express right to sue[59] (or an express exclusion from
suing),[60] the courts are left to construe the statute, and to infer whether Parliament
intended to provide a right to damages in tort. This gives the courts a considerable
amount of discretion, in the exercise of which they will consider the purpose of the
statute and whether, in all the circumstances, individuals such as the claimant could
have been intended to have a civil remedy.

The first question in dealing with breach of statutory duty is therefore to look at the
wording of the particular statutory provision which has been breached: construing it
according to the guidelines established by the courts, does it give a remedy in tort to
individuals who suffer harm as a result of its breach? If this is established, there are
four further matters to consider:

- Is the duty owed to this particular claimant?

- Has the defendant breached his or her statutory duty?

- Did the breach cause the damage in question?

- Was the injury of the kind which the statute intended to prevent?

Only if all five questions are answered in the affirmative will an action lie for breach of
statutory duty. It must be stated that much turns on the interpretative powers of the

---

[55] Although there are arguments to the contrary, most notably the argument of statutory negligence
forwarded by E.R. Thayer (1914) 27 Harv. L.R. 317. It should be noted that the tort of breach of statutory
duty is distinct from statutes which place liability in negligence in statutory form such as the Occupiers'
Liability Acts which are discussed in Ch. 8. See, generally, K. Stanton et al, *Statutory Torts* (Sweet and
Maxwell, 2003) and RA Buckley (1984) 100 L.Q.R. 204.
[56] See G. Williams (1960) 23 M.L.R. 233.
[57] [1982] A.C. 173 at 187, rejecting the majority judgment in *Ex p. Island Records Ltd* [1978] Ch. 122.
[58] Despite the plea by Lord du Parcq in *Cutler v Wandsworth Stadium Ltd* [1949] A.C. 398 at 410 that
Parliament should state explicitly whether it intended that there should be a civil remedy or not. See also
McCall v Abelesz [1976] Q.B. 585.
[59] *e.g.* see Consumer Protection Act 1987, s.41.
[60] *e.g.* Health and Safety at Work etc. Act 1974, s.47(1)(a) provides that the general duties under the Act do
not give rise to civil liability. S.47(2) provides, however, that breach of a duty imposed by the health and
safety *regulations* shall, so far as it causes damage, give rise to civil liability except in so far as the regulations
provide otherwise.

courts and whether or not they are willing to accept that a regulatory statute was intended to place an additional burden on defendants to pay civil damages. Generally, the courts have shown themselves willing to adopt such a construction in relation to employee safety, but have adopted a more restrictive view in other contexts. In considering the employment cases, it should be borne in mind that until 1948, breach of statutory duty formed one of the ways of circumventing the doctrine of common employment. Policy considerations have therefore been influential in deciding when to allow a remedy for breach of statutory duty—arguably this is inevitable when the courts are given a broad interpretative discretion. The Law Commission, in 1969,[61] attempted to limit this discretion by recommending the enactment of a general statute that would have created a presumption that a civil remedy was intended unless the contrary was stated. This did not become law. Such a provision would have greatly increased the role of this tort, in a way which does not reflect the current restrictive view taken outside industrial safety.

Although the courts exercise discretion in such cases, this discretion is not without limits. The courts have developed guidelines which they use in deciding whether a civil remedy was intended. These are examined below.

Construing Parliamentary intention

The courts have identified a number of factors which indicate whether Parliament   **7–011**
intended a remedy to lie for breach of statutory duty. The leading case of *Lonrho Ltd v Shell Petroleum Co. Ltd (No. 2)*[62] highlights the most significant factors. The case concerned the supply of oil in breach of certain sanctions following the unilateral declaration of independence by Southern Rhodesia in 1965. Lonrho brought an action for breach of statutory duty, alleging that it had suffered heavy losses when (unlike its competitors) it had complied with the sanctions. Lord Diplock, giving the leading judgment, held that the action failed. Whilst confirming that the overall test was one of identifying whether the purpose of the Act was to give the claimant a civil remedy, his Lordship identified a number of factors which assisted the courts in construing statutory provisions. His Lordship held that the courts should generally take a restrictive view where the Act provided its own penalties, but that there were two main exceptions to this rule. The first exception was where the claimant could show that the statute had been enacted for the benefit or protection of a particular class of individuals. The second exception was where the statute conferred a public right and a particular member of the public suffered special damage.[63] Neither exception was applicable in *Lonrho*. The sanctions had been imposed, as a matter of state policy, to destroy the illegal UDI regime and were not intended either to benefit a particular class of individuals, nor to establish a public right. Lonrho therefore had no valid claim for breach of statutory duty.

---

[61] See Law Commission Report No. 21, *The Interpretation of Statutes* (1969) para.38. This proposal did form part of the Interpretation of Legislation Bill 1980, but this was subsequently withdrawn. R.A. Buckley (1984) 100 L.Q.R. 204 at 231–232 argues that this provision would not, in any event, have resolved all the problems involved in construing statutes.

[62] [1982] A.C. 173 at 185.

[63] His Lordship's second exception is contentious and it is fair to say that it has not been taken up by the courts. The best example of liability in such circumstances is that of public nuisance (discussed in Ch. 10) which is clearly not statutory.

Whilst the considerations which influence the courts in construing Parliamentary intention are elusive, and difficult to examine in isolation, it is possible to identify and discuss a number of relevant points:

- whether the statute protects a specific "class" of individuals;
- the nature of the legislation;
- whether alternative remedies exist at law.

Each of these points will be examined below.

(1) Protection of a class

7–012 There is clear authority that if the statute is passed for the protection of a limited class of the public, rather than for the benefit of the public as a whole, a court will be more inclined to find that a civil remedy was intended.[64] Thus, in *Atkinson v Newcastle Waterworks Co.*,[65] the Court of Appeal rejected the claim of a householder whose premises had burnt down. The defendants had been in breach of their statutory duty to maintain water pressure in their pipes. As a result, when the fire broke out, there was insufficient water to extinguish it. Lord Cairns L.C. held that it would be a startling proposition to place an additional burden on a company supplying a town with water by making it liable to householders whose properties were damaged by fire.[66] The statutory scheme was for the benefit of the public as a whole and not individual householders, otherwise the company would be practically insuring householders against damage by fire.[67]

However, the fact that a particular provision refers to a certain class of individuals will not of itself give rise to an action in tort. As Lord Browne-Wilkinson stated in *X v Bedfordshire CC*, "a private law cause of action will arise if it can be shown, as a matter of construction of a statute, that the statutory duty was imposed for the protection of a limited class of the public *and* that Parliament intended to confer on members of that class a private right of action."[68] The *purpose* of the statute remains important. For example, in *Cutler v Wandsworth Stadium Ltd*,[69] section 11(2) of the Betting and Lotteries Act 1934 required the owner of a dog-racing track to provide space for bookmakers. The House of Lords held that although bookmakers were indeed an identifiable class, they could not sue for damages when excluded from the track. The purpose of the statute was to regulate the conduct of race tracks, and not to protect the livelihood of bookmakers, who might benefit incidentally from such regulation.

[64] See *X v Bedfordshire CC* [1995] 2 A.C. 633 at 731 and *O'Rourke v Camden LBC* [1998] A.C. 188 at 193. But note criticism of this approach by Atkin L.J. in *Phillips v Britannia Hygienic Laundry Co.* [1923] 2 K.B. 832 at 841.
[65] (1877) 2 Ex.D. 441. This marked a change from the more liberal approach first adopted by the courts, see *Couch v Steel* (1854) 3 E. & B. 402; 118 E.R. 1193.
[66] (1877) 2 Ex. D. 441 at 445–446.
[67] See also *Thames Trains Ltd v Health and Safety Executive* (2003) 147 S.J.L.B. 661, CA (duty owed by Health and Safety Executive to anyone affected by the railway being unsafe did not give rise to individual rights for passengers and train operators).
[68] [1995] 2 A.C. 633 at 731 (emphasis added).
[69] [1949] A.C. 398.

Similarly, in the more recent case of *R. v Deputy Governor of Parkhurst Prison, ex p. Hague*,[70] the House of Lords held that the Prison Rules 1964 were intended to regulate the administration of prisons and the management and control of prisoners. They did not give rise to any private rights for prisoners if they were breached.

(2) The nature of the legislation

This also seems to be significant in recent years. Where a statute has a "social welfare" goal, the courts have resisted imposing the burden of civil liability on usually a public authority defendant. It may be recalled that in the House of Lords decision in *X v Bedfordshire CC*[71] (discussed in Ch. 2) the plaintiffs brought actions against local authorities concerning the negligent performance of their statutory duties relating to education and child welfare. Actions were also brought for breach of statutory duty. The plaintiffs were unsuccessful in their claims in negligence and, unsurprisingly, their Lordships were also reluctant to impose liability for breach of statutory duty. Lord Browne-Wilkinson held that although the legislation was designed to protect children at risk and ensure adequate educational provision, it was nevertheless not Parliament's intention to allow individual children or their families to sue for damages. The plaintiffs were told to pursue their claims in administrative law, rather than the law of torts. In the later case of *Phelps v Hillingdon LBC*,[72] Lord Slynn re-iterated that, despite the existence of a valid claim for negligence, no remedy would lie for breach of statutory duty where the purpose of the legislation was one of social welfare: "The general nature of the duties imposed on local authorities in the context of a national system of education and the remedies available by way of appeal and judicial review indicate that Parliament did not intend to create a statutory remedy by way of damages."[73]

7–013

A similar position was taken in *O'Rourke v Camden LBC*[74] in relation to the local authority's statutory duty to house homeless persons. Lord Hoffmann in *O'Rourke* set out the reasoning of the court:

" . . . the Act is a scheme of social welfare, intended to confer benefits at the public expense on grounds of public policy. Public money is spent on housing the homeless not merely for the private benefit of people who find themselves homeless but on grounds of general public interest: because, for example, proper housing means that people will be less likely to suffer illness, turn to crime or require the attention of other social services. The expenditure interacts with expenditure on other public services such as education, the National Health Service and even the police. It is not simply a private matter between the claimant and the housing authority."[75]

On this basis, the statutes in both cases were passed for the benefit of society in general, and not for the benefit of individuals. This indicator is therefore perhaps

---

[70] [1992] 1 A.C. 58. Hague was more successful in his alternative claim in public law. The House of Lords held that prisoners' rights were adequately protected by alternative claims in public law and in the torts of misfeasance in public office, trespass to the person and negligence. For the significance of alternative remedies, see below.

[71] [1995] 2 A.C. 633.

[72] [2001] 2 A.C. 619.

[73] *ibid.*, at 652.

[74] [1998] A.C. 188. See R. Carnwath [1998] P.L. 407.

[75] [1998] A.C. 188 at 193.

better analysed as a particular example of (1) above: the courts rejecting liability where the statute is not for the benefit of a specific *class* of the public, but for the *public at large*. The courts are also very conscious of the wide discretion exercised by public authorities in such cases, and are reluctant to regulate this discretion through the law of tort. As Lord Hoffmann commented in *O'Rourke*: "the existence of all these discretions makes it unlikely that Parliament intended errors of judgment to give rise to an obligation to make financial reparation. Control by public law remedies would appear much more appropriate".[76]

(3) Alternative remedies

7–014   This overlaps with (2) in that the courts are influenced by the fact that public authorities are accountable in administrative law.[77] Moreover, where the statute sets up a system of fines, the court will be reluctant to assume that Parliament intended the additional burden of civil liability, unless, as stated by Lord Diplock in *Lonrho*,[78] it is apparent that the duty was imposed for the benefit or protection of a particular class.[79] In contrast, if there is no stated remedy for breach and there is an intention to protect a limited class, the court is more likely to hold that the statute gives rise to a civil action.[80]

Similarly, if adequate remedies are provided by the *common law*, or by *other statutory provisions*, this will indicate that no additional civil action exists. This, however, begs the question as to what is meant by "adequate". In *McCall v Abelesz*,[81] adequate remedies were said to exist against the harassment of tenants, which justified the refusal of liability, but it may be questioned whether this was in fact the case. The court in *Issa v Hackney LBC*[82] held that the adequacy of alternative remedies should be assessed at the date of enactment of the statute in question, and in that case refused to take account of the fact that the protection of tenants had diminished since the enactment of the Public Health Act 1936.

The common law position can impact in a further way. As well as suggesting that no liability should exist where there is an alternative remedy at law, it also indicates that

---

[76] [1998] A.C. 188 at 194.

[77] See *X v Bedfordshire C.C.* [1995] 2 A.C. 633 and *Phelps v Hillingdon LBC* [2001] 2 A.C. 619.

[78] *Lonrho Ltd v Shell Petroleum Co. Ltd (No.2)* [1982] A.C. 173 at 185.

[79] This may be unclear on the facts. Compare, for example, the Court of Appeal decisions of *Todd v Adams (The Maragetha Maria)* [2002] 2 Lloyd's Rep 293 (CA) and *Ziemniak v ETPM Deep Sea Ltd* [2003] 2 Lloyd's Rep 214, which both concerned breach of safety rules pursuant to the Merchant Shipping Act 1995. In *Todd*, the court somewhat reluctantly found that breach of rules made under the Act concerning the safety of fishing vessels did not give a right of action following a tragic fishing accident with the loss of all crew. The rules had specifically provided criminal sanctions and penalties and established a certification scheme which rendered civil liability inappropriate. However, in *Ziemniak* breach of rules in a different part of the Act did provide a civil remedy for a claimant seriously injured during a lifeboat test in harbour. Here, the claim was treated as one of safety in the workplace, thereby meriting the more generous treatment given to such claims. The rules did contain criminal sanctions, although they did not cover the accident in question. *Todd* was doubted, but nevertheless distinguished.

[80] See *Cutler v Wandsworth Stadium Ltd* [1949] A.C. 398 and *Kirvek Management & Consulting Services Ltd v Attorney General of Trinidad and Tobago* [2002] 1 W.L.R. 2792, PC. However, this did not assist the plaintiff in *R. v Deputy Governor of Parkhurst Prison, ex p. Hague* [1992] 1 A.C. 58.

[81] [1976] Q.B. 585 (the case concerned s.30(2) of the Rent Act 1965 which is no longer applicable) See also *Cullen v Chief Constable of the Royal Ulster Constabulary* [2003] 1 W.L.R. 1763 (HL(NI)): adequate public law remedies justified denying the claimant a private law claim when refused a reason for denial of access to solicitor in custody (note the strong dissent of Lords Bingham and Steyn concerning adequacy).

[82] [1997] 1 W.L.R. 956.

no liability should exist where it is for a type of damage irrecoverable at common law. The case of *Pickering v Liverpool Daily Post*[83] illustrates this point. Here, the plaintiff (a convicted murderer and sex offender) wished to prevent a newspaper from publishing information about his application to a mental health review tribunal to be discharged from a mental hospital. The House of Lords held that any breach of the Mental Health Review Tribunal Rules did not grant him a right to a civil remedy. There is no tort of breaching privacy in English law,[84] and, at that the court held that the defendants' actions were not capable of causing the plaintiff loss of a kind for which the law affords a remedy.[85] The courts also, in line with the common law position, seem far more willing to award damages for personal injury than for economic loss.[86]

The considerations discussed above are subject to the underlying policy decisions of the courts. As stated earlier, the courts have shown a notable leniency in finding civil liability for breaches of statutes involving industrial safety.[87] The questionable case of *Monk v Warbey*[88] is also a good example of the influence of policy on the courts. Despite clear authority that road-users did not form an identifiable class,[89] the court held that civil liability would be imposed on the owner of a vehicle who had allowed an uninsured driver to use it, contrary to s.35(1) of the Road Traffic Act 1930.[90] This was obviously an attempt to ensure that the victim received compensation. Nowadays such a problem is dealt with by the Motor Insurers' Bureau (see Ch. 1), although *Monk* remains good law.[91] A contrasting approach was taken by the Court of Appeal, however, in the more recent case of *Richardson v Pitt-Stanley*.[92] In this case, the plaintiff, who had been injured at work, had successfully sued his employers only to find that the company which employed him was in liquidation and unable to pay, and had failed to comply with its obligation under the Employers' Liability (Compulsory Insurance) Act 1969 to obtain insurance against liability. He therefore brought an action against the directors of the company for breach of statutory duty. The majority of the Court of Appeal rejected his claim. *Monk* was distinguished on a number of technical grounds.[93] Stuart-Smith L.J. also held, controversially, that the purpose of the Act was not solely to ensure injured employees could be compensated, but to protect employers from the risk of a heavy claim or loss.[94] Such a construction undoubtedly masked a policy decision not to render employers liable in tort for failing to comply with the insurance provisions of the Act.

[83] [1991] 2 A.C. 370.
[84] See *Wainwright v Home Office* [2003] 3 W.L.R. 1137, HL.
[85] "[T]hough [publication] may in one sense be adverse to the patient's interest" *per* Lord Bridge at 420. This is applied very narrowly in *Cullen v Chief Constable of the Royal Ulster Constabulary* [2003] 1 W.L.R. 1763 (HL(NI)). Privacy law has since developed following the implementation of the Human Rights Act 1998: see *Campbell v Mirror Group Newspapers Ltd* [2004] 2 W.L.R. 1232.
[86] See *Richardson v Pitt-Stanley* [1995] Q.B. 123 at 130 and 132.
[87] See, *e.g. Groves v Lord Wimborne* [1898] 2 Q.B. 402 and *Black v Fife Coal Co. Ltd* [1912] A.C. 149.
[88] [1935] 1 K.B. 75, CA.
[89] See *Phillips v Britannia Hygienic Laundry Co.* [1923] 2 K.B. 832.
[90] Now the Road Traffic Act 1988, s.143. See also *Roe v Sheffield City Council* [2003] 2 W.L.R. 848.
[91] See *Norman v Ali (Limitation Period)* [2000] R.T.R. 107 where the MIB required, pursuant to s.5(1)(d) of the Uninsured Drivers' Agreement 1988, that the claimant should bring the car-owner (Aziz) into the action, on a *Monk v Warbey* type action, for permitting Ali to drive the car when uninsured against third party risks. The limitation period for such actions is that of personal injury claims, namely, three years (see Ch. 14).
[92] [1995] Q.B. 123 (Sir John Megaw dissenting).
[93] Which have been described as "less than compelling": see J. O'Sullivan [1995] C.L.J. 241 at 242.
[94] [1995] Q.B. 123 at 131.

It is therefore impossible to divorce the decisions of the courts from the influence of policy. In fact, the whole task of finding whether Parliament intended civil liability has been dismissed by many writers as a fiction.[95] It is unlikely in many cases that parliamentary drafters actually *considered* whether a remedy should exist in tort and it might be suspected that, even if the issue was considered, it would have been avoided as politically contentious. This leaves a considerable amount of discretion with the courts. While this may be thought undesirable, the courts have little option until parliamentary drafters deal with the question of civil liability for breach of statutory obligations on a more regular basis. The law at present is unpredictable and reflects the policy choices of the court. It is important, however, not to over-exaggerate these problems. In practice, the number of claims made for breach of statutory duty is small and the significance of such problems is minimal.

Further considerations

7–015   If the statute is one for which the courts are prepared to find civil liability, then this is not the end of the matter. The claimant has to satisfy four further hurdles:

- Is the duty owed to this particular claimant?
- Has the defendant breached his or her statutory duty?
- Did the breach cause the damage concerned?
- Was the damage of the kind which the statute intended to prevent?

These will be examined below.

(1) Is the duty owed to this particular claimant?

7–016   The claimant must show that he or she is within the class of persons intended to benefit under the statute. This goes back to the construction of the statute. In *Knapp v Railway Executive*,[96] for example, a breach of regulations in maintaining a level crossing, which led to a gate swinging back to injure the driver of an oncoming train, was held not to be actionable. Although the statutory provisions did give a remedy at common law, they were only for the benefit of road-users and did not benefit persons travelling on the train.

(2) Has the defendant breached his or her duty to the claimant?

7–017   The defendant must have acted in breach of his or her duty as set out in the statute. Again, we must turn back to the wording of the statute and examine just what the defendant was required to do or not to do. Is the duty one of reasonable care or does the statute impose strict liability? The courts will examine the exact wording of the statute and, again, in the industrial context, have interpreted legislation in a pro-employee manner. For example, the provision that the employer must act "so far as is reasonably practicable" has been interpreted to place the legal burden on the employer

---

[95] G. Williams (1960) 23 M.L.R. 233 at 244 describes it as "this process of looking for what is not there".
[96] [1949] 2 All E.R. 508, CA.

to establish that it was not reasonably practicable to take the precautions in question.[97] However, the courts do respect the strict wording of the statute. In *Chipchase v British Titan Products Co. Ltd*,[98] a regulation required every working platform from which a person could fall more than six feet six inches to be at least 34 inches wide. The plaintiff fell from a platform that was nine inches wide, but only six feet from the ground. On this basis, no claim could arise under statute and the plaintiff was left to pursue a claim in ordinary negligence.

(3) Did the breach cause the damage concerned?

Causation must be proved, and a similar approach is taken to that adopted for the tort of negligence, which we discussed in Ch. 6.[99] One particular problem which has arisen is where the statutory duty is placed on both the employer and the employee, and although the employer has taken all reasonable steps, the conduct of the employee has caused the accident. In such cases, the courts are reluctant to find the employer liable for the employee's own breach of statutory duty. In *Boyle v Kodak Ltd*,[1] the plaintiff had been injured when he fell off a ladder which was required by law to be secured. Previous authority demonstrated that civil liability arose from breach, but the House of Lords held that it was not prepared to find the employer liable if only the plaintiff had been at fault. Lord Reid stated that "it would be absurd if, notwithstanding the employer having done all he could reasonably be expected to do to ensure compliance, a workman, who deliberately disobeyed his employer's orders and thereby put the employer in breach of a regulation, could claim damages for injury caused to him solely by his own wrongdoing".[2] On the facts, however, the court found that the employers had failed to show that the accident was solely due to the fault of the plaintiff and so liability would be divided 50:50, due to the contributory negligence of the plaintiff. The limitations of *Boyle* should be noted. Only if the duty is placed *both* on the employer and employee and the employee is the only person at fault will the courts refuse liability.

7–018

(4) Is the damage of the kind which the statute intended to prevent?

This, again, is a question of construction. The courts will examine the statute, and if the claimant has suffered an injury different from that mentioned in the statute, then the claimant will not be able to recover. It will therefore depend on how the court interprets "damage". In *Gorris v Scott*,[3] the Court of Exchequer adopted a strict line. Here, the Act in question required that animals be transported in pens to prevent the spread of contagious diseases. In violation of the Act, the plaintiff's sheep had been transported without pens and had been washed overboard in bad weather. The court held that such damage was "something totally apart from the object of the Act of Parliament"[4] and rejected the plaintiff's claim. Nowadays it is unlikely that a court

7–019

---

[97] *Nimmo v Alexander Cowan & Sons Ltd* [1968] A.C. 107, HL (admittedly by a slim majority of 3 to 2).
[98] [1956] 1 Q.B 545, CA.
[99] See, in particular, *McWilliams v Sir William Arrol Ltd* [1962] 1 All E.R. 623 which concerns breach of statutory duty.
[1] [1969] 1 W.L.R. 661; [1969] 2 All E.R. 439. See also *Ginty v Belmont Building Supplies Ltd* [1959] 1 All E.R. 414 at 423–424 and *Anderson v Newham College of Further Education* [2003] I.C.R. 212.
[2] [1969] 1 W.L.R. 661 at 665–666.
[3] (1874) L.R. 9 Exch. 125.
[4] *ibid.*, 129–130 *per* Kelly C.B.

would take such a strict approach. The courts (in line with the approach taken in *The Wagon Mound*) will simply examine whether the damage suffered is of the *kind* that the statute was designed to prevent.[5]

Defences

7–020 These will be discussed in more detail in Ch. 14. It is worth noting at this stage that there is some indecision as to whether the defence of voluntary assumption of risk (or *volenti non fit injuria*) applies to breach of statutory duty. The House of Lords in *ICI v Shatwell*[6] held that the defence would apply where the employer was not at fault and was only liable vicariously for the acts of its employees. Lords Reid and Pearce stressed that the defence should not apply if the employer is in some way at fault in failing to comply with the duty.[7]

Although the principle of contributory negligence clearly applies to the tort of breach of statutory duty,[8] there is some authority that it will be applied leniently towards employees injured in the course of their employment. In *Caswell v Powell Duffryn Associated Collieries*,[9] it was held that the courts should take account of any continual noise, strain and risk to which employees were exposed which might lead to their failure to take reasonable care. This seems to be another example of the preferential treatment given to industrial injury claims.

Breaches of European legislation (the "Eurotort")

7–021 This is an area of increasing importance, which we mentioned in our introductory chapter. Claimants have a right to a remedy in national law for a number of breaches of European law, and the House of Lords in *Garden Cottage Foods Ltd v Milk Marketing Board*[10] held that such remedies would arise under the tort of breach of statutory duty. Under s.2(1) of the European Communities Act 1972, the State has an obligation to ensure that national law should be consistent with EU law and, therefore, if it acts in breach of Treaty provisions, it can be said to "breach" this duty. The right to a national remedy has increased in recent years, with ground-breaking decisions such as *Francovich v Italian Republic*[11] and *Brasserie du Pêcheur v Germany; R. v Secretary of State for Transport, ex p. Factortame (No.4)*.[12] Reference should be made to

---

[5] *Donaghey v Boulton & Paul Ltd* [1968] A.C. 1 at 26 *per* Lord Reid, HL (who draws a clear comparison with the position in negligence under *The Wagon Mound* [1961] A.C. 388 discussed in Ch. 6).
[6] [1965] A.C. 656.
[7] Lord Pearce, *ibid.*, at 687, extends this to where the employer is vicariously in breach of statutory duty through the neglect of some person who is of superior rank to the claimant and whose commands the claimant was bound to obey.
[8] See s.4, Law Reform (Contributory Negligence) Act 1945.
[9] [1940] A.C. 152 at 166. It should be noted that this case was decided before the Law Reform (Contributory Negligence) Act 1945 when contributory negligence was an absolute defence to the employee's claim which may have encouraged a more generous approach.
[10] [1984] A.C. 130. See also Mann J. in *Bourgoin S.A. and Others v Ministry of Agriculture, Fisheries and Food* [1986] Q.B. 716 at 733.
[11] (C6/90) [1991] E.C.R. I-5357, [1993] 2 C.M.L.R. 66.
[12] (C46/93 and C48/93) [1996] Q.B. 404; [1996] 1 C.M.L.R. 889. See A. Downes (1997) 17 L.S. 286 and P. Craig (1997) 113 L.Q.R. 67.

works on EC law for detailed discussion of such developments,[13] but it should be noted that these developments in European law have led to a right to damages which is far wider than that provided by the traditional English tort of breach of statutory duty. In the leading case of *Brasserie du Pêcheur v Germany; R. v Secretary of State for Transport, ex p. Factortame (No.4)*,[14] the European Court of Justice indicated the scope of the right to damages in national law:

"Community law confers a right to reparation where three conditions are met: the rule of law infringed must be intended to confer rights on individuals; the breach must be sufficiently serious; and there must be a direct causal link between the breach of the obligation resting on the state and the damage sustained by the injured parties."[15]

The first and third conditions are very similar to those of breach of statutory duty. However, the second condition does differ. It is not intended to be a test of fault, but whether the State has shown a manifest and grave disregard to the limits of its discretion.[16] Where such conditions exist, States must provide remedies which are no less favourable than rules applying to similar claims based on national law, and the rules must not be such as in practice to make it impossible or excessively difficult to obtain reparation.[17] Subject to these principles of equality and effectiveness, it remains for the national court to find the facts, decide whether the breach of Community law is sufficiently serious[18] and determine whether there is a direct causal link between the breach and the damage suffered.[19]

It remains a moot point how this fits into the tort of breach of statutory duty. Three main options exist. Either breach of European legislation should be treated as a tort in its own right (which is unlikely), breach of statutory duty should evolve as a tort according to the demands of European law, or breach of European legislation should be treated as a separate category of liability within breach of statutory duty, whose rules should remain unchanged. At present, the third option seems to be adopted. The recent decision of *R. v Secretary of State for Transport, ex p Factortame (No.7)*[20] confirms that, for limitation purposes at least, the action will be treated as a claim for

---

[13] See P. Craig and G. de Burca, *EU law: Text, Cases and Materials* (3rd ed., Oxford, 2002) Ch. 6 and T. Tridimas (2001) 38 C.M.L.R. 301.

[14] [1996] Q.B. 404.

[15] *ibid.*, at 499, para.51. See also *Norbrook Laboratories Ltd v Ministry of Agriculture, Fisheries and Food* [1998] 3 C.M.L.R. 809 paras 106–111; *R. v H.M. Treasury, Ex parte British Telecommunications* [1996] 2 C.M.L.R. 217 para.39; *R. v MAFF, Ex parte Hedley Lomas* [1996] 2 C.M.L.R. 391, para.25, and *Dillenkofer and Others v Germany* [1996] 3 C.M.L.R. 469 para.24. See W. van Gerven (1996) 45 I.C.L.Q. 507. The court also warned at 503 (para.87) that a more flexible approach towards compensation might be required, notably in relation to damages for loss of profit.

[16] See *Brasserie du Pêcheur v Germany; R. v Secretary of State for Transport, ex p. Factortame (No.4)* [1996] Q.B. 404 and *R v Secretary of State for Transport, ex p Factortame (No.5)* [2000] 1 A.C. 524.

[17] *ibid.*, at 504, para.90.

[18] See *R v Secretary of State for Transport, ex p Factortame (No.5)* [2000] 1 A.C. 524, where the House of Lords found that the Government's breach of EC law in enacting the Merchant Shipping Act 1988 which prevented foreign nationals from fishing in British waters was "sufficiently serious".

[19] The national courts may also determine whether the European legislation provides individual rights provided that the interpretation amounts to an *acte clair*: *Three Rivers District Council v Bank of England (No. 3)* [2003] 2 A.C. 1.

[20] [2001] 1 W.L.R. 942, QBD (T & CC), Judge Toulmin Q.C.

breach of statutory duty, although Judge Toulmin Q.C. remarked that "[i]t may well be that the term 'Eurotort' is apt to describe the particular characteristic in *Brasserie du Pêcheur* to differentiate it from the somewhat different requirements under English domestic law."[21] The court rejected the argument that such claims could be classified as misfeasance in public office.[22]

VICARIOUS LIABILITY

7–022   This is a different concept from the two forms of liability examined above. It is not a tort in its own right, but a rule of responsibility which renders the defendant liable for the torts committed by another. The commonest example is that of an employer for its employees. It therefore fits neatly into this chapter and will be dealt with solely in this context. Other examples of vicarious liability include the liability of a firm for the torts of partners.[23]

Vicarious liability is essentially a rule of convenience. It does not mean that the tortfeasor (X) is not personally liable for his negligence, but that the claimant has the choice to sue X or his employer (Y) and generally, the claimant will sue Y, because Y has the deeper pocket. The House of Lords has confirmed that the employer may seek to recover damages from the employee who committed the tort,[24] but in practice, this does not happen. Employers' liability insurers have entered into a "gentlemen's agreement" not to pursue actions against employees except where there has been evidence of collusion or wilful misconduct.[25] This, of course, contradicts completely the idea of corrective justice, discussed in Ch. 1, that only those at fault should pay compensation in tort.

Yet, the vicarious liability of an employer is limited in application. It is confined first to "employees", and secondly to acts committed in the course of employment. An employer is not responsible if the employee's negligent act does not relate to his or her position, for example, where the employee (X) negligently crashes his car into the claimant whilst driving home from work. This has led to subtle distinctions, which will be discussed below.

To establish vicarious liability against an employer,[26] the claimant must show all three of the following:

- The employee committed a tort;

---

[21] [2001] 1 W.L.R. 942, QBD (T & CC), Judge Toulmin Q.C., para.176.
[22] See the now leading case on this intentional tort: *Three Rivers District Council v Bank of England (No.3)* [2003] 2 A.C. 1, which imposes liability for a deliberate abuse of power by a public official.
[23] Partnership Act 1890, s.10. See *Dubai Aluminium Co Ltd v Salaam* [2002] 3 W.L.R. 1913 (HL): firm of solicitors liable for partner's dishonest participation in a fraud. S.10 covers both common law and equitable wrongs. Vicarious liability has also been linked with the concept of agency. For an attempt to use agency to extend the liability of an (insured) car owner, see *Morgans v Launchbury* [1973] A.C. 127, HL.
[24] This may occur either for breach of an implied term in the contract of employment to use reasonable care and skill (*Lister v Romford Ice and Cold Storage Co.* [1957] A.C. 555), or, because vicarious liability is treated as joint and several liability, under the Civil Liability (Contribution) Act 1978 which entitles the employer to seek a contribution from the employee with respect to his or her responsibility for the damage caused. This Act is discussed in more detail in Ch. 15.
[25] See G. Gardiner (1959) 22 M.L.R. 652. Also R. Lewis (1985) 48 M.L.R. 275, 281–282.
[26] See, generally, P.S. Atiyah, *Vicarious Liability in the Law of Torts* (Butterworths, 1967).

- The existence of an employer/employee relationship;

- The employee acted in the course of his or her employment when committing the tort in question.

We examine these requirements below.

(1) The employee committed a tort

This may be considered obvious, but is worth noting. If the employee is not liable in tort, then it is pointless suing the employer, as there is nothing for the employer to be vicariously liable *for*. The claimant must therefore prove that the employee's conduct satisfies all the requirements of the tort in question.   **7–023**

(2) The existence of an employer/employee relationship

This has caused some confusion, which is aggravated by the fact that most cases on the employer/employee relationship do not arise in tort, but usually in relation to employment and tax law disputes.[27] It is not enough to say that the tortfeasor was employed by the defendant. The courts draw a distinction between, on the one hand, a *contract of service*[28] or employment—where the person employed is an "employee", and, on the other hand, a *contract for services*—where the person employed is an "independent contractor". Generally, an employer is not vicariously liable for the actions of independent contractors. So, if I employ a workman to fix the reception on my television, I have entered a contract for services with an independent contractor and I would not be liable for his torts. Unfortunately, this distinction is not always so easy to draw. In recent times, the nature of employment has changed, with workers far more insecure than they have been in the past. Workers may be employed on a casual basis, or via an employment agency, or on a government scheme, and it is difficult to ascertain their exact status.[29] This difficulty is compounded by the various arrangements undertaken by workers to limit their tax liability, frequently by labelling themselves as independent contractors for this purpose. The courts, therefore, face a real challenge in distinguishing between contracts of employment and contracts for services. A number of factors can be identified as important to the courts in deciding this question, but it is fair to state that the courts generally adopt a "broad brush" approach, dependent on the facts of each particular case.[30]   **7–024**

---

[27] See E. McKendrick (1990) 53 M.L.R. 770 and R. Kidner (1995) 15 L.S. 47, who both argue that the courts should recognise that the status of workers may vary according to the context in question.

[28] Readers will find reference to employees as "servants" in case law. We prefer to avoid this old-fashioned term, and, for the sake of clarity, we use the term "employee".

[29] See, for example, recently *Brook Street Bureau (UK) Ltd v Dacas* [2004] I.R.L.R. 358.

[30] The question of the existence of a contract of employment will, in most cases, be considered a mixed question of law and fact for the trial judge, and an appeal court will be reluctant to intervene in the absence of an error of law or perversity: see Lord Hoffmann in *Carmichael v National Power plc* [1999] 1 W.L.R. 2042.

Factors identifying "employees"[31]

7–025   **The terms of the contract.** The courts have clearly stated that they will not be governed by the wording of the contract, but will examine the *substance* of the contract. In *Ferguson v Dawson*,[32] for example, it had been agreed between the parties that workers employed on a building site would be "self-employed labour only sub-contractors". By this means, the workers avoided the deduction of income tax and national insurance contributions from their weekly payments.[33] The plaintiff, who worked on the defendants' building site, argued when injured that he was an employee and therefore able to sue for breach of statutory duty. The court held that in reality the relationship was one of employer and employee. The defendants could dismiss the workmen, move them between sites, tell them what work to do and had provided them with tools. These factors indicated that they were employees and not independent contractors.

However, the courts have experienced some disquiet in allowing a worker, who deliberately chooses to be employed as an independent contractor to avoid tax, to turn to the courts when he or she wishes to obtain the benefit of employee protection legislation.[34] The Court of Appeal in *Young and Woods v West*[35] was sympathetic to such concerns, but maintained that the court should look to the realities of the situation in the belief that "the Inland Revenue would [not] fail to discharge their statutory duty".[36]

7–026   **Control.** In the past, the control test was the primary indicator used by the courts.[37] An employer/employee relationship was held to exist when an employer could tell an employee what work to undertake and how it should be done. While this test is still used, it is clearly outdated in relation to modern work practices.[38] In an advanced technological age, employees are frequently expected to be able to exercise discretion and initiative in their performance. Professionals with skill and experience do not expect to be told what to do and how to act during each working day. A good example is that of a doctor in the Accident and Emergency department of a hospital.[39] It is clearly impossible for any employer to tell the doctor how to perform his or her duties. The doctor will be expected to exercise a large amount of discretion in deciding how to deal with patients. As Cooke J. commented in *Market Investigations v Minister of Social Security*[40]: "the most that can be said is that control will no doubt always have to be considered, although it can no longer be regarded as the sole determining factor".

---

[31] Chief Constables will be vicariously liable for the torts of police officers even though they are not strictly employees: see s.88(1), Police Act 1996. Due to the discretion given to police officers, such liability may be more extensive than that of the ordinary employer, provided that the police officer in question was at least apparently acting in the capacity of a police officer: see *Weir v Bettison* [2003] I.C.R. 708, CA.
[32] [1976] 1 W.L.R. 1213. See also *Mersey Docks and Harbour Board v Coggins and Griffith (Liverpool) Ltd* [1947] A.C. 1.
[33] The plaintiff further ensured his avoidance of PAYE tax by giving the false name, "Goff".
[34] Lawton L.J. dissenting in *Ferguson v Dawson* [1976] 1 W.L.R. 1213 at 1227 held that it was contrary to public policy to allow a worker to change his or her status in such a manner and that the worker should be held to the initial bargain. See also comments in *Massey v Crown Life Assurance* [1978] 1 W.L.R. 676, CA.
[35] [1980] I.R.L.R. 201.
[36] *ibid.*, at 207 *per* Stephenson L.J.
[37] Originating in the judgment of Bramwell L.J. in *Yewens v Noakes* (1880) 6 Q.B.D. 530.
[38] See O Kahn-Freud (1951) 14 M.L.R. 504 who criticises the control test as old-fashioned.
[39] See *Cassidy v Ministry of Health* [1951] 2 K.B. 343, CA.
[40] [1969] 2 Q.B. 173 at 185.

The relationship as a whole. This is the modern approach, which encompasses the   7–027
two earlier points. The cases reveal a number of factors which the courts will consider
in deciding whether an employer/employee relationship exists.[41] These include, in
addition to the terms of the contract and the control test:

- the payment of wages and National Insurance contributions, etc., on a regular
  basis;

- an indefinite term of employment;

- a fixed place and time of performance;

- the provision of equipment or materials by the employer;

- the degree of financial risk and investment taken by the worker;

- whether the worker can profit from his or her performance;

- whether the worker must hire his or her own assistants or replacements;

- whether the work is integrated into the business or accessory to it;[42]

- whether there are mutual obligations on both parties. (A contract of employment is indicated where there is an obligation on the employer to provide and
  pay for work and an obligation on the worker to be ready and willing for
  work).[43]

Recent cases in employment law have stressed that mutuality of obligation and control,
interpreted broadly in the light of modern employment practice, should form the
"irreducible minimum" of any contract of employment.[44]

On this basis, in *Market Investigations v Minister of Social Security*,[45] part-time
interviewers working under short-term contracts for a market research company were
held to be employees. Their employers exercised extensive control over their work and
Cooke J. held that the limited discretion given to employees to decide when they
would work, and the ability to work for others during the relevant period, were not
inconsistent with the existence of a series of contracts of employment. In contrast, in
Ready Mixed Concrete (South East) Ltd v Minister of Pensions and National Insurance,[46]
McKenna J. held that arrangements to deliver ready-mixed concrete by "owner-
drivers", paid at fixed mileage rates, were not contracts of employment. This difficult
case illustrates the problem often facing the court where there are indications both
ways. *Against* a contract of employment was the fact that the drivers had to buy their

---

[41] See, notably, Cooke J. in *Market Investigations Ltd v Minister of Social Security* [1969] 2 Q.B. 173, 184–185
("the matter had never been better put than by Cooke J.": Lord Griffiths in *Lee Ting Sang v Chung Chi-
Keung* [1990] 2 A.C. 374, 382, PC).
[42] See Denning L.J. in *Stevenson, Jordan and Harrison Ltd v Macdonald and Evans* [1952] 1 T.L.R. 101 at
111, although it is questionable whether this does any more than restate the question.
[43] Compare the application of this test in *Nethermere (St Neots) Ltd v Taverna and Gardiner* [1984] I.C.R.
612 and *O'Kelly v Trusthouse Forte* [1984] 1 Q.B. 90.
[44] See *Nethermere (St Neots) Ltd v Taverna and Gardiner* [1984] I.C.R. 612, 623 *per* Stephenson L.J.,
approved in *Carmichael v National Power plc* [1999] 1 W.L.R. 2042, 2047 *per* Lord Irvine L.C. and
Montgomery v Johnson Underwood Ltd [2001] I.C.R. 819 (CA).
[45] [1969] 2 Q.B. 173.
[46] [1968] 2 Q.B. 497.

own vehicles, which were maintained at their own expense, and the fact that the drivers were described in the contracts as independent contractors. Yet *in favour* of a contract of employment was the high level of control exercised by the company. Vehicles were bought on hire purchase from a company associated with the defendants and had to be painted in the company's colours. The drivers were obliged to wear the company uniform and comply with the company's rules, including a prohibition on using the vehicles for any other business. Nevertheless, McKenna J. felt that ownership of the vehicles, and the fact that the drivers took the chance of profit and bore the risk of loss, indicated that the drivers were in reality independent contractors.[47]

7–028   **Lending an employee.**   One particular problem which arises is the status of employees who are hired out to work for a different company. Do such employees remain the employees of their general employer, or do they become the employees of the hiring company? This will of course determine who is vicariously liable for the employees' torts. The leading case is that of *Mersey Docks and Harbour Board v Coggins and Griffith (Liverpool) Ltd.*[48] Here, the harbour board employed Newall as a crane driver. The board hired the crane, together with Newall, to a firm of stevedores on terms which stipulated that Newall was the employee of the firm, although the board continued to pay his wages and retained a power of dismissal. In loading a ship, Newall negligently injured one of the firm's employees and the question was who was liable for his actions. The House of Lords held that the harbour board remained liable. At the time of the accident, although the company instructed Newall in what work to do, they had no control as to how Newall operated the crane. Looking at all the circumstances of the case, the facts that the harbour board retained authority to control how the crane was driven, and paid the wages of Newall, indicated that they were still his employers. Further, it was held that the courts would generally assume that the general or permanent employer would remain the employer of the tortfeasor. Only in exceptional circumstances would the heavy burden of proof be satisfied to find the hirer liable.[49] This seems sensible on the facts. The harbour board lent the crane and Newall to various stevedores to unload ships, and it would be absurd if Newall had a different employer each day. Lord Porter indicated that in future cases, courts should consider a number of factors, including who pays the worker's wages, who has power of dismissal, how long the alternative work lasts and the complexity of the machinery used.[50] The more complex the machinery, the more unlikely that the employee will be deemed to work for the company hiring his or her services.

(3)   The employee acted in the course of employment

7–029   The employer will be liable for torts committed "in the course of employment".[51] This phrase has caused considerable problems in interpretation. It has been established that the employer cannot simply argue that the employee was not employed to commit torts

---

[47] See also *Todd v Adams (The Maragetha Maria)* [2002] 2 Lloyd's Rep 293 where the Court of Appeal held that an arrangement whereby remuneration of the crew of a fishing vessel depended solely on a share of the profits (or losses) of each trip should be characterised as a joint venture rather than a contract of service.
[48] [1947] A.C. 1.
[49] But see *Interlink Express Parcels Ltd v Night Trunkers Ltd* [2001] R.T.R. 23 (CA) where the court stressed the question of control.
[50] [1947] A.C. 1 at 17.
[51] To be actionable all necessary features of the tort must be committed in the course of employment: see *Credit Lyonnais NV v Export Credits Guarantee Department* [2000] 1 A.C. 486, HL.

and was therefore acting outside the course of his or her employment. This would effectively undermine the whole concept of vicarious liability. A broader test is therefore applied. The employee is held to be acting in the course of employment if his or her conduct is authorised by the employer, or is considered to be an unauthorised means of performing the job for which he or she is employed. Whilst it is obvious that an employer will be liable for actions it has authorised,[52] the second category has proven more difficult to explain. It has now been interpreted as covering actions *closely connected* to the job for which the tortfeasor is employed.[53] The "course" or "scope" of employment will depend on the facts of each particular case, but we outline below a selection of case law indicating the approach adopted by the courts.

Generally, the courts have taken a generous approach to this question. For example, in *Century Insurance v NI Road Transport Board*,[54] a driver of a petrol lorry was held to be acting in the course of his employment when he discarded a lighted match, which he had used to light a cigarette, while delivering petrol. This led to an explosion which damaged the tanker, a car, and several nearby houses. Lighting a cigarette was held to be an act of comfort and convenience which would not be treated as outside the scope of employment.

An equally broad approach was taken by the House of Lords in *Smith v Stages*.[55] This case raised the problem whether employees driving to and from work were acting within the scope of their employment. The court held that generally this will not be the case unless special circumstances exist, for example the employee is required under the contract of employment to use the employer's transport to work.[56] Equally, if the employee's job requires travel, for example because he or she is a sales rep or a gas-fitter, then such travel will be deemed to be within the course of his or her employment. However, a deviation or interruption from a journey taken in the course of employment will, unless incidental, take the employee out of the course of employment for the time being. This last point is illustrated by two cases involving tortfeasors employed to drive a horse and cart for their employers. In *Whatman v Pearson*,[57] the employee had, against strict instructions, chosen to travel home for dinner by horse and cart. His employers were held liable for the damage caused when the horse escaped due to the employee's negligence. Byles J. held that the employee was clearly acting within the general scope of his authority in dealing with the horse and cart during the day. In contrast, in *Storey v Ashton*,[58] the court held that an employee who, after business hours, had driven to a friend's house, was not in the course of employment. The trip had nothing to do with his employment and his employer was thus not held liable for the injuries suffered by the plaintiff due to the employee's negligent driving. We can see from these cases that the question is therefore one of degree.

---

[52] Although arguably the employer is primarily liable for such actions: see Lord Millett in *Lister v Hesley Hall Ltd* [2002] 1 A.C. 215.

[53] See *Lister v Hesley Hall Ltd* [2002] 1 A.C. 215.

[54] [1942] A.C. 509. See also *Bayley v Manchester, Sheffield and Lincolnshire Ry Co.* (1873) L.R. 8 C.P. 148: railway porter mistakenly pulling passenger from what he believed to be the wrong train just after the train had started to leave the station found to be in the course of his employment.

[55] [1989] A.C. 928.

[56] See Lord Goff *ibid.*, at 936–937 and Lord Lowry *ibid.*, at 955–956. This is subject, of course, to any express arrangements between employer and employee.

[57] (1868) L.R. 3 C.P. 422.

[58] (1869) L.R. 4 Q.B. 476.

The facts of *Smith v Stages* raised a different problem. Here, two employees who normally worked in Staffordshire had been sent to South Wales to undertake certain emergency works. They had been paid their ordinary salary to travel to and from Wales, together with their travel expenses. The employees decided to work non-stop and so return to Staffordshire earlier than anticipated. They drove back immediately on completion of the job without any sleep. A crash occurred in which both men were seriously injured. As the driver (Stages) was uninsured, his passenger sued their employer, claiming that the employer was vicariously liable for Stages' negligent driving.

The court held that the employer was vicariously liable. The employer had paid the men their wages and not merely a travel allowance for the time taken on the journey. This meant that the men were still acting in the course of their employment. This was despite the fact that the employer did not provide the car and left the mode of transport to the discretion of the men. This seems to be a policy decision ensuring that, in the absence of insurance, and in circumstances where the Motor Insurers Bureau will not provide cover,[59] the victim is fully compensated.

The line distinguishing conduct within and outside the scope of employment can be extremely fine. A good illustration is *Staton v NCB*.[60] Here, an employee at a colliery was held to be within the course of his employment while cycling across his employer's premises at the end of the working day to collect his wages from the pay office. Finnemore J. held that it was an act incidental to his employment and, if performed negligently, his employer would be vicariously liable.

Prohibited and criminal conduct by employees

7–030   Even if the conduct in question has been expressly prohibited by the employer, this does not mean that the employee has acted outside the scope of his or her employment. Whilst this may seem unfair to employers, it would be wrong if the employer could escape liability by simply prohibiting the commission of torts in the course of employment. The test is therefore whether the prohibition limits the scope of employment (as opposed to simply directing how the employee does his or her job). This is not particularly clear, and the courts' decisions provide limited assistance.

If the prohibited conduct can be found to *benefit the employer* in some way, then there is authority that the courts will be willing to find the employer vicariously liable. For example, in *Limpus v London General Omnibus Co.*,[61] the company's instructions not to race with, or obstruct, other buses had been disobeyed by one of its drivers who had obstructed a rival bus. This led to a collision with the plaintiff's bus, which overturned. The court found the company vicariously liable for the driver's negligent actions, on the basis that the employee's actions were simply an improper and unauthorised mode of doing an act which he was authorised to do, namely promoting the company's bus service.

More difficult are the cases where the driver of a company vehicle, contrary to express instructions, gives a lift to an unauthorised passenger. Will the employer be

---

[59] Lord Lowry [1989] A.C. 928 at 939 comments that the case arose because the driver was uninsured and the time limits under the Motor Insurers Bureau agreement had not been complied with.
[60] [1957] 1 W.L.R. 893.
[61] (1862) 1 H. & C. 526; 158 E.R. 993. See also *Ilkiw v Samuels* [1963] 1 W.L.R. 991 and *Kay v ITW Ltd* [1968] 1 Q.B. 140, but contrast *Beard v London General Omnibus Co.* [1900] 2 Q.B. 530 (bus conductor not in the course of employment when driving bus).

vicariously liable for any injury to the passenger in such circumstances? The courts'
approach has not been particularly consistent. In *Twine v Bean's Express Ltd*,[62] Lord
Greene M.R., arguably influenced by the fact that trespassers were owed a minimal
duty of care in 1946 (see Ch. 8), held that giving a lift to a hitchhiker was an act which
the driver was not employed to perform. A different approach was taken by the
majority of the Court of Appeal, however, in *Rose v Plenty*.[63] Here, a milkman had
been warned by his employer not to allow children to assist him, nor to allow
passengers on his float. In breach of these instructions, he engaged the plaintiff, aged
13, to help him. The plaintiff was injured due to the milkman's negligent driving. The
majority held that if the purpose of the prohibited act was to further the employer's
business, the act was in the course of employment. Scarman L.J. distinguished *Twine v
Bean's Express Ltd* on its facts. In that case, giving a lift to another had not been a
mode of doing something which the driver was employed to do. We can perhaps share
the doubts of Lawton L.J. (dissenting) as to the clarity of this distinction in practice,[64]
especially where there is clear authority that an act is not required to benefit an
employer to be in the course of employment.[65] The answer possibly lies in the
comment of Denning L.J., in *Rose v Plenty*, that following the introduction of
compulsory insurance in 1972, such cases are unlikely to arise in future. This does
suggest a policy decision to ensure that the injured boy obtained compensation. It must
be questioned whether *Rose v Plenty* leaves the law in a satisfactory state.

Further guidance may be found in a series of cases which deal with the question of
vicarious liability for criminal acts by employees. Whilst vicarious liability may seem
surprising in this context, it should be remembered that crimes such as assault, theft
and fraud are also torts, and employers have been found liable in such circumstances.
In *Poland v John Parr and Sons*,[66] for example, the defendants were found liable for
their employee assaulting a boy whom he believed had stolen a bag of sugar from his
employer's wagon. The court held that the employee had implied authority to make
reasonable efforts to protect his employer's property, and that the violence was not so
excessive as to take the act outside the scope of his employment. Equally, in *Lloyd v
Grace, Smith & Co.*,[67] a firm of solicitors was found vicariously liable for the fraudulent
activities of its managing clerk, who had defrauded a widow of her property. However,
the courts have stressed that for fraudulent misrepresentation, employers will only be
liable if they have given the employee actual or ostensible authority to make the
statements and this authority is relied upon by the claimant.[68] There is also authority

---

[62] (1946) 62 T.L.R. 458; 175 L.T. 131. Comment FH Newark (1954) 17 M.L.R. 102, 114. See also *Conway v
George Wimpey & Co. Ltd* [1951] 2 K.B. 266.
[63] [1976] 1 W.L.R. 141. See J. Finch (1976) 39 M.L.R. 575.
[64] His Lordship comments [1976] 1 W.L.R. 141 at 146 that "fine distinctions of that kind should have no
place in our law, particularly in a branch of it which affects so many employers and their insurers".
[65] See *Lloyd v Grace, Smith & Co.* [1912] A.C. 716 overturning *Barwick v English Joint Stock Bank* (1867)
L.R. 2 Ex. 259 on this point.
[66] [1927] 1 K.B. 236. See also *Dyer v Munday* [1895] 1 Q.B. 742 and FD Rose (1977) 40 M.L.R. 420 who
argues for a more liberal approach. The fact that the boy in *Poland* had fallen and had his leg amputated as
a result of the injury might have encouraged a more generous approach.
[67] [1912] A.C. 716. See also *Uxbridge Permanent Benefit Building Society v Pickard* [1939] 2 K.B. 248 and *Noel
v Poland* [2001] 2 B.C.L.C. 645.
[68] See *Armagas Ltd v Mundogas SA (The Ocean Frost)* [1986] A.C. 717, HL and *Kooragang Investments Pty v
Richardson & Wrench* [1982] A.C. 462 (PC), but see *Dubai Aluminium Co Ltd v Salaam* [2002] 3 W.L.R.
1913.

that an employer may be vicariously liable for the theft by an employee of goods entrusted to his or her care.[69]

The House of Lords in *Lister v Hesley Hall Ltd*[70] reviewed the application of vicarious liability in the context of serious criminal conduct amounting to an intentional tort. Here, the warden of a home for boys with emotional and behavioural difficulties had been found guilty of systematic sexual abuse of some of the boys under his care. In the earlier case of *Trotman v North Yorkshire County Council*,[71] the Court of Appeal had refused to accept that similar misconduct—the antithesis of what a carer was employed to do—could be deemed to be "in the course of his employment". The House of Lords took a broader view. Where the intentional tort was *closely connected* to the work the perpetrator was employed to do, it would be fair and just to find his employer vicariously liable.[72] The warden in *Lister* had been employed to provide a home for the boys and supervise them day-to-day in circumstances where he and his disabled wife were often the only members of staff on the premises. Such close contact was sufficient to satisfy the court that there was a close connection between what he had been employed to do and the acts of abuse committed. If, however, the acts of abuse had been committed by a groundsman, there would have been no close connection between his job and the torts in question.

To establish this connection, then the court will examine the nature and purpose of the job and the circumstances and context in which the acts took place. Their Lordships maintained, however, that this would not affect existing authority that private acts of passion, resentment or spite were outside the scope of employment.[73]

Lister has been followed by a number of cases in which the "close connection" test has been applied. In *Dubai Aluminium Co Ltd v Salaam*,[74] work undertaken by a solicitor for a client which assisted a fraud was found by the House of Lords to be closely connected to his work. In *Mattis v Pollock (t/a Flamingo's Nightclub)*[75] the Court of Appeal adopted a generous approach when a guest at a nightclub had been rendered paraplegic when stabbed by the bouncer outside the club. Although the act was one of revenge for injuries and humiliation inflicted on the bouncer some time earlier in the club by the victim's group of friends, the court held that since the

---

[69] Although the Court of Appeal in *Morris v Martin* [1966] 1 Q.B. 716 found an employer liable for the employee's theft on the basis of the principles of bailment for reward, it has been suggested that this case could simply have been decided on the basis that the act was in the course of the thief's employment. In *Lister v Hesley Hall Ltd* [2002] 1 A.C. 215, for example, Lord Steyn at 225 viewed the case as "the classic example of vicarious liability for intentional wrongdoing". The fact that the employee had been entrusted with the care of the fur was considered to strengthen the argument that the theft could be considered in the course of his employment.

[70] [2002] 1 A.C. 215. Comment P. Giliker (2002) 65 M.L.R. 269 and C.A. Hopkins (2001) 60 C.L.J. 458.

[71] [1999] L.G.R. 584.

[72] Adopting the test established by the Supreme Court of Canada in *Bazley v Curry* (1999) 74 D.L.R. (4th) 45 and *Jacobs v Griffiths* (1999) 174 D.L.R. (4th) 71 noted by P. Cane (2000) 116 L.Q.R. 21.

[73] See, for example, *Irving v Post Office* [1987] I.R.L.R. 289—Post Office not liable for postman writing racially offensive message on the back of an envelope addressed to his neighbours—and compare *Deatons Pty Ltd v Flew* (1949) 79 C.L.R. 370, HC Aus (beer and glass thrown in customer's face by barmaid found not to be in course of employment) with *Petterson v Royal Oak Hotel Ltd* [1948] N.Z.L.R. 136 where, in similar circumstances, the barman was found to be in the course of his employment.

[74] [2002] 3 W.L.R. 1913. Contrast *JJ Coughlan Ltd v Ruparelia The Times*, August 26, 2003, CA (no close connection between promotion of "preposterous" fraudulent scheme promising risk-free investment with return of 6000% *per annum* and ordinary course of solicitor's business).

[75] [2003] 1 W.L.R. 2158 (leave to appeal to HL refused: [2003] 1 W.L.R. 2838). See also *Vasey v Surrey Free Inns plc* [1996] P.I.Q.R. 373 and *Fennelly v Connex South Eastern Ltd* [2001] I.R.L.R. 390, CA.

employee had been encouraged by his employer to keep order by violent behaviour, the employer would be vicariously liable for an assault linked to the incident in the club.[76] Much would seem to turn on the court's condemnation of the employer's behaviour. He had known and encouraged the violent tendencies of the bouncer and so the court was able to find a close connection between the attack and what the bouncer had actually been employed to do.[77] The decision does, however, throw doubt on earlier cases such as *Warren v Henlys Ltd*[78] where the courts were more ready to classify acts of personal vengeance as outside the scope of employment.

It may be questioned, however, whether this test adds clarity to the law. Lord Nicholls commented in *Dubai* that: "This 'close connection' test focuses attention in the right direction. But it affords no guidance on the type or degree of connection which will normally be regarded as sufficiently close to prompt the legal conclusion that the risk of the wrongful act occurring, and any loss flowing from the wrongful act, should fall on the firm or employer rather than the third party who was wronged. . . . this lack of precision is inevitable, given the infinite range of circumstances where the issue arises."[79] In each case, therefore, the courts will face the difficult question whether the employee can "fairly" and "properly" be said to be acting in the course of employment. Some guidance may be obtained from pre-existing authority, but ultimately it will be a question of policy for the courts dependant on the extent to which they consider victims should receive the protection of vicarious liability.

Summary

We have seen that employers may find themselves liable for the tortious acts of their   **7–031** employees if they are deemed to be acting in the course of their employment. It is not necessary that the employee acts for the benefit of his or her employer, although this will support the conclusion that the employee is acting in the course of his or her employment, and not "on a frolic of their own".[80] If, however, the tortfeasor is not an employee, but an independent contractor, the employer will not generally be liable for his or her actions, unless the independent contractor has been taken on to perform a task for which the employer is directly responsible and cannot delegate responsibility. The extent of such liability will be examined below.

Liability for the actions of independent contractors[81]

Whilst an employer cannot be *vicariously* liable for the actions of independent   **7–032** contractors, employers may nevertheless find themselves liable for the actions of independent contractors if they place the employer in breach of a non-delegable duty

---

[76] Even where the employee in question had been chased out of the club by the group of friends, gone to his nearby home to fetch a knife and then had returned to the club to wreak revenge.
[77] The Court was even, in such circumstances, prepared to find the employer primarily liable for the attack.
[78] [1948] 2 All E.R. 935. (Assault by garage attendant following argument over payment for petrol. Customer had called the police and told the garage attendant that he would report him to his employers, whereupon the attendant hit him.) See similar decision in *Keppel Bus v Sa'ad bin Ahmad* [1974] 1 W.L.R. 1082, PC (comment FD Rose (1975) 91 L.Q.R. 17): bus passenger who criticised the conductor for being rude to an elderly female passenger insulted and then struck in the eye with the ticket punch acting outside the course of his employment. Doubt was also expressed on *Daniels v Whetstone Entertainments Ltd* [1962] 2 Lloyd's Rep 1.
[79] [2002] 3 W.L.R. 1913 at 1920. See also Judge L.J. in *Mattis* above at 2164: "a deceptively simple question."
[80] See Parke B. in *Joel v Morrison* (1834) 6 C. & P. 501; 172 E.R. 1338.
[81] See, generally, G. Williams [1956] C.L.J. 180.

to the claimant, or the employer has authorised the independent contractor to commit a tort.[82] Examples of such non-delegable duties include the employer's duty of care to its employees (discussed above), liability under the rule in *Rylands v Fletcher* (discussed in Ch. 10), and liability for works conducted on or over the highway, such as occurred in the odd case of *Tarry v Ashton*,[83] where a householder was found strictly liable when a lamp attached to his house, which was adjacent to the highway, fell on a person walking past.[84] On this basis, an employer will be liable to an employee if reasonable care is not taken in providing a safe place of work, even though the problem has been created by the negligence of an independent contractor.

It should be noted, however, that the courts are not prepared to find the employer liable, even when a non-delegable duty is owed, for collateral or casual negligence by the independent contractor which is unconnected with the job the independent contractor was engaged to perform.[85] The leading example is that of *Padbury v Holliday and Greenwood Ltd*.[86] Here, a sub-contractor, engaged to place casements in windows on a building site, had negligently placed an iron tool on a window sill. The tool fell and injured a passer-by. The Court of Appeal held that placing the tool on the sill was not an action taken in the ordinary course of doing the work he was employed to do, but was an act of collateral negligence for which the defendants were not liable. The case therefore limits the scope of the employer's duty to guard against risks which are not created by the work itself. This should be contrasted with the courts' more liberal treatment of the "scope of employment", discussed above.

Can vicarious liability be justified?

7–033   So far we have discussed the various criteria used by the courts to impose vicarious liability. In this section, we address a different issue: *should* we have a rule of vicarious liability in English law? It is plainly inconsistent with any idea that the person at fault should pay the claimant damages, and with the concept of retributive justice (see Ch. 1). It also diminishes the deterrent effect of tort law. Why should I take care at work if any harm I cause will be paid for by my employer?[87] A number of arguments have been put forward to justify vicarious liability.[88] It has been suggested that the employer has, in effect, caused the accident by setting the whole incident in motion by negligently employing a careless employee. Alternatively, the employer takes on the employee in the pursuit of profit, and one of the "costs" of employing the employee is his or her potential to cause harm.[89] Little credit is given now to early ideas that

---

[82] *Ellis v Sheffield Gas Consumers Co*. (1853) 2 E. & B. 767; 118 E.R. 955.
[83] (1876) 1 Q.B.D. 314. Contrast the two Court of Appeal decisions in *Salsbury v Woodland* [1970] 1 Q.B. 324 and *Rowe v Herman* [1997] 1 W.L.R. 1390, which adopt a narrow interpretation of this category.
[84] Other examples include withdrawal of support from neighbouring land: *Bower v Peate* (1876) 1 Q.B.D. 321 and cases involving ultra-hazardous acts: *Honeywill & Stein v Larkin Bros* [1934] 1 K.B. 102.
[85] But note the criticisms of this rule by Sach L.J. in *Salsbury v Woodland* [1970] 1 Q.B. 324 at 348.
[86] (1912) 28 T.L.R. 494. See also comments of Denning L.J. in *Cassidy v Ministry of Health* [1951] 2 K.B. 343 at 365 But contrast *Holliday v National Telephone Co*. [1899] 2 Q.B. 392.
[87] Apart from the fact that it is unlikely to boost my employment prospects! Arguably, such an argument may be countered by the deterrent effect on the employer in seeking to prevent such accidents occurring in the first place.
[88] See P.S. Atiyah, *Vicarious Liability in the Law of Torts* (Butterworths, 1967), Ch. 2 and the excellent article of G. Williams (1957) 20 M.L.R. 220, 228–235 and 437.
[89] See Lord Nicholls in *Dubai* above at 1919.

vicarious liability rested on the fact that the employee's acts were impliedly authorised, or that the employee should have been controlled by the employer.

The most realistic explanation, perhaps, rests with the two factors of compensation and insurance.[90] Professor Glanville Williams has commented: "However distasteful the theory may be, we have to admit that vicarious liability owes its explanation, if not its justification, to the search for a solvent defendant".[91] Vicarious liability ensures that the claimant sues a defendant with means, and that losses are spread efficiently via the network of compulsory employer insurance. Employers are free to spread the cost of insurance either through the price of their goods or by controlling other fixed costs, such as the level of wages.

The courts themselves have shown no particular concern as to the rationale behind vicarious liability. The best statement of principle is perhaps that of Scarman L.J., in *Rose v Plenty*, who commented: "It [is] important to realise that the principle of vicarious liability is one of public policy. It is not a principle which derives from a critical or refined consideration of other concepts in the common law".[92]

Employers' liability: conclusion

Employers' liability is a large subject. Tort law forms only a part of the potential liability of an employer. Nevertheless, it is important, particularly in the form of vicarious liability which plays a significant role in ensuring compensation in the law of torts. Although, following the abolition of the doctrine of common employment, the employer's personal liability is no longer as important, it is still a significant part of negligence liability in tort. Breach of statutory duty is a limited remedy, and until statutory drafters undertake to provide some clarity in this area of law, or a clear policy stance is taken by the government—such as that suggested by the Law Commission in 1969—this will continue to be a confusing area of law.   **7–034**

---

[90] See Lord Millett in *Lister* above at 243 who comments that vicarious liability "is best understood as a loss-distribution device." Note also his Lordship's comment in *Dubai* above at 1938.

[91] G. Williams (1957) 20 M.L.R. 220 at 232. See also H.J. Laski (1916) 26 Yale L.J. 105.

[92] [1976] 1 W.L.R. 141 at 147. See also Lord Pearce in *ICI v Shatwell* [1965] A.C. 656 at 685: "The doctrine of vicarious responsibility has not grown from any very clear, logical or legal principle, but from social convenience and rough justice".

Chapter 8

Occupiers' Liability

Introduction

An occupier of premises may be liable in tort to a claimant who, whilst on those **8–001** premises, suffers personal injury or property damage because the premises are in a defective or dangerous condition.[1] As in a common law negligence action, the claimant must prove the existence of a duty of care, breach of that duty, causation, and that the loss suffered is not too remote. Occupiers' liability, therefore, may be thought of simply as an aspect of the tort of negligence. The important difference, however, is that in this area of the law the question of whether or not a defendant owes a duty of care, and the question of the standard of care required of him or her are answered by reference to two statutes, namely the Occupiers' Liability Act 1957 and the Occupiers' Liability Act 1984. In summary, the 1957 Act regulates the duties owed by an occupier to "visitors" to his or her premises, whilst the 1984 Act applies to "others" who enter premises. Usually, these "others" will be trespassers.

This chapter examines both of these statutes in detail, beginning with the Occupiers' Liability Act 1957. Before considering this Act, however, it is appropriate to give an outline of the common law which prevailed before it was passed. The old law relating to occupiers' liability was complex and uncertain. It is useful to have some understanding of the problems associated with the old law, in order to appreciate the purpose of the modern legislation. Reference to the old law is also necessary to explain some of the terminology which the modern legislation employs.

The old law

Prior to the Occupiers' Liability Act 1957, the common law had distinguished between **8–002** four categories of persons who entered premises. Each category of entrant was owed a different standard of care by the occupier. The distinctions between these categories were extremely fine. The basic idea, however, was that the greater the benefit which accrued to the occupier by the person's presence on the premises, the higher would be the standard of care owed to that person. The four categories of entrant recognised by the common law were as follows:

---

[1] Liability of non-occupiers for defective premises, at common law and under the Defective Premises Act 1972, is discussed in Ch. 3.

(1) Contractual entrants

8–003   The highest standard of care was owed to persons who entered premises in accordance with the terms of a contract made with the occupier, for example guests staying in a hotel. The occupier had a duty to see that the premises were as safe as reasonable care and skill could make them for the purposes contemplated by the contract.

(2) Invitees

8–004   Invitees at common law were persons who entered premises to pursue some "common interest" with the occupier, for example customers entering the occupier's shop. Here, the occupier was obliged to use reasonable care to protect the invitee from unusual dangers of which he or she knew or ought to have known.[2]

(3) Licensees

8–005   Where the entrant could not be said to be pursuing any "common interest" with the occupier, but the occupier had simply given his or her permission (express or implied) for the entrant to be on the premises, the entrant was classified as a licensee. Friends invited to dinner by an occupier, for example, were classified as licensees at common law. Here, the occupier merely had a duty to warn the licensee about any trap or concealed danger on the premises of which he or she had actual knowledge.

(4) Trespassers

8–006   The lowest standard of care was owed to trespassers (*i.e.* those entering without the permission of the occupier). Trespassers generally entered premises at their own risk. The only duty which an occupier had was a duty to refrain from any deliberate act intended to cause bodily harm to the trespasser (firing a shotgun, for example) or done with reckless disregard for the presence of the trespasser (setting a man-trap, for example).[3]

The need for reform

8–007   The four categories of entrant described above were regarded by the common law as exhaustive, so that all entrants had to be classified as falling into one category or another. The case law, as it developed, presented a very muddled picture. In particular, the courts experienced difficulty in distinguishing between invitees, who had a "common interest" with the occupier, and licensees, who did not. The legalistic distinction between invitees and licensees eventually appeared artificial and unworkable. The need to revise the old rules prompted the government to appoint a Law Reform Committee, whose report was published in 1954.[4] The committee recommended that the fine distinctions under the old law should be abolished, in favour of a uniform standard of care owed to all *lawful* visitors to premises.[5] The tough attitude towards trespassers, however, was maintained, and it was not until the Occupiers' Liability Act 1984 that unlawful entrants were given statutory protection. The

---

[2] See *Indermaur v Dames* (1866) L.R. 1 C.P. 274 *per* Willes J. at 288.
[3] *Robert Addie & Sons (Collieries) Ltd v Dumbreck* [1929] A.C. 358.
[4] *Occupiers' Liability to Invitees, Licensees and Trespassers*, Cmnd 9305 (1954).
[5] *ibid.*, paras 78(i) and (ii).

committee's recommendations were given legal force in the Occupiers' Liability Act 1957.

OCCUPIERS' LIABILITY ACT 1957

Under the Occupiers' Liability Act 1957,[6] an occupier owes a single duty to all lawful visitors, irrespective of their purpose in entering the premises. Thus, s.2(1) of the Occupiers' Liability Act 1957 states:

> "An occupier of premises owes the same duty, the 'common duty of care', to all his visitors. . ."

Section 2(2) goes on to define the 'common duty of care', and the sections which follow set out various matters which are relevant in deciding whether the common duty of care has been discharged. Before we embark on a detailed analysis of those sections, however, it is appropriate to make a number of general observations.

The scope of the 1957 Act

(1) The Act covers damage to property as well as personal injury

Like the common law which it replaced, the Act covers both personal injury caused to a visitor and damage to his or her property. The Act also applies in respect of damage to property lawfully on the premises, even where that property does not belong to a visitor.[7] Thus, if a tile falls from the roof and damages a visitor's borrowed car parked on the premises, the owner of the car may sue for that damage. The Act does not, however, apply to property which is outside the boundaries of the premises. Mocatta J., in *AMF International Ltd v Magnet Bowling Ltd*,[8] remarked that, where property was damaged, there was no reason in principle why consequential economic loss should not be recoverable.[9]

(2) Liability under the Act may be limited by an express term of a contract, or by a notice given to visitors

It should be appreciated at the outset that, to a certain extent, the Act allows an occupier to limit his or her liability to visitors. An occupier can do this by displaying a notice on the premises, or, where visitors enter under a contract, by including a term in that contract which sets the standard of care he or she owes. These matters are considered more fully towards the end of this chapter.

(3) The Act is thought to apply only to the "occupancy duty"

It is unlikely that every careless act or omission which causes loss to a visitor on an occupier's premises will give rise to a claim under the Act. Thus, if a visitor is walking up the occupier's drive and is injured by a carelessly driven car, he or she will not sue

8–008

8–009

8–010

8–011

---

[6] See, generally, D. Payne, "The Occupiers' Liability Act" (1958) 21 M.L.R. 359.
[7] s.1(3)(b).
[8] [1968] 1 W.L.R. 1028.
[9] *ibid.*, at 1049 (on the basis that the Act makes no attempt to quantify or limit the damages recoverable).

under the Act, but in ordinary common law negligence. This is because the duty of care he or she is owed has nothing to do with the fact that the accident happened on the occupier's premises.

The old common law had distinguished between situations where the claimant suffered loss because he or she fell foul of some defect in, or dangerous object on, the premises (tripping over a loose floorboard, for example, or being electrocuted by a badly wired plug) and situations where the claimant's loss was caused by some *activity* carried out on the premises (the claimant was knocked down by a car, for example). The former situation was governed by the special rules of occupiers' liability, which laid down the "occupancy duty". This duty arose where the claimant's loss could be said to result from the *state of the premises*. The latter situation, however, was governed only by the ordinary rules of negligence, which laid down the "activity duty".

It is unclear whether this distinction has survived the 1957 Act. The wording of the Act does not make it clear whether the Act regulates only the "occupancy duty", or whether it also regulates the "activity duty", and the issue has been the subject of academic debate. The problem is that there are two relevant sections of the Act, each of which appears to give a conflicting answer to the question. Section 1(2) of the Act provides that the Act shall ". . . regulate the nature of the duty imposed by law in consequence of a person's occupation or control of premises". This implies that the Act covers only the "occupancy duty". Section 1(1), on the other hand, provides that the Act shall apply ". . . in respect of dangers due to the state of the premises or to things done or omitted to be done on them". This, then, implies that the modern law of occupiers' liability also covers situations where the claimant's loss is caused by a breach of the "activity duty".

Most academic commentary suggests that the 1957 Act applies only to the "occupancy duty".[10] In other words, it covers only those situations where the claimant's loss is due to the defective or dangerous state of the premises. It appears, however, that where an activity on premises gives rise to a continuing source of danger (use of the premises for motor racing, for example), the Act may apply.[11] The true position remains undecided by the courts because, whilst the debate may be of academic interest, the principles applied in a common law negligence action arising from a harmful *activity* on premises are so similar to those applied under the 1957 Act that nothing turns on the distinction between the "activity duty" and the "occupancy duty" under the modern law.

Having gained some appreciation of the general scope of the Act, then, our next task must be to examine its precise wording. It is this wording that provides the mechanism by which the interest of an occupier, in maintaining the premises as he or she wishes, is to be balanced against the safety of his or her visitors. It has been said that, under the Act, an "occupier" of "premises" owes a "common duty of care" to all his "visitors". These key terms require clarification.

[10] A view endorsed by the Law Commission in Report No. 75 *Report on Liability for Damage or Injury to Trespassers and Related Questions of Occupiers' Liability*, Cmnd 6428 (1976), para.23, cited by Neill L.J. in *Revill v Newbery* [1996] 2 W.L.R. 239 at 245. See also Stephen-Brown L.J, *obiter*, in *Ogwo v Taylor* [1988] A.C. 431 at 438.
[11] Law Commission Report No. 75 (above).

Definition of "Occupier"

Section 1(2) of the Act states that an "occupier" is simply a person "who would at   **8–012** common law be treated as an occupier". We must therefore examine the relevant case law. What emerges is that the courts have taken a broad approach, holding that a person will be an "occupier" if he or she has a *sufficient degree of control over the state of the premises*. A person need not have a legal estate in land to be the "occupier" of that land, nor need he or she have a right to exclusive possession.[12]

The leading case is *Wheat v E. Lacon & Co. Ltd.*[13] The defendants, a brewery, owned a public house. They allowed the publican and his wife, Mr and Mrs Richardson, to live in accommodation above the pub, not as tenants, but as mere licensees. The brewery had given Mrs Richardson permission to take in paying guests in part of the upstairs accommodation, access to which was gained by an outside staircase. The staircase was dangerous because its handrail did not go all the way to the bottom, and because it was unlit. One evening, the plaintiff's husband, who was a paying guest, fell down the staircase and was fatally injured. The plaintiff sued the brewery under the 1957 Act, and the question arose whether the brewery were "occupiers" of the private part of the building.

The House of Lords held that, in the circumstances, the brewery had retained sufficient control over the upstairs part of the premises to be regarded as occupiers. Although they had granted Mr and Mrs Richardson a licence to occupy the upstairs part of the premises, they had retained the right to access that part themselves. This meant that they could still exercise some control over the state of that part of the premises. Their Lordships found that the publican, his wife and the brewery were all "occupiers" under the Act. The standard of care required of each, however, was defined by the extent to which each had control over the premises. On the facts, neither the Richardsons nor the brewery had fallen below their respective standards of care. The short handrail did not by itself make the staircase unreasonably hazardous, and they were not responsible for a stranger having caused it to become unlit by removing a light bulb.

Two important points, then, emerge from the decision in *Wheat v E. Lacon & Co. Ltd*:

- There can be more than one occupier of premises;
- Where the owner of premises licenses others to occupy those premises, but retains the right to enter the premises, he or she remains an "occupier" for the purposes of the Act. This is to be contrasted with a situation where the owner grants a tenancy conferring on others exclusive possession of the premises. Here, the landlord will normally have given up control of the premises, so that he or she cannot be regarded as an occupier.

In all cases, the key question for the courts is not whether a person is in *actual occupation* of the premises, but whether he or she exercises *control* over the premises.

---

[12] *Humphreys v Dreamland (Margate) Ltd* (1930) 144 L.T. 529; *Hartwell v Grayson Rollo and Clover Docks Ltd* [1947] K.B. 901.

[13] [1966] A.C. 552. Compare *Bailey v Armes* [1999] E.G.C.S. 21 (no occupation of a flat roof to which children gained access without the defendants' knowledge.)

This is clear from the decision in *Harris v Birkenhead Corp*.[14] The defendant was a local authority which had made a compulsory purchase order on a house. It then served on the owner of the house, and on a tenant who occupied it, a notice of entry under the Housing Acts, which entitled it to take possession of the house within 14 days. The local authority did not in fact take possession of the house after that time, and the tenant remained there for many weeks. Eventually the tenant departed, leaving the house uninhabited, but the local authority took no steps to assert its possession of the house. A four and a half year-old child entered the house through an unsecured door and was injured when he fell from a second floor window.

In the Court of Appeal, the local authority argued that before it could be regarded as the "occupier" of the house, there must have been an actual or symbolic taking of possession of the house on its behalf, and that its mere *right* to take possession was insufficient. This argument was rejected. On the facts, the Court of Appeal held that the local authority became the occupier as soon as the premises were vacated. Although it could not be said that in every case a person with an immediate right to take possession of premises would be an "occupier", in these particular circumstances, actual physical possession of the premises was not necessary before the local authority could be regarded as having control of the premises.

Where an independent contractor enters premises to undertake work, whether or not this contractor becomes an occupier of the premises depends on the nature and scale of the work being undertaken. Thus, a contractor undertaking a large building development would become the occupier of the site, whilst a decorator painting a house would not.[15] Later in this chapter we shall see that where a visitor suffers loss because of a contractor's negligent work, an occupier can sometimes escape liability by arguing that he or she had delegated the work to a contractor. It does not follow, however, that entrusting work to a contractor automatically makes that contractor an *occupier*.

Definition of "premises"

8–013 There is no explicit definition of "premises" in the Act. Section 1(3)(a), however, states that the Act regulates the obligations of persons occupying or having control over "any fixed or moveable structure, including any vessel, vehicle or aircraft". Case law has established that "premises" covers not only land and buildings, but also such structures as lifts, ladders, diving boards, scaffolding and even large digging machines.[16]

Definition of "visitor"

8–014 Section 1(2) of the Act provides that a "visitor", under the Act, is simply someone who would have been either an "invitee" or a "licensee" at common law before the Act was passed. The position of contractual entrants is governed by s.5 of the Act. To a limited extent, an occupier is free to set his or her own standard of care in relation to

[14] [1976] 1 W.L.R. 279.
[15] *Page v Read* (1984) 134 N.L.J. 723.
[16] See *Haseldine v Daw* [1941] 2 K.B. 343; *Wheeler v Copas* [1981] 3 All E.R. 405; *Ewa Perkowski v Wellington Corp.* [1959] A.C. 53; *Bunker v Charles Brand* [1969] 2 Q.B. 480.

contractual entrants, but where he or she does not do so, such entrants are treated in the same way as visitors and are owed the "common duty of care".[17] As has been said, the Act gives no protection to trespassers. It should also be remembered, of course, that the Act has no application to persons who are outside the premises.

Under the Act, the troublesome distinction between invitees and licensees is replaced by a single test: has the occupier given the entrant *permission* to be on the premises? In cases where the occupier has expressly given permission to enter, the matter is straightforward. In other cases, the law will sometimes say that an occupier has given *implied permission* for a person to be on the premises. In addition, there are certain rules which govern the status of particular types of entrant. The issues which arise may be considered under the following headings:

Persons entering by authority of law

By s.2(6) of the Act, persons entering premises in the exercise of a right conferred by law, for example firemen attending a fire, or policemen executing a warrant, are treated as if they had been given permission to enter by the occupier. Strictly speaking, such cases are not cases of implied permission, but of *deemed* permission, because these persons are treated as visitors even where the occupier expressly states that he or she does not want them on the premises.   **8–015**

Persons exercising rights of way

Persons entering land in the exercise of a public[18] or private[19] right of way, or in the exercise of a right conferred under the National Parks and Access to the Countryside Act 1949,[20] are not "visitors" under the Act. Persons exercising *private* rights of way are owed a duty under the Occupiers' Liability Act 1984, which is discussed later in this chapter. Those exercising a *public* right of way, however, are only owed the limited duty which had been established at common law. Thus, the occupier is not under a duty to maintain public rights of way which run over his or her land.   **8–016**

Implied permission

It is clear that a person who enters premises in order to communicate with the occupier will be treated as having the occupier's implied permission to be on the premises. Thus, a postman or other individual has implied permission to walk up the occupier's drive to use the letterbox, or to call at the front door, unless he or she knows, or ought to know, that this is expressly forbidden (for example, by a sign posted on the gate).[21]   **8–017**

Much of the case law on implied permission, however, must nowadays be seen in the context of the state of the common law when it developed. As has been noted, the

---

[17] Occupiers' Liability Act 1957, s.5(1).
[18] *Greenhalgh v British Railways Board* [1969] 2 Q.B. 286; *McGeown v Northern Ireland Housing Executive* [1995] 1 A.C. 233 See J. Murphy, "Public Rights of Way and Private Law Wrongs" [1997] Conv. 362.
[19] *Holden v White* [1982] 2 Q.B. 679.
[20] S.1(4). See also Countryside and Rights of Way Act 2000, s.13, which amends the 1957 Act to make it clear that persons are not "visitors" when exercising rights of way conferred by the 2000 Act. The section also amends the 1984 Act to make it clear that such persons are owed no duty in respect of dangers arising from natural features of the landscape or when passing through walls, fences, etc. other than by making proper use of gates and stiles. At the time of writing, the section is not yet in force.
[21] *Robson v Hallett* [1967] 2 Q.B. 393.

common law was harsh in its treatment of trespassers. Many judges felt that the rules could produce injustice. They therefore sought to avoid the rigours of the common law in hard cases by classifying trespassers as implied licensees. This often entailed a strained interpretation of the facts.

In *Lowery v Walker*,[22] for example, the plaintiff was using a short-cut across a farmer's field when he was attacked by a horse. The farmer knew that the short-cut had been regularly used by the public for the past 35 years, and had protested about this, although he had never brought legal proceedings. Despite these protests, it was held that the farmer had given implied permission for people to use the short-cut. The plaintiff could therefore be classified as an implied licensee and was able to succeed in his claim. Similarly, in *Glasgow Corp. v Taylor*,[23] a council's failure to fence off a poisonous plant near a children's playground made it liable in respect of a seven-year-old child who died after eating berries from the plant. The berries looked like cherries or large blackcurrants and were tempting to children. Even though the boy had no right to take the berries, or even to approach the bush, and an adult doing so might have been treated as a trespasser, the boy was treated as an implied licensee.

Now that trespassers are afforded greater protection under the Occupiers' Liability Act 1984 than was the case at common law, there is less need for the courts to resort to the idea of implied permission to do justice in hard cases. The earlier authorities, therefore, are unlikely to be followed unless the court feels that, in a particularly meritorious case, even the protection afforded by the Occupiers' Liability Act 1984 would be insufficient.

Limitations on permission

8–018   The permission given by an occupier, whether express or implied, may be limited in three ways. First, the occupier may permit a person to be in some parts of the premises but not others. Secondly, the occupier may permit the person to remain on the premises only for a certain period of time. Thirdly, the occupier may permit the person to be on the premises only for certain purposes. It is clear that where a person enters premises with permission, but that permission is subsequently expressly revoked, the law will allow a reasonable time to leave the premises, during which he or she will still be treated as a visitor.[24]

Difficulties arise when visitors stray from the permitted area. In *Gould v McAuliffe*,[25] for example, a customer in a pub, looking for an outside lavatory, wandered through an unlocked gate into a private part of the premises where she was attacked by a dog. The argument that she had become a trespasser was rejected. It was held that where an occupier wishes to exclude a visitor from an area into which visitors are likely to wander, he or she must take reasonable steps to inform the visitor that the area is out of bounds. On the facts, because there was no notice informing the plaintiff that the area beyond the gate was private, this had not been done. Whether it is necessary to post a notice excluding visitors from a particular area will, of course, depend on the facts of each case. Such a notice will not be necessary in respect of a part of the premises to which no one would reasonably expect a visitor to go.[26]

[22] [1911] A.C. 10.
[23] [1922] 1 A.C. 44. Compare *Edwards v Railway Executive* [1952] A.C. 737.
[24] *Robson v Hallett* [1967] 2 Q.B. 393; *Kay v Hibbert* [1977] Crim. L.R. 226.
[25] [1941] 2 All E.R. 527, CA.
[26] *Mersey Docks and Harbour Board v Procter* [1923] A.C. 253.

In determining whether or not a person is a visitor, it is relevant to consider the *purpose* for which that person is permitted to be on the premises. As Scrutton L.J. put it, in *The Calgarth*[27]:

"When you invite a person into your house to use the staircase, you do not invite him to slide down the banisters."

Thus, where a person is invited for one purpose (to sleep in a bed) and starts to pursue an activity unrelated to that purpose (jump up and down on the mattress), that person may cease to be a visitor, even though he or she has not strayed from the permitted area. To understand why this is so, it must be remembered that the Act treats as "visitors" people who were, under the old law, licensees or invitees. A licence to be on premises will almost always have implied conditions. When a person breaches one of these conditions, he or she ceases to be a licensee. It therefore follows that he or she ceases to be a "visitor". It should be noted that the permission to use the premises for the purposes in question must be given *by the occupier*.[28] Permission given by someone else is not sufficient.

The "common duty of care"

Section 2(2) of the Act defines the "common duty of care" as follows:　　　　　**8–019**

"The common duty of care is a duty to take such care as in all the circumstances of the case is reasonable to see that the visitor will be reasonably safe in using the premises for the purposes for which he or she is invited or permitted by the occupier to be there."

It should be noted that it is the *visitor*, rather than simply the *premises* which must be reasonably safe. It follows that if the occupier invites or permits, say, a blind man to come onto the premises, he or she must take greater care to ensure that the visitor does not stumble over obstacles than would be the case in relation to a sighted person. In this regard, it should be noted that liability under the Act can arise where an occupier merely *fails to protect* a visitor from a danger on the premises. The occupier does not need to have created that danger in order to be liable. Thus, the Act imposes liability for mere omissions in a way which is unusual in English law. It imposes on an occupier a duty to his or her visitor which is very different from the duty owed at common law by a bystander to a stranger. It will be recalled that Lord Keith, in *Yuen Kun Yeu v Att.-Gen. of Hong Kong*,[29] made it clear that there is no liability at common law "on the part of one who sees another about to walk over a cliff with his head in the air, and forbears to shout a warning". This is because, although the danger is foreseeable, there is insufficient "proximity" (closeness of relationship) between the claimant and the defendant. In cases of occupiers' liability, however, the position is different. The fact that the occupier has invited or permitted the claimant to be on the

---

[27] [1927] P. 93 at 110.
[28] See Occupiers' Liability Act 1957, s.2(2), discussed below.
[29] [1988] A.C. 175 at 192 (see Ch. 2).

premises creates the necessary degree of proximity. Therefore, the occupier must protect the visitor from danger, even though he or she has not caused the danger by any positive act.

Discharging the common duty of care

8–020   In deciding whether or not the occupier is in breach of the common duty of care, the courts will have regard to the same general factors which would be considered in a common law negligence action. These general factors were discussed in Ch. 5. They include the likelihood of a risk materialising, the magnitude of the loss if the risk does materialise, and the cost and practicality of taking precautions. In addition, however, the Act expressly refers to a number of more *specific* factors which are to be considered when deciding the question of breach of duty. In particular, the Act contains a provision relating to warnings, and another governing the extent to which an occupier will be liable for dangers created by independent contractors. These provisions are discussed later in the chapter. First, we must examine the extent to which an occupier can rely on a visitor to look after his or her own safety on the premises.

Section 2(3) of the Act provides that, in deciding whether the common duty of care is discharged, it is relevant to consider "the degree of care, and of want of care, which would ordinarily be looked for in such a visitor". For good measure, however, that subsection goes on to refer to two specific types of visitor—children and professionals—and makes it clear what degree of vigilance for their own safety an occupier should expect from each type of visitor. It is convenient to deal with each type of visitor in turn.

Children[30]

8–021   Section 2(3)(a) of the Act provides:

> "an occupier must be prepared for children to be less careful than adults."

Children often fail to appreciate dangers that are obvious to adults. Their natural curiosity often leads them into dangerous situations. In discharging his or her duty of care, therefore, an occupier must bear in mind that children tend to be attracted to certain objects, unaware that they are dangerous. This, of course, was what happened in *Glasgow Corp. v Taylor*[31] (discussed above) where the poisonous berries, which looked like blackcurrants, were said to be an "allurement" to small children. Similarly, in *Jolley v Sutton LBC*,[32] the council was held to be in breach of its duty of care by allowing an old wooden boat, which was an enticing play area for children, to be left abandoned on its land. A 13-year-old boy (Jolley) and his friend had attempted to repair the boat to take it to Cornwall to sail, and Jolley had been injured when the

---

[30] See R. Kidner, "The Duty of Occupiers towards Children" (1988) 39 N.I.L.Q. 150.
[31] [1922] 1 A.C. 44.
[32] [2000] 1 W.L.R. 1082, HL; [1998] 1 W.L.R. 1546, CA.

boat, which had been jacked up, fell on him. Overturning the Court of Appeal decision which had held the activities of the boys too remote a consequence of breach,[33] the House of Lords took the view that the courts should not underestimate the ingenuity of children in finding unexpected ways of doing mischief to themselves and others. On this basis, their Lordships restored the view of the trial judge that the type of accident and injury which occurred was reasonably foreseeable in the context of teenage boys attracted to an obviously abandoned boat.

The decision in *Jolley*, then, makes it clear that the courts will apply the rules of occupiers' liability generously towards children, particularly in relation to serious personal injury.[34] However, an occupier will not be liable for every action of a child on his or her premises. This is especially true in the case of very young children, for whom even the most innocuous objects on premises may present a danger. An occupier cannot be expected to ensure that his or her premises are as safe as a nursery for any visiting toddler. If some provision were not made in law to limit the scope of an occupier's duty to very young visitors, the occupier might be apt to exclude them from the premises for fear of liability. Such a solution would not be socially acceptable. The law therefore provides that an occupier is entitled to assume that the behaviour of very young children will be supervised by a responsible adult. The leading case is *Phipps v Rochester Corp*.[35]

In *Phipps*, the plaintiff was a five-year-old boy. Accompanied by his sister, aged seven, he went out collecting blackberries on a large open space and fell into a deep trench, breaking his leg. The trench, which would have been an obvious danger to an adult, had been dug by the defendants, who were developing the site. Devlin J., after reviewing the relevant authorities, concluded that where children of "tender years" were concerned, an occupier was entitled to consider how a prudent parent or guardian of the child should behave. As Devlin J. remarked, "it would not be socially desirable if parents were, as a matter of course, able to shift the burden of looking after their children from their own shoulders to those of persons who happen to have accessible bits of land".[36] Prudent adults would not have allowed two small children to roam over the site unaccompanied. In the circumstances, therefore, the occupiers of the site escaped liability. Their only duty to very young children was to ensure that they were reasonably safe on the site when accompanied by a responsible adult, and on the facts, this duty had been discharged.

Whether or not an occupier is entitled to expect that very young children on his or her premises will be accompanied by an adult depends on the facts of any given case. Essentially, two matters are relevant, namely the age of the child and the nature of the premises. Thus, a prudent parent should realise that whilst only very young children will be at risk in a playground, a building site, such as that in *Phipps*, would present dangers to older children if unaccompanied. It appears from the decision in *Simkiss v Rhondda BC*,[37] however, that an occupier is required to take account of the social habits of the neighbourhood in which his or her premises are situated. Thus, where a piece of land becomes locally recognised as a playground for unaccompanied small children, an occupier must ensure that these children are reasonably safe.

---

[33] On remoteness generally, see Ch. 6.
[34] Justin Jolley had suffered serious spinal injuries rendering him paraplegic.
[35] [1955] 1 Q.B. 450.
[36] [1955] 1 Q.B. 450 at 472.
[37] (1983) 81 L.G.R. 460.

Professional visitors

8–022   Section 2(3)(b) of the Act provides:

> "an occupier may expect that a person, in the exercise of his calling, will appreciate
> and guard against any special risks ordinarily incident to it, so far as the occupier
> leaves him free to do so."

This subsection gives statutory force to the position which had been established at
common law.[38] An occupier may expect that a skilled visitor, employed to undertake
work on the premises, will take appropriate precautions against risks ordinarily
associated with his or her work. The subsection does not, of course, cover risks not
normally associated with the job. Thus, in *Eden v West & Co.*[39] the defendants were
liable where a carpenter removed a window and the brickwork above it collapsed on
him—the risk of this happening in a modern property was extraordinary and the
defendants ought therefore to have warned him that the brickwork was not properly
supported.

The leading case is *Roles v Nathan*.[40] (This is also an important case on *warnings*,
discussed below). Two chimney sweeps had been engaged to clean the flue of a boiler
and to seal up some vent holes in the flue so that it would operate more efficiently.
The defendant's heating engineer had repeatedly warned the sweeps about the dangers
of being overcome by carbon monoxide fumes if they worked on the flue while the
boiler was lit. He gave evidence, however, that the sweeps had been inclined to dismiss
his warnings, taking the view that they were the experts and could look after
themselves. The sweeps completed most of their work, telling the man in charge of the
boiler room that they would return to finish the job the following day. In fact, the
sweeps returned later that evening, by which time the boiler had been lit, and were
overcome by fumes while working in the flue.

A majority of the Court of Appeal held that the occupiers were not liable for the
death of the sweeps. As Lord Denning M.R. put it:

> "When a householder calls in a specialist to deal with a defective installation on his
> premises, he can reasonably expect the specialist to appreciate and guard against
> the dangers arising from the defect. The householder is not bound to watch over
> him to see that he comes to no harm."[41]

This view accords with common sense—an occupier would not receive a warm
reception if he or she began to tell a specialist contractor all about the usual risks
involved in his or her job. Therefore, since it would be inappropriate for the occupier
to give a warning of those risks, the occupier should not be liable if the risks
materialise. Both Harman L.J. and Pearson L.J. agreed with Lord Denning's statement
of principle, although Pearson L.J., who dissented, took a different view of the facts.

---

[38] See *Christmas v General Cleaning Contractors* [1952] 1 K.B. 141, affirmed [1953] A.C. 180, and *Bates v Parker* [1953] 2 Q.B. 231.
[39] [2003] P.I.Q.R. 2.
[40] [1963] 1 W.L.R. 1117.
[41] *ibid.*, at 1123.

On his Lordship's view, the risk of the boiler being lit was not a risk which was "ordinarily incident" to the sweeps' calling. Rather, it was a special and unusual risk. This was shown by the fact that the defendants had felt it necessary to give repeated warnings about its occurrence.

Sometimes, professional visitors will suffer injury as a result of a danger on the premises, even though they have exercised all due care and skill in taking care of their own safety. In such cases, the courts have held that the mere fact that the visitor is possessed of special skill will not, by itself, entitle the occupier to escape liability. The essential point to grasp is this: the fact that the visitor has special skill does not mean that he or she has *voluntarily assumed the risks* associated with the task, it simply means that he or she is expected to take greater care than would be taken by a lay person in relation to those risks. Thus, in *Ogwo v Taylor*,[42] a fireman injured whilst fighting a fire in a confined space was able to recover from an occupier who had negligently started the fire on the premises. The House of Lords held that whilst an occupier was entitled to expect that the fireman would use his professional skill in tackling a fire, if, despite exercising all due skill, the fireman suffered injury, the occupier would be liable. (It should be noted that *Ogwo v Taylor* was decided on the basis of common law negligence principles. The key finding was that the occupier had put the fireman at risk by negligently *creating* a danger on his premises.)

Giving a warning of the danger

Section 2(4)(a) of the Act provides that in deciding whether or not an occupier has **8–023** discharged the common duty of care, the fact that he or she has warned visitors of the danger is a relevant consideration. The subsection goes on to state, however, that:

"the warning is not to be treated without more as absolving the occupier from liability, unless in all the circumstances it was enough to enable the visitor to be reasonably safe."

Thus, a distinction must be drawn between a mere warning of the danger, which offers no assistance as to how to avoid the danger, and a warning which *enables the visitor to be reasonably safe*. Under the Act, only the latter type of warning will completely discharge the common duty of care. Again, the leading authority is *Roles v Nathan*,[43] in which Lord Denning M.R. explained the position as follows:

"Supposing, for instance, that there was only one way of getting into and out of premises, and it was by a footbridge over a stream which was rotten and dangerous. According to [the old law] the occupier could escape all liability to any visitor by putting up a notice: 'This bridge is dangerous', even though there was no other way by which the visitor could get in or out, and he had no option but to go over the bridge. In such a case, s.2(4) makes it clear that the occupier would nowadays be liable. But if there were two footbridges, one of which was rotten, and the other safe a hundred yards away, the occupier could still escape liability, even today, by putting

---

[42] [1988] A.C. 431, HL, approving *Salmon v Seafarer Restaurants Ltd* [1983] 3 All E.R. 729.
[43] [1963] 1 W.L.R. 1117 at 1124.

up a notice: 'Do not use this footbridge. It is dangerous. There is a safe one further upstream'. Such a warning is sufficient because it does enable the visitor to be reasonably safe."

The chimney sweeps in *Roles v Nathan* had been given clear warnings of the danger by the defendant's heating engineer. According to Lord Denning M.R., with whom Harman L.J. agreed, these warnings enabled the sweeps to be reasonably safe, by making it clear that the danger could be avoided if they desisted from working in the flue when the boiler was alight. Pearson L.J, however, took a different view, holding that the warnings were of little value to the sweeps, given that the defendant's agents had themselves ignored the advice of the heating engineer and had lit the boiler before the sweeps had completed their work.

Not only must the warning tell the visitor what to do in order to avoid the danger, it must be given in terms which are comprehensible to the visitor. It is recognised that children do not always give warnings the attention they deserve, so that an occupier may be required to take other steps, such as the erection of a barrier, to discharge the common duty of care.

A number of other points should be noted about s.2(4)(a). First, the section refers to a warning given *by the occupier*.[44] Strictly speaking, it must follow that a warning given by someone other than the occupier is prima facie insufficient to discharge the occupier's duty of care, even if it enables the visitor to be reasonably safe. This being said, a warning given to a visitor by a third party will, of course, form part of "all the circumstances of the case" and as such (according to s.2(2) of the Act) will be a relevant consideration. Secondly, it should be noted that the words "without more" raise the possibility that a warning which does not by itself enable the visitor to be reasonably safe might be regarded as sufficient to discharge the common duty of care when taken together with some other factor in the case (the presence of a guard rail, for example). Thirdly, note that a sign stating that "visitors enter at their own risk" is not a warning at all, but an attempt to evoke the defence of voluntary assumption of risk. Similarly, a sign declaring that "no responsibility is accepted for any loss or damage on the premises" is not a warning, but an attempt to exclude liability. These matters are discussed towards the end of this chapter.

Above, we have dealt with the effect of a warning in situations where the occupier has decided to give one. But warnings can be important in a different context: sometimes, the claimant's case is that the defendant's breach of the common duty of care consists of *failing to give a warning* in circumstances where one should have been given. In such cases, the courts have repeatedly stressed that an occupier has no duty to warn visitors about *obvious* risks. Thus, in *Darby v National Trust*[45] where the claimant drowned in a pond of deep murky water, the defendants were under no duty to place notices around the pond warning of this risk—there were no hidden dangers in the pond, and the risk of drowning in deep murky water was one which would have been obvious to any adult who went into the pond. Similarly, in *Blackpool and Fylde College v Burke*[46], when a pile of badly-stacked classroom chairs fell on a student, the

[44] In *Roles v Nathan* [1963] 1 W.L.R. 1117, this requirement was satisfied because the heating engineer who gave the warnings was the defendant's agent.
[45] [2001] P.I.Q.R. P 27.
[46] [2001] EWCA Civ 1679.

college was under no duty give warnings and instructions about how to stack the chairs, because the way the chairs should be stacked was obvious, as was the risk of their collapsing if this was not properly done.

Entrusting work to independent contractors

We have seen the extent to which independent contractors, who are possessed of   **8–024**
special skill, can be expected to look after their own safety while they are on the premises. Here, we are concerned with a different situation, namely where a visitor (other than the independent contractor) suffers loss because of the independent contractor's negligence in carrying out work for the occupier. The visitor's loss may result from the manner in which the contractors conduct themselves whilst on the premises (the visitor trips over a toolbox left in a corridor), or it may result from a defect in the premises left by poor workmanship (the visitor falls down a staircase negligently erected by the contractors). Under the doctrine of vicarious liability (discussed in Ch. 7) an employer is not normally responsible for the negligent actions of independent contractors. Can an occupier therefore escape all blame for dangers created by independent contractors on the premises? The House of Lords decision in *Thomson v Cremin*,[47] in 1941, had suggested that an occupier would usually remain personally responsible for the shortcomings of contractors employed on the premises, but this decision was criticised by the Law Reform Committee in 1954. The committee's recommendations were given statutory force in s.2(4)(b) of the Act.

In summary, s.2(4)(b) provides that where a visitor suffers damage due to "the faulty execution of any work of construction, maintenance or repair"[48] by an independent contractor, the occupier is not normally liable if, in all the circumstances of the case:

- it was reasonable to entrust the work to an independent contractor;

- the occupier took reasonable steps to satisfy himself or herself that the contractor was competent; and

- the occupier took reasonable steps to satisfy himself or herself that the work had been properly done.

The first of these requirements has posed few problems for the courts, who appear to have taken the view that it will be reasonable to entrust work to a contractor whenever that work is of a type which is normally undertaken by contractors. The second requirement, also, is rarely the focus of the courts' inquiry. Usually, a contractor will be taken to be competent unless the occupier is aware of facts which suggest incompetence (faulty work carried out in the past, for example). In some circumstances, it may be appropriate for an occupier to check a contractor's competence by seeing that he or she is a member of a relevant trade association, holds relevant qualifications, is suitably experienced and is insured. Such circumstances arose in *Bottomley v Todmorden*

---

[47] (1941) [1953] 2 All E.R. 1185.
[48] The courts have interpreted these words broadly. It was held in *Ferguson v Welsh* [1987] 1 W.L.R. 1553, for example, that the section is applicable to demolition work, even though this is, of course, the complete antithesis of "construction, maintenance and repair".

Cricket Club,[49] where the defendants were held liable for the activities of independent contractors providing a fireworks display—the hazardous nature of the activity placed the defendants under a duty to take positive steps to check the competence of the contractors, and, in particular, to check whether they were insured.

Most of the difficulty for the courts has arisen in deciding whether and when it will be reasonable for an occupier to inspect a contractor's work personally, to see that it has been properly done. Two matters are relevant, namely the nature of the work undertaken and the character of the occupier. Thus, the more complex and technical the work, the less reasonable it is for the occupier to inspect it in person. Where, however, the occupier is a specialist company or a local authority, a more detailed inspection may be called for than would be required of a lay person. Two cases, both decided prior to the 1957 Act, illustrate the principles which the courts will apply.

In *Woodward v Mayor of Hastings*,[50] a pupil was injured when he slipped on a snow-covered step at school. The local authority was not able to escape liability by claiming that it had delegated the task of cleaning the step to the school cleaner who, it was argued, was an independent contractor.[51] The cleaning of the step was not a specialist task, and the danger was obvious. The occupiers therefore had a duty to inspect the cleaner's work to see that it had been properly done. This seems a particularly harsh decision, but perhaps may be explained due to the obvious risk of danger to children on an icy day requiring the school to check that such work was properly done, and the courts' sympathy towards child visitors.

In *Haseldine v Daw*,[52] on the other hand, the plaintiff was fatally injured when a lift in a block of flats fell to the bottom of its shaft, due to the negligence of independent contractors employed to repair the lift. It was held that the occupier had discharged his duty to visitors by engaging an apparently competent firm of engineers to maintain the lift. Because the work carried out on the lift was of a technical nature, the occupier could not be expected to ensure that it had been properly done. It was reasonable for him to leave the maintenance of the lift to an expert. Scott L.J. observed that, if the occupier were made liable in such circumstances, this would effectively make him the insurer of the contractor's negligence.[53] Such a decision would be inconsistent with the principle discussed in Ch. 1 that the law of tort operates most efficiently when it places liability on the party who is able to avoid the risk at least cost.

A few words must be said about the limits of the decision in *Haseldine v Daw*. Clearly, it is authority for the proposition that where the work in question involves complex or technical tasks, the occupier cannot be expected personally to see whether these tasks have been properly performed. It is far from certain, however, that the decision will allow an occupier to wash his or her hands of all responsibility simply by arguing that the work requiring special skill has been delegated to a contractor. Whatever may have been the position when the case was decided, it must be remembered that the 1957 Act requires an occupier to take reasonable steps to check the work. Thus, if contractors were to remove a lift (a specialist task) but were to leave

---

[49] [2003] EWCA Civ 1575, but see *Naylor v Payling* [2004] EWCA Civ 560.
[50] [1945] 1 K.B. 174.
[51] The court in fact found that the cleaner was the agent of the local authority rather than an independent contractor.
[52] [1941] 2 K.B. 343.
[53] *ibid.*, at 356.

the entrance to the shaft unguarded, it would be difficult for the occupier to escape liability, because the danger would be obvious, even to a lay person. Where the occupier is a commercial concern, and the work in question is especially complex (such as the construction of a large building or ship), the occupier's duty to check each part of the work, as it is completed, may be onerous. In some cases, he or she may even have to engage independent experts to supervise the contractor's work.[54]

It is to be noted that s.2(4)(b) employs the past tense. It requires an occupier to "satisfy himself. . . that the work *had* been properly done". It follows from this that the section does not require an occupier to supervise a contractor's working practices on a day-to-day basis. However, an occupier may be held in breach of his or her duty to supervise the contractor's activities, not by virtue of s.2(4)(b), but because of a general breach of the "common duty of care", which requires an occupier to do what is reasonable "in all the circumstances of the case". Thus, an ordinary householder will not be expected to supervise the technical aspects of a contractor's day-to-day activities,[55] but may be under a duty to safeguard visitors against obvious dangers created by those activities.

It is clear from the House of Lords decision in *Ferguson v Welsh*[56] that an occupier has no general duty to supervise the system of work used by a contractor so as protect the contractor's employees from harm. Their Lordships stated that in very exceptional cases, an occupier who becomes aware that the contractor's employees are obviously in danger might be under a duty to ensure that dangerous working practices are stopped. Lord Goff, however, doubted whether an ordinary householder could really be expected to challenge the working practices of, for example, an electrician sent to work on his premises, even if he or she knew that those working practices were dangerous.[57]

Exclusion of liability

It was noted at the beginning of this chapter that an occupier may limit or exclude his or her liability under the Act. This is clear from the wording of s.2(1) of the Act, which imposes the "common duty of care" on an occupier "except in so far as he is free to and does extend, restrict, modify or exclude his duty . . . by agreement or otherwise". An occupier may exclude or limit his or her liability either by displaying a notice on the premises, or by an express term of a contract governing a visitor's entry. Both of these methods, however, are subject to the restrictions on exclusion of liability contained in the Unfair Contract Terms Act 1977. Before considering that Act, it is convenient to deal with each method of exclusion in turn.   8–025

(1) Displaying a notice on the premises

It has been noted that exclusion notices are conceptually distinct from warning notices. Although it is not uncommon to see notices which combine exclusion of liability with an element of warning, in such cases, each element of the notice should be treated separately.   8–026

---

[54] *AMF International Ltd v Magnet Bowling Ltd* [1968] 1 W.L.R. 1028.
[55] *Ferguson v Welsh* [1987] 1 W.L.R. 1553, *per* Lord Goff at 1564; *Green v Fibreglass Ltd* [1958] 2 Q.B. 245.
[56] [1987] 1 W.L.R. 1553.
[57] *ibid.*, at 1564.

The fact that the 1957 Act permits an occupier to exclude liability by a notice is a reflection of the position which had been established under the common law. In *Ashdown v Samuel Williams & Sons Ltd*,[58] a licensee was injured while using a short-cut over the defendants' land. The defendants were not liable because they had posted notices on the land stating that no person on the land would have any claim against the defendants for any injury whatsoever. The Court of Appeal held that, provided occupiers took reasonable steps to bring the exclusion of liability to the attention of persons on the premises, they were free to dictate their own terms of entry. The decision reflected the idea that "an Englishman's home is his castle"—it was based on the assumption that if the law allowed an occupier to exclude a person altogether from his or her premises, it followed that the occupier would be entitled to attach whatever conditions he or she liked to a person's permission to enter.

In *Ashdown*, the conflict between the freedom of an occupier to exclude liability and the right of a visitor to claim compensation for injury was resolved in favour of the occupier. Under modern law, however, this conflict is often resolved in favour of the visitor. Thus, if the case were decided today, the defendant would be unable to rely on the notice to exclude liability for personal injury, because the notice would be void under s.2(1) of the Unfair Contract Terms Act 1977. The relevant provisions of this Act are considered more fully below. Despite its title, the Act does not apply just to exclusion clauses in contracts, it also applies where the defendant attempts to restrict his or her liability in tort by displaying a notice. Section 1(1)(c) of the Unfair Contract Terms Act 1977 expressly states that the Act applies to notices excluding or limiting the common duty of care under the 1957 Act.

(2) An express term of a contract

8–027   Where a visitor enters premises in accordance with a contract governing his or her entry, occupiers may include in that contract a term which specifies the standard of care owed to their visitor. This standard may be lower (or higher) than the "common duty of care".[59] Where the contract in question contains no express term providing for a standard of care (or where it contains an express term which is void under the Unfair Contract Terms Act 1977, discussed below), s.5(1) of the Act operates to imply into the contract the "common duty of care". Thus, an occupier cannot argue that there is an *implied* term in the contract to the effect that the standard of care he or she owes is lower than the standard in the 1957 Act.

8–028   **The contract's effect on third parties.** It is important to note the effect of s.3 of the 1957 Act. The wording of this section is rather complex, but its effect is simple. The section deals with a situation where: (1) an occupier enters into a contract with A, under which the occupier permits A to use his or her premises, *and* (2) the contract contains an express term setting a standard of care in relation to A, *and* (3) the occupier agrees, by the terms of the contract, to let B enter the premises (even though the occupier has no contract with B). This situation may arise, for example, where a landlord occupier lets a room to A on terms which allow B to visit him.

In such cases, s.3 provides that if the relevant term of the contract sets a standard of care *lower* than the standard set in the 1957 Act, then that term does not apply to B.

---

[58] [1957] 1 Q.B. 409.
[59] *e.g.* such a term may exclude or limit liability for damage to the visitor's property.

This is a straightforward application of privity of contract. Instead, B is owed the "common duty of care" under the Act. The section also provides, however, that if the term in question sets a *higher* standard of care than the Act demands, B is entitled to the benefit of the term, unless the contract expressly provides to the contrary. Thus, if a person, while visiting a tenant, suffers loss because of some defect in a part of the building over which the landlord retains occupational control (the stairway, for example), he or she can sue the landlord irrespective of any exclusion clause in the lease, but will also be able to sue if he or she suffers injury because the landlord has not provided security lighting as promised in the lease.

The Unfair Contract Terms Act 1977

Section 2 of the Unfair Contract Terms Act 1977 provides that where the liability in question is "business liability", notices or contract terms which attempt to exclude liability for personal injury or death are void.[60] Notices or contract terms which attempt to exclude liability for other matters (damage to property, for example) are valid only if they are "reasonable".[61] The main difficulty, then, is to decide whether the occupier is attempting to exclude "business liability". Section 1(3) of the Act defines "business liability" as liability for the breach of an obligation arising from "things done . . . in the course of a business[62] . . . or . . . from the occupation of premises used for business purposes of the occupier". Clearly, then, an ordinary householder, unless he or she is using their house for business purposes, will not be affected by the 1977 Act. It is equally clear that where the occupier makes a personal profit by charging the visitor for admission, the Act will apply.

8–029

The Act's rather vague definition of "business liability", however, gave rise to uncertainty in cases where the occupier used his or her land for a business purpose (farming or forestry, for example) but allowed people to access that land for a purpose unrelated to the business (to view an ancient monument, for example). This uncertainty was resolved by s.2 of the Occupiers' Liability Act 1984. That section amended the definition of "business liability" to make it clear that in such cases the 1977 Act does not generally apply. According to the amended definition, liability to persons accessing premises for "recreational or educational purposes" is not "business liability" unless those persons are also accessing the premises for the business purposes of the occupier. Thus, a farmer can exclude liability to persons viewing an ancient monument on his land (unless he or she charges them a fee). It should be noted, however, that in such cases the occupier is only free to exclude liability resulting from the dangerous or defective *state* of the premises (*i.e.* liability for breach of the "occupancy duty"). The occupier cannot exclude liability for breach of the "activity" duty. Thus, if the visitor were hit by a negligently driven tractor, the 1977 Act would apply to prohibit exclusion of liability.

It remains unclear how far the words "recreational. . .purposes" can cover a situation where the occupier allows his or her premises to be used for charity fund-raising events. It is noteworthy that the word "charitable" is omitted from the description of purposes for which exclusion of liability is permitted. It is also

---

[60] S.2(1).
[61] S.2(2). For the test of reasonableness, see s.11 and Sch.2.
[62] "Business" includes the activities of professionals, government departments and local authorities: s.14.

noteworthy that the definition of "business" in s.14 of the 1977 Act includes activities which would not normally be thought of as "business", namely the activities of government departments and local authorities. This suggests that the courts would have little difficulty in extending the definition of "business" to cover charitable activities. "Professional fund raising", where only a proportion of the proceeds are donated to charity, is clearly a business activity, so the 1977 Act's prohibitions on excluding liability will apply. But do these prohibitions also apply even in cases where the use of the premises is wholly for a charitable purpose? The point is undecided, although some assistance may be derived from the pre-1977 decision in *White v Blackmore*.[63] Here, the plaintiff was killed because of defective barrier ropes at a charity motor-racing event. A majority of the Court of Appeal held that the organisers had effectively excluded liability by posting a notice outside the premises. The fact that the premises were being used for a charitable purpose, however, forms no part of the *ratio* of the case. Only Lord Denning M.R. (dissenting) refers to the point. In his view, the court should not be "over-anxious" about imposing liability on a charity where that liability is covered by insurance.

In cases where the Unfair Contract Terms Act 1977 does not prohibit exclusion of liability, it is unclear whether the occupier is entitled to exclude liability altogether, or whether he or she will always owe his or her visitors some minimum standard of care, such as the lesser duty owed to trespassers, discussed below. Certainly, the 1957 Act does not entitle an occupier to exclude liability where he or she would not have been allowed to do so under the pre-Act common law. Thus it has been suggested that there can be no exclusion of the common duty of care in relation to persons who enter premises under authority of law.[64] It is unlikely that a court would allow an occupier ever to exclude the duty of "common humanity"[65] because, as a matter of policy, this represents a minimum standard of care owed to all, and should therefore be unexcludable. The real question, then, is whether the higher standard of care owed under the 1984 Act is excludable. This, again, is unlikely. Unlike the 1957 Act, the 1984 Act does not expressly allow an occupier to modify or restrict the duty of care. The point remains undecided, however, because, in practice, it is quite easy to *discharge* the duty (rather than *exclude* it) by giving a warning of the danger.[66]

LIABILITY TO NON-VISITORS

We have seen that the 1957 Act applies only to "visitors", but that certain persons who enter premises are not "visitors", either because they were not invitees or licensees at common law, or because the Act specifically excludes them from its scope. All of these persons, however, with the exception of individuals exercising a public right of way,[67] are owed a duty under the Occupiers' Liability Act 1984.

---

[63] [1972] 3 All E.R. 158.
[64] W.H. Rogers, *Winfield & Jolowicz on Tort* (16th ed., Sweet and Maxwell, 2002), p.321.
[65] See the House of Lords in *British Railways Board v Herrington* [1972] A.C. 877.
[66] For further discussion, see Gower (1956) 19 M.L.R. 536, Jones (1984) 47 M.L.R. 713 and Buckley [1984] Conv. 413.
[67] *McGeown v Northern Ireland Housing Executive* [1995] 1 A.C. 233; Occupiers' Liability Act 1984, s.1(7).

The 1984 Act, then, applies to people who are on the premises without the occupier's permission. Usually, such people are trespassers, although it should be noted that a person who, for example, falls on to premises from other premises, is not, technically, a trespasser, because the tort of trespass requires that a defendant must intend to be on the land. It should also be noted that, especially in the case of children, it is not true to say that all trespassers are committing a moral wrong. People can become trespassers by accident if they wander on to an occupier's land not realising they need permission to be there.

Sometimes, a person enters premises as a visitor, but becomes a trespasser when he or she breaches some express or implied condition of his or her licence to be there. Thus, a visitor who strays from the permitted area, outstays his welcome, or begins to pursue some purpose unauthorised by the occupier will lose his protection under the 1957 Act and will be protected only by the 1984 Act.

The old law

In order to appreciate the scope of the 1984 Act, it is necessary to refer to the position **8–030** at common law before it was passed. This is useful not only by way of background, but because much of the reasoning of Lord Diplock in *British Railways Board v Herrington*,[68] the leading pre-Act case, has recently been approved by the Court of Appeal when interpreting the Act's provisions.

The law as it stood in 1929 was shortly stated by Lord Hailsham in *Robert Addie & Sons (Collieries) Ltd v Dumbreck*[69]:

> "The trespasser comes on to the premises at his own risk. An occupier . . . is liable only where the injury is due to some wilful act involving something more than the absence of reasonable care. There must be some act done with the deliberate intention of doing harm to the trespasser, or at least some act done with reckless disregard of the presence of the trespasser."

This approach reflected the idea that, as a matter of policy, an occupier should not be bound to protect a wrongdoer who violated his or her property rights by entering without permission. But the rule could produce some harsh results. In *Addie* itself, for example, a child trespasser, playing in a field owned by the colliery, got caught in the machinery and died. The boy could not, as in *Glasgow Corp. v Taylor*,[70] be classified as an implied licensee, because he had been repeatedly warned not to go into the field. The colliery therefore escaped liability.

In 1954, the Law Reform Committee, whose proposals formed the basis of the 1957 Act, stated that although it felt that the existing law relating to trespassers could be harsh when applied to children, it could find no adequate way of providing for child trespassers without imposing too great a burden on occupiers.[71] Trespassers were therefore omitted from the 1957 Act. In 1972, however, the law underwent a fundamental change with the decision in *British Railways Board v Herrington*.[72]

---

[68] [1972] A.C. 877.
[69] [1929] A.C. 358 at 365.
[70] [1922] 1 A.C. 44.
[71] *Occupiers' Liability to Invitees, Licensees and Trespassers*, Cmnd 9305 (1954), para.80.
[72] [1972] A.C. 877.

In *Herrington*, a six-year-old boy climbed through a gap in a fence beside an electrified railway line and was severely injured when he came into contact with the live rail. The defendants knew that children had been using the gap in the fence as a short-cut, but had taken no steps to deter them. The House of Lords held that the defendants were liable, observing that the policy considerations which had formed the basis of the old law on trespassers were no longer persuasive. Society's attitude towards trespassers had changed, so *Addie* was no longer good law. Their Lordships held that occupiers owed a duty of "common humanity" to trespassers. This was more than a duty to refrain from causing deliberate harm, but lower than the duty imposed by the 1957 Act. The precise scope of the duty, however, was unclear, because each of the Law Lords appeared to regard the matter slightly differently. In 1976, the Law Commission reported that it could not extract from the decision any single clear principle, and that legislation was required.[73] Eventually, this came in the form of the Occupiers' Liability Act 1984.

OCCUPIERS' LIABILITY ACT 1984

8–031   It is convenient to speak of the 1984 Act applying to "trespassers", because this covers the majority of cases, although, as explained above, technically it can apply to other people as well. In summary, the Act provides that an occupier must take reasonable care to see that a trespasser does not suffer personal injury on his or her premises.[74] No duty is owed in respect of a trespasser's property.[75] According to s.1(3), the duty in respect of personal injury is owed if:

- the occupier is aware of the danger, or has reasonable grounds to believe it exists; and

- the occupier knows or has reasonable grounds to believe that a trespasser is in the vicinity of the danger, or may come into that vicinity; and

- the risk of personal injury is one against which, in all the circumstances of the case, the occupier may be expected to offer the trespasser some protection.

An occupier may discharge his or her duty to trespassers either by giving a warning of the danger, or by taking other reasonable steps to discourage trespassers from encountering the danger,[76] for example by securing the premises behind a locked gate. Note that, in contrast to the 1957 Act, there is no requirement that the warning must enable the entrant to be reasonably safe. Thus, the duty can be discharged by a notice posted on the premises which gives a simple warning of the danger (for example "Danger—Rotten Footbridge"). The notice need not inform trespassers how to use the premises safely.

In applying these provisions, the courts have been anxious not to impose too onerous an obligation on occupiers. They have often held that there is no liability,

---

[73] Law Commission Report No. 75, Cmnd 6428 (1976).
[74] S.1(4).
[75] S.1(8), but see *Tutton v Walter* [1986] Q.B. 61.
[76] S.1(5).

either because no duty is owed under the Act, or because the duty has been discharged, or because the claimant voluntarily assumed the risk and is the author of his or her own misfortune. All three of these factors found favour with the House of Lords in *Tomlinson v Congleton Borough Council*[77] to produce a finding of no liability.

The defendant council was in charge of a piece of recreational land on the site of a disused quarry. A lake had formed in part of the old quarry, which attracted many visitors in hot weather. The defendant council had placed notices around the lake, reading: "Dangerous water: no swimming", and had employed rangers to warn visitors of the dangers of swimming in the lake. However, visitors would frequently swim in the lake, ignoring the notices, and were often rude to the rangers when asked to get out of the water. Following a number of serious incidents in which visitors nearly drowned, the council had resolved to make the beaches of the lake less attractive by dumping ballast on the shore to discolour the sand, and by planting vegetation at the lakeside, but, owing to financial constraints, this had not been done at the time of the claimant's accident. The claimant was an 18 year-old man, who entered the water, and, from a standing position in the shallows, executed a dive.[78] He hit his head on the sandy bottom, suffering severe injury which rendered him tetraplegic.

The House of Lords held that the risk of the claimant suffering injury had not arisen from the "state of the premises, or things done or omitted to be done on them" within the meaning of the 1984 Act. Rather, it had arisen from the claimant's own misjudgment in attempting to dive into shallow water. It followed that the risk was not one against which the Act obliged the council to offer him any protection. According to Lord Hoffmann[79], there was "an important question of freedom at stake" in the case. The Court of Appeal had held that the council, having been aware of the number of accidents suffered by irresponsible visitors swimming in the lake, was under a duty to safeguard those visitors by implementing its resolution to destroy the beaches. Lord Hoffmann pointed out, however, that the majority of people at the lakeside were behaving quite properly, enjoying themselves in a way which posed no risk to themselves or to others, and continued:

> "It is unjust that the harmless recreation of responsible parents and children with buckets and spades on the beaches should be prohibited in order to comply with what is thought to be a legal duty to safeguard irresponsible visitors against dangers which are perfectly obvious."[80]

Accordingly, the "social cost" involved in denying responsible visitors access to recreational facilities should have been taken into account in deciding whether it was reasonable for the council to have destroyed the beaches in order to discourage irresponsible visitors from harming themselves. In their Lordships' view, this "social cost" could not be justified.

The approach in *Tomlinson* was followed in *Simonds v Isle of Wight Council*.[81] Here, the claimant, a five year old child, broke his arm when he fell from a swing near to a

---

[77] [2004] 1 A.C. 46.
[78] There was some indecision as to whether he had become a trespasser by so doing—it was "swimming" that was prohibited by the notices, not entering the water.
[79] *Tomlinson v Congleton Borough Council* [2004] 1 A.C. 46 at 85.
[80] *ibid.*, at 85.
[81] [2004] E.L.R. 59.

playing field being used for a school sports day. It had been argued that the school was under a duty to immobilise the swings, or at least to place a cordon around them to discourage children from using them. In denying that the school was under such a duty, Gross J., referring to *Tomlinson*, pointed out that the result of a finding of liability might be that pleasurable sporting events such as the one in question would cease to be held, because of the high cost of liability insurance.

Whilst the general principles the courts adopt in applying the Act are illustrated by the reasoning in *Tomlinson*, there are few other noteworthy cases on the 1984 Act. This is largely because, as Lord Steyn observed in *Jolley v Sutton LBC*,[82] cases on occupiers' liability are "invariably very fact-sensitive". In other words, because the statutes (particularly the 1984 Act) are framed in such broad terms, the question of whether or not they produce liability in any given situation will depend heavily on the particular factual circumstances of each case. One interesting point of *law*, however, has arisen in respect of the words "has reasonable grounds to believe". The decision in *White v St Albans City and District Council*[83] made it clear that where an occupier erected a fence around the premises, this did not necessarily mean that he or she had "reasonable grounds" to expect trespassers, but uncertainty remained about how the words should be interpreted.

In *Herrington*, Lord Diplock had expressed the view that no duty to trespassers could arise unless an occupier had actual knowledge of facts as to the condition of his or her land, and actual knowledge of facts which suggested the likely presence of trespassers. An occupier was under no duty to make inquiry as to the state of the premises for the benefit of trespassers.[84] Under the 1984 Act, it was unclear whether this remained the position, or whether the words "reasonable grounds to believe" meant, for example, that an occupier who had no actual knowledge of a dangerous object on the premises could be liable in circumstances where a reasonable occupier *ought* to have known about its presence. However, in *Swain v Natui Ram Puri*[85] and *Ratcliff v McConnell*,[86] the Court of Appeal has expressly endorsed Lord Diplock's views, suggesting that, on a proper construction of the Act, an occupier must actually know the primary facts (from which a reasonable occupier would conclude that there was a danger, or a likelihood of trespassers) before he or she can be liable. The judgment in *Ratcliff* also endorses Lord Diplock's view that the financial resources of the particular occupier are relevant in deciding what level of protection he or she can reasonably be expected to offer to trespassers.

In *Swain*, a child trespasser had been seriously injured when, having scaled a seven foot fence and wall covered with barbed wire to reach a roof, he fell through a skylight. It was argued that although the occupier did not know of trespassers in the vicinity, he *should* have known that a large unoccupied factory, adjacent to an inner city council estate where many children lived, would be bound to attract child trespassers. The Court of Appeal rejected this view. A duty would only arise under the 1984 Act when the occupier had actual knowledge[87] of the relevant facts (here, that children would

---

[82] [2000] 1 W.L.R. 1082 at 1089.
[83] *The Times*, March 12, 1990.
[84] [1972] A.C. 877 at 941.
[85] [1996] P.I.Q.R. P442, CA,
[86] [1999] 1 W.L.R. 670
[87] This would extend to "shut eye" knowledge, that is, facts which are obvious but which the occupier chooses to ignore.

climb on the roof) or had known facts which gave reasonable grounds for this belief (*e.g.* had known about gaps in the barbed wire over the perimeter fence). Constructive knowledge would not suffice.

Although the Court of Appeal approved Lord Diplock's views in *Ratcliff*, the case itself turned on the defence of voluntary assumption of risk. In *Ratcliff*, the occupiers of a college swimming pool were not liable when a student trespasser broke into the pool and dived head first into the water, suffering severe injuries. The Court of Appeal held that the student had voluntarily assumed the risk of his activities. He knew that the pool was closed for the winter and had been partially drained, and ought to have realised that it was dangerous to dive into shallow water.

Finally, it should be noted that although the 1984 Act refers to liability for "things done or omitted to be done" on premises,[88] the decision in *Revill v Newbery*[89] makes it clear that the Act applies only to liability for the *state* of premises. It does not regulate the "activity duty". Thus, in considering whether the defendant was liable for accidentally injuring a trespasser, when firing a shotgun towards him intending to frighten him off, the Court of Appeal held that the provisions of the 1984 Act were not, strictly speaking, relevant, although they assisted greatly in determining the nature of the duty owed at common law, which was virtually identical to that owed under the Act.

DEFENCES

The various defences generally applicable to actions in negligence apply in the same way to actions brought under the Occupiers' Liability Act 1957 and the Occupiers' Liability Act 1984. In practice, voluntary assumption of risk is the most important defence in occupiers' liability cases (see *Ratcliff v McConnell*, noted above). This defence is expressly preserved in both Acts.[90] It is discussed, together with other defences, in Ch. 14.

8–032

Contributory Negligence

There is no explicit reference to the Law Reform (Contributory Negligence) Act 1945 in either the 1957 or the 1984 Act. This is surprising, because the matter was expressly mentioned in the Law Reform Committee's recommendations which led to the passing of the 1957 Act.[91] Nevertheless, the courts have regularly applied the principle of contributory negligence in deciding cases under both Acts.[92]

8–033

---

[88] S.1(1)(a).
[89] [1996] 2 W.L.R. 239.
[90] Occupiers' Liability Act 1957, s.2(5) and Occupiers' Liability Act 1984, s.1(6).
[91] *Occupiers' Liability to Invitees, Licensees and Trespassers*, Cmnd 9305 (1954), para.78(ix).
[92] See, *e.g. Stone v Taffe* [1974] 1 W.L.R. 1575 and *Bunker v Charles Brand* [1969] 2 Q.B. 480 where in both cases damages were reduced by 50%. See also *Kiapasha v Laverton* [2002] EWCA Civ 1656. For the 1984 Act, see *Revill v Newbery* [1996] 2 W.L.R. 239.

Chapter 9

STRICT LIABILITY STATUTES

In this chapter, we will examine two forms of strict liability imposed by statute: for defective products under the Consumer Protection Act 1987 and for damage caused by animals under the Animals Act 1971. In both cases, these forms of liability are in addition to the existing common law. The first part of this chapter will deal with the important provisions relating to defective products. This will be followed by a brief discussion of the Animals Act 1971.

9–001

(1) CONSUMER PROTECTION ACT 1987

Introduction

In this section, we examine liability for defective products in the law of torts. At common law, this is simply part of the tort of negligence, with which we should now be familiar. It should not be forgotten that *Donoghue v Stevenson*[1] involved an allegation that Mrs Donoghue's ginger beer bottle contained a snail, or, in other words, that Mrs Donoghue had been the victim of a defective product. The case is therefore not only the classic example of the duty of care in negligence, but the classic example of liability for a defective product. However, the common law has now been supplemented by the enactment of the Consumer Protection Act 1987, which was introduced to comply with EC Directive 85/374 on liability for defective products. The aim of the Act is to assist consumers in their claims against manufacturers of defective products by rendering the manufacturer (and associated parties) strictly liable. However, until recently, this change in the law has had less impact in practice than may have been expected.

9–002

We shall proceed by considering, first of all, the position at common law. This is of interest in highlighting why reform of this area of law was necessary and, more importantly, in understanding the position in law when the provisions of the 1987 Act do not apply. It is important to remember that the 1987 Act *supplements* the common law—it does not replace it. Secondly, we shall examine the provisions of the 1987 Act

[1] [1932] A.C. 562.

and the extent to which it imposes strict liability on manufacturers of products and on associated parties.

THE COMMON LAW POSITION

9–003   Prior to *Donoghue v Stevenson*, tort law provided little assistance to persons injured by a defective product. Most claimants were forced to rely on contract law, provided, of course, that they could establish the necessary contractual relationship. There are a number of benefits in bringing a contractual claim. First, the claimant is not required to show the fault of the seller, but simply that the seller is in breach of a term of the contract. The seller is therefore strictly liable for his or her breach. Secondly, contract law has no problem in awarding compensation for personal injury and property damage caused by the supply of a defective product.[2] It will also award compensation for the cost of replacing the defective product itself. The buyer's position is further improved by the existence of implied terms. For example, under the Sale of Goods Act 1979, it is implied that, where the seller sells the goods in the course of a business, the goods must be of satisfactory quality[3] and be fit for their purpose.[4] On this basis, the buyer can sue for breach of contract if the goods fail to satisfy these terms.

There are, however, a number of disadvantages in bringing a claim in contract law. First, there must be a term (express or implied) in the contract which provides that the product should not be defective. Secondly, subject to the provisions of the Contract (Rights of Third Parties) Act 1999,[5] the rules of privity of contract only allow the parties to the contract to take the benefit of such terms.[6] Thirdly, the seller may exclude or limit liability for breach, although this will be subject to the provisions of the Unfair Contract Terms Act 1977 and Unfair Terms in Consumer Contracts Regulations 1999. Fourthly, although the chain of contracts between the manufacturer and the buyer will ultimately pass liability back up the chain to the manufacturer, this chain is easily broken, for example, by exclusion clauses or the insolvency of one of the parties. Liability may therefore fall arbitrarily on one party in the chain, regardless of the fact that the fault is solely that of the manufacturer.

As stated earlier, prior to 1932, tort law had a very limited application to defective products. A manufacturer would only be liable in tort if the product was classified as "dangerous" (for example, dynamite) or was actually known to the manufacturer to be

---

[2] Subject of course to the rules of remoteness stated in *Hadley v Baxendale* (1854) 9 Ex 341. See *Grant v Australian Knitting Mills Ltd* [1936] A.C. 85 where the plaintiff sued the retailer under the contract of sale for the skin disease he suffered as a result of the defective state of the product sold.

[3] S.14(2) of the Sale of Goods Act 1979 (as amended by the Sale and Supply of Goods Act 1994).

[4] S.14(3) of the Sale of Goods Act 1979 (as amended by the Sale and Supply of Goods Act 1994). See also the Supply of Goods and Services Act 1982.

[5] S.1(1) provides that a third party may be able to enforce a term of a contract in his or her own right if either (a) the contract expressly provides for this or (b) the parties intend by a term of the contract to confer a benefit on him or her. The third party must be expressly identified in the contract by name, as a member of a class or as answering a particular description: s.1(3). These requirements will limit the number of possible claims under the Act.

[6] Unless, of course, the purchaser sues for his or her own loss, which includes that arising from the injury of a third party. For example, in *Frost v Aylesbury Dairy* [1905] 1 K.B. 608, the purchaser sued to recover the expenses to which he had been put by the illness and death of his wife due to typhoid fever caught from the milk supplied by the defendants.

dangerous, in which case he or she would then be obliged to warn the product's recipient of the danger. The distinction between "dangerous" and "non-dangerous" products was not particularly helpful and indeed made little sense. As Scrutton L.J. famously commented, "Personally, I do not understand the difference between a thing dangerous in itself, as poison, and a thing not dangerous as a class, but by negligent construction dangerous as a particular thing. The latter, if anything, seems the more dangerous of the two; it is a wolf in sheep's clothing instead of an obvious wolf".[7] The courts' reluctance to adopt a general principle of negligence liability and their adherence to the "privity of contract fallacy" (by which the contract between the manufacturer and the retailer was deemed to obstruct any other form of liability in favour of third parties)[8] prevented the emergence of a general defective product action in tort.

In *Donoghue v Stevenson*,[9] the majority of the House of Lords overturned the questionable distinction between dangerous and non-dangerous chattels and discarded the "privity of contract fallacy". The court saw no reason why the same set of facts should not give one person a right in contract and another a concurrent right to sue in tort.[10] It will be recalled that the case concerned the decomposed remains of snail, alleged to have been found in an opaque bottle of ginger beer that had been bought by Mrs Donoghue's friend. The existing rules of tort law seemed to preclude Mrs Donoghue's claim. A ginger beer bottle is not dangerous in itself and it was not known to contain a noxious substance. Mrs Donoghue had no contractual relationship with any of the parties and so could not rely on any implied terms as to quality. Nevertheless, the majority of the House of Lords held that where a manufacturer sells goods in such a manner that he intends them to reach the ultimate consumer in the form in which they have left him, with no reasonable possibility of intermediate examination, then the manufacturer will be liable for the absence of reasonable care in manufacturing the products.[11]

Three points may be noted about the decision in *Donoghue v Stevenson*. First, no distinction is drawn between different types of products. Logically, however, in assessing breach of duty (*i.e.* whether the manufacturer has exercised reasonable care), greater care would be required in the manufacture of explosives than in the manufacture of ginger beer. Indeed, the standard of care required for particularly dangerous products may be so high as practically to amount to a guarantee of safety.[12] Secondly, it should be noted that the manufacturer must intend the goods to reach the consumer intact. A reasonable possibility of intermediate examination would appear to exclude liability. Thirdly, the case deals with the manufacture of products and not with design. Design defects in products are of particular concern. Whereas a problem with manufacture may be limited to a particular batch, a design defect will affect many more products, thereby increasing the possibility of harm. We shall have to consider how *Donoghue v Stevenson*[13] applies to defects in design and what protection it gives to potential claimants.

[7] *Hodge & Sons v Anglo-American Oil Co* (1922) 12 Lloyd's Rep. 183 at 187.
[8] See *Winterbottom v Wright* (1842) 10 M & W 109, discussed in Ch. 2.
[9] [1932] A.C. 562.
[10] *ibid., per* Lord Macmillan at 610.
[11] *ibid., per* Lord Atkin at 599. Contrast Lord Buckmaster's strong dissenting judgment at 577–8.
[12] *ibid., per* Lord Macmillan at 612.
[13] *ibid.*

The scope of *Donoghue v Stevenson*

9–004   The burden will on the claimant to satisfy the ordinary rules of negligence *i.e.* to establish a duty of care, breach, causation and remoteness. Their application to defective product claims will be discussed below.

The duty of care

9–005   This is the ordinary common law duty of care, discussed in Ch. 2. It is not confined to the relationship between manufacturers and ultimate consumers. Makers of component parts, repairers, fitters, erectors, assemblers and even distributors may find themselves liable to the consumer for their failure to exercise reasonable care in dealing with a product. Equally, the range of claimants has extended beyond the ultimate consumer to parties coming into contact with the product. In *Stennett v Hancock and Peters*,[14] for example, a decision which followed shortly after *Donoghue*, the plaintiff suffered injury when part of a wheel from a passing lorry flew off and struck her on the leg. The lorry had recently been repaired by the second defendants, who were found to have re-attached the wheel negligently. The court rejected the claim against the owners of the lorry, but the claim against the second defendants succeeded. *Donoghue v Stevenson* was held to extend to repairers where a person suffered injury on the road as a result of their negligence. Moreover, it is clear that the duty may extend beyond the product itself to include its container, packaging, and directions or instructions for use.[15]

Breach

9–006   Whether the defendant has exercised reasonable care will obviously depend on the particular facts of each case, to which the general principles relating to breach will be applied. Obviously, once the manufacturer knows of the defect, he or she will be negligent if production and marketing of the unsafe product continues.[16] It has been held that even when using component parts, a manufacturer should exercise care in purchasing suitable parts and should not simply assume that the component part is sound.[17] It is a more difficult question whether the manufacturer's duty extends to taking steps to recall products found to be defective after the products have gone into circulation. The best view, perhaps, is that the manufacturer may find himself or herself liable for failing to recall products already in circulation, particularly if the products have just entered the market, and should recall the product line in question as soon as practicable. As Sir Michael Ogden Q.C. commented in *E. Hobbs v Baxenden Chemical Co*[18]:

> ". . . a manufacturer's duty of care does not end when the goods are sold. A manufacturer, who realises that omitting to warn past customers about something

---

[14] [1939] 2 All E.R. 578. See also *Haseldine v Daw* [1941] 2 K.B. 343 where a visitor using a lift in a block of flats was allowed to sue the repairers of the lift when the lift fell to the bottom of its shaft.
[15] *Watson v Buckley, Osborne, Garrett & Co* [1940] 1 All E.R. 174.
[16] *Wright v Dunlop Rubber Co Ltd* (1972) 13 K.I.R. 255 at 272.
[17] *Winward v T.V.R. Engineering* [1986] B.T.L.C. 366.
[18] [1992] 1 Lloyd's Rep. 54 at p.65. See also *Hamble Fisheries Ltd v L Gardner & Sons Ltd* [1999] 2 Lloyd's Rep. 1 at 9 *per* Mummery L.J.; *Hollis v Dow Corning* (1996) 129 D.L.R. (4th) 609; *Carroll v Fearon* [1998] P.I.Q.R. P416.

might result in injury to them, must take reasonable steps to attempt to warn them, however lacking in negligence he may have been at the time the goods were sold."

Breach will generally not cause the claimant particular problems. Although there is some authority that the *res ipsa loquitur* rule (see Ch. 5) does not apply to defective products,[19] the courts have shown themselves willing to infer the absence of reasonable care from the fact a defect exists. For example, in *Grant v Australian Knitting Mills Ltd*,[20] Dr Grant claimed that he had suffered a skin disease from wearing underpants manufactured by the defendants, because they contained an excess of sulphites. The fact that the manufacturers had specifically adopted precautions against excess sulphite did not assist them. Lord Wright inferred that, in such circumstances, the chemicals could only be present in the garment if someone had been at fault. The plaintiff was not required to identify the exact person responsible for the breach, or to specify what he or she did wrong. The burden was therefore on the manufacturer to rebut the inference of negligence with sufficient evidence. This sort of approach lightens the claimant's burden considerably. It would, for example, have been very difficult for Mrs Donoghue to specify exactly what was so wrong with the manufacturing process that a snail could have entered a ginger beer bottle. Equally, in *Mason v Williams & Williams Ltd*,[21] the court was prepared to infer negligence where a plaintiff had been injured using a chisel, which was too hard for its purpose. The chisel had come straight from the manufacturers and the court was prepared to find that the undue hardness must have been produced by carelessness in the course of manufacture, rather than by anything that had happened at the plaintiff's place of work. Finnemore J. stated that showing that the chisel was defective was "as far as any plaintiff can be expected to take his case." It should be noted, however, that his Lordship was careful to distinguish this approach from the doctrine of *res ipsa loquitur*. It should also be noted that the approach has only been applied in relation to manufacturing defects and appears to have little application to design defects.

Causation and remoteness

The ordinary rules of negligence apply and reference should be made to the principles outlined in Ch. 6. The ordinary "but for" test will apply. Note, however, that particularly in medical cases, it may be difficult to differentiate between different possible causes of the injury.   **9–007**

The type of loss recoverable

In defective product cases, the type of loss recoverable is limited by the same rules that apply in other negligence cases. A claimant, therefore, may recover foreseeable personal injury and property damage, but will not succeed in recovering pure economic loss. In *Murphy v Brentwood DC*,[22] the House of Lords emphasised that the cost of replacing a defective product will be classified as pure economic loss, and is therefore non-recoverable. It was noted in Ch. 3 that a claim for loss of profits is unlikely to   **9–008**

[19] Lord Macmillan in *Donoghue v Stevenson* [1932] A.C. 562 at 622: "There is no presumption of negligence in such a case at present, nor is there any justification for applying the maxim *res ipsa loquitur*."
[20] [1936] A.C. 85 at 101. See also *Carroll v Fearon* [1998] P.I.Q.R. P416.
[21] [1955] 1 W.L.R. 549. See also *Hill v Crowe* [1978] 1 All E.R. 812.
[22] [1991] 1 A.C. 398; [1990] 2 All E.R. 908.

succeed unless that loss of profits is consequential on property damage caused by the defective product supplied.[23] Whilst the "complex structure theory" was discussed in Ch. 3 in relation to defective buildings,[24] its relevance to defective products generally must be considered here.[25] Component parts installed at the time of manufacture will be considered part of the product supplied.[26] In contrast, it appears that replacement parts, such as a replacement wheel, will be regarded as a separate product.[27] The decision of the Court of Appeal in *M/S Aswan Engineering Establishment Co v. Lupdine Ltd*[28] highlights the difficulties of applying the complex structure idea to products. The plaintiffs in this case had shipped a consignment of a waterproofing compound (Lupguard) to Kuwait in plastic pails. The pails, which had been selected by the sellers of the compound, had collapsed in the high temperatures of Kuwait with the result that the entire consignment had been lost. As the seller of the compound was in liquidation, Aswan brought an action against the manufacturers of the pails for the loss suffered. The Court of Appeal dismissed the claim on the basis that the loss was not reasonably foreseeable, but Lloyd L.J. expressed the provisional view that there was damage to "other property", namely the Lupguard, which would be recoverable even though the compound had been purchased in the pails.[29] Whilst finding such reasoning logical, Nicholls L.J. expressed reservations as to a rule which would impose liability on the maker of a container—such as a bag, carton or bucket—for loss of its contents.[30]

Particular problems relating to defective products

(1) What is a product?

9–009   In *Donoghue v Stevenson*, Lord Atkin restricted himself to consideration of articles of common household use, where everyone, including the manufacturer, would know that the articles would be used by persons other than the actual ultimate purchaser.[31] The courts have been prepared to interpret "product" quite broadly to include tombstones,[32] hair dye,[33] industrial chemicals,[34] lifts[35] and motor cars.[36]

(2) Has there been intermediate examination or interference?

9–010   This is, in a sense, a question of causation. To find the defendant liable, the court must be satisfied that he or she caused the defect, and that it was not due to the fault of another party in the supply chain (or even the claimant). In *Grant v Australian Knitting*

---

[23] *Spartan Steel & Alloys Ltd v Martin & Co (Contractors) Ltd* [1973] Q.B. 27, CA.
[24] See *D & F Estates v Church Commissioners* [1989] A.C. 177.
[25] See A. Tettenborn [2000] LMCLQ 338.
[26] See, for example, *The Rebecca Elaine (Hamble Fisheries Ltd v L Garnder & Sons Ltd)* [1999] 2 Lloyd's Rep. 1 [defective pistons in an engine where the manufacturer of the engine was sued] cf. *Nitrigin Eireann Teoranta v Inco Alloys* [1992] 1 W.L.R. 498, May J.
[27] See *M/S Aswan Engineering Establishment Co v Lupdine Ltd* [1987] 1 W.L.R. 1 at 21.
[28] [1987] 1 W.L.R. 1.
[29] Fox L.J. in agreement.
[30] [1987] 1 W.L.R. 1 at 29.
[31] [1932] A.C. 562 at 583.
[32] *Brown v Cotterill* (1934) 51 T.L.R. 21.
[33] *Watson v Buckley, Osborne, Garrett & Vo* [1940] 1 All E.R. 174.
[34] *Vacwell Engineering Co v B.D.H. Chemicals* [1971] 1 Q.B. 88.
[35] *Haseldine v Daw* [1941] 2 K.B. 343.
[36] *Andrews v Hopkinson* [1957] 1 Q.B. 229 at 237.

Mills Ltd,[37] it was argued that the mere possibility that the goods might be tampered with after they had left the factory should enable the manufacturer to escape liability. The defendants claimed that because the garments had been wrapped in paper packets to allow shopkeepers to sell each garment separately, there was a possibility of interference with the goods, and this meant the defendants should not be liable. The Privy Council dismissed this argument. Interference was a question of fact, and here it was beyond question that the garment had reached Dr Grant subject to the same defect as when it left the manufacturer.

Where, however, there is a reasonable possibility or probability[38] of interference, the court will take a different line. In *Evans v Triplex Safety Glass Co Ltd*,[39] Mr Evans had bought a car which had been fitted with a "Triplex Toughened Safety Glass" windscreen. One year later, the windscreen suddenly shattered for no apparent reason whilst Mr Evans was driving the vehicle, injuring himself, his wife and his son. In an action against the manufacturers of the safety glass, Porter J. held that Mr Evans had not given sufficient evidence to satisfy the court that the manufacturers were at fault. His Lordship suspected that the real fault lay with the fitting of the windscreen into its frame. In addition, Mr Evans had owned the car for a year before the accident and either he or his supplier might reasonably have inspected the windscreen prior to the accident.

The question of inspection or examination may be a difficult one, particularly where one party in the contractual chain, other than the manufacturer, has had the opportunity to examine the product but chooses not to do so. There is no general obligation at law on such parties to subject all goods to exhaustive examination. The manufacturer will therefore remain liable where he or she has no reason to contemplate that the defect will be discovered before the product reaches the consumer. There may be circumstances, however, when the manufacturer may reasonably expect a third party to examine the product and, if such examination would have revealed the defect, assert that it is the third party's failure to examine the product adequately (rather than defective manufacture) which has caused the injury. In such circumstances, it will be the third party and not the manufacturer who is liable to the claimant.

This question did not arise in *Donoghue*. The ginger beer bottle was opaque and had been sealed, so no-one could have examined its contents prior to consumption. In *Andrews v Hopkinson*,[40] however, a second-hand car dealer, who did have the opportunity to check cars for defects, was held liable for failing to inspect his cars for obvious defects. In this case, which involved a hire purchase agreement for a second-hand car, the plaintiff brought an action against the dealer for injuries resulting from an accident due to the defective steering mechanism of the car. The car was around 18 years old and had been in the dealer's possession for a week. The court heard evidence that the steering mechanism was a particular danger in an old car, which could have

---

[37] [1936] A.C. 85.
[38] Goddard L.J. in *Haseldine v Daw* [1941] 2 K.B. 343 at 376 suggests that the word "probability" is more accurate. In that case, the engineers repairing the lift could not have reasonably contemplated any immediate inspection and so owed a duty to any person who, in the ordinary course of events, would be expected to make use of the thing repaired.
[39] [1936] 1 All E.R. 283.
[40] [1957] 1 Q.B. 229 at 237. See also *White v Warwick* [1953] 1 W.L.R. 1285; *Griffiths v Arch Engineering Co Ltd* [1968] 3 All E.R. 217.

been discovered on inspection. In such circumstances, McNair J. was in no doubt that the defendant was liable for failing to examine the vehicle, or at least for failing to warn the claimant that no examination had been carried out. Similarly, in *Vacwell Engineering Co v B.D.H. Chemicals*,[41] a party supplying chemicals was expected to inform himself about the potential hazards and warn the recipient accordingly.

The real question is whether the defendant can *reasonably expect* a third party or the consumer to undertake an inspection in the circumstances. For example, in *Griffiths v. Arch Engineering Co Ltd*,[42] a sub-contractor, who had hired a portable grinding tool which was in a dangerous condition, was not liable to an injured workman for failing to examine the tool. It was clear that the tool had been hired for immediate use, and because the plant hire company had no reason to suppose that an examination would be carried out, they would be liable. The defendant can secure his or her position by attaching a warning to the product that it must be examined prior to use. This places a duty on the third party to examine the product and, of course, renders intermediate examination reasonably probable. By this means, the seller of a dangerously defective car in *Hurley v. Dyke*,[43] who had warned that the car was sold "as seen and with all its faults", avoided liability to a claimant, who had been injured in a subsequent accident caused by the car's defective condition.

(3) The manufacture/design distinction

9–011   The cases we have discussed so far have been concerned with *manufacturing* defects where, due to a problem at the manufacturing stage, the product contains a particular defect which has injured the claimant. This is distinct from a *design* defect, which arises from the very nature of the product itself. The latter is obviously more potentially damaging. Whilst a bad batch of goods will affect a number of consumers, a design defect will affect *every* consumer of the product and may be impossible to discover on inspection or examination. In considering liability for defective goods, design defects must be given particular attention.

The case law, however, is primarily concerned with manufacturing defects. There are a number of reasons for this. First, *Donoghue*, the main precedent in this area of law, concerns a manufacturing defect. Secondly, and more fundamentally, liability for design defects is more difficult to establish on the common law rules of negligence, and presents particular problems for litigants. As shown above, the courts are prepared to *infer* negligence in respect of manufacturing defects, placing the burden on the defendant to rebut this inference by giving evidence that the defect has been caused by the fault of another party, or that its manufacturing system operates in a reasonable manner. This imposes a considerable burden on the defendant, which has been held to be close to strict liability. In contrast, the same reasoning does not apply to design defects. If a person develops cancer after taking drug X, which has been *manufactured* without fault, this may be caused by a multiplicity of different factors, for example, the claimant's genetic makeup, or environmental pollution. It will be for the claimant to establish that (a) a design fault in drug X causes cancer and (b) the design fault was a material cause of his or her cancer. This is a far from easy task and is rendered more

---

[41] [1971] 1 Q.B. 88.
[42] [1968] 3 All E.R. 217.
[43] [1979] R.T.R. 265, HL. See also *Kubach v Hollands* [1937] 3 All E.R. 907.

difficult if the person is taking other drugs, or undertaking other medical treatment. The claimant will only be able to obtain disclosure of the relevant design documentation *after* he or she has commenced the claim and incurred considerable costs. Without a clear admission by the manufacturer, or inside information, it will be difficult to bring a claim in the first place. In contrast where a person bites into a bar of chocolate and finds a lump of metal in it, the court will infer that the metal can only be present due to the fault of someone in the manufacturing process and, in the absence of evidence of interference, or a duty to inspect, will turn to the manufacturer to meet this claim.

The problems arising from design defects were only too apparent in the thalidomide cases.[44] Thalidomide was a drug used by mothers to counter morning sickness, but with appalling side-effects, in that between 1959 and 1962 an estimated 10,000 children were born with physical deformities. This was a classic example of a design defect. Yet, when the parents brought claims in negligence, they experienced difficulty in showing that the manufacturers had failed to take reasonable care in producing the drug. The manufacturer's conduct is judged by reference to what was reasonable at the time the product was put into circulation.[45] The manufacturer will not be judged with hindsight if the dreadful consequences were not foreseeable by the reasonable manufacturer at the time the product was put in circulation.[46]

The need for change?

Whilst the common law has reached a fairly satisfactory position in relation to manufacturing defects—with the courts willing to infer negligence and adopt a flexible approach towards liability—the thalidomide tragedy focussed attention on the problems litigants might experience in relation to *design* defects. This led to demands for a change in the law. At this time (the 1970s), the concept of strict liability as a means of ensuring loss distribution and compensation was particularly fashionable (see the Report of the Pearson Commission in 1978, discussed in Ch. 1). It was suggested that manufacturers should be strictly liable for defects in their products for the following reasons:

9–012

- The manufacturer created the product and therefore the hazard. Since this risk was created in the pursuit of profit, it was reasonable to expect the manufacturer to accept liability for the hazards caused;

- The manufacturer was best placed to insure against the risk, and the price of insurance could be distributed via the price of the product; *and*

- Liability would give the manufacturer a greater incentive to take safety precautions.

Such arguments are not without problems. For example, where individuals have contents insurance for their personal property, forcing manufacturers to take out

[44] See the excellent book by H. Teff and C. Munro, *Thalidomide: the legal aftermath* (Saxon House, 1976).
[45] See *Roe v Minister of Health* [1954] 2 Q.B. 66: "We must not look at the 1947 accident with 1954 spectacles".
[46] The legal issues were never decided as the thalidomide litigation was settled.

insurance against product liability would lead to double cover, which is economically inefficient. The Law Commission in its 1977 Report, *Liability for Defective Products*,[47] suggested that this could be dealt with by limiting strict liability to claims for personal injury and death, but this has not been implemented. A manufacturer is also likely to disagree fundamentally with the first argument which arguably penalises the manufacturer's initiative in placing a product on the market which may have enormous social benefits and responds to consumer choice.

Nevertheless, growing pressure for reform, combined with E.C. initiatives to harmonise the rules on defective products in Member States, resulted in a change in the law. EC Directive 85/374 of July 25, 1985 required Member States to bring into force, within three years, changes in their national laws to comply with the Directive.[48] The UK, on March 1, 1988, brought into force Part 1 of the Consumer Protection Act 1987, s.1(1) of which states that:

> "This Part shall have effect for the purpose of making such provision as is necessary in order to comply with the product liability Directive and shall be construed accordingly."

Therefore, if the wording of the Act appears to conflict with the Directive, this conflict should be resolved in favour of the Directive and any dispute settled by the European Court of Justice.

CONSUMER PROTECTION ACT 1987

9–013 The Product Liability Directive, in its preamble, states:

> ". . . liability without fault on the part of the producer is the sole means of adequately solving the problem, peculiar to our age of increasing technicality, of a fair apportionment of the risks inherent in modern technological production."

The Consumer Protection Act 1987 ("the Act") therefore seeks to make the manufacturer of a product (and others dealing with it) liable without proof of fault for personal injury and property damage caused wholly or partly by a defect in product. The provisions of the Act and the way in which they operate are set out below. It should be noted, however, that by granting the manufacturer certain defences and failing to give a precise definition of "defect", the Act has led many to question how "strict" the liability imposed by the Act actually is.[49]

Who can sue?

9–014 This obvious question is not dealt with expressly by the Act. However, reading ss.2(1) and 5(1), it clearly allows litigants to sue if they suffer damage as a result of a defective product.

[47] Report No. 82, Cmnd 6831.
[48] Art. 19. See OJ 1985 L210 p29.
[49] See, for example, J. Stapleton [(1986) 6 OJLS 392 and *Product Liability* (Butterworths, 1994)] and C. Newdick (1987) 103 L.Q.R. 288.

Who is liable?

Reference should be made here to s.1(2) and s.2 generally. The Act includes not only **9–015** manufacturers (or "producers"), but extends to own-branders and parties importing goods into the European Community. Suppliers are not generally liable, except under the special provisions of s.2(3). However, the Act does not, of course, prevent a supplier from being sued for breach of contract.

(1) Producer—ss.1(2) and 2(2)(a)

Section 1(2) gives three different meanings for a "producer". The first and simplest is **9–016** that of a manufacturer of a product.[50] It should be noted that a manufacturer of a *component part* of the product is equally classified as a producer, so that if the product fails due to a malfunction of a component part, both the manufacturer of the final product and the manufacturer of the component part will be liable.[51]

The second and third meanings relate to goods which have not been manufactured. If the defendant has "won or abstracted" the product[52] (for example, mined coal), or has carried out an industrial or other process on the goods to which the essential characteristics of the goods are attributable[53] (as in the case of canned peas or frozen fish, for example), he or she will be classified as a producer. This last category is not particularly clear and leaves a number of important questions (such as what are the "essential characteristics" of the goods) to the discretion of the court. Those involved in packaging will not be affected unless the packaging alters the essential characteristics of the product.

(2) Own-brander—s.2(2)(b)

Section 2(2)(b) states that liability may attach to "any person, who, by putting his name **9–017** on the product or using a trade mark or other distinguishing mark in relation to the product, has held himself out to be the producer of the product." The important question here is whether the person has *held himself out* as the producer. This will not be so in the case of a product in a supermarket marked "made for Safecos", but will be so where a product is marketed as "Safeco baked beans".

(3) Importer into E.C.—section 2(2)(c)

This is a provision to save claimants the time and expense of pursuing defendants **9–018** outside the European Community. Thus, the subsection provides that "any person who has imported the product into a member State from a place outside the member States in order, in the course of any business of his, to supply it to another" will be liable. This provision is confined to the importer into the EC. It does not affect those who import from one EC country to another, where liability will remain with the first importer. The product must be imported for supply "in the course of any business of his" and so if person X imports a car from Japan privately for his own use, he will not be liable to any person who is injured when it explodes due to a defect in its manufacture.

---

[50] S.1(2)(a).
[51] S.2(5). Liability is "joint and several". This is discussed in Ch. 14.
[52] S.1(2)(b).
[53] S.1(2)(c).

(4) Supplier—s.2(3)

9–019 The supplier is not generally liable under the Act. However, s.2(3) deals with the situation where the consumer has bought defective goods which do not indicate the identity of the producer. Where damage has been caused wholly or partly by a defect in a product, the supplier will be liable if:

- the claimant has requested the supplier to identify the producer/own-brander or importer of the product;

- the request is made within a reasonable period after the damage has occurred and at a time when it is not reasonably practicable for the person making the request to identify those persons; *and*

- the supplier fails within a reasonable period after receiving the request either to comply with the request or to identify the person who supplied the product to him.

The consumer can therefore trace the producer through the chain of supply. The supplier will be able to pass on liability, provided, of course, he or she has maintained proper records of his or her dealings. It should be noted that the mere supply of the end product does not mean that the supplier is deemed to have supplied all the component parts.[54] This means that the supplier will not be liable for failing to identify the producers of all the component parts.

Liability under the Act therefore extends beyond the manufacturer, but it should be noted that it is nevertheless not as wide as the common law, which extends to repairers, fitters, erectors and assemblers.

What is a product?

9–020 This is defined by s.1(2) to include any goods[55] or electricity and includes a product which is comprised in another product, whether by virtue of being a component part or raw material or otherwise. From December 4, 2000, "product" includes all primary agricultural products (that is, food sold in its raw state such as meat or vegetables) and game. Although these products were previously excluded from the Act,[56] it became desirable in the wake of the BSE crisis to include these products and "help restore consumer confidence in the safety of agricultural products".[57] Accordingly, following Directive 1999/34/EC, the Act has been modified.[58]

Buildings are not covered by the Act, although individual goods from which they are built (for example, bricks and beams) are covered. The Act is additionally not intended

---

[54] S.1(3).
[55] S.45(1) defines "goods" to include substances, growing crops and things comprised in land by virtue of being attached to it and any ship, aircraft or vehicle. It does not seem to include the land itself.
[56] Art. 15(1)(a) of the 1985 Directive rendered it optional to include primary agricultural produce and game within the definition of "product". Solely Greece, France, Luxembourg, Finland, Sweden and Austria (with respect to GMOs) chose to include such products.
[57] Recital 5 to Directive 1999/34/EC OJ 1999 L49 p1.
[58] See Consumer Protection Act 1987 (Product Liability)(Modification) Order 2000 (SI 2000/2771). Unfortunately, no corresponding alteration has been made to the definition of "producer" in s.1(2), although agriculture will no doubt often involve some form of "industrial process".

to extend to pure information, except in the case of printed instructions or warnings for a product, which will render the producer (not the printer) liable for errors or omissions in the instructions or warnings which make the product unsafe. The Department of Trade and Industry guidance on the Act[59] indicates that in relation to computer software supplied as an intrinsic part of a product, liability will rest on the producer of the product and not on the consultant who designed the package.

What is a defect?

This is the key concept in the Act.[60] The defendant is liable for damage caused wholly or in part by a "defect" in a product. Section 3 defines a defect as existing when "the safety[61] of the product is not such as persons generally are entitled to expect". The standard is thus set by "persons generally". This ambiguous term has led to some difficulty. It would appear to include the expectations not only of consumers, but also of the manufacturing community. Manufacturers, however, are likely to have lower expectations than those of consumers, who may view themselves as entitled to a product perfect in every way, despite its low market price. The manufacturers' view will inevitably reflect a cost/benefit analysis, whereby the product is only "defective" if the magnitude of the danger inherent in the product, and the cost of preventing the danger, outweighs its utility. It is not clear from the section which form of reasoning a court should utilise in deciding whether a product is "defective" under the Act. Subsequent case-law has, by reference to the wording of the Directive and its preamble, specified that the standard is "the safety which the public at large is entitled to expect."[62]

9–021

A further question is what the public are *entitled* to expect. For example, a knife, due to its very nature, has an obvious risk of danger, but it nevertheless provides a useful tool. It would clearly be unrealistic if the public could legitimately expect to be protected from any harm due to its sharp blade. Certain practical limits are therefore necessary in applying this test.

This test will ultimately be applied by the court. Section 3(2), does, however, provide that in assessing whether a defect exists, the court should take *all* the circumstances into account, including:

    (a)   (i)   the manner in which and purposes for which the product has been marketed;

          (ii) the get-up (or packaging) of the product;

        (iii) the use of any mark (for example the "kite mark") in relation to the product;

        (iv) any instructions for, or warnings with respect to doing or refraining from doing anything with or in relation to the product;

---

[59] *Guide to the Consumer Protection Act 1987* (HMSO, 2001), p.5.

[60] See A Stoppa (1992) 12 L.S. 210.

[61] "Safety" is defined to include safety with respect to products comprised in that product and safety in the context of risks of damage to property, as well as in the context of risks of death and personal injury: s.3(1).

[62] See *Abouzaid v Mothercare (UK) Ltd* [2000] Lloyd's Rep. Med. 280, where Pill L.J. relies on recital 6 to the Directive, and *A v National Blood Authority* [2001] 3 All E.R. 289 at 334: "the court will act as . . . the appointed representative of the public at large".

(b) what might reasonably be expected to be done with or in relation to the product; *and*

(c) the time when the product was supplied by its producer to another. It is irrelevant that products supplied after that time are generally safer than the product supplied to the claimant.

For many years, however, it was difficult, due to the absence of reported cases, to consider how this test would be applied in practice. Since 1999, a number of cases have been reported, which give valuable assistance in assessing the meaning of "defect" under the Act. Initially, the courts adopted an approach similar to that used in negligence (discussed in Ch. 5). In *Richardson v LRC Products*,[63] for example, Mrs Richardson brought an action under the Act when she became pregnant when a condom used by her husband failed. In the absence of any convincing explanation for its failure, the judge examined the care taken by the manufacturer in producing the goods and noted that its standards exceeded the relevant British Standard. It is difficult to reconcile such concerns with a regime of strict liability. A better explanation would be that public do not expect condoms to be 100 per cent effective and, on this basis, the product could not be said to be defective.

The Court of Appeal in *Abouzaid v Mothercare (UK) Ltd*,[64] in its first full judgment on the Act, was critical of such fault-based reasoning. In this case, a child of 12 had been injured when attempting to fasten a sleeping bag manufactured by the defendants to the back of a pushchair. The buckle on the elastic fastenings had sprung back, hitting him in the eye. As a result, the child suffered a significant loss of vision in his left eye. The Court of Appeal adopted a strict view of "defect". In examining the safety which the public at large is entitled to expect, Pill L.J. found that, although this was a borderline case, the severe consequences of injury indicated that the product was defective.[65] It was irrelevant whether this defect should have reasonably come to the manufacturer's attention. The fact that the court found that the defendants would not have been liable in negligence highlighted the distinction between fault-based liability and liability under the Act.

This distinction is further reinforced by the judgment of Burton J. in *A & Others v National Blood Authority*.[66] This was a class action brought by over 100 claimants who had been infected with the virus Hepatitis C through blood transfusions which had used blood or blood products obtained from infected donors. It was alleged that, although the risk of the virus had been known since at least the 1970s, it was, at the time of infection, impossible to detect. Screening for the virus was available only from September 1991. On that basis, the defendants argued that the most that the public could have legitimately expected up to that date was that all reasonable precautions

---

[63] [2000] Lloyd's Rep. Med. 280. See also *Worsley v Tambrands Ltd* [2000] P.I.Q.R. P95 [toxic shock syndrome resulting from use of tampon], the highly questionable decision of *Foster v Biosil* (2001) 59 B.M.L.R. 178 (CC (Central London)) [ruptured breast implant] and, even more recently, *Sam B v McDonald's Restaurants Limited* [2002] EWHC 490 (QBD) [spillage of hot drinks]. See R. Freeman [2001] JPIL 26.

[64] [2000] All E.R. (D) 2436; *The Times*, February 20, 2001 (CA), also known as the "Cosytoes" case.

[65] "Members of the public were entitled to expect better from the appellants": para.27.

[66] [2001] 3 All E.R. 289. Comment C Hodges (2001) 117 L.Q.R. 528; G. Howells and M. Mildred (2002) 65 M.L.R. 95.

would be carried out, not that the blood would be 100 per cent clean. In the view of the judge, this was a blatant attempt to re-introduce fault-based ideas which were contrary to the purpose of the Directive. Section 3 would be confined to *relevant* circumstances,[67] and the steps taken by the manufacturer to avoid the risk would not be relevant in a no-fault regime. On this basis, "avoidability" of the harmful characteristic would be ignored,[68] as would the impracticality, cost or difficulty of taking precautionary measures. Burton J. equally refused to take account of the fact that the defendants were obliged to supply blood to hospitals and patients as a service to society. There was no necessary reason why a public body should receive preferential treatment where a product was unsafe.[69] The public at large were entitled to expect that the blood transfusion would be free from infection. There was no material publicity or information to make them consider otherwise.[70]

This would suggest that the courts will in future take a stricter view of what will be   **9–022**
deemed "defective" under the Act. Burton J. drew a distinction between two categories of product—standard and non-standard. "Standard" products are those which perform as the producer intends. Any defect will thus show up in every product produced. A "non-standard" product, in contrast, is a rogue product, which differs from the normal product manufactured for use by the public, for example, a chocolate bar containing a piece of metal. Where a product is "non-standard", Burton J. noted that it will be easier to establish that it is defective unless it can be shown that the public have accepted its non-standard nature (for example, due to warnings, its presentation or publicity). In the judge's view, infected blood fell into the "non-standard" category.[71] It differed from the norm intended for use by the public. Further, the public (unlike the medical profession) had not been aware of the risk of Hepatitis C and could not be said to have accepted its non-standard nature. In contrast, a standard product will raise more complex issues. The courts will be forced to consider, and take expert evidence on, the relevant factors under s.3(2) and the nature of comparable products in the market (and their price) to ascertain the product's safety for foreseeable use. It remains unclear how the courts will apply strict liability to "standard" products and whether a cost/benefit analysis can be avoided, but it should be noted that in *Abouzaid*, a strict line was taken towards such a product.

In *Abouzaid* and *A*, therefore, the courts adopted a purposive analysis, favouring consumer protection in a no-fault regime, and Burton J. in *A* cast doubt on earlier decisions such as *Richardson*.[72] The factors expressly mentioned in s.3(2) will continue to be of assistance. For example, the use of warnings may still provide a means to avoid liability. In *Worsley v Tambrands Ltd*,[73] the fact that the risk of toxic shock syndrome had been mentioned on the packaging of the product, and in detail on a

[67] This is not obvious from the wording of section 3(2), which states that "all the circumstances shall be taken into account": see C. Hodges (2001) 117 L.Q.R. 528, 530.
[68] "Indeed . . . had it been intended that it would be included as a derogation from, or at any rate a palliation of, [the purpose of the Directive], then it would certainly have been mentioned" above at 336.
[69] Above at 318.
[70] Burton J. questioned at 338 whether, in any event, even express warnings would have been sufficient or whether they would have been ruled out as an attempt to exclude or limit liability which, under s.7, is not permitted.
[71] Burton J. above at 337 rejected the view that blood with a risk of virus could be treated as a "standard" product as too "philosophical".
[72] See Burton J. in *A v National Blood Authority* [2001] 3 All E.R. 289, 319.
[73] [2000] P.I.Q.R. P95.

leaflet which accompanied the product which the purchaser was advised to read and keep, led to a finding of no liability. It will be a question for the court whether the warning is sufficient. In *Worsley*, for example, the claimant suffered a near-fatal illness, but the risk of such an event was very small. The courts are likely to be particularly demanding in relation to products aimed at children or other vulnerable parties.

Further, s.3(2)(c) ensures that the defendants are not discouraged from making improvements in product safety. This subsection prevents the claimant from arguing that the very act of improving the product amounts to an admission that it was defective in the past. The product is judged at the time that it is supplied by the producer, not when it is received by the claimant. On this basis, the producer will not be liable for ordinary wear and tear to goods which may have lingered on the shelves for months or even years. It will not protect the producer, however, where safety expectations and the product design have not changed in the intervening years.[74]

What damage?

9–023   Section 5(1) provides that death and personal injury[75] are covered by the Act. The Act is more restrictive, however, in relation to property damage,[76] and does not include pure economic loss. This is consistent with the common law position, which excludes liability for pure economic loss resulting from a defective product. Section 5(2) excludes loss or damage to the product itself and loss or damage to the whole or any part of the final product which has been supplied with the product as a component. On this basis, if the windscreen of a vehicle shatters due to a defect and causes the vehicle to crash, the claimant cannot sue for the cost of the windscreen or the vehicle itself. If, however, the driver had purchased a replacement tyre for the vehicle, which burst due to a defect and caused the car to crash, the driver would be able to recover for damage to the car. The tyre was *not* supplied with the vehicle when purchased, and so recovery is not excluded by s.5(2).

Property claims are further excluded if the loss or damage suffered, excluding interest, does not exceed £275 (s.5(4)). By this means, the courts avoid having to consider very small claims. Claims are also excluded if the property at the time it is lost or damaged is not of a description ordinarily intended for private use, occupation or consumption, and not intended to be so used (s.5(3)). The Act therefore gives primary protection to the *consumer*. Again, there will be definitional problems. For example, if a lecturer buys a computer for use in his or her research, but also for the family to play games and surf the net, can it be viewed as property ordinarily intended for private use and intended to be so used?

The UK government chose not to implement an option in the Directive to set a maximum level of damages for which a defendant could be liable. Article 16(1) of the Directive states that the producer's total liability for damage resulting from death or personal injury caused by the product and identical items with the same defect may be

---

[74] See *Abouzaid v Mothercare (UK) Ltd* [2000] All E.R. (D) 2436; *The Times*, February 20, 2001.
[75] S.45(1) defines "personal injury" to include any disease and any other impairment of a person's physical or mental condition.
[76] Which includes damage to land: s.5(1).

limited to an amount not less than 70 million ECU. This has only been implemented in Germany, Spain and Portugal.

Defences

Section 4, or more specifically s.4(1)(e), of the Act has caused the most controversy and has even led to a reference to the European Court of Justice challenging the United Kingdom's implementation of the Product Liability Directive. Section 4 gives the defendant six possible defences. It is important to recognise that the mere existence of defences does not mean that the Act does not impose strict liability on the defendant. The aim of strict liability is simply to remove from the claimant the burden of proving that the defendant has been at fault. **9–024**

Let us examine the defences in turn.

(a) The defect is attributable to compliance with a requirement imposed by law

This is obviously necessary, otherwise the defendant would be torn between complying with two conflicting legal provisions. However, compliance with a legal requirement will only absolve a producer from liability if the defect was an *inevitable* result of compliance.[77] **9–025**

(b) The defendants did not at any time supply the product to another

This protects the defendants if they have not put the product in circulation, for example, the product is stolen or a counterfeit copy, and found to be defective. It should be noted, however, that "supply" is defined quite generously under the Act.[78] **9–026**

(c) Supply by the defendants was not in course of their business

Defendants can take advantage of this defence if the only supply of the product was *not* in the course of their business and either: **9–027**

   (i) section 2(2) does not apply (*i.e.* they are only suppliers), or

   (ii) they are within s.2(2) (*i.e.* they are producers, own-branders or importers into the EC), but are not acting at the time with a view to profit.

This is somewhat confusing and is best illustrated by examples. If I make a cake and sell it at the local craft fair, I am not acting in the course of business, but I am a producer and acting with a view to profit.[79] I cannot therefore use the defence. If, however, I wish to get rid of my old lawnmower and sell it to my neighbour for £50, I am not acting in the course of business and I am not a producer, own-brander or importer and so can rely on the defence if the lawnmower proves to be defective. It is irrelevant whether I have profited from the transaction or not.

---

[77] Department of Trade and Industry "Guide to the Consumer Protection Act 1987" (HMSO, 2001).
[78] "Supply" is defined in s.46 to include selling, hiring out or lending goods, entering into a hire-purchase agreement to furnish the goods, the performance of any contract for work and materials to furnish the goods or even giving the goods as a prize or otherwise making a gift of the goods.
[79] Query the situation if I sold it at the school fête for charity.

(d) The defect did not exist in the product at the relevant time, i.e. when it was put in circulation[80]

9–028 This makes the simple point that if the defect is due to wear and tear resulting from use of the product after the product has been put in circulation, the defendant will not be liable. It should be noted, however, that this is a *defence* and so the burden will be on the defendant to establish this.

(e) The development risk defence

9–029 This defence is optional to Member States (see Art. 15(1)(b)), although it has generally been implemented within the European Community.[81] Its implementation in English law has, however, proved controversial.[82] Section 4(1)(e) provides a defence where:

> ". . . the state of scientific and technical knowledge at the relevant time was not such that a producer of products of the same description as the product in question might be expected to have discovered the defect if it had existed in his products while they were under his control."

This may be contrasted with the wording of Article 7(e) of the Directive, which the Act seeks to transpose into English law:

> ". . . the state of scientific and technical knowledge at the time when [the producer] put the product into circulation was not such as to enable the existence of the defect to be discovered."

At first sight, there appears to be a substantive difference between the two defences. Whilst the Directive suggests that the producer must establish, objectively, that the knowledge available at the time of circulation would not have alerted the defendant to the particular risk, s.4(1)(e) appears more generous. Its wording suggests that the producer need only show that a "reasonable producer", *i.e.* another producer in the same market, would not have known of the risks in question. Such a test is reminiscent of the *Bolam* test for breach of duty, discussed in Ch. 5, and is hardly indicative of strict liability on the producer. Indeed, it seems to suggest simply that the defendant will not be liable if he or she can demonstrate that he or she has exercised the care of a "reasonable producer" in the market in assessing the risks associated with the product.[83]

[80] S.4(2) defines the "relevant time" to signify (a) if the defendant is within s.2(2), the time when he supplied the product to another, or (b) if the defendant is not within s.2(2) [for example, a supplier], the time when the product was last supplied by a person to whom s.2(2) does apply.
[81] Except in Finland and Luxembourg. Spain excludes the defence for food and medicinal products and France excludes the defence for products derived from the human body. Germany has permitted liability for development risks in the area of pharmaceutical products since 1978.
[82] The United Kingdom's implementation of the defence may be contrasted with the view of the Law Commission, in their 1977 report, *Liability for Defective Products* No. 82, Cmnd 6831 para.105, that if the product was found to be defective, in the light of the thalidomide case, the injured person should be compensated by the producer however careful the producer had been. The report of the *Royal Commission on Civil Liability and Compensation for Personal Injury*, Cmnd 7054 (1978), Vol 1, para.1259 also recommended that the defence should not be allowed.
[83] This provoked a considerable academic debate: see, for example, J. Stapleton, *Product Liability* (Butterworths, 1994) and C. Newdick [1988] C.L.J. 455.

The possible conflict between these two provisions was examined by the European Court of Justice in *European Commission v United Kingdom*.[84] The European Commission had initiated infringement proceedings against the U.K. in April 1989, alleging that the Act did not properly transpose the Directive into English law, as required by Art. 19 of the Directive. It was argued that s.4(1)(e) was broader than the defence in Art. 7(e). The European Court of Justice rejected this claim. It held that Art. 7(e) imposed an objective test on the producer as to the state of scientific and technical knowledge at the time the product was put in circulation, which would include the most advanced level of knowledge in the relevant field. The producer would be presumed to possess such knowledge, and it was not a question of the producer's subjective state of knowledge or the particular practices and safety standards of the producer's industrial sector. However, the Court was not prepared to go so far as to presume that the producer would be acquainted with *all* relevant scientific knowledge at the time the product was put into circulation. It approved the view of the Advocate General Tesauro that the knowledge in question must be *accessible*. It would thus be unfair to expect the producer to be familiar with research carried out by an academic in Manchuria who published in a local scientific journal in Chinese, which was not circulated outside the boundaries of the region. If the relevant scientific research is accessible, however, it will not be a valid excuse to argue that it represents an isolated opinion: the producer is expected to keep note of, and consider, all relevant research.

In the view of the Court, there was no clear indication that s.4(1)(e) was inconsistent **9–030** with a proper interpretation of the Directive. Whilst the section could be interpreted in a broader sense, the Court held that its wording did not suggest that the availability of the defence depended on the subjective knowledge of the producer. There was, in any event, no English decision which indicated that the English courts would interpret s.4(1)(e) in a way which would conflict with their duty, stated in s.1(1) of the Act, to construe the Act in accordance with the Directive. The Advocate General suggested that, in this light, the Commission's application had been "overhasty, to say the least".

One might consider that, due to the absence of case-law, English law had a fortunate escape, but the legacy of this case is that, in future, s.4(1)(e) will be interpreted in a manner consistent with the comments of the European Court of Justice. Indeed, in the leading case of *A & Others v National Blood Authority*,[85] Burton J. refers not to the sections of the Act, but to the Directive itself, in considering this defence. It is clear from this decision that the courts will, in future, adopt a strict approach to this defence and reject any approach based on fault.

As stated above, *A & Others v National Blood Authority* concerned a class action by over 100 claimants who had been infected with Hepatitis C through blood transfusions. At the time of infection, the relevant defendants had been aware of the risk of the disease, but did not possess the requisite technology to identify infected blood until a later date. They therefore sought to rely on the "development risk" defence on the basis that the state of scientific and technical knowledge was such that the existence of the defect in the product itself was undetectable. Burton J. adopted a firm line. The

[84] [1997] All E.R. (EC) 481; [1997] 3 C.M.L.R. 923. Comment C. Hodges (1998) 61 M.L.R. 560.
[85] [2001] 3 All E.R. 289. Comment C. Hodges (2001) 117 L.Q.R. 528; G. Howells and M. Mildred (2002) 65 M.L.R. 95.

defendants did know of the possible existence of a defect in blood generally. Their absence of knowledge related to the ability to devise a test to identify *which* blood was infected. In such circumstances, it would be inconsistent with the purpose of the Directive if the producer, knowing of a risk, continued to supply the product without liability simply because he or she could not identify in which of his products the defect would occur:

> "If there is a known risk, *i.e.* the existence of the defect is known or should have been known in the light of . . . accessible information, then the producer continues to produce and supply at his own risk. It would, in my judgment, be inconsistent with the purpose of the directive if a producer, in the case of a known risk, continues to supply products simply because, and despite the fact that, he is unable to identify in which if any of his products that defect will occur or recur."[86]

This firm line was also adopted by the Court of Appeal in *Abouzaid v Mothercare (UK) Ltd*.[87] It had been argued that since the defendants had been unaware of the potential problems with the buckle fastening, and no record of any comparable incident had been recorded by the Department of Trade and Industry accident database, the state of scientific and technical knowledge did not indicate a problem at the relevant time. The Court of Appeal gave this argument short shrift. The defence was present to deal with technical advances, not to deal with problems which no-one had thought about. A simple practical test would have identified how a buckle would spring back if extended. Equally, Pill L.J. doubted whether a DTI database fell within the category of "scientific and technical knowledge".[88]

The strict line taken in these cases would seem finally to allay fears that s.4(1)(e) has re-introduced negligence into the Act with a reversed burden of proof on the manufacturer.

(f) The defect was a defect in a finished product (X) in which the product in question had been comprised AND was wholly attributable to the design of X or to compliance with the producer of X's instructions

9–031   This protects the defendant who has supplied a component part of a product, and risks being found to be jointly and severally liable, under s.2(5), when a defect is found in the finished product. It is essentially a denial of causation: my product has no causal link with the injury caused to the claimant. The defence is somewhat complicated and best illustrated by an example. A instructs B to supply tyres which are suitable for a family car, which A decides would be ideal in constructing his new racing car. A is wrong, and the tyres burst at 100 mph, causing A to crash. B will be able to rely on this defence to deny liability. If, however, B was aware of the purpose for which A was purchasing the tyres (for which they were clearly deficient), it is likely that B would be liable in negligence for failing to warn A that they were not suitable for racing cars. Equally, if the tyres burst not because they were used for the wrong purpose, but because they were defectively manufactured, the defence would not apply. The defect

---

[86] Above at 340.
[87] [2000] All E.R. (D) 2436; *The Times*, February 20, 2001.
[88] Para.29.

must be *wholly* attributable to A's conduct and the burden will be on the component producer to prove this to the court.

Contributory negligence

Section 6(4) ensures that the principle of contributory negligence is also available to the defendant.[89] This may appear somewhat odd. The defendant is liable *without proof of fault*, but the claimant's damages may be reduced if the claimant's fault has increased the damage suffered by him or her. Section 1(1) of the Law Reform (Contributory Negligence) Act 1945 states that the defence applies "where any person suffers damage as the result partly of his own fault and partly of the fault of any other person", but "fault" is interpreted broadly by s.4 of that Act to include any "act or omission which gives rise to a liability in tort". The defendant, if liable, is therefore presumed to be at "fault", and the claimant's actual fault is balanced against the responsibility of the defendant. This again gives rise to concern as to the intrusion of fault into a strict liability statute. It should also be noted that the claimant's contributory negligence, for example in using a product in an unreasonable way, may indicate that the product is not *defective*, in any event, under the criteria set under s.3(2) (see, in particular, s.3(2)(b)).

9–032

Exclusion Clauses

In view of the aim of the Act to protect claimants from injury due to defective products, s.7 provides that such claims "shall not be limited or excluded by any contract term, by any notice or by any other provision". This avoids the technicalities of the Unfair Contract Terms Act 1977 and sends a clear message to defendants that exclusion clauses are not an adequate response to potential liability.

9–033

Limitation Periods

These are discussed in Ch. 14. A limitation period indicates the time period within which a claimant must bring a claim. If a claim is brought after this period, however good the claim, the courts will refuse to allow the claim to proceed. By this means, the courts avoid dealing with stale claims and claimants are encouraged to act promptly when the evidence is fresh. The Limitation Act 1980 contains the main provisions. Section 11A deals specifically with actions in respect of defective products. In relation to claims for personal injury or property loss, the claim must be brought within three years from the date on which the cause of action accrued.[90] The cause of action will accrue either when the damage is caused or, if later, when the damage is reasonably discoverable[91] by the claimant. Section 11A(3) provides that an action under Part 1 of the 1987 Act shall not be brought after the expiration of the period of 10 years from

9–034

[89] S.6 also renders the Fatal Accidents Act 1976 and the Congenital Disabilities (Civil Liability) Act 1976 applicable.
[90] S.11A(4).
[91] The date of knowledge is defined in s.14, Limitation Act 1980.

the time the product was put into circulation.[92] This long-stop provision will serve to protect defendants from claims in respect of design defects which come to light long after products have been in circulation.

Causation and Remoteness

9–035   There are no specific rules in the Act and so the ordinary rules described in Chapter 6 of this book will apply. The Act gives the claimant no further assistance in what, as stated earlier, may be a difficult task, particularly in cases of illness and disease. This was illustrated recently in relation to the third generation oral contraceptive pill. In a trial lasting three months and hearing the conflicting evidence of 10 experts, Mackay J. concluded, in a judgment of 200 pages, that there was insufficient evidential basis to establish that an increased risk of cardio-vascular injury was caused by the product. On this basis, there was therefore no need to examine the law under the Act.[93]

ASSESSMENT OF THE IMPACT OF THE ACT

Continuing practical problems

9–036   Whilst it has taken almost 12 years from the introduction of the Act for a claimant to bring a successful claim,[94] the two recent cases of *Abouzaid* and *A* have done much to allay fears that the Act provided little addition to the common law.[95] The ruling of the European Court of Justice in *European Commission v United Kingdom*[96] has proved an important milestone in affirming the objectives of the Directive and its goal in providing consumer protection. Nevertheless, as seen in the cases discussed above, litigation will often prove an expensive and lengthy process, particularly if complex medical evidence is involved. Further, the claimant receives no assistance in proving causation, which may be an onerous task. The claimant's position is moreover weakened by the strict time limitations on his or her action. It is entirely probable that it would take more than 10 years for certain injuries resulting from design defects to become apparent, and yet the long-stop provision bars the litigant's claim absolutely. The inclusion of primary agricultural products in the Directive is therefore unlikely to assist persons suffering v.CJD as a result of eating beef infected with BSE, due to the long incubation period of the illness.

Standard and non-standard products

9–037   It would seem that the different treatment of manufacture and design defects has survived the Act, although Burton J. in *A* prefers the similar, but not identical, terms of "standard" and "non-standard" product. In defining a "standard" product as one

---

[92] But see *Horne-Roberts v Smithkline Beecham plc* [2002] 1 W.L.R. 1662, CA (discretion to substitute new party even after expiry of the long-stop provision).
[93] *X v Schering Health Care Ltd* [2002] EWHC 1420; *Daily Telegraph*, August 1, 2002. See M. Mildred [2002] JPIL 428 and A. McAdams (2002) 146 S.J. 900.
[94] Our first edition in 2000 noted only one reported case which was directly in point: *European Commission v United Kingdom* [1997] 3 C.M.L.R. 923.
[95] See E. Deards and C. Twigg-Flesner (2001) 10 Nott L.J. 1.
[96] [1997] All E.R. (EC) 481; [1997] 3 C.M.L.R. 923, discussed above.

which performs as the producer intended, there is an obvious link with design defects. Equally, a clear example of a "non-standard" product would be a product subject to a manufacturing defect. Burton J. concedes that it will be easier to prove a defect in a non-standard product and that it would be more difficult to apply the "development risk defence" to non-standard products. Such a product may at most qualify once, *i.e.* where the problem, which led to an occasional defective product, was not known. Once the problem can be discovered by virtue of accessible information, the defence will no longer apply. Standards products, however, are likely to give rise to more complex litigation in ascertaining exactly what level of safety the public is entitled to expect. This mirrors the position at common law, where, it may be recalled, the courts are more willing to infer negligence in relation to manufacturing defects. The real deficiency in the common law lay in relation to claims for design defects, and it would appear that, despite the tough line taken towards strict liability by Burton J., the practical difficulties in bringing a claim for design defects will not disappear. It also remains to be seen whether the English courts will succeed in addressing the questions of defects in standard products and the degree of warning necessary to avoid liability without reference to cost/benefit analysis. For example, is it possible to ascertain what safety the public can legitimately expect from a product without considering what precautions the producer *could* have taken at the time it was put in circulation? The difficulties caused by the "standard"/"non-standard" distinction have already led two leading academics to question the merits of this distinction and what it positively contributes to our understanding of this area of law.[97]

Use of settlements

It is likely to remain the case that most litigation under the 1987 Act will be settled out of court.European Commission surveys indicate that this would seem to apply in most Member States, where few reported cases may be found.[98] It therefore remains difficult to assess the impact of the Act, particularly as settlements will frequently require the parties not to publicise the terms of the settlement. In contrast, in the United States, s.37 of the Consumer Protection Safety Act obliges producers to announce cases involving defective products and notify the Consumer Product Safety Commission.[99] If the product which has allegedly caused death or grievous bodily injury is the subject of at least three court cases in a two-year period, producers (and importers as well) have to notify the Commission of the circumstances of the case as soon as the cases have been settled, either by a ruling in favour of the claimant, or as the result of an out of court agreement.[1] There is no equivalent provision in the United Kingdom. Arguably, it would be in the public interest for greater information to be available on such settlements, which would enable a clearer assessment to be made of the impact of the

9–038

---

[97] See G. Howells and M. Mildred (2002) 65 M.L.R. 95, 101.

[98] See *Report from the Commission on the Application of Directive 85/374 on Liability for Defective Products*, Com (2000) 893, final, para 2.2 and Burton J. in *A v National Blood Authority* [2001] 3 All E.R. 289 at 319.

[99] This is an independent federal regulatory agency created in 1972 to "protect the public against unreasonable risks of injuries and deaths associated with consumer products". It covers about 15,000 types of consumer products used in home, schools and recreation, but does not regulate on-road motor vehicles, boats, aircraft, cosmetics, pesticides, alcohol, tobacco, firearms and medical devices. See *www.cpsc.gov*.

[1] See 15 USC Sec. 2085, "Notification of settlements or judgments".

Act on U.K. law. Certainly, it would assist the European Commission in its review of the operation of the product liability Directive within the European Community. Such measures, however, are likely to be opposed by manufacturers, who are far from willing to allow their competitors access to such information.

BREACH OF STATUTORY DUTY

9–039 Part II of the Consumer Protection Act 1987 provides for the Secretary of State to make safety regulations prescribing rules as to design, manufacture and packaging of certain classes of goods. This replaced earlier legislation in the Consumer Safety Act 1978. Although breach of such regulations generally incurs only criminal liability, s.41 expressly provides that an individual injured by a defect in a product resulting from breach of safety regulations has an action for breach of statutory duty. This provides a further option for litigants, although it should be noted that there are, as yet, no reported decisions in this area, and that the regulations only cover a limited class of goods.[2]

REFORM OF THE PRODUCT LIABILITY DIRECTIVE

9–040 The European Commission is required to undertake a review of the Product Liability Directive every 5 years.[3] In July 1999, it published a Green Paper on Liability for Defective Products,[4] in which it outlined the Commission's proposals to consult interested parties to assess the impact of the Directive on victims and on the sectors of the economy concerned, and to reflect on the need for reform. In particular, it sought views on:

- the burden of proof imposed on victims;
- the operation of the "development risks" defence;
- the existence of minimum and maximum values for claims and their justification;
- the 10-year deadline and the effects of a possible modification of this;
- assessment of the insurability of risks deriving from defective production;
- improved information on the settlement of cases concerning defective products;
- the supplier's liability;
- the type of goods and damage covered.

---

[2] See s.11(7).

[3] The Commission has to report regularly to the Community institutions on the state of the application of the Directive. Art. 21 of the Directive stipulates that it must report every 5 years on the general application of the Directive. Arts 15(3) and 16(2) stipulate that it must report every 10 years after notification of the Directive on development risks and financial limits.

[4] *http://europa.eu.int/comm/dg15/en/index.htm* (COM (1999) 396 final.)

In its report of January 2001,[5] the Commission resolved that in view of the belated transposition of the Directive in certain countries,[6] the possibility given to the Member States to apply their own national law, and the lack of available data, it would again not recommend any change to the Directive.[7] Nevertheless, the Commission has resolved actively to seek further information for future reforms. This will include setting up an expert group to gather information in the field of product liability, and launching a study into the economic impact of strengthening the current system of liability. It also proposes in the medium term to examine the practical effects of retaining a dual system of national law and liability under the Directive, thereby undertaking a complete overview of all applicable product liability laws in Member States. In addition, information will be collated in related areas such as general product safety and environmental liability. It is obviously hoped that in future reviews, the information will be available to form a basis for proposals for reform.

(2) ANIMALS ACT 1971

In this last part of the chapter, we will look briefly at the liability imposed by the Animals Act 1971. This was brought in to replace the rather complicated existing common law provisions which imposed strict liability on those responsible for wild and domestic animals.[8] The Act imposes strict liability for damage done by animals under the care of another. It should be noted that the Act applies *in addition to* ordinary common law principles. Therefore, a owner of a dog may still find himself or herself liable under occupiers' liability for injuries caused (see Ch. 8),[9] liable in nuisance (for example, for the smell caused by his or her pigs: see Ch. 10)[10] or liable in trespass (for example, for allowing hounds to stray onto another's land: see Ch. 11).[11] Owners may equally find themselves liable under the ordinary rules of negligence where they have failed to exercise reasonable care to prevent their pet causing foreseeable harm to another.[12]

9–041

The 1971 Act alone imposes strict liability. We set out below the main provisions. We do not deal with liability for injuries committed by dogs to livestock (s.3)[13] or

---

[5] COM (2000) 893, final.

[6] For example, France only implemented the Directive on May 23, 1998 (see law No. 389–98 of May 19, 1998).

[7] This is the second report of the Commission. In its first report of December 1995 (COM (1995) 617), the Commission concluded that, on the basis of the limited information available as to the operation of the Directive, it was not appropriate to submit any proposals for amendments.

[8] See s.1.

[9] See *Gould v McAuliffe* [1941] 1 All E.R. 515.

[10] See *Wheeler v JJ Saunders Ltd* [1996] Ch 19. Note also *Leeman v Montagu* [1936] 2 All ER 1677.

[11] See *League against Cruel Sports v Scott* [1986] Q.B. 240 (owner responsible for the damage caused if he or she intended animals to enter the claimant's land or, knowing that there was a real risk that they would enter, failed to take reasonable care to prevent their entry.)

[12] See *Fardon v Harcourt-Rivington* (1932) 146 L.T. 391, HL and *Draper v Hodder* [1971] 2 Q.B. 556. A further action may lie for a compensatory award from the Criminal Injuries Compensation Authority if the victim can establish that a criminal offence has taken place: see *Re C [CICA: Liability: 2002]* December 3, 2002; [2003] 7 C.L.10 (horses straying onto the highway amounting to a criminal offence under the Highways Act 1980, s.155).

[13] See also ss.5(4) and 9.

liability for damage caused by straying livestock (s.4),[14] which are not considered in most law courses.

Dangerous/non-dangerous species

9–042   The fundamental distinction in the Act is between wild animals (or dangerous species) and domestic animals (non-dangerous species). For example, a tiger will be classified as the former, a cat the latter. Different provisions apply according to the classification of the animal in question. Liability will be imposed on the "keeper" of the animal in both cases. "Keeper" is defined in s.6(3)[15] as the owner of the animal, someone who has it in his possession, or the head of a household where a minor under 16 owns or possesses the animal.[16]

Dangerous species

9–043   These are defined in s.6(2) of the Act. "A dangerous species[17] is a species—

   (a)   which is not commonly domesticated in the British Islands; and

   (b)   whose fully grown animals normally have such characteristics that they are likely, unless restrained, to cause severe damage or that any damage they may cause is likely to be severe."

This will therefore include animals such as tigers, elephants[18] and lions. As noted in the leading case of *Mirvahedy v Henley*,[19] cases will generally arise in the context of escapes from circuses or zoos. Section 2(1) provides that the keeper of the dangerous animal will be strictly liable for any damage caused by such an animal, subject to the defences outlined below. Liability will be regardless of fault and irrespective of any awareness of the animal's dangerous propensities. This appears to be entirely sensible. It is no excuse that your pet tiger escaped despite your reasonable efforts to fence it in. The risk of injury lies firmly on the keeper of any such animal.

Non-dangerous species

9–044   This is rather more complicated. It concerns domesticated animals and here liability is limited to circumstances where the keeper knows of the danger and severe injury is likely to arise due to the abnormal characteristics of the animal. Section 2(2) sets three conditions for liability which must all be satisfied:

   (a)   the damage is of a kind which the animal, unless restrained, was likely to cause or which, if caused by the animal, was likely to be severe; and

---

[14] See also ss.5(5), 5(6), 7 and 8.

[15] See also s.6(4): "Where an animal is taken into and kept in possession for the purpose of preventing it from causing damage or of restoring it to its owner, a person is not a keeper of it by virtue only of that possession."

[16] It should be noted that there may be more than one keeper: see *Flack v Hudson* [2001] Q.B. 698 where an action was brought on behalf of the person with possession of the horse against its owner. The Court of Appeal held that there was nothing in the Act to prevent one keeper suing another.

[17] "Species" includes sub-species and variety: s.11.

[18] See *Behrens v Bertram Mills Circus Ltd* [1957] 2 Q.B. 1, Devlin J. in which it was held to be irrelevant that the elephant in question was a trained circus animal rather than a wild animal. See also *Filburn v People's Palace and Aquarium Co* (1890) L.R. 25 Q.B.D. 258.

[19] [2003] 2 W.L.R. 882 at 913 *per* Lord Walker.

(b) the likelihood of the damage or of its being severe was due to characteristics of the animal which are not normally found in animals of the same species or are not normally so found except at particular times or in particular circumstances; *and*

(c) those characteristics were known to that keeper or were at any time known to a person who at that time had charge of the animal as that keeper's servant or, where that keeper is the head of a household, were known to another keeper of the animal who is a member of that household and under the age of sixteen."

The courts will generally consider each matter in turn. The first two conditions set an objective test. First of all, was the type of damage *foreseeable*? "Likely" has been interpreted as "to be reasonably expected".[20] It does not require probability, but equally a mere possibility will not suffice. Secondly, did the relevant characteristic of the animal *cause* the harm suffered? The third condition is subjective: did the keeper *know* of this characteristic? This requires actual knowledge of the potential danger by the keeper.[21] It does not, however, require the keeper to have actual knowledge of the particular circumstances in which the injury arose.

The application of these conditions has caused problems in practice, largely due to their wording, which has been described as giving rise to "several difficulties"[22], "remarkably opaque",[23] "somewhat tortuous",[24] and "inept".[25] The real difficulty arises in interpreting s.2(2)(b). The first limb is fairly straightforward: you will be liable if your animal has characteristics which other animals of the same species do not possess, for example, it is more vicious than usual. These have been called "permanent characteristics".[26]

The second limb deals with "temporary characteristics" and has been described by the House of Lords itself as "ambiguous" and "opaque". It contains a double negative: characteristics *not* normally found *except* at particular times or in particular circumstances. Does this mean:

(a) Normal characteristics which arise at particular times or in particular circumstances? *or*;

(b) Abnormal characteristics which only manifest themselves at particular times?

The House of Lords in the leading case of *Mirvahedy v Henley*[27] by a slim majority (3:2) chose the former explanation. On this basis, normal characteristics which only manifest themselves at particular times or on particular occasions might give rise to liability if the other two conditions are met. As Lord Nicholls indicated, as a matter of social

[20] Lord Scott in *Mirvahedy v Henley* at 903. See also Neill L.J. in *Smith v Ainger The Times*, June 5, 1990: "such as might happen" and "such as might well happen."
[21] It is not enough that the keeper ought to have known of the danger: see *Hunt v Wallis The Times*, May 10, 1991.
[22] Lord Denning M.R. in *Cummings v Granger* [1977] Q.B. 397 at 404.
[23] Ormrod L.J. in *Cummings v Granger* at 407.
[24] Slade L.J. in *Curtis v Betts* [1990] 1 W.L.R. 459 at 462.
[25] Nourse L.J. in *Curtis v Betts* above at 468.
[26] See Stuart-Smith LJ in *Curtis v Betts* above at 469.
[27] [2003] 2 W.L.R. 882.

policy, the choice is between placing the burden of liability on those who care for the animals and undertake any associated risks or forcing the public in general to accept that animals inevitably bring with them a risk of injury.[28] In adopting a broad interpretation of s.2(2)(b), the majority ensured that it would be easier in future to bring a claim under the 1971 Act without the necessity to show that the animal at that time was acting abnormally.

9–045
The case itself concerned a car accident caused by an alarmed horse bolting onto a busy dual carriageway. Mirvahedy suffered serious personal injuries and his car was badly damaged. The owners of the horse had taken reasonable care to fence in the horse and were not found to be liable on the basis of common law negligence. The case rested on the interpretation of s.2(2) of the Act. It was accepted that there was nothing abnormal in a horse bolting when frightened. It was entirely normal. However, horses would only bolt in particular circumstances, here where it had been terrified by some unknown event into escaping. The owners of the horse would therefore be strictly liable for the damage caused.

In reaching its decision, the majority affirmed the approach taken in two earlier Court of Appeal decisions in *Cummings v Granger*[29] and *Curtis v Betts*.[30] In *Cummings*, the plaintiff was attacked and seriously injured by an untrained Alsatian guard dog let loose in the defendant's scrap yard. But for certain defences discussed below, the plaintiff would have succeeded in her claim under the second limb of s.2(2)(b). This was not a ferocious dog possessed of characteristics not normally possessed by Alsatians, but just a typical guard dog which would be likely to attack any intruder into its territory. This was enough to establish the second limb.

Equally, in *Curtis v Betts*,[31] a bull mastiff named Max attacked a 10 year old child in the street while being transferred from the defendants' house to a Land Rover to be taken to the local park for exercise. The judge found that bull mastiffs[32] have a tendency to react fiercely at particular times and in particular circumstances, namely when defending the boundaries of what they regard as their own territory. Slade L.J. remarked that "The mere fact that a particular animal shared its potentially dangerous characteristics with other animals of the same species will not preclude the satisfaction of requirement (b) if on the particular facts the likelihood of damage was attributable to characteristics normally found in animals of the same species at times or in circumstances corresponding with those in which the damage actually occurred."[33]

On this basis where an animal is only aggressive in particular circumstances, for example, a dog guarding its territory or, if a bitch, when it has a litter of pups, the keeper may be found liable under s.2(2).

---

[28] Above at 884, although his Lordship indicated that where the law in question was governed by statute, such policy decisions must be deemed to have been dealt with by Parliament and it was not for the courts to intervene.
[29] [1977] Q.B. 397.
[30] [1990] 1 W.L.R. 469.
[31] [1990] 1 W.L.R. 469.
[32] The species here is treated as that of a "bull mastiff" rather than dogs in general. See also *Hunt v Wallis The Times*, May 10, 1991 (comparison with other border collies). From the case-law, this only seems to apply to breeds of dogs (except mongrels: *Smith v Ainger The Times*, June 5, 1990). Other animals are treated generally, *e.g.* horses.
[33] Above at 464.

Defences

As we saw in relation to the Consumer Protection Act 1987, strict liability does not **9–046** prevent defences arising. These are listed primarily in s.5 of the Act, although s.10 does provide a defence of contributory negligence.

(i) Fault of the victim

Section 5(1) provides that the keeper will not be liable where the damage suffered is **9–047** due wholly to the fault of the person suffering it, for example the claimant is bitten by a dog he has just kicked.

(ii) Voluntary acceptance of risk

Section 5(2) provides that the keeper will not be liable under s.2 where the victim has **9–048** voluntarily accepted the risk of injury or damage.[34] There is some possible overlap with 5(1). For example, a person who tries to escape despite being warned that a police dog will be released may be found to be at fault *and* to have voluntarily accepted the risk of being bitten.[35]

(iii) The victim is a trespasser

Section 5(3) is divided into two limbs. Under the first limb, the keeper will not be **9–049** liable for any damage caused by an animal kept on the premises to a trespasser if it is proved that the animal was not kept there for the protection of persons or property. If it is kept there for protection, the keeper will not be liable if it is kept for a purpose which is not unreasonable.

The operation of these defences is illustrated in *Cummings v Granger*.[36] Here, the plaintiff had been bitten when entering a scrap yard at night as a trespasser. Here, the Court of Appeal found s.2(2) to be satisfied, but that the defendant had good defences under ss.5(2) and 5(3). Section 5(1) was not satisfied as the incident had not *solely* been due to the plaintiff's fault. However, she had known that there was a fierce guard dog in the yard and could be taken to have knowingly accepted the risk of injury, satisfying s.5(2). Further it was held that a defence existed under s.5(3) as well: "Old scrap and bits of spares for motor cars are fair game in most parts of the country to anybody who is minded to steal that kind of thing. I do not think that it was in the least unreasonable to keep a guard dog in the yard."[37]

Conclusion

As a result of *Mirvahedy*, there are likely to be in future more claims brought under the **9–050** Act. Owning a pet is therefore not only a privilege, but a potential basis for liability.

---

[34] Note also s.6(5): "Where a person employed as a servant by a keeper of an animal incurs a risk incidental to his employment he shall not be treated as accepting it voluntarily."
[35] See *Dhesi v Chief Constable of West Midlands The Times*, May 9, 2000.
[36] [1977] Q.B. 397.
[37] Ormrod L.J. above at 408. This is now subject to the Guard Dogs Act 1975, which regulates the use of guard dogs.

Chapter 10

NUISANCE AND THE RULE IN *RYLANDS V FLETCHER*

Introduction

So far, we have examined torts which seek to protect the individual from harm inflicted **10–001** negligently. The only exception has been liability under certain statutes which, as discussed in Ch. 9, impose a form of strict liability on the producer of a defective product or the keeper of an animal. In this chapter, we consider the torts of nuisance and the rule in *Rylands v Fletcher*.[1] These torts have a different role from that discussed in earlier chapters: seeking to protect the claimant's ability to use and enjoy his or her land freely without undue interference by the defendant. Here, fault plays only a limited role. The main concern of the courts is to protect the claimant's rights in land. This chapter examines the rules governing the different types of nuisance recognised at law, the tensions between them, and their relationship with the rule in *Rylands v Fletcher*—which deals only with *isolated* cases of interference with the claimant's land. It also considers the impact of the House of Lords' judgments in *Hunter v Canary Wharf Ltd*[2] and *Cambridge Water Co v Eastern Counties Leather plc*,[3] which have had a dramatic effect on the law of private nuisance and the rule in *Rylands v Fletcher*. This is a developing area of law, impacting on the lives of ordinary individuals and the protection of the environment as a whole.[4] The continuing role of these torts, and their difficult relationship with negligence, will be discussed in this chapter. We begin by considering the role of nuisance in the law of torts, before considering liability under the rule in *Rylands v Fletcher*.

---

[1] (1865) 3 H & C 774 (Court of Exchequer); (1866) 1 LR 1 Ex 265 (Court of Exchequer Chamber), (1868) LR 3 HL 330 (House of Lords).
[2] [1997] A.C. 677.
[3] [1994] 2 A.C. 264. *See also Transco plc v Stockport MBC* [2003] 3 W.L.R. 1467, HL.
[4] There is, of course, a limit to what the private action of nuisance or *Rylands v Fletcher* liability can do to protect the environment and such protection is perhaps more efficiently dealt with on a national or international level by legislation in favour of the public at large. The role of tort in protecting the environment is discussed in *Environmental Protection and the Common Law* (J. Lowry and R. Edmunds ed.) (Hart, 2000).

NUISANCE

10–002 There are three main types of nuisance, which should be distinguished:

- Private nuisance
- Public nuisance
- Statutory nuisance

Private nuisance is generally defined as an "unlawful interference with a person's use or enjoyment of land, or some right over, or in connection, with it."[5] Consideration of this tort will form the main body of this chapter. Public nuisance, in contrast, is both a crime and a tort. An individual can bring an action where he or she has suffered particular harm from a nuisance which has materially affected the reasonable comfort and convenience of life of a sufficiently large number of citizens who come within the sphere or neighbourhood of its operation. Although the courts frequently draw comparisons between private and public nuisance, they are in reality very different torts, which seek to protect different interests. Whilst private nuisance seeks to protect private rights, public nuisance is primarily a crime, and acts as a general measure of public protection. Whilst the claimant may seek in his or her Statement of Case to allege that both torts have been committed,[6] it is important to recognise that in character, they have little in common bar their name.

Both private and public nuisance are distinct from statutory nuisances, which are nuisances which operate by virtue of particular statutes. The best example perhaps is that of Part III of the Environmental Protection Act 1990, which is primarily concerned with matters of public health. As statutory nuisances are unlikely even to provide a claim for breach of statutory duty,[7] they are not dealt with in this book. Readers are advised to consult specialist texts.[8]

PRIVATE NUISANCE

10–003 There are three main forms of private nuisance:

- Physical injury to land (for example, by flooding or noxious fumes);
- Substantial interference with the enjoyment of land (for example smells, dust and noise);
- Encroachment on a neighbour's land (for example, by spreading roots or overhanging branches).[9] This is of minor significance, but will be considered further in the section on remedies.

[5] W.V.H. Rogers, *Winfield & Jolowicz on Torts* (16th ed., Sweet and Maxwell, 2002), p.508. Winfield (1930–32) 4 C.L.J. 189 at 190.
[6] See, *e.g. Halsey v Esso Petroleum* [1961] 1 W.L.R. 683.
[7] *Issa v Hackney LBC* [1997] 1 W.L.R. 956.
[8] See, *e.g.* J. Thornton and S. Beckwith, *Environmental Law* (2nd ed., Sweet and Maxwell, 2004).
[9] See *Lemmon v Webb* [1895] A.C. 1, *Delaware Mansions Ltd v Westminster City Council* [2002] 1 A.C. 321 and *L.E. Jones (Insurance Brokers) Ltd v Portsmouth CC* [2003] 1 W.L.R. 427.

All three forms seek to protect the claimant's use and enjoyment of land from an activity or state of affairs for which the defendant is responsible. A fourth form of nuisance exists which is generally discussed in works on land law, namely where the defendant has interfered with a particular proprietary right the claimant possesses over the land, for example a right of way. Such interference is generally treated by analogy to trespass, in that provided a substantial degree of interference can be shown, the tort will be actionable *per se*.[10] By this means, the claimant's rights over land are vindicated, although where the right in question is simply a right to support, damage must be shown.[11]

The main distinction drawn by the courts is between physical damage to property and interference with one's enjoyment of land or personal comfort. The main impact of this distinction is that the courts are more willing to find a nuisance where physical damage to property has been caused. Mere personal discomfort will be treated with latitude unless the interference is such that it is "materially interfering with the ordinary comfort physically of human existence, not merely according to elegant or dainty modes and habits of living".[12] On this basis, loss of a view from one's property is a loss of "elegant" living and not such as to interfere with the ordinary comfort of human existence.[13] So, while the courts are willing to protect the claimant's personal comfort, they are more willing to protect the claimant's property. Thus, there is clear House of Lords authority that matters such as the nature of the locality will not be relevant where there has been material injury to property.[14]

What amounts to a private nuisance?

It must be self-evident that not *every* interference with the claimant's use and enjoyment of land can amount to a private nuisance. For example, I enjoy playing the piano, but of necessity must practise. Can my neighbour complain (a) because I play at all; or (b) because he or she enjoys fine music and the sound of my bad playing is unbearable? If either of the above were actionable, I would be severely limited in my ability to play the piano. My neighbour would be given the power to veto my choice of activity. However, if in a fit of enthusiasm, I decide to practice my scales between 2 a.m. and 4 a.m. every morning, my neighbour would appear to have legitimate grounds for complaint.[15] The tort of nuisance must balance my rights against those of my neighbour. Whilst it may be easy to say that noxious fumes which destroy every plant in my garden should be actionable, it is far more difficult to weigh up the complaints of a resident in an industrial area that lorries travelling to a factory cause noise and dust which affect his or her property. The test is one of "reasonable user", balancing the interest of the defendant to use his or her land as is legally permitted against the

10–004

---

[10] *Nicholls v Ely Beet Sugar Factory Ltd* [1936] 1 Ch. 343.

[11] *Midland Bank v Bardgrove Property Services* [1992] 37 E.G. 126.

[12] Sir Knight-Bruce V.C. in *Walter v Selfe* (1851) 20 LJ Ch 433 at 435.

[13] *Aldred's Case* (1610) 9 Co Rep 57b.

[14] *St Helen's Smelting Co v Tipping* (1865) 11 HLC 642 at 651.

[15] The neighbour might in practice prefer to rely on the procedures under Part III of the Environmental Protection Act 1990, ss.79–80 (duty on the local authority to abate a statutory nuisance where, *inter alia*, noise is prejudicial to health or a nuisance) and, if available, under the Noise Act 1996 (duty on local authorities to investigate complaints of excessive levels of noise from a dwelling house at night). See, further, texts on environmental law and F McManus (2000) 20 L.S. 264.

conflicting interest of the claimant to have quiet enjoyment of his or her land. The ordinary use of your home will not amount to a nuisance, even if it discomforts your neighbour due to poor soundproofing or insulation.[16] As Lord Wright states in the leading case of *Sedleigh-Denfield v O'Callaghan*[17]: "A balance has to be maintained between the right of the occupier to do what he likes with his own, and the right of his neighbour not to be interfered with".

"Reasonable User"

10–005   The first point to stress is that this is *not* a standard of reasonable care as in negligence. The rule is one of give and take. I do not expect my neighbours to be perfect or to exist in hermit-like silence and isolation, but neither do I expect my neighbours to use their property in such a way as to render my existence unbearable: I therefore expect them to use it reasonably. However, as in negligence, what is "unreasonable" is difficult to define. It does not require that the defendant's actions must be deliberate. Equally, it is clearly established that, in nuisance, the defendant's use of land can be "unreasonable" even though he or she has taken all reasonable care to prevent the nuisance occurring.[18] The courts' approach is therefore *results-based*: is the result of the defendant's conduct such that it is likely to cause unreasonable interference with the claimant's use and enjoyment of land? It is not a question of blaming the defendant, but of protecting the claimant's interest. There is, predictably, no set formula for determining what results are unreasonable. It is possible to list a number of circumstances which are clearly relevant to the courts' decisions in particular cases, but it is essentially a question of fact.

Factors Determining Reasonable User

10–006   The following factors are considered in turn below:

- The nature of the locality;
- The duration and frequency of the defendant's conduct;
- The utility of the defendant's conduct;
- Abnormal sensitivity of the claimant;
- Malice on the part of the defendant.

(1) The nature of the locality

10–007   As stated above, this is not relevant where material physical damage has been suffered by the claimant. Where the claimant has suffered personal discomfort and inconvenience, however, it is relevant. The classic quotation is that of Thesiger L.J. in *Sturges v*

---

[16] *Southwark LBC v Mills; Baxter v Camden LBC (No. 2)* [2001] 1 A.C. 1; approving Court of Appeal in *Baxter v Camden LBC (No. 2)* [1999] 1 All E.R. 237. See J. O'Sullivan 'Nuisance, local authorities and neighbours from hell' (2000) 59 C.L.J. 11.
[17] [1940] A.C. 880 at 903.
[18] *Rapier v London Tramways Co* [1893] 2 Ch. 588.

Bridgman: "What would be a nuisance in Belgrave Square would not necessarily be so in Bermondsey".[19] Therefore, in considering whether noise from a local factory causes a nuisance to local residents, the courts will examine the nature of the locality, and if it is an industrial area, will be less likely to find an actionable nuisance.

The nature of the locality may change over time from industrial to residential, and therefore the courts must have regard to the locality as it is today. Change may happen naturally, or may be due to deliberate development of the locality, as seen with the development of the London Docklands, which was classified as an urban development area. Indeed, in *Gillingham BC v Medway (Chatham) Dock Co. Ltd*,[20] Buckley J. held that planning permission to develop a disused naval dockyard as a 24–hour commercial dock had changed the character of the neighbourhood. Local residents therefore could not complain about the serious disruption caused to them by its operation. The question, however, is one of fact, not law. Planning permission is not a defence to nuisance. Where planning permission was given to expand a pig farm adjacent to holiday accommodation, this did not change the nature of the locality, and did not excuse the nuisance caused to the plaintiffs by the smell of the pigs.[21]

(2) Duration and frequency

It is a matter of common sense that the claimant will have to endure some inconvenience in his or her enjoyment of land.[22] What is unreasonable is when it occurs frequently and for long periods of time. Therefore, my neighbour undertaking DIY on Sunday morning must be endured, but my neighbour drilling for 24 hours, or every day between 12 p.m. and 2 a.m., is unreasonable.   **10–008**

Again, the courts will use a largely common-sense approach to this factor. In *De Keyser's Royal Hotel Ltd v Spicer Bros Ltd*,[23] the court was willing to grant an injunction for a temporary interference when it consisted of pile-driving in the middle of the night, but confined the injunction to forbidding work between 10 p.m. and 6.30 a.m. An action for physical damage to property, even if temporary, is likely to succeed, but in such a case the court will only award damages rather than an injunction. In *Crown River Cruises Ltd v Kimbolton Fireworks Ltd*,[24] the plaintiffs' vessels had suffered substantial fire damage caused by falling debris from a fireworks display to celebrate the fiftieth anniversary of the Battle of Britain. The display had only lasted about 20 minutes, but it was found to be inevitable that debris, some of it hot and burning, would fall on nearby property of a potentially flammable nature. The plaintiffs were therefore awarded damages.

Much ink has been spilt analysing whether an isolated escape can amount to an actionable nuisance. It is true that it is easier to obtain an injunction where the interference is continuous or recurrent, but this does not necessarily exclude an

---

[19] (1879) 11 Ch. D. 852 at 865. See also Veale J. in *Halsey v Esso Petroleum* [1961] 1 W.L.R. 683 and *Miller v Jackson* [1977] Q.B. 966 at 986.
[20] [1993] Q.B. 343.
[21] *Wheeler v J.J. Saunders Ltd* [1996] Ch. 19.
[22] See *Andreae v Selfridge* [1938] Ch. 1 at 5–6 per Lord Greene M.R. The Court of Appeal in *Clift v Welsh Office* [1999] 1 W.L.R. 796 held that there is no reason, however, why the law should expect the neighbour to put up with actual physical damage to his property, as opposed to discomfort and inconvenience, because it is temporary in nature (claim under s.10, Compulsory Purchase Act 1965).
[23] (1914) 30 T.L.R. 257.
[24] [1996] 2 Lloyd's Rep. 533.

isolated escape of sufficient gravity. The court in *S.C.M. (United Kingdom) Ltd v W.J. Whittal & Son Ltd*[25] accepted that such liability could arise where the plaintiff was affected by the *state* of the defendant's land or activities upon it, but excluded liability for a single negligent act, which it held would only found an action in negligence. Isolated escapes may, of course, be actionable in any event under the rule in *Rylands v Fletcher*, which will be considered later in this chapter.

(3) Utility of the defendant's conduct

10–009 This is not generally an important consideration. Private nuisance is concerned with the results of the defendant's conduct on the claimant and not on the community as a whole. It has been argued, however, that it should influence the court in exercising its equitable jurisdiction whether to grant an injunction, and will therefore be considered further in the section on remedies.

(4) Abnormal sensitivity

10–010 The result of the defendant's conduct must be such as to unreasonably affect the ordinary citizen. Discomfort resulting from personal sensitivity to noise or heat which would not affect the ordinary citizen will not found an action in nuisance. The leading case is *Robinson v Kilvert*,[26] where the defendant operated a business in the lower part of a building, which required hot and dry air. As a result, the temperature of the floor of the plaintiff's premises above rose to 80 F, which diminished the value of the brown paper stored there. The heat was not such as to affect ordinary paper or to cause discomfort to the plaintiff's workforce. The Court of Appeal refused the plaintiff damages. He had undertaken an exceptionally delicate trade and had not shown an actionable nuisance. This must be correct. It cannot be just to impose a burden on the defendant to compensate all claimants for interference, no matter how sensitive they are. This would unduly interfere with the defendant's own freedom to enjoy his or her property. It should be noted, however, that once an actionable nuisance is shown, the claimant may recover the full extent of his or her losses, even where they result from interference with an exceptionally delicate use of the land.[27]

10–011 Yet it may be difficult to determine what we would now regard as "unduly sensitive". It is clear that a person who cannot stand any noise or odours is more sensitive than normal. Does this extend, however, to the avid television viewer, which encompasses about 97 per cent of the population? Unfortunately, there are dicta suggesting exactly that. The root of the problem lies with the decision of Buckley J. in *Bridlington Relay v Yorkshire Electricity Board*.[28] The court in that case was unimpressed with the claim of a company, which relayed sound and television broadcasts, that its business would be interfered with by the erection of two pylons within 250 feet of its mast. Buckley J. refused an injunction because the defendants had given an assurance that the interference could be remedied, but his Lordship went further and doubted whether interference with a primarily recreational activity could ever found an actionable nuisance. This decision has been dismissed as out-of-date,[29] and Buckley J.

[25] [1970] 1 W.L.R. 1017 at 1031—point not considered on appeal [1971] 1 Q.B. 337. See also *British Celanese v Hunt* [1969] 1 W.L.R. 959 at 969 (liability for the way in which metal foil was stored on land).
[26] (1889) 41 Ch. D. 88. See also *Heath v Mayor of Brighton* (1908) 98 L.T. 718.
[27] *McKinnon Industries Ltd v Walker* [1951] 3 D.L.R. 577 at 581, PC
[28] [1965] Ch. 436.
[29] See *Nor-Video Services v Ontario Hydro* (1978) 84 D.L.R. (3d) 221.

expressly stated that he was not laying down an absolute rule. As our use of land changes with the advent of modern technology, it would be strange if an activity enjoyed by the majority of the population would not be regarded as an ordinary and natural use of one's premises. Nevertheless, the House of Lords in *Hunter v Canary Wharf Ltd*[30] gave no clear indication as to whether the case would be decided differently today, and Lords Goff, Hoffmann and Cooke expressly left the question open for future decision.

In the more recent decision of *Network Rail Infrastructure Ltd v Morris (t/a Soundstar Studio)*,[31] however, the Court of Appeal adopted a more considered approach. Here the claimant was complaining about electromagnetic interference from a section of Railtrack's signalling system to the music created by electric guitars in Mr Morris's recording studio. The Court recognised that, although this might have been dismissed as "extra-sensitive" in the past, the use of electric and electronic equipment was now a feature of modern life. It thus focussed on what was reasonable in the circumstances of the case. Buxton L.J. also went further to question the continued utility of *Robinson v Kilvert* when loss, in any event, must be reasonably foreseeable to be actionable in nuisance (see Remoteness below). It is to be hoped that the courts will in future take a more generous view of what can be regarded as actionable in nuisance.

(5) Malice

In assessing whether the defendant's use of his or her land is reasonable, regard will be **10–012** had to his or her frame of mind. This can be criticised for judging the defendant's conduct, which is not the role of nuisance, but there seems good authority for the fact that malice will encourage the courts to find an unreasonable user. The case of *Christie v Davey*[32] is the leading authority. The plaintiff was a music teacher who gave lessons at her home. The defendant, her neighbour, found the noise irritating and chose to express his displeasure by knocking on the party wall, beating trays, whistling and shrieking. The plaintiff succeeded in her claim for an injunction. North J. held that ". . . what was done by the defendant was done only for the purpose of annoyance and in my opinion, it was not a legitimate use of the defendant's house".[33] *Christie* was followed in *Hollywood Silver Fox Farm Ltd v Emmett*,[34] where Macnaghten J. granted an injunction against a defendant who had deliberately fired guns on his own land near its boundary with the plaintiffs' land. The plaintiffs carried on the business of breeding silver foxes on their land, and evidence was given that the discharge of guns during breeding time would frighten the vixens leading them to refuse to breed, miscarry, or kill their young. Although the use of land for breeding foxes was obviously sensitive, the presence of malice was sufficient to overcome this objection.

Such authority should be contrasted with that of the House of Lords in *Bradford Corp. v Pickles*.[35] The defendant had deliberately drained his land, with the intention of diminishing the water supply leading into the plaintiffs' land, and thereby forcing them to purchase his land. The House of Lords did not, however, grant an injunction, and

---

[30] [1997] A.C. 677.
[31] [2004] EWCA Civ 172.
[32] [1893] 1 Ch. 316.
[33] *ibid.*, at 327.
[34] [1936] 2 K.B. 468.
[35] [1895] A.C. 587.

refused to take note of the alleged malice of the defendant. This decision can nevertheless be distinguished from *Christie* in a number of ways. First, the plaintiffs in *Bradford* had no right to receive the water, and therefore no right had been interfered with on which to found the nuisance. Secondly, at least from the laissez-faire perspective of the nineteenth century, the defendant had done no more than exercise his right to appropriate or divert underground water to obtain a better deal from the plaintiffs. Could this really be regarded as malicious?

Malice will therefore be considered relevant by the courts in applying the test of "reasonable user". Caution should be adopted, however, towards comments in the leading case of *Hunter v Canary Wharf Ltd* (see below)[36] by Lord Cooke, who suggested that malicious erection of a structure for the purpose of interfering with television reception should be actionable in nuisance. These comments were based on Lord Cooke's minority belief that the interference caused by building the Canary Wharf tower was actionable, but could be justified on the ordinary principles of give and take. On this basis, malice (as in *Christie*) would be capable of converting a reasonable user into an unreasonable user. This was not, however, the majority view. On the majority view, as seen above, the claimant has no right to complain in such circumstances. The appropriate analogy would therefore be that of *Bradford Corp. v Pickles*: the defendant had a right to build the tower; the claimant had no right which had been interfered with, and so malice would be irrelevant.

Who can sue?

10–013　　The aim of private nuisance is to protect the claimant's use and enjoyment of land. It is therefore logical that the claimant must have some land which has been unreasonably interfered with. The more difficult question is: what link must the claimant have with the land? Does the law of tort demand an interest in land, as defined by property law, or simply some substantial link with the land? The traditional view was that an interest in land had to be shown. In *Malone v Laskey*,[37] the Court of Appeal refused the plaintiff's action for damages for personal injury when vibrations emitted from the defendant's premises caused an iron bracket supporting a cistern to fall upon her. She was a mere licensee without any interest in land, and so had no cause of action.

This position was challenged, however, by Dillon L.J. in *Khorasandjian v Bush*.[38] In this case, Miss Khorasandjian had been subjected to a campaign of harassment by a former boyfriend, for which he had spent some time in prison. She sought an injunction to prevent him "harassing, pestering or communicating" with her, particularly by means of persistent and unwanted telephone calls to her mother's home where she lived. Miss Khorasandjian, in common with Mrs Malone, had no proprietary interest in the home, but Dillon L.J. held that "the court has at times to reconsider earlier decisions in the light of changed social conditions" and therefore supported her claim in private nuisance.

Khorasandjian was in turn rejected by the majority of the House of Lords in the leading case of *Hunter v Canary Wharf Ltd*.[39] In this case, a number of local residents,

---

[36] [1997] A.C. 677.
[37] [1907] 2 K.B. 141. See also *Read v Lyons* [1947] A.C. 156 at 183.
[38] [1993] Q.B. 727 at 735, relying on the Canadian case of *Motherwell v Motherwell* (1976) 73 D.L.R. (3d) 62.
[39] [1997] A.C. 677.

who included homeowners, their families and other licensees, had complained about the Canary Wharf tower, which forms part of the Docklands development in London. The tower is nearly 250 metres in height and over 50 metres square, with a metallic surface, and, when erected, was found to interfere with the television reception of neighbouring homes. Two preliminary questions arose:

(1) Did an actionable nuisance exist?

The House of Lords held that the interference with television reception by the erection **10–014** of a building did not amount to an actionable nuisance. It was held, by analogy to cases which refused liability for blocking a view,[40] that the defendants were free to build what they wanted on their land, subject to planning controls and proprietary restrictions, such as easements, over the land. Complaints could thus only be made at the planning stage and not by means of the tort of private nuisance.[41]

(2) If an actionable nuisance existed, who could sue?

Their Lordships reasserted the traditional view stated in *Malone v Laskey*[42] and held **10–015** that only claimants with an interest in land or exclusive possession could bring an action for nuisance. In the words of Lord Goff: ". . . on the authorities as they stand, an action in private nuisance will only lie at the suit of a person who has a right to the land".[43] This represented a return to the historical roots of private nuisance as a tort to land. In so doing, the majority of the House of Lords (Lord Cooke dissenting) rejected the opportunity given in *Khorasandjian* to develop the tort to protect the personal interests of anyone occupying the land.

Rights in the Land

These were defined by the House of Lords in *Hunter* as consisting of interests in land **10–016** or exclusive possession. On this basis, if you are a landowner, tenant, grantee of an easement or *profit à prendre*, or simply have a right to exclusive possession of the land, you may sue, but any lesser right will not suffice. This division was justified by Lord Hoffmann in *Hunter*: "Exclusive possession distinguishes an occupier who may in due course acquire title under the Limitation Act 1980 from a mere trespasser. It distinguishes a tenant holding a leasehold estate from a mere licensee. Exclusive possession *de jure or de facto*, now or in the future, is the bedrock of English land law".[44]

The importance of exclusive possession may be seen in the Court of Appeal decision in *Pemberton v Southwark LBC*[45] In this case, a "tolerated trespasser", that is a former secure tenant, against whom an order for possession had been obtained but suspended whilst she continued to occupy the property and pay rent,[46] was allowed to sue for

---

[40] See *Dalton v Angus* (1881) 6 App Cas 740.
[41] However, in *Hunter*, due to the fact that the Secretary of State for the Environment had designated the area an enterprise zone, planning permission was deemed to have been granted for any form of development and no application for permission had to be made.
[42] [1907] 2 K.B. 141.
[43] *ibid.*, at 692, relying heavily on the classic article of Professor Newark 'The Boundaries of Nuisance' (1949) 65 L.Q.R. 480.
[44] *ibid.*, at 703.
[45] [2000] 1 W.L.R. 1672 (leave to appeal denied by the House of Lords: [2001] 1 W.L.R. 538).
[46] The term comes from *Burrows v Brent LBC* [1996] 1 W.L.R. 1448.

nuisance when her flat became infested with cockroaches. As stated by Roch L.J., "Possession or occupation by the tolerated trespasser may be precarious, but it is not wrongful and it is exclusive. . . . In those circumstances, in my judgment, the tolerated trespasser does have a sufficient interest in the premises to sustain an action in nuisance."[47]

You will not be able to claim, however, if you are simply a member of the landowner's family, a guest, lodger or employee. This does not, of course, stop you seeking alternative remedies in negligence, occupiers' liability, or resorting to the Protection from Harassment Act 1997 (which will be discussed further in Ch. 11) providing you can satisfy the necessary requirements to establish liability.

Losses incurred prior to acquisition of a right to land

10–017   It should be noted that, provided the nuisance is continuing, there is authority that the claimant may sue for his or her losses even if they began prior to acquisition of the premises. In *Masters v Brent LBC*,[48] Talbot J. held that the plaintiff was able to recover the losses incurred by him in remedying damage caused by encroaching tree roots, which caused subsidence to the house he had recently acquired. He could show a continuing actionable nuisance and so could recover the total cost of the works necessary to remedy the damage caused by the tree roots to the property. In *Delaware Mansions Ltd v Westminster City Council*,[49] the House of Lords approved this approach. Here, the roots of a tree on council land had caused damage to an adjoining building. Although most of the damage had occurred prior to the claimant's purchase of the property, their Lordships found that where there was a continuing nuisance of which the defendant knew or should have known, the purchaser would be able to recover reasonable remedial expenditure. The claimant was thus able to recover the cost of underpinning works which amounted to over £570,000. It should be noted that in both *Masters* and *Delaware*, there was no possibility of double recovery. Where, for example, the previous owner has incurred some remedial expenditure, a court would apportion the damages awarded between the two parties.

Landlords

10–018   A landlord whose property is leased retains only a "reversionary interest" in the premises, namely his or her right to possession at the end of the term of the lease. The landlord can only sue where the nuisance has harmed this interest in a permanent way, *i.e.* the value of the property will be diminished when the landlord comes back into possession.[50] Examples include vibrations which affect the structure of the property, and nuisances where there is a risk of the perpetrator gaining a legal right to commit the nuisance by prescription (see below). In contrast, the landlord cannot sue if the interference is of a temporary nature, such as noise or smoke which is unlikely to have any permanent effect on the land. In these circumstances, the action can only be brought by the tenant. The landlord can do nothing if the tenant decides instead to leave, or demands a decrease in rent.

[47] See above at 1682.
[48] [1978] Q.B. 841, although the close connection between the former owner (the plaintiff's father) and the plaintiff had placed doubt on the scope of this decision.
[49] [2002] 1 A.C. 321. Comment B Parker (2002) 61 C.L.J. 260.
[50] See *Jones v Llanrwst UDC* [1911] 1 Ch. 393 at 404.

The Human Rights Act 1998

It has been questioned whether the test in *Hunter v Canary Wharf* confining the right to **10–019** sue to those with rights to land is compatible with the Human Rights Act 1998. For example, Professor Wright in her book, *Tort Law and Human Rights*, suggests that "it is time for English law to move beyond the straitjacket of the forms of action, so that the boundaries of private nuisance are determined by the link with one's home."[51] The difficulty would seem to lie with Art. 8(1) of the European Convention on Human Rights. This states that "Everyone has the right to respect for his private and family life, his home and his correspondence."[52] This has been interpreted by the European Court of Human Rights in a broad sense, thereby permitting parties without rights in the home to sue.[53] For example, in *Khatun v United Kingdom*[54]—an appeal from part of the *Hunter* litigation in which the applicants had complained of dust arising from construction of the Limehouse Link Road—the European Commission of Human Rights found that:

"in domestic proceedings, a distinction was made between those applicants with a proprietary interest in the land and those without such an interest. For the purposes of Article 8 (Art 8) of the Convention, there is no such distinction. 'Home' is an autonomous concept which does not depend on classification under domestic law. Whether or not a particular habitation constitutes a "home" . . . will depend on the factual circumstances, namely, the existence of sufficient and continuous links."[55]

This suggests that in a suitable case, a court would be able to challenge the limitation in *Hunter* in favour of a test based on a sufficient link with the land. In *McKenna v British Aluminium Ltd*,[56] for example, Neuberger J. in a striking out decision was prepared to contemplate such a move. Here, over 30 children from a number of households had brought actions for private nuisance and under the rule in *Rylands v Fletcher*, alleging that emissions and noise from the defendants' neighbouring factory had caused them mental distress, physical harm and an invasion of privacy. The judge rejected the defendants' argument that their claims should be struck out unless they could point to a proprietary right.

"There is obviously a powerful case for saying that effect has not been properly given to Article 8.1 if a person with no interest in the home, but *who has lived in the house for some time* and had his enjoyment of the home interfered with, is at the mercy of the person who owns the home, as the only person who can bring proceedings."[57]

---

[51] (Hart, 2001), p.194.
[52] See Sch.1, Pt 1 of the Human Rights Act 1998.
[53] See, for example, D Feldman, *Civil Liberties and Human Rights* (2nd ed., OUP, 2002).
[54] (1998) 26 E.H.R.R. C.D. 212. The applicants complained that the work disrupted their rights under Art. 8 (home and family life) and Art. 14 (discrimination on the grounds of poverty in that due to the low value of their homes, any diminution of the market value was minimal).
[55] *ibid.*, at 215
[56] [2002] Env LR 30, Birmingham District Registry.
[57] Emphasis added. Neuberger J. leaves open the question whether the common law should be extended by reference to the law of nuisance, the rule in *Rylands v Fletcher*, negligence or a common law tort analogous to nuisance.

It remains to be seen whether the courts are prepared to change the rule in *Hunter* and ignore the evident intention of the House of Lords to provide a straightforward rule which sets out the boundaries of the tort and facilitates negotiated settlements of claims. It should also be noted that Article 8 is a qualified right and interference may, under Art. 8(2), be justified on the basis that it is "necessary in a democratic society in the interests of national security, public safety or the economic well-being of the country, for the prevention of disorder or crime, for the protection of health or morals, or for the protection of the rights and freedoms of others." On the facts of *Khatun*, the Commission ruled that the defendants' activities could be justified as pursuing a legitimate and important aim, given the importance of the public interest in developing the Docklands area of London and the limited interference to the applicants' homes.[58] The proposed change would alter the fundamental character of the tort, and it remains to be seen whether implementation of the Human Rights Act 1998 would have so drastic an effect.

Who can be sued?

10–020 The most obvious defendant is the person who *created* the nuisance. This is not contentious, but it is important to recognise that the liability of the creator of the nuisance is not dependent on occupation of the land. Even if the defendant no longer occupies the land, and cannot therefore abate (or "stop") any nuisance, he or she may still be liable.[59] However, if the creator cannot be traced or it is not financially viable to sue the creator, a number of other defendants exist:

- The occupier of the land;
- The landlord.

We deal with each of these potential defendants in turn.

(1) The occupier of the land

10–021 The occupier may find himself or herself liable for nuisances occurring during the period of occupancy even where he or she is not the creator. This will occur in four particular instances.

10–022 **(i) The occupier exercises control over the creator:** The occupier will be liable for a nuisance created by its employees in the course of their employment (under the principles discussed in Ch. 7), which will extend to independent contractors where the duty not to create a nuisance is non-delegable. Liability for independent contractors has caused some problems, and the concept of a non-delegable duty has been interpreted broadly. In *Matania v National Provincial Bank*,[60] the occupier of two floors of a building brought an action for nuisance against the occupier of the first floor in respect of the dust and noise caused by the work of his independent contractors. The

---

[58] The Commission additionally rejected the claim under Art. 14, on the basis that there were no other persons in "relevantly" similar situations to the applicants.
[59] See *Thompson v Gibson* (1841) 7 M. & W. 456.
[60] [1936] 2 All E.R. 633. See also *Bower v Peate* (1876) 1 Q.B.D. 321 and *Spicer v Smee* [1946] 1 All E.R. 489.

Court of Appeal held that the employer in such circumstances is liable for the damage occasioned by its independent contractors when their operations, by their very nature, involve a risk of damage to the claimant.

(ii) The occupier has adopted or continued a nuisance created by a trespasser: **10–023**
Here, the defendant is rendered liable for his or her omissions in failing to deal with a nuisance created by a trespasser. Liability is, however, far from strict. The defendant is only liable if he or she (i) *adopts* the nuisance, *i.e.* uses the state of affairs for his or her purposes or (ii) *continues* the nuisance, *i.e.* with actual or presumed knowledge of the nuisance, fails to take reasonably prompt and efficient steps to abate it. The same rule applies to private and public nuisance.[61] The leading case is the House of Lords decision of *Sedleigh-Denfield v O'Callaghan*.[62] A local authority, without the defendant's permission (and therefore as a trespasser), had placed a drainage pipe in a ditch on the defendant's land, with a grating designed to keep out leaves. The grating had not been fixed in the correct position, with the result that during a heavy rainstorm the pipe became choked with leaves and water overflowed onto the plaintiff's land. The House of Lords held the defendant liable. He had adopted the nuisance by using the drain for his own purposes to drain water from his land. He had also continued the nuisance because his manager should have realised the risk of flooding created by the obstruction and taken reasonable steps to abate it.

The rule can be justified as one of good sense and convenience. The occupier is best placed to deal with the nuisance, and the House of Lords rejected the idea that it was enough to give the claimant the right to enter on to the land to abate the nuisance. The Court of Appeal has more recently decided that there is no relevant distinction between a nuisance caused by the *state* of the property and one caused by the *activities* of trespassers upon it. Therefore, in *Page Motors Ltd v Epsom and Ewell BC*,[63] the local authority was found liable for failing to take reasonable steps to evict travellers whose activities had been harming the plaintiffs' businesses.

(iii) The occupier has adopted or continued a nuisance created by an act of nature: **10–024**
Until *Goldman v Hargrave*,[64] the courts had drawn a distinction between nuisances created by third parties and those resulting from acts of nature. Occupiers were under no duty to abate the latter, although they would have to allow their neighbours reasonable access to abate the nuisance. The Privy Council in *Goldman* refused to maintain this distinction, and held that the House of Lords decision in *Sedleigh-Denfield* should be applied equally to situations where the nuisance had been created by an act of nature. In *Goldman*, a 100 feet high redgum tree, growing in the centre of the defendant's land, was struck by lightning and caught fire. The defendant quite

---

[61] See *Attorney General v Tod Heatley* [1897] 1 Ch. 560, *R. v Shorrock* [1994] Q.B. 279 (liability for rave held on defendant's field) and *Wandsworth LBC v Railtrack plc* [2002] Q.B. 756 (Railtrack liable for failing to abate public nuisance caused by pigeons roosting under its railway bridge). It is not clear, however, whether the measured duty of care (see below) applies to public nuisance. *Wandsworth* states the law in objective terms and states that nothing in the later authorities should throw doubt on the law as stated in *Tod Heatley* in 1897. However, it also found that Railtrack had the means to abate the nuisance and, in view of its small cost of £9,000, liability would have been found in any event.
[62] [1940] A.C. 880.
[63] (1982) 80 L.G.R. 337.
[64] [1967] 1 A.C. 645.

properly cut down the tree, but left it to burn itself out when he could have simply eliminated any risk of fire by dousing the smouldering sections of the tree with water. The wind later picked up and rekindled the fire, which spread, causing damage to the plaintiff's land. In a significant judgment, Lord Wilberforce held that the defendant was liable for not acting against the foreseeable risk of fire.

The Court of Appeal approved Lord Wilberforce's judgment in *Leakey v National Trust*.[65] In this case, it was found that there was no valid distinction between an act of nature affecting something on the land and one deriving from the state of the land itself. In 1976, an exceptionally dry summer, followed by a very wet autumn, had led to subsidence of a hill above the plaintiffs' properties, causing damage to the properties. There was evidence that the defendants had been aware of this potential problem, indeed they had been warned by the plaintiffs, but had refused to act. The Court of Appeal held that they were liable. Megaw L.J. found that it would be a "grievous blot on the law"[66] if the law did not impose liability on the defendants in such circumstances. A duty is therefore placed on the occupier to take reasonable care to check his or her land for potential nuisances, as in *Sedleigh-Denfield*.

10–025 **The measured duty of care:** In finding liability in *Goldman*, Lord Wilberforce, however, limited this duty by making it clear that the defendant's conduct should be judged in the light of his or her resources and ability to act in the circumstances:

> "The law must take account of the fact that the occupier on whom the duty is cast has, ex hypothesi, had this hazard thrust upon him through no seeking or fault of his own. His interest, and his resources, whether physical or material, may be of a very modest character either in relation to the magnitude of the hazard, or as compared with those of his threatened neighbour. A rule which required of him in such unsought circumstances in his neighbour's interest a physical effort of which he is not capable, or an excessive expenditure of money, would be unenforceable or unjust . . . In such situations the standard ought to be to require of the occupier what it is reasonable to expect of him in his individual circumstances."[67]

Where, therefore, the defendant is poor, and abatement will require vast expense, the defendant will not be considered liable.[68] Equally, less will be expected of the infirm than of the able-bodied. This subjective approach would seem to extend to situations where the occupier is liable for the act of a trespasser or for a failure to support his or her neighbour's land. In *Page Motors Ltd v Epsom and Ewell BC*,[69] for example, the Court of Appeal applied and extended the test to include consideration of the particular character of the defendant. In that case, the defendant was a local authority.

---

[65] [1980] 1 All E.R. 17.

[66] *ibid*., at.35. See also *Bybrook Barn Garden Centre Ltd v Kent County Council* [2001] Env L.R. 30, CA. The House of Lords in *Marcic v Thames Water Utilities Ltd* [2003] 3 W.L.R. 1603, however, distinguished an ordinary occupier of land from statutory occupiers where the law of nuisance must be careful not to impose obligations inconsistent with the statutory scheme under which they operate.

[67] [1967] 1 A.C. 645 at 663.

[68] Although contrast *Abbahall Ltd v Smee* [2003] 1 W.L.R. 1472, CA (no allowance made for elderly flat-owner reliant on state benefits), although this may be distinguished on its facts—cost of repairs to communal roof to be shared equally amongst flat-owners.

[69] (1982) 80 L.G.R. 337.

The court, in deciding whether it had failed to take reasonable steps, therefore considered the responsibilities of the local authority to the public at large, for example, for the problems likely to be produced by moving the travellers to another site in the borough. Whilst this would justify it acting more slowly than a private individual, permitting the nuisance to continue for five years was clearly excessive. Equally, in *Holbeck Hall Hotel Ltd v Scarborough BC (No. 2)*,[70] the Court of Appeal applied the test to a local authority sued for loss of support. Here, a massive landslip in 1993 had led to the collapse of part of the four star Holbeck Hall Hotel, which was situated at the top of a cliff overlooking the North Sea. As a result, the hotel had to be demolished. The hoteliers sued the local council, who owned the land forming the undercliff between the hotel and the sea, for loss of support, claiming that they should have taken measures to prevent the damage caused. The council had been aware of the danger of landslips due to marine erosion, and had undertaken works in the past, but had not foreseen a landslip of this magnitude. The Court of Appeal rejected the claim. The Wilberforce test would apply to claims for loss of support,[71] but the council could not be found liable for failing to undertake measures which only a geological expert could have identified as necessary. The defendant would thus not be liable where he or she was unable to foresee the *extent* of the loss suffered. In any event, even if the loss had been foreseeable, in view of the extensive and expensive nature of the works necessary, "the scope of the duty may be limited to warning neighbours of such risk as they were aware of or ought to have foreseen and sharing such information as they had acquired relating to it."[72]

This subjective test may be contrasted with the objective standard of care adopted in negligence (discussed in Ch. 5). We may also note the more restrictive test of remoteness employed in *Holbeck Hall* in comparison to the more generous *Wagon Mound* test discussed in Ch. 6. The test is confined, however, to circumstances in which the defendant has not created the nuisance.

One final point of comparison may be drawn between *Sedleigh-Denfield* liability, and the duty of care imposed on landowners in negligence for omissions discussed in Ch. 2. It will be recalled that in *Smith v Littlewoods*,[73] the occupier was held not to be liable to adjoining occupiers for the acts of vandals who had set fire to a derelict cinema on its land. The court held that the occupier would not be responsible where it was no more than a merely foreseeable possibility that trespassers would gain access to land and cause damage to the property of neighbouring owners.[74]

(iv) The creator is the occupier's predecessor in title: Liability in this context is limited. It can only arise where the nuisance was created by a predecessor in title to the occupier and the occupier knew or ought reasonably to know of the existence of

---

[70] [2000] Q.B. 836. Comment M.P. Thompson [2001] Conv 177 and C.A. Hopkins (2000) 59 C.L.J. 438.
[71] Thereby overturning previous authority which indicated that there was no positive duty in such circumstances to provide support: *Sack v Jones* [1925] Ch. 235; *Macpherson v London Passenger Transport Board* (1946) 175 L.T. 279. *Holbeck Hall* was applied in *Rees v Skerrett* [2001] 1 W.L.R. 1541, CA where the owner of a terraced house had, when demolishing the house, failed to take reasonable steps to protect the party wall where it was reasonably foreseeable that, if not properly weatherproofed, the wall would suffer damage.
[72] See Stuart-Smith L.J. [2000] Q.B. 836 at 863.
[73] [1987] A.C. 241. See B.S. Markesinis (1989) 105 L.Q.R. 104.
[74] See Lord Griffiths [1987] A.C. 241 at 251.

the nuisance.[75] In this sense, it strongly resembles the *Sedleigh-Denfield* principle. Although there is no authority that the subjective standard of care applies, it would be illogical not to apply it in such a case.

(2) The Landlord

10–026   On the grant of a lease, the tenant will be in possession and will be liable for any nuisance he or she creates. However, there may be circumstances where an alternative action lies against the landlord. There are three main situations where this may occur.

10–027   **(i) Where the landlord expressly or impliedly authorises the nuisance**[76]:   To establish whether the landlord has authorised the tenant to commit the nuisance, the courts will examine the purpose for which the premises are let. The landlord will be liable if the necessary consequence of the letting is that an actionable nuisance will be produced. *Tetley v Chitty*[77] is a good example of such liability. The local authority had let a parcel of its land in a residential area to a go-kart club, in the full knowledge that the club intended to use and develop the land for go-karting. The local residents complained, however, at the noise which came from the track. The court found the local authority liable for the nuisance. The noise was the natural and necessary consequence of that activity, and by granting a lease for this purpose, the authority had given express or at least implied consent to the nuisance.

Such liability did not lie, however, in *Smith v Scott*.[78] Here, a dwelling house had been let to a family known by the landlord to be likely to cause a nuisance. The tenants proceeded to cause damage to the neighbouring property of an elderly couple, and caused such a nuisance that the couple were obliged to leave their home and seek other accommodation. The landlord had inserted in the tenancy agreement a clause expressly prohibiting the committing of a nuisance. The insertion of this covenant countered any arguments of implied authorisation, so that it could not be said that the nuisance was a necessary consequence of the letting.

This decision was recently approved by the Court of Appeal in *Hussain v Lancaster CC*.[79] Here, the claimants were shopkeepers in a council housing estate, who had been subjected to racial harassment and vandalism by other council tenants. Some individuals were prosecuted, but a total of 106 people had been involved in these actions. The council was held not to be liable for the racial harassment of a shopkeeper by its tenants on a housing estate. The council's standard form tenancy agreement included a clause instructing the tenant "not to discriminate against or harass any residents or visitors". In the circumstances, the council could not be said to have specifically authorised these acts. Equally, in *Mowan v Wandsworth L.B.C.*,[80] the Court of Appeal struck out a claim against the council on the basis that it could not be said to have authorised the conduct of a tenant suffering from a mental disorder, who lived above the home of the claimant. Reasonable foresight of the nuisance is not sufficient to impose liability on the landlord. As stated by the House of Lords in *Southwark LBC v*

[75] *St Anne's Well Brewery Co v Roberts* (1929) 140 L.T. 1; *Wilkins v Leighton* [1932] 2 Ch. 106.
[76] See *Harris v James* (1876) 45 L.J.Q.B. 545.
[77] [1986] 1 All E.R. 663.
[78] [1973] Ch. 314.
[79] [2000] Q.B. 1.
[80] (2001) 33 H.L.R. 56.

Tanner, "It is not enough for [landlords] to be aware of the nuisance and take no steps to prevent it. They must either participate directly in the commission of the nuisance or they must be taken to have authorised it by letting the property."[81]

This would seem to let the landlord off fairly easily.[82] In *Smith v Scott*, for example, **10–028** it was obvious that the tenants would not respect this clause, but foresight was not enough to establish liability. In reality, the courts are being asked to deal with difficult social problems through the imperfect medium of the tort of private nuisance. In *Hussain*, the Court of Appeal clearly regarded this as a matter for police and other agencies rather than the civil courts.Issues such as anti-social behaviour, racial harassment and care in the community cannot realistically be dealt with by the courts alone, and the test of express or implied authorisation thus masks a refusal by the courts to intervene. This provides little consolation, however, to those suffering as a result of these problems.[83]

The courts are, however, willing to make such judgments where the defendant is not the landlord, but a licensor of the premises.For example, in *Lippiatt v South Gloucestershire CC*,[84] the Court of Appeal was prepared to find a licensor liable for the acts of licensees on its property. In this case, travellers on the council's land had undertaken a number of acts which harmed the land of neighbouring farmers. Such activities included frequent acts of trespass, stealing timber, gates and fences, dumping rubbish and damaging crops. *Hussain* was distinguished on the basis that the licensor, unlike the landlord, retains control over the premises, and that licensees may be moved on more easily than tenants. The local authority was thus found liable for failing to exercise its powers to evict travellers from its land at an earlier stage. One may question this distinction. The treatment of travellers raises social issues not so different from those outlined in relation to landlords, rendering such a distinction artificial in practice.[85] Equally, the justification that the claimant may also sue the tenant directly, whilst he or she may have difficulties pursuing a licensee, ignores the problems in identifying the tenant in question (consider *Hussain*) or potential difficulties in obtaining a remedy against a particular tenant (for example, in *Mowan*, the court was not convinced that an injunction would be awarded against a person suffering from a mental disorder).[86] It must be questioned whether this distinction can be justified in practice.

It has been suggested that the claimants in the above cases may now be able to invoke Article 8 of the European Convention on Human Rights, namely the right to respect for their private and family life and their home.[87] However, it remains questionable how useful it will be in this context. Although Art. 8 imposes a positive duty on local authorities to ensure that this right is respected, it is a qualified right, and subject to the discretion of the court, which will consider any other remedies available.[88] In *Mowan*, Peter Gibson L.J. rejected the argument on the basis of Article

[81] [2001] 1 A.C. 1 at 22 *per* Lord Millett, relying on *Malzy v Eichholz* (1916) 2 K.B. 308.
[82] See M. Davey [2001] Conv 31 and J. Morgan (2001) 60 C.L.J. 382.
[83] See S. Bright and C. Bakalis (2003) 62 C.L.J. 305.
[84] [2000] Q.B. 51.
[85] The distinction is equally blurred by cases such as *Chartered Trust plc v Davies* (1998) 76 P. & C.R. 396, where a landlord was found liable for continuing the nuisance where it had retained control over the common parts in which the nuisance created by its tenant had taken place.
[86] See *Wookey v Wookey* [1991] Fam 121.
[87] D. Rook [2002] Conv 316.
[88] See s.8 of the Human Rights Act 1998.

8 where the complainant had an alternative action for judicial review of the local authority's decision not to take the neighbour into care or against the tenant herself, despite some misgivings as to the likely success of any such action. Equally, it has been conceded that provided the local authority adopts a decision-making process which satisfies proportionality and does not impose a disproportionate burden on the persons concerned, it may escape liability.[89]

10–029   **(ii) The landlord knew or ought to have known of the nuisance before letting:**   There is authority that where the nuisance consists of lack of repair, the landlord cannot avoid liability by simply inserting into the lease a covenant that the tenant must undertake the repairs. As Sachs L.J. commented in *Brew Bros Ltd v Snax (Ross) Ltd*[90]:

> "As regards nuisance of which [the landlord] knew at the date of the lease, the duty similarly arises by reason of his control before that date. Once the liability attaches I can find no rational reason why it should as regards third parties be shuffled off merely by signing a document which as between owner and tenant casts on the latter the burden of executing remedial work. The duty of the owner is to ensure that the nuisance causes no injury, not merely to get someone else's promise to take the requisite steps to abate it."

10–030   **(iii) The landlord covenanted to repair, or has a right to enter to repair:**   This may be express or implied.[91] Liability is based on the fact that the landlord has retained a degree of control over the condition of the premises. One particular example of implied retention of control is through ss.11 and 12 of the Landlord and Tenant Act 1985. If a dwelling house is let for a term of less than seven years, there is an implied and non-excludable covenant to keep in repair the structure and exterior of the house and certain installations for the supply of water, gas, sanitation and electricity. This is supplemented by negligence liability under s.4 of the Defective Premises Act 1972. Section 4(1) provides that:

> "Where premises are let under a tenancy which puts on the landlord an obligation to the tenant for the maintenance or repair of the premises, the landlord owes to all persons who might reasonably be expected to be affected by defects in the state of the premises a duty to take such care as is reasonable in all the circumstances to see that they are reasonably safe from personal injury or from damage to their property caused by the relevant defect."[92]

This duty is owed only if the landlord knows of the defect (whether as the result of being notified by the tenant or otherwise) or ought in all the circumstances to have known of the relevant defect.[93]

---

[89] See D. Rook [2002] Conv 316 at 340.
[90] [1970] 1 Q.B. 612 at 638–9.
[91] See *Mint v Good* [1951] 1 K.B. 517.
[92] "Relevant defect" is defined in s.4(3).
[93] S.4(2). See also s.4(4), which extends the duty to situations where the landlord has reserved the right to enter the premises to carry out any description of maintenance or repair of the premises.

Must the nuisance emanate from the defendant's land?

Lord Goff commented in *Hunter v Canary Wharf Ltd* that the nuisance would generally **10–031** arise from something emanating from the defendant's land.[94] He did, however, recognise that there were exceptions to this rule. Injunctions have been granted against brothels and "sex centres", where the complaint has been about the presence of prostitutes and clients visiting the premises, rather than an "emanation" from the land.[95] Some confusion has been caused, however, by the recent case of *Hussain v Lancaster CC*,[96] where the Court of Appeal rejected a claim for nuisance on the basis that the actions complained of did not involve a use of the defendants' land. This case was distinguished, however, by the Court of Appeal in the subsequent decision in *Lippiatt v South Gloucestershire CC*,[97] where the Court held that when the land on which the trespassers resided was used as a "launching pad" for repeated acts of damage, the council would be liable. *Hussain* was distinguished as relating to individual acts by perpetrators who happened to live in council property. Their conduct was in no sense linked to, nor did it emanate from, their homes. Whilst Evans L.J. suggested that there had thus been an "emanation" in *Lippiatt*—namely the travellers themselves—Staughton L.J. was less convinced: "It seems to me that there is not a great difference in such a case whether the offending act of the defendant takes place on his land, or on the public road outside his gate. But we need not rule on that today."[98] The question was therefore left open and we must await another occasion when an authoritative statement may be produced by the House of Lords.

Relevant defences

There are a number of defences which apply to an action for nuisance. The general **10–032** defences of voluntary assumption of risk and contributory negligence apply, but will be discussed in more detail in Ch. 14. It should be noted that although the Law Reform (Contributory Negligence) Act 1945 does not expressly mention nuisance, its provisions are generally accepted to apply. We confine our examination here to defences which are peculiar to nuisance. These are:

- Statutory authority;
- 20 years prescription;
- Inevitable accident;
- Act of a stranger.

The most significant defence is that of statutory authority.

(1) Statutory authority

Many nuisances are caused by activities undertaken by local authorities or other bodies **10–033** acting under statutory powers. If their actions are within the scope of the statute (or *intra vires*), they are authorised by Act of Parliament and cannot be challenged by the

[94] [1997] A.C. 677 at 685–686.
[95] *Laws v Florinplace* [1981] 1 All E.R. 659 and *Thompson-Schwab v Costaki* [1956] 1 All E.R. 652.
[96] [2000] Q.B. 1.
[97] [2000] Q.B. 51.
[98] *ibid.*, at 65.

courts. Parliament is presumed to have considered the competing interests, and to have determined which is to prevail in the public interest and whether or not compensation is to be paid to those adversely affected. It is important to distinguish this defence from planning permission, by which the applicant is given permission to construct a particular building. This does not mean that his or her actions have been authorised by Parliament. Planning permission is, at most, a matter to be considered in identifying the nature of the locality of the nuisance. The question here is very different: does the defendant have statutory authority to commit the nuisance?

The vital question is whether the operations causing the alleged nuisance are within the authority given by statute. Generally, this will be the case if the statute expressly or by necessary implication authorises the nuisance, or the nuisance is the inevitable consequence of the performance of the authorised operations. The leading case on statutory authority is *Allen v Gulf Oil Refining Ltd*.[99] Gulf Oil had obtained its own private Act of Parliament to authorise its expansion in Milford Haven, South Wales. The Act provided specifically for the acquisition of all necessary land and the construction of a refinery, but no express provision was made for the use and operation of the refinery once it had been built. Local residents complained about the noise and vibrations emitted by the refinery and *Allen* was brought as a test case. The House of Lords took the question to be one essentially of statutory construction. Was the nuisance authorised, expressly or implicitly, by the relevant statute? If so, the defendant would not be liable. The burden was, however, on the defendant to satisfy the court that this was in fact so. The court held, by a majority of four to one, that the operation of the refinery was implicitly authorised by the Act, the nuisances were inevitable, and so Gulf Oil had a good defence to the plaintiffs' action. The plaintiffs would only have a remedy to the extent to which any nuisance exceeded the statutory immunity.

The nuisance will not be inevitable if it has been caused by the negligence of the defendant. "Negligence" here is used in a special sense, so as to require the undertaker to carry out the work and conduct the operation with all reasonable regard and care for the interests of other persons.[1] It should be noted that an inevitable nuisance, even when committed without negligence, is unlikely to be considered authorised if the statute contains a "nuisance clause" providing that nothing in the Act shall exonerate the undertaker from liability for the nuisance.[2] Equally, if the defendant has a choice how to exercise a statutory power, and chooses an option which creates a nuisance when there are other options which would not have raised such problems, it is unlikely to be found to be authorised.[3]

The Human Rights Act 1998 may, additionally, have some impact on this defence. Section 3(1) of the Act provides that "So far as it is possible to do so, primary legislation and subordinate legislation must be read and given effect in a way which is compatible with the convention rights." It is possible that conduct authorised by statute may conflict with an individual's rights, for example, in relation to Article 8 (right to private and family life).The House of Lords' decision in *R. v A (No. 2)*[4]

---

[99] [1981] A.C. 1001.
[1] See *Wildtree Hotels Ltd v Harrow L.B.C.* [2001] 2 A.C. 1 at 13 *per* Lord Hoffmann.
[2] See *Department of Transport v N.W. Water Authority* [1983] 3 W.L.R. 105 at 109, approved [1984] A.C. 336 at 359. This only applies to statutory powers and will not apply to statutory duties.
[3] *Metropolitan Asylum District v Hill* (1881) 6 App. Cas. 193.
[4] [2002] 1 A.C. 45 (interpretation of s.41(3), Youth Justice and Criminal Evidence Act 1999 to comply with Art. 6). See D. Nicol [2002] P.L. 438.

indicates that the courts do possess broad interpretative powers to avoid all such conflicts without resorting to a declaration of incompatibility.

(2) 20 years' prescription

Prescription provides a means by which the defendant obtains a legal right to act in a **10–034** certain way, which would ordinarily be contrary to the law, due to the passage of time. In this context, it will be a valid defence for the defendant to show that the nuisance complained of had interfered with the claimant's interest in land for more than 20 years. It should be noted, however, that this applies only to private nuisance. It does not apply to public nuisance, on the basis that length of time should not legitimise a crime. The period is judged carefully, because the law does not easily diminish property rights, and starts from the time at which the nuisance is known by the claimant to affect his or her interests. The difficulties faced in successfully relying on this defence were shown in *Sturges v Bridgman*.[5] Here, a confectioner had used large pestles and mortars at the back of his premises for more than 20 years. His premises were adjacent to the garden of a doctor, who made no complaint until he decided to build a consulting room at the end of his garden. Then, for the first time, he found that the noise and vibration materially interfered with the pursuit of his practice. The court granted him an injunction, despite the fact that the noise and vibrations had existed for over 20 years and that he had chosen to build in his garden in the full knowledge of the defendant's operations (it was no defence that the plaintiff came to the nuisance—see below). This case shows the defence will only be successful where the interference has affected the claimant for the required period of time.

(3) Inevitable accident

The defence of inevitable accident is based on the fact that the damage suffered by the **10–035** claimant occurred despite the exercise of all reasonable care by the defendant. On this basis, this defence can only be relevant to torts where the exercise of reasonable care is necessary for liability. It therefore plays a minimal role in the tort of nuisance and is only relevant where liability is dependent upon proof of negligence. Reference should be made to Ch. 14.

(4) Act of a stranger

This defence is subject to the principle in *Sedleigh-Denfield v O'Callaghan*.[6] Reference **10–036** should therefore be made to the earlier part of this chapter.

Ineffective defences

The following are defences which have been rejected by the courts: **10–037**

- The claimant came to the nuisance;
- The defendant's conduct has social utility;

[5] (1879) 11 Ch. D. 852.
[6] [1940] A.C. 880.

- *Jus tertii*;
- The nuisance is due to many.

(1) Coming to the nuisance

10–038 It is a well-established rule that the claimant may sue even though the nuisance was, to his or her knowledge, in existence before he or she arrived at the premises. By upholding such a rule, the courts clearly favour the right of the claimant to freely enjoy his or her land. The claimant is able to attack the status quo on the basis of his or her own personal interests, despite the fact it may result in the closing down of established businesses, or put an end to activities which benefit the community as a whole. The classic case is that of *Bliss v Hall*,[7] in which the defendant's business of manufacturing candles gave off offensive smells. It was no defence to the plaintiff's action that the business had already been in existence for three years before the plaintiff moved in nearby. In more recent times, the rule has been criticised as being unduly favourable to the claimant. In *Miller v Jackson*,[8] the defendants had used a cricket ground for over 70 years. In 1972, the land to the north of the cricket ground was sold to developers, who built a line of semi-detached houses there. The plaintiffs bought one of these properties and complained that despite the fence around the ground (which was increased in height in 1975) cricket balls had been struck into their garden or against their house on a number of occasions. The Court of Appeal was sympathetic to the club. If the plaintiffs were granted an injunction, the club would be closed down at the instigation of parties who had chosen to move to a property adjoining a cricket club. Nevertheless, the majority held that *Sturges v Bridgman*[9] was still good law, and they were bound to hold that it was not a good defence that the plaintiffs had come to the nuisance. As Geoffrey Lane L.J. explained, ". . . it is not for this court as I see it to alter a rule which has stood for so long."[10] This did not prevent the majority ruling that it would not be equitable to award an injunction in such circumstances, thereby confining the plaintiffs' remedy to an award of damages. This case will be discussed further in the section on remedies below.

(2) Utility

10–039 The courts will not accept a defence that the nuisance caused by the defendant has a benefit to the public at large. This is a further example of the law's support for the property rights of the individual, as is clearly seen in the case of *Adams v Ursell*.[11] The defendant ran a fried fish shop in a residential part of a street. The court granted an injunction restraining the defendant from carrying on his fried fish business on the premises, and rejected the argument that the closure of the shop would cause great hardship to the defendant and to his customers, for whom it was a cheap source of nourishment.

(3) Jus Tertii

10–040 This rests on the allegation that a third party has a better title to the affected land than the claimant, and that the third party should therefore be bringing the action. It has been rejected in a number of cases.[12] It seems correct that where the claimant must

[7] (1838) 4 Bing. N.C. 183 at 185.
[8] [1977] Q.B. 966.
[9] (1879) 11 Ch. D. 852.
[10] [1977] Q.B. 966 at 987.
[11] [1913] 1 Ch. 269.
[12] *Nicholls v Ely Beet Sugar Factory Ltd* [1936] 1 Ch. 343.

show an interest in land or right to exclusive possession, this should be sufficient to found his or her claim.

(4) Due to many

It is no excuse that the defendant was simply one of many causing the nuisance in question. This will be so even if his or her actions in isolation would not amount to a nuisance. In *Lambton v Mellish*,[13] the plaintiff sought an injunction against two rival businessmen who operated merry-go-rounds accompanied by music on their premises. The combined noise was found to be "maddening". Chitty J. was not prepared to excuse one of the defendants on the basis that his contribution to the noise was slight: "if the acts of two persons, each being aware of what the other is doing, amount in the aggregate to what is an actionable wrong, each is amenable to the remedy against the aggregate cause of complaint."[14] Again, this seems to be a rule of convenience in favour of the claimant, although it may be justified on the basis that the defendant's conduct should be considered in the light of *all* the surrounding circumstances, including the conduct of others. Therefore, an act which would have been reasonable in isolation may, in the light of all the circumstances, amount to an unreasonable interference with the claimant's use and enjoyment of land.

10–041

RELATIONSHIP BETWEEN PRIVATE NUISANCE AND OTHER TORTS

It is important to distinguish private nuisance from other torts, such as negligence and trespass, which are commonly claimed in the same action. The relationship between private and public nuisance has already been dealt with above.

10–042

The relationship between private nuisance and negligence[15]

This has caused the most controversy over the years, primarily due to a number of cases which focus on negligence in determining whether the defendant has committed an actionable nuisance. The clearest example of this is the group of cases on continuing or adopting a nuisance. In *Goldman v Hargrave*,[16] Lord Wilberforce remarked that: "The present case is one where liability, if it exists, rests upon negligence and nothing else; whether it falls within or overlaps the boundaries of nuisance is a question of classification which need not here be resolved". However, Megaw L.J. in *Leakey v National Trust*[17] described the claim as one in nuisance, and, as stated earlier, such cases are distinct from ordinary claims in negligence in that (a) they impose liability for an omission, and (b) they impose a subjective standard of care.

The accepted position is that the two torts are conceptually distinct, and this was emphasised by the House of Lords in *Hunter v Canary Wharf Ltd*[18] and *Cambridge*

10–043

---

[13] [1894] 3 Ch. 163.
[14] *ibid.*, at 166.
[15] See C Gearty (1989) 48 C.L.J. 211; P Giliker in *Environmental Protection and the Law* (Hart, 2000).
[16] [1967] 1 A.C. 645 at 657.
[17] [1980] 1 All E.R. 17.
[18] [1997] A.C. 677.

Water Co. v Eastern Counties Leather plc.[19] The central concept of private nuisance is that of "reasonable user". This is distinct from negligence. There is clear authority that the defendant may be liable in spite of exercising reasonable care and skill.[20] As stated above, the concept of reasonable user is *results-based*: is the result of the defendant's conduct such that the claimant suffers unreasonable interference with the use and enjoyment of his or her property? This is a very different approach from that in negligence. For example, the classic case of negligence is that of a road traffic accident caused by the negligent driving of a motorist. The court does not consider the degree of injury suffered by the particular claimant, and weigh this against the right of the particular motorist to drive his or her car without restriction. Rather, it draws on case law which has established that the motorist owes a duty of care to pedestrians and other road-users, and ascertains whether he or she has driven below the standard of the ordinary reasonable driver, thereby causing the accident.

A further distinction is that while negligence primarily protects against personal injury, private nuisance seeks to protect interests in land. This is forcefully stated by the majority of the House of Lords in *Hunter*. The role of private nuisance is to remedy undue interference with rights in land—hence the only parties who can sue are those with an interest in land or exclusive possession which has been interfered with. Their Lordships, in *Hunter*, went further, suggesting that only negligence was capable of protecting against personal injury, as this is not the concern of private nuisance. The implications of this will be considered further in our section on remedies.

It is clear, therefore, that while the torts overlap, and the fact that the defendant's actions were committed negligently may encourage a court to find liability, the torts are distinct. This is not to deny that the growth of negligence in the twentieth century has influenced the development of the older tort of private nuisance. This influence may be seen in relation to the continuation or adoption of a nuisance and the fact that the rules of remoteness set out in *The Wagon Mound (No.1)*[21] are common to negligence, private and public nuisance.[22] This does not signify, however, that the courts will not continue to distinguish between the two different torts.

The relationship between private nuisance and trespass to land

10–044   Both torts have the common aim of protecting those with an interest in or exclusive possession of land. Trespass will be discussed in more detail in our next chapter: Ch. 11. For the moment, it should be noted that trespass involves an *intentional* and *direct* act which interferes with the land. It is actionable without proof of damage. In contrast, nuisance involves an *indirect* act which is only actionable on proof of damage. The distinction is historical, and results from the old rigid forms of action, which required that a claim had to be made in a certain form or not at all. Although the forms of action were abolished in the nineteenth century, the distinction between direct and indirect forms of interference with land persists. The distinction may be illustrated by the following classic example: I throw a log onto your land—this is a

[19] [1994] 2 A.C. 264.
[20] *Rapier v London Tramways Co.* [1893] 2 Ch. 588.
[21] [1961] A.C. 388.
[22] See *The Wagon Mound (No.2)* [1967] 1 A.C. 617. See below.

direct interference and therefore I am liable in trespass even if it does not cause you injury or property damage. (Obviously more damages will be recovered if it crashes through your greenhouse!) Alternatively, I pile up some logs on my land and one of them rolls off the pile and onto your land. Here, the interference is indirect and it will only be actionable in nuisance if you can show that it has caused some injury to your rights in the land.

PUBLIC NUISANCE[23]

It is important, before examining the rule in *Rylands v Fletcher*, to give an overview of the operation of public nuisance. It has a minor role to play in the law of torts and therefore this section will seek to give the reader a general idea of its impact, whilst acknowledging that its role has been largely overtaken by statute. The classic definition may be found in Romer L.J.'s judgment in *Att.-Gen. v P.Y.A. Quarries Ltd*[24]: "any nuisance is 'public' which materially affects the reasonable comfort and convenience of life of a class of Her Majesty's subjects. The sphere of the nuisance may be described generally as 'the neighbourhood'; but the question whether the local community within that sphere comprises a sufficient number of persons to constitute a class of the public is a question of fact in every case". It is not necessary to show that every member of the class has been affected, but the nuisance must be shown to injure a representative cross-section of the class.

    As Lord Denning remarked in *Southport Corp v Esso Petroleum Co. Ltd*,[25] "the term 'public nuisance' covers a multitude of sins, great and small." The tort has indeed been used to deal with a variety of situations including pollution from oil and silt, pigeon droppings, bogus bomb alerts, pirate radio broadcasting and raves. Its most common use, however, is in relation to claims for unreasonable interference with the claimant's use of the highway. Obviously, in such cases, it will be difficult to bring a claim in private nuisance unless the interference affects the use and enjoyment of the claimant's land, and here the complaint will generally relate to the claimant's right to pass along the highway.

10–045

Obstructions on the highway

Whilst complaints as to the *condition* of the highway itself will now largely be covered by the Highways Act 1980, the claimant may wish to bring an action relating to unreasonable *obstructions* on the highway. As noted in *Dymond v Pearce*,[26] some obstructions are inevitable. It is generally acceptable for vehicles to stop on the highway to deliver goods or to park in a lay-by, but a prima facie nuisance would be created where a vehicle is left for a considerable period without any valid justification. Equally, whilst it is reasonable for a person to put up scaffolding for works on his or

10–046

---

[23] See J. Spencer (1989) 48 C.L.J. 55.
[24] [1957] 2 Q.B. 169 at 184. See also Denning L.J. at 190–191.
[25] [1954] 2 Q.B. 182 at 196.
[26] [1972] 1 All E.R. 1142.

her house which obstructs the highway on a temporary basis, a nuisance would be created if the erection of the scaffolding was unreasonable in size or duration.[27] It is a matter of degree. It is still unclear whether fault is necessary to establish that the obstruction is unreasonable. Certainly the majority in *Dymond* were prepared to contemplate liability where an action for negligence would fail, despite statements to the contrary in *The Wagon Mound (No.2)*.[28] Lord Denning M.R. attempted a compromise in *Southport Corp. v Esso Petroleum Co. Ltd*[29] by suggesting that for public nuisance, unlike negligence, once the nuisance was proved, the legal burden would fall on the defendant who caused it to justify or excuse himself or herself. This would serve to keep the torts logically distinct, but as the House of Lords on appeal did not deal with this matter, the view of Lord Denning M.R. is not authoritative. The courts still experience difficulty in separating the question whether there is a nuisance (*i.e.* an unreasonable obstruction of the highway) from the question of fault.

Projections over the highway

10–047   There is further confusion whether fault is relevant when the claimant's injuries are caused by an object *projecting* onto the highway from the defendant's land. In *Tarry v Ashton*,[30] an occupier had been found liable when a heavy lamp, attached to the front of his building on the Strand, fell on a passer-by. The occupier was held to owe a positive, continuing and non-delegable duty to keep the premises in repair so as not to prejudice the public. In *Noble v Harrison*,[31] however, the court held that the defendant could only be liable if he or she knew, or should have known, of the circumstances which caused the injury. Here, a branch of a beech tree growing on the defendant's land, which overhung the highway, had suddenly broken and damaged the plaintiff's vehicle. The fracture had been due to a latent defect which could not have been detected by reasonable and careful inspection. Rowlatt J. held that the defendant was not liable and distinguished the earlier decision of *Tarry v Ashton*[32] on the basis that it applied to artificial rather than natural objects.

The Court of Appeal in *Wringe v Cohen*[33] continued to follow *Tarry* as imposing a rule of strict liability in respect of artificial structures projecting onto the highway:

> ". . . if, owing to want of repair, premises on a highway become dangerous and, therefore, a nuisance and a passer-by or an adjoining owner suffers damage by their collapse, the occupier, or owner if he has undertaken the duty of repair, is answerable whether he knew or ought to have known of the danger or not."

This line of authority was followed by the Court of Appeal in *Mint v Good*.[34] As a result of these decisions, the courts apply different rules depending on whether the

---

[27] *Harper v Haden* [1933] Ch. 298.
[28] *Overseas Tankships (UK) Ltd v Miller Steamship Co. Pty* [1967] 1 A.C. 617.
[29] [1954] 2 Q.B. 182 at 197.
[30] (1876) 1 Q.B.D. 314.
[31] [1926] 2 K.B. 332.
[32] (1876) 1 Q.B.D. 314.
[33] [1940] 1 K.B. 229 at 233.
[34] [1951] 1 K.B. 517.

projection onto the highway is artificial or natural. This distinction is difficult to justify on principle, but, as may be seen above, owes more to the court's willingness in *Noble* to distinguish a line of authority it preferred not to follow.

However, in practice, the distinction between the different rules is not great. The court in *Wringe v Cohen* recognised two defences which had been mentioned by Blackburn J. in *Tarry*: (i) where the danger had been caused by the unseen act of a trespasser, and (ii) where the damage is due to a "secret and unobservable operation of nature" (a latent defect) of which the occupier does not know or ought not to have known. Such defences largely undermine the idea of strict liability for projections on the highway and clearly inject an element of fault. Here, once again, we can observe the influence of negligence on the development of the tort of nuisance. It should also be noted that the Court of Appeal in *Salsbury v Woodland*[35] refused to extend *Tarry* to work undertaken *near* the highway in circumstances where, if care was not taken, injury to passers-by might be caused. The court held that no such category of strict liability existed, and that the ordinary rules of negligence would apply. The occupier would, however, have been strictly liable for the actions of his independent contractors if the work had been inherently dangerous (see our earlier discussion of this point under Private Nuisance, above).

Particular damage

It is not enough for the claimant to show that he or she is a member of the class whose reasonable comfort and convenience has been materially affected by the defendant. To bring an action in tort, the claimant must show that he or she has suffered "special" or "particular" damage in excess of that suffered by the public at large.[36] This is largely a measure to limit the number of claims and avoid the defendant being deluged with claims from every member of the class affected. Such special damage must be direct and substantial and includes personal injury, property damage, loss of custom or business and, it is claimed, delay and inconvenience. The latter category is contentious, and it has been suggested that the claimant must also show pecuniary loss due to the delay.[37] If the individual cannot prove special damage, the only other basis on which an action may be brought in tort is in the name of the Attorney-General by means of a relator action (for example, see *P.Y.A. Quarries* above). This is seldom used. Alternatively, the local authority may be persuaded to exercise its power under s.222 of the Local Government Act 1972 to bring proceedings for an injunction when it considers it "expedient for the promotion or protection of the interests of the inhabitants of their area".[38]

10–048

[35] [1970] 1 Q.B. 324 at 345, CA.
[36] See G. Kodalinye (1986) 2 L.S. 182.
[37] See *Winterbottom v Lord Derby* (1867) L.R. 2 Ex. 316 at 321–322.
[38] See, for example, *Stoke-on-Trent City Council v B & Q (Retail) Ltd* [1984] A.C. 754. In *Wandsworth LBC v Railtrack plc* [2002] Q.B. 756, the local authority was able to complain about the damage caused by pigeons roosting under the defendant's railway bridge under s.222 and, because the nuisance affected those using the highway when passing under the bridge, by virtue of s.130 of the Highways Act 1980 (highway authority empowered to bring legal proceedings in their own name to protect the public's right to use and enjoy the highway). There is no obstacle to the local authority bringing an action under both provisions in highway cases: *Nottingham City Council v Zain* [2002] 1 W.L.R. 607, CA. *Zain* additionally raises the interesting question as to what extent a local authority should be permitted to use s.222 to enforce criminal law, for example, by excluding a drug dealer from a housing estate. Such a use was found to be arguable in this case.

THE RULE IN *RYLANDS V FLETCHER*

10–049   So far, we have considered the way in which nuisance protects the claimant's ability to exercise his or her rights without undue interference by the defendant. In this section, we consider a particular cause of action which protects an occupier against interference due to an *isolated* escape from his or her neighbour's land. The particular rules relating to this cause of action, and its relationship with nuisance, will be considered below. First, let us examine the case which provides both the principle and the name for this cause of action: *Rylands v Fletcher*.[39]

The defendant was a millowner, who had employed independent contractors to build a reservoir on his land to provide water for his mill. During the course of building, the independent contractors discovered some old shafts and passages of an abandoned coalmine on the defendant's land, which appeared to be blocked. When the reservoir was filled, the water burst through the old shafts, which were subsequently found to connect with the plaintiff's mine. As a result, the plaintiff's mine was flooded and he sought compensation.

Although the independent contractors had clearly been negligent in failing to ensure that the mine shafts were blocked off securely, the plaintiff's action was against the millowner. The millowner had not been shown to be negligent. The plaintiff also faced the added obstacle that the courts had severe doubts whether an isolated escape, as opposed to a continuous state of affairs, could found an action in nuisance. This did not prevent his action succeeding. The case was finally resolved at House of Lords level, but the classic statement of principle was given by Blackburn J. in the Court of Exchequer Chamber:

> "We think that the true rule of law is that the person who for his own purposes brings on his lands and collects and keeps there anything likely to do mischief if it escapes, must keep it in at his peril, and, if he does not do so, is prima facie answerable for all the damage which is the natural consequence of its escape."

This was approved by the House of Lords, although Lord Cairns used the term "non-natural user" in explaining the principle.

What is the significance of *Rylands v Fletcher*?

10–050   This has caused some controversy. Blackburn J. reasoned by analogy to existing examples of liability, such as cattle trespass and nuisance, and clearly did not believe himself to be laying down any new principle of law. Liability under the rule is therefore closely related to these torts. However, in the first part of the twentieth century, *Rylands v Fletcher* liability developed as a separate "rule" with its own requirements, which will be outlined below. It has been suggested that the rule can be explained as a decision to impose strict liability on persons conducting ultra-hazardous activities. Certainly this idea has received support in the United States. The Tentative Draft of

---

[39] (1865) 3 H. & C. 774 (Court of Exchequer); (1866) 1 L.R. 1 Ex. 265 (Court of Exchequer Chamber); (1868) L.R. 3 H.L. 330 (House of Lords).

the Restatement (3d) on Torts imposes strict liability for abnormally dangerous activities,[40] when "(1) the activity creates a foreseeable and highly significant risk of physical harm even when reasonable care is exercise by all actors; and (2) the activity is not a matter of common usage."[41] This idea was not, however, accepted in England. The Law Commission, in its 1970 Report, *Civil Liability for Dangerous Things and Activities*,[42] expressed doubts as to its usefulness, finding that any benefits provided by its relative simplicity and flexibility would be outweighed by difficulties in application. The House of Lords sounded the death-knell for strict liability for ultra-hazardous activities in *Read v Lyons*,[43] where their Lordships clearly rejected this as an explanation of *Rylands v Fletcher* liability. (This case is discussed below). Lord Goff in *Cambridge Water* took the view that, as a general rule, strict liability for operations of high risk would be more appropriately imposed by statute than the courts and that, in any event, *Read v Lyons* served to preclude any such development.[44]

A further suggestion has been that the rule should be absorbed into the law of negligence. Whilst this may seem an odd suggestion, the High Court of Australia in *Burnie Port Authority v General Jones*[45] decided exactly that in 1984. The court held, by a majority of five to two, that the occupier was liable for fire damage caused by the negligence of his independent contractors under the ordinary rules of negligence, due to the existence of a non-delegable duty of care. The reasoning in this case, which relies heavily on the concept of non-delegable duties, is somewhat strained and, despite the growing influence of negligence in the twentieth century, received little support in England.

The English courts have questioned, however, the relationship between the rule in *Rylands v Fletcher* and private nuisance. Lord Goff in *Cambridge Water Co. v Eastern Counties Leather plc*,[46] relying on historical analysis,[47] commented that:

> "it would . . . lead to a more coherent body of common law principles if the rule were to be regarded as essentially an extension of the law of nuisance to isolated escapes from land".

The recent House of Lords ruling in *Transco plc v Stockport MBC*[48] confirmed that the **10–051** rule should be treated as a sub-species of private nuisance. In this case, their Lordships took the opportunity to review the scope and application in modern conditions of the

---

[40] Para.20, replacing para.519 of the Second Restatement. See, generally, KN Hylton 'The Theory of Tort Doctrine and the *Restatement (Third) of Torts'* (2001) 54 Vanderbilt Law Review 1413.
[41] This is a modification of paragraph 520 of the Second Restatement.
[42] Law Commission Report No. 32 (1970), Pt III. However, the idea did receive some support in the report of the Pearson Commission in 1978 (Report of the Royal Commission on Civil Liability and Compensation for Personal Injury, Cmnd 7054 (1978), Vol. 1, Ch. 31 para.1651) which recommended a statutory scheme making the controller of any listed dangerous thing or activity strictly liable for death or personal injury resulting from its malfunction. As discussed in Chapter 1, the broad views of the Pearson Commission on liability have never been adopted in this country.
[43] [1947] A.C. 156 at 167, 181, 186 (liability rejected in respect of a high explosive shell which exploded and injured a munitions inspector).
[44] [1994] 2 A.C. 264 at 305.
[45] (1994) 120 A.L.R. 42. For a discussion of the case, see R.F.V. Heuston and R.A. Buckley (1994) 110 L.Q.R. 506.
[46] [1994] 2 A.C. 264 at 306.
[47] Particularly, the article of FH Newark, "The Boundaries of Nuisance" (1949) 65 L.Q.R. 480.
[48] [2003] 3 W.L.R. 1467.

rule in *Rylands v Fletcher*. It therefore provides helpful guidance as to the future application of this tort. In particular, the court:

- Rejected the suggestion that it should be absorbed into the tort of negligence or fault-based principles, as in Australia and Scotland[49];

- Rejected the suggestion of a more generous application of the rule. Their Lordships favoured a more restrictive approach, confining the rule to exceptional circumstances where the occupier has brought some dangerous thing onto his land which poses an exceptionally high risk to neighbouring property should it escape, and which amounts to an extraordinary and unusual use of land; *and*

- Clarified that only those with rights to land could sue.

This decision ends a long period of speculation as to the relationship between this tort and private nuisance. It serves also to emphasise the residuary role of the rule in modern society where statutes and regulations largely cover the area of dangerous escapes which the rule once covered *e.g.* the discharge of water is now regulated by s.209 of the Water Industry Act 1991.[50] It remains to be seen, following such a review, how useful such a limited claim will now be.[51]

Liability under the rule in *Rylands v Fletcher*

10–052   There are four requirements which must be established for the claimant to sue under the rule. The first two derive from Blackburn J.'s statement of principle. The third derives from Lord Cairns in the House of Lords. The fourth requirement, namely foreseeability of the kind of damage suffered, is of more recent origin and comes from the leading judgment of Lord Goff in *Cambridge Water Co. v Eastern Counties Leather plc*.[52]

(1) The defendant brings on his lands for his own purposes something likely to do mischief

10–053   This requires a voluntary act of bringing something on the land. What is "likely to do mischief" is an interesting question. In *Rylands* itself, water was held to be within this category, and other case law has referred to electricity, oil, vibrations, noxious fumes and even a flagpole or a fairground ride.

This requirement seems to have been toughened up by *Transco*. Lord Bingham remarked that "I do not think the mischief or danger test should be at all easily satisfied. It must be shown that the defendant has done something which he recognised, or judged by the standards appropriate at the relevant place and time, he ought reasonably to have recognised, as giving rise to an *exceptionally high risk of*

---

[49] See *RHM Bakeries (Scotland) Ltd v Strathclyde Regional Council* [1985] S.L.T. 214.
[50] See also s.73(6), Environmental Protection Act 1990 (pollution by escape of waste) and s.7, Nuclear Installations Act 1965 (radio-active matter).
[51] Lord Hoffmann commented above at 1483 that "It is perhaps not surprising that counsel could not find a reported case since the second world war in which anyone had succeeded in a claim under the rule."
[52] [1994] 2 A.C. 264.

danger or mischief if there should be an escape, however unlikely an escape may have been thought to be."[53] This again will serve to restrict the application of the rule.

(2) If it escapes

This is one of the key features of liability. The rule in *Rylands v Fletcher* deals with isolated escapes and therefore proof of an actual escape is vital. The leading case is the House of Lords decision in *Read v Lyons*,[54] where their Lordships took the opportunity to review the law and establish clear rules of liability. In the case itself, an inspector of munitions had been injured by an explosion of a shell whilst inspecting the defendants' munitions factory. Their Lordships held that there had not been an "escape" within the rule. An escape would only occur when the object moved from the defendant's premises to a place which was outside his occupation or control. **10–054**

There is some debate whether an *intentional release* of an object is capable of being regarded as an "escape". Taylor J. in *Rigby v Chief Constable of Northamptonshire*[55] held that trespass would seem to be the correct action for the intentional and direct infliction of harm. However, this was questioned by Potter J. in *Crown River Cruises Ltd v Kimbolton Fireworks Ltd*,[56] at least where the intentional release was not deliberately aimed in the direction of the claimant, or with the intention of impinging on his or her property. With respect, Taylor J.'s view is probably more consistent with the traditional division between nuisance and trespass, and with Lord Goff's return to the traditional view of these torts in *Cambridge Water* and *Hunter v Canary Wharf*.

(3) Non-natural user

Blackburn J. in *Rylands v Fletcher* referred to the defendant bringing onto the property something "which was not naturally there", which Lord Cairns in the House of Lords interpreted as a "non-natural use". On this basis, thistledown, blowing from the defendant's land onto the plaintiff's land, has been held not to found an action.[57] Over time, however, the "non-natural" use requirement came to be interpreted as "non-ordinary" use, so as to limit the application of the rule in *Rylands v Fletcher*. As Professor Newark has remarked, "the result as applied in the modern cases is, we believe, one which would have surprised Lord Cairns and astounded Blackburn J."[58] The result has been unpredictability and confusion, and many would sympathise with Viscount Simon in *Read v Lyons*, who commented: "I confess to finding this test of 'non-natural' user (or of bringing on the land what was not 'naturally there', which is not the same test) difficult to apply".[59] **10–055**

The classic definition, however, is that of Lord Moulton in *Rickards v Lothian*,[60]:

> "It is not every use to which land is put that brings into play [the *Rylands v Fletcher*] principle. It must be some special use bringing with it increased danger to others, and must not merely be the ordinary use of the land or such a use as is proper for the general benefit of the community."

[53] See above at 1474 (emphasis added).
[54] [1947] A.C. 156.
[55] [1985] 2 All E.R. 983 at 996.
[56] [1996] 2 Lloyd's Rep. 533.
[57] *Giles v Walker* (1890) 24 Q.B.D. 656.
[58] FH Newark (1961) 24 M.L.R. 557 at 571.
[59] [1947] A.C. 156 at 166.
[60] [1913] A.C. 263 at 280.

This broad definition has allowed the courts to conclude that domestic water, electricity and gas supplies could be regarded as a "natural" use of land. "Natural user" has even controversially been extended to the manufacture of explosives during war-time,[61] although this was doubted in *Transco*.[62] Essentially, "natural" has been interpreted as any ordinary use of land. Whilst what is ordinary will change with time (for example keeping a car was "non-natural" in 1919,[63] but would not be so regarded today), interpreting the rule in this way clearly gives the courts considerable discretion in deciding whether to apply the rule to a given set of facts.

The meaning of "non-natural user" must now be viewed in the light of Lord Goff's comments in *Cambridge Water Co. v Eastern Counties Leather plc*[64] and the House of Lords ruling in *Transco plc v Stockport MBC*.[65] Lord Goff remarked in *Cambridge Water* that " ... the storage of substantial quantities of chemicals on industrial premises should be regarded as an almost classic case of non-natural use".[66] His Lordship held that this was regardless of any benefit the factory may give to the public by means of increased employment (thereby criticising the "general benefit of the community" test of Lord Moulton). Equally, his Lordship refused to accept that storing chemicals in industrial premises might be regarded as an "ordinary" use of such premises.

The House of Lords in *Transco* approved Lord Goff's judgment and expanded upon it. The case itself was primarily concerned with the nature of the "non-natural user" test. Stockport MBC were the owners of a block of flats and an adjacent disused railway embankment. A water pipe serving the flats leaked and the water percolated to the surface and onward into the embankment through a crack in the ground. There was no evidence that this was due to negligence. The embankment collapsed as a result of having become saturated with water, and the void left by the collapse exposed a high pressure gas main owned by British Gas (now Transco). The claimants wisely acted promptly to prevent a potential fracture of the pipe, incurring costs of around £94,000. The question arose whether the storage of water in pipes was a "non-natural" use of the land.

The House of Lords agreed with the Court of Appeal that the provision of a water supply to a block of flats by means of a connecting pipe was a natural use of land. This is consistent with prior authority. However, the tests used indicate that the "non-natural user" requirement will be more difficult to satisfy than previously. The court sought to find the creation of a special hazard constituting an extraordinary use of land, and noted the link between the first requirement (something likely to do mischief) and the question of non-natural use. All five judges sought some use which was extraordinary and unusual according to contemporary standards.[67] This clearly did

[61] *Read v Lyons* [1947] A.C. 156 at 174, 176.
[62] See Lords Bingham above at 1475 and Walker at 1502. Note also criticism of this decision by Lord Goff in *Cambridge Water Co. v Eastern Counties Leather plc* [1994] 2 A.C. 264 at 308 and contrast *Rainham Chemical Works v Belvedere Fish Guano Co.* [1921] 2 A.C. 465 where the manufacture of explosives during the First World War was regarded as "non-natural
[63] *Musgrove v Pandelis* [1919] 2 K.B. 43.
[64] [1994] 2 A.C. 264.
[65] [2003] 3 W.L.R. 1467.
[66] Above, at 309.
[67] Although Lord Bingham above at 1475 warned against a too inflexible approach. A use might be extraordinary and unusual at one time or place, but not so at another.

not exist on the facts. It was a routine function which would not have struck anyone as raising any special hazard. Lord Hoffmann suggested that "A useful guide in deciding whether the risk has been created by a 'non-natural' user of land is therefore to ask whether the damage which eventuated was something against which the occupier could reasonably be expected to have insured himself."[68] If it is, then the use is classified as ordinary and the test is not satisfied.

(4) Foreseeability of damage of the relevant type

This requirement comes from the review undertaken by the House of Lords of liability **10–056** under the rule in *Cambridge Water Co. v Eastern Counties Leather plc.*[69] In this case, the defendants had used a chemical called perchloroethene (PCE) for degreasing pelts at their tannery. There were regular spillages, which gradually seeped into and built up under the land. The chemical seepage was such that it contaminated the plaintiffs' water supply 1.3 miles away, forcing them to find another source at a cost of nearly £1 million. The plaintiffs sued in negligence, nuisance and under the rule in *Rylands v Fletcher*. By the time the case reached the House of Lords, only liability under the latter head was in issue.

The House of Lords held that the defendants were not liable. It was not foreseeable to the skilled person that quantities of chemical would cause damage to the plaintiffs' water, and foreseeability of damage was a requirement of liability under the rule in *Rylands v Fletcher*.[70] Lord Goff justified his conclusion by analogy to nuisance, and by reference to Blackburn J.'s statement of principle in *Rylands* itself, namely that the rule referred to "anything likely to do mischief if it escapes".

There has been some discussion as to how far this test of foreseeability goes. Must the escape also be foreseeable? Although Lord Goff's judgment is not entirely clear, the best view is that the escape need not be foreseeable. As Lord Goff commented, "the principle is one of strict liability in the sense that the defendant may be held liable notwithstanding that he has exercised all due care to prevent the escape from occurring".[71] This is certainly the interpretation adopted by Judge Peter Bowsher Q.C. in *Ellison v Ministry of Defence*,[72] although his comments were *obiter* on the facts.

Lord Goff also considered the position in relation to the *continuing* contamination by PCE. The problem had been identified. Could the defendants be liable for such ongoing damage now it was clearly foreseeable? His Lordship found this argument to be ill-founded. The chemical was now beyond the control of the defendants, and to impose liability would be to adopt a stricter position than that adopted in nuisance or negligence.

---

[68] See above at 1484.
[69] [1994] 2 A.C. 264.
[70] See also *Savage v Fairclough* [2000] Env L.R. 183, CA where pollution of a private water supply, which had arisen due to nitrate contamination from a neighbour's farm, was not considered foreseeable by a "hypothetical good farmer" running a farm such as the one in question. Note also *Hamilton v Papakura DC* [2002] UKPC 9; *The Times*, March 2, 2002, where the Privy Council held that damage caused to crops due to the presence of a herbicide in the town water supply (which remained fit for human consumption) did not lead to foreseeable loss.
[71] *ibid.*, at 302.
[72] (1996) 81 B.L.R. 101.

Who can sue?

10–057 Before the House of Lords' decision in *Transco*, it had been unclear in light of *Cambridge Water* and *Hunter* whether it was necessary to have an interest in land or exclusive possession to sue. Non-occupiers had in the past recovered damages under this head;[73] although this line of authority had been criticised in the leading case of *Read v Lyons*.[74] Yet, in view of Lord Goff's comment in *Cambridge Water* that the focus of both torts is the same—namely the protection of rights to land—logically, only claimants with a right to land should be able to sue.[75] *Transco* confirms the force of Lord Goff's logic: only parties with rights over land may bring an action under the rule in *Rylands v Fletcher*.

Who can be sued?

10–058 The occupier of land will be liable if he or she satisfies the requirements for establishing the tort. Therefore, if you have accumulated the mischief which has escaped, *etc.*, you may be liable. There is clear authority that licensees may be sued.[76] Indeed, in *Rylands* itself, although the millowner was treated as the owner of the land, on the facts of the case, the millowner had built the reservoir to serve his mill on land belonging to a certain Lord Wilton (with his Lordship's permission) and was therefore strictly only a licensee.

Defences

10–059 There are a number of relevant defences:

- Claimant's default;
- Unforeseeable act of a stranger;
- Act of God;
- Statutory authority;
- Consent.

The first three derive from the judgment of Blackburn J. in *Rylands*.

(1) Claimant's default

10–060 It is a valid defence that the escape was due wholly or partially to the claimant's fault. In *Ponting v Noakes*,[77] the plaintiff's horse had died when it had reached over the fence and eaten leaves from a poisonous tree on the defendant's land. The defendant was

---

[73] See, *e.g.* dicta in *Shiffman v Order of the Hospital of St John of Jerusalem* [1936] 1 All E.R. 557 (although decided on negligence) and *Perry v Kendricks Transport Ltd* [1956] 1 W.L.R. 85 at 92.
[74] [1947] A.C. 156 at 173 (per Lord Macmillan) and at 186 (per Lord Uthwatt). See also Widgery J. in *Weller & Co. v Foot and Mouth Disease Research Institute* [1966] 1 Q.B. 569 at 588.
[75] Such reasoning convinced Neuberger J. in *McKenna v British Aluminium Ltd* [2002] Env LR 30, Birmingham District Registry.
[76] See *Rainham Chemical Works v Belvedere Fish Guano Co.* [1921] 2 A.C. 465 at 479 *per* Lord Sumner, who cited *Eastern and South African Telegraph Co. v Cape Town Tramways Cos Ltd* [1902] A.C. 381 at 392; *Midwood v Manchester Corp.* [1905] 2 K. B. 597; *Charing Cross Electricity Supply Co. v Hydraulic Power Company* [1914] 3 K. B. 772.
[77] [1894] 2 Q.B. 281.

not found to be liable when the harm suffered was due to the horse's own conduct. (There had equally been no "escape"). Reference should also be made to the Law Reform (Contributory Negligence) Act 1945, s.1.

(2) Unforeseeable act of stranger

This is a well-established defence. In *Box v Jubb*,[78] the court again faced the consequences of a reservoir overflowing onto the plaintiff's land, but this time the defendant was not liable. The overflow had been due to the actions of another neighbouring reservoir owner, over which the defendant had no control, and of which he had no knowledge. In such circumstances, the defendant was not held liable for the flooding.

    10–061

This approach was followed in *Rickards v Lothian*.[79] Here, the plaintiff's premises had been flooded due to a continuous overflow of water from a sink on the top floor of the building. The overflow had been caused by a water tap being turned on full, and the wastepipe plugged, by the deliberate act of a third party. The defendant escaped liability as he could not reasonably have known of the act so as to prevent it.

The act of the third party must be *unforeseeable*. If the defendant should have foreseen the intervention, the defence will not be established. For example, in *Northwestern Utilities Ltd v London Guarantee Co.*,[80] it was held to be foreseeable that works undertaken by a third party near the defendants' gas mains might damage their mains and require remedial work. It was therefore no defence to claim that the gas leak, which caused the fire destroying the plaintiff's hotel, was due to damage to the mains by the acts of a third party. The defendants had left the matter to chance, and this was not sufficient to excuse them from liability.

Three points of contention remain. First, and simplest, there has been some debate as to who is a "stranger". It obviously includes trespassers, but it has been suggested that it should also include licensees over whom the defendant does not exercise control, in order to keep liability within reasonable bounds. This view received support in *Ribee v Norrie*.[81] Here, Miss Ribee, described as a sprightly 70-year-old lady, suffered property damage and personal injury when her home caught fire.[82] The fire had started in an adjoining property which had been divided into bedsit accommodation. It was suspected that the fire had been caused by one of the occupants leaving a smouldering cigarette on the settee in the common area. The Court of Appeal held the landlord of the hostel liable. He could have exercised some control over the persons occupying the hostel, for example, by putting up notices prohibiting smoking, and could have foreseen such an accident occurring. It could not be said that the fire was due to the unforeseeable act of a stranger.

Secondly, it is unclear whether the defence applies to the *negligent* act of a third party. It would seem, as a matter of logic, that the defence should not be defeated on

---

[78] (1879) 4 Ex. D. 76.
[79] [1913] A.C. 263. See also *Perry v Kendricks Transport Ltd* [1956] 1 W.L.R. 85.
[80] [1936] A.C. 108.
[81] [2001] P.I.Q.R. P8.
[82] She was saved, we are told, by her heroic spaniel, which jumped on her bed and whimpered until she awoke! It should be noted that it remains contentious whether liability for the escape of a fire is covered by the rule in *Rylands v Fletcher* or under a parallel rule of the common law: see *Musgrove v Pandelis* [1919] 2 K.B. 43 and *H&N Emanuel v Greater London Council* [1971] 2 All E.R. 835, 839 *per* Lord Denning M.R. See A. Ogus (1969) 28 C.L.J. 104.

proof that the third party did not act intentionally. The real emphasis should be on whether the defendant should have been able to foresee, and therefore react to, the actions of the third party. This takes us to our third problem. The formulation of this defence is sounding more and more like an action for negligence. Defendants will *not* be liable if they can show that they did not foresee, or should not have foreseen, the actions of the third party. *Street on Torts*[83] has gone so far as to say that despite clear authority for this defence, the cases are erroneously decided and have nothing to do with the rule in *Rylands v Fletcher*, but are cases decided in negligence. This, perhaps, is to take conceptual neatness a step too far. Undoubtedly, negligence principles have influenced the development of the rule as much as they have influenced nuisance, but it is still conceptually distinct.

(3) Act of God

10–062   This defence is, due to the advances in modern technology and science, largely defunct. The defendant will not be liable where the escape is due solely to natural causes, in circumstances where no human foresight or prudence could reasonably recognise the possibility of such an occurrence and provide against it. So far, there has been only one successful English case, which was decided in 1876. In *Nichols v Marsland*,[84] the defendant had some ornamental pools on his land, which contained large quantities of water. These pools had been formed by damming up with artificial banks a natural stream which flowed through his property. Due to extraordinary rainfall, the banks broke down, and the rush of escaping water carried away four bridges. The Court of Appeal held that the defendant should not be held liable for an extraordinary act of nature which could not have been reasonably anticipated.

A stricter view was taken in *Greenock Corp. v Caledonian Ry*,[85] in which the court was critical of the approach taken by the court in *Nichols*. In this case, a concrete paddling pool for children had been constructed by the local authority in the bed of a stream, requiring the course of the stream to be altered. Again, there was an extraordinary level of rainfall, which caused the stream to overflow at the pool. Due to the construction of the pool, water which would have otherwise flowed down stream flowed down a public street. The House of Lords held that such an event did not qualify as an act of God.

In view of *Greenock*, it is most unlikely that the defence would succeed today. However, it is possible that a situation may exist where modern precautions against exceptional natural conditions were defeated (for example, an earthquake in a London suburb) and the defence might come into play, but such circumstances would be very rare indeed.

(4) Statutory authority

10–063   Again, this defence is important, and the approach is the same as that taken in nuisance (see above). It will therefore be a question of construction in each case. The courts will examine whether the breach of the rule in *Rylands v Fletcher* was authorised by the statute in question. In *Green v Chelsea Waterworks Co.*,[86] the defendants, who

---

[83] J. Murphy (11th ed., Butterworths, 2003) p.446.
[84] (1876) 2 Ex. D. 1.
[85] [1917] A.C. 556.
[86] (1894) 70 L.T. 547.

were under a statutory duty to maintain a continuous supply of water, were not liable when, in the absence of negligence, the water main burst, damaging the plaintiff's premises, horse and stock. However, the defendants were liable for a burst water main in *Charing Cross Electricity Supply Co. v Hydraulic Power Co.*[87] Here, the defendants were operating under a statutory power to supply water for industrial purposes. These powers were subject to a "nuisance clause", which provided that nothing in the Act should exonerate the undertakers from liability for nuisance. On this basis, the defendants remained liable even in the absence of negligence.

The Court of Appeal in *Dunne v North Western Gas Board*[88] sought to clarify the different treatment of statutory duties and powers. In this case, there was a series of 46 explosions of coal gas in Liverpool, which resulted when a water main had leaked and water had washed away the soil supporting a gas main. The plaintiffs sued both the Gas Board and the Corporation which was responsible for the water main. The Gas Board had a statutory duty to supply gas and it had, in the absence of negligence, a good defence of statutory authority. The Corporation, in contrast, only acted under a statutory power. Here, unlike *Charing Cross*, the Act did not contain a nuisance clause, and so the Corporation would not be liable in the absence of negligence.

The House of Lords in *Transco* emphasised the significance of this defence in limiting the application of the rule by excluding claims for high risk activities arising from work constructed or conducted under statutory authority.[89]

(5) Consent

This may be express or implied. Consent will be implied where the escape results from something maintained for the common benefit, for example, in a block of flats, from the guttering, or from common utilities such as water, gas or electricity. The tenant in such circumstances is assumed to forego any rights against the landlord, due to the benefit he or she gains, provided the escape occurs without negligence.[90]   **10–064**

REMEDIES

There are three main remedies: **10–065**

- Injunctions;
- Abatement;
- Damages.

The main remedy for nuisance is the injunction. Where liability lies under the rule in *Rylands v Fletcher*, the escape has usually occurred, and the damage has already been caused, so the claimant will be seeking damages. Remedies will be discussed generally

---

[87] [1914] 3 K.B. 772.
[88] [1964] 2 Q.B. 806 at 833–837.
[89] See Lord Hoffmann above at 1480.
[90] *Kiddle v City Business Properties Ltd* [1942] 1 K.B. 269 at 274. See also *Carstairs v Taylor* (1871) L.R. 6 Ex. 217. See L. Kadirgamar [1973] Conv 179.

in Ch. 15, but we examine here their particular application in relation to nuisance and the rule in *Rylands v Fletcher*. We will also consider the possibility of a claimant recovering under the Human Rights Act 1998.

(1) Injunctions

10–066   As will be discussed further in Ch. 15, an injunction is an equitable and therefore a discretionary remedy. As a remedy, it is well suited to nuisance, because it can be adapted to meet the balance of competing interests. The courts are generally willing to grant an injunction, unless there are exceptional circumstances which mean that damages are seen as the most appropriate remedy. In such circumstances, damages are said to be given "in lieu of" (instead of) an injunction. Whilst section 50 of the Supreme Court Act 1981 is the section governing this matter, the leading case is that of *Shelfer v City of London Electric Lighting Co.*[91] In this case, A.L. Smith L.J. laid down the four conditions which would lead a court to grant damages in lieu of an injunction:

- Where the injury to the claimant's legal rights is small;

- Where the injury is capable of being estimated in money;

- Where the injury can be adequately compensated by a small money payment; *and*

- Where it would be oppressive to the defendant to grant an injunction.

In the case itself, the court granted an injunction against vibrations and noise caused by the defendant's machinery, even though the result would deprive many of its customers of electricity. The courts are unwilling to allow a defendant essentially to buy the right to commit the nuisance by paying damages to the claimant.[92]

The exercise of this discretion was discussed by the Court of Appeal in *Miller v Jackson*[93] and *Kennaway v Thompson*.[94] In the former case, the majority of the court held that an injunction was inappropriate, on the basis that the public interest in cricket should prevail (Lord Denning M.R.) and the plaintiffs had knowingly bought the property in the knowledge that a nuisance would be likely to occur (Cumming-Bruce L.J.). Damages were therefore awarded.[95] In *Kennaway*, Lawton L.J. held that the relevant authority remained that of *Shelfer*, which did not support either proposition. Accordingly, the plaintiff would be awarded an injunction against power boat racing on a nearby lake, regardless of any public interest in power boat racing, and regardless of fact that she had chosen to build a house near the lake in the knowledge that some racing took place.[96] Nevertheless, the injunction was awarded on terms. The court used its discretion to stipulate a strict timetable for international,

---

[91] [1895] 1 Ch. 287. For a recent application, see *Daniells v Mendonca* (1999) 78 P & C.R. 401, CA.
[92] See Lindley L.J. *ibid.*, at 315–316.
[93] [1977] Q.B. 966.
[94] [1981] Q.B. 88. See R.A. Buckley (1981) 44 M.L.R. 212.
[95] See also *Dennis v Ministry of Defence* [2003] Env L.R.34: damages appropriate when contrary to public interest to prevent RAF flying Harrier jets from its base. This was justified as consistent with developing human rights case-law.
[96] Although it had increased in volume and noise beyond tolerable levels in subsequent years.

national and club events, thereby allowing the racing to continue in a limited form. By such means, and also by using their power to suspend the injunction to give the defendant the opportunity to remedy the nuisance, the courts recognise and balance the competing rights of the litigants.[97]

(2) Abatement

This is a form of self-help, by which claimants intervene themselves to stop the nuisance. Generally, the courts are reluctant to encourage such actions. Claimants who wish to take the law into their own hands must do so at their peril, and run the risk of countervailing claims for trespass and conversion. Generally, however, it is an acceptable response towards encroaching roots and branches, where it would make little sense to go to court.[98] For example, in *Delaware Mansions Ltd v Westminster City Council*,[99] discussed under private nuisance, the House of Lords accepted that the claimant company was entitled to recover the costs of remedying a continuing nuisance caused to his property by tree roots when the defendant council had refused its request that the tree be removed. Even in the face of such obvious nuisances, however, claimants proceed at their own risk and their actions must be no more than necessary to abate the nuisance. Lord Cooke also warned against imposing unreasonable burdens on local authorities to pay for remedial works and advised that "as a general proposition, I think that the defendant is entitled to notice and a reasonable opportunity of abatement before liability for remedial expenditure can arise."[1] The claimant should therefore take care not to enter his or her neighbour's land, and give notice if entry is necessary, except in an emergency. Any branches or roots which have been lopped off remain the neighbour's property and if they are kept, the claimant may be held liable for conversion (civil theft). Abatement, therefore, is a remedy of limited utility.

10–067

(3) Damages

All of the three heads of liability we have discussed in this chapter become actionable only on proof of damage.[2] Special damage must of course be proved for the individual to claim a remedy for public nuisance.

10–068

Personal injury

Public nuisance, as discussed above, protects the individual who, as a member of the public, has suffered particular damage due to the defendant's actions. It seems clear that any damages award covers personal injury, damage to property, loss of custom, and perhaps even particular inconvenience caused to the individual. Private nuisance and the rule in *Rylands v. Fletcher*, in contrast, are aimed specifically at protecting the interests of claimants with rights to land. They therefore award damages for the diminution in the value of the land, or lesser enjoyment of the use of land or its fixtures. On this basis, this would seem to exclude damages for personal injury.

10–069

[97] See S. Tromans (1982) 41 C.L.J. 87 at 93–95, who argues for greater use of damages awards.
[98] See *Lemmon v Webb* [1895] A.C. 1.
[99] [2002] 1 A.C. 321.
[1] *ibid.*, at 334.
[2] Although the courts are sometimes generous in finding damage for certain types of private nuisance, *e.g.* interference with certain easements.

Professor Newark, in an article cited by Lord Goff in *Cambridge Water* and *Hunter*, explained that the land merely provided the *setting* for the injury, and therefore there was no special reason for distinguishing personal injury caused by a nuisance from other cases of personal injury to which the ordinary rules of negligence apply.[3]

This view seems to be followed in the leading authorities at the moment, namely *Hunter v Canary Wharf Ltd*[4] and *Transco plc v Stockport MBC*,[5] although the issue was not strictly in point in either case. The majority in *Hunter* held that only those with an interest in land or exclusive possession could sue in private nuisance, and Lords Lloyd and Hoffmann held expressly that compensation should not be awarded for personal injury, as it represents harm to the person, not the land. This view was also taken by the House of Lords in *Transco*, despite mixed authority in the past where damages for personal injury had been awarded for breach of the rule in *Rylands v Fletcher*,[6] although not without challenge.[7] Lord Bingham, however, affirmed that "the claim cannot include a claim for death or personal injury, since such a claim does not relate to any right in or enjoyment of land."[8]

The logical consequence of their Lordships' decision is that damages are awarded to vindicate the rights of property-owning claimants to enjoy their land. Compensation is therefore awarded for the injury to the land, not the person, and the sum awarded should not differ, however many people reside on the land. Personal injury is therefore protected by the tort of negligence, not nuisance, and should not be confused with personal discomfort, which is related to the diminished utility of the land. *Bone v Seale*[9] has cited as an illustration of this distinction. Here, damages were awarded to compensate for the personal discomfort caused by smells from an adjacent pig farm. The award represented the diminished utility value of the land "suffering" from the smells. Such an award could be made even in the absence of evidence that the value of land had diminished, and irrespective of the number of people affected and any injury the smell may have caused them.

This is not entirely convincing. It is hard to persuade non-lawyers that damages are awarded not for their twitching nostrils, but for the "suffering" of the land on which they are standing. Equally, if such "suffering" cannot always be converted into market loss (*i.e.* diminution of value of the land), it is difficult to say on what basis such damages are awarded, if not on a personal basis. Lords Lloyd and Hoffmann suggest that the loss is one of "loss of amenity". This was recognised by the House of Lords in the contract law case of *Ruxley Electronics and Construction Ltd v Forsyth*.[10] In this case, Mr Forsyth had required a swimming pool of a certain depth, and this had not been provided, although this did not diminish the actual value of the pool. The House of Lords in *Ruxley* approved the trial judge's award of damages for loss of amenity, although Lord Mustill clearly awarded such damages on the basis that the consumer's subjective preference, expressed in the contract, had not been satisfied. It is questionable whether this case establishes a principle under which damages can be assessed

---

[3] (1949) 65 L.Q.R. 480 at 489.
[4] [1997] A.C. 677.
[5] [2003] 3 W.L.R. 1467.
[6] *Hale v Jennings* [1938] 1 All E.R. 579; *Shiffman v Order of the Hospital of St John of Jerusalem* [1936] 1 All E.R. 557 (although decided on negligence) and *Perry v Kendricks Transport Ltd* [1956] 1 W.L.R. 85 at 92.
[7] See *Read v Lyons* [1947] A.C. 156.
[8] See above at 1473. See also Lord Hoffmann at 1481.
[9] [1975] 1 All E.R. 787.
[10] [1996] A.C. 344.

independently of the personality of the occupants of land and indeed, its exact status in contract law remains uncertain.

Economic loss

In *Hunter*, Lord Hoffmann recognised that loss of profits was recoverable as consequential loss when it resulted from the claimant's inability to use the land for the purposes of his or her business.[11] Recovery of such losses has been accepted in a number of cases. For example, in *Andreae v Selfridge & Company Ltd*[12] the owner of a hotel was allowed to recover damages for the loss of custom suffered by her business due to noise and dust caused by the defendants' construction work. More recently, in *Jan de Nul (UK) Ltd v AXA Royale Belge S.A. (Formerly N.V. Royale Belge)*,[13] the Court of Appeal permitted the Hampshire Wildlife Trust to recover over £100,000 for an investigation into silting of feeding grounds at the head of an estuary. Although the report had indicated no long-term damage would occur, the court found that it had acted reasonably in commissioning such a report and the cost of the survey was consequential on physical interference with its property rights.

10–070

Damage to chattels

By chattels, we mean personal property which happens to be on the land. One would expect that if the courts are reluctant to award damages for personal injuries, they would be equally reluctant to award damages for loss of chattels. If you cannot recover for your own broken leg, it would seem incongruous if you could recover for the broken leg of your poodle. Certainly this is the view of Professor Newark in his much-cited article.[14] Unfortunately, this point is not dealt with in *Hunter*, except by Lord Hoffmann, who supports a continuing right to sue for damage to chattels and livestock in nuisance as consequential loss. There is clear authority in support of this position. In *Halsey v Esso Petroleum Co. Ltd*,[15] damage to laundry hanging in the garden was deemed actionable in private nuisance and under the rule in *Rylands v Fletcher*. Equally, damage to the paintwork of the plaintiff's car on the highway was held to be actionable in public nuisance and under the rule in *Rylands v Fletcher*.

Whilst the position seems difficult to justify, it may, perhaps, be explained if we consider the practical impact of not allowing recovery for damage to chattels. For example, a farmer complains that the defendant emits noxious fumes over his land. These fumes have ruined his crops and trees, and harmed the health of his livestock. If only damage to land is recoverable, the farmer will only be awarded damages for his crops and the trees.[16] Yet, these are simply alternative means of farming one's land, and why should the law draw an arbitrary distinction between the different modes of farming? This would certainly not appear to be consistent with the approach of the court in *St Helen's Smelting Co. v Tipping*.[17] It remains to be seen how this problem might be resolved in the future.

10–071

---

[11] [1997] A.C. 677 at 706.
[12] [1938] Ch. 1. See, also, Lawton J. in *British Celanese v Hunt* [1969] 1 W.L.R. 959.
[13] [2002] 1 Lloyd's Rep. 583.
[14] (1949) 65 L.Q.R. 480 at 490.
[15] [1961] 2 All E.R. 145.
[16] Crops and trees are, of course, treated as part of the land in question.
[17] (1865) 11 H.L.C. 642.

Remoteness

10–072   Damages under private nuisance, public nuisance and the rule in *Rylands v Fletcher* are all subject to the test set out in *The Wagon Mound (No.1)*,[18] namely that the defendant is only liable for damages of a type which can be reasonably foreseen. Reference should be made here to Ch. 6. Lord Reid, in *The Wagon Mound (No.2)*, held foreseeability to be an essential element in determining liability in both public and private nuisance: "It would not be right to discriminate between different cases of nuisance".[19] In *Cambridge Water*, Lord Goff clarified that the *Wagon Mound* test would apply to the rule in *Rylands v Fletcher*. The reader should therefore ignore Blackburn J.'s statement, in the case itself, that the defendant will be liable for all the natural consequences of the escape.

The Human Rights Act 1998

10–073   The case of *Marcic v Thames Water Utilities Ltd*[20] provides a useful illustration of the potential for the Act to supplement and change the law of nuisance, but also of the reluctance of the courts to overwhelm public bodies with excessive liability. Peter Marcic brought a claim against his statutory water and sewage undertaker, Thames Water Utilities Ltd (TWUL). He complained of TWUL's failure since 1992 to prevent persistent external flooding and back flow of foul water from its sewer system into his home at times of heavy rain.Although it was reasonably practicable for TWUL to prevent the flooding, it had refused to do so. Under its present scheme of priorities, there was no prospect of such works being undertaken in the foreseeable future. After 9 years, Marcic turned to law and brought this action for damage to his property in nuisance and under the 1998 Act.

   Although his claim in private nuisance was rejected at first instance as contrary to existing authority, Judge Havery Q.C. approved the claim under the Human Rights Act 1998 founded on infringement of the claimant's rights to private and family life (under Art. 8) and peaceful enjoyment of his possessions (Art. 1 of Protocol 1).[21] TWUL was a public authority under s.6 of the Act, and the case-law of the European Court of Human Rights supported use of Art. 8 and Art. 1 of Protocol 1 in this context.[22] Although both Art. 8 and Art. 1 of Protocol 1 are qualified rights—the court must consider "the protection of the rights and freedoms of others"[23] and "the public

---

[18] *Overseas Tankship (UK) Ltd v Morts Dock and Engineering Co. Ltd* [1961] A.C. 388 at 427.
[19] *The Wagon Mound (No.2) (Overseas Tankship (UK) Ltd v Miller Steamship Co. Pty)* [1967] 1 A.C. 617 at 640.
[20] [2003] 3 W.L.R. 1603 (HL); [2002] Q.B. 929 (CA).
[21] Where there is a demonstrable and significant fall in the value of the property, without proper compensation, this amounted to a partial expropriation: see *S v France* (1990) 65 D.R. 250 at 261. See D Anderson [1999] E.H.R.L.R. 543.
[22] The court relying on *Baggs v UK* (1987) 9 E.H.R.R. 235, (a case of nuisance by noise from Heathrow airport affecting the applicant's enjoyment of his home); *S v France* (1990) 65 D.R. 250 (effect of nuclear power station near home); *Guerra v Italy* (1998) 26 E.H.R.R. 357 (toxic emissions from factory); *López Ostra v Spain* (1994) 20 E.H.R.R. 277 (fumes and smells from waste treatment plant).
[23] Art. 8, para.2: "except such as is in accordance with the law and is necessary in a democratic society in the interests of national security, public safety or the economic well-being of the country, for the prevention of disorder or crime, for the protection of health or morals, or for the protection of the rights and freedoms of others."

interest"[24]—in view of the frequent flooding of Marcic's property and TWUL's unsatisfactory system of prioritisation, the judge supported Marcic's claim under the Act.

The Court of Appeal in supporting Marcic's claim in private nuisance rendered any claim under the Act unnecessary. Section 8(3) of the Act provides that "No award of damages is to be made unless, taking account of all the circumstances of the case, including—(a) any other relief or remedy granted, or order made, in relation to the act in question (by that or any other court) . . . the court is satisfied that the award is necessary to afford just satisfaction to the person in whose favour it is made." Nevertheless, the Court of Appeal supported the reasoning of the first instance judge. The court suggested that even if the court had decided that a fair balance had been struck between the competing interests of Marcic and TWUL's other customers, the defendant might, in any event, be required to pay compensation to ensure that one person did not bear an unreasonable burden.[25]

The Court of Appeal ruling in *Marcic* was applied by Buckley J. in *Dennis v Ministry of Defence*.[26] This involved a claim for compensation by Mr and Mrs Dennis whose property was adjacent to an RAF base and who had suffered deafening noise due to the flying of Harrier jets over their land. Although the court again found a nuisance at common law, it held that the noise and the resultant reduction in the value of the estate did amount to a breach of the Dennis's rights under Article 8 and Article 1 of Protocol 1, although any breach would be balanced by the state's interest in national security and the cost and inconvenience of uprooting a military base. Nevertheless, the court saw no reason why the Dennis's should bear the cost of this disturbance alone and that damages of £950,000 would have been payable under the Act to cover the period until 2012 when Harrier training was expected to be phased out. This sum was thus awarded for common law nuisance.

When *Marcic* reached the House of Lords, the award in *Dennis* of £950,000 and the potential liability of Thames Water for £1 billion if it compensated every customer in Marcic's position[27] did not go unnoticed. Their Lordships rejected liability either at common law or under the Act. Where Parliament had established an elaborate scheme of regulation in which an independent regulator sought to balance the competing interests of the parties involved, liability would not be imposed. It would be inconsistent with the statutory scheme and, given the need to balance competing interests and the availability of judicial review, this scheme was compatible with Art. 8 and Art. 1 of Protocol 1 of the Convention. Following the European Court of Human Rights decision in *Hatton v United Kingdom*,[28] which confirmed the margin of appreciation given to States in matters of general policy, the House found that the scheme did strike a reasonable balance: "Parliament acted well within its bounds as policy maker."[29] The reluctance of the House to intervene on the basis of the Human

[24] Art. 1, Protocol 1.
[25] See *S v France* (1990) 65 D.R. 250 at 263 and *James v United Kingdom* (1986) 8 E.H.R.R. 123, para 54: "under the legal systems of the contracting states, the taking of property in the public interest without payment of compensation is treated as justifiable only in exceptional circumstances."
[26] [2003] Env L.R.34.
[27] In the financial year 1999–2000, the profits of the whole group (of which TWUL formed only a part) amounted to only £344 million after tax.
[28] Application No. 36022/97, (2003) 37 E.H.R.R. 28.
[29] See above at 1616.

Rights Act 1998 is particularly notable in view of its criticism of the treatment of Mr Marcic. Such concerns, however, did not persuade the House of Lords to support his claim.[30]

Conclusion

10–074   The House of Lords' decisions in *Hunter v Canary Wharf Ltd*,[31] *Cambridge Water Co. v Eastern Counties Leather plc*[32] and *Transco plc v Stockport MBC*[33] cast new light on the nature of the torts of private nuisance and *Rylands v Fletcher* liability. In so doing, their Lordships clearly distinguish these torts from the tort of negligence, examined earlier in this book, although in practice the line is not so clear. Nevertheless, these decisions are highly significant in indicating the future development of these torts, and their importance should not be underestimated. In contrast, public nuisance has received minimal attention, and should be noted primarily in connection with obstruction of the highway.

In the next chapter, we examine the tort of trespass in its many forms: trespass to the person, goods and land. In considering trespass to land, readers should note our earlier discussion of its relationship with private nuisance.

---

[30] Although Lord Hoffmann notes that Thames Water had agreed with the Regulator in 2002 to free 250 properties (including that of Marcic) from the risk of external flooding.
[31] [1997] A.C. 677.
[32] [1994] 2 A.C. 264.
[33] [2003] 3 W.L.R. 1467.

Chapter 11

TRESPASS

Introduction

The tort of trespass is one of the oldest torts in English law. In modern law, it takes **11–001** three forms—trespass to the person, to land and to goods. All three torts have the same characteristics: they must be committed intentionally, cause direct and immediate harm and are actionable *per se*, *i.e.* without proof of damage. Although these three criteria have not always been followed—for example in the past, the courts have been willing to impose liability for trespass to the person where the tort has been committed negligently[1]—they are generally followed today. They serve to distinguish trespass from other actions, such as negligence and nuisance, which were traditionally called "actions on the case" and deal with indirect harm.

It is important to recognise that the tort of trespass operates in a different manner from torts such as nuisance and negligence. These torts, which we have already looked at, compensate the claimant for harm incurred unintentionally or indirectly, and act as a form of loss-spreading. The aim of trespass, however, is to vindicate the claimant's right to be free from interference either to his or her person, property or goods. On this basis, the torts are actionable *per se*. Damage is not the trigger for compensation. The wrongful actions of the defendant in interfering with a recognised legal interest possessed by the claimant trigger compensation. Of course, in awarding damages the courts will examine whether any loss or damage has been suffered. They will generally only award nominal damages in trespass to land or goods if no damage exists, but the existence of aggravated and exemplary damages in these fields highlights the willingness of the courts to acknowledge the importance of protecting these interests in modern society.

The tort of trespass does, however, have a close connection with other areas of law. Trespass to the person, in dealing with interference with the person in terms of personal integrity and freedom of movement, bears a close relationship with criminal law and the offences found in the Offences against the Person Act 1861. Trespass to land, in contrast, deals with interference with the claimant's possession of land and therefore bears a close relationship with the tort of private nuisance, discussed in the previous chapter. Trespass to goods is also very closely connected to the tort of conversion. The significance of this will be discussed below.

[1] See *Weaver v Ward* (1617) Hob. 134 and *Scott v Shepherd* (1773) 2 W. Bl. 892.

This chapter will concentrate on trespass to the person and trespass to land. Trespass to goods will be dealt with briefly at the end of the chapter.

TRESPASS TO THE PERSON

11–002 As stated above, trespass to the person protects the claimant against interference with his or her person. This may be attempted by means of assault, battery or false imprisonment. These torts possess the classic "trespass" characteristics in that they must be committed intentionally, by direct and immediate actions and are actionable without proof of damage.[2] To the reader, these torts are perhaps better recognised as criminal offences and indeed, the defendant will normally face criminal, rather than civil, charges for such actions. There are a number of reasons for this. First of all, the police will usually be called in, which makes criminal proceedings more likely. Secondly, the claimant may not wish the pressure of further civil proceedings brought at his or her own instigation when the defendant may not have the means to satisfy judgment. Thirdly, the criminal courts now possess at least some means of awarding compensation to a victim of crime,[3] and victims may also recover under the Criminal Injuries Compensation Scheme[4] which is a national fund, granting compensation for personal injury caused by crimes of violence. The Scheme will award compensation to any person who has sustained personal injury directly attributable to a crime of violence or to the apprehension of an offender or the prevention of an offence. Such compensation is unlikely to be as high as that awarded in a successful tort action, but is undoubtedly an easier option for the victim.

A tort action will generally be motivated by more than just a desire for compensation. It may be pursued to highlight a refusal of the Director of Public Prosecutions to bring a criminal prosecution[5] or in the face of an unsuccessful prosecution. As the burden of proof is lower in the civil courts, the claimant may succeed in proving his or her case on the balance of probabilities where the prosecutor has failed to prove the allegations in a criminal court beyond reasonable doubt. In the American case concerning O.J. Simpson, for example, the defendant, an ex-football star and celebrity, was found not guilty of the murder of his ex-wife and her lover, but was nevertheless subsequently found liable to pay damages by a civil court. A tort action may also be brought to highlight abuse of power by public bodies such as the police, and a successful claimant may have his or her point reinforced by an award of exemplary damages.[6] In seeking to gain compensation where criminal proceedings have failed, litigants should note the limitations in sections 44 and 45 of the Offences against the Person Act 1861.[7] These sections relate to assault and battery charges heard in the magistrates' courts.[8] Section 45 provides that where a summary hearing brought by or

---

[2] See F.A. Trindade (1982) 2 O.J.L.S. 211.
[3] See Powers of the Criminal Courts (Sentencing) Act 2000, ss.130–134.
[4] See generally the Criminal Injuries Compensation Act 1995.
[5] See, *e.g.* Halford v Brookes [1991] 1 W.L.R. 428.
[6] See, *e.g.* the guidelines given by Lord Woolf in *Thompson v Commissioner of Police of Metropolis* [1998] Q.B. 498.
[7] The Law Commission Report No. 218, *Criminal law: Legislating the criminal code: Offences against the person and general principles* (1993) recommended the repeal of these sections.
[8] Note that common assault and battery are summary offences by virtue of the Criminal Justice Act 1988, s.39.

on behalf of the party aggrieved has been held and has ended, after a hearing on the merits, either with a certificate of dismissal,[9] or with the accused being convicted and fined or imprisoned, civil proceedings for the same cause will be barred.[10] As most criminal offences, save the most serious, are tried in the magistrates' court, this in practice limits the situations in which the victim can sue for compensation in tort.

Most cases are therefore decided by the criminal courts and for this reason, the civil courts will often reason by analogy to criminal cases. We shall also use criminal cases, where appropriate, to illustrate the likely treatment of a tort claim. Criminal law authorities, however, should be treated with caution. They are not authority in the law of tort and can therefore only be treated as guidance. Proper regard must be had to the differing concerns of criminal law (which are largely punitive) and trespass to the person (which protects the personal integrity and right to self-determination of the claimant). We shall examine battery, assault and false imprisonment in turn.

Battery

This has a number of components. Force must be applied intentionally by immediate   **11–003**
and direct means to another individual. This can vary from the most minor contact with the claimant or his or her clothing, such as an unwanted peck on the cheek, to a violent blow in the chest. Because the tort is actionable without proof of damage, both types of battery render the defendant liable to pay damages. The requirements of battery are examined below.

(1) It must be intentional

This means that the act of force must be *voluntary*. For example, Y has not committed   **11–004**
a battery if X grasps his arm and pulls it to strike Z. Intention relates *only* to the action of the defendant. It is not necessary that the defendant intends the consequences of his or her actions. On this basis, the defendant will be liable for all the consequences flowing from the tort, whether or not they are foreseeable.[11] Equally, if I intend to hit A and instead hit B, I commit a battery against B.[12] This rule, which is essentially one of convenience, has been explained as the concept of "transferred intent".

The tort may be committed even if the original action was unintentional, if the defendant at some point intends to apply force. For example, in *Fagan v Metropolitan Police Commissioner*,[13] the defendant unintentionally stopped his car on a policeman's foot. At this stage, no tort had been committed. However, by deliberately failing to move until the police officer had shouted "Get off my foot" several times, he committed a battery. It seems likely that, as in criminal law, recklessness in the use of force is sufficient to establish intent in battery.[14]

[9] This cannot be given when the defendant has pleaded guilty: *Ellis v Burton* [1975] 1 W.L.R. 386.
[10] See *Wong v Parkside Health NHS Trust* [2003] 3 All E.R. 932 at 937, CA. The question focuses on the conduct in question, for example an assault. The courts will not allow the claimant to circumvent s.45 by framing the claim under a different cause of action *e.g.* under the rule in *Wilkinson v Downton*. See also *Masper v Brown* (1876) 1 C.P.D. 97.
[11] See *Williams v Humphrey*, *The Times*, February 20, 1975 where the defendant was liable for deliberately pushing a guest in his swimming pool, although he clearly did not intend to cripple the plaintiff, who broke his ankle and foot.
[12] *James v Campbell* (1832) 5 C. & P. 372; 172 E.R. 1015, and *Bici v Ministry of Defence, The Times*, June 11, 2004.
[13] [1969] 1 Q.B. 439.
[14] *R. v Venna* [1976] Q.B. 421. Subjective recklessness will suffice: see *R. v Savage* [1992] 1 A.C. 699, HL.

(2) It must be direct

11–005   It is a basic requirement of any trespass that the injury must be direct. If the injury is indirect, the claimant must find another basis for recovery. However, this requirement has been interpreted flexibly. In the eighteenth century case of *Scott v Shepherd*,[15] for example, the defendant was found liable for battery when he had thrown a lighted squib into a market place. This was despite the fact that the squib had been thrown on by two stallholders, to protect themselves and their wares, before it had exploded in the face of Scott. The majority of the court found the battery to be sufficiently direct. Equally, in *DPP v K*,[16] the force was considered sufficiently immediate and direct where a schoolboy had poured some concentrated sulphuric acid, stolen from a chemistry lesson, into a hand-dryer which was later used by another pupil with horrific results. The court held that the boy had known full well that he had created a dangerous situation, but had nevertheless taken the risk of injury to another. It was no excuse that he had panicked and had intended to remove the acid as soon as he was able.

(3) Immediate force

11–006   The tort of battery applies to any form of bodily contact. This causes a potential problem. If applied literally, it would cover all forms of contact. For example, A would commit a battery by tapping B on the shoulder to get his attention. It would clearly be a nonsense if an actionable battery was committed in such circumstances, and the law would, in effect, provide a charter for vexatious litigants to sue. Whilst this is common sense, the courts have experienced difficulties in finding a theoretical basis on which to draw a line between actionable batteries and ordinary social contact. Lord Holt C.J.'s comments in *Cole v Turner*[17] have been cited, where his Lordship held that "the least touching of another in anger is a battery". On this basis, the Court of Appeal in *Wilson v Pringle*[18] held that battery must be committed with "hostile" intent. On the facts of the case, a boy had suffered serious injury due to the antics of a fellow pupil. The defence alleged that the defendant had merely pulled the schoolbag off the schoolboy's shoulder, which had led him to fall on the ground and injure himself. The court held that liability depended on whether the pupil's actions had been "hostile" and not simply a schoolboy prank. It can be questioned whether this is helpful. What is hostile to one person may seem quite the opposite to another. For example, should an over-enthusiastic slap on the back or a surgeon's mistaken amputation of a leg be regarded as non-hostile and therefore not a battery? Even if an objective interpretation is adopted, it simply seems to mean that the reasonable person would view the action as contrary to the ordinary rules of social conduct. If this is so, then the view of Robert Goff L.J. in *Collins v Wilcock*[19] is preferable. His Lordship took the entirely sensible view that instead of adopting complicated legal rules based on implied consent to the battery, or hostile intent, the law should just exclude liability for conduct generally acceptable in the ordinary conduct of daily life—a view which he reiterated in *Re F*.[20]:

[15] (1773) 2 W. Bl. 892.
[16] [1990] 1 W.L.R. 1067. See also *Haystead v Chief Constable of Derbyshire* [2000] 3 All E.R. 890, QBD.
[17] (1704) 6 Mod. Rep. 149.
[18] [1987] Q.B. 237.
[19] [1984] 1 W.L.R. 1172. See also Lord Goff in *Re F*. [1990] 2 A.C. 1.
[20] [1990] 2 A.C. 1 at 72–73.

"... a broader exception has been created to allow for the exigencies of everyday life: jostling in a street or some other crowded place, social contact at parties and such like. This exception has been said to be founded on implied consent, since those who go about in public places, or go to parties, may be taken to have impliedly consented to bodily contact of this kind. Today this rationalization can be regarded as artificial: and, in particular, it is difficult to impute consent to those who, by reason of their youth or mental disorder, are unable to give their consent. For this reason I consider it more appropriate to regard such cases as falling within a general exception embracing all physical contact which is generally acceptable in the ordinary conduct of everyday life."

Assault

This tort protects the claimant in *fear* of battery. Where the defendant's actions cause the claimant reasonably to apprehend the direct and immediate infliction of force on him or her, the tort is committed. It is important to stress first of all that this is distinct from the popular meaning of "assault", which in tort equates with the tort of battery. So, if I point a gun at you, I have only committed an assault. It is irrelevant that the gun is unloaded—you do not know that, and have every reason to apprehend battery.[21] Only when I shoot the gun and hit you have I committed a battery. If my aim is poor and I miss, only an assault has been committed. **11–007**

The requirements of assault are as follows:

(1) Reasonable apprehension of harm

The key to assault is the reasonable apprehension of harm. If I creep up and strike you from behind without your knowledge, I have only committed a battery. It is only assault if you are aware of my approach. Equally, if you are lucky enough to be saved from physical harm by the intervention of a third party, or if I change my mind, I have only committed an assault. In *Stephens v Myers*,[22] for example, the plaintiff was threatened with violence whilst attempting to expel the defendant from a parish meeting. The defendant had approached the plaintiff threatening violence, but, due to the intervention of the churchwarden, was liable only for assault. Passive obstruction, however, such as that seen in *Innes v Wylie*,[23] where a policeman stopped the plaintiff from entering a room, will not amount to assault. If the human obstruction is passive, like a door or a wall preventing entry, the claimant has no reason to anticipate the direct and immediate infliction of force, so the defendant cannot be liable. The test of reasonable apprehension is an objective one. It is irrelevant whether the particular claimant was *actually* in fear, or could have defended himself or herself successfully. **11–008**

(2) It must be intentional

This is a basic requirement of the tort and here signifies that the defendant intended the claimant to apprehend reasonable force would be used or was reckless as to the consequences of his or her actions.[24] **11–009**

---

[21] *R. v St George* (1840) 9 C. & P. 483 at 493. See also *Logdon v DPP* (unreported, 1976).
[22] (1840) 4 C. & P. 349.
[23] (1844) 1 C. & K. 257 at 263. Contrast *Chief Constable of Thames Valley Police v Hepburn, The Times*, December 19, 2002, CA.
[24] *R. v Venna* [1976] Q.B. 421.

(3) It must be immediate and direct

11–010   This is really part of the test of reasonable apprehension. If the claimant can see that the defendant is not in a position to inflict immediate and direct harm on the claimant, then the claimant has nothing to fear and so the defendant is not liable for assault. Therefore, if I threaten you with violence as I am passing you in a train, I have not committed assault. More controversially, in *Thomas v National Union of Miners (South Wales Area)*,[25] striking miners, who hurled insults at working miners who had been transported into work in vehicles, were not held liable for assault, because the vehicles had been protected by a police cordon.

10–011   **Can words amount to an assault?:**   There is old authority that words by themselves cannot amount to an assault.[26] This may now be challenged in the light of the House of Lords case of *R. v Ireland*.[27] Here, three women had been harassed by Ireland. He was alleged to have made repeated telephone calls to them, generally at night, during which he remained silent. The women suffered psychiatric illness as a result. The House of Lords rejected the proposition that an assault could never be committed by words as unrealistic and indefensible. Liability would in fact depend on whether the claimant, in the circumstances before the court, reasonably believed that the oral threat could be carried out in the sufficiently near future to qualify as an immediate threat of personal violence. On the facts, the court was prepared to accept that silence would be capable of giving rise to such fears. This seems sensible and it is to be hoped that although the decision was made in criminal law, it will be applied by analogy to tort law. Whilst the old saying goes that "sticks and stones may break my bones, but words will never hurt me", this seems to require an unduly high level of courage by the reasonable person. Few amongst us would not experience fear if telephoned by a stalker. As recognised by the court in *R. v Ireland*, whilst the recipient of the call may have no knowledge of the stalker's whereabouts, the fear lies with the knowledge that the stalker, in contrast, knows exactly where the recipient is at the time of the call.

    Conversely, it has long been accepted that words may *negative* an assault. In the classic case of *Tuberville v Savage*,[28] the defendant placed his hand on his sword and stated that "If it were not assize time, I would not take such language from you". It was assize time and so, in reality, the defendant was stating that he did not intend to strike the plaintiff. This must be distinguished from a conditional threat, where the claimant is merely given an option to avoid violence. It was no excuse for the highwayman to claim that his victims had a viable alternative option when he stated "stand and deliver, your money or your life!" On this basis, in *Read v Coker*,[29] the defendant was liable for assault when he and his servants threatened to break the plaintiff's neck unless he left the defendant's workshop.

False imprisonment

11–012   This tort is concerned with the claimant's right to freedom of movement. A complete restriction of this freedom, unless it is expressly or impliedly authorised by the law, will render the defendant liable. It is necessary to exclude conduct expressly or impliedly

---

[25] [1986] Ch. 20 at 65.
[26] See *Mead's v Belt's Case* (1823) 1 Lew. C.C. 184: "no words or singing are equivalent to an assault".
[27] [1998] A.C. 147.
[28] (1669) 1 Mod. Rep. 3.
[29] (1853) 13 C.B. 850.

authorised by the law from this tort in view of the custodial powers of the state and the powers of the police force, provided, of course, these bodies act within the powers given them by law. It is no excuse that the defendant had wrongfully assumed in good faith that he had a legal right to detain the claimant.[30] In this sense, false imprisonment is a strict liability tort. It is not the conduct of the defendant which is judged, but the injury to the claimant. "False" simply means wrongful. Equally, "imprisonment" does not require the defendant to put the claimant in prison, but will extend to any actions which deprive the claimant of his or her freedom of movement. It should be noted that it need not be shown that force has been used.

One question which has arisen is this: where A has given orders to B to restrain C, is A or B liable for false imprisonment? Generally, the actor (here B) will be liable, unless B exercises no discretion in the matter and is forced to obey the instructions of A. An example of this may be found in *Austin v Dowling*.[31] Here, a police inspector had refused to take the responsibility for arresting the plaintiff on a charge made by the defendant's wife, but finally did arrest the plaintiff when the defendant signed the charge sheet. It was held that the defendant was liable for false imprisonment. In modern times, however, the courts have taken the view that the police, as professionals, are expected to exercise their own judgment and not simply follow the instructions of others. This view formed part of the reasoning of the Court of Appeal in *Davidson v Chief Constable of North Wales and Another*,[32] where a store detective had given evidence to the police which led to the arrest of Davidson for shoplifting. Davidson and a friend were detained by the police for two hours before it became clear that the store detective's suspicions were unfounded. Davidson sued the store detective for false imprisonment. The Court of Appeal held that no action lay against the store detective where she had merely given information to the police, who could act as they saw fit. Only if the detective had been the instigator, promoter and active inciter of the action would the detective be liable.

The requirements of false imprisonment are examined below:

(1) A complete restriction of the claimant's freedom of movement

This requirement does not refer simply to putting the claimant in prison, but to any **11–013** actions which restrict the claimant's freedom of movement in every direction. It is not satisfied, however, if the claimant is able to move in one direction. For example, in *Bird v Jones*,[33] the plaintiff had insisted on passing along the public footway on Hammersmith Bridge in London, which the defendants had partially enclosed without due permission. The plaintiff had climbed over a fence erected by the defendants to close off the footway on one side of the bridge, but was prevented from moving along the footway by the defendants. He was told that he might go back and use the public footway on the other side of the bridge, but the plaintiff would not do so. The court held that the defendants were not liable for false imprisonment. They had not imposed a *complete* restriction on the plaintiff's freedom of movement.

---

[30] See *R v Governor of Brockhill Prison, ex p Evans (No. 2)* [2001] A.C. 19 (prison governor liable for unauthorised detention of prisoner when his sentence (calculated by him on the law as then understood) was subsequently found to be incorrect). See P. Cane (2001) 117 L.Q.R. 5. Contrast *Quinland v Governor of Swaleside Prison* [2003] Q.B. 306, CA (sentence miscalculated by judge, but detention by prison governor under warrant of commitment was legally justified until warrant set aside).
[31] (1870) L.R. 5 C.P. 534.
[32] [1994] 2 All E.R. 597, CA.
[33] (1845) 7 Q.B. 742.

It is therefore a question of fact. If the claimant is able to return in the same direction in which he or she came, or is given reasonable means of escape, the defendant will not be liable. The means of escape must be reasonable—a rope left by the window of a seven storey building will clearly not suffice. The question of confinement divided the House of Lords, however, in *R. v Bournewood Community and Mental Health NHS Trust, ex p. L.*[34] The majority found that a mentally disordered patient who had been placed voluntarily in an unlocked ward and showed no desire to leave had not been detained, despite the fact that the hospital gave evidence that he had been sedated and would have been detained compulsorily had he sought to leave. One must have sympathy with the view of Lord Steyn dissenting that, "The suggestion that L was free to go is a fairy tale."[35]

11–014   It is a matter of contention whether a reasonable means of escape exists when the defendant imposes conditions on the manner in which visitors leave his or her premises. There is authority that, provided the conditions are reasonable, the defendant is not liable if he or she refuses to allow the claimant to leave until these conditions are satisfied. In *Robinson v Balmain Ferry Co. Ltd*,[36] for example, the plaintiff had contracted to enter the defendants' wharf to catch a ferry boat to cross the river. For reasons of efficiency, the fee of one penny was paid on one side of the river, on entering and exiting the wharf. Having a 20 minute wait for the next boat, the plaintiff changed his mind and tried to exit the wharf. He refused to pay the stipulated charge of one penny to leave the wharf, as required by a notice above the turnstile. The defendants refused to let him leave until the charge was paid. In an action for false imprisonment, the Privy Council held that a penny charge was a reasonable condition for leaving by a route different from the one stipulated in the contract: "There is no law requiring the defendants to make the exit from their premises gratuitous to people who come there upon a definite contract which involves their leaving the wharf by another way".[37]

This approach was taken a step further by the House of Lords' decision five years later in *Herd v Weardale Steel, Coal and Coke Co. Ltd*.[38] Here, a miner had refused to do certain work, on the basis that it was dangerous, and had demanded to be taken to the surface before the end of his shift. His employer refused. Their Lordships held that the employer was not liable for false imprisonment. The miner had voluntarily entered the mine under a contract of employment, and was deemed to have impliedly consented that he would not be brought to the surface until the end of the shift.

These cases involve a worrying invasion of the civil liberties of those involved.[39] However, there is clearly a line to be drawn. As Viscount Haldane points out in *Herd*, a claimant cannot expect to be able to stop an express train because he or she now wishes to get off the train. The traveller consents to a restriction on his or her freedom of movement for the duration of the journey. If this consent is withdrawn, logically he or she should be permitted to alight at the first reasonable opportunity, which will usually be the next designated stop. It does not entail a right to stop the train

---

[34] [1999] 1 A.C. 458.
[35] *ibid.*, at 495.
[36] [1910] A.C. 295, PC.
[37] *ibid.*, at 299.
[38] [1915] A.C. 67.
[39] See generally K.F. Tan (1981) 44 M.L.R. 166.

immediately. On this basis, the miner in *Herd* quite rightly limited his claim for false imprisonment to the period during which the lift was available to take him out of the mine. It is when the defendant refuses to allow the claimant to leave in such circumstances that a claim for false imprisonment should lie.

Robinson may, however, be defended on the basis that the plaintiff's restraint was not complete, as he could have crossed the river (subject to a query as to whether this is reasonable). *Herd* is more difficult to defend. It is difficult to see the decision as anything but a harsh ruling in favour of an employer's rights over his employees. It is scarcely legitimate to suggest imprisonment as a reasonable response to the employee's breach of contract. A better explanation of *Herd* (and certainly one more palatable to modern industrial relations) is to view it as an omission case. Trespass is concerned with intentional, immediate and direct *actions*, not omissions, and therefore the employee had suffered no trespass to his person. It is questionable, however, whether this should apply where the defendant is, albeit lawfully, responsible for the detention of the claimant in the first place. It is hoped that a modern court would accept that where the claimant has withdrawn consent to the restriction on his or her freedom, he or she should be released at the earliest reasonable opportunity.

It is unnecessary to show the claimant knew of the imprisonment

Here the point is simply that the tort protects the claimant's freedom of movement, because it is a recognised interest the legal system wishes to protect. Proof of damage is not required, and so it is not necessary that the claimant has *suffered* from the knowledge of his or her false imprisonment. *Grainger v Hill*[40] established that the tort exists even if the claimant is too ill to move, and in *Meering's case*,[41] the Court of Appeal held that the tort can be committed even where the claimant does not know that he or she is being detained. In this case, the plaintiff had been suspected of stealing from his employer, the defendants, and so he had been asked to accompany two of his employer's private police force to the company's office. He had agreed and waited as instructed in the waiting room. Unknown to the plaintiff, the two policemen remained nearby and had been instructed not to let him leave the waiting room until the Metropolitan Police arrived. He later sued for false imprisonment. The court held that the tort had been committed as soon as the defendant was under the control of the defendants' police. Atkin L.J. stated the legal position:

11–015

> "It appears to me that a person could be imprisoned without his knowing it. I think a person can be imprisoned while he is asleep, while he is in a state of drunkenness, while he is unconscious, and while he is a lunatic . . . Of course the damages might be diminished and would be affected by the question whether he was conscious of it or not." [42]

This is a strong statement, indicating the courts' disapproval of any unjustified and complete restriction on the claimant's freedom of movement.[43] As Lord Griffiths

---

[40] (1838) 4 Bing. N.C. 212.
[41] *Meering v Grahame-White Aviation Co. Ltd* (1920) 122 L.T. 44.
[42] *ibid.*, at 53.
[43] There is authority to the contrary in *Herring v Boyle* (1834) 1 Cr. M. & R. 377 which was not cited in *Meering*. This was criticised, however, by Lord Griffiths in *Murray v Ministry of Defence* below at 701.

commented in *Murray v Ministry of Defence*[44]: ". . . the law attaches supreme importance to the liberty of the individual and if he suffers a wrongful interference with that liberty it should remain actionable even without proof of special damage".

(2) Without legal authorisation

11–016 *The burden of proof lies on the defendant* to justify the lawfulness of the arrest and the claimant is only required to show that he or she has been denied freedom of movement. On this basis, this requirement should be treated as a defence to be established by the defendant and will be so treated in a later section, below. Again, we can see that the rule seeks to protect the civil liberties of the claimant.

THE RULE IN *WILKINSON V DOWNTON*

11–017 In all three torts above, the three characteristics of a trespass action are apparent: *intentional* acts which *directly* harm the claimant, which are actionable *without proof of harm*. They do not include intentional harm which has been *indirectly* caused. This gap is filled by the so-called rule in *Wilkinson v Downton*. Like the rule in *Rylands v Fletcher* seen in the previous chapter, the rule is named after its leading case, where the relevant legal principles were set out. In *Wilkinson v Downton*[45] the defendant falsely told the plaintiff that her husband had been involved in an accident in which he had been seriously injured. The defendant later claimed that it had been a practical joke, but the shock suffered by the plaintiff as a result led her to suffer weeks of illness. She sued the defendant for damages. His actions had been intentional, but the harm had been indirect. Nevertheless, Wright J. held that where the defendant had wilfully undertaken an act calculated to cause physical harm to the plaintiff, there was a good cause of action. It is clear, however, that, unlike trespass, harm must be proved.

The case was applied by the Court of Appeal in *Janvier v Sweeney*.[46] In this case, a private detective had pretended to be a police officer, and, in order to obtain access to her employer's correspondence, had threatened the plaintiff that she was in danger of arrest for association with a German spy (her fiancé was German). The plaintiff suffered psychiatric illness as a result, and was allowed to recover damages under the rule in *Wilkinson v Downton*.

However, despite such a rapid start, and the potential breadth of the rule, it has not been much relied upon by the courts, due to the increasing role of the tort of negligence in recent times. Yet, it was resurrected by the Court of Appeal in the 1993 case of *Khorasandjian v Bush*[47] to deal with the problem of harassment. In the absence of a tort of harassment,[48] the court resorted to existing tortious actions (private nuisance and the rule in *Wilkinson v Downton*) to protect a young woman who had been suffering from a campaign of harassment undertaken by a former boyfriend. The

---

[44] [1988] 1 W.L.R. 692 at 703 (although the comment was *obiter*). See also Sedley L.J. in *Chief Constable of Thames Valley Police v Hepburn The Times*, December 19, 2002, CA.
[45] [1897] 2 Q.B. 57.
[46] [1919] 2 K.B. 316.
[47] [1993] Q.B. 727.
[48] *Patel v Patel* [1988] 2 F.L.R. 179.

rule was relied upon by the court to support the grant of an injunction against the defendant for wilful actions calculated to cause physical harm to the plaintiff. But one problem existed. In both *Wilkinson* and *Janvier*, the plaintiffs had suffered physical or psychiatric injury. In contrast, in *Khorasandjian*, the plaintiff had merely suffered from stress. Nevertheless, Dillon L.J. took a broad approach. His Lordship held that there was "an obvious risk that the cumulative effect of continued and unrestrained further harassment such as she has undergone would cause [psychiatric] illness",[49] which would suffice for a *quia timet* injunction (an injunction given to prevent an apprehended tort).

The courts have subsequently disapproved of such a broad approach. Harassment is now dealt with specifically by means of the Protection from Harassment Act 1997 (see below). In *Hunter v Canary Wharf*,[50] the House of Lords found that, in view of the Act, the decision in *Khorasandjian* granting the plaintiff a remedy in private nuisance should be overruled. Whilst their Lordships did not overturn the alternative ground for the decision based on the rule in *Wilkinson v Downton*, Lord Hoffmann in the recent decision in *Wainwright v Home Office*[51] favoured a narrower interpretation of the law. Whilst expressly questioning the continued need for this tort, he was unwilling to see it extended beyond claims for indirectly inflicted physical and recognised psychiatric injury. Both he and Lord Scott expressed concern that to do so would encourage unwarranted litigation: "In institutions and workplaces all over the country, people constantly do and say things with the intention of causing distress and humiliation to others. This shows lack of consideration and appalling manners but I am not sure that the right way to deal with it is always by litigation."[52] The view of the court was clearly that, in view of the expansion of the tort of negligence, this tort was effectively defunct.

The 1997 Act will be examined later in this chapter.

TRESPASS TO THE PERSON: DEFENCES

Defences generally are dealt with in Ch. 14. Here, we highlight the defences which are of particular importance in actions for trespass to the person.   **11–018**

(1) Consent

This is an obvious defence. If I expressly consent to contact or implicitly lead the defendant to believe that I am consenting, I cannot later sue the defendant. It would be highly inconvenient if no such rule existed. On this basis, hospitals can ensure that they commit no torts against patients whilst operating by asking them to sign consent forms. Equally, a patient who presents his or her arm for an injection is clearly consenting to the infliction of immediate and direct force on their person. Team sports similarly rely on the ability of the individual to consent to the rough and tumble which may ensue (but not, of course, to a violent blow by an opposing team member contrary to the rules of the game). In this way, the self-determination of the individual is protected.   **11–019**

[49] See above at 736.
[50] [1997] A.C. 677.
[51] [2003] 3 W.L.R. 1137, HL. See also *Wong v Parkside Health NHS Trust* [2003] 3 All E.R. 932, CA.
[52] *ibid.*, at 1149.

The consent must, of course, be real and not induced by fraud, misrepresentation or duress. So, in *R. v Williams*,[53] the defendant, a singing tutor, was liable in battery for sexually assaulting a naive plaintiff who had been falsely informed that this would improve her voice. The fraud must go to the very nature and quality of the act or to the identity of the assailant.[54] Fraud as to the effect and consequences of the act is not deemed sufficient to nullify consent,[55] although it is submitted that this may lead to unduly harsh results in practice.

It is not necessary in English law for the claimant to be aware of all the relevant facts in giving his or her consent. As may be recalled from Ch. 5, the House of Lords in *Sidaway v Bethlem Royal Hospital*[56] held that a medical practitioner was not obliged to inform the patient of all the risks of a medical procedure, but simply to provide a reasonable level of information, judged according to the practices of a respectable body of opinion in that sector of the medical profession. The patient will therefore usually be given a broad understanding of the procedure, but no more. But if the patient specifically asks a question, the doctor is expected to answer both truthfully and as fully as the questioner requires.[57] Provided the patient is informed in broad terms of the nature of the procedure to be undertaken and of any significant risks which would affect the judgment of a reasonable patient,[58] real consent is given. If the claimant believes the information given is deficient, the remedy lies in the tort of negligence, not trespass to the person.[59] It has been suggested, however, that in the light of the Royal Bristol Infirmary Report, which emphasised the central role of consent in the provision of medical care, and the Human Rights Act 1998, more detailed information may be required.[60] It must therefore be questioned whether *Sidaway* now goes far enough to meet these concerns.

One peculiar aspect of consent is that for trespass to the person, but *not*, it should be noted, for trespass to land, the burden is on the *claimant* to prove absence of consent. Generally, the burden is on the defendant to establish any defences. This suggests that in trespass to the person, consent is not a defence at all but part of the cause of action to be proved on the balance of probabilities by the claimant. At first instance, in *Freeman v Home Office (No.2)*,[61] McCowan J. held that the burden of proof was on the claimant, because the tort consists of a trespass against the will of the party. In practice, however, the issue of consent will usually be raised by the defendant and is therefore generally treated as a defence.

---

[53] [1923] 1 K.B. 340.
[54] *R. v Linekar* [1995] Q.B. 250, CA.
[55] *Hegarty v Shine* (1878) 14 Cox C.C. 124; *R. v Clarence* (1888) 22 Q.B.D. 23; *R. v Linekar* [1995] Q.B. 250, CA.
[56] [1985] A.C. 871. Approved in *Creutzfeldt-Jakob Disease Litigation (No. 1)* (2000) 54 B.M.L.R. 1 (QBD).
[57] *Chester v Afshar* [2003] Q.B. 356, CA.
[58] *Pearce v United Bristol Healthcare* [1999] P.I.Q.R. P53, CA. Although it is impossible to state how significant this risk may be, Lord Bridge in *Sidaway* above indicated that it would be something in the region of 10 per cent.
[59] See *Chatterton v Gerson* [1981] Q.B. 432, 443 *per* Bristow J. Note that if the patient has consented to one procedure, it does not mean that the patient has consented to any further invasion unless the doctor has ensured that the terms of consent authorise such further treatment as the doctor considers necessary or desirable.
[60] See A Hockton, *The Law of Consent to Medical Treatment* (Sweet and Maxwell, 2002) at 1–006. Indeed, the guidance given to doctors by the General Medical Council goes beyond that stated in *Sidaway*: www.gmc-uk.org/standards/default.htm.
[61] [1984] 1 Q.B. 524, affirmed [1984] 1 Q.B. 548. Contrast majority view of the Supreme Court of Canada in *Non-Marine Underwriters v Scalera* (2003) 185 D.L.R. (4th) 1.

Refusal of consent

It seems logical that if I have a right to consent to a trespass to my person, I have a   **11–020**
corresponding right to refuse consent to such actions. But whilst it is clearly desirable
that I have the right to *refuse* consent to your violent actions, it is more contentious
when I wish to refuse to consent to life-saving medical treatment. The idea of self-
determination implies that the doctor should not be allowed to overrule my express
wishes, even with my best interests at heart. Therefore, if a Jehovah's Witness clearly
states that, because of her religious beliefs, she is not prepared to authorise a blood
transfusion, the doctor will commit a battery if he administers blood against her will.[62]

It has been held that an adult of sound mind and full understanding should be able
to decide to refuse treatment, even if the treatment is necessary to save his or her life
or even, controversially, that of her unborn child.[63] Capacity will be presumed unless
shown otherwise.[64] Only where there is doubt as to the patient's free will and capacity
will no trespass take place. For example, in *Re T. (Adult: Refusal of Treatment)*,[65] a
patient had refused a blood transfusion, following a road traffic accident and
subsequent Caesarian section to deliver her premature baby. She was not a Jehovah's
Witness, but had been brought up by her mother, who was a devout Witness, to believe
that blood transfusions were wrong. Her refusal followed time alone with her mother.
It was held that in the light of her illness, the incomplete information she had been
given, and the perceived influence of her mother, the doctors had acted lawfully in the
circumstances in giving her a transfusion. This case shows how narrow the line between
autonomy and lack of capacity may sometimes be.

This does not mean that a patient suffering from some mental disability cannot
refuse consent. The question remains one of capacity. In *Re J.T. (Adult: refusal of
medical treatment)*,[66] the patient had a learning disability which in the past had been
associated with extremely severe behavioural disturbance. She was currently being
detained under the Mental Health Act 1983. Wall J. held that, nevertheless, she was
capable of comprehending and retaining the information given, believing it, and
making a choice in the light of it.[67] She was therefore competent to refuse the renal
dialysis necessary to keep her alive. These cases will never be easy to decide, but the
courts are reluctant to deny the right of the individual to retain self-determination over
his or her body.

Difficult problems arise in determining the extent to which a child may be able to
refuse to give consent to medical treatment. In relation to consent, s.8(1) of the Family
Law Reform Act 1969 permits children of 16 and over to consent to surgical, medical

---

[62] *Malette v Shulman* (1990) 67 D.L.R. (4th) 321.

[63] *St George's Healthcare NHS Trust v S.* [1999] Fam 26. Scott (2000) 20 O.J.L.S. 407 highlights the
difficulties in determining the nature of moral and legal duties in such situations. See also *Re AK (Adult
patient)(Medical Treatment: Consent)* [2001] 1 F.L.R. 129 (victim suffering from motor neurone disease but,
although severely disabled, intellect unimpaired). Note also the guidance set out in *Re B v NHS Hospital
Trust* [2002] 2 All E.R. 449, 473–474 by Dame Elizabeth Butler-Sloss.

[64] *Re MB* [1997] 2 F.C.R. 541 at 553 *per* Butler-Sloss L.J.

[65] [1993] Fam. 95.

[66] [1998] 1 F.L.R. 48.

[67] Applying the test stated in *Re C. (Refusal of medical treatment)* [1994] 1 F.L.R. 31. See also *Re MB* [1997]
2 F.C.R. 541 (fear of needles rendered patient temporarily incompetent) and *Re W* [2002] EWHC 901,
Independent, June 17, 2002 (psychopathic disorder, but sufficient mental capacity to weigh the information
required to reach a decision as to treatment).

or dental treatment without the consent of a parent or guardian. In relation to children below 16, the House of Lords in *Gillick v West Norfolk Area Health Authority*[68] held by a majority that a child below 16 is capable of giving valid consent, provided that the child is of sufficient intelligence and understanding to appreciate what is proposed. This is regardless of the feelings of his or her parents. However, this is not the same as giving the child a right to *refuse* consent. In *Re W*,[69] W was a girl of 16 who was suffering from anorexia nervosa. She opposed the local authority's decision to move her to a unit specialising in the treatment of eating disorders. The Court of Appeal held that even if the child is 16 or over, or "Gillick competent", a parent or guardian may nevertheless consent on the minor's behalf. The court warned doctors to listen to the objections of minors, whose objections would increase in importance according to the age and maturity of the minor, but held that such objections were not an absolute bar to treatment. In any event, the court has an inherent jurisdiction to intervene to protect minors irrespective of their wishes. This allows the court to intervene and overrule a minor's objection to treatment.

In the case of younger children, parental consent will suffice for general medical treatment. Even where the parents refuse consent, the court's inherent power may be invoked to ensure the child receives the appropriate treatment.[70] In the recent case of *Re C*,[71] Wilson J. overruled parental objections to HIV testing of their baby girl. The mother was HIV positive and the child had a 20 to 25 per cent chance of infection. Whilst the court was prepared to accord great importance to the wishes of her parents, the arguments in favour of testing the baby were overwhelming. This view was approved by the Court of Appeal,[72] in which Butler-Sloss L.J. emphasised that the welfare of the child was the paramount concern of the court.

Limits to consent

11–021   Criminal law has refused to accept the defence of consent where the defendant has inflicted bodily harm on the claimant: ". . . it is not in the public interest that people should try to cause, or should cause, each other actual bodily harm for no good reason".[73] The House of Lords decision in *R. v Brown*,[74] which held a group of sado-masochists liable for acts of violence in which they had willingly and enthusiastically participated, was challenged in the European Court of Human Rights. The Strasbourg court held that the decision was not contrary to Art. 8 of the European Convention on Human Rights, which grants everyone a right to respect for their private and family

---

[68] [1986] A.C. 112.
[69] [1993] Fam. 64. See also *Re M (A child)(Medical treatment)* [1999] 2 F.L.R. 1097.
[70] The recent judgment of the European Court of Human Rights in *Glass v United Kingdom* [2004] 1 F.C.R. 553 stresses the role of the court in protecting the personal integrity of the child under Art. 8, even where emergency procedures are involved if sufficient time exists.
[71] [2000] Fam. 48, Fam. Div. See also *Re B (A child) (Immunisation: Parental rights)* [2003] Fam Law 731, CA (immunisation ordered despite mothers' objections) and the more drastic *Re A (Children) (Conjoined Twins)* [2001] Fam 147, CA (parents' objections to separation of conjoined twins overruled, although the inevitable result was that one of the girls would die).
[72] [1999] 2 F.L.R. 1004; [2000] Fam. Law 16, CA.
[73] *Att.-Gen.'s Reference (No.6 of 1980)* [1981] Q.B. 715 at 719 *per* Lord Lane C.J., except in the course of properly conducted games and sports or the lawful chastisement or correction of children.
[74] [1994] 1 A.C. 212. See also *R. v Emmett, The Times*, October 15, 1999, but contrast *R. v Wilson* [1997] Q.B. 47, CA (wife able to consent to branding buttocks with hot knife on the basis that it was analogous to tattooing!)

life.[75] The United Kingdom government was permitted under Art. 8(2) to take measures necessary to protect its citizens from personal injury and its response had not been disproportionate to the need in question. The same approach has been adopted towards terminally ill patients who, unable to act due to their disability, wish to seek the assistance of another to commit suicide. In *Pretty v United Kingdom*,[76] Diane Pretty had sought an undertaking from the Director of Public Prosecutions that her husband would not be prosecuted under the Suicide Act 1961 for helping her to commit suicide. She was suffering from motor neurone disease and wished to avoid the extremely distressing and undignified final stages of the disease. The DPP refused her request. The European Court of Human Rights found that this refusal did not conflict with Mrs Pretty's human rights. Limiting her right to self-determination might interfere with her rights under Article 8, but this could be justified as "necessary in a democratic society"[77] due to the need to safeguard life and protect the weak and vulnerable in society, who might be exploited by permitting assisted suicide. Whilst there was no evidence to suggest that Mrs Pretty fell into this category, this broader social goal was found to justify the DPP's position.[78]

It remains an open question whether such policy arguments will extend to tort. Much no doubt will depend on the nature of the injury inflicted: is the claimant consenting to a tattoo, ear-piercing, or serious physical injury? Lord Denning M.R., in *Murphy v Culhane*,[79] suggested that a defence of voluntary assumption of risk (or *volenti non fit injuria*, see Ch. 14) might still apply, for example where a burglar had taken upon himself the risk that the householder might defend his or her property, but there is little real authority on this point, and a court is unlikely to wish to be seen to condone disproportionate physical injury. In any event, such a question is unlikely to arise often in practice.

Necessity

This is a limited defence. It allows the defendant to intervene to prevent greater harm   **11–022**
to the public, a third party, the defendant or the claimant. The courts are careful to keep this defence within strict bounds and generally the defendant must act reasonably in all the circumstances. This defence solves a particular practical problem experienced by the emergency services. If a patient is brought into the accident and emergency section of a hospital unconscious, or is mentally ill and incapable of consenting, when can the medical practitioners involved be certain that their intervention is legal? It would be absurd and discriminatory if they were permitted to refuse to treat such patients in the absence of express evidence of consent.[80] This problem was addressed by the House of Lords in *Re F.; F. v West Berkshire Health Authority*.[81] Lord Goff held

[75] *Laskey, Jaggard and Brown v UK* (1997) 24 E.H.R.R. 39.
[76] (2002) 35 E.H.R.R.1 (see also UK proceedings: *Pretty v DPP* [2002] 1 A.C. 800).
[77] Art. 8(2).
[78] The Strasbourg court also found no violation of Art. 2 (right to life) and Art. 3 (right not to be subjected to degrading treatment).
[79] [1977] Q.B. 94. See also Lord Mustill in *Airedale NHS v Bland* [1993] 1 All E.R. 821.
[80] The situation is exacerbated by the absence of any wardship jurisdiction for adults or the mentally ill in this context.
[81] [1990] 2 A.C. 1. See also *R. v Bournewood Community and Mental Health NHS Trust, ex p. L* [1999] 1 A.C. 458, HL.

that the doctors may intervene in the best interests of the patient where (a) it is necessary to act in circumstances where it is not practicable to communicate with the patient; and (b) the action taken is such as a reasonable person would in all the circumstances take. On this basis, where a patient is unconscious but otherwise competent and not known to object to the treatment, treatment may be legally justified. Where the incapacity is temporary, the doctor should do no more than is reasonably required in the best interests of the patient before he or she recovers consciousness.

The situation where the incapacity is permanent, for example where the patient is in a permanent coma or permanently mentally ill,[82] is more difficult. In *Re F.* itself, an application was made to the court to authorise a sterilisation operation on a woman of 36, with a mental age between five and six years old, who was clearly incapable of consenting to the operation. The House of Lords held that treatment would be justified if it would be in the patient's best interests and would be endorsed by a reasonable body of medical opinion. Where a number of reasonably suitable treatments were available, treatment should, however, be determined according to the best interests of the patient, taking into account broader ethical, social, moral and welfare considerations.[83] On this basis, hospitals will be permitted to undertake treatment necessary to preserve the life, health and wellbeing of the patient. This may extend beyond surgical operations or substantial treatment to include routine medical and dental treatment, provided it is in the best interests of the patient. Their Lordships held in *Re F* (Lord Griffiths dissenting) that the law should not require judicial approval to be sought on each occasion treatment was given, although they felt it would be "highly desirable" to seek judicial approval for operations such as sterilisations. The sterilisation of a minor or a mentally handicapped adult will in virtually all cases require the prior sanction of a High Court judge.[84]

A good example of the dilemmas involved in such decisions is given in the well-known case of *Airedale NHS v Bland*.[85] This involved another victim of the tragic Hillsborough disaster. Tony Bland had been in a persistent vegetative state (PVS) for three and a half years following injuries suffered by him at the match, which had caused him to suffer irreversible brain damage. He continued to breathe unaided and his digestion continued to function, but he could not see, hear, taste, smell or communicate in any way. He was given no prospect of recovery. The doctors, with the support of his parents, applied to the court to withhold all life-sustaining treatment. Lord Goff, in the House of Lords, again applied the principles stated in *Re F*. His Lordship held that there was no absolute rule that a patient's life had to be prolonged by treatment or care regardless of all the circumstances and the quality of the patient's life. Treatment could be withdrawn if the patient had no hope of recovery and a

[82] Certain limited provision is made under the Mental Health Act 1983 for psychiatric treatment of persons formally detained in a mental hospital. The government is also proposing significant reforms under the Mental Capacity Bill, which will provide statutory definitions of "capacity" and "best interests" and a statutory form of the common law defence of necessity to care for persons of 16 or over suffering from lack of capacity: see *www.dca.gov.uk*.
[83] *Re S (Adult Patient: Sterilisation: Patient's Best Interests)* [2001] Fam 15, CA. See also *Re A (Mental Patient: Sterilisation)* [2000] 1 F.L.R. 549, CA and *Simms v Simms* [2003] Fam 83, Fam Div.
[84] *Practice Note (Official Solicitor: Declaratory Proceedings: Medical and Welfare Proceedings for Adults who lack Capacity)* [2001] 2 F.L.R. 158.
[85] [1993] 1 All E.R. 821.

reasonable medical practitioner would hold that it was not in the patient's best interests to prolong the patient's life. If an adult of full understanding has the right to withhold consent to medical treatment due to his right to self-determination, his Lordship held that it would be inconsistent if there was no corresponding rule to deal with the refusal of consent where the patient is incapable of indicating his wishes.

This is, with due respect, a questionable analogy. It is difficult to consider a right to self-determination in terms of an individual who lacks capacity. The justification for intervention must surely be a paternalistic concern for the best interests of the individual concerned. One can further criticise the court's distinction between a doctor actively taking life (*i.e.* euthanasia, which is prohibited) and one in which the doctor discontinues life-saving treatment (which is allowed provided that the court's approval is sought). In the latter, the patient is allowed to die of his or her pre-existing condition, which the court classifies as an omission for which the doctors will not be judged responsible. Yet, in both cases the doctor may be acting in the best interests of the patient to relieve the patient's condition, and indeed, the latter option will generally result in the patient starving to death or dying from infection, which is a far from dignified end.

In *NHS Trust A v M*,[86] the court was asked to consider whether discontinuance of treatment did, in fact, violate Art. 2 (right to life) and Art. 3 (right not to suffer degrading treatment) of the European Convention on Human Rights. The court held that, generally, Art. 2 would require a deliberate act, not an omission, by someone acting on behalf of the State, which results in death. Where treatment has been discontinued in the best interests of a patient, in accordance with the views of a respectable body of medical opinion, the State's positive obligations under Art. 2 were discharged. Equally, there was no violation of Art. 3. It could not in any event be invoked where the patient was unable to experience pain and was unaware of the nature of the treatment. The court thus approved Lord Goff's distinction in *Re F* as convention-compatible. Such rulings amount to a compromise whereby the judiciary avoid ruling on the controversial question of euthanasia, but provide patients and their families with a limited remedy in extremely distressing circumstances. The court's approval should be sought in virtually all such cases.[87]

(3) Self-defence

This seems to be a valid defence by analogy with criminal law. Section 3 of the **11–023** Criminal Law Act 1967 provides that a person has right to use "such force as is reasonable in the circumstances in the prevention of crime". The key consideration, of course, is whether the defendant's force is reasonable and not out of proportion to force exerted against him or her. This will be a question of fact. In *Lane v Holloway*,[88] where an elderly plaintiff had struck the young defendant on the shoulder during an argument, and the defendant had responded with an extremely severe blow to the

---

[86] [2001] Fam. 348 (Fam Div). Followed by *Re G (Adult incompetent: Withdrawal of treatment)* (2002) B.M.L.R. 6.
[87] *Practice Note (Official Solicitor: Declaratory Proceedings: Medical and Welfare Proceedings for Adults who lack Capacity)* [2001] 2 F.L.R. 158 and *Practice Note (Family Division: Incapacitated Adults: Declaratory Proceedings)* [2002] 1 W.L.R. 325, Fam Div.
[88] [1968] 1 Q.B. 379.

plaintiff's eye, the defendant was held liable. The blow in the circumstances was out of proportion to the plaintiff's actions. This may be contrasted with the more recent case of *Cross v Kirkby*.[89] Here a farmer, who had been struck by a hunt saboteur with a baseball bat, wrestled the bat from him and struck a single blow to the head which, unfortunately, caused him serious injuries. In finding self-defence, the Court of Appeal took into account the anguish of the moment in assessing whether this was an excessive and disproportionate response to the threat posed, and held that the law did not require the defendant to measure the violence to be deployed with mathematical precision. It should be noted that the right to defend oneself in self-defence extends to defence of one's spouse, and, if the analogy with s.3 of the Criminal Law Act 1967 is correct, to defence of others.

(4) Provocation

11–024   The general view, stated in *Lane v Holloway*,[90] is that provocation is not a valid defence. It may reduce or extinguish the claimant's entitlement to exemplary damages, but will not reduce ordinary compensatory damages. This was followed by May L.J. in *Barnes v Nayer*[91] where the court held that prolonged abuse and threats from a neighbouring family was insufficient provocation to justify the defendant attacking the mother with a machete. Lord Denning, in *Murphy v Culhane*,[92] modified his view in *Lane*, holding that it could reduce the compensatory measure where the victim is at least partly responsible for the damage suffered. This seems questionable and is really an argument for reducing the damages for contributory negligence (see below). It is submitted that the view in *Lane* is to be preferred.

(5) Contributory negligence

11–025   There is some authority that the principles of contributory negligence apply to battery. In *Murphy v Culhane*,[93] Murphy was alleged to have been part of a gang which had set out to attack Culhane. Murphy had been killed when Culhane struck him on the head with a plank. Lord Denning saw no reason why the deceased's fault should not result in a reduction in his widow's damages under ss.1(1) and 4 of the Law Reform (Contributory) Negligence Act 1945. This was approved by May L.J. in *Barnes v Nayer*.[94] It is nevertheless difficult to see fault as a defence to an intentional tort, which is distinct from negligence (see below) and is concerned with the individual's right to personal integrity, rather than the apportionment of loss. It is suggested that any concerns as to the "worthiness" of the claimant have no place in assessing ordinary compensatory damages for trespass against the person.

(6) Lawful authority

11–026   This defence is generally applied in relation to false imprisonment where the defendants have specific statutory authority to deprive the claimant of his or her complete freedom of movement. It should be noted that even Art. 5 of the European

[89] *The Times*, April 5, 2000.
[90] [1968] 1 Q.B. 379.
[91] *The Times*, December 19, 1986.
[92] [1977] Q.B. 94.
[93] *ibid*.
[94] *The Times*, December 19, 1986. See also *Ward v Chief Constable of the Royal Ulster Constabulary* [2000] N.I. 543.

Convention on Human Rights, which gives a right to liberty and security and which, under the Human Rights 1998, can now be enforced against public authorities such as the police, recognises that this will be limited in accordance with procedures prescribed by law.[95] This is obviously an important defence—without it our criminal justice system would fall apart. Section 12(1) of the Prison Act 1952 authorises the imprisonment of persons sentenced to imprisonment or committed to prison on remand pending trial. Equally, a lawful arrest will not render a police officer or citizen liable for false imprisonment. Reference should be made here to the provisions of the Police and Criminal Evidence Act 1984, particularly ss.24, 25 and 28. Readers are advised to consult specialist texts for detailed study of the requirements of a lawful arrest.[96] Basically, a police officer may legally arrest a person under a warrant. Section 24 makes provision for both a police officer and private citizen to arrest an individual without a warrant if the individual is in the act of committing an arrestable offence, or if he or she has reasonable grounds for suspecting the individual to be in the act of committing such an offence. Arrestable offences are serious offences which include, for example, offences for which the sentence is fixed by law, for example murder, or offences carrying a penalty of five or more years.[97] Individuals undertaking a "citizen's arrest" should, however, take care to ensure that they have not stepped outside the legal limits. Section 24(5) of the Act provides that where an arrestable offence *has been* committed, any person may arrest without warrant anyone guilty of the offence, or in relation to whom there are reasonable grounds for suspecting guilt. This latter provision should be noted carefully. Private individuals will not be protected from civil liability if no offence has in fact been committed.[98] In contrast, a police officer will not be liable, even if no offence has in fact been committed, provided he or she reasonably suspected that such an offence had been committed and had reasonable cause to suspect the individual to be guilty of that offence: s.24(6). Section 25 provides the general police powers of arrest. Reference should also be made to s.3 of the Criminal Law Act 1967, which allows a person to use such force as is reasonable in the circumstances to prevent crime or in effecting or assisting in the lawful arrest of offenders, suspected offenders or persons unlawfully at large. There are also common law powers to intervene and take reasonable steps to prevent breaches of the peace.[99]

CAN TRESPASS TO THE PERSON BE COMMITTED NEGLIGENTLY?

As stated in the introduction, early authority does seem to indicate the existence of a **11–027** tort of negligent trespass to the person. It is doubtful, however, whether this tort has survived the growth and dominance of the tort of negligence outlined in earlier

[95] Art. 5(1) lists six cases where an individual may legitimately be deprived of his liberty and these include detention after conviction by a competent court and lawful arrest for the purpose of bringing a person before a competent legal authority on reasonable suspicion of having committed an offence.
[96] *e.g.* see M. Zander, *The Police and Criminal Evidence Act 1984* (4th ed., Sweet and Maxwell, 2003).
[97] This also includes offences under ss.24(2) and (3) of the Act and under Criminal Justice and Public Order Act 1994, s.85.
[98] See *R. v Self* [1992] 3 All E.R. 476 at 480.
[99] See *Albert v Lavin* [1982] A.C. 546 at 565. See also police powers to enforce public order under the Public Order Act 1986 and the Criminal Justice and Public Order Act 1994.

chapters of this book. Nevertheless, Diplock J. in *Fowler v Lanning*[1] did not rule out the existence of such a tort. In this case, his Lordship held that a pleading which simply stated that "the defendant shot the plaintiff" disclosed no cause of action. The plaintiff should have pleaded either intention or negligence on the part of the defendant and if negligence was alleged, the burden of proof generally lay on the plaintiff. Diplock J. therefore left open the question whether the plaintiff could have brought an action for negligent trespass to the person.

Lord Denning, in *Letang v Cooper*,[2] was perhaps predictably more forthright. Here, the plaintiff had suffered injuries when the defendant had driven over her legs whilst she was sunbathing outside a hotel on a piece of grass which was used as a car park. Her obvious course of action would have been to sue in negligence, but due to the three year limitation period for personal injuries (see Ch. 14), she was out of time. She therefore tried to claim within the six year limitation period allocated for trespass, by framing her case as one of unintentional trespass to the person. The Court of Appeal rejected her claim, drawing a distinction between intentional and unintentional trespass to the person. Although Diplock L.J. was more cautious, suggesting that it was irrelevant whether the tort was described as unintentional trespass or negligence, Denning L.J. refused to accept the existence of a tort of unintentional trespass:

". . . when the injury is not inflicted intentionally but negligently, I would say the only cause of action is negligence and not trespass."[3]

If this is correct, then any claims for injury to the person which are not intentional must be brought in negligence. This does not seem to involve a dramatic step. It is difficult to see, in any event, why negligent conduct should be actionable without proof of damage. Lord Denning's view consolidates the position of trespass in the law of torts as a tort seeking to compensate for *intentional* conduct which unduly interferes with the personal integrity and autonomy of the individual.

Before moving on to consider trespass to land, there are two further related torts which should be considered. Harassment has been discussed above, and here we outline the provisions of the Protection from Harassment Act 1997, which are likely to be relevant to litigants considering an action for intentional injury by another. Equally, malicious prosecution, although not a form of trespass and only actionable on proof of damage, is frequently pleaded in common with false imprisonment and it is therefore convenient to consider its operation in this chapter.

PROTECTION FROM HARASSMENT ACT 1997

11–028 Until recently, harassment was not a recognised tort[4] and litigants were forced to frame their claims in trespass or nuisance.[5] However, s.3 of the Protection from Harassment Act 1997 creates a statutory tort of harassment. Yet, despite the

[1] [1959] 1 Q.B. 426 at 433.
[2] [1965] 1 Q.B. 232.
[3] *ibid.*, at 240. Approved in *Wilson v Pringle* [1987] Q.B. 237. Note also the distinction drawn in *Stubbings v Webb* [1993] A.C. 498. Here, an adult, who alleged that she had been sexually abused as a child, argued that, although her action for trespass was out of time, she could sue for personal injury caused by "negligence, nuisance or breach of duty" under s.11, Limitation Act 1980. This argument, which had received support in *Letang*, was rejected by the House of Lords (see Ch. 14).
[4] *Patel v Patel* [1988] 2 F.L.R. 179, CA.
[5] See *Khorasandjian v Bush* [1993] Q.B. 727.

importance of these provisions, it has been the criminal provisions of the Act which have so far received the most attention.[6]

What is "harassment"?

"Harassment" is described in s.1(1) as a course of conduct which amounts to   **11–029** harassment of another, and which the defendant knows or ought to know amounts to harassment of the other. Section 1(2) further provides that the defendant ought to know that his or her conduct amounts to harassment if a reasonable person in possession of the same information would think the course of conduct amounted to harassment of the other. This is an objective test. The court will not take account of any mental disorder from which the defendant is suffering, or any other characteristics, as this would substantially lessen the protection given to victims by the Act.[7]

The description of "harassment" in s.1(1) is somewhat circular, but clearly goes beyond mere stalking which was the principal target of the Act. Section 7 provides some assistance. "Harassment" is defined as conduct which includes "alarming the person or causing the person distress."[8] "Course of conduct" is stated to involve conduct on at least two occasions,[9] and may include speech.[10] Although the cases now give some guidance, the general feeling stated in *Thomas v News Group Newspapers Ltd* is that "'Harassment' is . . . a word which has a meaning that is generally understood."[11]

Claims will be restricted in a number of ways. First, a "course of conduct" must be proved. Secondly, s.1(3) provides that a valid defence exists when the conduct was pursued for the purpose of detecting crime, under any legal requirement, or was reasonable in the circumstances. Thirdly, it has also been doubted in a number of cases whether injunctions may be granted in favour of limited companies as opposed to individuals.[12] Despite the fact that the Act has been used to curb the activities of activists, for example animal rights protesters, the courts have indicated that the Act should not be used to restrict the citizen's right to protest in the public interest.[13]

Remedies

If harassment is shown, s.3 allows the claimant to sue for damages and/or an   **11–030** injunction. An injunction may be granted for actual or apprehended acts of harassment. Damages here may include a sum for anxiety and any financial loss resulting

---

[6] Ss.2 and 4. In 1998, for example, there were nearly 6,000 prosecutions under the Act: J Harris, *Home Office Research Study 203* (2000).
[7] *R. v C (Sean Peter)* [2001] 2 F.L.R. 757, CA (Crim).
[8] S.7(2).
[9] S.7(3). See *Lau v DPP* [2000] 1 F.L.R. 799 (the fewer the number of incidents and the wider the time lapse, the less likely a finding of "course of conduct").
[10] S.7(4). It may even on rare occasions extend to press articles which provoke reader hostility to a particular individual, although the courts are very conscious of the risk of violating Art. 10 of the Convention (freedom of expression): *Thomas v News Group Newspapers Ltd* [2002] E.M.L.R. 4.
[11] *Thomas v News Group Newspapers Ltd* [2002] E.M.L.R. 4, para.30 *per* Lord Phillips M.R.
[12] *DPP v Dziurzynski* [2002] EWHC 1380; (2002) 166 J.P. 545 and *Daiichi UK Ltd v Stop Huntingdon Animal Cruelty* (2003) *The Times,* October 22, QBD.
[13] See *Huntington Life Sciences Ltd v Curtin, The Times,* December 11, 1997, but also *DPP v Moseley, The Times,* June 23, 1999.

from the harassment.[14] If the defendant breaches the injunction, s.3(3) controversially permits a civil court to issue a warrant for the arrest of the defendant.[15]

MALICIOUS PROSECUTION

11–031   This tort has much in common with the tort of false imprisonment. Both torts focus on loss of liberty. Whilst, in false imprisonment, the defendant exercises direct restraint over the movements of the claimant, malicious prosecution may be seen as *indirect* restraint by means of setting the prosecution in motion. This tort is not, however, actionable *per se* and damage must be proved. The classic definition of damage was given by Holt C.J. in *Savile v Roberts*,[16] namely damage to a man's fame (or reputation), person or property. It is clear that an unwarranted prosecution may damage a person's reputation. Harm to the person has been interpreted broadly to include both the threat of imprisonment and actual imprisonment. Harm to property signifies the costs incurred by the claimant in defending the charges.

The tort has four requirements:

- the defendant has prosecuted the claimant;

- maliciously (*i.e.* with some wrongful or improper motive);

- without reasonable and probable cause;

- the prosecution ended in the claimant's favour. (This may be by acquittal, discontinuance by the prosecution, conviction quashed on appeal or on technical grounds.)

Actions will generally be against the police. Actions may be brought against private individuals, however, if they can be shown to have falsely and maliciously given information to the police, in circumstances where the police had no effective discretion whether to prosecute. This will not be established simply on the basis that the defendant has given information to the police, or prepared a report for the police. A recent example is that of *Martin v Watson*,[17] where the defendant maliciously made a groundless accusation of indecent exposure against the plaintiff, who was subsequently prosecuted. Lord Keith, in his leading judgment, held that:

> "Where an individual *falsely and maliciously* gives a police officer information indicating that some person is guilty of a criminal offence and states that he is willing to give evidence in court of the matters in question, it is properly to be

---

[14] S.3(2).
[15] The court in *Silverton v Gravett* (unreported, October 19, 2001, QBD) held that this did not breach Article 10 (freedom of expression) nor Art. 11 (freedom of association) of the European Convention on Human Rights as such restrictions could be justified as being "for the prevention of disorder or crime" or " for the protection of the reputation or rights of others": see Arts 10(2) and 11(2).
[16] (1698) 1 Ld. Raym. 374.
[17] [1996] 1 A.C. 74 at 86–87. Emphasis added. Note further guidance given by Brooke L.J. in *Mahon v Rahn (No 2)* [2000] 1 W.L.R. 2150 at 2205–2206. *Martin* was applied recently in *Sallow v Griffiths* [2001] F.S.R. 15, CA.

inferred that he desires and intends that the person he names should be prosecuted. Where the circumstances are such that the facts relating to the alleged offence can be within the knowledge *only* of the complainant, as was the position here, then it becomes virtually impossible for the police officer to exercise any independent discretion or judgement, and if a prosecution is instituted by the police officer the proper view of the matter is that the prosecution has been procured by the complainant."

This is not an easy tort to establish and the courts are careful not to allow the tort to be used to discourage the prosecution of suspected criminals. The most difficult obstacle for a claimant is to prove that the defendant had no reasonable and probable cause for the prosecution. This involves proving a negative, which is always problematic. The claimant must establish on the balance of probabilities that the defendant did *not* have an honest belief in the guilt of the accused, founded on objective facts which gave reasonable grounds for the existence of this belief.[18] Malice alone will not suffice. This is particularly difficult to establish if, for example, the defendant has taken legal advice (provided of course the legal adviser was given all the relevant facts). It will be for the jury to decide whether the defendant honestly believed the guilt of the accused.[19] Malicious prosecution is usually heard by a judge and jury[20] and while it is for the judge to determine whether the prosecutor had reasonable and probable cause, it remains nevertheless for the jury to determine any disputed facts relevant to that question. The jury will also determine whether the defendant was malicious.

11–032

Malicious prosecution only relates to prosecution, *i.e.* criminal charges. It remains questionable whether there is an equivalent tort of malicious institution of civil proceedings. This was doubted in *Metall und Rohstoff v Donaldson, Lufkin & Jenrette Inc.*[21] and in the recent House of Lords case of *Gregory v Portsmouth CC.*[22] Even if it does exist, it will rarely succeed, due to difficulties in proving damage.[23] Equally, it has been held that such proceedings do not affect the claimant's reputation, because his or her fair name is protected by the trial and judgment of the court.[24] Lord Steyn in *Gregory v Portsmouth CC* saw no reason change the current legal position:

"I am tolerably confident that any manifest injustices arising from groundless and damaging civil proceedings are either already adequately protected under other torts or are capable of being addressed by any necessary and desirable extensions of

[18] See *Herniman v Smith* [1938] A.C. 305 and, more recently, *Isaac v Chief Constable of the West Midlands Police* [2001] EWCA Civ 1405.
[19] *Glinski v McIver* [1962] A.C. 726.
[20] In common with false imprisonment.
[21] [1990] 1 Q.B. 391.
[22] [2000] 1 A.C. 419, which held that the tort does not apply to internal disciplinary proceedings. Lord Steyn held that the law, by providing adequate alternative remedies in defamation, malicious falsehood, conspiracy and misfeasance in public office, made it unnecessary and undesirable to extend this tort. For comment, see P. Cane (2000) 116 L.Q.R. 346. Note also *Strickland v Hertfordshire CC* [2003] EWHC 287.
[23] It is assumed that if the claimant succeeds in the initial action, the order for costs in the claimant's favour will cover any financial loss (this, unfortunately, is untrue unless the court awards indemnity costs, which is exceptional).
[24] Generally, see *Quartz Hill Gold Mining Co. v Eyre* (1883) 11 Q.B.D. 674 at 689–690. Note the comments of Lord Steyn in *Gregory v Portsmouth C.C.* [2000] 1 A.C. 419 at 428: "However realistic this view may have been in its own time, it is no longer plausible".

other torts. Instead of embarking on a radical extension of the tort of malicious prosecution I would rely on the capacity of our tort law for pragmatic growth in response to true necessities demonstrated by experience."[25]

There does, however, seem to be a tort of malicious abuse of process. This is really a form of the tort of misfeasance in a public office, which applies where an official knowingly acts in excess of his powers, or acts with malice towards the claimant. The claimant must show special damage, and examples include malicious procurement of a search-warrant[26] and malicious presentation of a winding up order or petition for bankruptcy[27] without reasonable or probable cause.

TRESPASS TO LAND

11–033   Trespass to land is clearly a different type of tort from those examined above. Its rationale is not to protect the integrity or reputation of the claimant, but to protect the claimant against direct and unjustifiable interference with his or her possession of land. There is an obvious similarity here with the tort of nuisance which equally deals with an unjustifiable interference with the claimant's use and enjoyment of land. However, there is a notable distinction. Trespass to land, in common with all forms of trespass, must be *direct* and *immediate* and is actionable *without* proof of damage. In contrast, nuisance, as discussed in Ch. 10, involves an indirect act which is only actionable on proof of damage. The distinction, which derives from the old rigid forms of action, survives despite the abolition of the forms of actions over 100 years ago. On this basis, if I throw a brick and destroy your prize flowers, I have committed an actionable trespass. If, however, I build a fire in my garden and noxious fumes blow over and harm your prize flowers, I have only committed a nuisance.

Unlike trespass to the person, trespass to land does not generally lead to criminal liability, although there are a number of statutory exceptions.[28] It is actionable *per se*, which may seem surprising. Tort law in the twenty-first century is generally more concerned with protecting personal interests, such as those discussed above, than with protecting interests in land, but historical concerns that trespass would lead to a breach of the peace led the courts to find liability without proof of harm.[29] Nevertheless, a claimant is likely to receive only nominal damages without proof of loss. Trespass also serves a useful function in determining boundaries to land (although claimants may alternatively seek a declaratory judgment) and in dealing with persistent trespassers by means of injunctive relief.

---

[25] [2000] 1 A.C. 419 at 432–433.
[26] *Reynolds v Commissioner of Police of the Metropolis* [1985] Q.B. 881; *Gibbs v Rea* [1998] A.C. 786, PC. See, recently, *Keegan v Chief Constable of Merseyside* [2003] 1 W.L.R. 2187 where the Court of Appeal found, on the facts, no improper motive, but noted that had the Human Rights Act 1998 been in force, Article 8 might have made a difference.
[27] *Johnson v Emerson* (1870–71) L.R. 6 Ex 32; *Quartz Hill Gold Mining Co. v Eyre* (1883) 11 Q.B.D. 674. See, more recently, *Tibbs v Islington LBC* [2002] EWCA Civ 1682 [2003] B.P.I.R. 743.
[28] *e.g.* "aggravated trespass" under Criminal Justice and Public Order Act 1994, s.68 (as amended), where persons have trespassed on the land to disrupt a lawful activity taking place on the land (*e.g.* hunt saboteurs).
[29] See *Clerk & Lindsell on Torts* (18th ed., Sweet and Maxwell, 2000), para.18–09.

In common with trespass to the person, it is an intentional tort, but it is the act of entry which must be intentional and not the act of trespass. On this basis, provided your actions are voluntary, you are a trespasser whether you know you are trespassing or not.[30] It is therefore no excuse that you are utterly lost, although the courts will not impose liability where you were forcibly thrown or pushed onto the land.[31] Where animals stray onto another's land, Park J. in *League against Cruel Sports v Scott*[32] indicated that the owner will be responsible for the damage they cause if he or she intended them to enter the claimant's land or, knowing that there was a real risk that they would enter, failed to take reasonable care to prevent their entry. On this basis, the master of a hunt was liable when his hounds entered land belonging to the League against Cruel Sports, who were, unsurprisingly, not prepared to tolerate such a trespass. This case raises the question whether, in spite of *Letang v Cooper*,[33] a defendant may commit a trespass to land negligently. It is submitted that a consistent approach should be adopted to trespass, which should be confined to intentional voluntary acts. It is contrary to the general development of the law for a tort actionable *per se* to be committed negligently.

Trespass is therefore established where the claimant can show a direct and unjustifiable interference with the claimant's possession of land. The nature of these two requirements will be examined below.

(1) Direct and unjustifiable interference

This can occur in a number of ways. The obvious examples are walking on my lawn or entering my house without my permission, but it will also include such diverse examples as throwing a CS gas canister on my land[34] or allowing sheep to stray onto my land.[35] Trespass may be committed by interference with the subsoil and even airspace if it is within the height necessary for the ordinary use and enjoyment of the land and structures on it.[36] On this basis, the defendants in *Bernstein v Skyviews & General Ltd*[37] were not liable for taking aerial photographs of the landowner's home at a height of many hundreds of metres above the ground. This is re-affirmed by the Civil Aviation Act 1982, s.76(1), which provides that civil aircraft flying at a reasonable height do not commit a trespass. A reasonable height will be determined by the court with regard to the wind, weather and all the circumstances of the case. A claimant may recover damages, however, from the owner of the aircraft for property damage or personal injury caused by something falling from an aircraft while in flight, taking off or landing. The claimant need not prove negligence or intention, or establish any other

11–034

---

[30] *Conway v George Wimpey & Co. Ltd* [1951] 2 K.B. 266 at 273–274.
[31] *Smith v Stone* (1647) Style 65.
[32] [1986] Q.B. 240.
[33] [1965] 1 Q.B. 232 (which of course only deals with trespass to the person).
[34] *Rigby v Chief Constable of Northamptonshire* [1985] 1 W.L.R. 1242.
[35] This was recently found to extend to the discharge of water into a canal without permission: *British Waterways Board v Severn Trent Water Ltd* [2002] Ch. 25, CA.
[36] See *Kelsen v Imperial Tobacco Co Ltd* [1957] 2 Q.B. 334 and, more recently, *Anchor Brewhouse Developments Ltd v Berkley House (Docklands Developments) Ltd* (1987) 38 B.L.R. 82 (injunction awarded to stop a developer's cranes oversailing the plaintiff's land, even though they were high enough not to affect the normal use of that land).
[37] [1978] Q.B. 479.

cause of action, provided that the loss or damage was not caused or contributed to by the negligence of the claimant.[38]

It should also be noted that the public have a right to use the public highway for any reasonable purpose, which will extend to peaceful assembly, provided their acts do not amount to a public or private nuisance and do not obstruct the highway by unreasonably impeding the public's primary right to pass and repass.[39]

(2) Possession of land

11–035 This is the interest protected by the tort of trespass. Only those with possession of the land can sue for trespass. It is not enough to be physically on the land or to have control over the land. A mere licensee, such as a lodger or guest in a hotel, cannot sue for trespass. The claimant must have an interest in land in possession or at least exclusive possession to maintain an action for trespass.[40] An interest in land without possession will not suffice. For example, when a landlord has leased his property, the tenant is the party in possession. The landlord will only be able to sue if the trespasser injures the interest he or she has in possession, namely the reversionary interest in land, *i.e.* the landlord's right to possession at the end of the term of the lease.[41] Ordinarily, it will be the tenant who sues for trespass. The similarities with the right to sue in nuisance, discussed in Ch. 10, should be noted. The claimant will be able to sue regardless of the fact that he or she was out of the premises at the time the trespass took place or had only just acquired the right to possession. The concept of "trespass by relation" allows the claimant to sue for trespass even if the trespass took place between the time when the right to possession was obtained and actual entry into possession.[42]

TRESPASS TO LAND: DEFENCES

11–036 The defences bear a clear resemblance to the defences discussed above for trespass to the person, namely consent, necessity and lawful authority. Similarly to nuisance, there is generally no defence of *jus tertii* to trespass. *Jus tertii* alleges that the claimant cannot succeed because a third party has a better title to the land than the claimant and should therefore be bringing the action instead of the claimant. It has been rejected in a number of cases.[43]

(1) Licence

11–037 The defendant will not be liable for trespass where he or she has permission to act, be it express or implied, from the party in possession. A licence should be distinguished from interests in property, such as easements or *profits à prendre* which give the

---

[38] S.76(2).
[39] *DPP v Jones* [1999] 2 A.C. 240, HL (peaceful assembly on highway did not amount to trespass necessary to invoke police powers against trespassory assembly under the Public Order Act 1986).
[40] *Nicholls v Ely Beet Sugar Factory* [1931] 2 Ch. 84.
[41] See *Jones v Llanrwst U.D.C.* [1911] 1 Ch. 393 at 404.
[42] See *Clerk & Lindsell on Torts op. cit.* para.18–026.
[43] *Nicholls v Ely Beet Sugar Factory* [1931] 2 Ch. 84; *Chambers v Donaldson* (1809) 11 East. 65. It may, however, be used in relation to actions for the recovery of land: see below.

grantee a proprietary right to enter the land. These are dealt with in the standard works on land law.[44] Although a licence to act is a good defence, it has two notable limitations. It may be restricted by express or implied terms and if they are exceeded, the defendant has committed a trespass. As noted in Ch. 8, "When you invite a person into your house to use the staircase, you do not invite him to slide down the banisters".[45] Equally, permission can be withdrawn, thereby rendering the defendant a trespasser if he or she fails to leave within a reasonable period of time.

Express or implied limits on permission to enter have been discussed above and in Chapter 8. However, the ability to withdraw or *revoke* the licence is more complicated. The licence cannot be revoked where the claimant has also been granted a property interest such as a *profit à prendre*,[46] or has a licence coupled with an equity.[47] In other circumstances, it will depend on whether the claimant has been given permission to enter under a bare licence (*i.e.* in the absence of consideration), or under a contractual licence (*i.e.* in return for consideration, for example by purchasing a ticket to watch a football match). A bare licence may be revoked at any time,[48] although public law may impose some limits on the power of a public body to revoke its licence.[49] A contractual licence may be revoked (although this may result in a claim for breach of contract) unless (a) there is an express or implied term in the contract limiting the power to revoke the licence for a defined or reasonable time, and (b) the court would be prepared to grant an injunction to prevent breach of contract.[50] The existence of any implied term will be a question of construction on the facts of the case. For example, if I buy a ticket for the cinema, it is implied that (provided I behave myself) I can stay in the cinema until the end of the film.[51] If the licence is revocable, the defendant must be given reasonable time to leave and remove his or her goods.

(2) Necessity

Necessity is also a valid defence to trespass to land. The necessity may be public or private, but in both cases, there must be an actual or reasonably perceived danger in relation to which reasonable steps are taken. For example, if there is a fire and the defendant enters another's land or destroys another's property to stop the spread of the fire, the defence will be one of public necessity if the actions are in the public interest. If the defendant has intervened to save his or her own person or property from imminent danger, the defence will be one of private necessity.[52] In *Rigby v. Chief*

11–038

---

[44] Note also that such rights may be acquired by prescription (see Ch. 10.)
[45] See Scrutton L.J. in *The Calgarth* [1927] P. 93 at 110.
[46] A right to take goods from the land—see *Thomas v Sorrell* (1673) Vaughan 330.
[47] See *National Provincial Bank Ltd v Hastings Car Mart Ltd* [1964] Ch. 665 and Gray and Gray, *Elements of Land Law* (Butterworths, 2001) 3rd ed. No. 2.16.
[48] See *CIN Properties Ltd v Rawlins* [1995] E.G.L.R. 130 which applied this rule even to quasi-public places such as a shopping centre and survived a challenge to the European Commission on Human Rights (*Anderson v United Kingdom* [1998] E.H.R.L.R. 218). This was applied in *Porter v Commissioner of Police for the Metropolis* (unreported, 20 October 1999), despite the highly critical academic response of Gray and Gray [1999] E.H.R.L.R. 46.
[49] See *Wandsworth v A* [2000] 1 W.L.R. 1246, CA (attempt to deny parent access to a primary school).
[50] *Winter Garden Theatre (London) Ltd v Millennium Products Ltd* [1948] A.C. 173.
[51] Compare *Hurst v Picture Theatres Ltd* [1915] 1 K.B. 1. There is also authority that if the court is prepared to award an order for specific performance, the licence cannot be revoked even where the licensee has yet to enter into possession of the premises: *Verrall v Great Yarmouth BC* [1981] Q.B. 202.
[52] Although it has been held that it is no excuse to an action in trespass that you entered due to threats to your life: *Gilbert v Stone* (1647) Style 72.

Constable of Northamptonshire,[53] a young psychopath broke into a gun shop and armed himself. To end the siege, the police fired a canister of CS gas into the shop to smoke out the intruder. Unfortunately, it set the shop alight. The shopkeeper sued the police for damages. Taylor J. held that the police could rely on the defence of necessity provided they could show that they had not been negligent in creating or contributing to the necessity. On the facts, the intruder had been a clear threat to the public and the police had clearly not caused or contributed to the problem at hand. They were therefore not liable in trespass.[54]

In recent years, the Court of Appeal has expressed concern as to the operation of this defence and advocated that it should be confined to very limited circumstances. Lord Denning M.R. in *Southwark LBC v Williams*[55] highlighted the concern that it could be used to justify public unrest. Here, a group of individuals in dire need of accommodation had relied on necessity to justify taking over a number of empty houses belonging to the local authority which were due for development. Lord Denning M.R. held that such behaviour was not acceptable in society and that the defence should only apply to urgent situations of immediate peril:

> "If homelessness were once admitted as a defence to trespass, no one's house could be safe. Necessity would open a door which no man could shut. It would not only be those in extreme need who would enter. There would be others who would imagine that they were in need or would invent a need, so as to gain entry . . . So, the courts must for the sake of law and order take a firm stand. They must refuse to admit the plea of necessity to the hungry and the homeless, and trust that their distress will be relieved by the charitable and the good."[56]

This approach was approved by the Court of Appeal in *Monsanto plc v. Tilly*.[57] Here, campaigners against genetically modified (G.M.) crops had entered onto land and destroyed some of the G.M. crops growing there. Monsanto, a company licensed by the Department of the Environment to carry out trials on G.M. crops, sought injunctions against the defendants prohibiting them from trespassing on the land. The defendants claimed that they had a valid defence of necessity, but this was dismissed by the Court of Appeal. The court held that the real purpose of the campaign was to attract publicity for their cause, and their actions did not fit within the very narrow defence of necessity. The defence would only apply where the defendants faced an emergency where it was necessary for the defendants to act in the face of immediate and serious danger to life or property, and where their actions were reasonable. In any event, there was a public authority responsible for the public interest in relation to G.M. crops, namely the Department of Environment. Again, the Court of Appeal stressed that the defence of necessity should not be used to justify "all sorts of wrongdoing".

---

[53] [1985] 1 W.L.R. 1242.
[54] They were, however, liable for negligence, as discussed in Ch. 2.
[55] [1971] 1 Ch. 734.
[56] *ibid.*, at 744.
[57] [2000] Env. L.R. 313; *The Times*, November 30, 1999.

(3) Justification by law

It is a valid defence that the defendant was legally authorised to enter onto the claimant's land. The most obvious example is that of a police officer entering premises under warrant. Reference should be made again to the Police and Criminal Evidence Act 1984 (ss.16 to 18) and the Criminal Justice and Public Order Act 1994.[58] One particular problem, which has now been resolved by statute, is the difficulty experienced by householders who needed access to neighbouring land to undertake repairs to their property. Their neighbours at common law were quite entitled to refuse, or charge a premium. The Access to Neighbouring Land Act 1992 now provides that the court may make an order allowing access to land for the purpose of carrying out works which are reasonably necessary for the preservation of adjoining or adjacent land and which cannot be carried out, or would be substantially more difficult to carry out, without entry upon the land. The scope of the Act is limited, however, by the fact that the court cannot make such an order if it would cause unreasonable interference with the neighbour's enjoyment of the land or unreasonable hardship. Equally, it is confined to work to "preserve" the land, although it will extend to improvement work incidental to such works: s.1(5).

11–039

Abuse of such legal authority is treated severely. Where the defendant has entered the property with legal authority, but subsequently abuses that authority, the trespass is deemed to have taken place from the moment of entry (the so-called doctrine of trespass *ab initio*).[59] This only applies, however, to positive acts of abuse and does not apply to omissions. It also does not seem to apply to cases of partial abuse. In *Elias v. Pasmore*,[60] the police had lawfully entered the plaintiff's premises to arrest a man, and had seized a number of documents, some of them unlawfully. Horridge J. held that the original entry was not a trespass to land. The only action was for trespass to the goods unlawfully seized. It is submitted that, despite criticism of trespass *ab initio*,[61] the doctrine is sound and should be preserved. Trespass protects the claimant's right to possession, and any abuse of legal authority which interferes with this right should not be tolerated.

TRESPASS TO LAND: REMEDIES

The ordinary remedies of damages and/or an injunction may be obtained for trespass. The trespass may consist of a single act or be continuous. If the trespass is continuous, the claimant will have a right to sue for as long as it lasts. On this basis, the claimant may bring a second action for damages if the trespass persists.[62] The assessment of

11–040

---

[58] See also s.2 , Countryside and Rights of Way Act 2000.
[59] See the *Six Carpenters' Case* (1610) 8 Co. Rep. 146a.
[60] [1934] 2 K.B. 164.
[61] The doctrine has been criticised as antiquated and for failing to recognise that a lawful act should not be rendered unlawful by subsequent events: see the Court of Appeal *obiter* in *Chic Fashions (West Wales) Ltd v Jones* [1968] 2 Q.B. 299 at 313, 317, 320. Lord Denning is critical of the doctrine in *Chic Fashions* when it is used against the police, but nevertheless uses it against taxi-drivers in *Cinnamond v British Airports Authority* [1980] 1 W.L.R. 582 at 588 who had abused their right to set down passengers at London airport by touting for business.
[62] *Holmes v Wilson* (1839) 10 A. & E. 50.

damages will be discussed in more detail in Chapter 15. Here, therefore, we confine our study to remedies which are particularly relevant to the tort of trespass. Further details may be found in texts on land law.

(1) Self-help

11–041 This is mentioned to stress its limits. A party in possession may use reasonable force to resist wrongful entry or attempted entry by a trespasser. Such people are therefore perfectly within their rights to erect fences or put up barbed wire fences. The force must be reasonable and any force in excess of what is reasonably necessary will render the person liable for trespass to the person.

A guard dog is equally permissible, provided that it is reasonable to keep the dog on the premises for that purpose: s.5(3) of the Animals Act 1971. Section 1 of the Guard Dogs Act 1975 further provides, however, that a guard dog should not be used unless the dog is secured, or his handler is on the premises and the dog is under the control of the handler at all times. In any event, a notice containing a warning that a guard dog is present should be clearly exhibited at each entrance to the premises.

Although anyone in possession of land has a right to re-enter at all times,[63] this is limited by the Criminal Law Act 1977.[64] Section 6 renders it an offence for anyone without lawful authority (other than a displaced residential occupier[65]) to use or threaten violence for the purposes of securing entry to any premises occupied by another. Readers should also note the restrictions on entry contained in the Protection from Eviction Act 1977, which renders it an offence to unlawfully evict or harass any person with a right to remain in occupation of the premises.

(2) Order for possession of land

11–042 This is an action for the recovery of land (formerly called "Ejectment"), by which the person entitled to possess the land seeks a court order to recover the land. This is usually achieved by the claimant proving his or her own title to land.[66] There is now a special summary procedure the claimant can use against persons entering or remaining on their premises without the claimant's licence or consent, whether or not the claimant is able to identify them.[67] This permits the claimant to take action against squatters within a short period of time. This is essentially a proprietary action, but is mentioned because it has evolved from the tort of trespass.

[63] Note *Ropaigealach v Barclays Bank plc* [2000] Q.B. 263, CA (mortgagee permitted to exercise right to take possession without court order).
[64] As amended by the Criminal Justice and Public Order Act 1994.
[65] This is defined by s.12(3) as any person who was occupying the premises as a residence immediately before being excluded from occupation by a trespasser.
[66] On this basis, there is authority that the defence of *jus tertii* applies to an action for recovery of land. But note the extension of recovery to contractual licensees in *Manchester Airport Plc. v Dutton* [2000] Q.B. 133, CA (licensee with right to occupy land entitled to bring action for possession against trespasser even when not in actual occupation), although applied restrictively in *Countryside Residential (North Thames) Ltd v T (A Child)* (2001) 81 P. & C.R. 2, CA.
[67] See the Civil Procedure Rules, Part 55.

(3) Mesne[68] *profits*

These will usually be claimed in addition to the action for recovery of possession of   **11–043**
land. They are a form of consequential damages, given to the claimant for the time he
or she has been kept out of possession of his or her land. By this means, the claimant
can seek a reasonable rent for the defendant's possession of the property, damages for
deterioration, and the reasonable costs of getting possession. The remedy is usually
used against a tenant who has refused to leave at the end of the lease. It is irrelevant
that the claimant cannot show that the property could have been let during this period
or that the defendant did not profit from the property. The damages are for the lost
use of the property. Therefore, in *Inverugie Investments Ltd v Hackett*,[69] the Privy
Council held that the plaintiff could recover a reasonable rent for every apartment in a
hotel block, in spite of the defendants' objections that they had never been fully
booked and indeed had an average occupancy of 35 to 40 per cent. Lord Lloyd held
that it was not a question of the actual loss suffered, or whether the defendants had
derived any actual benefit from the use of the premises, but of assessing a reasonable
rate for the 15$\frac{1}{2}$ years the plaintiff had been out of possession:

> "If a man hires a concrete mixer, he must pay the daily hire, even though he may
> not in the event have been able to use the mixer because of rain. So also must a
> trespasser who takes the mixer without the owner's consent. He must pay the going
> rate, even though in the event he had derived no benefit from the use of the
> mixer."[70]

On this basis, it was acceptable to calculate the sum due on the wholesale rate paid by
tour operators, which took into account seasonal variations in the booking fee.

TRESPASS TO GOODS

Finally, we shall briefly examine the tort of trespass to goods. This tort is now largely   **11–044**
covered by the Torts (Interference with Goods) Act 1977, which brings together torts
dealing with wrongful interference with goods, such as trespass and conversion
(essentially theft in civil law[71]). Reference should be made to other texts for a full
understanding of wrongful interference with goods.[72] Here, we confine ourselves to a
general discussion of trespass to goods.

This form of trespass deals with intentional and direct interference with the
possession of goods. This includes removing or damaging goods—in fact, any act
interfering with the claimant's possession of the goods. It is unnecessary to show the

---

[68] Pronounced "mean".
[69] [1995] 1 W.L.R. 713.
[70] *ibid.*, at 718.
[71] Conversion is defined as wilfully dealing with the claimant's property in a way which amounts to a denial
of the claimant's rights over it, whereby the claimant is deprived of the use and possession of the property.
The Act also abolishes the old tort of detinue: s.2(1).
[72] See, *e.g.* MG Bridge, *Personal Property Law* (OUP, 2002) 3rd ed., and S Worthington, *Personal property
law: Text, cases and materials* (Hart, 2000).

defendant has removed the goods to establish this tort. Scraping your keys on the side of a vehicle would amount to trespass to goods.[73] In contrast to the other forms of trespass discussed above, the requirements of this tort are not particularly clear. They will be examined below.

The requirements of trespass to goods

(1) It must be intentional

11-045   Generally, it would seem that the interference with the goods must be intentional. It is irrelevant whether the defendant realised that he or she was committing a trespass. For example, in *Wilson v Lombank Ltd*,[74] a car had been sent to a garage for repair. The defendant, believing wrongly that the car was his, removed it from the garage. It was held that the defendant was liable in trespass. He had intentionally removed the vehicle and it was irrelevant that it was due to a mistake.

However, in a number of cases, intentional conduct does not appear to be a sufficient condition of liability. In *National Coal Board v JE Evans & Co. (Cardiff) Ltd*,[75] for example, the court excused the intentional conduct of the defendants who, in digging a trench, had damaged an underground cable belonging to the plaintiffs. The court found that the defendants had not been negligent—there was no way they could have known of the presence of the cable, which had been laid by the plaintiffs or by the plaintiffs' predecessors in title without informing the landowner. The cable was not visible and had not been marked on the plan given to the defendants by the landowners. On this basis, where the claimant cannot reasonably know of the existence of the goods, but nevertheless harms them, a court will not find liability for trespass. Whilst this case seems to rest on the fundamental unfairness of finding such a defendant liable, the case law on road traffic accidents is more difficult to explain. Here, the courts again look for negligence even when the action is brought in trespass.[76] This raises the "*Fowler v Lanning*[77] question" of whether there is a parallel claim for unintentional trespass to goods. It must be doubted whether such a claim is necessary and it may be preferable simply to treat such claims as negligence. Nevertheless, there is still some support for a tort of unintentional trespass to goods. For example, s.11(1) of the Torts (Interference with Goods) Act 1977 refers to "intentional trespass to goods", which suggests that it should be distinguished from "unintentional" trespass to goods.

(2) It must be direct

11-046   The interference must be direct. This raises all the questions we have seen considered above in relation to the other forms of trespass. For example, if I put out poison for my neighbour's dog, is this direct enough to amount to trespass to goods? It may be

---

[73] See the example given by Alderson B. *obiter* in *Fouldes v Willoughby* (1841) 8 M. & W. 540 at 549: "Scratching the panels of a carriage would be a trespass".
[74] [1963] 1 W.L.R. 1294.
[75] [1951] 2 K.B. 861.
[76] *Holmes v Mather* (1875) 133 L.T. 361 where Bramwell B. at 363 attributes it to "the convenience of mankind in carrying on the affairs of life".
[77] [1959] 1 Q.B. 426.

argued that it is no more indirect than the acid put in the hand-dryer in *DPP v K*,[78] discussed above. Nevertheless, the general view is that it is probably not direct enough.[79]

(3) Actionable per se?

This tort is generally regarded as actionable without proof of damage. Thus, it covers **11–047** activities such as the unauthorised touching of museum exhibits, which would not otherwise be protected in tort. There is some authority in favour of proof of damage, but these cases can generally be explained as highway cases based on negligence.[80]

(4) Possession

The key to this tort is interference with the possession, not the ownership, of goods. In **11–048** *Wilson v Lombank Ltd*,[81] for example, the plaintiff was found not to be the true owner of the car, having purchased the vehicle from a person who had no right to sell the car. Nevertheless, he was found to be in possession at the time of the trespass, and was therefore able to bring an action for trespass to goods. The question is therefore whether the claimant was in possession at the time the interference took place. Bailees,[82] trustees, executors, administrators of estates and owners of franchises will all satisfy this requirement.

Defences

The defences are similar to those mentioned for other forms of trespass. It is a valid **11–049** defence that the claimant has consented to the interference. Equally, if the trespass in question was necessary for the preservation and protection of the goods and reasonable steps were taken,[83] the defendant has a good defence. Readers should note that under the Police and Criminal Evidence Act 1984,[84] the police are given specific powers to search for and seize property without liability. Section 11(1) of the 1977 Act states that contributory negligence is no defence to proceedings based on "intentional" trespass to goods. Again, this begs the question whether contributory negligence could be a defence should unintentional trespass to goods be recognised, but as this is essentially a claim for negligence, the answer is obviously yes. Section 8 of the 1977 Act also provides a further defence:

> "The defendant in an action for wrongful interference shall be entitled to show, in accordance with rules of court, that a third party has a better right than the plaintiff in respect of all or any part of the interest claimed by the plaintiff, or in right of which he sues."

Under this provision, the defendant may protect himself or herself against double liability by identifying who had the interest protected by the tort at the relevant time.

---

[78] [1990] 1 W.L.R. 1067.
[79] See *Clerk & Lindsell on Torts op. cit.* paras 14–134.
[80] *Everitt v Martin* [1953] N.Z.L.R. 298 and *Slater v Swann* (1730) 2 Stra. 872.
[81] [1963] 1 W.L.R. 1294.
[82] See *Owen and Smith (trading as Nuagin Car Service) v Reo Motors (Britain) Ltd* (1934) 151 L.T. 274, CA.
[83] See *Kirk v Gregory* (1876) 1 Ex. D. 55 where the defence failed because, although the defendant had acted *bona fide*, it was not proved that the interference was reasonably necessary.
[84] See ss.8–22.

Rules of court now provide that the claimant should give particulars of title and identify any other person who, to his or her knowledge, has or claims to possess an interest in the goods.[85] Readers should also note that the 1977 Act gives the claimant a wider range of remedies than the common law remedies of damages and/or injunction, which include a final order for special delivery, or for delivery or damages, if the defendant is in possession or control of the goods.[86]

Trespass to goods is therefore a means by which the claimant's possession of goods can be protected from unwarranted interference by others. It is limited in scope, but presents an example of one of the many varied interests protected by the law of torts.

---

[85] CPR rule 19.5A.
[86] See Torts (Interference with Goods) Act 1977, s.3.

Chapter 12

DEFAMATION

Introduction

Defamation is a different type of tort from those examined in earlier chapters. It does **12–001** not protect the personal safety of the individual or even the personal integrity and right to self-determination of the claimant. It protects something far more indistinct: the reputation of the claimant. On this basis, while abuse of the claimant in private can only give rise to liability for harassment or possibly assault, unjustified criticism of the claimant to *another*, which makes society think less of the claimant, gives rise to the tort of defamation. It is the claimant's reputation, not injured feelings, which the tort aims to protect.

The tort raises a number of difficult problems. For example, a basic democratic right stated in Art. 10 of the European Convention on Human Rights is the right to freedom of expression, which includes the right to "hold opinions and to receive and impart information and ideas without interference by public authority". Article 10 is now incorporated into English law by the Human Rights Act 1998 and s.6 of the Act provides that it is unlawful for a public authority (which includes courts) to act in a way which is incompatible with a Convention right.[1] Freedom of expression includes the right to criticise, and is particularly important in relation to politicians and officials who occupy positions of power. This is further supported by s.12 of the 1998 Act which provides that when a court is considering whether to grant any relief which, if granted, might affect the exercise of freedom of expression, it must have particular regard to the importance of this right and, *inter alia*, the public interest in publishing such material by the press.[2] To what extent therefore should a politician, such as Albert Reynolds, the former Prime Minister of the Republic of Ireland, be able to rely on the tort of defamation to sue *The Times* newspaper for criticising his actions whilst Prime Minister?

On the other hand, the reader will be fully aware of the frequent complaints of press intrusion and irresponsible reporting where journalists, anxious for a "scoop" in a very competitive media market, publish without fully checking their facts. Unfortunately the old adage that "there is no smoke without fire" still applies, and a person mistakenly

---

[1] The Act came into force on October 2, 2000.
[2] See ss.12(1) and (4).

named as a serial rapist is unlikely to fight the corner of freedom of expression. Article 10(2) of the Convention recognises that the right to freedom of expression cannot go unchallenged. Such a right "carries with it duties and responsibilities [and so] may be subject to such formalities, conditions, restrictions or penalties as are prescribed by law and are necessary in a democratic society . . . for the protection of the reputation or rights of others". The law of defamation must therefore attempt to balance the competing rights of freedom of expression and protection of one's reputation. This is a far from easy task and, unfortunately for the reader, has led to a complex and frequently confusing area of law. This will be examined below.

We will approach defamation in four logical stages. This aids clarity and helps to minimise the difficulties outlined above. Four main questions must be addressed:

(a) Is the statement defamatory?

(b) Does it refer to the claimant?

(c) Has it been published?

(d) Do any of the defences apply?

These will be considered in this and the following chapter. This chapter will focus on the first three stages, establishing when a claimant can bring an action for defamation and who can sue and be sued. Ch. 13 will set out the defences available to defendants, particularly in the light of the Defamation Act 1996 and the recent House of Lords decision in *Reynolds v Times Newspapers Ltd*.[3] It will also consider alternatives to defamation law (for example the tort of malicious falsehood[4]) and the ability of regulatory bodies such as the Press Complaints Commission to deal with complaints of media excess.

The first step must, however, be to examine the long-standing division of defamation into two parts: libel and slander. Both are examples of defamation, but for historical reasons are treated separately. It would make life easier for all if this distinction were abolished (unless the reader has a particular desire to maintain a distinction logical in Tudor times, but sadly not our own), but this does not appear to be imminent. Abolition has been suggested from 1843 without success[5] and it is therefore unlikely to occur in the near future. The distinction will therefore be examined below.

LIBEL AND SLANDER

12–002   These torts are generally distinguished on the basis that libel takes permanent form, for example, an article or a photograph published in a daily newspaper,[6] while slander is temporary, for example words shouted across a classroom or gestures made to a crowd.[7] The permanency of libel is deemed to make it more serious—more people will

[3] [2001] 2 A.C. 127.
[4] A claimant may also wish to consider an action in negligence or breach of confidence. See Ch. 2.
[5] See, in particular, Ch. 2 of the report of the Faulks Committee in 1975 (Report of the Committee on Defamation, Cmnd 5909).
[6] Or even a waxwork: *Monson v Tussauds Ltd* (1894) 1 Q.B. 671, CA.
[7] It is generally suggested that sign language would be treated as slander.

possibly see it and it will not be forgotten. Damage is presumed, and libel is therefore actionable *per se* (*i.e.* without proof of damage). Slander, in contrast, requires proof of special damage, which can be proved by evidence of financial loss or any other material loss capable of estimation in financial terms. Being shunned by friends is not sufficient. However, being shunned by clients will suffice, due to the financial impact on your business.[8] The damage must, as always, not be too remote. In defamation cases, the test for remoteness, as stated by *Lynch v Knight*,[9] is that the loss is such as might fairly and reasonably on the facts of the case have been anticipated and feared to result. Libel, unlike slander, is also a crime, although few prosecutions are made.

Unfortunately, the distinction between libel and slander is far from watertight. A spoken insult in the presence of your peers may do more harm to your reputation than insults in a disreputable newspaper. The distinction may also be quite complicated. For example, I dictate a letter to my secretary who then posts it. It contains defamatory material. On the current case law, the letter once sent amounts to libel for which I am responsible, but my dictation to the secretary is merely slander.[10] Further problems arise if you consider what happens if the spoken words are recorded on tape: do they now amount to libel? What about insulting words in a long-running play—can they really be considered slander when repeated every night? In the latter case, Parliament has helpfully intervened and stated that performances of a play (except when given on a domestic occasion in a private dwelling) shall be treated as publication in permanent form and therefore libel.[11] Equally, broadcasts on television or on radio are treated as libel.[12] *Youssoupoff v MGM Pictures Ltd*[13] deals somewhat confusingly with our first problem. Here, a Russian Princess complained about words used in the film soundtrack to "Rasputin, the Mad Monk", which she claimed had falsely suggested that she had been raped or seduced by Rasputin. The court took the view that speech which was synchronised with the film took a permanent form and should be treated as libel. Logically, therefore, if the film broke down but the words continued it would be slander. Yet, this ignores the fact that although the words are merely heard, they are permanently recorded which, it is submitted, suggests that they should be considered to be libel. Further examples of unresolved problems include whether writing in chalk on a wall[14] or sky-writing by aeroplanes[15] amounts to libel or slander. Such uncertainty, it is submitted, is as good a reason as any for abolishing the distinction between libel and slander.

Types of slander actionable *per se*

Further remnants of the past are the four occasions where slander is actionable without proof of damage. These represent occasions where the court feels safe in *presuming* damage, because of the nature of the allegations made. **12–003**

---

[8] See *Storey v Challands* (1837) 8 C. & P. 234.
[9] (1861) 9 H.L.C. 577 at 600 (Lord Wensleydale).
[10] *Osborn v Thomas Boulter & Son* [1930] 2 K.B. 226.
[11] Theatres Act 1968, s.4(1).
[12] Broadcasting Act 1990, s.166.
[13] (1934) 50 T.L.R. 581.
[14] See *Monson v Tussauds Ltd* (1894) 1 Q.B. 671 at 692 which suggests it should be treated as libel.
[15] The Faulks Committee at para.76 suggested that it would be libel due to the fact that the vapour takes some time to disperse.

(1) Imputation of a criminal offence punishable by imprisonment

12–004   There must be an imputation that a criminal offence has been committed. For example, in *Webb v Beavan*,[16] it was stated that "I will look you up in Gloucester gaol next week. I know enough to put you there". This was held to imply that a criminal offence had been committed and so was actionable *per se*. An allegation that an individual is *suspected* of a criminal offence will not suffice.[17]

(2) Imputation of a contagious disease

12–005   This, with the rise of AIDS, could have some contemporary relevance. An accusation that a physician has AIDS or is HIV positive would clearly harm the reputation of the physician. However, the last reported case brought under this head was in 1844,[18] which removes its topicality somewhat. The rule has been used in relation to diseases such as venereal disease, leprosy and plague, but it must be questioned whether, with advances in medicine, this exception ought to survive when it can no longer be assumed that people with contagious diseases will be shunned.

(3) Imputation of unchastity or adultery by a female

12–006   This is stated to be actionable *per se* under section 1 of the Slander of Women Act 1891. In modern times, it seems very outdated.

(4) Imputation of professional unfitness or incompetence

12–007   This is the only exception with any contemporary relevance (and on which there are reported cases in the last 100 years). A statement criticising a person's professional competence or fitness for office may affect his or her reputation and will be difficult to brush off. The only question which has arisen here relates to the scope of the exception. At common law, it was held that the accusation had to relate directly to the person's professional competence. The exception therefore did not apply where the accusation was unrelated to the post, for example where a headmaster was accused of committing adultery with one of the school's cleaners.[19] The exception was broadened by s.2 of the Defamation Act 1952 to include all words likely to disparage the claimant's official, professional or business reputation, whether or not the words relate to the claimant's office, profession, calling, trade or business.

As may be seen, the distinction between libel and slander still has a basis at law, although its rationale is questionable. It has been suggested that it excludes minor claims for slander where the claimant has suffered little harm, but in reality the cost of bringing a defamation claim, and procedural rules against vexatious litigants, are likely to deter such claimants in any event.

THE GENERAL REQUIREMENTS OF DEFAMATION

12–008   As stated above, the best way of approaching defamation is by logically answering the following four questions:

---

[16] (1883) 11 Q.B.D. 609.
[17] *Simmons v Mitchell* (1880) 6 App. Cas. 156, PC.
[18] *Bloodworth v Gray* (1844) 7 Man. & Gr. 334 (venereal disease).
[19] *Jones v Jones* [1916] 2 A.C. 481. Applied in *Hopwood v Muirson* [1945] K.B. 313 (solicitor criticised whilst acting as referee for friend).

- Is the statement defamatory?
- Does it refer to the claimant?
- Has it been published to a third party?
- Can the defendant rely on any of the defences?

The role of the judge and jury

An action for defamation, unlike one for negligence, will usually be heard by a judge   **12–009**
and jury, unless the court is of the opinion that the trial requires any prolonged
examination of documents or accounts, or any scientific or local investigation which
cannot conveniently be made with a jury.[20] The judge will determine, as a matter of
law, whether the words are capable of being defamatory, that is, could a reasonable
jury come to the conclusion that the statement was capable of bearing a defamatory
meaning?[21] The jury will determine whether, as a matter of fact, the words in the case
are defamatory. The jury will also determine the level of damages and may, if
appropriate, award aggravated or punitive damages.

The first three questions will be examined in this chapter. Defences will be examined
in Ch. 13.

(1) Is the statement defamatory?

The statement is defamatory if it harms a person's reputation. It is more difficult,   **12–010**
however, to state exactly *when* a person's reputation will be harmed. The classic
definition is found in *Sim v Stretch*,[22] where statements were held to be defamatory and
therefore to harm a person's reputation when they "tend to lower the plaintiff in the
estimation of right-thinking members of society generally".[23] This has been extended
by *Youssoupoff v MGM Pictures Ltd*[24] to circumstances where the claimant is "shunned
or avoided" as a result of the statements. The question is therefore whether your
reputation has been harmed in the eyes of "right-thinking members of society".
Essentially, this is the standard of the "reasonable person", who is, of course, a fiction,
but this sets at least an objective standard to be applied by the courts. The reasonable
person, we are told, is fair-minded, neither unduly suspicious nor unduly naive, nor
avid for scandal, nor bound to select one defamatory meaning when non-defamatory
meanings are available.[25] In practice, it will be determined partly by the judge, who

---

[20] Supreme Court Act 1981, s.69. See *Beta Construction Ltd v Channel Four Television Co Ltd* [1990] 1
W.L.R. 1042, CA.
[21] *Capital and Counties Bank Ltd v Henty* (1882) 7 App. Cas. 741, although the application of the test in this
case is less than satisfactory. See also *Mark v Associated Newspapers Ltd* [2002] E.M.L.R. 38, CA.
[22] [1936] 2 All E.R. 1237.
[23] *ibid.*, at 1240, HL *per* Lord Atkin.
[24] (1934) 50 T.L.R. 581. See L Treiger-Bar-Am (2000) 20 L.S. 291.
[25] See *Lewis v Daily Telegraph* [1964] A.C. 234 at 259–260 per Lord Reid. Society would appear to signify
society as a whole and not simply a section of the community: *Tolley v Fry* [1930] 1 K.B. 467 at 479. It has
been suggested that, in view of the more diverse nature of society today and the fact that the reputation of a
person within his or her own racial or religious community may be damaged by a statement which would not
be regarded as damaging by society at large, this may need to be re-addressed in future: *Arab News Network
v Al-Khazen* [2001] EWCA Civ 118.

decides whether the statement in question is capable of being defamatory before it can be put before a jury. This can raise questions as to the ability of the courts to relate to the standards of society in general. For example, in *Byrne v Deane*,[26] a verse had been placed on the notice-board of a golf club which stated: "But he who gave the game away, may he byrnne [*sic*] in hell and rue the day". Mr Byrne, who was a member of the club, alleged that it implied that he had informed the police of certain illegal gambling machines which had been on the premises and which had been removed as a result. The Court of Appeal held that the verse was not defamatory. An allegation that he had reported a crime to the police could not be regarded as lowering the reputation of Mr Byrne, certainly not in the eyes of a "good and worthy subject of the King". The resulting distress and perhaps isolation suffered by Mr Byrne as a result of the verse was regarded as irrelevant. There is therefore a distinct danger that the standard of "right-thinking people" may rise far above the general standards of society, and fail to protect the claimant's reputation adequately by assuming that right-thinking people could not possibly conclude that a particular statement is defamatory.

Further difficulties may be seen when this test is applied to allegations of adultery and homosexuality. Whilst clearly defamatory in the past, it might be suggested that in more liberal times, they would no longer affect a person's reputation. The court must choose between a liberal approach and an appreciation that such a view may not be shared by every member of society. Who, then, is the right-thinking member of society? In *R. v Bishop*,[27] the court recognised that the legalisation of homosexuality in the Sexual Offences Act 1967 did not necessarily change the views of society, and that, in 1975, many still regarded homosexuality as immoral. It is an open question whether this is still the case today. Arguably, the situation is different for adultery. In a society where one in three marriages fail, one might expect a more tolerant view of adultery and sex outside marriage. On this basis, a statement that X is an adulterer should not be regarded as defamatory, unless it suggests that X is a hypocrite, for example, he is a clergyman or the Minister for the Family. It should be remembered, however, that provided the judge rules that the statement is *capable* of being defamatory, it is the jury who finally resolves whether the statement *is*, in fact, defamatory. It is to be hoped that the jury will reflect current trends in society when reaching its decision.

12–011   It should also be noted that it is no excuse that the defendant did not intend the words to be defamatory.[28] The law protects reputation and it cannot be said that the statement does not affect the claimant's reputation just because the insult was unintentional. The test is objective, and it is irrelevant that the defendant did not intend to defame the claimant, or even whether the people to whom the statement was communicated actually believed the statement to be true.[29] The defendant may, however, be able to claim that the words should not be treated as defamatory because the statement was mere abuse uttered in rage ("You idiot!") and was not intended to be taken seriously. This is a very fine line. While the courts may be prepared to disregard words spoken in the heat of the moment, which the hearer must have understood to be mere abuse, they are unlikely to dismiss written words on this basis.

---

[26] [1937] 1 K.B. 818 at 833.
[27] [1975] Q.B. 274 at 281 The case itself concerned the admissibility of character evidence.
[28] The intention of the defendant may, however, be relevant in relation to possible defences (see Ch. 13) or at least diminish the award of damages.
[29] See *Morgan v Odhams Press* [1971] 1 W.L.R. 1239 at 1246 and 1252.

The general view is that the writer will generally have had the opportunity to cool down and repent, so that if the words are published nevertheless, they cannot be dismissed as mere abuse. In *Berkoff v Burchill*,[30] the majority of the Court of Appeal held that a published description of the actor, director and writer Steven Berkoff as "hideously ugly" was capable of being defamatory and could not be dismissed as mere abuse. He was a person in the public eye and it was held that such a description would expose him to ridicule as it suggested that he had a repulsive appearance.

Defamation is not confined to direct attacks on the claimant's reputation. If this were so, a defendant could easily resort to indirect attacks, safe in the knowledge that the audience would be well aware of what was actually being alleged, and yet the claimant could do nothing. To protect the claimant's reputation, defamation must also include implied or veiled attacks, which are generally known as "innuendo".

Innuendo

An innuendo consists of an implied attack on a person's reputation. The test is **12–012** objective: what view would a reasonable person take of the statement? There are two types of innuendo: true (or legal) and false (or popular). A true innuendo is one where the attack is truly hidden in the absence of special facts and circumstances, which the claimant must show are known by some of the people to whom the statement is published. The court will obviously have to be informed in the Statement of Case what special meanings are alleged and what facts support this meaning.[31] A false or popular innuendo is one which a reasonable person guided by general knowledge would infer from the natural and ordinary meaning of the words.[32] The court does not have to be informed of any specific facts to draw this inference. This is a complicated distinction, and an example will help the reader to understand the distinction between true and false innuendo. Suppose that A publishes a statement that B works for "the family business". By itself, this is not defamatory *unless*:

(i) B's father has been arrested for involvement with the Mafia. With this extra knowledge, we now know that A is implying that B works for the Mafia and is involved in organised crime. This is defamatory as a true innuendo

(ii) B can show that the term "family business" is known to be a slang term for the Mafia. This is unlikely here, but if B were successful, he would be relying on a false or popular innuendo.

A true innuendo was relied upon in *Tolley v J.S. Fry & Sons Ltd*,[33] where a famous amateur golfer alleged that a caricature of him had appeared without his knowledge or consent in an advertisement for Frys Chocolate. This, in itself, was not defamatory. However, Tolley claimed that for people who knew of his amateur status it would

---

[30] [1996] 4 All E.R. 1008. Contrast *Norman v Future Publishing Ltd* [1999] E.M.L.R. 325, CA.
[31] Pt 53, r.2.3 of the Civil Procedure Rules (CPR): "(1) The claimant must specify in the particulars of claim the defamatory meaning which he alleges that the words or matters complained of conveyed, both (a) as to their natural and ordinary meaning; and (b) as to any innuendo meaning (that is a meaning alleged to be conveyed to some person by reason of knowing facts extraneous to the words complained of) and (2) In the case of an innuendo meaning, the claimant must also identify the relevant extraneous facts."
[32] See, generally, *Lewis v Daily Telegraph Ltd* [1964] A.C. 234 at 271–272 *per* Lord Hodson.
[33] [1931] A.C. 333.

imply that, contrary to acceptable amateur conduct, he had accepted money. The House of Lords held the advertisement to be capable of bearing the meaning alleged in the innuendo. People knowing of Tolley's amateur status might think less of him and therefore his reputation would be diminished.[34] Equally, in *Cassidy v Daily Mirror Newspapers* Ltd,[35] there was nothing defamatory in publishing a photograph depicting Cassidy and a young woman announcing that they were engaged. However the fact that Mr Cassidy was still married led the majority of the Court of Appeal to recognise that the words were defamatory of the existing Mrs Cassidy, on the basis that a reasonable person knowing of their relationship might assume that she had cohabited with Cassidy outside marriage. This, in 1928, would be regarded in a negative light. It was no excuse that the newspaper did not know that Cassidy was already married, and had in fact been told by Cassidy that he was engaged to the woman with whom he had been photographed.

Lewis v Daily Telegraph Ltd[36] is a good illustration of how courts deal with a false innuendo. Here, the defendants had published a paragraph in their newspaper which indicated that the Fraud Squad was investigating the affairs of a company and its chairman, Mr Lewis. This was in fact true, and so the claim for defamation on the literal meaning of the words failed. However, it was also claimed that the paragraph contained an innuendo—it indicated that the company was being operated in a fraudulent and dishonest way. The majority of the House of Lords held that the words were not capable of bearing that meaning. The test was an objective one: what would an ordinary and reasonable person infer as the natural and ordinary meaning of these words? The court held that a reasonable person might infer from the paragraph that the company and Lewis were *suspected* of fraud, but held that a reasonable person would not assume that a police investigation indicated that Lewis and the company were *guilty* of such conduct. This has to be correct, otherwise newspapers would be unable to report investigations prior to their final result. The court also recommended that, for clarity, claimants should set out the meaning of the false innuendo on which they wish to rely if it does not speak for itself.[37] This will enable the defendant to be fully aware of the case against him or her and will clarify issues prior to trial.

12–013   The general test is therefore: would the reasonable person view the statement as defamatory on the particular facts of the case? The courts do look at the statements in context. It is not enough to point to a particular sentence or isolated paragraph. The court will look at the article as a whole. This is illustrated by the approach of the House of Lords in *Charleston v News Group Newspapers Ltd*.[38] *The News of the World* had run a story about a computer game, which featured near-naked bodies of models in pornographic poses, on which the heads of two characters from the Australian soap

---

[34] Evidence was given that he would have been called on to resign the membership of any reputable golf club.
[35] [1929] 2 K.B. 331.
[36] [1964] A.C. 234 at 258. See also *Mapp v News Group Newspapers Ltd* [1998] Q.B. 520. Contrast *Hayward v Thompson* [1982] Q.B. 47, where the words "connected with" a murder plot were held to be plainly capable of conveying to ordinary persons the imputation of Hayward's guilt.
[37] [1964] A.C. 234 at 281 and 273. Note Lord Denning M.R. in *Allsop v Church of England Newspaper Ltd* [1972] 2 Q.B. 161 at 167 who stated that, in most cases, it is not only desirable but necessary for the claimant to set out in the Case Statement the meaning which he or she says the words bear unless there is only one ordinary meaning which is clear and explicit. See now CPR, Part 53.
[38] [1995] 2 A.C. 65.

"Neighbours" (Madge and Harold Bishop) had been superimposed. The headline read "Strewth! What's Harold up to with our Madge?" and was accompanied by photographs of the characters as depicted in the game. The actors complained that the photographs suggested that they had participated in some way in the making of the game. Although the accompanying article made it clear that the actors had not participated in any way, it was argued that a significant proportion of readers skimming through the newspaper would only read the headlines and look at the photographs, and would come to the wrong conclusions. The court refused to approach the case in this way. "Defamatory" was judged by the standard of the ordinary reasonable person, who would have taken the trouble to discover what the article was about. It was therefore irrelevant that the *News of the World* may have some readers who only read the headlines.[39] Lord Nicholls did warn newspapers, however, that they were "playing with fire", and that if the explanatory text were tucked away further down the article or on a continuation page, the court would be likely to take a different view.[40]

Once the claimant has shown that the words used were defamatory, he or she must move on to the second requirement and show that the words in fact referred to him or her.

(2) Does the statement refer to the claimant?

This is obviously not a problem if the claimant is mentioned by name, but otherwise the question is again the view of the reasonable person: would the reasonable person, having knowledge of the special circumstances, understand the words to refer to the claimant?[41] This was considered by the House of Lords in *Morgan v Odhams Press Ltd*.[42] A newspaper article in *The Sun* had reported that a girl had been kidnapped by a dog-doping gang. This was incorrect and the girl had been staying at Mr Morgan's flat at the relevant time. Morgan produced a small number of witnesses who had seen the two together and who claimed that, having read the article, they assumed it to suggest that Morgan was part of the dog-doping gang. The majority of the House held that on the facts there was sufficient material for a jury to find that the statement referred to him. It was not necessary to find a specific "pointer" in the article, or a "peg" on which to hang such a reference. Although a careful study of the article would have suggested that it could not refer to Morgan, it was held that the ordinary, reasonable reader did not have the forensic skills of a lawyer. The majority of the House held that, taking account of the sensationalist nature of the article, and the fact that the average reader was likely to read the story casually, gaining a general impression of it, the ordinary reasonable person would, on the facts, have drawn the inference that the article referred to Morgan.[43] A new trial was ordered nevertheless, due to the judge's misdirection to the jury on the assessment of damages.

It is generally the rule that the meaning of any statement must be judged at the time of publication. Liability will not arise where an innocent statement is later rendered

12–014

---

[39] [1995] 2 A.C. 73 *per* Lord Bridge.
[40] *ibid.*, at 74.
[41] *Morgan v Odhams Press Ltd* [1971] 1 W.L.R. 1239.
[42] *ibid.*, at 1245 and 1269–1270.
[43] Note the contrast with the approach taken by the House of Lords in the more recent case of *Charleston v News Group Newspapers Ltd* [1995] 2 A.C. 65, discussed above.

defamatory by subsequent events.[44] However, the courts will not allow this rule to be used to "cover up" defamatory statements where the defendant has made a defamatory statement, but only identified the claimant in a later article. Therefore, in *Hayward v Thompson*,[45] the Court of Appeal admitted in evidence a later article identifying the plaintiff where the first article had merely referred to "a wealthy benefactor of the Liberal party". On this basis, both articles were found to be defamatory of the defendant. [46]

12–015   As stated above, it is irrelevant whether the defendant intended the words to be defamatory. It is equally irrelevant whether the defendant intended to refer to the claimant. Provided reasonable persons would find the statement defamatory, and to refer to the claimant, the defendant who publishes the statement will be liable. *Hulton & Co. v Jones*[47] is the classic example. The defendant newspaper had published a humorous account of a motor festival in Dieppe, featuring the antics of a fictional churchwarden from Peckham called Artemus Jones. Unfortunately for the newspaper, this was also the name of a barrister, who sued for libel. The real Mr Jones was not a churchwarden, had not gone to the Dieppe festival and did not live in Peckham, but friends of his swore that they believed the article to refer to him. The House of Lords held that there was evidence upon which the jury could conclude that reasonable people would believe Mr Jones was referred to and it was irrelevant that the defendants had no intention to defame him.[48]

It is of no assistance to the defendant that the words were true of another individual. In *Newstead v London Express Newspaper Ltd*,[49] a report of the conviction for bigamy of a Harold Newstead, aged 30, of Camberwell, London provoked an action for defamation from another Harold Newstead who also lived in Camberwell and who was about the same age. The Court of Appeal upheld his claim against the newspaper. *Newstead* is perhaps a more meritorious case than *Hulton*. Such a coincidence was obviously prejudicial to the reputation of the innocent Mr Newstead, and the newspaper should therefore have made greater efforts to identify the real culprit. The decision does impose a considerable burden on newspapers, however, which cannot possibly check every story to ascertain whether there is any chance of confusion as to the identity of the person involved. This was recognised by the court, but it was held that it was not unreasonable to place a burden on the party who puts the statements into circulation to identify the person so closely that little or no risk of confusion arises.[50]

The question arises, however, whether it is reasonable to expect newspapers to bear the risk of a person being mistaken for another individual in a photograph in the paper. This problem arose in *O'Shea v MGN Ltd*,[51] where the *Sunday Mirror* had

[44] *Grapelli v Derek Block (Holdings) Ltd* [1981] 1 W.L.R. 822.
[45] [1982] Q.B. 47.
[46] In any event, there was evidence that a number of people had identified Mr Hayward from the context of the first article, including his family, other members of the Liberal party and innumerable journalists.
[47] [1910] A.C. 20. The Faulks Committee recommended no change in the rule of *Hulton v Jones* (para.123).
[48] W.V.H. Rogers, *Winfield & Jolowicz on Torts* (16th ed., Sweet and Maxwell, 2002), p.422, notes that Jones had once worked for the newspaper. This might have influenced the jury, even though his counsel accepted that the author of the article and the newspaper editor did not know of the existence of the respondent.
[49] [1940] 1 K.B. 377.
[50] *ibid.*, at 388 *per* Greene M.R.
[51] [2001] E.M.L.R. 40 (QBD).

published an advertisement for an adult internet service featuring a "glamour" model, who resembled the claimant. Ms O'Shea complained that ordinary sensible readers, who were aware of her resemblance to the model, would have concluded that she had consented to appear on a highly pornographic website. Whilst concluding that, as a matter of law, the image was defamatory,[52] Morland J. held that liability would be contrary to Art. 10 of the European Convention on Human Rights. Protection of Ms O'Shea's reputation could not be said to meet a "pressing social need"[53] and to be necessary in a democratic society for the protection of the reputation of others.[54] The judge distinguished *Hulton* and *Newstead* on the basis that the existence of the claimants could have been discovered in those cases, whereas it would have been impossible in *O'Shea*. Liability would impose an "impossible burden" on the publisher, which could not be justified.[55]

It may be questioned whether such a distinction is valid. Ms O'Shea had been accidentally defamed, as had Mr Jones, and it may be challenged whether the *form* the statement takes should be of such crucial importance. If the true objection is to liability for unintentional defamation, can the Art. 10 right to freedom of expression be confined to photographs? It remains to be seen whether *O'Shea* will found a basis to challenge this form of liability or will be treated in future as an isolated exception. At present, the general rule remains. If confusion does arise, the defendant has only two options:

(i) To argue that there is not enough evidence for a reasonable person to find confusion as to identity (which must have been a close call in *Hulton*).

(ii) To adopt a defence of unintentional defamation. This will be discussed in the next chapter, but generally involves an apology and offer to pay some compensation.

Group defamation

If the statement in question relates to a group of individuals, it will be difficult for the **12–016** claimant to establish that the words refer to him or her directly. Unless the group in question has legal identity, for example is a company, and can therefore sue for loss of the group's reputation, no action will stand *unless*:

(i) the class is so small that the claimant can establish that the statement must apply to every member of the class; or

(ii) the claimant can show that the statement refers to him or her directly.

The leading case on group defamation is the House of Lords case of *Knuppfer v London Express Newspaper Ltd*.[56] In this case, an article had been published which

---

[52] See *Dwek v Macmillan Publishers Ltd* [2000] E.M.L.R. 284, CA, (photograph described as Dodi Fayed with a prostitute was, in fact, of the claimant).
[53] See Lord Keith in *Derbyshire CC v Times Newspapers* [1993] A.C. 534 at 550.
[54] See Art. 10(2).
[55] Para. 43. Morland J. was additionally concerned that liability would inhibit investigative journalism into drug dealing, corruption, child abuse and prostitution.
[56] [1944] A.C. 116.

criticised the Young Russian political party, Mlado Russ. The party consisted of several thousand members, but they were mainly overseas and the British branch consisted of only 24 members. Knuppfer was one of these members. To establish that the libel referred directly to him, he alleged that because he was the head of the British branch, British readers would assume the remarks referred to him. This argument was rejected by the House of Lords. It was held that the article was not capable of referring to Knuppfer. There had been no mention of the activities of the party in the United Kingdom and their Lordships found no evidence to infer that the article referred to Knuppfer. Lord Porter advised that in deciding whether the article was capable of referring to the claimant, the court should examine the size of the class, the generality of the charge and the extravagance of the accusation.[57] The true test was whether a reasonable jury could find that the article was capable of referring to the claimant.

As a general rule, therefore, a statement aimed at a group will not be considered to refer to its individual members. On this basis, a politician could not sue a newspaper which printed "All politicians are liars" unless he or she could show something which referred specifically to him or her.[58] It will depend on the facts of the case. Obviously, the smaller the group and more specific the charge, the easier it will be to show that the article refers to the claimant. For example, a statement that the local five-a-side team are utterly incompetent obviously refers to five particular individuals.[59]

(3) Has the statement been published to a third party?

12–017   This third requirement is vital. It is not enough, for example, that the defendant sends a letter to the claimant making lurid accusations against him or her. This will not harm his or her reputation, although he or she may be distressed by it. It is only when the letter is seen by a third party (or "published") that the claimant's reputation will be harmed.[60] It can be seen that "publication" has nothing to do with printing presses, but signifies that the libel or slander has come to the knowledge of a third party. The claimant's reputation will only suffer harm when the offending words are communicated to someone other than the claimant and the defendant. Insulting words spoken to the claimant in private by the defendant are not defamatory, although they may of course give rise to claims for harassment or assault. Although readers may see the term "malicious publication" used, this should not be taken literally. Malice is not required. We therefore use the simple term "publication".

The requirement of publication is obviously met by printing an article in a newspaper or book, or by shouting a remark in a lecture theatre, and will not generally be a problem. It is really a matter of common sense. For example, if I make defamatory statements in my lecture and the students (a) cannot understand me because I am speaking in old Norse,[61] or (b) cannot hear me because my microphone is not working, I have not published my statements. Publication requires that the words

---

[57] [1994] A.C. 124.
[58] It would seem that although political parties cannot sue for defamation, politicians can sue in their own right. This is discussed below under "Who can sue?"
[59] See also *Aspro Travel v Owners Abroad Group plc* [1996] 1 W.L.R. 132, where directors of a limited family company were allowed to sue for defamation in their own right.
[60] This is not the case, however, for criminal libel, where publication to the prosecutor alone will suffice.
[61] Unless I am very unlucky and one of my audience understands old Norse!

must be intelligible and reach the third party. Problems have arisen when the defendant alleges that he or she did not intend to publish the words. For example, A sends a letter defamatory of B to B. B alleges in court that it was opened by his wife, Mrs B, and it has therefore been published to a third party enabling him to sue for defamation. A states that he did not intend the letter to be published and therefore he should not be liable. The courts deal with this by having a test of reasonable foresight: if it is reasonably foreseeable that a third party would see the statement, then the defendant will be liable. On that basis, in *Theaker v Richardson*,[62] the defendant was liable for sending a defamatory letter to a married woman, which had been opened by her husband. The letter, which had been addressed to the wife, had been sealed in a brown envelope which looked like an election circular. The court upheld the view of the jury that it was foreseeable that the husband would open the letter. In contrast, in *Huth v Huth*,[63] it was found that it was not foreseeable that a butler would open his employer's mail. Defendants wishing to avoid publication should ensure that the document is in a sealed envelope marked "private and confidential". Making defamatory remarks on a postcard or telegram is obviously unwise and the court will presume, in the absence of evidence to the contrary, that someone will have read the remarks along the way.[64] Similarly, a careless defendant who leaves documents open on his or her desk runs the risk of publication to visitors or perhaps cleaners, but not, it would seem, to a burglar who steals the document from a locked drawer.[65]

A few odd rules remain. It is still the rule (despite the fact that the law no longer regards husband and wife as one person) that a husband does not publish words by telling his wife (or vice versa).[66] A modern explanation for this rule may be a concern for "marital harmony" whereby the courts are reluctant, save in exceptional circumstances, to see spouses give evidence against one another. It also seems to be the rule that while an author who dictates a document to a typist is liable for publication,[67] a typist or printer who hands back to the author a document containing defamatory statements made by the author is deemed not to be liable for publication. This is easier to explain. The typist can hardly publish the document to the author of the document itself.[68] The typist and printer are effectively acting as the author's agents, and an agent repeating back the statements of the principal cannot be treated as publication to a third party. However, if the documents are shown to anyone else, the typist or printer (as well as the author) *may* be liable for publication of the statements.

In this regard, it should be noted that it is no defence that the defendant is merely repeating the defamatory statements of another.[69] Repetition will increase the harm to the claimant's reputation, for which the defendant will be obliged to pay compensation.

[62] [1962] 1 W.L.R. 151.
[63] [1915] 3 K.B. 323.
[64] See, *e.g. Sim v Stretch* [1936] 2 All E.R. 1237.
[65] *Pullman v Hill* [1891] 1 Q.B. 524 at 527 *per* Lord Esher M.R.
[66] *Wennhak v Morgan* (1888) 20 Q.B.D. 635.
[67] *Osborn v Thomas Boulter & Son* [1930] 2 K.B. 226.
[68] See *Eglantine Inn Ltd v Smith* [1948] N.I. 29 at 33 and *Osborn v Thomas Boulter & Son* [1930] 2 K.B. 226 at 237 *per* Slesser L.J.
[69] *Weld-Blundell v Stephens* [1920] A.C. 956. See also *Stern v Piper* [1997] Q.B. 123 and *Shah v Standard Chartered Bank* [1999] Q.B. 241. This rule was strongly affirmed in *Mark v Associated Newspapers Ltd* [2002] E.M.L.R. 38, CA, where it was held to be consistent with Article 10 of the European Convention on Human Rights.

The fact that the person repeating the libel or slander expresses a doubt or disbelief as to the truth of the statement is irrelevant—repetition is sufficient to incur liability.[70]

There are a limited number of situations, however, where the original defamer, rather than the repeater, will remain liable, namely:

(a) Where the original defamer has authorised or requested publication;[71]

(b) Where he or she intended that the statement should be repeated or republished;

(c) Where he or she has informed a person who is under a moral duty to repeat or republish the statement,[72] or, generally,

(d) Where the re-publication is, on the facts, the natural and probable result of the original publication.

12–018 This last point was argued in *Slipper v BBC*.[73] Slipper, a former detective superintendent, had complained about a film made and broadcast by the BBC which dealt with his abortive efforts to bring back one of the Great Train Robbers, Ronnie Biggs, from Brazil. Slipper claimed that a press review of the film and its later public broadcast portrayed him in a defamatory light, and that the BBC were responsible for the repetition of the libel in the newspaper reviews of the film. The Court of Appeal treated the matter as one of causation and remoteness, rather than turning on any particular rule relating to defamation: did the reviews amount to a *novus actus interveniens* breaking the chain of causation? Therefore, if repetition of the libel was the natural and probable consequence of the original publication, the original publisher would remain liable. On the facts, the court held that this was a question for the jury and refused to strike out this part of Slipper's case.

The application of this test was discussed more recently in *McManus v Beckham*.[74] Here, McManus had complained that Victoria Beckham, wife of footballer David Beckham, had entered his memorabilia shop and had advised customers that a signed photograph of her husband for sale in the shop was a forgery. The incident received extensive press coverage, and McManus brought a claim based on subsequent damage to his business. The question remained whether it was a natural and probable consequence of her outburst that it would receive media attention. The Court of Appeal rejected a test of reasonable foresight, which had been suggested in *Slipper*. This would impose an unfair burden on the defendant. A just and reasonable result would be achieved by imposing liability:

(a) Where the defendant is *actually aware* that what she says or does is likely to be reported, and, that if she slanders someone that slander is likely to be repeated in whole or in part; *or*

(b) Where she *should have appreciated* that there was a *significant* risk that what she said would be repeated in whole or in part in the press and that that would increase the damage caused by the slander.[75]

---

[70] *Slipper v BBC* [1991] 1 Q.B. 283.

[71] *e.g.* by requesting journalists present to note allegations made during a parish meeting: see *Parkes v Prescott* (1869) L.R. 4 Ex. 169 at 179.

[72] *Slipper v BBC* [1991] 1 Q.B. 283 at 301 *per* Slade L.J.

[73] [1991] 1 Q.B. 283.

[74] [2002] 1 W.L.R. 2982.

[75] Waller L.J. above at 2998.

In other words, she will be liable where it was foreseeable that further publication would probably take place and that, in consequence, increased harm to the claimant would ensue.[76] On the facts of the case, it could not be said that it was impossible for the claimants to satisfy this test.[77]

One last question is whether it is possible to publish by omission. For example, in *Byrne v Deane*,[78] discussed earlier, the question arose whether the club could be liable for failing to remove the notice in question. The court held that those responsible for the club would be liable if they failed to remove defamatory matter attached to the club notice-board within a reasonable time. However, if the defamatory matter was not readily removable (for example, carved deep into stonework) and could only be removed at great inconvenience and expense, its non-removal would not amount to publication. Equally, the host of a phone-in show might find himself or herself liable for failing to take reasonable care to prevent controversial guests making defamatory statements. It is therefore a question of control. In this last case, however, the host may now have a defence of innocent dissemination under section 1 of the Defamation Act 1996 (see Ch. 13).

Who can sue?

(1) Any living human being

We have seen numerous examples of this already, such as Princess Youssoupoff and   **12–019**
Artemus Jones. It should be noted, however, that the action does not survive death,[79]
so the estate of a person who has been defamed has no cause of action.

(2) Companies

This is more controversial. A company is a corporate entity, not a real person, and is   **12–020**
incapable of having its "personal feelings" injured by the defendant's statements. Yet, as we stated at the start of this chapter, the tort of defamation is concerned with *reputation*, not personal feelings. A company does have a business reputation to protect. Despite arguments that this interest is not sufficient to merit the benefit of a tort actionable *per se*, and is sufficiently protected by other torts, such as malicious falsehood and deceit, it is clear that companies can sue for defamation. The classic authority is *South Hetton Coal Co. v North-Eastern Association Ltd*,[80] where the Court of Appeal held that the company was entitled to sue a newspaper which had alleged that properties in which the company housed its employees were highly insanitary. A libel calculated to injure the company's trading reputation was held to be actionable. Readers may remember the more modern example in the long-running "McLibel" trial[81] in which the fast-food chain McDonalds brought a case against two environmental campaigners for allegedly defamatory statements about the company. The Faulks

---

[76] Laws L.J. above at 3001. This arguably is an easier test, although Clarke L.J. found no disagreement between the two judges and concurred with both.
[77] The case was ultimately settled, Mrs Beckham paying the claimants £55,000 for the hurt and damage suffered together with a set of official merchandise signed by her husband: Statement in Open Court, March 11, 2003 (QBD, Gray J.).
[78] [1937] 1 K.B. 818.
[79] Law Reform (Miscellaneous Provisions) Act 1934, s.1(1).
[80] [1894] 1 Q.B. 133.
[81] *McDonalds Corp. v Steel (No.4)* [1995] 3 All E.R. 615. The trial itself lasted 313 days (the longest trial in English history). See J. Vidal, *McLibel—Burger culture on trial* (Pan, 1997).

Committee recommended that companies should not be able to sue unless they had suffered financial loss or the words were likely to cause the company financial damage.[82] This has not been implemented.

Who cannot sue?

(1) Governmental bodies

12–021 The House of Lords in *Derbyshire CC v Times Newspapers Ltd*[83] held that institutions of central or local government, such as local authorities, could not sue for defamation. This is an important decision. The plaintiff, a local authority, had brought an action for damages for libel against *The Times* in respect of two newspaper articles which had questioned the propriety of its financial dealings. On a preliminary issue as to whether the plaintiff had a cause of action against the defendants, the House of Lords upheld the view of the Court of Appeal that a local authority could not bring an action for libel. Lord Keith, giving the leading judgment, commented that:

> "It is of the highest public importance that a democratically elected governmental body, or indeed any governmental body, should be open to uninhibited public criticism. The threat of a civil action for defamation must inevitably have an inhibiting effect on freedom of speech."[84]

The decision is therefore significant in recognising that it is in the public interest that individuals are free to question and criticise central and local government. It would be contrary to the democratic process and freedom of expression for such bodies to have a right to sue in defamation, and would "place an undesirable fetter on freedom of speech".[85] In reaching this conclusion, the House of Lords, unlike the Court of Appeal,[86] did not rely on the European Convention on Human Rights, but relied on English and United States case law.[87] In future, however, with the incorporation of the Convention into English law by the Human Rights Act 1998, it can be expected that Article 10 will form the main focus of any discussion of freedom of expression. The decision marks welcome recognition that open government is a valuable part of modern democratic society and that any restrictions of freedom of expression in this context should be examined very carefully.

(2) Political parties

12–022 The logic of (1), namely the requirement that the public should be able to question the executive, applies equally to political parties. Buckley J. in *Goldsmith v Bhoyrul*[88]

[82] Para.342.
[83] [1993] A.C. 534. See B. Bix and A. Tomkins (1993) 56 M.L.R. 738; S. Palmer [1993] C.L.J. 363, and E. Grant and J.G. Small (1994) 14 O.J.L.S. 287.
[84] [1993] A.C. 534 at 547.
[85] *ibid.*, at 549 *per* Lord Keith.
[86] [1992] Q.B. 770.
[87] Lord Keith commented ([1993] A.C. 534 at 541): "My Lords, I have reached my conclusion upon the common law of England without finding any need to rely upon the European Convention . . . I can only add that I find it satisfactory to be able to conclude that the common law of England is consistent with the obligations assumed by the Crown under the Treaty in this particular field".
[88] [1998] Q.B. 459 at 463.

applied *Derbyshire* to exclude a claim for defamation by the Referendum Party.[89] Despite the fact that the party had yet to be elected, Buckley J. held that defamation actions, or the threat of such actions, would restrict free speech, which would be contrary to the public interest. The public should be free to discuss and criticise political parties putting themselves forward for election.

It is important, however, to note the limited effect of these two decisions. These decisions do not prevent individual politicians from suing, and indeed a number of politicians have sued in recent years (for example, former Conservative M.P.s Rupert Allason and Neil Hamilton) with mixed success. There is an obvious argument that politicians, involved in the democratic process, should also be prevented from suing for defamation for the reasons stated in *Derbyshire*, at least when the statements relate to their performance as Members of Parliament.[90] This does not appear to be the legal position at present. There is no English equivalent to the United States restrictions on the ability of public figures to sue for defamation, stated by the United States Supreme Court in *New York Times v Sullivan*.[91] In that case, the Supreme Court held that in the light of the protection of free speech in the First Amendment, public figures may only sue if they can present clear and convincing evidence of actual malice by the publisher. Actual malice is shown by proving that the defendant published the piece with knowledge that the defamatory statement was false or at least with reckless disregard as to its falsity. The rule in *Derbyshire* is further undermined by the fact that governmental bodies still have the right to sue for malicious falsehood (see Ch. 13) and to prosecute for criminal libel. The impact of the decision must therefore be questionable when the restriction can so easily be circumvented in this way.[92] In *Derbyshire* itself, the council leader, Bookbinder, was able to sue in his own right for damages. Mr Bookbinder's earlier action against Norman Tebbit, former Chairman of the Conservative party, will be discussed in the next chapter.

Conclusion

In this chapter, we have examined the necessary elements which the claimant must establish to bring an action for defamation. The next chapter will concentrate on the defences available to the defendant. As we shall see, it is with the defences that the real tensions between the right of freedom of speech and the need to protect the claimant's reputation show themselves. Whilst recognising that a claimant should have a right to defend his or her reputation against publication of defamatory words, the courts nevertheless consider whether publication can be defended, either on the basis that the words are true, or that publication is in the public interest. The defences available in defamation are somewhat complicated and therefore warrant a chapter of their own.

12–023

---

[89] The Referendum party had been founded by the late Sir James Goldsmith. It sought to secure a referendum on Britain's future in Europe and put up 547 candidates in the 1997 election.
[90] See E. Barendt [1993] P.L. 449.
[91] 376 U.S. 254 (1964). See also *Lingens v Austria* (1986) 8 E.H.R.R. 407 in which the European Court of Human Rights adopted an approach towards public figures similar to that adopted in the U.S. For a comparison, see D. Elder (1986) 35 I.C.L.Q. 891.
[92] See B. Bix and A. Tomkins (1993) 56 M.L.R. 738.

Chapter 13

DEFENCES TO DEFAMATION

Introduction

In the last chapter we examined the basic requirements of a defamation action. The burden is on the claimant to establish (a) that the statement is defamatory, (b) that it refers to the claimant and (c) that it has been published to a third party. In this chapter, we examine the defences open to the defendant once the claimant has established these three requirements. The main defences are justification (or truth), fair comment and privilege. These defences protect the defendant in two ways: first, where he or she has told the truth, and, secondly, where the words have been published in circumstances where it is in the public interest that the defendant should be free to publish. These defences must now also be considered in the light of the Human Rights Act 1998. The Act places particular importance on freedom of expression (Art. 10) and requires the courts to balance the protection of a party's reputation against the public interest in allowing individuals to "hold opinions and to receive and impart information and ideas without interference" by the courts. Section 12(4) of the Act further provides that the courts "must have particular regard to the importance of the Convention right to freedom of expression." Although the law of defamation has always recognised these two conflicting interests, it cannot be denied that the 1998 Act has brought this debate to the fore.

It should be also noted that although justification, fair comment and privilege are the most important defences, other defences exist. It is a defence if the claimant has expressly or impliedly consented to the publication of the defamatory matter,[1] and under the Defamation Act 1996[2] a number of further options arise: unintentional defamation and innocent dissemination. Consent will be discussed generally in Ch. 14, but the other five defences will be examined below. If all the defences fail, the defendant has one final option. This is to mitigate the level of damages (to be assessed by the jury) by raising arguments in his or her favour, for example that an apology was made or that the defamatory material was not shown to a large number of people.

13–001

---

[1] *Cookson v Harewood* [1932] 2 K.B. 478n; *Chapman v Lord Ellesmere* [1932] 2 K.B. 431 at 463–465 *per* Slesser L.J.

[2] See K. Williams (1997) 5 Tort L. Rev. 206.

Such arguments will not amount to a defence, but may at least lead the jury to award a lesser amount of damages against the defendant.

We shall discuss each defence in turn.

(1) JUSTIFICATION (OR TRUTH)[3]

13–002   It is a valid defence to show that the defamatory statements were in fact true. Two points should be noted here. First, defamatory statements are presumed to be *untrue*. The claimant does not have to show that the statements were false. The burden therefore will be on the defendant to show that the statements were true and so justified. Secondly, the claimant has no right to complain about true statements which lower his or her reputation. Logically, such statements merely bring the individual's reputation down to its appropriate level.[4] It is also irrelevant whether the statements are published out of malice or to let others know the truth. The only exception to this is contained in s.8 of the Rehabilitation of Offenders Act 1974. Section 8(5) provides that where the claimant complains that the defendant has published information concerning his or her spent convictions, the defendant cannot rely on the defence of justification if the publication is proved to have been made with malice. The burden will be on the claimant to show the presence of malice.[5]

The difficulties in proving that a particular allegation is true should not be underestimated. The defendant will have to justify, on the balance of probabilities, not only the express meaning of the words, but any innuendoes deriving from the statement. In *Wakley v Cooke*,[6] for example, the defendant had called the plaintiff a "libellous journalist". He was able to show that a judgment had once been obtained against the plaintiff for libel. However, because the words, by innuendo, were capable of meaning that the plaintiff was in the *habit* of libelling people, the comment could not be justified by referring to only one previous incident of libel. The defendant's claim of justification therefore failed.

The burden on the defendant is reduced, however, by the fact that the defendant is only required to show that the words used were *substantially* true. In *Alexander v North Eastern Railway Co*,[7] the defendants had stated that the plaintiff had been convicted of an offence of dishonesty and sentenced to three weeks' imprisonment in default of payment of a fine. In fact, they could only prove the conviction and a sentence of two weeks' imprisonment. Nevertheless, the court found the statement to be substantially true and the defendants therefore succeeded in their defence of justification.

Section 5 of the Defamation Act 1952 also assists the defendant when several allegations have been made against the claimant. Section 5 provides that:

[3] The term favoured by the Faulks Committee (Report of the Committee on Defamation, 1975, Cmnd 5090) para.129, who believed that it would save confusion.
[4] *M'Pherson v Daniels* (1829) 10 B. & C. 263 at 272. It is irrelevant that the defendant did not know the statements to be true at the time they were made, provided they are of course in fact true.
[5] Eady J. in *Silkman v Heard* (February 28, 2001, QBD) raises the question whether this is compatible with the right to freedom of expression in Art. 10 of the European Convention on Human Rights in that the information is in the public domain and this section has been relied on so rarely in defamation actions.
[6] (1849) 4 Exch. 511; 154 E.R. 1316.
[7] (1865) 6 B. & S. 340; 122 E.R. 1221.

" . . . in an action for libel or slander in respect of words containing two or more distinct charges against the plaintiff a defence of justification shall not fail by reason only that the truth of every charge is not proved if the words not proved to be true do not materially injure the plaintiff's reputation having regard to the truth of the remaining charges."

On this basis, if the defendant has made a number of *distinct* charges against the claimant and the defendant cannot prove the truth of all the charges, this does not necessarily mean that the defendant cannot establish the defence. It will be sufficient that the defendant has proved the truth of the most serious charges such that the other statements do not injure the claimant's reputation *materially*. An example will help: X has published an article which alleges that Y (i) had stolen all the Christmas presents from a children's home, (ii) had written on the wall "Santa Claus does not exist", and (iii) had spelt "Santa Claus" incorrectly. If X could justify allegation (i) and (ii), his defence would not fail because he could not also prove allegation (iii).

13–003

The burden is therefore on the defendant to justify the substantial truth or "sting" of the allegations. To achieve this, the defendant may also wish to raise matters with a "common sting" in support of his or her claim of justification. For example, in *Williams v Reason*,[8] a Welsh amateur rugby player sued in respect of an article which accused him of writing a book for profit, contrary to his amateur status. The defendants claimed justification and were permitted to allege in support of the article that the player had previously taken money for wearing a particular brand of boots. The sting of the defamatory words was that Williams had compromised his amateur status (so-called "shamateurism") and the evidence of the boots money went to justify that charge. However, if the allegation against the claimant is *specific*, then the claimant can simply sue on the basis of this individual allegation and the defendant will not be permitted to raise matters with a "common sting".[9] On this basis, the Court of Appeal in *Bookbinder v Tebbit*[10] struck out part of the defence put forward by Norman Tebbit, the former chairman of the Conservative party, which referred to general examples of irresponsible spending by Derbyshire City Council. The court found that Tebbit had made a specific allegation against Bookbinder that the council, under his leadership, had squandered public money by overprinting stationery with a political message. He would therefore have to justify that particular allegation.

The defendant can also, when appropriate, rely on s.13 of the Civil Evidence Act 1968 (as amended by s.12(1) of the Defamation Act 1996). This provides that if the defendant has alleged that the claimant has committed an offence, this can be proved to be true simply by giving evidence of the conviction. It is not necessary to prove that the claimant was rightly convicted.

If the defendant cannot show that the statements were substantially true, the defence fails. Partial justification will not constitute a defence, although it may serve to reduce the jury's assessment of damages. Should the defendant fail completely in the defence of justification, it is likely that a jury will award the claimant a higher level of

---

[8] [1988] 1 W.L.R. 96 at 103 *per* Stephenson L.J.
[9] *Polly Peck (Holdings) plc v Trelford* [1986] Q.B. 1000. See also *Cruise v Express Newspapers plc* [1999] Q.B. 931, CA (where the article in question contains two separate and distinct allegations, the defendant will not be permitted to rely on the other allegation to support a defence of justification or fair comment.)
[10] [1989] 1 W.L.R. 640.

damages. An unsuccessful attempt to justify the defamatory statement aggravates the injury to the claimant by giving the statement extra publicity at trial, and so merits a higher award.[11] It is therefore a calculated risk whether to raise this defence. Where the defendant raises a defence of justification or fair comment, the defendant must make it clear which of the words complained of are statements of fact, and must set out the facts and matters relied upon to support the allegation that the words are true.[12] The defendant must also state the meaning he or she seeks to justify.[13]

(2) FAIR COMMENT

13–004   This is a very different defence to justification. Here, the defendant does not have to show that his or her words are true, but that he or she has exercised the right to criticise the claimant. Inevitably, however, the defendant's right to freedom of expression will be kept within bounds. The difficult question for the court is where the law should draw the line between the defendant's democratic right to comment and the claimant's right to protect his or her reputation. In applying the defence, the courts have imposed three main limitations on the extent to which a defendant can escape liability for criticism: (a) it must be in the public interest, (b) it must be "comment", and (c) it must be fair and honest. These limitations are discussed below.

In the public interest

13–005   This is the first limitation on the defence: it is only acceptable if the defendant comments in the "public interest" or in relation to a matter submitted for public criticism (for example, a book). This raises the obvious question of what is meant by the "public interest". A mere glance at the tabloid press indicates that the public are interested in all sorts of things! "Public interest" is therefore not interpreted as what interests the public, but rather what a judge considers it is in the public's interest to know. In other words, matters which affect people generally, in which they are *legitimately* interested or concerned.[14] Such matters range from the conduct of politicians,[15] to the insanitary conditions in which employees are housed,[16] to the sudden closure of a West End play.[17]

It must be comment

13–006   The defendant must be able to show that the words in question consist of a comment on a given set of facts. Whereas for justification, the defendant must prove that the words used are true, the defendant is not required to show that the comment is true,

[11] See Lord Diplock in *Broome v Cassell & Co. Ltd* [1972] A.C. 1027 at 1125.
[12] See Practice Direction to Part 53, para.2.5 to the Civil Procedures Rules.
[13] *Lucas-Box v News Group Newspapers Ltd* [1986] 1 W.L.R. 147.
[14] See Lord Denning M.R. in *London Artists v Littler* [1969] 2 Q.B. 375 at 391.
[15] *Seymour v Butterworth* (1862) 3 F. & F. 372; 176 E.R. 166.
[16] *South Hetton Coal Co. v North-Eastern Association Ltd* [1894] 1 Q.B. 133.
[17] *London Artists v Littler* [1969] 2 Q.B. 375.

merely that it is fair. It is important, however, that the comment should be based on a true set of facts. (The defendant will obviously not be able to invent facts and then "comment" on them). The only exception to this rule is where the facts commented upon have been published by a person on a privileged occasion, for example where a witness has made a statement in court.[18] Otherwise, the facts on which the comment is made must be shown to be true.

It is sometimes a difficult question whether the defendant has sufficiently stated or indicated the facts on which the comment is made. The case law provides no clear answer. In *Kemsley v Foot*,[19] Lord Kemsley (a well-known newspaper proprietor at the time) complained about an article entitled "Lower than Kemsley", which criticised the quality of a newspaper unconnected with him. The article contained no other reference to Kemsley, but the inference was obviously that Kemsley produced low quality newspapers. The defendants claimed fair comment, but it was questioned whether the defendants could rely on this defence when there were no facts in the article to "comment" upon. The House of Lords took a very broad view of the headline and held that where a "substratum of fact" could be inferred from the words used, the defence of fair comment could be put to the jury. Here, the defendants had clearly referred to Lord Kemsley, who was well-known to the public generally. This decision seems very generous on the facts, and a far stricter line was taken by the House of Lords in the more recent case of *Telnikoff v Matusevitch*.[20] In this case, a letter was published in the *Daily Telegraph* which criticised an article by the plaintiff, published in the same newspaper, concerning recruitment to the BBC Russian service. The letter suggested that the plaintiff was racist. The plaintiff brought an action against the letter writer for libel. The question arose whether, in considering the letter writer's defence of fair comment, the letter should be considered in the context of the article it criticised. The majority of the House of Lords held that in considering whether the letter amounted to "comment", the court should *not* look at the article, since many readers of the letter would not have read the article or, if they had read it, would not have had its terms fully in mind. If, in isolation, remarks in the letter were adjudged to be statements of fact rather than comment, then the defence of fair comment would not lie, and the defendant would have to resort to the alternative defence of justification. Lord Keith denied that this would require future letter writers to include the entire text of the article in the letter. The onus would simply be on the letter writer to make it clear that he or she was writing comment and not making statements of fact. His Lordship thought that newspaper editors would not have any difficulty in observing whether this had in fact been achieved.[21]

There is, therefore, a fine line between a statement of fact (to which the defence of fair comment does not apply) and comment based on ascertainable facts. Generally, it would seem that if the statement in question refers to a given set of facts which are common knowledge, or are referred to directly, then it is comment. So, if I state that "X has just been convicted of murder. His conduct has been disgraceful", I will be able to rely on the defence of fair comment, provided I can prove that X has been convicted

---

[18] *Mangena v Wright* [1909] 2 K.B. 958; *Brent Walker Group plc v Time Out Ltd* [1991] 2 Q.B. 33, CA (provided the report is fair and accurate).
[19] [1952] A.C. 345.
[20] [1992] 2 A.C. 343.
[21] Note, however, Lord Ackner's vigorous dissenting judgment in favour of freedom of speech.

of murder. Equally, it would seem, if X is well-known to the public as a murderer, on the basis of *Kemsley*, I could still rely on fair comment if I simply stated "X's conduct is disgraceful". In contrast, if I stated "Y is untrustworthy", this would be treated as a statement of fact, because there is no factual basis upon which I can claim to be commenting. We can see, therefore, that the issue is far from straightforward. It will fall to the judge to decide whether the words are capable of amounting to comment (the jury will decide ultimately whether the words *do* amount to comment). The defendant may be assisted, however, by section 6 of the Defamation Act 1952. This states:

".. . in an action for libel or slander in respect of words consisting partly of allegations of fact and partly of expressions of opinion, a defence of fair comment shall not fail by reason only that the truth of every allegation of fact is not proved if the expression of opinion is fair comment having regard to such of the facts alleged or referred to in the words complained of as are proved."

This means that the truth of every statement of fact need not be proved. For example, A publishes an article which states that schoolteacher B failed his examinations at university, is always late and is therefore incompetent to teach at the local school. B sues for libel. A is able to prove that B failed his examinations, but finds that B is noted for his punctuality. Here, A can rely on section 6 to show that his comment is fair, and it will not matter that he cannot show the truth of all the allegations of fact.

Fair and honest

13–007   This final limitation is difficult to define. The courts apply the following test: was the opinion, however exaggerated, obstinate or prejudiced, honestly held by the person expressing it?[22] The judge will decide whether a hypothetical person *could* honestly express the commentator's views on the assumption that he knew the facts accurately stated in the article (the objective test).[23] The jury will decide whether the defendant acted honestly and not maliciously (the subjective test). It should be noted that the jury need not *agree* with the comment, but must decide whether the statement is within the bounds of fair comment. The fact that the comment is expressed strongly, provided it does not descend to mere abuse, will make no difference.[24]

The defence of fair comment, unlike the defence of justification, will be defeated by malice. (As we will see later, malice also defeats the defence of qualified privilege) It is for the claimant to allege malice, and the judge will only put the allegation to the jury where he or she is satisfied that the claimant can adduce evidence to support a finding that the defendant was malicious. It has been assumed in the past that "malice"

[22] See *Reynolds v Times Newspapers Ltd* [2001] 2 A.C. 127 at 193 *per* Lord Nicholls; *Slim v Daily Telegraph* [1968] 2 Q.B. 157 at 170; *Merivale v Carson* (1887) 20 Q.B.D. 275 at 281; *Turner v Metro-Goldwyn-Mayer Pictures Ltd* [1950] 1 All E.R. 449 at 461; *Silkin v Beaverbrook Newspapers Ltd* [1958] 1 W.L.R. 743 at 747.
[23] Eady J. in *Branson v Bower (No.2)* [2002] Q.B. 737 at 750 found that it would be unnecessary and confusing to consider whether the defendant could or should have discovered other facts that would have led a hypothetical observer to the conclusion that his or her comment was unwarranted. The judge therefore rejected any attempt to introduce negligence into the defence of fair comment.
[24] *Merivale v Carson* (1887) 20 Q.B.D. 275.

possesses the same meaning for the defences of fair comment and qualified privilege, namely that the courts are required to consider whether the defendant was acting under some indirect or improper motive. However, Lord Nicholls in a recent judgment in the Court of Final Appeal in Hong Kong took a different view. In *Cheng v Tse Wai Chun*,[25] his Lordship focussed on the key question of honesty, which he found to be the touchstone of this defence.[26] Regardless of motive, if the defendant honestly believed the truth of his comment, then a court would not find malice. Spite, animosity, intention to injure or other motivation would only be relevant as evidence that the defendant did not genuinely believe the view expressed. Although only persuasive in English law, Eady J. has supported this development in two judgments.[27] In *Branson v Bower (No.2)*, he emphasised the rationale for this change:

"It is necessary to acknowledge that if a defendant does indeed have to pass any more restrictive test, going beyond that of honesty, then the consequence would be a significant inhibiting effect on freedom of expression on matters of public interest . . . As Lord Nicholls makes clear, the whole point about a defence of fair comment is that it is to allow citizens to express hard-hitting opinions on matters of public interest honestly without fear of being brought before the courts."[28]

One final difficulty lies in reconciling the *Campbell v Spottiswoode*[29] line of authority with the Lord Nicholls test. In this case, Cockburn C.J. held that where the defendant has alleged that the claimant has "corrupt, base, or dishonest motives" for acting in a certain way, he could not rely on fair comment "unless there is so much ground for the imputation that a jury shall find, not only that he had an honest belief in the truth of his statements, but that his belief was not without foundation".[30] This additional requirement of "without foundation" has caused some problems in interpretation. It would appear to indicate that the defendant must prove the truth of the comment, but this was denied by Buckley L.J. in *Peter Walker Ltd v Hodgson*[31] who found that it would be satisfied where a fair-minded man might, upon the facts, *bona fide* hold that opinion. It remains an unjustifiable anomaly, and has been rightly criticised by the Faulks Committee who recommended that it should be removed and the ordinary rules of fair comment should apply.[32] This view was supported recently by Eady J. in *Branson v Bower (No.2)*,[33] and it is to be hoped that this recommendation will finally be acted upon.

[25] Also known as *Tse Wai Chun Paul v Albert*, [2001] E.M.L.R. 777 at 797; 10 B.H.R.C. 525 (CFA (HK)). Comment F.A. Trindade (2001) 117 L.Q.R. 169.
[26] Indeed, his Lordship favoured the name "honest comment" to that traditional title of "fair comment": above at 782.
[27] *Branson v Bower (No.2)* [2002] Q.B. 737 and *Sugar v Associated Newspapers Ltd* (unreported) February 6, 2001.
[28] See above at 746. Lord Nicholls had held that the right to express comments honestly held lay at the heart of the defence and so would allow politicians, social reformers, busybodies, those with or without political or other ambitions to "grind their axes": above at 789.
[29] (1863) 3 B. & S. 769.
[30] See above at 776.
[31] [1909] 2 K.B. 239 at 253.
[32] See Faulks Committee (Report of the Committee on Defamation, 1975, Cmnd 5090), para.169.
[33] [2002] Q.B. 737 at 746.

(3) PRIVILEGE

13–008   This is the third main defence. Here, we are concerned with a list of occasions when the public interest in freedom of expression is such that it overrides any concerns as to the effect of this freedom on the claimant's reputation. A defendant who makes a defamatory statement on such an occasion may raise the defence of privilege. The defence is somewhat technical: the defendant must show the court that the occasion on which the statement was made falls within an established head of privilege.

There are two types of privilege in English law. Absolute privilege is the stronger form of privilege and applies on occasions where the need to protect freedom of speech is so important as to create an *absolute* defence to any action for defamation, irrespective of the motives or words of the author. Qualified privilege is the weaker form of privilege. It applies on occasions where it is desirable that freedom of speech should be protected, but only where the author is acting honestly and without malice. If the claimant can show that the defendant has acted maliciously, the qualified privilege is lost. The judge decides whether the occasion is a privileged one, and whether a reasonable jury could find that the author's dominant motive was malice. The jury will decide whether any allegation of malice has been proved.

Decisions determining the occasions which merit absolute or qualified privilege have been taken over the last 500 years and represent the policy choices of Parliament and the judiciary at particular moments in history. The most recent consideration of privilege by the legislature has resulted in the Defamation Act 1996. The House of Lords also recently considered privilege in the case of *Reynolds v Times Newspapers*.[34] Both are discussed below.

Absolute privilege

13–009   Absolute privilege applies to statements made in Parliament, in court and by certain officers of state. There are five main occasions when the defence will apply.

(1) Statements in Parliament

13–010   Article 9 of the Bill of Rights 1688 provides that "the freedom of speech and debates or proceedings in Parliament ought not to be impeached or questioned in any court or place out of Parliament". This preserves parliamentary autonomy, and allows Members of Parliament freely to criticise individuals as they feel appropriate. It also prevents the courts from inquiring into the conduct of parliamentary business. On this basis, in *Church of Scientology of California v Johnson-Smith*,[35] the plaintiff was not permitted to rely upon statements made by an M.P. in Parliament as evidence of malice, even though the action was based on comments made by the M.P. outside Parliament. The rule can be a mixed blessing for M.P.s. When the former Conservative M.P., Neil Hamilton, sued *The Guardian* for libel, the action was stayed by May J., on the basis that the defendants would be unable to mount an effective defence because of parliamentary privilege.[36] This left Hamilton unable to clear his own name and

[34] [2001] 2 A.C. 127.
[35] [1972] Q.B. 522.
[36] *Hamilton v Guardian Newspapers, The Times*, July 22, 1995, following the Privy Council decision in *Prebble v Television New Zealand* [1995] 1 A.C. 321 (see A. Sharland and I. Loveland [1997] P.L. 113).

pressure mounted for a change in the law. In an attempt to avoid any unfairness, Parliament passed s.13 of the Defamation Act 1996, which provides that an M.P. may waive privilege for the purpose of defamation proceedings.[37] However, even with the benefit of this section, Mr Hamilton later chose to withdraw his action against *The Guardian*. This section has been criticised for unduly favouring M.P.s over their opponents. The section gives no corresponding right to the opponent to ask for Parliamentary privilege to be removed.

(2) Reports, papers, votes and proceedings ordered to be published by either House of Parliament

Statements in these documents are absolutely privileged by virtue of section 1 of the Parliamentary Papers Act 1840. Absolute privilege does not extend, however, to extracts from, or abstracts of, Parliamentary papers, or to reports of Parliamentary proceedings, but all of these are covered by qualified privilege, which will be discussed below.

13–011

(3) Judicial Proceedings

It is important that the court should hear all relevant and admissible evidence, and it would be contrary to public policy if witnesses were reluctant to give evidence for fear that they may subsequently be sued for defamation. To ensure a fair trial, absolute privilege is therefore given to all oral and written statements made in the course of judicial proceedings. "Judicial proceedings" are defined broadly, and cover all tribunals exercising functions equivalent to a court of justice.[38] The privilege extends to statements made by the judge, jury, advocates, the parties and witnesses.[39] This freedom to comment may be abused, but it is for the judge to regulate the conduct of the case in court. The defence also applies to statements made on occasions that can be regarded as a step in judicial proceedings, for example witness statements.[40] Whilst the defence applies to the solicitor/client relationship in connection with litigation, it is not clear whether it applies to communications between a solicitor and client which are not related to judicial proceedings. Logically, perhaps, it should not. In *More v Weaver*,[41] however, the Court of Appeal held that all relevant communications between solicitor and client were absolutely privileged. The question was left open by the House

13–012

[37] S.13 came into force on September 4, 1996. s.13(1) provides "(1) Where the conduct of a person in or in relation to proceedings in Parliament is in issue in defamation proceedings, he may waive for the purposes of those proceedings, so far as concerns him, the protection of any enactment or rule of law which prevents proceedings in Parliament being impeached or questioned in any court or place out of Parliament." See *Hamilton v Al Fayed (No.1)* [2001] 1 A.C. 395, where the House of Lords applied s.13 in Hamilton's favour—a short lived victory for Mr Hamilton whose claim ultimately failed. Comment A.W. Bradley [2000] P.L. 556.
[38] See *O'Connor v Waldron* [1935] A.C. 76 and *Trapp v Mackie* [1979] 1 W.L.R. 377, HL. This has recently been found to include the Authorisation Tribunal of the self-regulatory Securities Association: *Mahon v Rahn (No.2)* [2000] 1 W.L.R. 2150.
[39] *Royal Aquarium and Summer and Winter Garden Society v Parkinson* [1892] 1 Q.B. 431 at 451 *per* Lopes L.J.
[40] *Watson v McEwan* [1905] A.C. 480 at 487. This avoids the potential difficulty of individuals being reluctant to make witness statements due to their fear of being sued for defamation.
[41] [1928] 2 K.B. 520, CA.

of Lords in *Minter v Priest*,[42] and it is more likely that such communications are covered by qualified privilege (discussed below).

(4) Reports of United Kingdom court proceedings

13–013 Section 14 of the Defamation Act 1996[43] provides that absolute privilege is accorded to all fair and accurate *contemporaneous* reports of public proceedings in a court in the United Kingdom, in the European Court of Justice (or any court attached to that court) and in the European Court of Human Rights.[44] Thus, a newspaper can give an account of court proceedings without fearing actions for defamation. "Contemporaneous" is the main limiting factor. This seems to mean as soon as practicable.[45] It is for the jury to decide whether the report is a fair and accurate one.

(5) Communications between certain officers of state

13–014 The argument here is that officers of state will perform their duties better if they are not acting under fear of litigation. This is essentially the familiar public policy argument that is used in the tort of negligence to justify not imposing liability on the police and other public bodies (see Ch. 2). The leading case on this category of absolute privilege is *Chatterton v Secretary of State for India*.[46] Here, the Court of Appeal held that an action for libel based on a letter written by the Secretary of State for India to his parliamentary under-secretary, to enable the latter to answer questions in Parliament concerning the plaintiff, was rightly dismissed by the trial judge. To allow any judicial inquiry into such matters would tend to deprive officers of state of their freedom of action. The scope of this immunity is a matter of some debate, and it has been narrowly construed in more recent times. The immunity does not, for example, extend to communications between civil servants. Henn-Collins J. in *Szalatnay-Stacho v Fink*[47] suggested that it does not extend to officials below the rank of Minister, and in *Merricks v Nott-Bower*[48] the Court of Appeal refused to strike out a claim simply because the report was written by high-ranking police officers.

Qualified Privilege

13–015 This is the more limited form of privilege, and again largely consists of a list of occasions when the defendant has a valid defence to an action for defamation. The defendant must establish that the statement was made on such an occasion, or that he or she can satisfy the general test at common law. The privilege will be lost, however, if the claimant[49] can show either that the statement was made maliciously (for example,

---

[42] [1930] A.C. 558 (see Lord Buckmaster at 570, Viscount Dunedin at 575 and Lord Atkin at 586). Note also the judgments of Brooke L.J. (with whom Nourse L.J. and Sir Brian Neill agreed) in *Waple v Surrey County Council* [1998] 1 W.L.R. 860 and Gray J. in *Clarke v Davey* [2002] EWCA 2342, 8 November 2002, who found a realistic prospect that Ms Clarke would be able to establish at trial that *More v Weaver* could no longer stand in the light of subsequent authority.

[43] This replaces the very similar Law of Libel Amendment Act 1888, s.3 (as amended) which was confined to television, newspapers and the radio.

[44] It also extends to certain international criminal tribunals: s.14(3).

[45] S.14(2).

[46] [1895] 2 Q.B. 189.

[47] [1946] 1 All E.R. 303 at 305; not considered by Court of Appeal [1947] K.B. 1.

[48] [1965] 1 Q.B. 57.

[49] Although the burden of proving malice is usually on the claimant, the burden will be on the defendant in cases of qualified privilege under the Parliamentary Papers Act 1840, s.3 (see below) to prove that the extract was published bona fide and without malice.

the defendant abused the privilege by using it for some purpose other than that for which the privilege was given) or that the defendant has exceeded the privilege (for example by publishing the statements more widely than necessary). In *Horrocks v Lowe*,[50] Lord Diplock considered the meaning of "malice", and held that the defendant is entitled to be protected by the privilege unless a "dominant and improper" motive is proved. His Lordship emphasised, however, that judges and juries should be slow to find a defendant malicious on the sole ground that the publication of the defamatory words (even though he believed them to be true) was prompted by the dominant motive of injuring the claimant. Generally the defence of qualified privilege would be lost if it could be shown that the defendant did not honestly believe that what he or she said was true, or was reckless as to its truth or falsity.[51]

The occasions when qualified privilege exists are listed below. Generally, these occasions are prescribed by statute. The Defamation Act 1996 put on a statutory basis a number of miscellaneous occasions on which qualified privilege had previously arisen at common law. Nowadays, there is only one important surviving example of qualified privilege at common law. We consider this first, before turning to the statutory examples.

Qualified privilege at common law

Here, we are concerned with qualified privilege which arises in situations where there **13–016** is a "reciprocal duty and interest" between the defamer and the person to whom the statement is published. Unfortunately, as we shall see, it has proved difficult to define precisely *when* such situations will arise. The defence has a number of forms, but in its basic form has two requirements:

- X has a duty or interest in communicating with Y (this duty may be legal, moral or social); *and*

- Y has a corresponding interest or duty in receiving the information in question.[52]

The element of reciprocity is essential. On this basis, if X writes a letter to Y which contains false defamatory statements about Z, but (a) X has a duty to inform Y, and (b) Y has an interest in receiving this information, X has a good defence of qualified privilege.

Qualified privilege will also extend to situations where X publishes a statement to Y who shares a "common interest" with X, for example in the business in which they both work.[53] Further, it will include the situation where X has published the statement to defend his or her own interests and it is in the interest of Y to receive and consider the statement. For example, in *Osborn v Boulter*[54] the plaintiff had claimed that he had been supplied with poor quality beer. The defendant's response—that the plaintiff watered down his beer—was sent to meet this accusation and was therefore privileged.

---

[50] [1975] A.C. 135 at 149–150.
[51] Except where the person is under a duty to pass on, without endorsing, defamatory reports made by some other person.
[52] See *Adam v Ward* [1917] A.C. 309 at 334 *per* Lord Atkinson.
[53] See, *e.g. Bryanston Finance Ltd v de Vries* [1975] Q.B. 703.
[54] [1930] 2 K.B. 226 at 233–234.

The courts have found that the law will generally attach privilege more readily to communications within an existing relationship rather than one between strangers.[55] The privilege will not be lost by dictating a letter to a secretary or delivering a circular to a printer.[56] These are reasonable and ordinary means of communication in business and are therefore privileged. It is not clear, however, whether they are covered by an ancillary form of privilege, which is dependent on the defendant establishing qualified privilege between the defendant and the intended recipient of the letter, or whether they form their own head of qualified privilege because of the common interest between the author and the typist in getting the letter written. Divergent views were expressed in *Bryanston Finance Ltd v de Vries*,[57] and the point therefore remains open.

The rationale for this head of qualified privilege is said to be the "common convenience and welfare of society".[58] In other words, it is necessary at times for people to be free to communicate without fear of litigation, in order to protect their own interests or because they are under a duty to communicate. The law will respect this freedom as being in the public interest provided it is not abused (*i.e.* exercised with malice).[59] A few examples will assist. On applying for a job, your new employer will generally require a reference from your former employer. Your former employer is under no legal duty to provide the reference, but is under a social duty to do so. It is very much in the interest of your new employer to see your reference. Therefore the reference will be protected by qualified privilege: *Spring v Guardian Assurance*.[60] The same reasoning will apply in respect of complaints made or information given to the police or appropriate authorities regarding suspected crimes.

A more graphic example may be seen in the case of *Watt v Longsdon*.[61] In this case, the plaintiff was managing director of a company overseas. The defendant was also a director of the company. The defendant had been informed by a manager (B) of various allegations of misconduct relating to the plaintiff. The defendant wrote back to B, adding his own suspicions, and asking B to obtain sworn statements to support the allegations. Without waiting to verify the complaints, the defendant wrote to the chairman of the board of directors, and to the plaintiff's wife (who was an old friend of his), informing them of the allegations. The allegations proved to be false and the plaintiff sued the defendant for libel. The question arose whether publication of the allegations to the chairman of the board and to the plaintiff's wife were covered by qualified privilege. The Court of Appeal held that the defendant's letter to the chairman of the board of directors was covered by qualified privilege. Employees of a company would have a common interest in the affairs of the company, which entitled them to discuss the behaviour and conduct of another employee. Additionally, there was a possibility that the chairman might be asked to provide a reference for the plaintiff at a future date. The qualified privilege did not extend, however, to the

---

[55] See *Kearns v The General Council of the Bar* [2003] 2 All E.R. 534, CA.
[56] *Osborn v Boulter* [1930] 2 K.B. 226 at 234.
[57] [1975] Q.B. 703—Lord Denning M.R. arguing for original privilege at 719 and Lawton L.J arguing for ancillary privilege at 736–738.
[58] *Toogood v Spyring* (1834) 1 C.M. & R. 181 at 193 *per* Parke B.; 149 E.R. 1044 at 1049–1050; *Davies v Snead* (1870) LR 5 QB 608 at 611 *per* Blackburn J.
[59] See Lord Nicholls in *Reynolds v Times Newspapers* [2001] 2 A.C. 127 at 194.
[60] [1995] 2 A.C. 296. In this case, the plaintiff relied on negligence and breach of contract following a finding that none of the persons involved in the giving of the reference had acted maliciously.
[61] [1930] 1 K.B. 130.

defendant's letter to the plaintiff's wife. Here, the defendant was held to have no duty to pass this information to the wife, particularly when it had not been verified. Yet, this is not clear-cut. Arguably, a wife has an interest in hearing about the misconduct of her husband, and there may sometimes be a "moral" or "social" duty to inform her of his misconduct. The court held it that it would depend on the circumstances of each case. If the defendant had known the information to be genuine, it may have been found that the defendant had a moral duty to pass the information to the wife.[62] This case illustrates the problems of dealing with vague concepts of "duty" and "interest". The law's attempt to define these concepts will be examined below.

What is a legal, moral or social duty? The observations of Lindley L.J., in *Stuart v* **13–017** *Bell*,[63] make it clear that the law simply leaves this question to be answered at the discretion of the judge:

> "The question of moral or social duty being for the judge, each judge must decide it as best as he can for himself. I take moral or social duty to mean a duty recognised by English people of ordinary intelligence and moral principle, but at the same time not a duty enforceable by legal proceedings, whether civil or criminal."

This provides little assistance. At best, we can say that the law applies an objective test, having regard to the moral and social duties prevalent in society. This inevitably raises a question as to the ability of the courts to ascertain the views of modern society. In practice, it will be a matter of looking at past case law and ascertaining what situations in recent times have given rise to such duties.

What is an interest? Generally, this is easier to define. The courts will interpret **13–018** "interest" broadly to include, for example, financial and business interests such as an interest in the financial stability of an individual or company. Again, an objective test will be applied, and the question will be decided by the judge, who will ascertain whether the interest is legitimate and should be protected for the common convenience and welfare of society.

The duty/interest test and the media: The leading case on common law qualified **13–019** privilege is now the House of Lords decision in *Reynolds v Times Newpapers*,[64] in which the relationship between qualified privilege and the press was called into question. The House of Lords recognised that in a democracy the press play a vital role in ensuring that the public are informed and aware of the laws and regulations which affect their daily lives. This fact is recognised expressly in the Human Rights Act 1998, which came into force on October 2, 2000. Section 12(4) of the Act provides that the courts should have a particular regard to the importance of freedom of expression in deciding cases which concern journalistic, literary or artistic material, and should examine (i) the extent to which the material has, or is about to, become available to the public; (ii) the extent to which it is, or would be, in the public interest for the material to be

---

[62] See Scrutton L.J. *ibid.*, at 149–150.
[63] [1891] 2 Q.B. 341 at 350.
[64] [2001] 2 A.C. 127 (HL); [1998] 3 W.L.R. 862 (CA). Comment F.A. Trindade (2000) 116 L.Q.R. 185; I. Loveland [2000] P.L. 351; K. Williams (2000) 63 M.L.R. 748; I Loveland [2000] E.H.L.R.L. 476.

published; and (iii) any relevant privacy code.[65] This section was introduced by the government in response to concern that the Act might undermine press freedom and result in the introduction of a privacy law "through the back door". The Act was therefore amended by the government to include section 12, which was "designed solely to ensure that free speech, free expression, is abundantly safeguarded after the Bill becomes law".[66]

In view of such advocacy of press freedom, there is a clear argument that the defence of qualified privilege should be extended to all statements published in the public interest. Society has a clear interest in such stories, and the press may regard itself as under a duty to publish such material. Such an extension would ensure that the press, provided it acted without malice, would have the freedom to discuss important issues without the "chill" of a potential libel claim. This argument is particularly strong in relation to political discussion. Political matters are of direct concern to the electorate. Therefore it can be argued that the electorate has a "right to know". The courts have nevertheless traditionally opposed qualified privilege in this context, except in extreme circumstances such as a national emergency.[67] In *Reynolds v Times Newpapers*, the House of Lords reiterated that the media did not possess its own head of qualified privilege, even when dealing with matters of political information. However, a more liberal stance was suggested. This decision, and its implications, will be examined below.

In *Reynolds*, the former Prime Minister of the Republic of Ireland, Albert Reynolds, brought an action against *The Times* over an article which he claimed implied that he had deliberately misled the Irish Parliament and his cabinet colleagues during a political crisis in Ireland in 1994. He succeeded at first instance, but the jury awarded him one penny in damages. He appealed. *The Times* also appealed, claiming that it was protected by qualified privilege. The Court of Appeal set aside the jury's verdict and ordered a retrial, but held that the article was not covered by qualified privilege. *The Times* appealed to the House of Lords, but the majority of the House rejected its appeal. It was held that there was no special head of qualified privilege for the media based on the public interest in political information and discussion. On this basis, the ordinary "duty/interest" test outlined above would apply. However, their Lordships were of the view that this test was flexible enough to include consideration of diverse factors such as the nature, status and source of the material published and the circumstances of publication.[68] The court disagreed that such factors formed a third test of their own (the "circumstantial test" which had been adopted by the Court of Appeal). Lord Nicholls, who gave the leading opinion, held that:

> "With all due respect to the Court of Appeal, this formulation . . . gives rise to conceptual and practical difficulties and is better avoided . . . These factors are to

---

[65] S.12(1) provides that "This section applies if a court is considering whether to grant any relief which, if granted, might affect the exercise of the Convention right to freedom of expression". S.12(5) adds that "relief" includes any remedy or order (other than in criminal proceedings).

[66] Lord Williams of Mostyn, Hansard, H.L. col. 2113, October 29, 1998.

[67] See *Blackshaw v Lord* [1984] Q.B. 1 at 27 *per* Stephenson L.J.: "There may be extreme cases where the urgency of communicating a warning is so great, or the source of the information so reliable, that publication of suspicion or speculation is justified; *e.g.* where there is danger to the public from a suspected terrorist or the distribution of contaminated food or drugs; but there is nothing of that sort here".

[68] See *Blackshaw v Lord* [1984] Q.B. 1 at 27.

be taken into account in determining whether the duty-interest is satisfied, or, as I would prefer to say in a simpler and more direct way, whether the public are entitled to know the particular information."[69]

Applying this test, the majority agreed with the Court of Appeal that the article did **13–020** not contain information which the public had a right to know.[70] Their Lordships particularly focused on the fact that the article had failed to mention Mr Reynolds' own explanation of his conduct to the Irish Parliament. The case nevertheless marked a clear recognition by the House of Lords of the importance of Article 10 of the European Convention on Human Rights, and of the need to balance the countervailing interests of reputation and freedom of speech. It also gave the press some hope, in recognising that, in the right circumstances, the press could rely on qualified privilege when discussing political matters. Lord Nicholls advised future courts to consider a number of factors (which are not exhaustive) in deciding whether a duty to publish political discussion could be established, namely:

   (i) The seriousness of the allegation—the more serious the charge, the more the public is misinformed and the individual harmed if the allegation is not true;

  (ii) The nature of the information—whether it is a matter of public concern;

 (iii) Its source;

  (iv) What steps had been taken to verify the information;

   (v) The status of the information, *i.e.* the reliability of the report;

  (vi) The urgency of the matter (news being a perishable commodity);

 (vii) Whether comment is sought from the claimant;

(viii) Whether the gist of the claimant's side of the story has been told;

  (ix) The tone of the article; *and*

   (x) The general circumstances and timing of the publication.

Such a flexible approach leaves the courts free to weigh up the competing interests of freedom of expression and reputation on the facts of each case. Yet such flexibility brings also uncertainty. While Lord Nicholls asserted that courts should be slow to find that publication is not in the public interest, particularly in relation to political discussion,[71] it remains for the courts to determine how his Lordship's ten guidelines will be applied. As Lord Lester of Herne Hill Q.C. commented following judgment in *Reynolds*:

"What matters now is for the media to develop and monitor their own codes of responsible journalism so that they are able to take advantage of the new

---

[69] [2001] 2 A.C. 127 at 197.
[70] The minority felt that the issue of qualified privilege should be re-considered in the light of their Lordships' judgments at the re-trial.
[71] Lord Nicholls [2001] 2 A.C. 127 at 205.

opportunities created by *Reynolds*. The temptation is for the media to follow the easy line of least resistance and to censor themselves rather than to meet the challenge of *Reynolds*: namely, to maintain the high professional and ethical standards that they expect of those who govern on our behalf. To avoid that professional challenge would not be in the best interests of free expression and an informed public."[72]

13–021   **The application of *Reynolds*:**   In a number of judgments, the courts have sought to establish guidance for defendants seeking to rely on the *Reynolds* test for qualified privilege.It should be stressed that this test only applies in relation to the media, who are required, unlike other defendants, to justify their conduct in order to rely on the defence. It does not, however, seem to be confined to political matters, but extends to any question of interest to the public, although most cases have some political element.[73] The test, as formulated, is one of responsible journalism. Whilst there is a public interest in a modern democracy in free expression and the promotion of a free and vigorous press, it will only be the duty of the press to publish in circumstances in which it has acted responsibly. Equally, it will be a question of fact in each case, and it should be noted that the ten *Reynolds* factors are not exclusive and need not all be satisfied. For example, verification may not be necessary (factor iv) where both sides to a political dispute have been fully, fairly and disinterestedly reported in their respective allegations and responses. The public, in such circumstances, may be entitled to be informed of such a dispute which is of real interest to them without having to wait for the publisher, following an attempt at verification, to commit himself to one side or the other.[74] The ongoing litigation between *The Times* newspaper and a Russian business-man, Mr Loutchansky, has served to highlight many of these points.

The complaint related to two articles which appeared in *The Times* in 1999. It was alleged, amongst other things, that the claimant was a Russian mafia boss, and that he was involved in money laundering and the smuggling of nuclear weapons. The first article, which contained the majority of the allegations, was based on information from a variety of sources, including media cuttings and unidentified sources. The second article relied on allegations made by the estranged wife of a person alleged to have been associated with the claimant. The defendants had not approached the claimant to seek his side of the story or to put any of the allegations to him. *The Times* did not attempt to deny that the articles were defamatory, but sought to support publication largely on the basis of qualified privilege, contending that the allegations were of great public interest and contained information which the public had a right to know.

In the first case, *Loutchansky v Times Newspapers Ltd (No.1)*,[75] *The Times* sought to strengthen its defence by including certain facts of which it had been unaware at the time of publication, but which supported its case. The question arose whether all the factors identified by the court for consideration in *Reynolds* had to be determined on

---

[72] *The Times*, December 7, 1999. Lord Lester Q.C.. represented *The Times* in *Reynolds*.
[73] Contrast *GKR Karate (UK) Ltd v Yorkshire Post Newspapers Ltd* [2000] 1 W.L.R. 2571, which concerned allegedly sub-standard karate courses!
[74] See *Al-Fagih v HH Saudi Research & Marketing (UK) Ltd* [2002] E.M.L.R. 13 (Mantell L.J. dissenting). Contrast *James Gilbert Ltd v MGN Ltd* [2000] E.M.L.R. 680, where verification would have been very easy and involved utilising an existing channel of communication.
[75] [2002] Q.B. 321.

the basis of the defendant's state of knowledge at the time of publication. The Court of Appeal affirmed that this was the case. Factors such as 'the steps taken to verify the information', 'the urgency of the matter' and 'the circumstances of publication' would, in the words of Brooke L.J., "lose a lot of their potent effect if the law permitted a publisher to publish untrue defamatory matter without sufficient inquiry and then to justify that publication . . . by being allowed to rely on after-acquired information."[76]

The Court of Appeal again dealt with this case in the consolidated hearing of **13–022** *Loutchansky v Times Newspapers Ltd (Nos. 2–5)*.[77] In ruling on a number of matters (including internet defamation and s.8 of the Defamation Act 1996 which will be considered later in this chapter), the court stressed that the *Reynolds* test was one of the responsible journalism. If the newspaper could satisfy the *Reynolds* criteria and demonstrate that it had acted responsibly, the defence of qualified privilege would apply. In determining the public interest, the Court of Appeal noted three matters of individual and public concern which would be predominant in the mind of the court:

(i) If qualified privilege was allowed, then, to all intents and purposes, the publisher would have a complete defence and the claimant would be denied a remedy;

(ii) Setting the standard of journalistic responsibility too low would inevitably encourage too great a readiness to publish defamatory matter; *and*

(iii) Setting the standard too high would deter newspapers from their proper function of keeping the public informed.

The court additionally recognised that where privilege is found, little room is left for a finding of malice: a responsible journalist will not act maliciously.[78] The ten factors thus incorporate both the test for privilege and the question of malice, thus limiting the role of the jury in this context. In stipulating the test to be one of responsible journalism, the Court rejected the test applied by Gray J. below—whether a publisher would be open to legitimate criticism if he failed to publish the information in question—as too stringent.

The case was remitted to Gray J., who, applying the above principles, found against *The Times*.[79] The judge held that although money laundering and the other international criminal activities mentioned in the first article were matters of legitimate public concern, the implication of the claimant in such misconduct, which was of the utmost gravity, was manifestly likely to be highly damaging to his reputation. Therefore, a proportionate degree of responsibility was required of the editor and the journalist before giving currency to such allegations. In the circumstances, the defendants had *not* met the requisite standard of responsibility. Notably, the allegations made were vague, the sources were somewhat unreliable, insufficient steps had

---

[76] See above at 336. See also May L.J. in *GKR Karate (UK) Ltd v Yorkshire Post Newspapers Ltd* [2000] 1 W.L.R. 2571 at 2577. Note that the same rule applies to fair comment, but that further facts may be pleaded for justification: see *Cohen v Daily Telegraph* [1968] 1 W.L.R. 916.
[77] [2002] Q.B. 783.
[78] See also *GKR Karate (UK) Ltd v Yorkshire Post Newspapers Ltd* [2000] 1 W.L.R. 2571 at 2580 *per* May L.J.
[79] *Loutchansky v Times Newspapers Ltd and others* [2002] EWHC 2490 (QB); [2002] All E.R. (D) 371 (Nov), (Approved judgment).

been taken to verify the information, and no steps had been taken to call for a comment from the claimant before publication. In respect of the second article, in view of the questionable nature of the source, the judge held that to reiterate the allegations without any verification or corroboration fell well below the standard of responsible journalism.

In contrast, in *Bonnick v Morris*,[80] Lord Nicholls was prepared to adopt a more flexible approach where the words used were ambiguous and could have conveyed either a defamatory and non-defamatory meaning to the ordinary reasonable reader. Here, the article had referred to the dismissal of Mr Bonnick in the context of contractual litigation in which irregularities had been alleged. Mr Bonnick alleged that the article suggested that there was a connection between his dismissal and the irregularities stated. In the view of the court, the defamatory meaning was not obvious. Here, the article related to a matter of considerable public concern and was generally well-balanced and, in such circumstances, it was prepared to overlook the failure of the journalist to inquire into the truth of the statement or refer to the claimant's own explanation in the article. Lord Nicholls emphasised, however, that the court would not have been so generous if an expressly defamatory statement had been made.

It remains a moot point whether *Reynolds* could be subject to challenge under the Human Rights Act 1998. The European Court of Human Rights in *Lingens v Austria*,[81] in finding that the conviction of a journalist for defamation was in breach of Art. 10 (freedom of expression), strongly advocated the right of the press to impart information and ideas on political issues in the public interest. The court drew a distinction between public and private figures and found that public figures must accept a greater degree of scrutiny than private individuals. This mirrors the position in the United States where, following *New York Times v Sullivan*,[82] public figures may only recover damages for defamation if they are able to show by clear and convincing evidence that the defendant published with malice. Yet, the English courts have so far embraced *Reynolds* as a valid compromise between freedom of expression and protection of reputation, consistent with the requirements of Article 10.[83] In the words of Lord Nicholls in the Privy Council case of *Bonnick v Morris*,[84] "Responsible journalism is the point at which a fair balance is held between freedom of expression on matters of public concern and the reputations of individuals . . . It is the price journalists pay in return for the privilege." This may lead to harsh results. It may be recalled that non-media defendants do not have to demonstrate that they have acted responsibly. In *Kearns v The General Council of the Bar*,[85] a letter circulated to the 10,000 members of the Bar did not have to satisfy the *Reynolds* test, and a defence of qualified privilege was successful. Yet in *Al-Fagih v HH Saudi Research & Marketing (UK) Ltd*,[86] a Saudi Arabian newspaper with a circulation of around 1,500 readers in the UK did have to meet such a test. It may be questioned whether *Reynolds* does strike an adequate balance between freedom of speech and protection of reputation, or whether English

---

[80] [2003] 1 A.C. 300.
[81] (1986) 8 E.H.R.R. 407. See also *De Haes and Gijsels v Belgium* (1997) 25 E.H.R.R. 1 and *Castells v Spain* (1992) 14 E.H.R.R. 445.
[82] 66 376 U.S. 254 (1964).
[83] See, for example, Eady J. in *Baldwin v Rusbridger* [2001] E.M.L.R. 1062.
[84] [2003] 1 A.C. 300 at 309.
[85] [2003] 2 All E.R. 534, CA.
[86] [2002] E.M.L.R. 13.

law is reaping the result of allegedly possessing the worst tabloid newspapers in the world. The English position may be contrasted with that of New Zealand, in which the New Zealand Court of Appeal rejected *Reynolds* as too uncertain and restrictive and favoured the generic head of privilege rejected so firmly by the House of Lords.[87] In so doing, the court commented that this could be justified on the basis that New Zealand newspapers were more responsible than their English counterparts.[88]

Qualified privilege under statute.

The Defamation Act 1996 provides for numerous occasions on which qualified privilege will arise. Section 15(1) provides that "The publication of any report or other statement mentioned in Sch.1 to this Act is privileged unless the publication is shown to be made with malice."[89] Some of the most important examples in Sch.1 are considered below.   **13–023**

(i) Reports of Parliamentary proceedings: Absolute privilege only extends to reports, papers, votes and proceedings ordered to be published by either House of Parliament. It does not include fair and accurate reports of parliamentary proceedings, which were covered by common law qualified privilege[90] and are now covered by the Defamation Act 1996. Schedule 1, para.1 provides that there is privilege for a fair and accurate report of proceedings in public of a legislature anywhere in the world. Schedule 1, para.7 also provides that a fair and accurate copy of, or extract from, matter published by or on the authority of a government or legislature anywhere in the world is privileged. This expands the previous privilege granted under s.3 of the Parliamentary Papers Act 1840.[91] In both cases, publication is covered by qualified privilege "without explanation or contradiction" (the meaning of this phrase is discussed later).   **13–024**

(ii) Reports of judicial proceedings: As stated above, absolute privilege is accorded to fair and accurate *contemporaneous* reports of court proceedings in public. Fair and accurate *non-contemporaneous* reports of public judicial proceedings are covered by qualified privilege.[92] The common law is now replaced by the Defamation Act 1996 (Sch.1, para.2) which provides that a fair and accurate report of proceedings in public before a court anywhere in the world is privileged without explanation or contradiction.   **13–025**

(iii) Registers: Likewise, publications of a fair and accurate copy of or extract from a register required by law to be open to public inspection, for example the register of county court judgments, was privileged under the common law[93] and is now privileged without explanation or contradiction under the Defamation Act 1996 (Sch.1, para.5).   **13–026**

---

[87] See *Lange v Atkinson* [2000] 3 N.Z.L.R. 385, which affirmed and elaborated its original decision in *Lange v Atkinson* [1998] 3 N.Z.L.R. 424 after the Privy Council ([2000] 1 N.Z.L.R. 257) had remitted the case for rehearing in the light of *Reynolds* (comment N.W. Barber and A.L. Young (2001) 117 L.Q.R. 175). All that had to be proved was the absence of malice and that a genuine political discussion was involved. Consider also the different Australian test set out in *Lange v Australian Broadcasting Co* (1997) 189 C.L.R. 520 based on a test of reasonableness.

[88] See above at 398.

[89] Sch. 1 and s.15 only came into force on April 1, 1999: Defamation Act 1996 (Commencement No.1) Order SI 1999/817.

[90] *Wason v Walter* (1868) L.R. 4 Q.B. 73.

[91] As amended by Defamation Act 1952, s.9(1).

[92] This does not extend to fair and accurate reports of judicial proceedings in foreign courts: *Webb v Times Publishing Co.* [1960] 2 Q.B. 535.

[93] *Searles v Scarlett* [1892] 2 Q.B. 56.

13–027   **(iv) Other matters covered by s.15 and Sch.1 to the Defamation Act 1996:**   We have already seen the operation of Sch.1 in the examples above. Schedule 1 replaces previous statutory provisions for privilege in the Law of Libel Amendment Act 1888 and the Defamation Act 1952. It also covers some of the common law examples of qualified privilege. It is divided into two sections. Part I deals with reports which are privileged "without explanation or contradiction". Part II deals with reports which are privileged "subject to explanation or contradiction". This distinction is important. Qualified privilege may be lost (for Pt II reports *only*) if it is proved that the defendant has been requested, by the claimant, to publish in a suitable manner[94] a reasonable letter or statement by way of explanation or contradiction, and has refused or neglected to do so: s.15(2). In other words, the claimant must be given the right of reply with respect to Part II reports. However, the courts will not permit Sch.1 to be abused. Section 15(3) provides that the privilege will not extend to matters which are not of public concern and the publication of which is not for the public benefit. It will equally not protect the publication of matters prohibited by law.[95]

We shall refrain from repeating the long list of reports and statements given in Schedule 1. Readers are advised to look at the Defamation Act 1996. Generally, Pt I covers fair and accurate reports of legislative, court or government body proceedings anywhere in the world, as may be seen from the examples given above. The Pt II list consists of a number of different types of reports, including fair and accurate copies of or extracts from documents made available by a court in any Member State, or by the European Court of Justice[96] (para.10); fair and accurate reports of proceedings at any public meeting held in a Member State (para.12); and fair and accurate reports of proceedings at a general meeting of a UK public company (para.13).

13–028   **Schedule 1 and freedom of expression:**   It is inevitable that, following *Reynolds*, the courts would be asked to consider the relationship between freedom of expression and statutory qualified privilege. In *McCartan Turkington Breen v Times Newspapers Ltd*[97] (a case heard the day after the Human Rights Act 1998 came into force), the court considered the meaning of the term "public meeting" in the Northern Irish equivalent to para.12 (see above).[98] Did it include a press conference? It was alleged that defamatory statements had been made against the plaintiffs in a report of a press conference organised by an informal committee, which sought to secure the release from prison of a British serviceman, Private Lee Clegg. At first instance, Girvan J. had found that the issue of invitations to members of the press, but not to the general public, indicated that the press conference was not a "public meeting" and accordingly no privilege attached to the report. The Northern Ireland Court of Appeal affirmed this view. The House of Lords rejected such a narrow definition. "Public meeting" was to be interpreted in the context of contemporary conditions, and a meeting would be public if its organisers opened it to the public or, by issuing a general invitation to the

---

[94] That is, in the same manner as the publication complained of or in a manner that is adequate and reasonable in the circumstances: s.15(2).

[95] S.15(4)(a).

[96] Or by a judge or officer of any such court.

[97] [2001] 2 A.C. 277. Comment I Loveland [2001] P.L. 233.

[98] S.7 and para.9 of the Schedule to the Defamation Act (Northern Ireland) 1955 granted qualified privilege to "a fair and accurate report of the proceedings at any public meeting. " These provisions have now been repealed and replaced by the Defamation Act 1996.

press, manifested an intention to communicate the proceedings to a wider public. A meeting did not lose its public character because admission was subject to some restriction. The organisers' object had been to stimulate public pressure to rectify a perceived injustice, and a press conference was an important vehicle to promote discussion and furtherance of matters of public concern. There was nothing in its nature to exclude it from the ordinary meaning of a "public meeting".[99]

Lord Bingham emphasised the importance of the media in keeping the public informed:[1]

> "It is very largely through the media, including of course the press, that [the public] will be so alerted and informed. The proper functioning of a modern participatory democracy requires that the media be free, active, professional and enquiring. For this reason the courts, here and elsewhere, have recognised the cardinal importance of press freedom and the need for any restriction on that freedom to be proportionate and no more than is necessary to promote the legitimate object of the restriction."

Such statements must give hope to journalists that the courts will adopt a more generous interpretation of qualified privilege in future. Nevertheless, the courts will, as seen in *Loutchansky*, still seek to ensure that the standard of responsible journalism is maintained, and will continue to be alert to any suggestion that they have given a green light to a general media head of qualified privilege. The *Reynolds* criteria will be monitored, and it should be recalled that whilst *The Times* newspaper was successful in *McCartan Turkington Breen*, it failed to satisfy a court that it should be awarded qualified privilege in *Loutchansky*.

(4) OFFER OF AMENDS UNDER THE DEFAMATION ACT 1996

This defence applies to unintentional defamation. It may be recalled that the **13–029** publication of a statement may amount to defamation even though the defendant did not intend to harm the claimant's reputation. For present purposes, there are two senses in which the publication of a defamatory statement might be said to be "unintentional". First, there is the situation where, for example, a newspaper publishes a defamatory statement, *knowing* that it refers to the claimant, but honestly and reasonably believing that the statement is true (as in *Cassidy v Daily Mirror*, discussed in Ch. 12). Secondly, there is the "mistaken identity" situation, where a newspaper publishes a statement which is false and defamatory in relation to the claimant, but intends the statement to refer to *someone else*, about whom it is true (as in *Newstead v London Express*, also discussed in Ch. 12).

Section 4 of the Defamation Act 1952 did provide some mechanism whereby a defendant could, in such circumstances, make an "offer of amends" which, if accepted, would end proceedings, and if not accepted would amount to a defence. But this

---

[99] The House of Lords also ruled that a press release issued at the press conference, but not read aloud, could be part of the relevant proceedings.
[1] See above at 290–291.

provision was little used, mainly because of the difficulties defendants had in proving that the statement was published "innocently", as required by s.4(5). A revised version appears in the Defamation Act 1996.[2] Sections 2 to 4 set out the new procedure for making an offer of amends.

Under s.2, the defendant must be prepared:

   (i) To admit that he or she was wrong (or partly wrong);

  (ii) To offer in writing to make a suitable correction and apology;

 (iii) To publish the correction and apology in a manner that is reasonable and practicable in the circumstances; *and*

 (iv) To pay the claimant such compensation (if any) and such costs as may be agreed or determined to be payable.

The offer may relate to the statement generally, or only to a specific defamatory meaning (known as a "qualified offer"). Timing is important. The offer must be made *before* service of a defence.[3] This forces the defendant to decide whether to fight the action or admit that he or she is wrong. If the offer is accepted, the claimant must discontinue the action against the defendant. If the parties cannot agree the amount of compensation to be paid, s.3(5) provides that it will be settled by the court, sitting without a jury, "on the same principles as damages in defamation proceedings".[4] If the offer is not accepted, the action may continue, but the defendant may use the making of the offer as a defence unless the claimant is able to show that the defendant knew or had reason to believe that the statement referred to the claimant (or was likely to be understood as referring to him) *and* was both false and defamatory of him. The test is one of bad faith, not negligence.[5] In other words, the burden is on the claimant to show that the defamation was intentional or reckless. Section 4(4) provides that the defendant cannot rely on an offer of amends by way of defence in combination with any other defence. The defence is therefore of limited use, and a defendant would be wise to consider his or her tactical position before resorting to an offer or qualified offer of amends. It should be noted that even if the offer is not accepted, or not relied upon as a defence, it may be relied upon in mitigation of damages.[6]

On a historical note, the defendant still has a defence under s.2 of the Libel Act 1843 (as amended by the Libel Act 1845). This provides that it is a defence, when a libel is published in a newspaper without actual malice or gross negligence, for the defendant to publish a full apology in the newspaper and pay money into court by way of amends. This has not been repealed by the Defamation Act 1996, but has been little used due to substantial procedural disadvantages to the defendant. The Faulks Committee in 1975 recommended its repeal "with a view to simplifying this aspect of

---

[2] As recommended by the Neill Committee on Practice and Procedure in Defamation, 1991, Ch. VII.
[3] S.2(5).
[4] See *Abu v MGN Ltd* [2003] E.M.L.R. 21. This will involve questions such as mitigation, aggravation and causation of loss.
[5] S.4(3). See *Milne v Express Newspapers Ltd* [2003] 1 W.L.R. 927: "reason to believe" means choosing to ignore or shutting one's mind to information which should have led to a belief, not merely a suspicion, that the allegation was false. Approved *Milne v Express Newspapers* [2004] EWCA Civ 664.
[6] S.4(5).

the law of defamation",[7] but this sensible suggestion has not been taken up. After the 1996 Act, it is likely to be of only historical interest.

(5) INNOCENT DISSEMINATION

This defence applies to parties involved in the distribution process, who inadvertently **13–030** become involved in the publication of defamatory material. It therefore has no application to the actual author of the defamatory material, or to the publisher who actively produces the defamatory material. An example will help us understand the problem. I write a defamatory article for the Daily Rag. I have published the libel and will be liable, but so have the editor, publisher and the distributors of the Daily Rag, including Mr X, the newsagent. Each repetition of the libel is actionable by the claimant. It seems harsh to allow the claimant to sue all of the above parties. Therefore the defence of innocent dissemination seeks to draw a distinction between those who produce the libel (here myself, my editor and publisher) and those who "disseminate" or distribute it (here the distributors and Mr X). Until recently, the defence was part of the common law, as stated in *Vizetelly v Mudie's Select Library Ltd*.[8] The court in this case held that the mechanical distribution of defamatory material by agencies such as newsagents or libraries would be protected against claims for defamation *provided* they could show that:

(i) They did not know that the work contained a libel of the claimant;

(ii) It was not by negligence that they did not know of the libel; *and*

(iii) The defendants did not know, nor ought to have known, that the works were of such a character that they were likely to contain defamatory material.

In the case itself, the defendants were held liable for defamation because they had overlooked a publisher's circular which had requested the return of copies of the book in question, and in fact had no procedure for checking whether the books they lent contained defamatory material. They therefore failed to satisfy requirement (ii).

The common law has now been replaced and updated by section 1 of the Defamation Act 1996. It is now a defence to show that:

(i) The defendant is not the author,[9] editor or commercial publisher (in the sense of issuing material to the public in the course of business)[10] of the statement;

(ii) The defendant took reasonable care in relation to the publication; *and*

(iii) The defendant did not know, or had no reason to believe, that what he or she did caused or contributed to the publication of a defamatory statement.

---

[7] Para. 373.
[8] [1900] 2 Q.B. 170, applying *Emmens v Pottle* (1885) 16 Q.B.D. 354.
[9] S.1(2) defines "author" as originator of the statement, but does not include a person who did not intend that his or her statement be published at all.
[10] S.1(2).

In assessing the above criteria, the court will have regard to the extent of the defendant's responsibilities for the content of, or decision to publish, the statement; the nature and circumstances of the publication; and the previous conduct or character of the author, editor or publisher (s.1(5)). For example, if the defendant distributes work by an author renowned for controversy, the defendant will be expected to vet the work carefully for defamatory material.

Sections 1(3)(a) to (e) list a number of individuals who do *not* qualify as "authors", "editors" or "publishers". These provisions are not comprehensive, and do not prevent the courts reasoning by analogy. Section 1(3)(a) provides that distributors and printers[11] can rely on a s.1 defence. Interestingly, broadcasters of live programmes may also rely on the defence if, in the circumstances, they have no effective control over the maker of the statement, for example in live phone-in programmes.[12] Again, however, if controversial guests are invited, editors would be wise to employ some kind of screening process, and consider devices such as a delay mechanism on the transmission of material, if they wish to show that they have taken reasonable care.

13–031   Even the internet is provided for, in ss.1(3)(c) and (e). Section 1(3)(e) covers the "operator or provider of access to a communications system by means of which the statement is transmitted, or made available, by a person over whom he had no effective control"—essentially an internet service provider or "ISP". This particular provision was considered in the case of *Godfrey v Demon Internet Ltd*.[13] The defendants were an ISP which provided a particular newsgroup, which stored postings for about a fortnight. In January 1997, an unknown person made a posting to the newsgroup which was defamatory of Dr Godfrey. Godfrey contacted the defendants four days later, requesting that the posting be removed from their news server. The defendants failed to do so, and the posting remained on the server for the full two week period. It was accepted that the defendants could have removed the posting had they chosen to do so. Godfrey sued the defendants for libel. Morland J. struck out the defendants' s.1 defence. The defendants had known of the posting's defamatory contents and, by failing to remove the statements, lost the protection of s.1 of the Act. While the defendants were not the author, editor or commercial publisher of the statement, they could not show that they had taken reasonable care in relation to the publication, or that they did not know that what they did caused or contributed to the publication of a defamatory statement. Morland J. also refused to accept that an ISP could not "publish" information.[14] An ISP which transmitted a defamatory posting on a news server would, by analogy to a bookseller, be deemed to publish the information contained in the posting.[15]

The implications of *Godfrey* remain to be seen, but fears have been expressed that it will restrict freedom of speech on the internet. Faced with an allegation that a posting is defamatory, most ISPs will simply withdraw the posting to avoid potential litigation and will not bother to check whether the allegation is well-founded. Arguably, this will

---

[11] Ch. 11 of the report of the Faulks Committee in 1975 (*Report of the Committee on Defamation*, Cmnd 5909) recommended that the defence of innocent dissemination should be extended to printers.
[12] S.1(3)(d).
[13] [2001] Q.B. 201.
[14] In effect, rejecting the "mere conduit" argument that has gained acceptance in the US.
[15] Dr Godfrey's claim against Demon was finally settled, with much publicity, with an agreement to pay Godfrey £15,000 in damages plus costs which amounted to almost £250,000: *The Times*, March 31, 2000. As a result, a number of servers were closed down to avoid potential defamation claims.

give individuals the opportunity to "veto" any posting which contains information they do not wish to be published and consequently limit free speech. It is notable that the United States Supreme Court, when faced with a similar case in *Lunney v Prodigy*,[16] chose to find in favour of the ISP. The new Electronic Commerce (EC Directive) Regulations 2002[17] offer little comfort to ISPs. These Regulations, implementing EC Directive 2000/31/EC, limit the potential liability of ISPs in relation to a number of legal claims, including defamation, obscenity and copyright. Regulation 19 grants immunity to the ISP which hosts the relevant site, but only if two conditions are met:

(i) The ISP does not have actual knowledge of the unlawful activity or information and is not aware of facts or circumstances from which it would have been apparent to the ISP that the activity or information was unlawful; *and*

(ii) It acts expeditiously to remove such information on obtaining any such knowledge.

The Law Commission in the report discussed below concluded that this would act in the same manner as s.1, again leaving the ISP potentially liable where it has been notified of an allegedly defamatory posting.[18]

Loutchansky v Times Newspapers Ltd (No.2),[19] mentioned above under "Qualified Privilege", highlights a further risk of liability. Here, the article in question had been posted as part of *The Times'* publicly accessible online archive. The Court of Appeal held that every hit of the article on this site would amount to publication. This is consistent with *Godfrey*, but must be considered in the light of the established rule of English law that every publication will give rise to a cause of action.[20] On this basis, the claimant would be able to sue every time someone accessed the article. It was argued that such ongoing liability would be contrary to free speech, place an unfair burden on the ISP and totally undermine the one year limitation period for defamation claims (see below under "Limitation").The Court rejected these arguments. As "stale news", such information had limited public interest value and, in any event, the Court concluded that the attachment of an appropriate notice, warning that any suspected article should not be treated as the truth, would remove the sting from the material. In any event, any claims for damages would be modest. The court thus refused to change the law in favour of the US "single publication" rule, whereby an article is published only once when it is first posted on the archive.

---

[16] See 529 US 1098 (2000), *The Times*, May 3, 2000, where the US Supreme Court let stand a decision of the New York Court of Appeals (94 N.Y. 2d 242; 701 N.Y.S. 2d 684; 723 N.E. 2d 539) that Prodigy was a "common carrier" who would not be responsible for what appeared on its site.
[17] SI 2002/2013, in force from August 21, 2002.
[18] *Defamation and the Internet: A preliminary investigation*: para.2.23.
[19] [2002] Q.B. 783.
[20] *Duke of Brunswick v Harmer* (1849) 14 Q.B. 185. Upheld in *Berezovsky v Michaels* [2000] 1 W.L.R. 1004, HL.

Reform

13–032   Doubts have been expressed whether the current state of the law is satisfactory. The Law Commission in its preliminary report, *"Defamation and the Internet: A preliminary investigation,"*[21] found a "strong case" for changing the law. It had been given evidence that ISPs were receiving over a 100 complaints each year, and concluded that, under the present law, the safest course for any ISP in such circumstances would be to remove the material, whether or not the alleged defamatory material was in the public interest or true. This caused a potential conflict with Article 10. Equally, although it agreed with the view expressed above that damages arising from online archives would generally be modest, it noted concerns as to the costs and difficulties facing publishers in defending such cases if brought many years after the original publication.

A number of options for reform have been suggested:

- Giving ISPs in Britain the same immunity from libel claims they have in the US.

- Extending the innocent dissemination defence under s.1, possibly coupled with an industry code of practice.

- Adopting the US "single publication" rule for online archives, or developing a separate archive defence.

The Commission also considered the possibility of global claims against a web-site, but resolved that any solution would require an international treaty and was thus beyond the scope of the report. It remains to be seen what action, if any, the Government— who commissioned this report—will take in response to the Commission's findings.

(6) LIMITATION

13–033   This is not really a defence, but an assertion that the claimant has run out of time to bring his or her claim for defamation. As will be discussed in Ch. 14, the claimant has a limited time in law to bring a claim. In defamation the time limit is very short. Sections 5 and 6 of the Defamation Act 1996 amend the Limitation Act 1980 to reduce the time limit from three years to *one year*. Section 4A of the Limitation Act 1980 now provides that the ordinary six year time limit for claims in tort does not apply. After one year has expired, the claimant cannot normally sue, however bad the injury to his or her reputation. The assumption is that if your reputation has been injured, you should have realised this and be sufficiently incensed to bring the claim within a short period of time.[22] The court does, however, have a largely unfettered discretion to hold that the time limit should not apply under s.32A of the Limitation Act 1980.[23] In so

---

[21] Scoping study No.2, December 2002. See *The Guardian*, December 18, 2002. See also Scoping Study No.1, "Aspects of Defamation Procedure" (May, 2002) which also highlights the need to reform s.1 of the Defamation Act 1996 to ensure that the right balance is struck between claimants and defendants in defamation cases.

[22] Although it should be noted that in the case of slander not actionable *per se*, the one year time limit will only start to run from the date on which the special damage occurs. These points are dealt with in more detail in Ch. 14.

[23] See *Steedman v BBC* [2002] E.M.L.R. 17.

doing, it must balance the interests of the parties with regard to all the circumstances of the case. Section 32A(1) provides that "If it appears to the court that it would be equitable to allow an action to proceed having regard to the degree to which—(a) the operation of s.4A of this Act prejudices the plaintiff . . . and (b) any decision of the court under this subsection would prejudice the defendant . . . the court may direct that that section shall not apply to the action." The court will consider the length of the delay, why it occurred and, if it is due to lack of knowledge of certain facts, how soon the claimant acted once these facts were known.[24] The court will also examine the extent to which the delay has weakened the evidential basis for the claim.[25]

It should be noted that the one year time limit also applies to claims for malicious falsehood, which will be examined below.

THE NEED FOR REFORM

In this section, we examine some of the problems which have arisen in the tort of defamation, and the continuing need for reform in this area of law. Criticism of the operation of the law of defamation is nothing new. We have already mentioned some of the criticisms contained in the Faulks Committee report of 1975.[26] The Neill *Report on Practice and Procedure in Defamation* of July 1991 made a number of further recommendations, many of which formed the basis for the 1996 Act. Nevertheless, problems remain.[27] Readers will have noted how complicated many of the rules of the tort are, but there remain fundamental difficulties in its application and procedure. There have been a number of high profile cases, for example the case brought by Jeffrey Archer against the *Daily Star*,[28] where the media publicised the extravagant awards given by juries in libel trials. Such awards are particularly questionable when compared with the level of personal injury awards, which are strictly controlled by the courts and considerably less in value. Readers may also note that the claimants are usually people of means. Legal Aid has never been available for defamation, and a recent complaint to the European Court of Human Rights that this contravened the right to a fair trial (Art. 6) has been unanimously rejected.[29] Even in these days of conditional fees, individuals will have the problem of finding a firm prepared to take their case on such a basis, and dealing with the expenses not covered by the conditional fee arrangement. Defamation is therefore a tort which protects the reputation of those with the means to invoke it. As such, it is a far from efficient means of ensuring the right balance between protection of reputation and freedom of speech in modern society.

13–034

---

[24] See s.32A(2)(a) and (b).

[25] See s.32A(2)(c).

[26] *Report of the Committee on Defamation*, Cmnd 5909.

[27] See I. Loveland (1997) 46 I.C.L.Q. 561.

[28] This decision is perhaps now better known for providing the basis for Mr Archer's later conviction for perjury. The sum awarded was later repaid by Mr Archer: see *The Guardian*, October 2, 2002.

[29] *McVicar v United Kingdom* (2002) 35 E.H.R.R. 22, although it was a decision on its facts and does not exclude a future claim should the applicant be able to show real injustice arising from the decision to deny him or her legal aid: (2002) E.H.L.R.L. 693.

Procedural reforms

13–035   Much of the cost of defamation cases comes from the complicated trial process. The Defamation Act 1996 therefore contemplates that some cases should be dealt with by a summary non-jury procedure.[30] Under s.8(2), where the claimant has no realistic prospect of success, and there is no reason why it should be tried, a judge without a jury may dismiss the claim. Alternatively, where there is no defence which has a realistic prospect of success, and there is no other reason why the claim should be tried,[31] a judge may give judgment for the claimant and grant the claimant summary relief.[32] The remedies open to the claimant are limited, however. Under s.9(1), the court has a range of options which consist of: (i) a declaration that the statement was false and defamatory; (ii) an order that the defendant publish a suitable correction and apology; (iii) an award of damages not exceeding £10,000; and (iv) an injunction restraining publication. It is for the parties to arrange the correction and apology. If they cannot agree on its content, s.9(2) provides that the claimant must be satisfied by a summary of the court's judgment. The advantages to the parties are obvious: a speeded-up procedure which avoids a long-winded and costly trial. The claimant can ensure that the statement is corrected and may obtain a certain amount of damages. The judge is given a discretion under s.8(3) to force the claimant to follow the summary route if it "will adequately compensate him for the wrong he has suffered".

Use of this provision will inevitably be confined to straightforward cases where the claimant is prepared to accept an award not exceeding £10,000. Additionally, in the light of the European Convention on Human Rights, which (under Art. 6) grants the defendant a right to a fair trial, it must be questioned to what extent courts *should* restrict the defendant's ability to assert his or her right to freedom of expression in a full trial. It is a first step, however, in trying to simplify the complicated and costly procedure involved in defamation cases.

Control of damages

13–036   This has been one of the main complaints about the law of defamation in recent years. Damages are assessed by the jury, not the judge, and in the past the Court of Appeal has been reluctant to interfere with jury awards. However, after a series of notoriously high awards, this attitude has had to change.[33] Section 8 of the Courts and Legal

---

[30] The new procedure was brought into force (together with all the other provisions of the Defamation Act 1996 which apply in England and Wales and which had not so far been brought into force) by the Defamation Act 1996 (Commencement No.2) Order 2000 (SI 2000/222), on February 28, 2000.

[31] In deciding whether the claim should be tried, the judge will consider, amongst other things, how serious the defamation is and whether it is justifiable in the circumstances to proceed to a full trial: s.8(4).

[32] S.8(3). See *James Gilbert Ltd v MGN Ltd* [2000] E.M.L.R. 680 and, generally, CPR 53.2. The test is the same as that under CPR Part 24, which allows for summary disposal of cases generally. In *Loutchansky v Times Newspapers Ltd (Nos 2–5)* [2002] Q.B. 783, the Court of Appeal held that there was no reason why the summary procedure should not also be used for disposing of questions of quantum alone once liability had been determined or admitted.

[33] In *Tolstoy Miloslavsky v United Kingdom* (1995) 20 E.H.R.R. 442, the European Court of Human Rights found the law prior to the Courts and Legal Services Act 1990 and *Rantzen v Mirror Group Newspapers (1986) Ltd* [1994] Q.B. 670 to be contrary to Art. 10 of the European Convention on Human Rights. The jury's award of £1.5 million in damages (which was three times the size of the highest libel award previously made in England) was therefore a violation of Art. 10.

Services Act 1990 now empowers the Court of Appeal to substitute its own figure of damages for that of the jury without the need for a retrial.[34] More fundamentally, the Court of Appeal has recognised that the judge must exercise some degree of control over jury awards, by ensuring that they receive appropriate guidance in the summing-up.

This can be seen in the 1994 case of *Rantzen v Mirror Group Newspapers (1986) Ltd*,[35] where the newspaper had accused the television presenter Esther Rantzen, who had founded the children's charity ChildLine, of knowingly protecting a person guilty of sexual abuse. The jury had awarded £250,000. The Court of Appeal set this aside under s.8 of the Courts and Legal Services Act 1990 and substituted the figure of £110,000. Neill L.J. held that:

> "We consider therefore that the common law if properly understood requires the courts to subject large awards of damages to a more searching inquiry than has been customary in the past. It follows that what has been regarded as the barrier against intervention should be lowered. The question becomes: 'Could a reasonable jury have thought that their award was necessary to compensate the plaintiff and to re-establish his reputation?'"[36]

The Court held that the judge should refer to previous Court of Appeal decisions under s.8 for guidance, but was not prepared to say that the judge should refer the jury to other awards in libel actions or personal injury cases. It acknowledged that it would take some time for case law to develop under s.8 and, in the meantime, the jury should be invited to consider the purchasing power of their award (for example, could it buy a house, a car or a holiday?) and whether the award was proportionate to the damage suffered. A sum should be awarded which ensured that the claimant was provided with adequate compensation.[37] The court's judgment, which the court held to be consistent with Art. 10 of the European Convention on Human Rights, provided some guidance for juries, but was taken a step further in the now leading case of *John v Mirror Group Newspapers Ltd*.[38]

In this case, which was brought by the entertainer Elton John against the *Daily Mirror*, the Court of Appeal provided juries with further guidance. Despite the ruling in *Rantzen*, the court found that there was still evidence of disproportionate libel awards, and thought further action was necessary. On this basis, the court finally accepted that juries should be informed, by way of guidance, of the level of damages awarded in personal injury cases. While it was clearly impossible to compare severe brain damage with an attack on a person's reputation, it did give the jury some guidance as to the level of damages necessary in the circumstances. The judge, and advocates for both sides, would now be permitted to address the jury on what they considered to be the correct level of damages. Such changes, it was hoped, would make the assessment of damages "more rational and so more acceptable to public

---

[34] Note also that in *Grobbelaar v News Group Newspapers Ltd* [2002] 1 W.L.R. 3024, the House of Lords exercised its inherent power to alter the award.
[35] [1994] Q.B. 670.
[36] [1994] Q.B. 670 at 692.
[37] *ibid.*, at 696.
[38] [1997] Q.B. 586. Applied in *Kiam v MGN Ltd* [2003] Q.B. 281.

opinion".[39] The courts would continue to refer to decisions under the 1990 Act (as suggested in *Rantzen*) and would continue to refuse to allow references to defamation awards which had been made on different sets of facts. On this basis, the Court of Appeal reduced the jury's award of compensatory damages from £75,000 to £25,000.

13–037   Two further points should be made here. First, any compensatory sum awarded may be supplemented by aggravated or exemplary damages, which will be discussed generally in Ch. 15. Aggravated and exemplary damages play a significant role in defamation, which remains one of the few occasions when exemplary or punitive damages may be awarded in tort law. Aggravated damages will be awarded for additional injury to the claimant's feelings. The court will award exemplary damages where the defendant, either knowing a statement to be false or careless whether it be true or false, has deliberately published the statement because the profit gained from publication will outweigh any financial penalties.[40] This obviously is particularly apposite to newspapers publishing sensational stories such as the one concerning Elton John in *John*. Nevertheless, such sums are controlled, and the Court of Appeal reduced the exemplary damages in *John* from £275,000 to £50,000. Sir Thomas Bingham M.R. warned that "principle requires that an award of exemplary damages should never exceed the minimum sum necessary to meet the public purpose underlying such damages, that of punishing the defendant, showing that tort does not pay and deterring others".[41]

Secondly, the main problem here is still the jury. In the recent case of *Kiam v MGN Ltd*,[42] Sedley L.J. dissenting complained that the *John* case had failed in its purpose of limiting damages: "the train has left the station again and is now accelerating".[43] The Court of Appeal noted that whatever guidance is given to juries, the sums awarded remain large. This has been exacerbated recently by changes in personal injury law which have increased awards for non-pecuniary loss—to which libel juries are asked in *John* to refer.[44] Yet, however one refines the guidance given to juries, ultimately the question must arise whether it would be simpler just to abolish the jury in defamation cases or, less drastically, place assessment of damages in the hands of the judge. It is the judge, after all, who assesses damages in personal injury cases. This ensures a roughly coherent framework which at least allows parties some means of predicting the level of damages to be awarded. Uncertainty makes it difficult to settle defamation cases, which the general rules of civil litigation seek to encourage. The Faulks Committee in 1975 recommended removing the right to trial by jury and permitting only a judicial discretion to allow trial by jury if necessary.[45] This has not occurred.[46] The Law Commission, in its recent report on damages for non-pecuniary loss, decided that it was not appropriate at the present time to take assessment of damages away from the jury.[47] In the light of the changes likely to result from full implementation of the Defamation Act 1996 and the incorporation of the European Convention on

---

[39] See above at 616 *per* Sir Thomas Bingham M.R.
[40] See *Broome v Cassell* [1972] A.C. 1027.
[41] [1997] Q.B. 586 at 619.
[42] [2003] Q.B. 281.
[43] See above at 302.
[44] See Ch. 15; *Heil v Rankin* [2001] Q.B. 272.
[45] Para.516.
[46] Subject to the rules for summary disposal of cases by a single judge provided by Defamation Act 1996, s.8.
[47] Law Commission Report No. 257, *Damages for personal injury: Non-pecuniary loss* (1999), para.4.23.

Human Rights into English law, the Commission decided to wait, believing that such a change would require, in any event, a full examination of how defamation cases are tried. It nevertheless thought that it should never be left to a jury to decide whether exemplary damages should be awarded, or their amount.[48]

A graphic illustration of the difficulties invoked by the use of juries in libel trials may be seen in *Grobbelaar v News Group Newspapers Ltd*.[49] Grobbelaar—a well-known goalkeeper—had complained about articles which appeared in *The Sun*, based on covert audio and video recordings in which he was recorded agreeing to a proposed match fixing conspiracy, accepting £2,000 in cash, and claiming that he had previously accepted bribes for fixing particular games. The trial jury had found in his favour and awarded him damages of £85,000. The Court of Appeal, however, overturned the verdict as perverse in view of the evidence presented in court. In so doing, it demonstrated a clear lack of faith in the reasoning of the jury and re-affirmed the doubts of many as to the ability of the jury to act objectively in the course of such trials. The House of Lords (Lord Steyn dissenting) reinstated the jury's verdict and held that only exceptionally should the verdict of a jury be overturned as perverse. Lord Bingham found it "a very serious thing to stigmatise as perverse the unanimous finding of jurors . . . that is not a conclusion to be reached lightly or if any alternative explanation not involving perversity presents itself."[50] The majority found such an alternative explanation: the article contained two stings—first, that Grobbelaar had taken bribes and, secondly, that he had actually fixed matches. Whilst the first had been proved, the evidence at trial had not supported the latter. On this basis, the jury's finding of liability could be explained on the basis that it found insufficient justification for this latter allegation. However, the majority was unable to accept that this justified an award of £85,000. It again refused to declare this perverse, but reduced the award to £1. By accepting bribes, Grobbelaar had acted in a way in which no decent or honest footballer would act and had undermined the integrity of the game. Lord Millett found it an "affront to justice"[51] to award more than derisory damages to a sportsman whose reputation had been so destroyed. **13–038**

The current problem therefore remains unsolved. Arguably, the willingness of the present government to consider limiting the right of the accused to trial by jury in criminal law might suggest a greater openness to review of the merits of the jury system in defamation cases. However, at present, change does not appear imminent.

INTERIM INJUNCTIONS

It is worth noting briefly that although the claimant may wish to obtain an injunction to prevent publication of the statement in question, the courts will only rarely grant an injunction prior to a full hearing of the trial. Therefore, even if the claimant is given prior notice of publication of statements which may diminish his or her reputation, it will be difficult to prevent publication. The court's discretion to grant interim relief will **13–039**

---

[48] Para.4.32.
[49] [2002] 1 W.L.R. 3024, HL.
[50] See above at 3034–3035.
[51] Above at 3050.

not ordinarily be exercised to restrain a libel where the defendant alleges a defence or claims justification, unless the claimant can prove that the libel is plainly untrue.[52] In *Holley v Smyth*,[53] the majority of the Court of Appeal upheld this rule as supporting the right to free speech, even where the defendant's motives were questionable.[54]

In view of the problems associated with a defamation action, litigants may wish to consider two alternative options. Where the defamatory material has been published by the media, the individual may wish to send a complaint to the Press Complaints Commission or Broadcasting Standards Commission and take advantage of the remedies they provide. This is cost effective, but it should be considered whether the remedies are sufficient. Alternatively, the claimant may wish to sue for malicious falsehood. The advantages and disadvantages of these two options will be examined below.

COMPLAINTS TO REGULATORY BODIES

13–040   A person aggrieved by inaccurate statements in the media may complain to the Press Complaints Commission (the self-regulating body of the press) or Ofcom, the regulator for the UK communication industries. These bodies do not award compensation, but may require the offending newspaper or broadcaster to publish a summary of any adjudication. The Press Complaints Commission (PCC) follows a Code of Practice which protects "the rights of the individual and upholds the public's right to know".[55] The Code deals specifically with issues such as accuracy, the right to reply, privacy, harassment and intimidation and the treatment of children and other vulnerable parties. In 2002, the PCC dealt with 2,630 complaints. Where the complainant is successful, the PCC will generally try to negotiate the publication of an agreed correction and/or apology, a letter from the journal to the complainant, or a follow-up article. If this fails, it can require the publication of a critical adjudication in full and with due prominence. A copy of the adjudication will be published on the PCC website. The complaint must be brought, however, within one month of publication, and the procedure cannot be used if legal action has commenced.

Ofcom has more extensive powers.[56] Operating under the Communications Act 2003 and the Broadcasting Acts 1990 and 1996 (as amended), it is concerned with broadcasting standards (matters of taste and decency) and fairness (unfair or unjust treatment and the infringement of privacy). If it deems it necessary, Ofcom may issue a Direction not to repeat a programme, to broadcast a correction or a summary of the adjudication, or even fine the broadcaster. Again, short time limits apply. Because of restrictions on the period for which broadcasters have to retain recordings, complaints

---

[52] See *Bonnard v Perryman* [1891] 2 Ch. 269, C.A. See also *Williams Coulson & Sons v James Coulson and Co.* [1887] 3 T.L.R. 46: an interim injunction should only be used in the clearest of cases.
[53] [1998] Q.B. 726. (Staughton L.J. dissenting.)
[54] The defendant had used the threat of publication as a means of putting pressure on the claimant to compensate him for an alleged wrong.
[55] Preamble to the Code of Practice: see *www.pcc.org.uk*.
[56] Web site: *www.Ofcom.org.uk*. Ofcom replaced the Broadcasting Standards Commission in December 2003, and, in addition to regulating standards of taste and decency on all TV and radio channels, licences, commercial TV and radio and oversees the telecommunications industry.

must be brought within 42 days (radio), 90 days (television) and 60 days (satellite and cable) after the relevant broadcast.

These are therefore very limited provisions, both in terms of the remedies available and the time limits, but they provide some means of redress for complainants who feel that they have been misrepresented by the media. A further option which the claimant should consider, however, is whether he or she would be able to bring a claim for malicious falsehood.

MALICIOUS OR INJURIOUS FALSEHOOD

This is a different tort from defamation and can be classified as an economic tort, *i.e.* a **13–041** tort which specifically protects the economic interests of the claimant. Here, the claimant is complaining that the defendant has made a false statement to a third party which has damaged his or her business interests. This is distinct from defamation. Defamation protects the business *reputation* of the claimant. Malicious falsehood protects the *financial interests* of the claimant. This distinction is illustrated in the following example. The defendant has told X that the claimant's shop does not sell paper. This is untrue. X, as a result, buys his paper from the defendant's shop. Such a statement does not affect the claimant's trading reputation but will obviously reduce the income of the shop, and affect the claimant's financial position. On this basis, the Court of Appeal in *Ratcliffe v Evans*[57] held that the plaintiff had a valid action when a newspaper published a statement that the plaintiff's firm had gone out of business. It was held that the statement did not reflect on the plaintiff's character, but nevertheless the plaintiff could sue for the general loss of business which resulted from publication.

To bring a case for malicious falsehood, there are four main requirements:

  (i)   The defendant made a false statement concerning the claimant or his or her property;

  (ii) Maliciously;

  (iii) To some person other than the claimant; *and*

  (iv) As a result the claimant suffered economic loss.

The tort is therefore not actionable *per se*. Special damage must be proved, such as loss of business.[58] However, the claimant may be assisted by s.3(1) of the Defamation Act 1952. This provides that it is no longer necessary to allege or prove special damage if the words complained of:

"... are calculated to cause pecuniary damage to the plaintiff and are published in writing or other permanent form or if the said words are calculated to cause pecuniary damage to the plaintiff in respect of any office, profession, calling, trade or business held or carried on by him at the time of the publication."

---

[57] [1892] 2 Q.B. 524.
[58] *Royal Baking Powder Co v Wright Crossley & Co* (1900) 18 R.P.C. 95 at 99: "The damage is the gist of the action and therefore ... it must be especially alleged and proved."

This provision covers many of the occasions giving rise to the action and makes the tort largely actionable without proof of damage, provided the words are calculated to cause the claimant financial loss. The other requirements must, however, be met. The statement must be proved to be false.[59] This, unlike in defamation, will not be presumed. The claimant must also show that the statement was made maliciously, *i.e.* that the defendant knew that the statement was false, or was reckless as to whether it was true or not,[60] or was actuated by some indirect, dishonest or improper motive.[61] It is always a defence that the statement was made in good faith.[62]

13–042   Damages may extend to distress and injury to feelings consequential on financial loss. In *Khodaparast v Shad*,[63] an Iranian woman had lost her part-time job as a teacher in a religious school and found it difficult to gain employment when a former lover had distributed mock-up advertisements for telephone sex services using her photograph. At trial, he had persisted in insisting that these were genuine advertisements and such behaviour was typical of her loose morals. The trial judge had found in favour of the claimant and awarded additional aggravated damages[64] to reflect the injury to the claimant's feelings from the defendant's conduct prior to and during the trial. The Court of Appeal approved this award. As stated by Stuart-Smith L.J.: "once the plaintiff is entitled to sue for malicious falsehood, whether on proof of special damage or by reasons of s.3 of the 1952 Act I can see no reason why, in an appropriate case, he or she should not recover aggravated damages for injury to feelings . . . justice requires that it should be so."[65] It should be noted that this is an additional claim. It does not permit a claimant to obtain damages solely for emotional distress or injury to his or her reputation. Any claim for the latter must be brought under the tort of defamation.

Generally, therefore, defamation will be easier (depending of course on the facts) for the claimant to prove, so few actions are brought for malicious falsehood. The claimant will also have the benefit of a jury in defamation, which he or she will not have for malicious falsehood, which will be heard by a judge alone. There may nevertheless be advantages to suing for malicious falsehood. First, the claimant does not have to show an attack on his or her business reputation, but simply that the false statement has resulted in the business losing money. Secondly, the defence may prove useful where other causes of action fail. For example, in *Kaye v Robertson*,[66] the court, horrified by the behaviour of the newspaper in question, relied on malicious falsehood to support Kaye's claim. Gorden Kaye, a popular actor, had been seriously injured when a piece of wood smashed through his car windscreen during a bad storm in 1990. He was in a critical condition for many days, and a special notice was placed on his door to keep out visitors. A journalist and photographer from the *Sunday Sport* newspaper nevertheless entered the room, obtained a picture of Mr Kaye using a flash camera, and claimed that Kaye had consented to an "interview". The paper alleged

---

[59] It does not include mere advertising "puffs": *White v Mellin* [1895] A.C. 154.
[60] *Shapiro v La Morta* (1923) 40 T.L.R. 201.
[61] *Balden v Shorter* [1933] Ch. 427.
[62] *Spring v Guardian Assurance* [1995] 2 A.C. 296.
[63] [2000] 1 W.L.R. 618. Applied in *Smith v Stemler* [2001] C.L.Y. 2309 (Central London County Court).
[64] See Ch. 15: Damages.
[65] See above at 630–631, relying heavily on dicta from Nicholls V.C. and Sir Michael Kerr in *Joyce v Sengupta* [1993] 1 W.L.R. 337 and distinguishing previous negative dicta in *Fielding v Variety Inc* [1967] 2 Q.B. 841.
[66] [1991] F.S.R. 62.

that it had obtained "a great old-fashioned scoop". In fact, Kaye was in intensive care and could not remember the incident 15 minutes after the event. The Court of Appeal took a dim view of such conduct, but struggled to find a basis for liability in tort. Trespass to the person (see Ch. 12) did not work. The use of a flash by itself did not amount to battery.[67] The judges were tempted by libel, on the basis that it was defamatory to state falsely that Kaye had consented to give an exclusive interview to the *Sunday Sport*. However, the court adhered to the rule that interim injunctions (*i.e.* injunctions before the final hearing) should be used sparingly in libel.[68] The court therefore resorted to malicious falsehood: the paper's allegation that the story and photograph had been taken with Kaye's consent was clearly false, and Kaye had lost the right to sell his first interview after the accident for profit.[69] Bingham L.J. commented that "this case nonetheless highlights, yet again, the failure of both the common law of England and statute to protect in an effective way the personal privacy of individual citizens".[70]

Defamation: Conclusion

As may be seen, defamation is a difficult and complex area of law, but one which is of considerable interest to anyone who is concerned how the law of tort deals with the difficult issues of freedom of expression and the rights of individuals to protect their reputation from attack. The best way to approach this area of law is in stages, following the method indicated above. In this way, the reader can understand the reasoning adopted by the courts and appreciate the problems inherent in this area of law. Although the Defamation Act 1996 has attempted to deal with these problems, there is clearly a long way to go. The incorporation of the European Convention on Human Rights into English law by the Human Rights Act 1998 will ensure the continuation of this debate. **13–043**

---

[67] Although Glidewell L.J. suggested at 68 that a bright light deliberately shone into another's eyes which injured his sight or damaged him in some other way might at law be a battery.
[68] See above.
[69] The Court of Appeal also considered the economic tort of passing off, in which the claimant sues for a misrepresentation made to the claimant's prospective or existing customers which is calculated to injure the business or goodwill of the claimant and which has caused or threatened actual damage to the business or goodwill of the claimant. The claimant must be a "trader". The court held that the possibility of Kaye selling the story of his accident did not make him a "trader".
[70] [1991] F.S.R. 62 at 70. Arguably, this deficiency has now been met by the courts' development of breach of confidence to protect an individual's right to privacy.

Chapter 14

GENERAL DEFENCES AND EXTINCTION OF LIABILITY

Introduction

In this chapter, we examine defences generally and the ways in which the defendant's **14–001** liability can be extinguished. We have already considered a number of defences in this book, for example defences to defamation claims in Ch. 13, defences such as act of God or statutory authority in our Nuisance chapter, and necessity in our Trespass chapter. These will therefore not be considered here. This chapter will examine the remaining general defences in tort and should therefore be used in conjunction with earlier chapters outlining the requirements of the tort in question. We examine each defence in turn. It should be noted that, in general, the burden of proof in establishing a defence will rest on the defendant on the balance of probabilities. There is no limit on the number of defences a defendant may allege.

The second half of this chapter deals with ways in which the defendant's liability can be extinguished. The primary method is limitation. The Limitation Act 1980 imposes strict time limits within which the claimant must start his or her action. If these time limits are missed, then, subject to certain statutory discretions, the court will refuse to hear the claimant's action, however strong the claim. This ensures that claimants do not bring stale claims which it would be difficult for the defendant to defend. We shall also consider the effect of death of either party to the action, and the more technical grounds of waiver, and accord and satisfaction. We begin by examining the main general defences in the law of torts.

DEFENCES

Consent

We saw the defence of "consent" in our chapter on trespass to the person where the **14–002** surgeon, for example, operates on a patient. The surgeon is not committing a trespass if he or she has obtained the patient's consent to the procedure in question. In negligence, the terminology is different, and the courts prefer the term *volenti non fit* *injuria* or "voluntary assumption of risk". In relation to property, it is usually termed "leave" or "licence". Although the courts may use the terms interchangeably,[1] the defence is applied differently and we shall therefore divide consent into three categories:

   (i) consent;

   (ii) voluntary assumption of risk; and

   (iii) leave or licence.

We shall examine each category in context. Therefore, consent will be examined in the context of trespass to the person, voluntary assumption of risk in relation to negligence and leave or licence in relation to property torts.[2]

(i) Consent

14–003   The defendant will not be liable for trespass to the person where the claimant has consented to such actions. Consent may be express or implied. For example, by presenting your arm for an injection, you are impliedly showing that you consent to the physical contact involved. Following *Freeman v Home Office (No.2)*,[3] the burden is on the claimant to show the absence of consent. Although ordinarily the burden is on the defendant to establish a defence, the nature of trespass to the person is such that the claimant must show that the physical contact was incurred without his or her consent. In practice, however, the defendant is unlikely to rely on the claimant's failure to establish the absence of consent and will produce evidence to show consent. Practically, therefore, it works as a defence. This topic is discussed fully in Ch. 11 and therefore readers are advised to refer further to the section on "Consent" in that chapter.

(ii) Voluntary assumption of risk

14–004   In the tort of negligence, consent takes the form of an agreement to run the risk of the defendant's negligence. It may be express or implied and forms an absolute defence. There are traditionally said to be three main requirements for the defence:

   (a) agreement to the risk;

   (b) full knowledge of the nature and extent of the risk; *and*

   (c) voluntary choice by the claimant.

The three requirements will be examined below.

14–005   **(a) Agreement:**   There is mixed authority as to what is meant by "agreement". Lord Denning in *Nettleship v Weston*[4] took a very formalistic view, holding that "nothing will suffice short of an agreement to waive any claim for negligence".[5] This clearly did not

---

[1] See, *e.g. Arthur v Anker* [1997] Q.B. 564 at 572.
[2] By "property torts", we mean torts protecting land such as nuisance and trespass to land.
[3] [1984] Q.B. 524 at 539. Affirmed [1984] 1 Q.B. 548, CA.
[4] [1971] 2 Q.B. 691.
[5] *ibid.*, at 701.

exist on the facts of the case. It may be recalled from earlier chapters that a friend, who had been teaching the defendant to drive, had been injured by the defendant's negligent driving. The court held that the friend had not agreed to take the risk of this happening as he had specifically asked, prior to the lesson, whether he would be protected by the car-owner's insurance policy. It is unclear, however, whether such a stringent test for agreement applies generally. Such a test would rarely be satisfied, and his Lordship's view would severely limit the application of this defence. A more flexible approach was clearly evident in the House of Lords' decision in *ICI v Shatwell*.[6]

In this case, the plaintiff and his brother worked together at the defendant's quarry. With complete disregard to their employer's safety instructions (and certain statutory duties imposed on them) which required them to test detonators from a proper shelter, they decided to test the detonators in the open to save time. There was an explosion in which the plaintiff was seriously injured. He sued his employer as vicariously liable for his brother's negligence. The House of Lords was not prepared to allow him to recover damages. It was held that the plaintiff had voluntarily assumed the risk, having fully appreciated the potential danger which led to the injury. Although it is possible to explain this decision in terms of an implied agreement between the two brothers, little attention was paid by their Lordships to the requirement of agreement.[7] A clearer example of the artificiality of a formal requirement of express or implied agreement may be found in the House of Lords case of *Titchener v British Railways Board*.[8] In this case, a 15-year-old girl had been struck by a train while crossing a railway line. She was seriously injured. She was a trespasser, having passed through a gap in the boundary fence, and it was held that she clearly knew of the risk of being hit by trains when crossing the line. She had nevertheless taken that risk and, had the train driver been negligent, a defence of voluntary assumption of risk would have applied. In this case, it is difficult to see how any agreement (express or otherwise) could be found between the plaintiff and the train driver. The defence seemed to be based simply on her free acceptance of the risks involved.

"Agreement" should thus be interpreted loosely to mean that the claimant has clearly consented to the risk.[9] Obviously this will be easier to establish where the claimant has openly agreed with the defendant to undertake the risk, but this is not a necessary requirement. On this basis, "agreement" cannot be considered as a separate requirement. It is simply part of the question whether the defendant has fully consented to the risk, which also involves an examination of the claimant's knowledge and understanding of the risks involved. It is submitted therefore that (a) and (b) should be merged to form a single requirement that the claimant has full knowledge of and has accepted the nature and extent of the risks involved.

(b) Full knowledge and acceptance of the nature and extent of the risk: This is the **14–006** key issue. To lose the right to sue for negligence, it is not sufficient that the claimant simply consented to the defendant's activities. Such consent will only provide a defence if it is of a particular quality: it is given with a full understanding and acceptance of the nature and extent of the risks involved. For example, if I agree to attend your

[6] [1965] A.C. 656, see in particular Lord Reid.
[7] Although Lord Pearce referred to a genuine full agreement at 687.
[8] [1983] 1 W.L.R. 1427.
[9] Note, however, A.J.E. Jaffey (1985) 44 C.L.J. 87.

barbecue, I accept the risk of smoke and perhaps even the risk of food poisoning. However, unless you tell me, I do not accept the risk that you will try to set the barbecue alight with petrol, causing a massive explosion. My agreement to attend the barbecue was not with the full knowledge of the risks involved. This can lead to difficult questions of fact and has given rise to a number of controversial decisions, none more so than the Court of Appeal decision in *Dann v Hamilton.*[10]

In this case, the plaintiff and her mother had accepted a lift from Hamilton to see the coronation decorations. During the evening, Hamilton had consumed a certain amount of alcohol, but the plaintiff nevertheless accepted a lift home. This was despite the warning from a fellow passenger, who refused to travel any further in the car, that she should find an alternative means of transport. Due to Hamilton's negligent driving, the vehicle was involved in an accident in which Hamilton was killed and the plaintiff injured. The question arose whether the plaintiff had voluntarily assumed the risk of negligent driving. When warned by her friend, she had merely responded: "You should be like me. If anything is going to happen, it will happen". Was this statement sufficient to establish the defence?

Perhaps surprisingly, Asquith J. held that it was not. He distinguished between knowledge of a risk and consent to the risk. The plaintiff clearly knew that the driver was intoxicated, but his Lordship held that this did not mean that she had accepted the risk of him driving negligently. However, his Lordship did concede that if the drunkenness of a driver was so extreme and glaring that to travel with him would be to engage in an intrinsically and obviously dangerous occupation, such as meddling with an unexploded bomb, or walking on the edge of an unfenced cliff, the defence would be established.

This decision draws the defence very narrowly indeed.[11] One explanation is the fact that it is a driving case where, of course, the driver is required to be insured. The insurance cover ensures that the victim is fully compensated whilst the cost is spread evenly throughout the driving community. This explanation is nowadays further supported by s.149 of the Road Traffic Act 1988, which excludes the defence of voluntary assumption of risk in all road traffic cases. It provides that when a person uses a motor vehicle which is required by law to be insured:

> "any antecedent agreement or understanding between them (whether intended to be legally binding or not) shall be of no effect so far as it purports or might be held:
>
> (a) to negative or restrict any such liability of the user in respect of persons carried in or upon the vehicle as is required . . . to be covered by a policy of insurance, *or*
>
> (b) to impose such conditions with respect to the enforcement of any such liability of the user."

The defence will therefore never work against car passengers, who should be regarded as in a category of their own. This provision does not, however, prevent other defences

[10] [1939] 1 K.B. 509. See D.M. Gordon (1966) 82 L.Q.R. 62 for criticism.
[11] The decision was questioned by the Court of Appeal in *Pitts v Hunt* [1991] 1 Q.B. 24 who suggested that riding pillion on a motorbike after the plaintiff and the driver had been drinking for hours would, but for s.149 of the Road Traffic Act 1988, have amounted to voluntary assumption of risk. In any event, the court found a good defence of illegality and the case will be considered fully in that section.

applying, such as contributory negligence. In *Owens v Brimmell*,[12] for example, the plaintiff had accompanied the defendant to a number of public houses and finally to a club. Both men had drunk about eight to nine pints of beer. Driving home, the defendant lost control of the car, which collided with a lamp-post. The plaintiff suffered severe injuries and brain damage. Watkins J. held that where a passenger rides in a car with a driver whom he knows has consumed enough alcohol to impair to a dangerous degree his ability to drive properly and safely, the passenger will be found to be contributorily negligent. This will obviously apply where a passenger, knowing that he is relying on the driver for a lift home, accompanies him on a bout of drinking which diminishes the driver's ability to drive properly and safely. On this basis, although the defence of voluntary assumption of risk was not available, damages were reduced by 20 per cent.

In addition, s.149 does not mean that the defence of voluntary assumption of risk will not work in relation to other types of vehicle. Here, the leading modern case on the nature and extent of the risk is now *Morris v Murray*.[13] In this case, the plaintiff chose to fly in a light aircraft piloted by his friend, with whom he had consumed a considerable amount of alcohol prior to the flight.[14] The aircraft crashed shortly after take-off, killing the pilot and badly injuring the plaintiff. The Court of Appeal found in such circumstances that the defence had been established. The plaintiff was well aware of the extreme risk involved in flying with his friend. It was so dangerous that it amounted to an intrinsically dangerous activity, such as that outlined by Asquith J. in *Dann v Hamilton*. Such an adventure was wildly irresponsible.[15]

(c) Voluntary choice by the claimant: Even if the claimant has clearly consented, **14–007** with full knowledge of the risks involved, the defence will not be established if the consent cannot be said to be voluntary. Whilst this may seem obvious, the question of "voluntary choice" has at times been contentious. For example, in the nineteenth century the courts held that the defence applied to employees working under dangerous conditions, and refused to acknowledge that an employee's desire to keep his or her job might force him or her to agree to work under appalling conditions. In such circumstances, the employee, in the absence of statutory rights, was in no position to threaten the employer that unless working conditions improved, he or she would leave. The employer would simply accept the employee's resignation. The House of Lords' decision in *Smith v Charles Baker & Sons*[16] marked welcome recognition of the injustice of this approach. Here, the plaintiff was an employee, who worked on the construction of a railway where a crane would swing heavy stones above his head without warning. The employee was fully aware of the danger of stones falling, but carried on working. He was seriously injured when a stone fell from the crane. The House of Lords (Lord Bramwell dissenting) held the employer liable. Their Lordships refused to accept the argument that by continuing to work, the employee had voluntarily accepted the risk of the stones falling. Nevertheless, it was recognised that a balance had to be struck. If the work was intrinsically dangerous, despite reasonable

[12] [1977] Q.B. 859.
[13] [1991] 2 Q.B. 6. Comment K Williams (1991) 54 M.L.R. 745.
[14] The pilot was found to have consumed 17 whiskies.
[15] See Fox L.J. at 17.
[16] [1891] A.C. 325, HL.

steps by the employer to minimise risks, the employee would be deemed to accept those risks.[17] Here, this was not the case, and so the employer would be found liable.

No such risk of pressure was found in *ICI v Shatwell*[18] where the brothers, testing the detonators in the quarry, had been clearly instructed to take precautions, but nevertheless chose to accept the risk. The court held that, in the light of *Smith v Baker*, it would apply the rule very carefully to employees and be alert to pressure from employers. However, on the facts of this case, no such pressure had been exerted.

14–008   Consent is equally not voluntary if the claimant is so drunk that he or she is incapable of understanding the nature and extent of risk. Again this is a fine line. In *Morris v Murray*, despite his consumption of alcohol, it seems that the plaintiff was capable of realising the risks of flying with an intoxicated pilot,[19] but if he had drunk even more, the defence might not have been established. It has equally been questioned whether a defendant should be liable where, due to the defendant's negligence, the claimant has been given the opportunity to commit suicide. There is a clear argument that where the claimant has deliberately decided to end his or her life, the defence of voluntary assumption of risk should stand. This issue has been raised in two cases where the suicide took place when the deceased was under the care of the police or custodial authorities. In *Kirkham v Chief Constable of Greater Manchester*,[20] the plaintiff's husband had committed suicide while in a remand centre. The plaintiff had warned the police at time of his arrest of her husband's suicidal tendencies, but the police had negligently failed to pass on this information to the remand authorities. The Court of Appeal held that in the light of her husband's clinical depression, he could not be held to have voluntarily accepted the risk. This must be correct. If you are found to be of unsound mind, then an argument that you weighed up and decided to assume the risks of injury can hardly stand.

However, Lloyd L.J. indicated (*obiter*) that the defence would apply if the deceased had been of sound mind at the time of the suicide.[21] This was not followed by the House of Lords in the later case of *Reeves v Metropolitan Police Commissioner*.[22] In this case, Martin Lynch had committed suicide in police custody by hanging himself from a cell door. Although a doctor had found Lynch to be of sound mind, the police had known that he was a suicide risk and had kept him under frequent observation. Nevertheless, they had failed to take all adequate precautions to prevent the suicide. In an action for negligence under the Fatal Accidents Act 1976, the majority of the House of Lords (Lord Hobhouse dissenting) found the police liable. They had undertaken a specific duty to protect Lynch from the risk of suicide and this they had failed to do. Any defence of voluntary assumption of risk would be inconsistent with such a duty:

"If the defence were available in circumstances such as the present where a deceased was known to have suicidal tendencies it would effectively negative the effect of any duty of care in respect of such suicide."[23]

---

[17] See Lord Herschell *ibid.*, at 360.
[18] [1965] A.C. 656.
[19] He had in fact driven from the public house to the airfield and had helped start the aircraft and fuel it.
[20] [1990] 2 Q.B. 283.
[21] *ibid.*, at 290.
[22] [2000] 1 A.C. 360, HL.
[23] Lord Jauncey *ibid.*, at 375–376.

It made no difference whether the victim was of sound or unsound mind at the time of the suicide.

The limitations of this decision should be noted:

- The police admitted to owing a specific duty to protect Lynch from the risk of suicide. If it was simply a duty to take reasonable care of him, voluntary assumption of risk could still be argued. This duty will only arise where the police knew or ought to have known that the individual was a suicide risk.[24]

- The House of Lords stressed that such a specific duty of care would be rare.

- Their Lordships were far from happy in treating Lynch as being of sound mind (the main reason for departing from the view of Lloyd L.J. in *Kirkham*). Lord Hoffmann remarked that "I confess to my unease about this finding, based on a seven minute interview with a doctor of unstated qualifications".[25] This highlights the practical difficulties which would arise if liability were held to depend on whether the deceased was of sound or unsound mind.

- The damages were reduced in any event by 50 per cent for contributory negligence (see below).

A final example of where the courts have considered the "voluntariness" of the assumption of risk is in relation to rescuers. We have considered liability towards rescuers in Ch. 4, but one argument against liability would be that, in relation to non-professional rescuers at least, they have chosen to act. They are under no obligation to intervene, but have chosen to do so freely and so (arguably) have voluntarily accepted the risk of injury involved. If I choose to go into a burning building to save a baby, I must have appreciated the risk of injury and so (arguably) I have voluntarily accepted the risk and cannot sue. The courts have rejected this argument. It is obviously contrary to public policy, but the courts have chosen to analyse it as a situation where the rescuer is not acting voluntarily. The legal, social or moral duty which forces the rescuer to intervene is such that he or she does not act voluntarily in the circumstances. On this basis, the defence of voluntary assumption of risk will not work against rescuers.

A good example is the well-known case of *Haynes v Harwood*.[26] Here, a police officer had been injured whilst stopping runaway horses attached to a van in a crowded street. The defendant had negligently left the horses unattended on the highway and they had bolted when a boy had thrown a stone at them. The Court of Appeal held that the police officer's reaction had been reasonably foreseeable in the circumstances and refused to accept a defence of voluntary assumption of risk.[27] It was also held that the reaction need not be instinctive to be reasonable. This seems sensible. It is surely better to intervene having considered the dangers than to jump in immediately.

Other uses of "consent" in negligence

The courts have not always approached consent in negligence on a consistent basis. In addition to the defence of voluntary assumption of risk, the claimant's consent has been used by the courts in two further ways. First, the claimant's consent may limit the   **14–009**

---

[24] See *Orange v Chief Constable of West Yorkshire Police* [2002] Q.B. 347, CA. *Cf. Keenan v United Kingdom* (2001) 33 E.H.R.R. 38 concerning Art. 2 of the European Convention on Human Rights.
[25] *ibid.*, at 372. See also Lord Hope at 385.
[26] [1935] 1 K.B. 146.
[27] Greer L.J. *ibid.*, at 156–157. See also *Baker v T.E. Hopkins* [1959] 1 W.L.R. 966.

standard of care owed to the claimant by the defendant. Secondly, the claimant's consent may amount to an exclusion clause. These will be examined below. In both situations, the courts deny that they are applying the defence of voluntary assumption of risk, but the dividing line, as will be seen, is far from clear.

14–010   **(a) Setting the standard of care in negligence:**   Here, the claimant's acceptance of risk does not go to establish a defence but lowers the standard of care owed by the defendant to the claimant. This is illustrated by the case of *Wooldridge v Sumner*.[28] In this case, a professional photographer at a horse show had been knocked down by a galloping horse whose rider had taken the corner too fast.[29] The Court of Appeal held that the question in issue was the standard of care expected of a jockey in a race. In setting the standard, regard would be had to the fact that any reasonable spectator would: (a) expect the jockey to concentrate his attention on winning the race, and (b) accept the existence of certain risks, provided the jockey stayed within the rules of the race and was not reckless. On this basis, the jockey was not in breach of his duty of care to the spectator. The dividing line between "no breach of duty" and the defence of voluntary assumption of risk is unclear. The principle on which they rest is the same: the defendant is not liable where the claimant knows and assents to a particular risk. The courts utilise both approaches, and Fox L.J. in *Morris v Murray*[30] held that the gap between the two approaches is not a wide one.

14–011   **(b) Exclusion clauses:**   There is an obvious similarity between an express agreement to assume the risk of negligence and an exclusion clause, in which the claimant agrees to exclude or limit the defendant's liability. However, they are treated as distinct. *White v Blackmore*[31] is a good example of this distinction in operation. The plaintiff's husband had been killed in an accident at a race meeting for old cars. He had been thrown in the air when the rope behind which he was standing had been pulled away by an accident some distance away. Buckley L.J. held that the defendants (who organised the meeting) had successfully excluded liability by notices which absolved them from all liability for accidents howsoever caused. The circumstances did not, however, support the defence of voluntary assumption of risk. By simply standing behind a rope to observe a race, the spectator did not accept the risk of such injury due to the defendants' negligence. His Lordship nevertheless admitted the close relationship between the defence and the operation of exclusion clauses.

The distinction between voluntary assumption of risk and exclusion clauses is nevertheless important, particularly in the light of the strict legal requirements applied to exclusion clauses. For example, to be valid an exclusion clause must be incorporated either by writing, custom or reasonable notice. Equally, exclusion clauses are now regulated by statute. The Unfair Contract Terms Act 1977[32] limits the ability of the defendant to rely on exclusion clauses to exclude or limit liability for negligence as follows[33]:

---

[28] [1963] 2 Q.B. 43. See also *Condon v Basi* [1985] 1 W.L.R. 866, C.A. and C. Gearty (1985) 44 C.L.J. 371.
[29] Who went on to win!
[30] [1991] 2 Q.B. 6 at 15.
[31] [1972] 2 Q.B. 651.
[32] See also Unfair Terms in Consumer Contracts Regulations 1999 (SI 1999/2083). However, these regulations apply to standard form terms in consumer contracts and are unlikely to be relevant here.
[33] We list here only the main provisions of the Act relevant to this topic. Further reference should be made to works on the law of contract.

- The Act regulates exclusion clauses dealing with business liability, *i.e.* where liability arises:

  (a) from things done or to be done by a person in the course of a business (whether his own business or another's); *or*

  (b) from the occupation of premises used for business purposes of the occupier.[34]

  Clauses not dealing with business liability are not affected by the 1977 Act.[35]

- Negligence is dealt with in s.2. This provides that a person cannot by reference to any contract term or notice exclude or restrict liability for death or personal injury resulting from negligence.[36] If the claim is for property or other damage, s.2(2) provides that a person cannot exclude or restrict liability for negligence except in so far as the term or notice satisfies the requirement of reasonableness.

- The reasonableness test is set out in s.11 and Sch.2. These provide that the term must be reasonable having regard to all the circumstances at the time liability arose, including the relative bargaining positions of the parties, any inducement to agree to the clause and, where liability is limited, the resources available to the defendant to meet such liability and the ability of the defendant to obtain insurance cover.

- Section 2(3) deals specifically with the defence of voluntary assumption of risk and distinguishes the defence from exclusion clauses generally. It states: "Where a contract term or notice purports to exclude or restrict liability for negligence, a person's agreement to or awareness of it is not of itself to be taken as indicating his voluntary acceptance of any risk". Therefore, the defendant cannot exclude all possibility of the defence by means of a notice excluding liability. It will remain a question of fact, although it may be questioned what extra element is required to establish the defence of voluntary assumption of risk where the claimant has by notice or contract agreed to exclude liability.

(ii) Leave or licence

Consent in relation to claims for property torts such as trespass to land or nuisance has been mentioned in earlier chapters. As stated earlier, the courts prefer to use the terms "leave" or "licence" in this context. Reference should be made to the relevant chapter. 14–012

(2) Public policy and illegality

This defence is also known by its Latin name, *ex turpi causa non oritur actio*, which means that an action cannot be founded on a base cause.[37] It is essentially founded on policy. The law of tort is not prepared to assist parties whose claims arise directly out 14–013

---

[34] Unfair Contract Terms Act 1977, s.1(3).
[35] Except where the contrary is stated in s.6(4) [sale and hire purchase contracts under s.6] or where ss.2 to 7 do not apply [see misrepresentation under s.8].
[36] *ibid.*, s.2(1).
[37] The classic statement is by Lord Mansfield in *Holman v Johnson* (1775) 1 Cowp. 341 at 343: "No Court will lend its aid to a man who founds his cause of action upon an illegal or an immoral act".

of criminal activity or immoral conduct. It is obviously a matter of degree. If you are attacked when your car is parked on a double yellow line, then a court is not going to dismiss your claim because you were parked illegally. However, if you were involved in a burglary and seriously injured by your fellow burglar negligently handling explosives while trying to blow open the safe, the court would not tolerate your claim.[38] It is clearly a question whether the criminal or immoral act is the basis for the claim or simply background information. This can be a matter of degree. In *Ashton v Turner*,[39] the plaintiff and two other men had been in a car crash which was due to the negligent driving of the defendant. All three men were involved in a burglary, and the crash occurred while driving away from the scene of the crime. The court held that any negligence during the course of the burglary and the subsequent flight in the getaway car would be met by the defence of illegality. The plaintiff's claim was therefore rejected.

The leading case is *Pitts v Hunt*.[40] In this case, the plaintiff and Hunt had been drinking together and then set off home together on a motorbike. The plaintiff knew that Hunt was under age, drunk, uninsured and did not even possess a licence to drive the motorbike. Nevertheless, the plaintiff rode pillion and encouraged Hunt to drive recklessly and deliberately frighten other road-users. There was an accident in which the defendant was killed and the plaintiff seriously injured. The Court of Appeal refused the plaintiff's claim against Hunt's personal representatives on the basis of illegality. However, three lines of reasoning are evident from the court's decision. Illegality will be a defence when:

- due to the nature of the joint illegal activity undertaken by the claimant and Hunt, it is impossible for the court to determine the standard of care which is appropriate to this situation (the Balcombe argument);

- the claimant's cause of action arises directly *ex turpi causa* or "from a base cause" (the Dillon argument); and

- it is contrary to public policy and an affront to the public conscience to compensate the claimant (the Beldam argument).

As indicated, the first argument is that of Balcombe L.J. His Lordship held the term *ex turpi causa* to be "more likely to confuse than to illuminate"[41] and the real question to be whether the circumstances of the case preclude the court from finding a cause of action. On the facts of the case, both the plaintiff and Hunt were involved in reckless driving and the court was not prepared to assess the standard of care appropriate in such circumstances. The facts therefore prevented the court from finding that the Hunt owed a duty of care to the plaintiff.[42]

---

[38] See *National Coal Board v England* [1954] A.C. 403 at 429. Contrast, however, the approach of criminal law which is prepared to find manslaughter due to gross negligence where the victim has participated in the unlawful activity: see *R v Wacker* [2003] Q.B. 1207, CA (Crim) where a lorry driver was convicted for the manslaughter of 58 illegal immigrants who suffocated when he closed the air vent in the back of his lorry.
[39] [1981] Q.B. 137.
[40] [1991] 1 Q.B. 24.
[41] *ibid.*, at 49.
[42] His Lordship was influenced by the majority view in *Jackson v Harrison* (1978) 138 C.L.R. 438 at 455–456 *per* Mason J., (HC Aus). In this case, the court was able to assess the standard of care where the only illegality had been driving whilst disqualified and unlicensed.

Dillon L.J. preferred a test which focused on the basis for the claimant's action. A claimant should fail when his or her action arises directly *ex turpi causa*.[43] However, if the criminal activity is incidental to the wrong suffered, the defence will not stand.

Beldam L.J., however, followed the third argument outlined above. Rather than **14–014** refusing to examine any claim which is directly *ex turpi causa*, his Lordship held that it is the nature or quality of the illegality which determines whether the claim is to be barred. This would give rise to two questions:

(1) Has there been any illegality of which the court should take notice?

(2) Would it be an affront to the public conscience to allow the claimant to recover in such circumstances?[44]

Here, both questions were answered positively. The conduct of the parties was such that it would have amounted to manslaughter by unlawful act if it had caused the death of any third party and this, together with the policy underlying road traffic legislation, should bar the civil claim between the participants.

There is therefore a divergence of approach in the Court of Appeal. Does it matter? The Beldam test is the most flexible, but also the more uncertain. Dillon L.J. warns that the "affront to public conscience" test is likely to be very difficult to apply, since it leaves it wholly to the individual judge to decide what level of illegality is required to satisfy this test. It must be questioned whether it is satisfactory to leave the trial judge to determine the content of the modern social conscience. Dillon L.J. also warned that it would be difficult to divorce the public conscience from matters of an emotional nature relating to the circumstances of the accident. The other tests may seem to provide greater certainty, but questions remain. What type of criminal activity is required so that the court will refuse to assess the standard of care? When is the claim directly *ex turpi causa*? This of course will again depend on the view taken by the court. The Balcombe test is additionally limited in that it can have no applicability outside the tort of negligence.

Subsequent case-law has generally favoured the Dillon test.[45] In *Tinsley v Milligan*,[46] the House of Lords was openly critical of the uncertainty inherent in the public conscience test. Nevertheless there remain a few isolated decisions which still continue to adopt the broader approach, for example, the Court of Appeal decision in *Reeves v Metropolitan Police Commissioner*.[47] (Illegality was not raised in the House of Lords.) It may be recalled that the police were sued for negligence following a death in police custody. It was held that the police had a duty of care to prevent Lynch from committing suicide, which they had breached. The Court of Appeal considered whether such liability should be denied due to illegality. Although suicide has not been a crime since the Suicide Act 1961, the court considered whether there was sufficient

---

[43] [1991] 1 Q.B. 24 at 56 relying on the test in *Saunders v Edwards* [1987] 1 W.L.R. 1116.

[44] Using the test set out by Hutchison J. in *Thackwell v Barclays Bank plc* [1986] 1 All E.R. 676.

[45] See the Court of Appeal decisions in *Clunis v Camden & Islington H.A.* [1998] Q.B. 978, *Webb v Chief Constable of Merseyside Police* [2000] Q.B. 427, *Cross v Kirkby*, *The Times*, April 5 2000 and *Hewison v Meridian Shipping PTE* [2003] P.I.Q.R. 17 (where the same test was applied where the illegality applied not to the question of liability, but to a particular head of damages).

[46] [1994] 1 A.C. 340.

[47] [1999] Q.B. 169, CA.

evidence to conclude that ordinary citizens would be shocked or affronted by an award of damages in respect of the death of a man (known to be a suicide risk) while involuntarily in police custody. The court concluded that there was not and, according to the majority, such a defence would be invalid as contradicting the police's duty of care to prevent the risk of suicide in the first place.

14–015   This decision may be contrasted with the later Court of Appeal decision in *Vellino v Chief Constable of the Greater Manchester Police*,[48] where the Court drew a distinction between claims from prisoners in custody and on arrest. Here, the police had attempted to arrest Vellino at his second floor flat. He had previously evaded arrest by climbing out of a window and lowering himself onto the ground. On this occasion, however, his escape had tragic consequences when he fell badly and was left with severe brain damage and tetraplegia. The majority of the Court gave his claim short shrift: "To suggest that the police owe a criminal the duty to prevent the criminal from escaping, and that the criminal who hurts himself while escaping can sue the police for the breach of that duty, seems to me self-evidently absurd."[49] Only Sedley L.J. was prepared to contemplate a duty on the police not to afford both the temptation to escape and an opportunity to do so where there is a known risk that the prisoner will do himself real harm, and even so, damages under this limited duty would have been substantially reduced for contributory negligence.

The defence of illegality is most significant where it is only the claimant who is involved in criminal activity at the time of the tort. In *Clunis v Camden & Islington Health Authority*,[50] for example, Clunis had been convicted of manslaughter on the grounds of diminished responsibility. He had for no reason attacked and killed a man at an underground station. He had a long history of mental illness and seriously violent behaviour, but had been discharged from hospital, with after-care services in the community to be provided by the defendant health authority. The plaintiff claimed that, due to the negligence of the health authority, his condition had not been properly assessed and he was therefore not prevented from committing the attack. The Court of Appeal rejected this claim. It would be contrary to public policy to support such a claim arising out of commission of a crime. The criminal court had found Clunis to be of diminished responsibility, rather than insane, which indicated that he had appreciated what he was doing and that it was wrong. A claimant would not be allowed to rely on a criminal or immoral act to support his or her claim for compensation.[51] In any event, the health authority was not found to owe Clunis a duty of care.[52]

Nevertheless, illegal activities will not always obstruct the claimant's action in tort. In *Revill v Newbery*,[53] for example, the plaintiff was a burglar who had been shot whilst attempting to enter the defendant's shed to steal his property. The owner of the shed, who was 76, had been concerned about the spate of burglaries in the area and had

---

[48] [2002] 1 W.L.R. 218. Comment CA Hopkins (2002) 61 C.L.J. 257. See also *Sacco v Chief Constable of the South Wales Constabulary* (Unreported, May 15, 1998) CA.

[49] See Schiemann L.J. above at 224.

[50] [1998] Q.B. 978.

[51] The court refused to follow *Meah v McCreamer* [1985] 1 All E.R. 367 where a convicted rapist had been allowed to recover damages when a head injury in a road accident had led to a dramatic personality change. *Clunis* was applied in *Wilson v Coulson* [2002] P.I.Q.R. 22 where the court refused to allow a head of damages based on an illegal act, *i.e.* injuries resulting from a heroin overdose.

[52] Relying on *X v Bedfordshire C.C.* [1995] 2 A.C. 633, discussed in Ch. 2.

[53] [1996] Q.B. 567.

resolved to wait in his shed with a shotgun to defend his property. The burglar sued the defendant for negligence and the court rejected the defence of illegality. Parliament, in enacting the Occupiers' Liability Act 1984,[54] had clearly indicated that in future trespassers, including burglars, should not be treated as outlaws by the occupiers of land. Whilst an occupier might use reasonable force to defend his property, it was clearly an overreaction to shoot the burglar, who had not displayed any intention of resorting to violence. The illegal activities of the burglar therefore did not affect his claim. It should be noted, however, that the decision is confined to the duty owed by an occupier to a trespasser and that the court did reduce the damages awarded to the burglar by two thirds, under the principle of contributory negligence.

Reform

Despite some clear-cut cases, the defence of illegality remains shrouded in uncertainty. **14–016**
The best that can be said is that the defence will work when the claim is clearly founded on an illegal act, which is sufficiently serious (*e.g.* a crime leading to imprisonment), and the illegality in question cannot be dismissed as incidental. The Court of Appeal in *Vellino* saw no need to distinguish cases which dealt with illegality: (a) to deny a duty of care on the basis that it would not be fair, just and reasonable, and (b) as an absolute defence. In the case itself the majority adopted different approaches, but such a distinction was dismissed as irrelevant. On a basic level this is true—either way, the claimant's action will not succeed—although this is to ignore the different burdens of proof applicable to the duty of care (burden on claimant) and defence (burden on defendant). The Law Commission in its Consultation Paper "*The Illegality Defence in Tort*"[55] was critical of the current state of the law. It found it to be sometimes confusing, lacking a clear rationale. It therefore proposed a structured statutory discretion directing the court to ask itself whether the claim should be allowed in the light of the rationale behind the illegality defence—in general, to maintain the internal consistency of the law in the interest of promoting the integrity of justice[56]—and taking certain factors into account. These factors would be:[57]

(i)   the seriousness of the illegality;

(ii) the knowledge and intention of the claimant;

(iii) whether denying relief would act as a deterrent;

(iv) whether denying relief would further the purpose of the rule which renders the claimant's conduct illegal;

(v)   whether denying relief would be proportionate to the illegality involved; *and*

(vi) the degree of connection between the illegal act and the facts giving rise to the claim.

The Law Commission Report is unlikely to appear until late 2004. It must be questioned, however, whether a statutory discretion would in fact render this area of law more predictable or lead simply to uncertainty arising *via* a different route.

---

[54] See Ch. 8.
[55] Law Commission Consultation Paper No. 160 (2001).
[56] Relying on the test stated by McLachlin J. in *Hall v Herbert* (1993) 2 S.C.R. 159 at 178, Supreme Court of Canada.
[57] See paras 6.23–6.45.

(3) Contributory negligence[58]

14–017   It is convenient to refer to the principle of contributory negligence as a "defence", although, as will be seen, it can no longer operate as a complete defence to a claimant's action. Contributory negligence is generally raised in cases involving the tort of negligence, although it has a wider application, for example in breach of statutory duty, and there is some authority that it may even be used in relation to intentional torts such as trespass to the person.[59] It permits a defendant to argue that the damages awarded in favour of the claimant should be reduced because some of the damage was caused by the fault of the claimant. It has obvious links with causation, examined in earlier chapters. Indeed, it is impossible to have 100 per cent contributory negligence for the very reason that this in fact amounts to a statement that the claimant is the cause of the accident (or the *novus causa interveniens*) and has no right to sue the defendant.[60]

The principle of contributory negligence is now found in s.1(1) of the Law Reform (Contributory Negligence) Act 1945. The common law position prior to 1945 was complicated. The rule at common law was that the claimant could recover nothing if he or she was contributorily negligent.[61] The obvious injustice of this rule led the courts to modify this rule to:

- First, the rule of last opportunity. This was where the court found that although both parties were negligent, the defendant had the last chance to avoid the accident.[62] If so, the claimant would recover in full.

- Secondly, the rule of constructive last opportunity. This is where the defendant would have had the last opportunity to avoid the accident, but for his or her own negligence.[63] If proved, the claimant again would recover in full.

Such solutions served only to complicate the law, and of course did not remove the injustice of the former rule. Instead of the claimant's action failing, the claimant recovered full damages. This ignored his or her fault entirely. Neither the old rule nor the courts' modifications were fair to both parties. The law is now stated in the Law Reform (Contributory Negligence) Act 1945 (the Act).

The statutory position

14–018   Section 1(1) of the Act provides:

"Where any person suffers damage as the result partly of his own fault and partly of the fault of any other person or persons, a claim in respect of that damage shall not

---

[58] See N. Gravells (1977) 93 L.Q.R. 581.
[59] See *Murphy v Culhane* [1977] Q.B. 96, although this was doubted by Lord Rodger in *Standard Chartered Bank v Pakistan National Shipping Corpn (Nos 2 and 4)* [2003] 1 A.C. 959 at 975, HL. But not deceit: *Alliance and Leicester B.S. v Edgestop Ltd* [1994] 2 All E.R. 38 and *Standard Chartered Bank v Pakistan National Shipping Corpn (Nos 2 and 4)* above. The Torts (Interference with Goods) Act 1977, s.11(1) also provides that it is not a defence to proceedings founded on conversion or intentional trespass to goods.
[60] See *Pitts v Hunt* [1991] 1 Q.B. 24.
[61] See *Butterfield v Forrester* (1809) 11 East 60.
[62] *Davies v Mann* (1842) 10 M. & W. 546.
[63] *British Columbia Electric Ry v Loach* [1916] 1 A.C. 719.

be defeated by reason of the fault of the person suffering the damage, but the damages recoverable in respect thereof shall be reduced to such extent as the court thinks just and equitable having regard to the claimant's share in the responsibility for the damage."

This section finally allowed the courts to apportion damages as they felt "just and equitable" and marked a welcome move away from the technicalities of the common law. Damages will be reduced according to the claimant's responsibility for the damage (not the accident). On this basis, damages may be reduced in a car crash when the claimant has failed to wear a seatbelt.[64] This may not have led to the accident, but may have added to the injury suffered.

"Damage" is defined in s.4 to include loss of life and personal injury, and it continues to include property damage. It would also appear to cover claims for pure economic loss.[65] Section 4 also defines "fault" as:

". . . negligence,[66] breach of statutory duty or other act or omission that gives rise to liability in tort or would, apart from the Act, give rise to the defence of contributory negligence."

This is not particularly clear. The accepted view is that s.1 refers to "fault" both in relation to the claimant and the defendant. On this basis, the first part of the definition refers to the nature of the claim against the defendant, which can be for negligence, breach of statutory duty or any other act or omission giving rise to liability in tort. The second part of the definition refers to the act or omissions of the claimant which would at common law have given the defendant an absolute defence. On this basis, negligence by the claimant which would *not* at common law have given rise to a defence of contributory negligence—the classic example being deceit/fraud—would not affect the claim.[67]

A very broad interpretation of s.4 was adopted recently by the majority of the House of Lords in *Reeves v Metropolitan Police Commissioner*,[68] where their Lordships held that it included intentional acts by the claimant. On this basis, the deliberate act of the deceased in committing suicide in police custody amounted to contributory negligence within the Act. This is a very generous interpretation of "fault"—it can hardly be termed "negligent" to deliberately commit suicide—and it is somewhat artificial to

---

[64] See *Froom v Butcher* [1976] Q.B. 286.
[65] See *Platform Home Loans v Oyston Shipways Ltd* [2000] 2 A.C. 190, HL.
[66] This has raised problems whether contributory negligence can be a defence when the claimant alleges that the defendant's negligence amounts to breach of contract. The leading case of *Forsikringsaktieselskapet Vesta v Butcher* [1989] A.C. 852 limits the defence to where the defendant's liability in contract is the same as his liability in the tort of negligence independently of the existence of any contract. See also *Barclays Bank plc v Fairclough Building Ltd* [1995] Q.B. 214 and *Raflatac Ltd v Eade* [1999] 1 Lloyd's Rep 506, Colman J.
[67] This was confirmed recently by the House of Lords in *Standard Chartered Bank v Pakistan Shipping Corpn (Nos 2 and 4)* [2003] 1 A.C. 959 noted by N Beresford (2002) 62 C.L.J. 17, approving earlier authority in *Alliance and Leicester B.S. v Edgestop Ltd* [1993] 1 W.L.R. 1462, *Corporacin Nacional del Cobre de Chile v Sogemin Metals Ltd* [1997] 1 W.L.R. 1396 and *Nationwide B.S. v Thimbleby & Co* [1999] Lloyd's Rep PN 359. In deceit, it is irrelevant that the claimant may have allowed himself or herself to be influenced by other factors or has failed to verify the statement in question: *Edgington v Fitzmaurice* (1885) L.R. 29 Ch. D. 459 and *Redgrave v Hurd* (1881–82) L.R. 20 Ch. D. 1.
[68] [2000] 1 A.C. 360, HL.

claim that a person's act of suicide "contributed" to the damage, *i.e.* his death. However, the section is broadly phrased, and in view of the defendant's duty to prevent this very act occurring, the majority held that a "common sense" approach should prevail. Both the deceased's intentional act and the negligence of the police had contributed to his death and so a 50:50 division of responsibility was appropriate.

It should be noted that the aim of this section is not to show that the claimant owes the defendant a duty of care to protect him or her against liability, but to show that the claimant failed to exercise reasonable care and this added to his or her injuries.[69] It will be a question of fact in each case. There are three main questions the court should address:

(i) Was the claimant acting negligently?

(ii) Did his or her actions contribute to the damage suffered?

(iii) To what extent should his or her damages be reduced?

These questions will be examined below.

(i) Was the claimant acting negligently?

14–019　As we have seen above, the question is whether the claimant has exercised reasonable care. As Lord Denning stated in *Jones v Livox Quarries*: "A person is guilty of contributory negligence if he ought reasonably to have foreseen that, if he did not act as a reasonable, prudent man, he might hurt himself; and in his reckonings, he must take into account the possibility of others being careless".[70] It is clearly an objective test, but the courts will make allowances for children[71] and the aged and infirm. The courts will equally recognise that in an emergency (which is due to the fault of the defendant), some allowance must be made for decisions taken in the heat of the moment. In *Jones v Boyce*,[72] for example, the plaintiff was a passenger on top of the defendant's coach. In realising correctly that the coach was in danger of being overturned due to a defective coupling rein, he decided to jump off and broke his leg. The coach, in fact, did not overturn. The court nevertheless held that it was a question of whether the plaintiff had acted reasonably, and allowances should be made for the actions of parties placed in such a dangerous predicament. However, the reaction must be reasonable and respond to some danger. In *Adams v Lancashire and Yorkshire Ry Co.*,[73] for example, it was not deemed reasonable to deal with the inconvenience of a draft from an open train door by leaning out of the moving train to close it. The court held that the plaintiff should simply have moved seats or waited until the next station.[74] He therefore had no right to sue the defendant for negligence when he fell out of the train.

The same restrictions apply to rescuers. Whilst allowances will be made for the heat of the moment, the rescuer cannot claim for injuries which are due to his or her

---

[69] *Nance v British Columbia Electric Ry Co. Ltd* [1951] 2 All E.R. 448.
[70] [1952] 2 Q.B. 608 at 615.
[71] See *Yachuk v Oliver Blais Co Ltd* [1949] A.C. 386 and *Gough v Thorne* [1966] 3 All E.R. 398, depending on the age of the child.
[72] (1816) 1 Stark 493.
[73] (1869) L.R. 4 C.P. 739.
[74] The next station was three minutes away.

unreasonable response to the danger. For example, in *Harrison v British Railways Board*,[75] a misguided guard attempted to assist a passenger who was trying to join a moving train by signalling the driver to stop. Unfortunately, he gave the wrong signal and the driver continued to accelerate. He then tried to pull the passenger into the rapidly accelerating train, but both of them fell out. The guard sued the passenger for negligence. The court held that the passenger did owe the guard a duty of care when, through lack of care for his own safety, he had put himself in a situation of danger in which it was reasonably foreseeable that someone would intervene to help, but that a reasonable guard would have applied the emergency brake. On this basis, the guard's damages were reduced by 20 per cent. Boreham J. warned, however, that rescuers should be treated leniently: "One has a feeling of distaste about finding a rescuer guilty of contributory negligence. It can rarely be appropriate to do so".[76]

(ii) Did the claimant's actions contribute to the damage suffered?

The classic case is that of *Stapley v Gypsum Mines Ltd*.[77] Stapley had been killed in a mining accident when a large piece of the roof where he was working fell upon him. He, and another miner, Dale, had been instructed earlier to make that part of the mine safe by bringing down a section of the roof. The men tried unsuccessfully to bring down the roof and then carried on working. In an action by Stapley's widow, it was argued that Stapley's own negligence had been the substantial cause of his death. The majority of the House of Lords held that Dale had also been responsible for the accident, for whom the employers were vicariously liable, but that damages should be reduced by 80 per cent for contributory negligence. Lord Reid found the question of who had contributed to the damage to be one of common sense, depending on the facts of each particular case. Where a number of people had been at fault, it would be a matter of isolating those parties whose fault had led to the accident and was not too remote. Here, the question was whether the fault of Dale was so mixed up with the accident that, as a matter of common sense, his actions must be regarded as having contributed to his accident.[78] On the facts, there was insufficient separation of time, place or circumstance to find that Dale had not contributed to the accident.

It is also important that the claimant's negligence exposed him or her to the particular type of damage suffered. For example, if I drive without a seatbelt and suffer injuries whilst stationary when a lorry negligently drops its load on my car, it cannot be said that my failure to wear a seatbelt exposed me to that particular risk of damage. Conversely, the damages were reduced in *Jones v Livox Quarries*,[79] where the plaintiff had been injured when, whilst riding on the back of a vehicle to the works canteen, he was struck from behind by the driver of a dumper truck. Riding on the back of the vehicle was contrary to his employers' express instructions and what materialised was precisely the type of danger to be expected from such conduct. However, if a passing sportsman had negligently shot him in the eye, he could hardly be said to be

14–020

---

[75] [1981] 3 All E.R. 679.
[76] *ibid.*, at 686.
[77] [1953] A.C. 663. Note, however, PS Atiyah (1965) 43 Can. Bar. Rev. 609, who criticises the court's analysis of causation, and our discussion of this point in Ch. 6.
[78] See *Casey v Morane* [2001] I.C.R. 316, CA, which equally adopts a "common sense" approach to causation.
[79] [1952] 2 Q.B. 608.

contributorily negligent since this was not a risk to which his negligent actions exposed him.[80]

(iii) To what extent should the claimant's damages be reduced? What is "just and equitable" in these circumstances?

14–021   This is generally a matter of the court's discretion and therefore will depend on the facts of the case. The wording of the Act gives the courts considerable flexibility, which they utilise to the full.[81] Indeed, it is difficult critically to evaluate the court's assessment of contributory negligence, because the courts generally give a bald figure, with little guidance as to the reasoning underlying the sum. The courts have given some indications that they will be influenced by the relative blameworthiness of each party in addition to considering the degree to which their fault contributed towards the damage suffered,[82] but this will not always be the case. However, in certain circumstances, guideline figures have been given to provide some certainty and consistency, and these are generally followed.

14–022   **(a) Failure to wear a seatbelt:**   Guidelines were given by the Court of Appeal in *Froom v Butcher*.[83] In this case, despite driving carefully, Mr Froom had been struck head-on by a speeding car overtaking in the opposite direction. He suffered head and chest injuries, which were found to have been caused by his failure to wear a seatbelt. At the time, it was not compulsory to wear a seatbelt, and Froom had argued that he had made a conscious decision not to wear one, having seen a number of accidents where drivers wearing seatbelts had been trapped in the vehicle following an accident. The Court of Appeal held that his failure to wear a seatbelt did amount to contributory negligence. It had added to the injury suffered and it was irrelevant that *Froom* believed that it would be safer not to wear a seatbelt—the test was of the reasonable person who would, according to the court, wear a seatbelt. Damages were therefore reduced by 20 per cent.

The court gave general guidance as to the appropriate reduction for not wearing a seatbelt:

- 25 per cent if the injury would have been prevented altogether;
- 15 per cent if the injury would have been less severe; and
- 0 per cent if wearing the seatbelt would not have prevented injury.

This will tend to be followed save in exceptional cases; the courts acknowledging the value of having clear guidelines which will encourage parties to reach sensible settlements.[84] It should be noted that seatbelt wearing is now compulsory for front and back seats (where available). Although Lord Denning also suggested in *Froom* that

---

[80] Lord Denning's somewhat graphic example *ibid.*, at 616.
[81] An appeal court will only overturn a finding of contributory negligence where it finds that the judge had gone wrong in principle, misunderstood the facts or was clearly wrong: see *Kerry v Carter* [1969] 1 W.L.R. 1372 at 1376.
[82] See *Davies v Swan Motor Co. (Swansea) Ltd* [1949] 2 K.B. 291 at 326 *per* Lord Denning.
[83] [1976] Q.B. 286.
[84] See Keene L.J. in *Jones (a minor) v Wilkins* [2001] P.I.Q.R. 12.

exceptions may be made for pregnant women or "unduly fat" passengers,[85] pregnant women are not exempt, unless their doctor certifies that they should be for medical reasons.[86] A doctor may exempt any party if he or she decides that it is warranted and issue a formal "Certificate of Exemption from Compulsory Seat Belt wearing".[87] This must be produced on request by the police.

(b) **Failure to wear a crash helmet:** *Capps v Miller*[88] applied the *Froom* guidelines to crash helmets, although the majority held that a reduction of only 10 per cent would be appropriate where a crash helmet had been worn but not fastened. Section 16 of the Road Traffic Act 1988 now provides that it is compulsory to wear protective head gear when riding a motor bike. It should be noted that exceptions are made for Sikhs wearing turbans.[89]   **14–023**

Apart from this guidance, the court is free to assess what is just and equitable. It should be remembered that the reduction cannot be 100 per cent, as this is essentially a denial of causation.[90] Croom-Johnson L.J. in *Capps v Miller*[91] also advised the courts against making fine distinctions in percentages, although he disapproved of dicta indicating that an award of less than 10 per cent should not be given.[92]

Multiple defendants

One final problem we must address before moving on to the next defence is how to approach a situation where the claimant is suing more than one defendant. For example, the claimant (C) is suing two defendants (D and T) for negligence. C's contributory negligence is assessed at 20 per cent. How will this sum be deducted from the defendants' liability for damages?   **14–024**

The first point is that the two defendants are treated as jointly and severally liable at law.[93] This means that the claimant is entitled to sue one or both of the defendants for the full sum due. Under s.1 of the Civil Liability (Contribution) Act 1978, if only one defendant is sued, he or she is fully liable, but is entitled to claim a contribution from any other person liable in respect of the same damage. The contribution, under s.2, will be assessed by the court as the sum which is "just and equitable having regard to the extent of that person's responsibility for the damage in question". This is therefore a matter for the defendants to sort out and not for the claimant to worry about. Secondly, the contributory negligence of the claimant will be compared with the total responsibility of the defendants. In our example, the 20 per cent contributory negligence of C would be compared with the 80 per cent liability of D and T, and C would be awarded 80 per cent of the damages due. This is irrespective of whether C is suing D, T, or D and T together. It is irrelevant at this stage to what extent D and T are individually responsible. Thirdly, it is for D and T to argue their individual degree of responsibility.

---

[85] See above at 295.
[86] See Regs 5 and 6 (exemptions), Motor Vehicles (Wearing of Seat Belts) Regulations 1993 SI 1993/176.
[87] See Sch.1 of 1993 Regulations.
[88] [1989] 1 W.L.R. 839. See also *O'Connell v Jackson* [1972] 1 Q.B. 270.
[89] S.16(2).
[90] See *Pitts v Hunt* [1991] 1 Q.B. 24 at 48 per Beldam L.J. and *Anderson v Newham College of Further Education* [2003] I.C.R. 212 (breach of statutory duty).
[91] [1989] 1 W.L.R. 839 at 849.
[92] As suggested by the Court of Appeal in *Johnson v Tennant Bros Ltd*, November 19, 1954 (unreported).
[93] This is discussed more fully in Ch. 15.

By this means, the claimant is fully compensated and it is for the defendants to sort out the division of responsibility between them. This is seen in practice in *Fitzgerald v Lane*,[94] a case mentioned in Ch. 6. Here, the plaintiff had stepped out into traffic on a busy road when the lights at the pedestrian crossing had been against him. He had been struck by a vehicle driven by the first defendant, which pushed him into the path of the second defendant's car. Both the defendants were negligent, but the plaintiff had also been contributorily negligent in not looking properly before crossing the road. The House of Lords adopted the reasoning outlined above. First of all, to what extent was the plaintiff contributory negligent in comparison with the fault of both defendants? Here, it was found to be 50 per cent. Secondly, how should the remaining 50 per cent be divided between the two defendants?

Contributory negligence is a popular defence. Under the statute, the courts now have flexibility to allocate damages according to the fault of the parties involved. Unlike the defences of voluntary assumption of risk and illegality, this defence gives the courts the power to reduce damages without removing the claim altogether, and therefore is more readily used than the former, more drastic, defences.

(4) Inevitable accident

14–025   This is a little used defence, although readers may find reference to the defence in earlier case law. It is essentially a defence that, despite using all reasonable care, the accident nevertheless happened: "People must guard against reasonable probabilities, but they are not bound to guard against fantastic possibilities".[95]

In negligence, a claim that all reasonable care has been used will not tend to be treated as an independent defence, but as a matter relevant to the claimant's allegation that reasonable care has not been used. The allegation therefore goes to the question of breach of duty. It equally can have no application to torts where the defendant is liable *despite* the exercise of reasonable care, for example the tort of defamation. It is difficult therefore to see a modern role for this defence, except perhaps where the claimant is relying on the doctrine of *res ipsa loquitur* to establish breach of duty.[96] Here, the claimant relies on the circumstances of the accident to place the burden on the defendant to establish that reasonable care was taken. Yet, even this use has been criticised as an over-simplification of the doctrine,[97] and we must conclude that the role of this defence in the twenty-first century is highly questionable.

(5) Mistake

14–026   The fact the defendant made a genuine mistake is not generally a defence. It is no defence that the surgeon mistakenly believed that the patient had consented to open heart surgery, or that the defendant mistakenly believed that it was perfectly safe to drive at 100 mph in a residential area at night.

---

[94] [1989] A.C. 328. See also *Jones (a minor) v Wilkins* [2001] P.I.Q.R. 12, where the Court of Appeal, in assessing apportionment under the 1978 Act, drew an analogy with the *Froom v Butcher* guidelines under the 1945 Act. However, Sedley L.J. in the later case of *Pride Valley Foods Ltd v Hall & Partners* (2001) 76 Con L.R. 1 stressed that this was just one of the three questions to be addressed in contributory negligence and therefore 1978 Act case-law was unlikely to prove helpful in dealing with questions under the 1945 Act.
[95] *Fardon v Harcourt-Rivington* (1932) 146 L.T. 391 at 392 *per* Lord Dunedin.
[96] See earlier chapters and Lord Denning in *Southport Corp. v Esso Petroleum Co. Ltd* [1954] 2 Q.B. 182 at 200, CA, (reversed HL [1956] A.C. 218).
[97] WVH Rogers, *Winfield & Jolowicz on Torts* (16th ed., Sweet & Maxwell, 2002), p.869.

General defences: conclusion

We can therefore conclude that out of the defences referred to in this chapter, **14–027** contributory negligence is the most flexible, permitting the courts to limit the claimant's damages, but to not disallow the claim altogether. This is preferred by the courts to more drastic defences which provide a full defence to the claimant's action for damages. As stated earlier, these are not the only defences, and reference should be made to defences which apply to particular torts, discussed in the relevant chapters.

We now move on to consider the means by which the claimant's right of action can be lost. If a claim is extinguished, there is no further scope for the claim, however strong the claim may be. The main grounds for extinction will be set out below. The primary example is that of limitation, essentially where the claimant has run out of time to bring his or her claim. It should be noted that this is a significant source of negligence claims against solicitors, who are frequently sued by their clients for failing to commence proceedings within the time limits set by law.

EXTINCTION OF LIABILITY

(1) Limitation of Actions

Limitation is the main reason why claims in tort are extinguished.[98] It would cause **14–028** obvious problems if there were no time limit within which the claimant should bring an action in tort. For example, if the victim of a car accident were able to claim damages in tort 20 years after the accident, a number of problems would arise:

- Witnesses would be unlikely to remember the event;
- Witnesses may have disappeared or have died;
- Documentation would be lost; and
- The defendant, for an indeterminate time, would have to live with the possibility of being sued.

In view of such objections, the law sets a time limit on such claims.[99] The Limitation Act 1980 contains the main provisions.[1] Section 2 of the Act provides that actions founded on a tort[2] should be brought within six years of the date when the cause of action accrued, *i.e.* when the cause of action arises against a potential defendant.

---

[98] We use the term "extinguished" for convenience, but technically, except for real property and under Limitation Act 1980, ss.11A(3) and (2), limitation only amounts to a statutory bar to the claim.

[99] It should be noted that limitation periods are purely statutory and have been part of English law since the first Limitation Act of 1623. There were no time limits imposed at common law.

[1] The Act is subject to amendments, in particular by the Latent Damage Act 1986 and the Consumer Protection Act 1987.

[2] "Tort" is defined widely by Toulmin QC in *R v Secretary of State for Transport Ex p. Factortame* [2001] 1 W.L.R. 942, QBD (T & CC) at para.171 to cover: "breach of non-contractual duty which gives a private law right to the party injured to recover compensatory damages at common law from the party causing the injury." This broad definition includes the so-called Eurotorts, discussed in Ch. 7.

Where the tort is actionable on proof of damage, for example negligence, then the cause of action will only arise when the damage has taken place. Where the tort is actionable *per se* (*i.e.* without proof of damage), the cause of action will arise on the date of the defendant's act or omission.

However, not all tort claims are within s.2. There are special provisions for personal injury claims (s.11), defamation (s.4A) and defective products (s.11A). We shall examine each in turn.

Personal injury claims—ss.11, 12, 14 and 33 of the Limitation Act 1980

14–029   **Section 11**: provides that where, due to negligence, nuisance or breach of duty,[3] the claimant's action for damages consists of or includes damages for personal injury, the claim must be brought within three years from the date on which:

        (a) the action accrued; or

        (b) the date of knowledge (if later) of the injured person.[4]

"Personal injury" is defined in s.38 as including any disease or impairment of a person's physical or mental condition and will thus extend to psychiatric injuries, including the failure to mitigate the effects of dyslexia.[5] If the injured person dies before the expiration of either of these periods, then the action will run for the benefit of the estate for three years from: (a) the date of death; or (b) the date of the personal representative's knowledge; whichever is later.[6] It should be noted that s.11 covers claims which *include* damages for personal injury. The time limit will therefore apply to any additional claims, for example for property damage.

14–030   **Section 14**:   Section 14 defines "the date of knowledge".[7] This is deemed to be the date on which the claimant first had knowledge:

        (a) that the injury in question was significant; *and*

        (b) that the injury was attributable in whole or in part to the act or omission which is alleged to constitute negligence, nuisance or breach of duty; *and*

        (c) of the identity of the defendant; *and*

        (d) if it is alleged that the act or omission was that of a person other than the defendant, of the identity of that person and the additional facts supporting the bringing of an action against the defendant.

---

[3] This can be breach of statutory duty or contractual duty or any other breach of duty. It covers breach of contract, whether the duty is strict or to take reasonable care: *Foster v Zott GmbH & Co* (unreported, 24 May 2000), CA.

[4] S.11(4). This does not apply to damages under s.3 of the Protection from Harassment Act 1997—s.11(1A) inserted by Protection from Harassment Act 1997, s.6—which will be governed by s.9. S.9 deals with sums recoverable by statute and sets a six year limitation period. It equally does not apply to intentional trespass for which the ordinary six year period applies: *Stubbings v Webb* [1993] A.C. 498.

[5] See *Phelps v Hillingdon LBC* [2001] 2 A.C. 619 and *Robinson v St Helens MBC* [2003] P.I.Q.R. 9.

[6] S.11(5).

[7] For guidance, see *Spargo v North Essex District Health Authority* [1997] P.I.Q.R. 235, CA.

It is irrelevant that the claimant is unaware that, as a matter of law, the acts or omissions in question gave him or her a legal right to sue.[8] Section 14(2) provides that the injury is significant if the claimant would reasonably have considered it sufficiently serious to justify instituting proceedings for damages against a defendant who did not dispute liability and was able to satisfy judgment.[9] "Knowledge" is deemed to include knowledge which the claimant might reasonably be expected to acquire from facts observable or ascertainable by the claimant, or from facts ascertainable with the help of medical or other professional advice it is reasonable to expect the claimant to seek.[10]

Section 12: Section 12 makes special provision for dependants claiming under the   **14–031**
Fatal Accidents Act 1976 (which will be discussed in Ch. 15).[11] Section 12(1) requires the dependant to show that the deceased had a valid cause of action on death. If the action had been lost, for example due to a time limit or any other reason, the claim under the Fatal Accidents Act is lost. If the deceased did have a valid cause of action on death, then the dependant has three years to bring the action starting from:

(a) the date of death; *or*

(b) the date of knowledge of the person for whose benefit the action is brought; whichever is the later. ("Knowledge" is as defined in s.14, discussed above.)

Section 33: It can be seen that, generally, claims for personal injury, or under the   **14–032**
Fatal Accidents Act 1976, are subject to the short time limit of three years. This, however, must be considered in the light of the discretion provided under s.33 of the Act. Section 33 permits the court to override the statutory time limits if it appears equitable to the court to allow the case to proceed, having regard to the prejudice of denying the claim to the claimant[12] and the prejudice of allowing the claim to the defendant.[13] Section 33(3) directs the court, in considering whether to exercise its discretion, to have regard to all the circumstances of the case and in particular to:

(a) the length of, and the reasons for, the delay on the part of the claimant;

(b) the extent to which, having regard to the delay, the evidence in the case is likely to be less cogent;

(c) the conduct of the defendant after the cause of action arose, including (when relevant) the response made to any reasonable request by the claimant for

---

[8] S.14(1).
[9] This encompasses both a subjective and objective element, requiring the court to consider whether it would reasonably occur to this particular claimant, given the circumstances of the case, to bring a civil action: *McCafferty v Receiver for the Metropolitan Police District* [1977] 1 W.L.R. 1073 and *Stubbings v Webb* [1993] A.C. 498. It was designed to provide for cases of late diagnosis of physical diseases, such as asbestosis, and has proven more difficult to apply to cases of child abuse where the child is unlikely to consider instituting proceedings and where the effect may only be appreciated in later life: see *KR v Bryn Alyn Community (Holdings) Ltd (In Liquidation)* [2003] 3 W.L.R. 107.
[10] S.14(3). The claimant will not be fixed with expert knowledge which he or she has failed to obtain despite taking all reasonable steps to consult (and, where appropriate, to act on) expert advice.
[11] See also s.13.
[12] Or any person he or she represents.
[13] Or any person he or she represents.

information or inspection for the purpose of ascertaining facts which were or might be relevant to the claimant's cause of action against the defendant;

(d) the duration of any disability[14] of the claimant arising after the date of the accrual of the cause of action;

(e) the extent to which the claimant acted promptly and reasonably once he or she knew that there was a possible action for damages; and

(f) the steps, if any, taken by the claimant to obtain medical, legal or other expert advice and the nature of any such advice he or she may have received.

The House of Lords, in *Thompson v Brown*[15] and *Donovan v Gwentoys*,[16] indicated that s.33 was not confined to exceptional cases and that the courts could adopt a broad approach to its provisions. The judge is therefore given an unfettered discretion to assess the matter generally with reference to the factors highlighted in s.33(3).[17] The burden, however, of showing that it would be equitable to disapply the limitation period lies on the claimant and the courts have re-iterated that it is a heavy burden.

It should be noted that s.33 only applies to claims for personal injury or under the Fatal Accidents Act 1976 under s.11. It has no application to torts outside these sections, for example actions for trespass to the person.[18] This has led to some difficulties in relation to claims by adults for child abuse. Even with the provision under s.28 (see below) that time will only run from the age of majority, the trauma of childhood sexual abuse may take many years to manifest itself or be appreciated by the victim. However, the courts will *only* have the discretion to extend the time limit under s.33 if it is classified as a personal injury claim and not as an intentional act of battery. In *KR v Bryn Alyn Community (Holdings) Ltd (In Liquidation)*,[19] the Court of Appeal drew a distinction between claims for systematic negligence and abuse. Whilst the former would be regarded as a personal injury claim, the latter would not.[20] Therefore only those claimants able to frame their claims as being for negligently-incurred personal injuries (be they physical or psychiatric) could rely on s.33 of the Act. This does seem unjust and arbitrary, and has been criticised by the courts. In *Bryn Alyn*, Auld L.J. warmly commended the proposal of the Law Commission in its report, *Limitation of Actions* (No.270), that both actions should be subject to the same core regime of an extendable three years limitation period with discretion to disapply (see

[14] S.38(2) provides that "For the purposes of this Act a person shall be treated as under a disability while he is an infant, or of unsound mind".
[15] [1981] 1 W.L.R. 744.
[16] [1990] 1 W.L.R. 472. See also the Court of Appeal in *Nash v Eli Lilly & Co*. [1993] 1 W.L.R. 782 and *Firman v Ellis* [1978] Q.B. 886.
[17] For example, in *Robinson v St Helens MBC* [2003] P.I.Q.R. 9, the Court of Appeal refused to exercise its discretion to support a claim by a 33-year-old claimant that the local authority had negligently failed to treat his dyslexia during his primary and secondary schooling where there was no cogent medical evidence showing serious injury and the long delay would place the defendant in great difficulty in contesting the claim. See also *Rowe v Kingston upon Hull City Council* [2004] P.I.Q.R. P16.
[18] See *Stubbings v Webb* [1993] A.C. 498. The ordinary six-year limit will apply. *Stubbings* was upheld by the European Court of Human Rights in *Stubbings v United Kingdom* (1997) 23 E.H.R.R. 213.
[19] [2003] 3 W.L.R. 107.
[20] See also *Seymour v Williams* [1995] P.I.Q.R. 470 where a victim of childhood sexual abuse by her father was able to sue her mother for failing to protect her from the abuse even though her claim against her father was out of time. This was considered to be an action for personal injury.

below). It would, in the words of the judge, "obviate much arid and highly wasteful litigation turning on a distinction of no apparent principle or other merit."[21]

Defamation—ss.4A and 32A of the Limitation Act 1980

We looked at s.4A in Ch. 13. This section was introduced by s.5 of the Defamation Act 1996. Section 4A provides a one year time limit for claims for defamation. Under s.32A of the Act, however, the court retains a discretion to allow a claim out of time if it would be equitable, having regard to the prejudice to the claimant and defendant respectively.[22] This operates in the same manner as s.33 above. The provisions also apply to malicious falsehood.[23]   **14–033**

Defective products—s.11A of the Limitation Act 1980

Section 11A makes special provision for defective products and was set out in Ch. 9. Generally, it provides a three year period of limitation when the claim consists of or includes damages for personal injury or loss of or damage to any property, starting from: **14–034**

(a) the date on which the cause of action accrued; *or*

(b) if later, the date of knowledge of the injured person or, in the case of loss of or damage to property, the date of knowledge of the claimant.[24]

This is similar to s.11 above, but it should be noted that the date of knowledge is specifically dealt with under s.14(1A), which applies the s.14(1) criteria to defective products. Section 11A(3) provides for a 10-year long-stop, preventing any claim 10 years after the date on which the product was supplied to another or when the product was last supplied by a person.[25] The courts have a discretion under s.33 to override the statutory limitation period for death and personal injury claims, but the 10 year long-stop will continue to apply.[26]

Limitation problems

(i) Deliberate concealment: One obvious problem with limitation periods is where the defendant has concealed the damage. Section 32 deals directly with this problem. If the action is based on fraud or mistake, or where the defendant has deliberately concealed any fact relevant to the cause of action from the claimant, the limitation period will only start when the claimant has discovered the fraud, mistake or concealment or could, with reasonable diligence, have discovered it. An example of concealment may be found in the case of *Kitchen v RAF Association*[27] where a claim   **14–035**

---

[21] See above at 143.
[22] See, for example, *Steedman v BBC* [2002] E.M.L.R. 17 (extension rejected where good claim against solicitor and absence of any contemporary complaint).
[23] See *Cornwall Gardens Pty Ltd v RO Garrard & Co Ltd* [2001] EWCA Civ 699; *The Times*, June 19, 2001.
[24] Or (if earlier) of any person in whom the claimant's cause of action was previously vested.
[25] See Consumer Protection Act 1987, s.4.
[26] s.33(1A) provides that "The court shall not under this section disapply—(a) subs.3 of s.11A". S.11A(3) also applies regardless of the provisions for extension of time due to fraud, concealment or mistake (see s.32(4A)) or disability (see s.28(7)(a)).
[27] [1958] 1 W.L.R. 563 (although the case concerned s.26 of the Limitation Act 1939, the statutory predecessor of s.32).

was made against a firm of solicitors for negligence. It was held that the solicitors' failure to inform Mrs Kitchen of her possible claim against the local electricity board, when her husband had been electrocuted by a defectively installed cooker, did not amount to concealment. It was certainly negligent, but there was no evidence to show deliberate concealment of this fact. However, their failure to inform her of an offer by the electricity board to pay £100 was within the relevant section, as it amounted to deliberate concealment (basically to cover up for their mistake).

This interpretation of s.32 was confirmed by the House of Lords in *Cave v Robinson Jarvis & Rolf*,[28] which overturned the Court of Appeal ruling in *Brocklesby v Armitage & Guest*.[29] In *Brocklesby*, the Court had interpreted s.32 very broadly, notably relying on s.32(2) which defines deliberate concealment as the "deliberate commission of a breach of duty in circumstances in which it is unlikely to be discovered for some time." The Court of Appeal held that, in view of s.32(2), deliberate concealment could be proved by showing simply that the defendant's negligence consisted of an intentional act or omission in circumstances where the negligence would not be immediately apparent. It was not necessary to show that the defendant was aware of the breach of duty in question.[30] The House of Lords in *Cave* rightly pointed out that this would disapply the limitation period in every case where a professional had acted on behalf of a client and was subsequently found to be negligent. This would extend dramatically professional liability,[31] and force such defendants to defend every action, however stale. Lord Millett considered such a result to be "neither just, nor consistent with the policy of the Limitation Acts".[32] "Deliberate concealment" should therefore be interpreted as requiring the defendant to be aware of the breach of duty, and to conceal or fail to disclose the wrongdoing in circumstances where it is unlikely to be discovered for some time.

The section does also seek to protect innocent third parties. Section 32(3)(b) states that nothing in the section shall extend the limitation period for actions (a) to recover property or recover its value or (b) to enforce a charge against any property or set aside a transaction affecting property, when the action is brought against an innocent third party who purchased the property for valuable consideration after the fraud, mistake or concealment had taken place. Section 32(5) also provides that the s.14B time limit for latent damage (discussed below) does not apply to cases of deliberate concealment.

14–036   **(ii) Disability:** A further problem arises where the claimant cannot sue due to a disability. This is dealt with in s.28 which provides that if the person is under a disability on the date on which the action accrues, the six year limitation period will

---

[28] [2003] 1 A.C. 384, HL. See T. Dugdale (2002) 18 P.N. 156.

[29] [2002] 1 W.L.R. 598. Applied and extended by Laddie J. in *Liverpool Roman Catholic Archdiocese Trustees Inc v Goldberg (No.1)* [2001] 1 All E.R. 182.

[30] In *Brocklesby*, for example, the solicitors' negligence in failing to secure the claimant's release from his mortgage obligations had not become apparent until much later. The solicitors had not been aware that they had been negligent, but were nevertheless found to have acted "deliberately" in that they had intended to act for the claimant.

[31] Particularly in view of s.32(5) (discussed below) which denies the defendant the benefit of the 15-year long-stop provision of s.14B.

[32] See above at 392. The Law Commission in its report, *Limitation of Actions* (2001), was also critical at 3.136: "*Brocklesby* . . . ignores the rationale of s.32, which is that the defendant should not be able to profit from his own behaviour in concealing facts relevant to the claimant's claim."

only start when he or she has ceased to be under a disability or has died (whichever occurs first). By "disability", we mean that a person is under 18 or of unsound mind.[33] The main problem arises when the disability affects the claimant after the cause of action has arisen. In such cases, there is nothing in s.28 to stop the ordinary limitation period applying.[34]

(iii) **Latent damage: property damage or financial loss**[35]: "Latent damage" signifies **14-037** damage which cannot be detected immediately. Prior to *Murphy v Brentwood*,[36] such claims raised considerable limitation problems. *Anns v Merton LBC*[37] had established that structural damage to a building—for example defective foundations—would be recoverable. On this basis, the limitation period for latent damage would start from the time the defect came into existence, even though the defect might not be detectable until many years later.[38] This served to exclude a large number of claims. The Latent Damage Act 1986 therefore added ss.14A and 14B into the Act to deal specifically with this problem.

Subsections 14A(4) and (5) provide that the action for negligence[39] must be brought within:

(a) six years of the cause of action; *or*

(b) if later, three years from the earliest date on which the claimant[40] first had both the knowledge required for bringing the action for damages for the relevant damage and a right to bring such an action.

The test for knowledge mirrors that set out in s.14 above, namely knowledge of the material facts about the damage in respect of which damages are claimed, and any other facts relevant to the current action.[41] Section 14A is subject to an overriding time limit, stated in s.14B to be 15 years from the date of the last negligent act or omission which caused the damage in question. Section 3 of the Latent Damage Act 1986 also provides that where the property with the latent defect has changed ownership before the material facts about the damage are known, the new owner will have a fresh cause of action, to which ss.14A and B will apply.

Post-*Murphy*, where claims for defective premises are regarded as non-recoverable pure economic loss, these sections may seem somewhat defunct. There is no longer a

---

[33] S.38(2). S.38(3) provides that "For the purposes of subs.(2) above a person is of unsound mind if he is a person who, by reason of mental disorder within the meaning of the Mental Health Act 1983, is incapable of managing and administering his property and affairs".

[34] See s.28(1) and (2) and *Purnell v Roche* [1927] 2 Ch. 142. However, disability is expressly mentioned as a ground for extending the time limit for personal injury under s.33 above.

[35] See N. Mullany (1991) 54 M.L.R. 349. For personal injury and death, see s.11 above.

[36] [1991] 1 A.C. 398. See also Ch. 3.

[37] [1978] A.C. 728.

[38] See, *e.g. Pirelli General Cable Works Ltd v Oscar Faber & Partners* [1983] 2 A.C. 1.

[39] This is interpreted strictly. The sections will not apply to other torts such as nuisance or even claims in contract where the breach is founded on negligent conduct: see *Iron Trades Mutual Insurance Co. Ltd and Others v J. K. Buckenham Ltd* [1990] 1 All E.R. 808, approved by the Court of Appeal in *Société Commerciale de Réassurance v Eras International Ltd (formerly Eras (UK))* [1992] 2 All E.R. 82 (Note).

[40] Or any person in whom the cause of action was vested before him or her.

[41] See ss.14A(6)–(10).

cause of action to put a time limit on. However, they are still worth noting because they apply generally to negligence claims for latent damage (although not for personal injury and death, which is covered by s.11). They would therefore still apply to claims for property damage, for example, under the complex structure argument outlined in Ch. 3, or for financial losses resulting from negligent advice.[42]

The burden of proof

14–038 The issue of limitation will generally be raised by the defendant. However (although the law is not clear on this point), it seems that it is the claimant who bears the burden of proof, and who has to establish that the cause of action arose during the limitation period.[43] Claimants should note that it is not always enough to start the action within the limitation period. The court retains the power to dismiss a claim for want of prosecution where there has been prolonged or "inordinate and inexcusable" delay in the prosecution of the action. It should be noted that this is now governed by r3.4(2) of the Civil Procedure Rules and the courts have discouraged judges from seeking guidance from case-law prior to the implementation of the Rules.[44] In practice, it would seem that, in keeping with the strict timetables established by the Rules, the courts will be less tolerant of delays in pursuing a claim. Further, a court may find that a failure to proceed promptly amounts to an abuse of process, for example, where the claimant has commenced and continued litigation which he or she has no intention of bringing to a conclusion.[45]

Reform

14–039 There has been much criticism of the limitation regime. It is complicated, leads to uncertainty and, on a number of occasions, unjust results. In its 1998 Consultation Paper, the Law Commission came to the conclusion that "the present law on limitation suffers from a number of defects: it is incoherent, needlessly complex, outdated, uncertain, unfair and wastes costs."[46] In its 2001 Report (No.270), *Limitation of Actions*, the Commission put forward a simplified regime based on a primary limitation period of three years for the majority of claims, subject to a long-stop of 10 years. Its main recommendations are outlined below:

- The primary or "core" limitation period of three years should run from the date on which the claimant knows, or ought reasonably to know: (a) the facts which give rise to the cause of action, (b) the identity of the defendant, and (c) that

---

[42] See, *e.g. Henderson v Merrett Syndicates* [1995] 2 A.C. 145, discussed in Ch. 3. For a recent example, see *Babicki v Rowlands* [2002] Lloyd's Rep PN 121, CA where the defendant firm of solicitors had been negligent whilst acting for the Babickis in the purchase of business premises.

[43] See *Crocker v British Coal Corp.* (1996) 29 B.M.L.R. 159 and the Law Commission Report No.270 (2001), *Limitation of Actions*, 5.29, although it is for the defendant in his or her defence to raise the question of limitation: Practice Direction to Civil Procedure Rules Part 16, 13.1.

[44] In, for example, *Biguzzi v Rank Leisure Inc* [1999] 1 W.L.R. 1926 (Lord Woolf M.R. himself), *Axa Insurance Co Ltd v Swire Fraser Ltd* [2001] CP Rep 17 and *Securum Finance Ltd v Ashton* [2001] Ch. 291, the Court of Appeal has warned against restricting the wide discretion to strike out granted by rule 3.4(2) by reference to earlier authorities such as *Allen v Alfred McAlpine & Sons Ltd* [1968] 2 Q.B. 229 and *Birkett v James* [1978] A.C. 297.

[45] *Grovit v Doctor* [1997] 1 W.L.R. 640 *per* Lord Woolf. See also *Arbuthnot Latham Bank Ltd v Trafalgar Holdings Ltd* [1998] 1 W.L.R. 1426.

[46] Law Commission Consultation Paper No. 151 (1998), *Limitation of Actions*, para.11.1.

the injury suffered is significant. This will cover claims in most torts (including defamation), contract, restitution and trust law.

- The long-stop period of 10 years should normally run from the date on which the cause of action arises.[47]

- Personal injury should continue to be treated differently. The Commission backed down on its more radical proposals in the Consultation Paper that personal injury claims should be included within the core regime, subject only to an extended long-stop of 30 years.[48] It now proposes that the courts should continue to have a discretion to disapply the three-year limitation period and that no long-stop should apply.[49] In future, claims in negligence and trespass to the person will be treated in the same way under the core regime, thereby overturning the unjust distinction seen in *Stubbings v Webb* and in the *Bryn Alyn* litigation above.

- For minors, the core limitation period should not run until the minor is 18. However, the long-stop period should apply, although it will not bar an action before the claimant reaches 21. Adult disability will similarly suspend the core limitation period, but not the long-stop period.

- The long-stop should not apply to deliberate concealment, but only where the concealment is dishonest.

These recommendations have been accepted in principle by the Government in 2002.[50] Some caution is needed, however. Consultation has watered down a number of the proposals of the Consultation Paper and the suggested scheme will continue to raise uncertainty as to the "date of knowledge", the personal injury discretion and the meaning of "dishonesty". The judiciary has also been critical of the decision to reverse the one year limitation period for defamation and malicious falsehood. This was only introduced recently under the Defamation Act 1996 and the Commission has been accused of failing to appreciate "that a major, if not the major, objective of a defamation action is the vindication of the claimant's reputation, an objective which in most cases can only be attained by swift remedial action."[51] It remains to be seen if, and in what form, such recommendations are enacted.

---

[47] Where (as in negligence) loss or damage must be proved, time would run from the date of the act or omission that gives rise to the cause of action. This would also apply to claims for breach of statutory duty.
[48] This was largely due to evidence which indicated that the long-term effects of sexual abuse and mesothelioma, caused by exposure to asbestos, could manifest themselves over a period greater than 30 years: paras 3.102–3.104.
[49] This is subject to a number of exceptions, for example, where an adult claimant is suffering from a disability (paras 3.127–3.133) and under the Consumer Protection Act 1987 (para.4.37). Claims under the Fatal Accidents Act 1976 and under the Law Reform (Miscellaneous Provisions) Act 1934 will equally be subject to the statutory discretion to disapply the primary limitation period and will not be subject to a long-stop.
[50] See Lord Chancellor's Department Press Release of 16 July 2002: *www.gnn.gov.uk.*
[51] See Hale L.J. at para 32 in *Steedman v BBC* [2002] E.M.L.R. 17. Note also Brooke L.J. at para 46: "While I can understand the Commission's desire to remove the anomalies to which they draw their attention in their report, it appears to me that the experience of judges in this highly specialist field of practice needs to be taken carefully into account before there is any question of re-introducing a more relaxed limitation regime for defamation cases in this jurisdiction."

(2) Waiver

14–040 Waiver provides a further means by which a claimant may lose the right to bring his or her action. The term itself may lead to some confusion, as it has a number of legal meanings. First of all, waiver can be used to signify a choice between two inconsistent rights. The claimant cannot take advantage of both rights, and if the claimant, expressly or by unequivocal conduct, with full knowledge, indicates his or her intention to adopt one of these inconsistent rights, the other right will be lost. For example, A (an agent) commits a tort against his principal (P), for whom he works. P has not authorised such conduct. P then has a choice: ratify A's conduct or sue A in tort. If P ratifies the defendant's actions, P no longer has a claim against A in tort, but may have an action under the agency contract.[52]

The second meaning forms the basis for the doctrine of "waiver of tort". This term is misleading because it does not mean that the remedy in tort is extinguished, but that for certain torts,[53] the claimant may sue and receive either tortious damages (for reliance loss) or restitutionary damages (to recover the gain obtained by the defendant at his or her expense). The claimant cannot obtain both forms of damages, as they overlap. The claimant's action in tort will only be extinguished once final judgment has been given for restitutionary damages.[54]

(3) Accord and satisfaction

14–041 This is where the parties have agreed, for valuable consideration or by deed, to extinguish liability. "Accord" means agreement and "satisfaction" is the consideration and performance of that agreement. The agreement may be conditional, for example: I will accept £30,000 as compensation for my claim, subject to the right to return to court if my condition worsens; or may simply be in full satisfaction of the claim. If the defendant fails to pay the sum stipulated, the claimant may return to court, but it is a moot point whether the claimant goes to court to enforce the accord or to restart his or her claim. The answer depends on the nature of the agreement reached. If the agreement is to discharge the previous liability, the claimant must sue on the new agreement. If, however, the agreement can be construed as an agreement to discharge liability provided the sum is paid, then the claimant has a choice: pursue the original claim or the new agreement.

(4) Judgment

14–042 A final judgment in a case will extinguish the right of future action. The action effectively merges into the judgment. This is primarily on public policy grounds, and prevents the parties to litigation disputing the validity of the decision. The rule only

---

[52] See *United Australia Ltd v Barclays Bank Ltd* [1941] A.C. 1 at 28 *per* Lord Atkin.

[53] *e.g.* deceit and trespass to land, but contrast the nuisance case of *Stoke-on-Trent v W. and J. Wass Ltd* [1988] 1 W.L.R. 1466.

[54] See *United Australia Ltd v Barclays Bank Ltd* [1941] A.C. 1 at 30 *per* Lord Atkin. Further reference should be made to S Hedley and M Halliwell (eds), *The Law of Restitution* (Butterworths, 2002), Ch. 12 (by D Howarth). Note the recent cases of *Island Records Ltd v Tring International plc* [1995] 3 All E.R. 444, *Tang Man Sit v Capacious Investments Ltd* [1996] A.C. 514, PC and *Westminster CC v Porter (No. 2)* [2003] Ch. 436, Hart J.

applies where the decision is final, and it does not of course prevent either party appealing that the decision is wrong, in terms of law or fact, up until final judgment.

(5) Survival of actions on death

At common law, the general rule was that the death of either party extinguished any existing cause of action in tort (*actio personalis moritur cum persona*). It was not until 1934 that the problems arising from this rule forced the legislature to act. The growth of road traffic, and its accompanying accidents, led to complaints that it was unjust that where the defendant's negligent driving had led to an accident in which the defendant had been killed, the claimant would receive nothing from the defendant's estate or insurers. Section 1(1) of the Law Reform (Miscellaneous Provisions) Act 1934 now provides for the general survival of actions in tort. It states that:

14–043

". . . all causes of action subsisting against or vested in [any person on death] shall survive against, or, as the case may be, for the benefit of [the] estate."

This does not provide a cause of action for death itself. It is simply a question of the survival of actions existing at the time of death. This leaves one remaining problem. The claimant is penalised if the defendant dies before the claimant suffers damage due to the defendant's wrongful actions. For example, I negligently bake a cake which is contaminated, but die before you eat it. An action for negligence is dependent on proof of damage and so your action would only arise *after* my death. Section 1(4) deals with this problem. It provides that where damage has been suffered as a result of a wrongful act which would have allowed the claimant to sue the defendant if the wrongdoer had not died before or at the same time as the damage was suffered, an action will nevertheless subsist against him as if he had died after the damage had been suffered.

Section 1(1) does not apply to defamation claims. It was deemed too controversial to allow an action for defamation once the person defamed had died. However, there is no real reason why an action should not continue just because the defendant making the defamatory remarks is deceased. The harm to the reputation may still continue. The Faulks Committee[55] made some proposals for the survival of claims against the estate of the deceased defamer, and for limited recovery when the defendant has defamed a person now dead, but such recommendations have not been implemented.[56]

Extinction of liability: conclusion

In this chapter, we have examined a number of defences and considered ways in which the claimant can lose his or her claim due to extinction of liability. The courts, as we have seen, have a number of alternatives open to them when considering defences, and will tend to favour those defences which allow them to take a flexible approach to the claim. The Limitation Act 1980 forms a considerable barrier to claims where the claimant has delayed and, as we have shown, provides rules of considerable complexity.

14–044

---

[55] Cmnd 5909 (1975), Ch. 15.
[56] The Neill Committee on defamation found the recommendations problematic and resolved that the law should not be changed.

It is to be hoped that the proposals forwarded by the Law Commission will be considered seriously by the present government.

In our final chapter, we consider the matter most important to claimants: what remedies will the law award them for the torts committed against them?

Chapter 15

REMEDIES

Introduction

In this chapter, we examine the remedies available to claimants in actions in tort. We **15–001** concentrate on three main remedies: damages, injunctions and self-help. Readers will note that other remedies specific to particular torts have been discussed in earlier chapters. The main subject of this chapter will be damages. The courts have developed a complex framework of rules which govern the assessment of damages, which will be set out below. Readers should not forget, however, that for certain torts, such as nuisance, the equitable remedy of an injunction may prove more effective than damages, for example where the claimant wishes to prevent further interference with his or her enjoyment of land.

DAMAGES

Damages are the most commonly sought remedy in the law of tort. They provide a **15–002** means by which the courts can vindicate the rights of the claimant against the defendant by means of a financial award. They can therefore be awarded for torts which are actionable without proof of damage, such as trespass and libel, where they vindicate the claimant's right to be free from interference with his or her person, land and goods, or vindicate the claimant's reputation. They are equally significant, however, where the claimant has suffered actual damage or loss. Here, the claimant seeks not only to vindicate his or her rights, but a financial award which compensates the claimant for his or her losses (provided they are not too remote). The claimant may also seek a sum which further compensates for any additional distress, or which punishes the defendant for his or her appalling misconduct. The rules as to the assessment of such awards are complex and will be set out below, but first we shall outline the different types of damages available to the claimant. Although the claimant will generally seek compensatory damages, these are not the only form of damages available.

Types of Damages

The court may award seven different kinds of damages: **15–003**

- Compensatory;
- Contemptuous;
- Nominal;
- Aggravated;
- Exemplary or punitive;
- Restitutionary; and
- Damages under the Human Rights Act 1998.

We shall examine all seven types of damages in turn.

(1) Compensatory

15–004   Tort law seeks to fully compensate the victim. The underlying principle is expressed by the term *restitutio in integrum*. This is explained by Lord Blackburn in *Livingstone v Rawyards Coal Co*[1] as:

> "the sum of money which will put the party who has been injured, or who has suffered, in the same position as he would have been in if he had not sustained the wrong for which he is now getting his compensation or reparation."

The aim is therefore to award a sum in compensation to the claimant which puts the claimant in his or her pre-tort position. Obviously this is not always possible. If the claimant has suffered personal injury, a court cannot literally return the claimant to his or her pre-tort position. The court therefore seeks to find a financial sum which, as far as possible, will compensate the claimant. This is an inexact science. It is impossible to state the precise sum necessary to achieve this aim, and therefore the court seeks an approximate figure. While financial losses before trial can be estimated with some exactitude, the claimant may seek damages for future financial loss due to the tort, and again the court is forced to produce an approximate figure which it believes will cover this head of loss.

15–005   Assessing compensation is therefore often a far from easy task. The main problems arise in relation to personal injury claims and those consequent on a victim's death. This chapter will therefore concentrate on these particular claims. It should not be forgotten, however, that damages may also be available in tort for other types of loss, and reference should be made to the discussion in earlier chapters. There is also generally a duty to mitigate loss in tort. The courts will not allow a claimant to recover losses which he or she could have reasonably avoided. Although the main authorities on mitigation are in contract law (where the same rule applies), it seems clear that a court in tort will not require strenuous attempts by the claimant to reduce the loss suffered.[2] The old rule that losses incurred due to lack of funds were irrecoverable, *e.g.* expensive hire charges where it would have been more economical to purchase a new vehicle[3] has recently been overturned.[4]

---

[1] (1880) 5 App. Cas. 25 at 39 *per* Lord Blackburn.
[2] See *British Westinghouse Electric & Manufacturing Co Ltd v Underground Electric Railways Co of London Ltd (No.2)* [1912] A.C. 673, HL; *Andros Springs v World Beauty (The World Beauty)* [1970] P. 144.
[3] See *The Liesbosch* [1933] A.C. 449.
[4] *Lagden v O'Connor* [2003] 3 W.L.R. 1571.

The courts will generally award damages in one lump sum. This gives a claimant one chance to go to court to obtain damages, and the court will not allow a claimant to go back to court to recover a further award of damages, even if his or her loss has significantly increased, *unless*:

(i) the claimant is suing for breach of a separate and distinct legal right;[5]

(ii) the injury continues, such as under a continuing nuisance where a fresh cause of action occurs (see Ch. 10);

(iii) a provisional award of damages has been made under s.32A of the Supreme Court Act 1981 (see below); *or*

(iv) the first award was an interim award prior to trial (see below).

Compensatory damages are often divided in personal injury claims into special and general damages. These are terms used by the parties in their case statements. General damages are damages which cannot be precisely quantified, for example loss of future earnings or pain and suffering. Special damages are claimed for particular forms of pre-trial loss resulting from the tort, which the claimant can quantify, for example medical expenses and loss of earnings prior to trial. These should be set out clearly in the case statements.

(2) Contemptuous

This is a derisory award of the lowest coin in the land—now one penny—by which the court indicates that although the claimant has a good cause of action, it is a bare technical victory. Such awards are often found in libel actions.[6] The court, more drastically, can deny the claimant his or her costs, and this imposes a greater penalty on the claimant. In English law, costs usually follow the event, so the losing defendant will have to pay not only his or her own costs but also those of the claimant. However, under s.51 of the Supreme Court Act 1981, the award of costs is at the discretion of the court, and contemptuous damages may lead a court to exercise its discretion to order the claimant to pay his or her own costs. In such circumstances, any victory is wholly illusory.

15–006

(3) Nominal

Nominal damages are a token amount which recognises that the claimant's legal right has been infringed, but that no actual damage has been caused.[7] They therefore generally will apply to torts actionable *per se* (*i.e.* without proof of damage) such as trespass to the person or land and libel. An award of nominal damages should not affect the ordinary rule as to costs, as it does not indicate any negative finding.

15–007

[5] See *Brunsden v Humphrey* (1701) 1 Ld. Raym. 339 where the plaintiff was able to claim for damage to his vehicle and later for personal injury. However, note the rule in *Henderson v Henderson* (1843) 3 Hare 100 that it would be an abuse of process if the claimant did not bring forward their whole case in the first action. The court in *Talbot v Berkshire CC* [1994] Q.B. 290 cast doubt on *Brunsden* for not considering *Henderson* in its decision. For a more recent application of the *Henderson* rule, see *Johnson v Gore Wood & Co* [2002] 2 A.C. 1, notably Lord Bingham at 30.
[6] See the jury award in *Reynolds v Times Newspapers Ltd* discussed in Ch. 13.
[7] See, *e.g. Constantine v Imperial Hotels Ltd* [1944] K.B. 693.

(4) Aggravated

15–008   These form a further level of compensatory damages granted by the courts to compensate for additional mental distress inflicted on the claimant due to the malicious, high-handed, insulting or oppressive conduct of the defendant.[8] The manner in which the tort is committed or the motives of the defendant may therefore justify an award of aggravated damages.[9] For example, in libel, if the defendant has published the statement out of malice, or has persisted at trial with an insupportable plea of justification, an additional sum on top of compensatory damages may be awarded to the claimant. Such damages are not available for all torts. The courts will award aggravated damages for torts where the injury to the claimant's feeling and self-esteem are an integral part of the damage for which compensation is awarded.[10] On this basis, they are not awarded for negligence[11] or, arguably, nuisance,[12] but are commonly awarded for intentional torts such as trespass[13] and for libel.[14] The sum awarded is at the discretion of the court, but is usually moderate. Some guidelines exist. For example, the Court of Appeal in *Thompson v Metropolitan Police Commissioner*[15] indicated the level of awards suitable for damages against the police for false imprisonment and malicious prosecution. Indeed, claims against the police form a major reason for the award of aggravated damages.

(5) Exemplary or punitive

15–009   The leading case here is that of *Rookes v Barnard*.[16] In this case, Lord Devlin distinguished punitive damages[17] from aggravated damages and set out when punitive damages would be granted in English law. The concept of punitive damages may seem odd in tort. They are a form of damages which punish the defendant for his or her conduct, and attempt to deter the defendant and others from undertaking such conduct in future. Punitive damages are concerned with the conduct of the defendant rather than the damage suffered by the claimant. Although they are sometimes confused with aggravated damages, there is a clear division. Aggravated damages seek to compensate the claimant for any additional injury due to the manner in which the tort was committed. In contrast, punitive damages aim to punish the defendant.

    In *Rookes v Barnard*, Lord Devlin restricted punitive damages to three kinds of case. His Lordship doubted the legitimacy of such damages, which, in his view, confused the

---

[8] See Law Commission Report No.247, *Aggravated, exemplary and restitutionary damages* (1997) which recommended at para.6.1 that for clarity, these damages should in future be termed "damages for mental distress".

[9] See Lord Devlin in *Rookes v Barnard* [1964] A.C. 1129 at 1221 and Lord Diplock in *Cassell v Broome* [1972] A.C. 1027 at 1124.

[10] See Judge Toulmin Q.C. in *R. v Secretary of State for Transport, ex p Factortame (No.7)* [2001] 1 W.L.R. 942 where he rejected a claim for aggravated damages for the Government's breach of EC legislation providing for freedom of establishment of nationals in Member States, although he expressly left open the question whether the revisions of the Treaty under the Treaty of Amsterdam would affect his decision.

[11] *Kralj v McGrath* [1986] 1 All E.R. 54.

[12] *AB v South West Water Services* [1993] Q.B. 507.

[13] *e.g. Appleton v Garrett* [1996] 5 P.I.Q.R. P1 where a dentist had deliberately undertaken unnecessary dental work on unsuspecting young patients.

[14] See *John v MGN Ltd* [1997] Q.B. 586 at 607. Pearson L.J. gives an excellent summary of the law in *McCarey v Associated Newspapers Ltd* [1965] 2 Q.B. 86 at 104–105.

[15] [1998] Q.B. 498.

[16] [1964] A.C. 1129. See PR Ghandhi (1990) 10 L.S. 182.

[17] The Law Commission recommended that the term "punitive" should be used in future rather than "exemplary" in their 1997 Report No.247. It will therefore be used in this section.

civil and criminal functions of the law, and brought punishment into civil law without the procedural safeguards of criminal law. However, his Lordship admitted that punitive damages were firmly established in English law and therefore decided not to abolish this head of damages, but held that a restrictive approach should be taken in future. Further, juries (if present) should be directed that they should only award punitive damages when ordinary compensatory damages are inadequate to punish the defendant for his or her outrageous conduct, to show that tort does not pay, and to deter others.[18] The means of the parties would be taken into consideration in determining any award. This approach was approved by the House of Lords in the later case of *Cassell v Broome*.[19]

The three kinds of punitive damages.

Lord Devlin recommended that punitive damages should only be awarded in the three following situations:

15–010

- oppressive, arbitrary or unconstitutional actions by government servants;
- conduct calculated by the defendant to make a profit, which may well exceed any compensation payable to the claimant; and
- when expressly authorised by statute.

These will be examined below.

(i) Oppressive, arbitrary or unconstitutional actions by government servants: Here, the defendant is penalised for the abuse of executive power. It is therefore no excuse, as in *Huckle v Money*,[20] that the claimant was only wrongfully detained for no more than six hours, had been treated well, and provided with beefsteaks and beer. The court held that "to enter a man's house by virtue of a nameless warrant, in order to procure evidence, is worse than the Spanish Inquisition".[21] However, punitive damages will not be awarded on this basis against private individuals or corporations, however powerful they may be. They will also not be awarded against public bodies such as a nationalised water authority which is not exercising an executive function.[22] However, they may be awarded against the police or local government officials.[23] The court in *Holden v Chief Constable of Lancashire*[24] held that not all false arrests will merit punitive damages and that this will be a matter for the jury.[25] The court did find, however, that the claimant was not required to show oppressive, arbitrary *and* unconstitutional conduct by the official. Punitive damages could therefore be awarded where there was no oppressive behaviour by the arresting officer.

15–011

There is no clear reason why punitive damages under this head should be confined to misconduct by the executive. In modern times, where much power lies with private

[18] [1964] A.C. 1129 at 1228.
[19] [1972] A.C. 1027.
[20] (1763) 2 Wlls. K.B. 206; 95 E.R. 768.
[21] *ibid.*, at 207.
[22] *AB v South West Water Services* [1993] Q.B. 507.
[23] See *Cassell v Broome* [1972] A.C. 1027.
[24] [1987] Q.B. 380.
[25] False imprisonment being one of the few torts usually heard by a judge and jury.

individuals or corporations, the distinction between public and private bodies seems increasingly arbitrary. This, however, is the inevitable result of the approach taken by Lord Devlin in *Rookes v Barnard*, which sought to limit punitive damages to the bare minimum required by existing case law. It would be too much to expect analytical consistency from such an approach.

15–012   **(ii) Conduct calculated by the defendant to make a profit which may well exceed any compensation payable to the claimant:**   The aim here is to teach the defendant that tort does not pay and to deprive the defendant of the fruits of his or her tort. However, it is approached in a rough and ready way, and the court will not require the claimant to set out the profit obtained by the defendant from the tort. The real question is whether the conduct of the defendant was "calculated" to make a profit. To prove this, the claimant must show something calculated and deliberate in the defendant's actions, although it is not necessary that the defendant engaged in any precise balancing of the chances of profit and loss.[26] The most frequent example is found in libel.[27] In *Cassell v Broome*,[28] the House of Lords held that the court should investigate whether the defendant was aware of the fact that what he was planning to do was against the law (or had shown reckless disregard as to whether the proposed conduct was legal or illegal) and had nevertheless decided to carry on because the prospects of material advantage outweighed the prospects of material loss.

15–013   **(iii) Expressly authorised by statute:**   This is very rare. It has been argued that s.97(2) of the Copyright, Designs and Patents Act 1988[29] authorises punitive damages by virtue of its reference to "additional damages",[30] although its statutory predecessor did not.[31] The House of Lords in *Redrow Homes Ltd v Bett Brothers plc*[32] left this question expressly open, although Lord Clyde suggested *obiter* that they should be regarded as aggravated only.[33] More recently, Pumfrey J. in *Nottinghamshire Healthcare National Health Service Trust v News Group Newspapers Ltd*[34] has found that the section permits only aggravated damages, but on a basis far wider than that admitted at common law, and contains an element of restitutionary damages. It may be questioned whether "a wider form of aggravated damages" which expressly addresses the flagrancy of the breach can be viewed as distinct from exemplary damages or, more

---

[26] See *Cassell v Broome* [1972] A.C. 1027 at 1094 *per* Lord Morris.
[27] Although such awards are frequently made against landlords evicting tenants to obtain a higher level of rent from a new tenant: see *Drane v Evangelou* [1978] 1 W.L.R. 455 and *Asghar v Ahmed* (1985) 17 H.L.R. 25.
[28] [1972] A.C. 1027. See also *John v MGN Ltd* [1997] Q.B. 586 at 618 *per* Bingham M.R.
[29] "(2) The court may in an action for infringement of copyright having regard to all the circumstances, and in particular to—(a) the flagrancy of the infringement, and (b) any benefit accruing to the defendant by reason of the infringement, award such additional damages as the justice of the case may require."
[30] See also Reserve and Auxiliary Forces (Protection of Civil Interests) Act 1951, s.13(2). The High Court in *R. v Secretary of State for Transport, Ex p. Factortame (No.5)* [1998] C.M.L.R. 1353 held that liability for breach of European legislation did not entitle the claimants to exemplary damages. The European Communities Act 1972 simply did not provide for punitive damages: para.176. This finding was not appealed.
[31] S.17(3) of the Copyright Act 1956. This is the accepted view. However, cases such as *Williams v Settle* [1960] 1 W.L.R. 1072 do little to clarify this question.
[32] [1999] 1 A.C. 197.
[33] *ibid.*, at 207. For a contrary view, see C. Michalos (2000) 22 E.I.P.R. 470.
[34] [2002] E.M.L.R. 33.

likely, the statute in reality gives a discretion to award damages which include an exemplary element.

The "cause of action" test

The Court of Appeal decision in *AB v South West Water Services*[35] imposed one further **15–014** restriction on punitive damages: they should only be awarded for torts which had received punitive awards at the time of *Rookes v Barnard* (the "cause of action" test). If no such case had been reported, then no award would be given. This excluded punitive damages awards for torts such as negligence, public nuisance, deceit and for sex and race discrimination. This rule had no basis in principle and was simply a crude method of limiting claims. It predictably received well-deserved criticism in the Law Commission report on *Aggravated, Exemplary and Restitutionary Damages*.[36] The House of Lords in *Kuddus v Chief Constable of Leicestershire Constabulary*[37] finally overturned this "arbitrary and irrational restriction".[38] In future, the court would examine the facts of the case and would not be deflected by the claimant's cause of action. In the case itself, the fact that no-one had received punitive damages for the tort of misfeasance in public office prior to *Rookes v Barnard* did not preclude the claimant from recovering such damages.

The House in *Kuddus* expressed concern, however, that Counsel had not raised the fundamental question of the role of punitive damages in English tort law. Views varied from the critical approach of Lord Scott[39] to the more positive view of Lord Nicholls who considered that punitive damages perform an important function in buttressing civil liberties, for example in relation to claims of false imprisonment and wrongful arrest by the police.[40] It is an ongoing question whether punitive damages should continue to be part of English law. The Law Commission felt that they still played a valuable role and that they should be available for all torts or equitable wrongs (but not for breach of contract) where the defendant, in committing the tort, or by his or her subsequent conduct, has deliberately and outrageously disregarded the claimant's rights.[41] The Law Commission recommended, nevertheless, that punitive damages should remain a last resort remedy, and should not be awarded when other remedies adequately punish the defendant for his or her conduct. The Commission also noted the problem of high jury awards in libel and false imprisonment. Despite cases such as *John v MGM*[42] and *Thompson v Metropolitan Police Commissioner*,[43] where the Court of Appeal set down guidelines for awards, the Commission sensibly advocated that punitive awards should in future be dealt with by the judge.

Such suggestions are helpful, although the Government has stated that it does not intend to implement the reforms.[44] Although the primary aim of the law of tort is

---

[35] [1993] Q.B. 507. In any event, the defendants had been convicted for contamination of the water supply and fined (see *Archer v Brown* [1985] Q.B. 401, below). See generally A.S. Burrows (1993) 109 L.Q.R. 358.

[36] Law Commission Report No. 247 (1997).

[37] [2002] 2 A.C. 122.

[38] See Lord Nicholls *ibid*., at 142.

[39] *ibid*., at 159. Note also the recent article of A. Beever (2003) 23 O.J.L.S. 87, who argues that exemplary damages are an anomaly which should be expunged from the law.

[40] *ibid*., at 144.

[41] See above at para.6.3.

[42] [1997] Q.B. 586.

[43] [1998] Q.B. 498.

[44] Hansard (HC Debates), November 9, 1999, col. 502. The Government suggested that further judicial development of the law in this area might help clarify the issues.

(handwritten: Problems with (extending) punitive damages.)

compensation, this does not mean that tort law cannot have other objectives, including deterrence of particularly reprehensible behaviour. Indeed, other Commonwealth countries, such as Canada,[45] Australia[46] and New Zealand[47] have adopted a more generous treatment of punitive damages. However, a number of problems remain. First, with vicarious liability, the person who pays damages is not necessarily the guilty party. The Law Commission did not seek to change this rule, but Lord Scott in *Kuddus* was extremely critical of such a result.[48] Secondly, the punishment sum goes, not to the state, but to the claimant, who receives a windfall irrespective of his or her actual loss. Thirdly, there is the potential for double or excessive punishment if the defendant's conduct amounts to a crime for which he or she has been prosecuted. This problem was addressed by the court in *Archer v Brown*,[49] which held that if the defendant had already been prosecuted and sentenced in a criminal court for precisely the conduct which forms the basis of the suit, no punitive award should be made. Peter Pain J. stated that a man should not be punished twice for the same offence.[50] The Law Commission, in their 1997 report, proposed that the courts should have a discretion in such circumstances to refuse to consider or make an award of punitive damages where a defendant had already been convicted by a criminal court.[51]

(6) Restitutionary

15–015 We looked at the doctrine of "waiver of tort" briefly in Ch. 14, where the claimant has the option to choose between compensatory and restitutionary damages. Here, damages are assessed not on the loss caused to the claimant, but on the gain obtained by the defendant at the claimant's expense. It should be noted that not all torts allow for restitutionary damages, and further reference should be made to works on the law of restitution.[52] The Law Commission, in their 1997 report, decided that no attempt should be made at present to state comprehensively in legislation the situations in which torts should trigger restitutionary damages, and this should be left to common law development.[53] They nevertheless proposed legislation which would allow the courts to award restitutionary damages as an alternative to punitive damages.[54]

---

[45] *Hill v Church of Scientology of Toronto* (1995) 126 D.L.R. (4th) 129 and *Whiten v Pilot Insurance Company* (2002) 209 DLR (4th) 257. See M. Graham [2002] L.M.C.L.Q. 453.
[46] *Uren v John Fairfax & Sons Pty Ltd* (1966) 117 C.L.R. 118, High Court of Australia.
[47] *Television New Zealand v Quinn* [1996] 3 N.Z.L.R. 24 and *A v Bottrill* [2003] 1 A.C. 449 (Privy Council for New Zealand). See A. Phang and P-W Lee (2003) 62 C.L.J. 32.
[48] See above at 160–163. The other Law Lords did not express a concluded view on this point.
[49] [1985] Q.B. 401, but contrast *Messenger Newspapers Group Ltd v National Graphical Association* [1984] I.R.L.R. 397 where Caulfield J. refused to take into account a £675,000 fine imposed for contempt of court and ordered the defendant to pay an additional £25,000 as punitive damages.
[50] [1985] Q.B. 401 at 423.
[51] Law Commission Report No.247, paras 5.112–5.115.
[52] See, *e.g.* S. Hedley and M. Halliwell (eds), *The Law of Restitution* (Butterworths, 2002).
[53] Para.6.2.
[54] Paras 3.48–3.57. See para.3.51: "We therefore recommend that: legislation should provide that restitutionary damages may be awarded where: (a) the defendant has committed: (i) a tort or an equitable wrong, or (ii) a civil wrong (including a tort or an equitable wrong) which arises under an Act, and an award of restitutionary damages would be consistent with the policy of that Act, and (b) his conduct showed a deliberate and outrageous disregard of the plaintiff's rights. (Draft Bill, cl.2(1), 12(3))".

(7) Damages under the Human Rights Act 1998 ("the Act")[55]

Section 8(1) of the Act sets out the judicial remedies which arise when a public **15–016** authority has acted in a way which is incompatible with a Convention right (see s.6 and Ch. 2).[56] It states that, in such a case, the court "may grant such relief or remedy, or make such order, within its powers as it considers just and appropriate." This broad discretion, which includes the award of damages, has three main limitations:

(i) damages can only be awarded where the court has the power to award damages in civil proceedings;[57]

(ii) no award of damages can be made unless, taking account of all the circumstances of the case,[58] the court is satisfied that the award is *necessary* to afford just satisfaction to the claimant; *and*

(iii) in determining whether to award damages or the amount of the award, the court must take into account the principles applied by the European Court of Human Rights.[59]

There is thus no right to damages. The courts will examine all the circumstances of the case and consider whether "just satisfaction" has been achieved, even in the absence of an award of damages under the Act. Damages are thus a residual remedy. There is some dispute as to the extent these damages will differ from ordinary compensatory damages discussed above. It has been suggested that damages would be moderate and lower than for any comparable tort.[60] This view, however, has been recently rejected by the courts,[61] and the Law Commission in its Report expressed the view that "in the majority of cases under the HRA, the courts in England and Wales will find it possible and appropriate to apply the rules by which damages in tort are usually assessed to claims under the HRA."[62] Section 8(4) instructs the court to take account of the principles applied by the European Court of Human Rights, but this is unlikely to be of great assistance. This Court rarely gives guidance as to the principles adopted or even a breakdown of the award in question.[63] Nevertheless, a number of observations may be made. The primary principle (in common with English law) is that the victim should, as far as possible, be placed in the same position as if the violation of his or her rights had not occurred. Further, the Court is clearly more willing to award damages

---

[55] See, generally, the Law Commission Report No.266, *Damages under the Human Rights Act 1998* (2000) and J. Wright, *Tort Law and Human Rights* (Hart, 2001) pp.39–42.

[56] See also s.7.

[57] S.8(2).

[58] These include: (a) any other relief or remedy granted, or order made, in relation to the act in question (by that or any other court), and (b) the consequences of any decision (of that or any other court) in respect of that act: s.8(3).

[59] s.8(4). These are set out under Art. 41 of the Convention.

[60] See Lord Woolf C.J.,"The Human Rights Act 1998 and Remedies" in M. Andenas and D. Fairgrieve (eds), *Judicial Review in International Perspective: II* (Kluwer Law International, 2000), pp.429—436.

[61] *R (KB) v Mental Health Review Tribunal* [2003] 3 W.L.R. 185, QBD and, now the Lord Chief Justice himself in *Anufrijeva v London Borough of Southwark* [2004] Fam Law 12 para.73.

[62] *op. cit.* at para.4.26.

[63] See Law Commission *op. cit.* para.3.4: "Perhaps the most striking feature of the Strasbourg case-law, to lawyers from the U.K., is the lack of clear principles as to when damages should be awarded and how they should be measured."

for distress and disappointment than the English courts, although it has been suggested that such injury must be significant and of sufficient intensity before it could sound in damages.[64] The Court is equally willing to consider the character and conduct of the parties and the scale and manner of the violation of rights in deciding on the most appropriate response. The Court does not, however, award exemplary damages.[65] It should also be noted that proceedings for damages must be brought quickly under the Act, normally within one year of the act complained of.[66]

ACTIONS FOR PERSONAL INJURY

15–017   Having discussed the different kinds of damages available to claimants, we now focus on a specific type of action: a claim for compensation for personal injury. As highlighted above, the courts experience particular problems in assessing such awards. It is impossible to put a financial price on the loss of a limb, or the pain and suffering endured during an accident. Further, even financial losses cause difficulties when future financial loss is claimed. The courts are required to predict the future financial position of the claimant *if* the tort had not taken place. For example, if the claimant wishes to recover future loss of earnings, a court should take account of the fact that he or she may have been dismissed or made redundant, or taken a career break, or even promoted to run the company. Such prospects *should* be brought into any compensatory sum, but achieving this with any degree of accuracy is obviously difficult. As Lord Scarman commented in *Lim v Camden Area Health Authority*[67]: "There is really only one certainty: the future will prove the award to be either too high or too low".

The courts have adopted a number of principles which seek to achieve the goal of full compensation, which will be considered below, but a number of matters should be noted. First, the courts assess the claimant's loss on an individual basis. They therefore have no problem with the fact that claimant X, who is a company director living in a large house in Surrey, will receive far more damages than claimant Y, a worker in a fast food outlet living in rented accommodation, even though they have received exactly the same injuries due to the tort.[68] X will have suffered greater financial losses than Y and will therefore deserve a larger award. The courts have also traditionally been wary of the use of actuarial evidence in the calculation of awards. Actuarial evidence is used by insurance companies to calculate premiums, and it has been suggested that it may form a more accurate basis for assessing future financial losses in

---

[64] *R. (KB) v Mental Health Review Tribunal* [2003] 3 W.L.R. 185, Q.B.D., relying on *Silver v United Kingdom* (1983) 6 E.H.R.R. 62. The Court is equally more willing to award damages for negligently-incurred pure economic loss than in English law: see Ch. 3.
[65] See Law Commission *op. cit.* para.3.47 which examines the case-law of the European Court of Human Rights. Note also s.9(3): "In proceedings under this Act in respect of a judicial act done in good faith, damages may not be awarded otherwise than to compensate a person."
[66] See s.7(5): "Proceedings under subs.7(1)(a) must be brought before the end of—(a) the period of one year beginning with the date on which the act complained of took place; or (b) such longer period as the court or tribunal considers equitable having regard to all the circumstances, but that is subject to any rule imposing a stricter time limit in relation to the procedure in question."
[67] [1980] A.C. 174 at 183.
[68] See *West v Shepherd* [1964] A.C. 326.

tort. The courts have been reluctant to embrace such evidence, a judge commenting in 1985 that "the predictions of an actuary can be only a little more likely to be accurate (and will almost certainly be less interesting) than those of an astrologer".[69] Nevertheless, in the House of Lords in *Wells v Wells*[70] (which will be discussed in more detail below), Lord Lloyd adopted a far more positive view of actuarial evidence, holding that whilst such evidence should not govern personal injury claims, it should certainly be referred to, and used as a starting-point rather than a check. It would seem that, in future, actuarial tables will have an active role in setting the level of awards for pecuniary loss.[71]

We shall look first at how the courts assess past and future financial losses (or pecuniary loss). This will be followed by an examination of the most difficult category to assess: non-pecuniary loss.

Pecuniary Loss

If the claimant has suffered severe injuries, the largest part of the claim is likely to be for financial loss, including loss of earnings, cost of care and expenses. As stated above, while financial losses before trial can be assessed with some degree of accuracy, future losses are very difficult to calculate. This is not assisted by the general rule that the courts will award a once-and-for-all lump sum. The court must find a sum which, if properly invested, will cover the claimant for all future losses incurred due to the tort. The best the courts can do is to make a "guesstimate" of future losses. The difficulties in assessing the different types of financial loss suffered by the claimant will be examined below.

15–018

(1) Loss of earnings

While loss of earnings before trial can be assessed with a degree of accuracy, calculation of loss of future earnings is obviously more difficult. The method used by the courts is known as the "multiplier/multiplicand method". Essentially, a figure is reached by the court multiplying the multiplier by the multiplicand.

15–019

$$\text{MULTIPLIER} \times \text{MULTIPLICAND} = \text{future loss of earnings}$$

The *multiplicand* is the claimant's net annual loss.[72] This is his or her gross annual salary, less income tax and National Insurance.

The *multiplier* is the number of years for which this loss will continue. However, this is not a question of the difference between the claimant's age at the time of the accident and the age he or she resumes work or retires. The courts will take account of the possibilities of unemployment, redundancy and other factors reducing salary (although they will also take account of promotion prospects *etc.* to increase the figure). They will also note the fact that the claimant is being paid "up front". On this basis, the multiplier will be discounted to take account of these contingencies. The

---

[69] *Auty v National Coal Board* [1985] 1 All E.R. 930 at 939 *per* Oliver L.J.
[70] [1999] A.C. 345.
[71] See, *e.g. Worrall v Powergen plc* [1999] Lloyd's Rep. Med. 177 which followed Lord Lloyd's dictum.
[72] See *British Transport Commission v Gourley* [1956] A.C. 185, HL.

multiplier will therefore usually be set at a rate far lower than the actual number of years during which the injury will be suffered.

This formula is stated to give a lump sum sufficient, if invested, to produce an income equal to the loss of income suffered by the claimant.[73] Whether in fact this is achieved is highly questionable and in fact most unlikely. However, this myth persists in tort law.

Pressure has mounted, however, for the courts to adopt a more scientific approach. The Ogden Tables, which first appeared in 1984, have made considerable impact in persuading the courts of the merits of actuarial evidence. These are a set of actuarial tables, prepared by a working party of lawyers and actuaries for use in personal injury and fatal accident cases, which are published by the Government Actuary's Department. They are now regularly cited in court, and s.10 of the Civil Evidence Act 1995 provides that they are admissible as evidence in court. Although s.10 is not yet in force, the courts (particularly the lower courts) do refer to the Ogden Tables, but this has only added to the criticism of the courts' refusal to take account of inflation when establishing the multiplier.[74] In setting up the multiplier, the courts assume that the interest on the lump sum will cover inflation, and so this can be ignored.[75]

15–020   The courts had in the past presumed a return on investments of 4 to 5 per cent.[76] It was questioned whether this was a realistic figure, since it assumed that the successful claimant would invest in equities which, in an unstable stock market, could prove a risky investment. With the advent of index-linked government securities (I.L.G.S.) a safer alternative existed. These are bonds under which the return on capital is fully protected against inflation. On this basis, if inflation increases and so the lump sum is worth less, the claimant will be protected by the bond. However, greater security comes at a price, and the interest on such bonds is less than the general commercial rate. The Law Commission, in its 1994 report *Structured Settlements and Interim and Provisional Damages*,[77] recommended that the courts, in assessing the multiplier, should use the rate for index-linked government securities unless there are special reasons affecting the individual case. Section 1 of the Damages Act 1996 would seem to resolve this problem. Section 1 provides that the court is to "take into account such rate of return as may from time to time be prescribed by an order made by the Lord Chancellor". Until recently, however, the Lord Chancellor had failed to act on this provision.

In the absence of legislative intervention, the House of Lords intervened in July 1998 in the important case of *Wells v Wells*.[78] Their Lordships overruled the Court of Appeal, which had adhered to the recognised practice of assuming a 4 to 5 per cent return on investments. It was held that it was no longer appropriate to act on the assumption that the claimant will invest his or her damages in equities and to apply a discount rate of 4 to 5 per cent. Rather, the courts should recognise the suitability of

---

[73] Assuming the claimant will draw on the income and part of the capital from the sum invested so that the lump sum is exhausted at the end of the relevant period.

[74] In *Lim Poh Choo v Camden and Islington Area Health Authority* [1980] A.C. 174 at 193 Lord Scarman held that only in exceptional circumstances would any allowance be made for inflation.

[75] This process was affirmed recently by the Court of Appeal in *Cooke v United Bristol Health Care* [2004] P.I.Q.R. Q2.

[76] Since *Mallett v McMonagle* [1970] A.C. 166, HL.

[77] Law Commission Report No.224 para.2.25–2.28.

[78] [1999] 1 A.C. 345, HL. See D Kemp (1998) 114 L.Q.R. 570 who, at p.571, describes it as "one of the most important decisions in personal injury litigation since the Second World War".

index-linked government securities for a prudent investment of a large lump sum of damages, and, in the light of this, their Lordships applied a discount rate of 3 per cent.

This led to a dramatic increase in multipliers, previously capped at 18. In the case of *Thomas v Brighton Health Authority* (which was joined in *Wells*), serious injuries had been suffered by a child at birth, and the court raised the multiplier from 17 to 26.58. The Court of Appeal held in *Warren v Northern General Hospital Trust*[79] that the discount rate should remain at 3 per cent until the Lord Chancellor set a rate under s.1 of the Damages Act 1996. This was regardless of the fact that the net yield of index-linked government securities was found to have dropped to 2.5 per cent.

The Court was influenced by the imminent intention of the Lord Chancellor to prescribe a rate under s.1,[80] and, in 2001, this rate was indeed set at 2.5 per cent.[81]

Yet, this has not prevented a number of challenges to this rate. Section 1(2) of the Damages Act 1996 provides that the setting of the rate of return "shall not however prevent the court taking a different rate of return into account if any party to the proceedings shows that it is more appropriate in the case in question" and, as might be expected, litigants have relied on this provision to question the rate used. Guidance was finally given by the Court of Appeal in *Warriner v Warriner*.[82] A departure would only be justifiable if the case:

(i) fell into a category which the Lord Chancellor had not taken into account when setting the rate; *and/or*

(ii) had special features which were material to the choice of rate of return and were shown not to have been taken into account when the rate was set.

In the court's view, it would be appropriate to alter the rate in comparatively few cases. Here, the mere fact that Ms Warriner, who had suffered serious brain damage in a road accident, had a long life expectancy would not justify any alteration of the rate and, indeed, such claims were included in the category which the Lord Chancellor had in mind in setting the 2.5 per cent rate. Generally, then, the court will stick to 2.5 per cent in the interests of certainty to facilitate settlements and save the expense of expert evidence at trial. Whilst this is admittedly a "rough and ready" approach, such policy reasons would be undermined if every shift in market conditions required the courts to revise the rate.

The impact of *Wells* and the Lord Chancellor's intervention has been dramatic. Damages for future pecuniary loss have risen considerably. It should not be forgotten

---

[79] [2000] 1 W.L.R. 1404. See also *Jenkins v Grocott* [2000] P.I.Q.R. Q17 (Hale J.) and *Barry v Alberex Construction (Midlands) Ltd* [2001] EWCA Civ 433, *The Times* March 4, 2001 (CA) in which both courts affirm that the House of Lords in *Wells* clearly contemplated that the rate would remain at 3 per cent until the Lord Chancellor set a rate under the Act in the absence of significant economic changes. The lowering of the I.L.G.S. rate did not constitute such a change.

[80] See Consultation Paper, *The discount rate and alternatives to lump sum payments* (March 2000) (*http://www.dca.gov.uk/consult/general/damagesfr.htm*). Publication is noted by Stuart-Smith L.J. in his leading judgment in *Warren v Northern General Hospital Trust* [2000] 1 W.L.R. 1404.

[81] Damages (Personal Injury) Order 2001/2301, Art. 2. This was affirmed in the subsequent consultation paper, *Setting the discount rate: Lord Chancellor's Reasons* (July 2001) (*http://www.dca.gov.uk/civil/discount.htm*).

[82] [2002] 1 W.L.R. 1703. Note also *Cooke v United Bristol Health Care* [2004] P.I.Q.R. Q2, where the Court of Appeal rejected an indirect challenge to the discount rate by means of increasing the multiplicand.

that this carries with it a consequential rise in liability insurance premiums.[83] It should also be noted that the courts do not check what the claimant actually does with the sum awarded, and it is generally accepted that, in reality, it is unlikely that a claimant would place the entire award of damages in index-linked government securities. Nevertheless, if the claimant chooses to invest all the lump sum in the stock market or in his or her bank account, this is disregarded and will not affect the court's calculation of damages.[84]

(2) Lost years

15–021   This is a claim for loss of earnings during the period the claimant would have been able to work, but for the fact that his or her life has been shortened by the defendant's tort. In other words, suppose that claimant A was expected to live to 80. Following the tort, A will only live to 40. The claim will be for the loss of earnings from the age of 40. In the past, A could have claimed damages for loss of expectation of life for which the courts awarded a small sum, even though the claimant might be unaware of the loss or had been killed instantaneously.[85] In view of this award, the court in *Oliver v Ashman*[86] held that no additional award for loss of earnings during the "lost years" would be allowed. However, damages for loss of expectation of life were abolished by s.1(1)(a) of the Administration of Justice Act 1982. In 1980, the majority of the House of Lords in *Pickett v British Rail Engineering Ltd*[87] finally overturned *Oliver v Ashman* and accepted that a claim for loss of earnings during the "lost years" should stand. Their Lordships were influenced by the predicament of dependants, for whom the victim would have provided financial support during this period. If the victim cannot claim, and they are unable to bring a claim in their own right under the Fatal Accidents Act 1976 (see below),[88] then this head of damage would go uncompensated. This was held to be contrary to logic and justice.[89] In assessing the award, the court will look at the claimant's life expectancy before the accident and deduct the sum the claimant would have spent on supporting him or herself, including a proportion of the household bills.[90] The sum awarded will vary, but for a very young child any such loss is highly speculative and the court is likely to award nil damages.[91]

---

[83] The Lord Chancellor's Department March 2000 Consultation Paper para.14, reports that insurance industry sources estimate that reducing the guideline rate of return from 4.5 per cent to 3 per cent increased by £115 million the sum needed to be paid out in damages.

[84] See Lord Lloyd [1999] 1 A.C. 345 at 365. The Court of Appeal in *Warren* [2000] 1 W.L.R. 1404, for example, noted that the Court of Protection generally invested 70 per cent of the fund in equities, which was likely to give a higher rate of return than index-linked government securities. This was not treated as a relevant concern, although it may have influenced the court's adherence to the then 3 per cent rule when it seemed clear that the claimant would not be under-compensated.

[85] *e.g.* £200 in *Benham v Gambling* [1941] A.C. 157.

[86] [1962] 2 Q.B. 210.

[87] [1980] A.C. 136.

[88] A claim by dependants under the Fatal Accidents Act 1976 can only stand when the deceased's claim has not proceeded to judgment or settled.

[89] This action does not, however, survive for the benefit of the claimant's estate. s.1(2)(a) of the Law Reform (Miscellaneous Provisions) Act 1934 (as amended by the Administration of Justice Act 1982, s.4) provides that the estate cannot recover any damages for loss of income in respect of any period after the victim's death. This prevents any possibility of double recovery by the claimant as the executor of the estate and dependant.

[90] See *Harris v Empress Motors Ltd* [1984] 1 W.L.R. 212. This is far stricter than the approach under the Fatal Accidents Act 1976 which will be discussed below.

[91] *Croke v Wiseman* [1982] 1 W.L.R. 71. See P.J. Davies (1982) 45 M.L.R. 333.

(3) Loss of earning capacity

This is a claim for losses due to the fact that, although the claimant can carry on   **15–022**
working, his or her ability to obtain employment is hindered by the continuing effects
of the accident. For example, claimants disabled due to the accident may find it more
difficult to obtain a new job if their employment ends for some reason, particularly if
they were employed in a physically demanding job. This is often difficult to assess[92]
and, particularly in relation to children,[93] highly speculative.

(4) Deductions

In assessing the claimant's compensation, the court seeks to compensate the victim   **15–023**
fully, but is also careful to avoid over-compensation, which may unnecessarily penalise
the defendant for his or her tort and be a wasteful use of resources. This problem of
over-compensation arises when it is shown that, following the accident, the claimant
has received sums of money which also compensate him or her for the loss suffered.
The obvious example is where the defendant's tort stops the claimant working. Prior to
trial, unless the claimant can obtain an interim award or has savings, the claimant may
be dependent on income support. Alternatively, the claimant might have an insurance
policy providing critical illness cover, or be entitled to statutory sick pay. If the
claimant is awarded damages covering losses suffered prior to trial regardless of such
sums, he or she will be compensated twice for some of these pre-trial losses. There are
a number of options open to the courts to avoid over-compensation:

- Make the defendant liable only for the actual losses suffered by the claimant,
  deducting income support, *etc.*, received. This option means that the state,
  employer or insurance company which has provided financial support is
  effectively subsidising the defendant who is at fault.

- Ignore other benefits and make the defendant fully liable. Here, it is accepted
  that the claimant is over-compensated.

- Make the defendant liable only for the actual losses suffered by the claimant,
  but render the defendant liable to repay all those who supported the claimant
  prior to trial.

The courts confusingly adopt all three approaches. Lord Reid in *Parry v Cleaver*
explains the rules as depending on justice, reasonableness and public policy,[94] but this
takes us little further. We therefore set out in this section how these rules work.
Essentially, it depends on the nature of the benefit received by the claimant. The
principles involved are not particularly clear. The general approach seems to be that
when the claimant has received a benefit which reduces the actual loss suffered, it
should be deducted, but that the claimant should keep all "collateral payments". This
distinction is not, however, always apparent. The simplest way is to examine each
individual benefit in turn.

---

[92] See *Smith v Manchester Corpn* (1974) 17 K.I.R. 1, CA.
[93] See, *e.g. Croke v Wiseman* [1982] 1 W.L.R. 71 where the plaintiff was 21 months old at the time of the accident.
[94] [1970] A.C. 1 at 13.

(i) Charity

15–024 The law is reluctant to reduce the damages payable to the claimant due to receipt of charitable payments. There is a no doubt realistic fear that individuals would be reluctant to donate money to charity if the net result was to reduce the defendant's liability for damages at trial. Policy therefore dictates that such sums should not be deducted.[95]

(ii) Voluntary payments by the defendant

15–025 If the defendant has given any money to the claimant, or provided facilities such as a wheelchair, this will be deducted from the award. This will not include a company pension, as this is distinguishable from compensation for lost wages.[96] In the recent case of *Williams v BOC Gases Ltd*,[97] an *ex gratia* payment from the defendant employers, given as an advance against any damages awarded, was deducted. The Court of Appeal held that, as a matter of public policy, employers ought to be encouraged to make payments of this kind. This would not be treated as a charitable payment, even if given for benevolent reasons, unless the employer explicitly spelt out that it should be ignored if damages were awarded in future litigation.[98]

(iii) Insurance

15–026 Again, if the claimant has had the foresight to purchase an insurance policy to cover some of his or her losses, the courts are reluctant to penalise the claimant.[99] It would seem wrong that a claimant who has paid no premiums should obtain a higher damages award. Arguably this could be met by giving the claimant a credit for the premiums paid, but the courts have not chosen this path. In any event, if the insurance policy is one of indemnity (for example property insurance is usually indemnity insurance), the insurer is likely to seek to recover the monies paid by exercising its right of subrogation. The action will then be brought by the insurance company in the claimant's name. However, personal injury insurance is not generally indemnity insurance, and the claimant will be able to recover both the proceeds of the policy and the damages awarded by the court.[1]

(iv) Sick pay

15–027 This is deductible from damages for loss of earnings, whether or not it is paid by the defendant. It is not treated as insurance against loss of earnings, but as a substitute for wages. This extends to long-term sickness benefit paid by the employer.[2]

(v) Pension

15–028 If, as a result of the injury, the claimant retires from his or her job and receives a pension, this is not deductible from the claim for loss of earnings, because the pension is not deemed to be of the same nature as lost wages, but a form of insurance. In *Parry*

[95] See *Parry v Cleaver* [1970] A.C. 1: *Hussain v New Taplow Paper Mills Ltd* [1988] A.C. 514: and *Pirelli General plc v Jan Gaca* [2004] EWCA Civ 373; *The Times*, April 2, 2004.
[96] See *Parry v Cleaver* [1970] A.C. 1.
[97] [2000] I.C.R. 1181.
[98] See *Pirelli General plc v Jan Gaca* [2004] EWCA Civ 373; *The Times*, April 2, 2004, overruling *McCamley v Cammell Laird Shipbuilders Ltd* [1990] 1 W.L.R. 963.
[99] See *Bradburn v Great Western Rail Co* [1874] L.R. 10 Ex 1.
[1] See, generally, P. Cane, *Atiyah's Accidents, Compensation and the Law* (6th ed., Butterworths, 1999), pp.324–325.
[2] *Hussain v New Taplow Paper Mills Ltd* [1988] A.C. 514.

v Cleaver, a 35–year-old policeman had been severely injured in a road accident and was discharged from the police force. However, whilst in employment, he had made compulsory contributions to a police pension fund, and he became entitled to a pension for life on being discharged. The question was whether this pension should be taken into account when assessing the policeman's loss of earnings following the accident. The majority of the House of Lords held that it should be ignored. A contributory pension scheme was treated as a form of insurance, rather than sick pay, and should not be taken into account when assessing future loss of earnings. It would, however, be taken into account in assessing the loss suffered on reaching police retirement age, when there would be a diminution in pension entitlement. Lord Reid stressed that it was simply a case of comparing "like with like".[3] The minority favoured deduction. Lord Morris (dissenting) held that where there is no discretionary element, and the arrangements leading to the pension are an essential part of the contract, then the pension payments should be taken as a form of deferred pay, and deducted.[4] The majority view, however, was approved by the House of Lords in *Smoker v London Fire and Civil Defence Authority*.[5] Lord Templeman approved Lord Reid's statement in *Parry* that "a pension is the fruit, through insurance, of all the money which was set aside in the past in respect of [an employee's] past work".[6]

The House of Lords, in *Hussain v New Taplow Paper Mills Ltd*,[7] however, distinguished payments under a permanent health insurance scheme set up by the employer, to which employees were not required to contribute. Lord Bridge, delivering the unanimous opinion of the House, viewed such payments as the very opposite of a pension, and indistinguishable from long-term sick pay. On this basis, such payments were deductible. His Lordship commented: "It positively offends my sense of justice that a plaintiff, who has certainly paid no insurance premiums as such, should receive full wages during a period of incapacity to work from two different sources, his employer and the tortfeasor".[8] It would therefore seem that, in his Lordship's view at least, the claimant must have contributed to the pension to avoid any deduction of this benefit.

(vi) Social security benefits

For political reasons, deduction of social security benefits is largely governed by statute. At the commencement of the National Health Service, this matter was governed by the Law Reform (Personal Injuries) Act 1948.[9] Section 2 provided for a deduction from damages for loss of earnings of one-half the value of certain benefits, such as sickness benefit and invalidity benefit, receivable by the claimant in the five years following the accident. This did not include all benefits, however, and the

15–029

---

[3] [1970] A.C. 1 at 21.
[4] *ibid.*, at 32.
[5] [1991] 2 A.C. 502. See also *Longden v British Coal Corpn* [1998] A.C. 653, HL: contributory incapacity and disability pensions are non-deductible.
[6] *ibid.*, at 543.
[7] [1988] A.C. 514.
[8] *ibid.*, at 532.
[9] This still applies to torts which occurred before January 1, 1989 and which are not statutory barred by the Limitation Act 1980.

common law developed complementary rules deducting these other benefits in full for the period of the disability.[10]

The current legal position modifies the rules to resemble the third option mentioned above.[11] It represents a political decision to ensure that the overstretched welfare state is not subsidising defendants, and that social security payments made to claimants should be recovered whenever possible. Section 6 of the Social Security (Recovery of Benefits) Act 1997 now provides for the defendant to pay to the Department for Work and Pensions an amount equal to the total amount of specified social security benefits[12] payable to the victim in respect of his or her injury during the five years immediately following the accident (or until the making of the compensation payment whichever is earlier[13]). The claimant will get the difference (if any) between the damages awarded and recoverable benefits.[14] Section 4 provides that the defendant should not make any compensation payment in consequence of an accident, injury or disease suffered by the claimant until he or she has applied to the Secretary of State for a certificate of recoverable benefits.[15] These are processed by the Compensation Recovery Unit of the Department for Work and Pensions.[16] The provisions apply not only to court judgments, but extend to out-of-court settlements.[17]

The 1997 Act is more generous to claimants than the earlier Social Security Act 1989.[18] Benefits are now deducted only from certain heads of damages, namely loss of earnings, cost of care and loss of mobility, which are set out in Sch.2. This Schedule helpfully lists the relevant benefits to be deducted from each individual head. On this basis, income support will be deducted from any award for loss of earnings, and attendance allowance from damages for the costs of nursing and care. The state can no longer deduct any sum from damages awarded for pain and suffering and loss of amenity, because there is no equivalent state benefit. The defendant, who remains liable to the Secretary of State for "an amount equal to the total amount of the recoverable benefits",[19] may therefore be in a difficult position. Consider the following example. The claimant suffers injuries in an accident caused by the defendant's negligence. Damages are assessed at £10,000 (£7,000 loss of earnings and £3,000 non-pecuniary losses). The claimant has received £8,000 in income support. Under the 1997

---

[10] See *Hodgson v Trapp* [1989] A.C. 807. These rules still apply for benefits not covered by the 1997 Act, *e.g.* statutory payments under the Pneumoconiosis *etc* (Workers' Compensation) Act 1979 (*Ballantine v Newalls Insulation Co Ltd* [2001] I.C.R. 25, CA) or housing benefit (*Clenshaw v Tanner* [2002] EWCA Civ 1848).

[11] Namely that the defendant is liable only for the actual losses suffered by the claimant, but the defendant is rendered liable to repay all those who supported the claimant prior to trial.

[12] They are listed in Sch. 2, col. 2 and cover most benefits. There are exemptions, however, such as payments made under the Criminal Injuries Compensation Scheme and charitable trusts: see Sch. 1, Pt I. Claims under the Fatal Accidents Act 1976 are also excluded: Social Security (Recovery of Benefits) Regulations 1997 (SI 1997/2205), reg.2(2)(a).

[13] S.3. This is inserted to encourage early settlements.

[14] S.8(2).

[15] S.4.

[16] Note also the right of the NHS to recover the cost of treatment at a NHS hospital for victims of road traffic accidents: Road Traffic (NHS Charges) Act 1999. This has recently been extended and replaced by the Health and Social Care (Community Health and Standards) Act 2003, which now permits the NHS to recover the cost of hospital treatment and/or ambulance services from a person liable to pay compensation: see Pt 3 and ss.150–169.

[17] See s.1(3) of the 1997 Act.

[18] Later incorporated in the Social Security Administration Act 1992. The 1997 Act came into force on October 6, 1997.

[19] S.6(1).

Act, the defendant is liable to pay £8,000 to the state, although the claimant's award will only be reduced by £7,000 as no deduction can be made against non-pecuniary losses. The claimant will in such circumstances receive £3,000 damages (£10,000 minus £7,000). The defendant will be liable to pay £11,000 in total (£8,000 to the state and £3,000 to the claimant).[20]

The 1989 Act had separate provisions for damages for £2,500 or less, but at present, there is no provision for small payments under the 1997 Act.[21]

The current law on deductions therefore demonstrates no clear overall policy. Whilst trying to prevent over-compensation, the courts are generous in relation to charitable donations, insurance and pensions, but tough in relation to sick pay. The current distinction between a disablement pension and sick pay also demonstrates the confusion existing in this area of law.[22] The strict line taken in relation to recovery of social security benefits may additionally be criticised. The system involves administration costs, and may leave the successful claimant without any damages and the defendant incurring considerable costs in ascertaining his or her liability to the state. In examining the current legal position, the Law Commission concluded that in view of the lack of consensus as to any reform, it could not at present recommend any changes to the law.[23] Nevertheless, the Commission hoped that its report might assist the judiciary, and also the government, in developing this area of law. The confusion is therefore likely to continue in the immediate future.

(5) Expenses

The claimant can also recover *reasonably* incurred expenses, which will include medical expenses, increased living expenses and the cost of transport to and from hospital.[24] These will include past and future expenses incurred due to the injury. It is not unreasonable to choose private medical treatment instead of treatment under the National Health Service. Section 2(4) of the Law Reform (Personal Injuries) Act 1948 provides that the claimant is not obliged to use the NHS to mitigate loss. However, any saving the claimant makes due to being wholly or partly maintained at public expense in a hospital, nursing home or other institution will be set off against any loss of income due to the injury.[25] The courts are careful to avoid overcompensation, and therefore will deduct the cost of food, heating, *etc*. from the award.[26]

15–030

[20] See *Clerk & Lindsell on Torts* (18th ed., Sweet and Maxwell, 2000), para.29–34. The Court of Appeal in *Griffiths v British Coal Corpn* [2001] 1 W.L.R. 1493 modified this result slightly by allowing defendants to offset their liability to the State against any award of interest under each head. Further potential difficulties arise due to the failure of the 1997 Act to make allowances for any reduction in the claimant's damages for contributory negligence.
[21] Although it is possible for the Secretary of State to make regulations exempting payments below a certain amount: Sch.1, Pt 2.
[22] See Law Commission Report No.262, *Damages for Personal Injury: Medical, Nursing and Other Expenses; Collateral Benefits* (1999). The Commission rejected (at paras 11.51–11.52) treating pensions and sick pay alike and deducting both. It felt that there would be practical difficulties in distinguishing between some disablement pensions and some insurance policies.
[23] Law Commission Report No.262, *Damages for Personal Injury: Medical, Nursing and Other Expenses; Collateral Benefits* (1999), para.11.53.
[24] *Cunningham v Harrison* [1973] Q.B. 942. The courts will reject "unreasonable" expenses, for example, the costs of surrogacy with a slim chance of success: *Briody v St Helen's & Knowsley HA* [2002] Q.B. 856, CA.
[25] Administration of Justice Act 1982, s.5. *Lim Poh Choo v Camden and Islington Area Health Authority* [1980] A.C. 174 applies the same rule to private care.
[26] See *Housecroft v Burnett* [1986] 1 All E.R. 332.

Cost of a carer

15–031   A further expense following a serious accident may be the cost of a carer. The court again will award compensation for the cost of a carer if such expense is reasonably incurred. However, the carer in question may not be a professional carer, but a close relative or partner who wishes to care for their loved one. Such relatives are unlikely to charge a fee, but of course make considerable sacrifice in both financial and emotional terms. The Court of Appeal in *Donnelly v Joyce*[27] recognised that such carers should not go unrewarded.

In *Donnelly v Joyce*, the victim's mother had given up her part-time job to nurse her six year-old son. The court awarded a sum for her nursing services, but held that the loss was suffered by the victim, namely the need to receive nursing services due to the tort. It was not the loss of the mother which was being compensated. The court held, however, that it was unnecessary to show a contract between the victim and his mother to obtain the award.[28]

Donnelly was taken a step further by the House of Lords in *Hunt v Severs*.[29] In this case, the victim had been injured when riding as a pillion passenger on a motorbike driven by the defendant, who later became her husband. In claiming damages, she requested a sum for her carer, namely her husband. The House of Lords held that although the sum was awarded to the victim, it would be held on trust for the carer.[30] Here, the carer and the defendant were the same person. On this basis, the court held that there was no ground in public policy or otherwise to justify requiring the defendant to pay a sum to the claimant to be held on trust for himself.

On its face, the decision of the House of Lords seems entirely correct. It would be ridiculous to force the defendant to pay a sum to the claimant to be paid back to the defendant, but this ignores the reality of the situation. The husband was insured, and therefore the person paying the money (the real defendant) was not the husband, but his insurance company.[31] On this analysis, there is nothing wrong with an insurance company paying a sum to the wife to compensate her carer, whoever he or she may be. Following *Hunt v Severs*, if the carer is the tortfeasor, in order to obtain full compensation, the victim is forced to contract for a carer or use a different relative, even though the best person to care for the victim may be the tortfeasor. Certain disabilities render the victim very wary of strangers, and it seems a worrying development for the law to penalise a victim financially for choosing to be cared for by a loved one who happened to have caused the accident in question. The Law Commission, in their 1999 report, recommended that there should be a legislative

---

[27] [1974] Q.B. 454.
[28] The Court of Appeal in *Hardwick v Hudson* [1999] 3 All E.R. 426 distinguished this situation from where the victim's wife had provided commercial services for the claimant's business. Different considerations apply in a commercial environment where such services are usually paid for and the victim could only recover if there was evidence of an express or implied contract for the work. This approach is approved by the Law Commission in their Report No. 262, *Damages for Personal Injury: Medical, Nursing and Other Expenses; Collateral Benefits* (1999).
[29] [1994] 2 A.C. 350. See D. Kemp (1994) 110 L.Q.R. 524.
[30] Adopting the view of Lord Denning M.R. in *Cunningham v Harrison* [1973] Q.B. 942, 951–952. Watson and Barrie highlight the practical difficulties that might arise if this was treated strictly as a trust: see (2003) 19 PN. 320.
[31] Lord Bridge held that at common law the fact that the defendant is insured can have no relevance in assessing damages: [1994] 2 A.C. 350 at 363.

provision reversing the result in *Hunt*, and that the carer should have a legal entitlement to the claimant's damages for past (although not future) care.[32]

The cost of a carer is generally assessed at the commercial rate for such services.[33] If a mother gives up a highly paid employment, the loss will be capped at the commercial rate for the services provided.[34] Equally, if, due to the accident, a person cannot undertake the household tasks undertaken prior to injury, the reasonable cost of substitute services should be awarded.[35]

(6) Other damages

The examples of expenses listed above are not exhaustive, and damages claims will often consist of a large number of claims, depending on the particular facts of the case. For example, a claimant may wish to sue for the loss of pension rights or the inability to continue a profitable hobby. Subject to the rules of remoteness, the claimant may sue for any losses which are due to the defendant's tort.

15–032

Non-Pecuniary Loss

(1) Pain and suffering

The court will award a sum which represents the pain and suffering experienced by the claimant. The two are generally considered together. The Law Commission in 1995 defined "pain" as "the physical hurt or discomfort attributable to the injury itself or consequent on it", whilst "suffering" was defined as "mental or emotional distress which the plaintiff may feel as a consequence of the injury: anxiety, worry, fear, torment, embarrassment and the like".[36] It is a subjective test, and no sum will be awarded if the claimant is unconscious or unable to experience pain or suffering due to his or her condition.[37] The courts will concentrate on the actual condition of the victim and consider past, present and future suffering.

15–033

Section 1(1)(b) of the Administration of Justice Act 1982 also permits an award of damages to victims suffering or likely to suffer on the realisation that their expectation of life has been reduced as a result of the injuries.[38] This will form part of the award for pain and suffering. As the award is subjective, the claimant must be aware of his or

---

[32] Law Commission Report No.262 (1999) paras 3.76 and 3.62 . The High Court of Australia has refused to follow *Hunt* and followed the principle of *Donnelly v Joyce*: *Kars v Kars* (1996) 141 A.L.R. 37.

[33] This is usually subject to a discount to represent non-payment of tax and national insurance and the belief that care provided out of love and care makes commercial considerations less relevant: *Evans v Pontypridd Roofing Ltd* [2002] P.I.Q.R. Q5, CA.

[34] *Housecroft v Burnett* [1986] 1 All E.R. 332 at 343 *per* O'Connor L.J.

[35] See *Daly v General Steam Navigation Co. Ltd* [1981] 1 W.L.R. 120. In *Lowe v Guise* [2002] Q.B. 1369, the Court of Appeal extended recovery to a claimant who, due to the injury, was unable to continue to provide gratuitous care for his disabled brother on which the family depended.

[36] Law Commission Consultation Paper No. 140, *Damage for Personal Injury: Non-Pecuniary Loss* (1995), para.2.10. The Law Commission Report No. 257, *Damages for Personal Injury: Non-Pecuniary Loss* (April 1999) recommends that the present system of assessment by judges should continue and makes no proposals for reform. In *A v National Blood Authority* [2001] 3 All ER 289 at 382 (discussed in Ch. 9), Burton J. was prepared to award the claimants damages under this heading for the social handicap of carrying the Hepatitis C virus.

[37] *H. West & Son Ltd v Shephard* [1964] A.C. 326; *Lim Poh Choo v Camden and Islington Area Health Authority* [1980] A.C. 174 in contrast to loss of amenity which is assessed objectively.

[38] Administration of Justice Act 1982, s.1(1)(a) abolished a claim for loss of expectation of life *per se*.

her condition. Damages will be refused if the victim is rendered permanently unconscious either immediately or within a short time of the injury. In *Hicks v Chief Constable of South Yorkshire*,[39] for example, where medical evidence indicated that the plaintiffs' daughters, crushed in the Hillsborough disaster, would have lost consciousness within a matter of seconds and would have died within five minutes, the court rejected a claim for the distress suffered by the girls in their last moments.

(2) Loss of amenity

15–034   This is distinct from pain and suffering and is a claim for the loss of enjoyment of life experienced after the injury. For example, suppose that due to an injury to her leg, the claimant cannot play tennis or go for long country walks as she could prior to the accident. This is an objective test, and the fact that the claimant is unable to appreciate this loss is irrelevant. This is clearly seen in *H. West & Son Ltd v Shepherd*.[40] Here, the plaintiff had been badly injured in a road traffic accident and had sustained severe head injuries, resulting in cerebral atrophy and paralysis of all four limbs. Due to her injuries, her ability to appreciate her condition was severely limited. She was 41 at the time of accident, but had no prospect of improvement, and required full-time hospital nursing for the rest of her life, which was estimated as five years. The majority of the House of Lords held that she had suffered loss of amenity and approved the trial judge's award of £17,500.[41] The court was not prepared to treat such a victim as dead and reduce the damages on this basis.

This was approved by the House of Lords in *Lim v Camden Area Health Authority*.[42] In this case, a 36–year-old senior psychiatric registrar had suffered extensive and irremediable brain damage following a minor operation. As a result, Dr Lim was barely conscious and totally dependent on others. She was awarded £20,000 for pain and suffering and loss of amenity. This was approved by the House of Lords, which held that *West* could only be reversed by a comprehensive Act of Parliament which dealt with all aspects of damages for personal injury. The court was not prepared to overturn a decision which had formed the basis for settlements and damages awards for almost 20 years. A review of the position was undertaken by the Law Commission who, in its April 1999 Report No.257, *Damages for Personal Injury: Non-Pecuniary Loss*, did not recommend changing the rules for damages for non-pecuniary loss in respect of permanently unconscious or conscious but severely brain-damaged claimants.[43]

The same report stated that damages for non-pecuniary loss in cases of serious personal injury were generally too low, and should be increased generally by a factor of at least 50 per cent for awards over £3,000.[44] It was recommended that this should be achieved by guidelines set down by the Court of Appeal or House of Lords, but if this was not achieved within a reasonable period, then legislation should follow. A five judge Court of Appeal responded in March 2000 in *Heil v Rankin*.[45] In dealing with

[39] [1992] 2 All E.R. 65.
[40] [1964] A.C. 326 at 368–369 *per* Lord Pearce. See also *Wise v Kaye* [1962] 1 Q.B. 638.
[41] The minority (Lords Reid and Devlin) favoured a far smaller award.
[42] [1980] A.C. 174.
[43] See paras 2.19 and 2.24.
[44] See para.5.8.
[45] [2001] Q.B. 272. Comment R. Lewis (2001) 64 M.L.R. 100.

eight conjoined appeals, Lord Woolf M.R. proposed a more modest increase in awards than that suggested by the Law Commission. His Lordship suggested that in seeking to make compensation awards for non-pecuniary losses which were fair, reasonable and just, the awards should be subject to a tapered increase, from a maximum of one third, to nil when the award was below £10,000. Such increases would take account of the fact that people now live longer, but his Lordship also noted the impact of any increase on the level of insurance premiums.[46] This decision has given rise to a considerable increase in the level of awards. However, the threshold of £10,000, rather than the £3,000 suggested by the Law Commission, has limited the impact of the decision and excluded a large number of claims for minor injuries. In the case itself, *Heil* lost his appeal because the award was less than £10,000.

(3) Injury itself

This is difficult to assess. The courts have developed a system of tariffs which guide judges. Reference is made to previous case law and to the Judicial Studies Board guidelines,[47] with the stated aim of ensuring uniformity whilst keeping the level of such claims within reasonable bounds.   **15–035**

Interest

Interest will be added to damages depending on the nature of the injury suffered.   **15–036** Unless the claimant is awarded interim damages, he or she will be deprived of the damages award until the case is finally heard in court, which unfortunately may take a considerable amount of time. Section 35A of the Supreme Court Act 1981 provides for interest in actions for personal injuries in which the claimant recovers more than £200, unless the court is satisfied that there are special reasons why interest should not be given.[48] The rates are as follows.

(1) Pecuniary loss

No interest will be awarded for future pecuniary loss, because there has been no delay   **15–037** in receipt. For sums due from the date of the accident up to the date of trial, interest will be awarded at half the current short-term rate during that period to reflect the gradual nature of the loss.[49]

---

[46] *The Times*, March 24, 2000 reported that the Association of British Insurers believe that, following *Heil v Rankin*, the likely rise in premiums will be less than 10 per cent.

[47] Since 1992, the Judicial Studies Board has published *Guidelines for the Assessment of General Damages in Personal Injury Cases* (OUP, 2002) 6th ed, and summaries of awards may be found in *Kemp & Kemp on the Quantum of Damages* and in *Current Law*.

[48] County Courts Act 1984, s.69 makes similar provision for actions in the county court. The interest awarded will be simple interest, although the Law Commission has recommended that the court should have a discretion to award compound interest: Law Commission Consultation Paper No.167, *Compound Interest* (2002) and Report No.287, *Pre-judgment Interest on Debts and Damages* (2004).

[49] Giving typically a rate of 4 per cent. See *Jefford v Gee* [1970] 2 Q.B. 130 at 151. *Cookson v Knowles* [1979] A.C. 556 applies the decision to fatal accident cases.

(2) Non-pecuniary loss

15–038   Interest will be awarded at 2 per cent from the date of service of proceedings to the date of trial.[50] The figure is deliberately low, because the only loss suffered is the inability to use the money prior to trial.[51]

Alternatives to Lump Sum Payments

15–039   Damages will usually be awarded, as stated earlier, in the form of a lump sum. This does possess, however, a number of disadvantages. There is a distinct danger that a lump sum may run out due to poor investment, reckless spending, a higher than expected life expectancy, or inflation, leaving the claimant with insufficient funds to meet his or her needs. The lump sum is a "once-and-for-all" payment. This has led to calls for alternative forms of award which more closely reflect the actual needs of the claimant. Although there is already provision for provisional damages and interim awards, Parliament has recently shown its support for the use of periodic payments in certain cases and its ongoing support for structured settlements. These will be examined below.

(1) Provisional damages

15–040   Section 32A of the Supreme Court Act 1981[52] provides for provisional damages where it is proved or admitted that there is a chance that, at some definite or indefinite time in the future, the injured person will develop some serious disease, or suffer some serious deterioration in his or her physical or mental condition. Damages will be awarded on the basis that the claimant's condition will not deteriorate, but that the claimant can return to court for further damages if this occurs. The claimant is only entitled, however, to apply once for further damages, and these must be for a disease or type of injury specified in the original action.[53]

In *Willson v Ministry of Defence*,[54] the plaintiff sued his employer following an injury to his ankle at work when he slipped on a polished floor. He applied for an award of provisional damages on the basis that there was a possibility that he would develop arthritis, which might require surgery. Scott Baker J. refused to award provisional damages. His Lordship asked three questions:

(i) Was there a chance of deterioration?

(ii) Would the deterioration be serious?

---

[50] See *Birkett v Hayes* [1982] 1 W.L.R. 816 and *Wright v British Railways Board* [1983] 2 A.C. 773. Affirmed in *L (a patient) v Chief Constable of Staffordshire* [2000] P.I.Q.R. Q349, CA, which rejected the argument based on Lord Lloyd's reasoning in *Wells v Wells* [1999] 1 A.C. 345 that the rate should also be set at the I.L.G.S. rate.

[51] Damages for non-pecuniary loss being assessed as at the date of trial.

[52] Inserted by Administration of Justice Act 1982, s.6. See also CPR r.41.

[53] Damages Act 1996, s.3 provides that a provisional award will not stop the victim's dependants from bringing a claim under the Fatal Accidents Act 1976, but any part of the provisional award which was intended to compensate the victim for pecuniary loss during a period that in the event falls after his or her death shall be taken into account in assessing the amount of any loss of support suffered by the dependants under the Act.

[54] [1991] 1 All E.R. 638.

(iii) Should the court exercise its discretion in the claimant's favour in the circumstances of the case?

Whilst the plaintiff had shown a chance of deterioration which was measurable, rather than fanciful, his Lordship held that "serious deterioration" required more than the ordinary progression of a disease. A clear and severable risk was required which would trigger entitlement to further compensation. Arthritis following an ankle injury was not such an event. Epilepsy following a head injury would, however, seem to satisfy this test.[55] In practice, therefore, provisional damages will very rarely be awarded.

(2) Interim payments

The court has also, under s.32 of the Supreme Court Act 1981, a discretion to make an interim award prior to trial where the defendant has admitted liability to pay damages, the claimant has obtained judgment against the defendant with damages to be assessed, or where it is satisfied that claimant will obtain substantial damages at trial.[56] The court may order an interim payment to be paid in one sum or by instalments.[57] For personal injuries claims, however, the court may only make such an award if the defendant is insured in respect of the claim or is a public body.[58]

15–041

(3) Periodic payments

A more radical proposal for change is to replace a lump sum award with periodic payments. These could respond to changes in the claimant's condition and ensure that the claimant has sufficient funds long-term. The majority of the Pearson Commission recommended that the court should be obliged to award damages for future pecuniary loss caused by death or serious and lasting injury in the form of periodic payments, unless it is satisfied, on the application of the claimant, that a lump sum award would be more appropriate.[59] This proposal has not been adopted. At present, under s.2 of the Damages Act 1996, such awards may only be made with the consent of both parties.[60]

15–042

Yet, this is about to change. The Lord Chancellor's Department in two recent Consultation Papers has recommended that the courts should be given the power to order periodic payments for significant future financial loss, which should be reviewable in the light of changing medical or other exceptional circumstances.[61] These proposals now form the basis of ss.100–101 of the Courts Act 2003, although, at the

---

[55] See *Wan v Fung* [2003] 7 CL 113 (QBD)—1–2 per cent risk sufficient on the facts.
[56] See CPR 25.6–25.9.
[57] CPR r.25.6(7).
[58] CPR r.25.7(2). An award may also be made where the defendant is an insurer under s.151 of the Road Traffic Act 1988 or acting under the Motor Insurers' Bureau agreement.
[59] *Royal Commission on Civil Liability and Compensation for Personal Injury*, Cmnd 7054 (1978), Vol. 1, para.576.
[60] S.2(1): "A court awarding damages in an action for personal injury may, with the consent of the parties, make an order under which the damages are wholly or partly to take the form of periodical payments." Lord Steyn commented in *Wells v Wells* [1999] 1 A.C. 345 at 384 that the consent of both parties is never, or virtually never, forthcoming and that the present power to order periodic payments is a dead letter.
[61] *The discount rate and alternatives to lump sum payments* (March 2000) *(http://www.dca.gov.uk/consult/general/damagesfr.htm)* and *Damages For Future Loss: Giving the Courts the Power to Order Periodical Payments for Future Loss and Care Costs in Personal Injury Cases* (March 2002) *http://www.dca.gov.uk/consult/general/periodpay.htm.*

time of writing, they are not yet in force. A revised s.2 of the Damages Act 1996 will state that a court, in awarding damages for future pecuniary loss due to personal injury, "(a) may order that the damages are wholly or partly to take the form of periodical payments, and (b) shall consider whether to make that order."[62] With respect to other forms of damages, the rule remains that the consent of the parties is required.[63] One major concern has been the security of these future payments. What will happen, for example, if the defendant (or his or her insurers) becomes insolvent? Section 2(3) of the Act will provide that no order should be made unless the court is satisfied that the continuity of payments is reasonably secure.[64] The payment will be varied according to the retail price index[65] and specified circumstances yet to be ordered by the Lord Chancellor.[66]

The aim of these reforms is to promote the widespread use of periodic payments for awards for future pecuniary loss in personal injury cases. It has been described as a "revolutionary change".[67] It is important to recognise, however, that such payments are aimed at claimants with long term or permanent personal injuries where a significant award for future care costs and loss of earnings will be made. They offer few advantages where the level of future loss is low or where the care is only needed for a short time. Most claimants will thus continue to be awarded lump sums.

These reforms are largely based on the success since 1988 of structured settlements. Over 100 very seriously injured people each year now receive part of their compensation in the form of a pension derived from a structured settlement.[68] With the majority of personal injuries cases being settled, they provide an important alternative to the lump sum.

(4) Structured settlements[69]

15–043 This alternative is based on replacing the traditional lump sum with annuities purchased by the tortfeasor and managed by an assurance company. This concept received a boost in 1987 when the Inland Revenue indicated that the revenue from such annuities would not be taxed. On this basis, the recipient would receive income free from tax, and, if an index-linked annuity is chosen, protected against inflation. If the claimant's disability continues for a long time, there is also the possibility that the annuity might exceed any lump sum. It would also benefit the defendant's insurers, who might be able to negotiate a lower settlement to produce the necessary annual income.

Its operation, however, is somewhat complex. Once the settlement is agreed, two contracts are entered into[70]:

---

[62] S.2(1).
[63] S.2(2).
[64] See also ss.2(4)–(5) and the provisions of s.101, which amends ss.4 and 5 of the Damages Act 1996 to extend to claimants the same protection provided for structured settlements (see below).
[65] Ss.2(8) and 2(9).
[66] S.2B (Variation of orders and settlements).
[67] H. McGregor, *McGregor on Damages* (17th ed., Sweet and Maxwell, 2003).
[68] See R. Lewis (2003) 19 P.N. 297.
[69] See R. Lewis, *Structured Settlements: the Law and Practice* (Sweet and Maxwell, 1993) and Law Com. No. 224 (1994), *Structured Settlements and Interim and Provisional Damages*. They are now defined in Damages Act 1996, s.5. Useful guidance may also be found in the Practice Direction on Structured Settlements found in CPR Part 40C.
[70] There is some flexibility here. Parties may wish to consider whether to structure on a "top down" or "bottom up" approach and what type of annuity should be purchased.

- Contract one: between the defendant and the claimant to pay a lump sum, but on the basis that the bulk of this will be paid by instalments. Some money will still be paid "up front" to deal with expenses already incurred and financial loss, and a sum may be set aside for further contingencies.

- Contract two: between the defendant and a life assurance company for an annuity on the claimant's life. The annuity is paid to the defendant (or in reality his insurer) who pays it to the claimant free of tax.

The structured settlement is not suitable for all. For minor injuries, the costs of setting it up are prohibitive, and, on one view, a victim who dies soon after the injury is likely to be under-compensated. However, following Law Commission Report No.224,[71] structured settlements have received some legislative support. The Finance Act 1995 allowed the defendant's insurer to assign the benefit of the annuity to the claimant, while preserving the tax advantage. The claimant can therefore now receive payment directly from the life assurance office. Equally, the Damages Act 1996 provides protection for the claimant against the liquidation of the life assurance office[72] and preserves the possibility of a structured settlement if the case goes to trial. The structured settlement may thus provide an attractive alternative for claimants suffering from long-term injuries. Following the Courts Act 2003,[73] courts may now force parties to organise payment by means of periodic payments and this is likely to do much to promote use of this form of settlement.

Nevertheless, it is important to recognise that despite recent reforms promoting the use of periodic payments in personal injury cases, damages will in general continue to be awarded by means of a lump sum and will indeed be favoured by claimants who wish to be able to choose how to deal with the consequences of the tort.

ACTIONS ON DEATH

The death of a victim of a tort gives rise potentially to two different claims: claims from the deceased's estate and from those who were financially dependant on the deceased. Both will be examined below.   **15–044**

(1) Action by the deceased's estate

In Ch. 14, we looked at the survival of actions for or against the deceased's estate. Such claims are governed by the provisions of the Law Reform (Miscellaneous Provisions) Act 1934. Section 1(1) of the 1934 Act provides for the general survival of actions in tort: **15–045**

". . . all causes of action subsisting against or vested in [any person on death] shall survive against, or, as the case may be, for the benefit of [the] estate."

[71] *Structured Settlements and Interim and Provisional Damages* (1994).
[72] S.4, as amended by the Financial Services and Markets Act 2000 (Consequential Amendments and Repeals) Order SI 2001/3649, Pt 8 Art. 350 (d).
[73] See sections 100–101 above. Note also recommendations of the Master of the Rolls' Working Party on Structured Settlements in August 2002.

It is important to remember that this does not give the estate a cause of action for death itself. It simply means that the estate may pursue actions existing at the time of victim's death.

Damages for pecuniary and non-pecuniary losses up to the date of death may be recovered under the 1934 Act. Any claim for non-pecuniary loss will consist of pain and suffering and loss of amenity during any significant period between injury and death. No sum will be awarded if death is instantaneous or quick.[74] Pecuniary loss may be claimed, but s.1(2)(a) excludes a claim for damages for loss of income in respect of any period after a person's death. Section 1(2)(a) also excludes any award of punitive damages.[75] Any loss or gain to the estate consequent on death will not be taken into account, but a sum in respect of funeral expenses may be claimed.[76] The Law Reform (Contributory Negligence) Act 1945 will also apply to such claims.

(2) Action by the deceased's dependants

15–046   There is a second possible claim arising from the death of the victim. This is a claim not by the deceased's legal representatives, but by those for whom the deceased provided financial support. For example, the death of a victim who is a father is likely to affect his family financially as well as emotionally. At common law, the rule was that the victim's death would not give a cause of action to other persons, even when they were financially dependent on the deceased.[77] However, legislation has intervened, first in the Fatal Accidents Act 1846 (also known as Lord Campbell's Act) and more recently in the form of the Fatal Accidents Act 1976.

Fatal Accidents Act 1976

15–047   This consolidates earlier legislation. Sections 1(1) and (2) provide that:

"(1) If death is caused by any wrongful act, neglect or default which is such as would (if death had not ensued) have entitled the person injured to maintain an action and recover damages in respect thereof, the person who would have been liable if death had not ensued shall be liable to an action for damages, notwithstanding the death of the person injured.

(2) . . . every such action shall be for the benefit of the dependants of the person ("the deceased") whose death has been so caused."

This is not particularly clear, but s.1 essentially provides an action for damages for the deceased's "dependants", *i.e.* the group of persons, defined in s.1(3), who were financially dependent on the deceased. The statute creates a hybrid action: it is the

---

[74] *Hicks v Chief Constable of South Yorkshire* [1992] 2 All E.R. 65.
[75] Law Commission report No.247, *Aggravated, exemplary and restitutionary damages* (1997), para.6.3 proposed that this should be repealed and the Act amended to allow claims to survive for the benefit of the estate of a deceased victim, but that they should not be available against a wrongdoer's estate.
[76] S.1(2)(c).
[77] See *Baker v Bolton* (1808) 1 Camp. 493; 170 E.R. 1033 where the plaintiff failed despite the fact that he "was much attached to his deceased wife and that, being a publican, she had been of great use to him in conducting his business". See also *The Amerika (Admiralty Commissioners v S.S. Amerika)* [1917] A.C. 38, HL.

action of the dependants, but relies on the fact that the deceased could have sued the tortfeasor. If the deceased's action would have failed, for example because the defendant had a good defence or could rely on a valid exclusion clause (unlikely in the event of death),[78] the dependants have no claim. Equally, if the deceased had settled the claim[79] or obtained judgment[80] prior to death, then the dependants have no right of action. Under s.5 of the Act, any damages will be reduced due to the contributory negligence of the deceased. If the dependant has also contributed to the accident, the share of that particular dependant will also be reduced, but this will not affect other dependants.[81]

The dependants will not usually sue in their own right. Section 2 provides for the action to be brought by and in the name of the executor or administrator of the deceased. If there is no such person, or no action has been brought within six months after the demise of the deceased, then an action may be brought by and in the name of all or any of the dependants.[82]

The action, as stated above, is brought on behalf of the deceased's dependants. The court must be satisfied that each dependant:

(1) is a dependant within s.1(3) of the Act; *and*

(2) was, as a matter of fact, financially dependent on the deceased.

Only if the court is satisfied on (1) and (2) will any sum be awarded. We therefore examine each question in turn.

(1) Is the claimant a dependant within s.1(3) of the Act?

Section 1(3) (as amended by the Administration of Justice Act 1982) gives a statutory **15–048** list of those parties classified by law as dependants, namely:

(i) the spouse or former spouse of the deceased;[83]

(ii) a common law spouse, *i.e.* a person who was living with the deceased in the same household immediately before the date of the death and had been living with the deceased in the same household for at least two years before that date and was living during the whole of that period as the husband or wife of the deceased (a restrictive definition);

(iii) the deceased's parents, ascendants or anyone treated by the deceased as a parent;

(iv) the deceased's children (including any person treated as a child of the family in relation to a marriage to which the deceased was at any time a party) and other descendants; *and*

---

[78] Unfair Contract Terms Act 1977, s.2(1) renders invalid terms excluding liability in negligence for personal injury and death if the clause concerns business liability.
[79] *Read v Great Eastern Ry* (1868) L.R. 3 Q.B. 555.
[80] *Murray v Shuter* [1976] Q.B. 972.
[81] *Dodds v Dodds* [1978] Q.B. 543.
[82] S.2(2), although not more than one action shall lie for and in respect of the same subject matter of complaint (s.2(3), but see now *Cachia v Faluyi* [2001] 1 W.L.R. 1966, CA.
[83] Including a person whose marriage to the deceased had been annulled or declared void as well as a person whose marriage to the deceased has been dissolved: s.1(4).

(v) any person who is, or is the issue of, a brother, sister, uncle or aunt of the deceased.

Section 1(5) adds that "for the purposes of subs.(3) above:

(a) any relationship by affinity (*i.e.* marriage) shall be treated as a relationship of consanguinity (*i.e.* blood), any relationship of the half blood as a relationship of the whole blood, and the stepchild of any person as his child; *and*

(b) an illegitimate person shall be treated as the legitimate child of his mother and reputed father."

As can be seen, although the above list has been extended to cover stepchildren, adopted and illegitimate children and some cohabitees, it remains a restrictive provision. The provision in relation to cohabitees, brought in under the 1982 amendment, leaves much to chance and is further weakened by s.3(4), which states that in assessing damages "there shall be taken into account . . . the fact that the dependant had no enforceable right to financial support by the deceased as a result of their living together". This means that the award for a cohabitee is likely to be lower than for a lawful spouse. The Law Commission, in its 1999 report, *Claims for Wrongful Death*, recommended adding a further class of claimant to the s.1(3) list, namely any individual "who was being wholly or partly maintained by the deceased immediately before the death or who would, but for the death, have been so maintained at a time beginning after the death".[84] This is a considerable improvement, which fits neatly with the Commission's stated aim of bringing this area of law into line with the values of modern society, and it is disappointing that such an amendment has yet to be made.

(2) Was the claimant financially dependent on the deceased?

15–049 Even if the individual is within s.1(3), the court will only make an award if it is shown that the individual was financially dependent on the deceased. It is the financial, not emotional, dependency of the claimant on the deceased which is in question.[85] The assessment of damages is dealt with under s.3, which provides that damages should be awarded "as are proportioned to the injury resulting from the death to the dependants respectively". This is far from clear. It seems that the courts will examine whether the individual had a reasonable expectation of pecuniary benefit, as of right or otherwise, from the deceased.[86] Public policy will exclude some forms of benefit, for example if the deceased provided for his family by means of armed robberies.[87] It will be a matter of common sense. For example, if the deceased child helped out in the family business, or the deceased spouse cared for the children and the home, the court will award a sum representing the benefit given to the family. However, if the child was employed

[84] Para.3.45; Draft Bill, cl.1. A person is treated as being wholly or partly maintained by another if that person "otherwise than for full valuable consideration, was making a substantial contribution in money or money's worth towards his reasonable needs".
[85] See Latham L.J. in *Thomas v Kwik Save Stores Ltd, The Times*, June 27, 2000.
[86] See, *e.g. Davies v Taylor* [1974] A.C. 207 where a wife, who had deserted her husband, failed to show some significant prospect, rather than a mere speculative possibility, of a reconciliation with her husband had he lived.
[87] See *Burns v Edman* [1970] 2 Q.B. 541.

by the family business and received a wage, then it would be a different matter, since the family has not suffered any financial loss.[88] The court will have to look at the prospects of the deceased (as we saw in personal injury claims), but also this time the prospects of the dependants. For example, if a husband dies and leaves an elderly wife who was financially dependent on him, then the length of the dependency is unlikely to be long. Equally, children are (hopefully) not financially dependent forever, and account must be made for their increasing independence as they grow older.

One point of controversy has been in estimating the likely period of dependency of a widow. If she remarries, then she has a right to be supported by her new husband and would be overcompensated if she could also claim loss of dependency under the Act. However, the only way to prevent this overcompensation was for the court to estimate the widow's likelihood of remarrying and reduce damages accordingly. It is clearly somewhat objectionable for the court to be seen to assess the widow's possible value on the marriage market, and in view of this, the law was changed by the Law Reform (Miscellaneous Provisions) Act 1971. Section 3(3) of the Fatal Accidents Act 1976 now provides that the court should not take into account the remarriage of the widow or her prospects of remarriage. Arguably, this goes too far in ignoring the fact that the widow may have remarried prior to trial, but if this was not included, the inevitable result would be the postponement of such marriages until after the trial.

Again, this problem was addressed by the Law Commission in their 1999 report, *Claims for Wrongful Death*. The Commission recommended that s.3(3) should be repealed, and the fact of a marriage or financially supportive cohabitation taken into account when relevant.[89] This removes the problem of overcompensation, but does not mean a return to pre-1971 law. The Commission proposes that unless a person is engaged to be married at the time of trial, the prospect that he or she will marry, remarry, or enter into financially supportive cohabitation with a new partner, should not be taken into account when assessing the claim.[90] Neither should the prospect of divorce or breakdown in the relationship be taken into account, unless the couple were no longer living together at the time of death, or one of the couple had petitioned for divorce, judicial separation or nullity.[91] This seems a valid compromise and would be a welcome development.

Assessment

The courts adopt an approach similar to that used in the assessment of awards for future pecuniary loss in a personal injury claim. Again, the claimant will receive a lump sum, which represents the loss of dependency of that particular claimant (although a court in practice will tend to determine the total liability of the defendant and then apportion damages between the various dependants). The court will use the multiplier/ multiplicand method. This time the multiplicand will be the net loss of support, namely the deceased's net income less expenditure on his or her own behalf.[92] This will be multiplied by the multiplier. The multiplier will take account of the possible duration

15–050

---

[88] *Sykes v North Eastern Ry* (1875) 44 L.J.C.P. 191.
[89] Note also the compromise position taken by the High Court of Australia in *De Sales v Ingrilli* (2002) 193 A.L.R. 130.
[90] Para.4.53, Draft Bill, cl.4 and 6(5).
[91] Para.4.66, Draft Bill, cl.4.
[92] See *Harris v Empress Motors* [1984] 1 W.L.R. 212 at 216–217 *per* O'Connor L.J.

of the support, based on the likelihood of continued provision by the deceased and factors such as the life expectancy of the dependant (for example, if the dependant is a widow) or likely period of dependency (for example, if the dependant is a child). It will also be reduced for accelerated receipt.

The multiplier will be set at the date of death, not the date of trial as is the case in personal injury claims.[93] This is because, in contrast to personal injury claims, the court has the added uncertainty of what would have happened to the deceased prior to trial. The multiplier therefore is set at the earlier date to meet this uncertainty. Whilst this is straightforward, it does create a problem of under-compensation for pre-trial losses which, under the multiplier, will also be discounted for early receipt which, of course, does not in fact occur.[94] In any event, the courts will treat the period between death and trial differently and take the deceased's average rate of earnings in the past as the relevant factor on which loss of dependency is assessed.

Deductions

15–051   Again, concerns as to overcompensation arise when the deceased's dependants receive money, such as insurance or a widow's pension, from other sources which reduce their financial losses. Here the position is far simpler than for personal injury. Section 4 of the Act provides that "benefits which have accrued or will or may accrue to any person from his estate or otherwise as a result of his death shall be disregarded".[95] This is very generous and whilst it may be welcomed for its simplicity, it leaves the dependants overcompensated at the expense of the state or insurance company.

Unfortunately the apparent simplicity of s.4 has been thrown into question by two Court of Appeal decisions which interpret the meaning of "benefit" in that section somewhat differently. In *Stanley v Saddique*,[96] the Court of Appeal was asked whether, in awarding a child damages under the Act following the death of his mother, account should be taken of the fact that his father had remarried soon after his mother's death, and that he received better care from his stepmother. It was argued that this was a benefit which accrued as a result of his mother's death and should be disregarded under s.4. Such a benefit is indirect at best, but the court was prepared to give "benefit" a wide meaning and held that it was not confined to direct payments in money or money's worth. It would include the benefit of absorption into a new family unit of father, stepmother and siblings. On this basis, the child was able to recover damages for the loss of his mother's care, even though he was currently receiving better care from his stepmother. A further implication of *Stanley* is that the benefit of a widow or widower remarrying should be regarded as a "benefit" under s.4 and disregarded. This renders s.3(3) defunct.

Stanley can be contrasted with the Court's decision in *Hayden v Hayden*.[97] Here, the child's mother had been killed in an accident caused by the negligent driving of the

---

[93] See *Cookson v Knowles* [1979] A.C. 556 and *Graham v Dodds* [1983] 1 W.L.R. 808.

[94] See Nelson J. in *White v ESAB Group (UK) Ltd* [2002] P.I.Q.R. Q6 who agreed with the criticisms of the Law Commission that a multiplier which has been discounted for the early receipt of damages should only be used in the calculation of post trial losses, but held that he was bound by House of Lords authority to maintain the current legal position.

[95] As amended by Administration of Justice Act 1982, s.3(1). Reg.2(2)(a) of the Social Security (Recovery of Benefits) Regulations 1997 (SI 1997/2205) also provides that the recovery provisions for social security benefits do not apply to fatal accidents claims.

[96] [1992] Q.B. 1.

[97] [1992] 1 W.L.R. 986.

defendant, the child's father. As a result, the defendant gave up work and looked after the child himself, who was four years old at the time of the accident. The majority (McCowan L.J dissenting) held that s.4 did not apply in this case, and therefore the care given by the father would be taken into account when assessing loss of care. The majority judges adopted different reasoning, however. Croom-Johnson L.J. (who had also given judgment in *Stanley*) held that *Stanley* could be distinguished on the facts. In *Stanley*, death had led to an unstable relationship being replaced by a successful marriage, whereas in *Hayden* the child remained in the family home with her father, who continued to look after her. The continuing care of a father could not be regarded as a benefit accruing as a result of death. Parker L.J., in contrast, chose not to follow *Stanley* in reaching his conclusion,[98] and found that no loss had in fact been suffered when the child enjoyed uninterrupted care.

The law was left far from clear after *Hayden*. The Divisional Court in *R. v Criminal Injuries Compensation Board, Ex p. K*[99] reviewed the conflict between the two cases and preferred the decision in *Stanley*. *Hayden* was distinguished on its own particular facts, namely that it concerned a situation where the replacement care was provided by the tortfeasor who was an existing carer, who had been caring for the child prior to her mother's death. *Hayden* was further isolated by the Court of Appeal in the later case of *H v S*.[1] Again, the children had been cared for by their father after the death of their mother, but in this case, the parents had been divorced, and the father had lived separately with his new wife. He had, in fact, offered no financial support to the children prior to their mother's death. The Court distinguished *Hayden*. It could not be argued that the father was discharging pre-existing parental obligations where he had not supported his children in the past and had shown no real likelihood of doing so in the future. On such a basis, his care was a "benefit" resulting from death which could be disregarded by the Court. The situation would have been different, however, if the parents had been living together before the death, or there had been a financial order[2] or actual/potential support in place before the mother died.[3]

15–052

H v S thus supports the general proposition that the tortfeasor should not allowed to benefit from the generosity of a third party volunteering to care gratuitously for the victim's dependants by a reduction in the damages awarded. The term "benefit" is thus a disguised claim for the cost of care to be held on trust for the carer by the claimant (see *Hunt v Severs*, above). Yet, in this light, it becomes increasingly difficult to understand why an immediate family member (as in *Hayden*) undertaking greater parental duties should be denied the cost of his care whilst an uncle or estranged father will succeed, unless his claim is to be excluded due to the fact he or she is the tortfeasor.[4] It would seem to penalise parents taking their parental responsibilities

---

[98] Relying on the pre-section 4 case of *Hay v Hughes* [1975] Q.B. 790, CA. This was disapproved by the Divisional Court in *R. v Criminal Injuries Compensation Board, Ex p. K* [1999] Q.B. 1131. His Lordship also added as a postscript that difficulties would arise in any event where the carer was in fact the tortfeasor; a reason which the Divisional Court did support (see below).

[99] [1999] Q.B. 1131. It may be noted that the case concerned a claim to the Criminal Injuries Compensation Board. However, the courts use similar criteria to those adopted in ordinary civil claims for damages and so the issue was in point.

[1] [2003] Q.B. 965. Comment M. Lunney [2002] K.C.L.J. 219.

[2] There was a maintenance order in place against the father, but solely for a nominal sum which the court decided to ignore.

[3] See also *L v Barry May Haulage* [2002] P.I.Q.R. Q35.

[4] Assuming, of course, the correctness of *Hunt v Severs* [1994] 2 A.C. 350.

seriously. Clarification of the status of cost of care claims for dependants, removed from the artificial wording of s.4, would be a welcome addition to the law.

The operation of s.4 was examined by the Law Commission in *Claims for Wrongful Death*. The Commission's proposal was radical. Section 4 should be repealed and the position in fatal accident claims made consistent with that in personal injury claims. On this basis, charity, insurance, survivors' pensions and inheritance would continue to be non-deductible.[5] The Commission also recommended extending the recoupment of social security benefits to claims under the Fatal Accidents Act. Whilst this makes economic sense and would clarify the law, it is unlikely to prove popular with the public, as it would have a significant impact on the level of dependants' claims. It would take a strong government to implement such recommendations.

Damages for bereavement

15–053   It should be noted that under s.1A of the Act (as inserted by s.3 of the Administration of Justice Act 1982), the spouse of the deceased or the parents of an unmarried minor (the mother only if the child is illegitimate) will be awarded damages for bereavement. This is a rare example of a third party succeeding in a claim for mental distress, which is rarely compensated in the law of torts, although it is important to note that the claimant need not prove actual distress.[6] It is in reality a form of consolatory damages. This is shown by the relatively low amount awarded, which is now set at £10,000.[7] The sum will be awarded to the spouse or between the parents equally[8] and the claim does not survive for the benefit of the recipient's estate on death.[9]

The Law Commission, in *Claims for Wrongful Death*, proposed a significant reform of bereavement damages. First of all, their availability should be extended to include the child of the deceased (including adoptive children), the parents of the deceased (including adoptive parents), a fiancé(e), a brother or sister of the deceased (including adoptive brothers and sisters) and a cohabitee who lived with the deceased for not less than two years immediately prior to the accident.[10] This latter provision would include same sex relationships. Secondly, the Commission recommended that the sum should increase to £10,000, and should be linked to the Retail Prices Index. Such damages would be capped at £30,000 and, if there are more than three claimants, apportioned accordingly.[11] The award would be reduced if the deceased had been contributorily negligent.

The 1999 Law Commission report therefore proposed significant changes to the nature of actions on death. Whilst the sum awarded has indeed been increased, there are, at present, no proposals to extend the list of recipients.

ACTIONS FOR LOSS OR DAMAGE TO PROPERTY

15–054   This will be dealt with briefly. Loss or damage to property is subject to the same compensatory principles outlined above: to put, as far as possible, the claimant in the

---

[5] Para. 5.39, Draft Bill, cl.5.

[6] For claims for mental distress in tort generally, see P. Giliker (2000) 20 L.S. 19.

[7] Increased from £3,500 to £7,500 by the Damages for Bereavement (Variation of Sum) (England and Wales) Order 1990 (SI 1990/2575) from April 1, 1991, and now to £10,000 under the Damages for Bereavement (Variation of Sum) (England and Wales) Order 2002 (SI 2002/644) from April 1, 2002.

[8] S.1A(4).

[9] Law Reform (Miscellaneous Provisions) Act 1934, s.1A.

[10] Para. 6.31, Draft Bill, cl.2.

[11] Para. 6.41–6.51, Draft Bill, cl.2.

position as if the tort had not taken place.[12] Where the property has been totally destroyed, the courts will assess the market value of the property at the time and place of its destruction. The market value is the sum of money required to enable the claimant to purchase a replacement in the market at the price prevailing at the date of destruction or as soon thereafter as is reasonable. The claimant will also be able to claim consequential damages, provided they are not too remote. A good example may be found in the case of *Liesbosch Dredger v S.S. Edison*.[13] Here, the plaintiffs' dredger had been sunk as a result of the defendants' negligence. The court awarded the plaintiffs the market value of a comparable dredger, the cost of adapting the new dredger, insuring it and transporting it to where they were working, and compensation for disturbance and loss in carrying out their contract work from the date of the loss until a substitute dredger could reasonably have been available for use. A claimant will also be able to claim for such things as the reasonable amount of hire of a substitute until a replacement can be bought.[14] The claimant is unlikely to be awarded the cost of restoration of the property, unless there are exceptional circumstances, for example that there is no market for the property destroyed.[15]

If the property is merely damaged, then the court will award a sum for the diminution in value of the property, normally assessed as the cost of repair.[16] The cost of repair will normally be calculated at the time of damage, but there are exceptions to this rule where it would lead to injustice,[17] for example where it is reasonable for the claimant to postpone repairs to a later date.[18] The cost of repair will only be awarded if reasonable in the circumstances. Consistent with the duty to mitigate, the court will not award such damages if they exceed the market value of the goods, although allowance is made if the goods are unique.[19] If the claimant reasonably intends to sell the property in its damaged state, the court will not award the cost of repair, but a sum representing the diminution in capital value of the property. Consequential damages may be awarded, such as cost of substitute hire[20] and loss of use during the period of repairs.

---

[12] *Livingstone v Rawyards Coal Co* (1880) 5 App. Cas. 25 at 39 *per* Lord Blackburn.

[13] [1933] A.C. 449. The case is also authority for the rule that losses incurred due to impecuniosity are not recoverable. This rule has been overturned recently by the House of Lords in *Lagden v O'Connor* [2003] 3 W.L.R. 1571 on the basis that the law has moved on and that such a rule would be inconsistent with the general rules of remoteness: see Lord Hope at 1590.

[14] See *Moore v DER Ltd* [1971] 1 W.L.R. 1476.

[15] *Hall v Barclay* [1937] 3 All E.R. 620.

[16] *The London Corporation* [1935] P. 70.

[17] See Lord Wilberforce in *Miliangos v George Frank (Textiles) Ltd* [1976] A.C. 443, 468.

[18] *Dodd Properties (Kent) Ltd v Canterbury City Council* [1980] 1 W.L.R. 433 where it made commercial good sense to delay repairs until the time when the action had been heard and liability decided. See also *Alcoa Minerals of Jamaica Inc v Broderick* [2002] A.C. 372 (PC), applied by the CA in *Smith v South Gloucestershire DC* [2002] 38 E.G. 206.

[19] See *O'Grady v Westminster Scaffolding* [1962] 2 Lloyd's Rep. 238: 1938 MG car known as Mademoiselle Hortensia!

[20] Although the court will seek proof that the goods were indeed hired and that the price paid was reasonable: *H.L. Motorworks (Willesden) Ltd v Alwahbi* [1977] R.T.R. 276, CA. On the use of credit hire companies, see the House of Lords in *Dimond v Lovell* [2002] 1 A.C. 384 and *Lagden v O'Connor* [2003] 3 W.L.R. 1571 (cost of credit hire agreement recoverable when claimant could not afford hire of a private car while his car was being repaired).

JOINT AND SEVERAL LIABILITY

15–055   So far we have looked at damages generally. This section will examine the legal position where two or more defendants are liable for the same damage,[21] that is, where two or more defendants have committed concurrent torts which lead to a single indivisible injury.[22] This is distinct from the situation where the claimant has suffered different injuries due to the independent actions of two or more people—here it is for the claimant to bring independent claims against each of them. Our situation is where A has suffered one set of injuries resulting from an incident where both D1 and D2 are at fault, for example A was hit when crossing the road because of a car crash between two cars negligently driven by D1 and D2. Here the defendants are said to be jointly and severally liable. This means that the claimant has the choice to sue one or all of the defendants. In either case, the claimant will receive the full amount of damages. Therefore, if A suffered damages assessed at £300,000, A could sue D1 or D2 or both D1 and D2 for this sum. This means that the claimant can sue any of the defendants without worrying whether all the possible defendants are in court, and is able to avoid defendants who have no funds or are uninsured. It is of no concern to the claimant that one defendant is paying for liability for which he or she is only partially at fault.

It will, however, be seen differently from the perspective of the defendant who is the only person sued, but in fact only partially at fault. This situation is now governed by the Civil Liability (Contribution) Act 1978.[23] Section 1(1) provides that "any person liable in respect of any damage suffered by another person may recover a contribution from any other person liable in respect of the same damage". Liability includes liability in tort, for breach of contract, breach of trust or otherwise.[24] The defendant (D1) may therefore claim a contribution from any other wrongdoer (D2) responsible for the "same damage" for the amount by which his payment to the claimant exceeds his responsibility for the loss.[25] The contribution must be claimed, however, within the limitation period of two years.[26]

Assessment

15–056   Section 2 deals with assessment of contribution. Section 2(1) provides that "in any proceedings under s.1 above the amount of the contribution recoverable from any person shall be such as may be found by the court to be just and equitable having

---

[21] "Same damage" is be interpreted according to its natural and ordinary meaning and does not extend to substantially or materially similar damage: *Royal Brompton Hospital NHS Trust v Hammond (No. 3)* [2002] 1 W.L.R. 1397, HL.
[22] *Rahman v Arearose Ltd* [2001] Q.B. 351 (CA), although the application of the rule in this case is questionable: see T. Weir [2001] C.L.J. 237.
[23] See generally T. Dugdale (1979) 42 M.L.R. 182 and Law Commission, *Report on Contribution* No. 79 (1977).
[24] S.6(1).
[25] D1 is entitled to recover a contribution " . . . notwithstanding that he has ceased to be liable in respect of the damage in question since the time when the damage occurred, provided that he was liable immediately before he made or was ordered or agreed to make the payment in respect of which the contribution is sought": s.1(2).
[26] S.10, Limitation Act 1980. Time runs from the date on which the right to a contribution accrues, which is the date on which the judgment is given, the date of the arbitration award or the date on which the amount of settlement is agreed between the defendant and the person to whom the payment is to be made: ss.10(3), (4) of the Limitation Act 1980.

regard to the extent of that person's responsibility for the damage in question". This is very similar to the wording of s.1 of the Law Reform (Contributory Negligence) Act 1945 and the same principles seem to apply. The courts will look at causation, and at times, the blameworthiness of the defendants involved. The court has a considerable discretion and may even, if it considers it appropriate, at one extreme, exempt the defendant from any liability to make a contribution or, at the other extreme, direct that the contribution to be recovered from any person shall amount to a complete indemnity.[27] The court will also take into account any defence of contributory negligence, any enforceable exclusion clause[28] and any statutory limits on liability which the other wrongdoer could have used against the original claimant.[29] The Act also does not stop any tortfeasor contracting to indemnify him or herself against liability for contribution.[30]

By this means, the claimant is fully compensated and it is for the defendants to sort out the division of responsibility between them. A good example is *Fitzgerald v Lane*,[31] discussed in Chs 6 and 14, where the plaintiff had negligently stepped out into traffic on busy road and had been struck by a vehicle driven by the first defendant, which pushed him into the path of the second defendant's car. Both the defendants were negligent, but the plaintiff had also been contributorily negligent in not looking properly before crossing the road. The House of Lords held the plaintiff to be 50 per cent contributorily negligent. It then examined the position of the two defendants and found that they were jointly and severally liable, but that each of them was 25 per cent responsible for the injuries. Thus, if only one defendant had been sued, he would have been liable to the claimant for 50 per cent of the damages due, but could have claimed a contribution from the other driver of 25 per cent. In practice, the parties will attempt to get all other relevant parties before the court, and a defendant may take advantage of the "third party" procedure to add a defendant to the case, even when that person has not been mentioned in the claimant's statement of case.[32]

Settlements

The 1978 Act also makes special provision for settlements. A settlement does not deprive a defendant, who has agreed to make a payment in bona fide settlement or compromise of the claim, from seeking a contribution from any other parties he or she believes liable for the same damage.[33] However, a settlement with one defendant which is "full and final and in satisfaction of all causes of action" may prevent the claimant from pursuing other tortfeasors responsible for the same damage,[34] although much depends on the context and the actual words used.[35]

15–057

[27] S.2(2). Apportionment by the trial judge will only be interfered with on appeal where it is clearly wrong or where there has been an error in principle or a mistake of fact: *Kerry v Carter* [1969] 1 W.L.R. 1372 at 1376.
[28] Subject to the Unfair Contract Terms Act 1977, discussed in Ch. 14.
[29] S.2(3).
[30] S.7(3).
[31] [1989] A.C. 328.
[32] See now Civil Procedure Rules 1998, Pt 19.
[33] Provided the defendant would have been liable assuming that the factual basis of the claim against him could be established: see s.1(4). For the impact of a settlement on potential claims by the victim's dependants, see *Jameson v CECB (No.1)* [2000] 1 A.C. 455.
[34] See *Jameson v CECB (No.1)* [2000] 1 A.C. 455, HL, which was applied in *Rawlinson v North Essex HA* [2000] Lloyd's Rep Med 54.
[35] *Heaton v Axa Equity & Law Life Assurance Society plc* [2002] 2 A.C. 329, HL.

OTHER REMEDIES

15–058 Reference should be made to earlier chapters where we have discussed other remedies available for specific torts. Readers should specifically note occasions where the claimant can resort to self-help. In Ch. 10, we looked at abatement in nuisance, and in Ch. 11 we saw that the claimant may use reasonable force to resist trespass. However, such rights should to be exercised with extreme caution. Overstepping the mark can lead to legal action, as the householder found in *Revill v Newbery*[36] when he was found liable to a burglar while seeking to defend his allotment shed with a gun (see Chs 8, 11 and 14). Here, we will concentrate on the equitable remedy of an injunction.

Injunctions

15–059 Injunctions are an important tool by which the court can order the defendant to stop a continuing or recurring act, or order the defendant to act in a certain way. The courts will only grant an injunction if the claimant has a good cause of action, for example in nuisance or trespass. It is an equitable remedy and so lies at the discretion of the court. An injunction cannot be demanded as of right, and will not be awarded where damages are an adequate remedy, or where the claimant's conduct is such that it would not be equitable to make such an award. The court has the option to award damages in addition to or in substitution for an injunction,[37] but a court will only award damages instead of (or "in lieu of") an injunction in exceptional circumstances. The leading case is that of *Shelfer v City of London Electric Lighting Co.*[38] where A.L. Smith L.J. laid down the four conditions which would lead a court to grant damages in lieu of an injunction:

(i) where the injury to the claimant's legal rights is small;

(ii) where the injury is capable of being estimated in money;

(iii) where it can be adequately compensated by a small money payment; *and*

(iv) where it would be oppressive to the defendant to grant an injunction.

The court in *Shelfer* was keen to resist greater use of damages in lieu of an injunction, as it would amount to a licence to commit a nuisance. For example, if drilling at night entitled the claimant to an injunction, but the court chose to award damages of £5,000, this would entitle the defendant to drill at a cost of £5,000. The court felt that damages should not be used to legalise a wrongful act by placing a premium on the right to injure the claimant's legal rights.[39]

There are a number of different types of injunction, which will be discussed below.

Prohibitory and mandatory injunctions

15–060 A prohibitory injunction is an injunction which orders the defendant not to act in a certain way. This is the most common injunction granted, and deals with situations where, unless it is granted, the defendant is likely to continue acting in a tortious

---

[36] [1996] Q.B. 567.
[37] See now Supreme Court Act 1981, s.50.
[38] [1895] 1 Ch. 287. See also J.A. Jolowicz [1975] C.L.J. 224 and our discussion in Ch. 10.
[39] But see *Jaggard v Sawyer* [1995] 1 W.L.R. 269.

manner. A mandatory injunction, in contrast, is an injunction ordering the defendant to act in a certain way, and is granted more rarely. The courts will look at the facts of the case and decide whether damages would be appropriate. For example, it has been held that where the defendant has obstructed the claimant's right to light, or the defendant has erected a building in breach of a restrictive covenant, the court is more likely to award damages in lieu of an injunction.[40] The court must also be careful that, in granting an injunction, it ensures that the defendant knows exactly what in fact he or she has to do or not to do.[41]

Interim injunctions[42]

Prohibitory and mandatory injunctions can be given provisionally, prior to the final hearing (interim injunctions), or at the final hearing (perpetual injunctions). The court, faced with an application for an interim injunction, is in a difficult position. The rights of the parties have yet to be determined, and the full facts of the case have yet to be set out. Nevertheless, due to the likely harm of letting the defendant's conduct continue, the court may award an interim injunction but place conditions on its grant. For example, it is common for the court to require the claimant to give an undertaking to pay damages to the defendant for any loss suffered while the injunction is in force, should it prove to be wrongfully issued. This may be expensive. For example, the claimant (C) obtains an interim injunction which prevents the defendant (D) from operating his car plant during the night. At the full hearing of C's claim for nuisance, it is found that the area is classified as an industrial zone and the conduct does not amount to a nuisance. C therefore had no right to an interim injunction, and may find himself liable for the loss of profits experienced by D during the period of the injunction. The principles for the grant of an interim injunction are set out in *American Cyanamid Co. v Ethicon Ltd*,[43] and reference should be made to specific practitioners' texts. It should be noted that, as seen in Ch. 13, the courts are very reluctant to impose interim injunctions for claims for libel, despite *American Cyanamid*.[44] In *Kaye v Robertson*,[45] the Court of Appeal, although horrified at the conduct of the *Sunday Sport* which had intruded on Kaye whilst he was in intensive care to obtain an "exclusive", had nevertheless refused to grant an interim injunction for libel.[46] Relying on *Williams Coulson & Sons v James Coulson and Co.*,[47] it was held that such an injunction would only be awarded where there is a clear case in favour of the claimant. If the defendant has pleaded justification, fair comment or qualified privilege, the court will again only grant such an injunction when convinced that the defence will fail.

15–061

---

[40] *ibid.*, at 284.
[41] *per* Lord Upjohn in *Redland Bricks Ltd v Morris* [1970] A.C. 652 at 666.
[42] See Pt 25, Civil Procedure Rules.
[43] [1975] A.C. 396.
[44] Note also s.12(3) of the Human Rights Act 1998 which provides that "No such relief is to be granted so as to restrain publication before trial unless the court is satisfied that the applicant is likely to establish that publication should not be allowed", and its recent interpretation by the Court of Appeal in *Cream Holdings Ltd v Banerjee* [2003] Ch. 650 (test to be applied is one of the "real prospect of success convincingly established" which remains stricter than the ordinary *American Cyanamid* test (see Simon Brown L.J. at 670)). *Cream* is to be appealed to the House of Lords.
[45] [1991] F.S.R. 62 (discussed in Ch. 13).
[46] It was argued that it was defamatory to state falsely that Kaye had consented to give an exclusive interview to the *Sunday Sport*.
[47] [1887] 3 T.L.R. 46 which states that an interim injunction should only be used in the clearest of cases.

Quia timet injunctions

15–062   These are injunctions granted to prevent a legal wrong before it occurs. This is obviously an extreme remedy, and the courts will be careful to ensure that the conduct of the defendant is such that substantial damage to the claimant is almost bound to occur, and that damages are not an adequate remedy. As may be expected, the court uses the power to grant such an injunction rarely. The main authority here is Lord Upjohn's judgment in *Redland Bricks Ltd v Morris*,[48] which held that *quia timet* injunctions are granted in two particular types of case:

(1) Where the defendant has, as yet, not harmed the claimant, but is threatening and intending to do so, and if the defendant acts it will cause irreparable harm to the claimant or his or her property; and

(2) Where the claimant has been compensated for past damage, but alleges that the earlier actions of the defendant may lead to future causes of action.

Remedies: conclusion

15–063   The courts therefore employ a number of remedies in dealing with claims in tort. Although the primary remedy is that of compensatory damages, the courts will also use injunctions to meet the needs of claimants, or use damages to punish the misconduct of the defendant or vindicate his or her rights. Equally, the claimant may seek to use self-help remedies, but should be careful to stay within the remit of the law. In the field of damages for personal injury and death, the Law Commission's proposals for reform should be noted, particularly in the light of the major changes proposed for damages for death. It remains our hope that their recommendations will be carefully reviewed by the present government.

The Law Commission's recommendations also reflect the fact that tort law must continue to evolve in line with developments in modern society. As medical science improves and life expectancies increase, compensatory principles must adapt to these new conditions. Equally, as non-marital relationships become more common, legal recognition is a necessary step forward. A system of tort law which is responsive to such needs, and sufficiently flexible to change, is one which will hopefully thrive and continue to develop in the twenty-first century and beyond.

---

[48] [1970] A.C. 652 at 665–666.

INDEX